The Internet University

Professor D. Quinn Mills

BNi Publications, Inc.

EDITOR-IN-CHIEF

William D. Mahoney

TECHNICAL SERVICES

The Staff
of
New Promise, Inc.

COVER DESIGN

Debora Valencia

BNI Publications, Inc.

LOS ANGELES
10801 National Blvd. Suite 100
Los Angeles, CA 90064

ANAHEIM
1612 S. Clementine St.
Anaheim CA 92802

BOSTON
629 Highland Ave.
Needham, MA 02494

WASHINGTON, D.C.
502 Maple Ave. West
Vienna, VA 22180

1-800-873-6397

ISBN 155701258X

Copyright ® 1998 by BNI Publications, Inc. All rights reserved. Printed in the United States of America. Except as permitted under the United States Copyright Act of 1976, no part of this publication may be reproduced or distributed in any form or by any means, or stored in a data base or retrieval system, without the prior written permission of the publisher.

While diligent effort is made to provide reliable, accurate and up-to-date information, neither BNI Publications Inc., nor its authors or editors, can place a guarantee on the correctness of the data or information contained in this book. BNI Publications Inc., and its authors and editors, do hereby disclaim any responsibility or liability in connection with the use of this book or of any data or other information contained therein.

Table of Contents

Course Listings and Descriptions

Taking College Courses by Computer

The Internet University is a *virtual* campus. Not a university in the traditional sense, the campus of the Internet University exists solely in its connections. Colleges and universities that offer online courses have created this community that lives and operates in the combination of personal computers, Internet servers and a roster of thousands of courses. Thousands of students attend this virtual 'University' every day, and many more are signing on as the years fly by.

Some of these students are first-timers who have gotten their Internet connections to take a few courses; some are resuming their academic careers where they left off to address the demands of life and family. Perhaps some need a particular course — accounting, composition or management — to advance a career. Others may be exploring a subject area for curiosity or personal fulfillment. For any number of reasons there are many candidates for whom the principle of an Internet University is ideal.

Scope of this book

This book gives you an introduction to college courses online.

We consider a course to be online if:

- **the primary link between student and professor occurs via the Internet**

- **student enrollments are accepted from the general public**

- **no campus visits are required**

What You Need for the Internet University

All that the electronic student needs to participate in this once-elite process is a computer, online access, academic prerequisites where necessary, and for courses that are not free, the tuition. People with young children, a career, living in remote locations, physical disability, etc. are now able to move freely in the world of college education. The essentials:

Computer - An IBM-compatible or Macintosh computer is recommended, and just about any of these will work. There are stories of people who have attended class on a Commodore 64, but this book assumes use of a relatively current model of personal computer, and the basic skills necessary to turn the thing on and get to work with it (primarily word processing and 'Web surfing').

Online Access - Modem connection to a service provider is another prime ingredient — commercial online services, dial-up lines or links to connected local networks are the main sources. An alternative route to the Internet is a corporate, local library or other institutional network.

Academic Prerequisites - Standards parallel those in traditional schools this information is generally established through consultation with individual schools or guidance counselors. Where possible, this book assists in determining these prerequisites during the process of selecting a college, university or other institution.

Tuition - Credit course tuition is roughly comparable to fees paid at a campus, from $100 to $300 per credit or more. If the course is related to skill development for work requirements, these costs may be tax deductible. Corporations often extend tuition support to their employees, and colleges often will provide financial assistance, even for online courses. Many noncredit courses and 'freelance' educational opportunities (unstructured personal development courses) are free; these abound on the Internet.

Schooling of any sort in the late '90's generally involves use of computers. If you are equipped to take courses at your local college, or if you could take them if you had a local college, chances are you'll be able to attend online. The revolution in education-delivery brought about by the Internet is bringing access to college to the widest population ever.

The Nature of the Virtual Classroom

A *virtual* experience differs from a *real* experience in that it occurs primarily in the minds of the participants. When we participate in a telephone conversation it can be said that we are involved in a synchronous virtual event — that is, we are not actually with the other person, but we are nonetheless involved in a genuine real-time conversation. We experience the familiarity of the other person's voice, their interaction with our voice; and in our minds we mutually create a communications event. By using the telephone infrastructure, and despite the physical distance, we are virtually face-to-face (or 'mouth-to-ear'). Distance is a state of mind.

Similarly, correspondence by mail, with interactions separated by days, can be said to be an asynchronous virtual conversation. Again, as in the example of the phone conversation, we are exchanging information with our correspondent from different locations, though not at the same time. We substitute the 'mental' senses of our imagination for our real-world senses during the course of this virtual conversation. If our correspondent writes something funny, we laugh as if they are telling it to us in 'real-time': if the conversation turns sour, we experience it directly.

Creating the Virtual Classroom: With every instance of communication, those in communication create a mutually-imagined virtual 'place', whether this communication involves two or twenty persons. From within this 'place' a transfer of knowledge, technique and perspective can occur. With paper mail, a more primitive technology, it naturally takes longer for this 'place' to be established, and effective group interaction is quite limited. The Internet lends immediacy; a powerful educational environment.

In the virtual classroom, the effect of closeness and participation between those attending can be as real and engaging as with traditional class structures. Some participants even report an improved performance because the asynchronous nature of the discussion allows for a more studied and reflective analysis of the course materials.

Whether by email or paper mail, the students of the virtual classroom enter a cooperative conceptual event — they create a 'classroom' that is all their own. With email and a class mailing list, students 'attend' by logging on, downloading the day's correspondence and uploading responses they have written in response to yesterday's mail. This interplay of statements, moderated by the instructor, creates a rich academic experience.

Adding to Traditional Approaches: In many ways the experience of the virtual classroom parallels that of the traditional classroom. Students establish personal relationships with each other, and study groups are arranged. This academic discourse reaches a high level due in part to the effect of the correspondence being text-based. This format induces participants to compose their interactions, which leads to careful consideration in writing and rewriting of submissions.

Unlike with direct perception, reading conveys information to the mind through common understanding of symbols and graphics. Words must be 'decoded' in order for the individual to gather meaning from them. However, once we are literate, information from print tends to be absorbed almost immediately into memories, creating knowledge which is often indistinguishable from that gathered directly from reality.

Paper mail can carry 'words' quite well. Thus, the original paper basis of distance education worked quite well. Imagine though, the early days when mail was long delayed, and arrived irregularly. Even under those conditions distance learning worked, and with the tools of the Internet the process is enhanced. The immediacy and incredible variety of online communications and at a sources of the Internet brings people wanting to return to school many unanticipated benefits.

The new world of the Internet University, with email, ftp, Telnet and the Web, provide us with an accelerated and much broadened educational experience. As more people and educational institutions understand the benefits to providers of distance electronic education, and as greater technologies that increase speed and bandwidth evolve, the use of the Internet in education will become commonplace.

Internet Tools Used by the Student

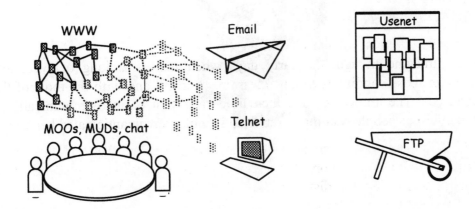

Class Mailing List in Operation

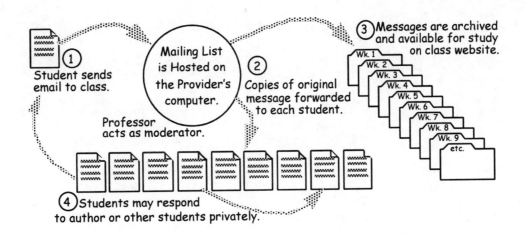

Choosing Your Online Course Provider

CASO's database lists over two hundred accredited colleges or universities which offer (or are planning to offer) online courses. Some of these offer fewer than ten courses, some over 100. Tuition ranges from $60 per credit to $300 or more. Undergrad, postgrad, CEU and certificate courses are available. Some providers will decrease tuition for non-credit option. Choosing which of these many providers to attend will be a matter of identifying where your needs correspond with what they are offering. So, you can see, with the wide range of options available, some study will be needed to choose your course provider:

We've identified each provider according to:

1. **Names of the courses they offer, with credits, dates, platform**
2. **Tuition and other costs**
3. **Which degrees (if any) they offer online**
4. **Level of courses offered; undergrad, graduate, certificate, CEU**
5. **Mode of course transmission; email, web, specialty**
6. **Accrediting agency**

The usual route that persons visiting our website take is to study the COURSE INDEX. Match a particular course to our requirements, taking note of the course number. The CASO indexing system places a four-character provider code before the institution's course number. In the following example, the University of Massachusetts - Dartmouth is offering the course. Note the 'MADA' appended before the "#" sign and the course number:

Online Interpersonal Communications
University of Massachusetts - Dartmouth

| MADA#CMP302 | Undergraduate | 0 credits | $135 |

The Internet now offers a fascinating (and bewildering) variety of interpersonal communications tools ranging from Email to the exciting new collaborative environments using phone, whiteboards, and interactive video. In this course we will examine these choices, as well as the effect they have on the quality of the interaction that takes place. This is a basic course in the Online Communications Skills Program and should be taken before, at the same time, or right after the WebCraft course.

This course can be tracked in our index using this code, and it is listed in the Catalog with the other courses that UMass-Dartmouth offers.

Identifying Course Provider Particulars

The CASO Internet University Guide identifies accredited colleges and universities in the US which offer courses that can be taken over the Internet. Some of these course are strictly email-based, and in that way are really just a modern version of traditional distance education. Others employ the most current tools of the Internet. Our selection criteria state that in order to be included a provider must be accredited, not require campus visits, and open the courses to public enrollment. The list in this book includes providers which meet these criteria, and lists courses that we've verified before the publishing date.

Accreditation: Courses listed in our Catalog are provided by colleges or universities accredited by one of the following agencies as recognized by The Council for Higher Education Accreditation (CHEA). To learn about the accreditation process visit the CHEA website (http://www.chea.org/).

> Middle States Association of Colleges and Schools
> North Central Association of Colleges and Schools
> New England Association of Schools and Colleges
> Northwest Association of Schools and Colleges
> Southern Association of Colleges and Schools
> Western Association of Schools and Colleges
> Distance Education and Training Council

Courses offered: The particulars for each course are identified: number of credits: (some may be quoted in 'quarter-credits'), dates, platform and tuition and mode.

Tuition and other costs: Institutional policies and expected costs are outlined. Remember that there may be additional costs, and that this is only a guide; for your own protection discuss the matter of costs fully with the provider. In virtually all cases it will be necessary to meet all costs before the course starts.

Online degrees (if any), and level of courses offered: A relatively few providers will offer the complete range of courses necessary for a degree, though this is growing in popularity. Some providers offer undergraduate-level courses only while others offer grad courses. Some offer both.

The
Internet
University

Your Guide To On-Line College Courses

Arts and Humanities

American Literature

Art History

Drama

TV and Film

Folklore

General

Music

Other

Philosophy and Ethics

Religion

US History

Visual Arts

Writing

19th Century American Literature
California State University - Dominguez Hills
CADO#HUX575 Undergraduate 3 credits $405
Studies in the American literary tradition focusing on classic fiction by Hawthorne, Twain, Howells, and James, writers who established the mainstream of our creative aesthetic. Their novels, exploring evil, guilt and sin, chronicle America's spiritual uncertainties and social turbulence. Prerequisite: HUX502 is recommended.

Advanced Ceramic Processing
State University of New York
SUNY#CES510001 Graduate 3 credits $1038*
This course provides a review of all relevant issues concerning the processing and sintering of advanced ceramic materials - discussing powder preparation and characterization, colloidal and sol-gel techniques, powder consolidation and forming, sintering theory and practice, and microstructure evolution. The course shows the importance of each step, and the critical interconnections among steps, in the overall fabrication of ceramics...focuses on the formation of ceramics by firing consolidated powders...reveals which ceramic manufacturing methods are easier to employ and why...covers the properties of colloidal suspensions...elucidates the fundamentals of sintering polycrystalline ceramics...and more.
* NY residents tuition: $137 per credit

Advanced Screenwriting
University of Colorado
CUON#ENGL3418 Undergraduate 3 credits $1953*
Offers students opportunities at advanced levels to conceptualize, structure, and write screenplays . Building upon the structural and stylistic elements in that course, students will complete an original feature-length screenplay. Prerequisite: ENGL2418.
* CO residents tuition: $136 per credit.

African-American Literature
University of Minnesota
MINN#GC1816 Undergraduate 4 credits $356
In this course, students will study and evaluate the poetry, drama, folklore, short stories, and longer fiction of black authors. Students will assess the artists' perceptions and interpretations of black culture in America from colonial times to the present.

African-American Literature
University of Missouri
MOCE#LI104A Undergraduate 3 credits $387
Using a socio-historical approach, this course surveys the writing of black authors from the mid-19th century to the 1960s. Perquisites: English 20 or equivalent.

Age of Enlightenment
Western Illinois University
WEIL#HIS426G Undergraduate 3 credits $795*
Explores the evolution of enlightenment in Europe, 1648-1789, and those modern secular attitudes toward religion, politics, and society associated with the names of John Locke, Frederick the Great, Voltaire, and the French philosophers. The course surveys the most significant events and personalities of the era and examines closely Voltaire's Candide as well as selected works of art and architecture.
* IL residents tuition: $88 per credit.

Agents, Managers, Producers and Others
University of Colorado
CUON#MUS3760 Undergraduate 3 credits $1953*
A study of the various individuals who comprise the artist's 'team' those who act as 'intermediaries' between the artist and the various buyers, from the multinational entertainment conglomerate to the ultimate consumer. To include a study of the functions of the personal manager, business manager, booking agent, producer, merchandiser and attorney from the artist's perspective and the perspective of each professional. The "in's and out's" of touring, (setting up a tour, artist compensation, tour promotion, etc.) and tips on 'deal shopping' will also be provided.
* CO residents tuition: $136 per credit.

Air Photo Interpretation
University of South Florida
FLSO#GEO4124 Undergraduate ?? credits $???
This course will offer a comprehensive overview of photographic and non-photographic remote sensing. It will look at the different systems utilized to collect remotely sensed information and what techniques are used to classify and interpret the imagery. Applications of air photo interpretation will be studied and evaluated for their usefulness as a problem-solving tool. The course material will concentrate heavily on the theory of remote sensing and the importance of understanding how different sensor platforms operate. Lab materials will be used to give the students a 'hands-on' approach as to how photo interpretation is carried out.

America Since 1970, The Mirror of the Movies
State University of New York
SUNY#AHI315585 Undergraduate 4 credits $1038*
As Americans, we never seem to tire of asking ourselves: Who are we' As our nation approaches a multiracial, multiethnic twenty-first century, the answers to our questions have never been more infinite nor more unsettled. As art and as commerce, as calculated entertainment and as auteur-driven vision, film has consistently offered intriguing and provocative answers to the puzzle of the American identity, past and present. Special Requirements: Students will need to have access to a VHS videotape deck and monitor, and will need to rent films specified in the syllabus from their local video store.
* NY residents tuition: $137 per credit

America, 1945 to the Present
University of Missouri
MOCE#HI308B   Undergraduate   3 credits $387

This course traces the role of America since World War II. Topics include aid to Europe; the Korean War; domestic, political, and cultural changes through the Eisenhower years; the New Frontier; the Great Society; the changes in the 1970s and early 1980s; the civil rights crisis; and the development of the welfare state.

American Cinema
Thomas Edison State College
THED#OLFIL110   Undergraduate   3 credits $397*

Introductory course in film studies, and in a broader sense, a language course-the language of the motion picture. Students will learn to become more active and critical viewers as they question the images of America they see on the movie screen and redefine their own relationship to those images. The course covers films as art, as cultural artifacts, as an economic force and as a system of representation and communication. It also includes the invention of the motion picture camera, the studio system, and different types of films, and the evolution of characters.

* NJ residents tuition: $33 per credit.

American Civilization
University of Missouri
MOCE#HI3   Undergraduate   3 credits $387

An introduction to U.S. history through the Civil War, this course surveys the political, economic, social, and cultural development of the American people.

American Civilization Since 1865
University of Missouri
MOCE#HI4   Undergraduate   3 credits $387

An introduction to U.S. history since 1865, this course surveys political, economic, social, and cultural development of the American people.

American Constitutional History I
University of Minnesota
MINN#HIST5331   Undergraduate   4 credits $391

The origins and developments of constitutional government in America with emphasis on the role of constitutional politics in the evolution of public policy. This course focuses on the English and colonial background through the Reconstruction period.

American Constitutional History II
University of Minnesota
MINN#HIST5332   Undergraduate   4 credits $391

Continuation of HIST5331, but need not be taken in sequence. Emphasizes the Constitution and the rule of law in modern America. Includes an optional videocassette with discussions of the Constitution by eminent judges and scholars. Students must indicate whether they want to take the course with or without the optional videocassette.

American Culture
UCLA
UCLA#X325F   Undergraduate   2 credits $300

The majority of foreign students who study English--both in their respective countries and in the United States--are interested in learning not only about the language but the culture as well. From baseball to literature, popular music to the animated films of Walt Disney, slang to debates about social, legal, and moral issues, American culture is a surprisingly rich, constantly evolving proposition.

American Cultures II
University of Minnesota
MINN#AMST1002   Undergraduate   4 credits $356

Interdisciplinary study of the diversity of American cultures, 1890-1945. Major topics: urban life and leisure, changing family and gender roles, race and national identity. Explores experiences and cultural products of European Americans, Native Americans, African Americans, Asian Americans, and Chicanos.

American Cultures III
University of Minnesota
MINN#AMST1003   Undergraduate   4 credits $356

Interdisciplinary study of diversity of American cultures, 1945 to present. Major topics: family practices and gender roles, social change movements (civil rights movement, American Indian movement, women's movement), and the politics of popular culture (music, television, fashion, art). Explores experiences and cultural products of European Americans, Native Americans, African Americans, and Chicanos.

American History I
University of Minnesota
MINN#HIST1301   Undergraduate   5 credits $445

An investigation of U.S. history from colonial times through Reconstruction. This course emphasizes political, economic, social, and diplomatic history. The assignments cover a wide variety of topics, including the witchcraft trials of Salem, slavery and the American Republic, the Revolution, and the Civil War. Students are required to view two videocassettes, Glory and Drums along the Mohawk.

American History I
New York Institute of Technology
NYIT#SS2500   Undergraduate   3 credits $???

The political, social, cultural, and economic factors pertaining to American history and civilization up to the year 1865. Two major areas of study are the colonial era through the American Revolution, and the nineteenth century.

American History I to 1865
Rogers State University
ROGE#HIST2483 Undergraduate 3 credits $495*
The great drama of the discovery of America and the founding of our nation as a series of tiny, struggling colonies marks the beginning of this course. The course explores how European settlers, seeking religious freedom and economic opportunity, shaped our nation out of the wilderness, developed a culture, and set a revolution in motion. It takes us through the shaping of our political system, the burgeoning of the industrial revolution, through the years before the Civil War and the war itself. Video: The American Adventure (Coast Community College Telecourses).
* OK residents $315.

American History II
University of Minnesota
MINN#HIST1302 Undergraduate 5 credits $445
An investigation of American history from 1880 to the present. Students will study "Captains of Industry" and the rise of industrial America; the populist and progressive reform movements; the world wars; the depression and the New Deal; the cold war, the civil rights movement, the women's movement, the Vietnam War, and the Reagan years.

American History II
New York Institute of Technology
NYIT#SS2510 Undergraduate 3 credits $???
A survey of American history from 1865 to the present. Particular attention is given to the various political movements and the four major wars. The American position as a world power and its role in international affairs. Effects of the growth of labor unions and corporations as integrated into merging historical patterns. Prerequisite: SS2500.

American History II from 1865
Rogers State University
ROGE#HIST2493 Undergraduate 3 credits $495*
The drama of the development of American society continues as the country grows into a world power. Topics include: Reconstruction, closing of the frontier, industrialism, overseas expansion, progressivism, the Twenties, depression and the New Deal, world leadership. Video: The American Perspective (Coast Community College Telecourses).
* OK residents $315.

American History since 1877
Mercy College
MERC#HI106 Undergraduate 3 credits $900
A general survey from the end of Reconstruction to the recent past. Major themes will be the development of American domestic politics; the nation's emergence as a world power; changes in American society, economy and culture; and the influence of past events on contemporary life.

American History Since 1877
Western Illinois University
WEIL#HIS106 Undergraduate 3 credits $795*
Traces events from the end of the Reconstruction era to the present. Module I (1877-1900) includes the growth of industry during the Gilded Age, the politics of the era, protest efforts of wage earners and farmers, American overseas expansion, and the emergence of American cities. Module II (1900-1938) covers the evolution of the Progressive Movement, America's entry involvement in World War I, the paradoxical nature of the 1920s, and the New Deal response to the Great Depression. Module III (1938-present) highlights the historical developments of this era, including America's deepening involvement in international affairs.
* IL residents tuition: $88 per credit.

American History through 1877
Mercy College
MERC#HI105 Undergraduate 3 credits $900
A general survey from the Age of Discovery through the end of Reconstruction, covering such major developments as the emergence and growth of the thirteen colonies; the founding and organization of the nation state; changing political, social, and economic patterns; and the origins and impact of the Civil War.

American History to 1877
University of North Alabama
NOAL#HIST201 Undergraduate 3 credits $258
This course is the first in a two-semester sequence dealing with the history of the United States, from the "discovery" of the so-called New World through the American Civil War--what Bernard De Voto has termed "the crux of our history." Most assuredly, this course is not about everything that happened up until then. Rather it is designed to introduce students to the significant people and events that influenced social, intellectual, economic, and political developments in the United States.

American History to 1877
Western Illinois University
WEIL#HIS105 Undergraduate 3 credits $795*
Surveys the history of the United States through the Civil War and Reconstruction. People--how they lived and why they made the choices they did--figure prominently in the story. Emphasis is on causes, meaning, insight into significant episodes, and relevance for the present. Where historians differ, alternative interpretations are presented. After successfully completing this course, you will be a wiser conversationalist and a more effective voter and citizen-lobbyist.
* IL residents tuition: $88 per credit.

American Immigration 1884-1984
University of Minnesota
MINN#HIST3910 Undergraduate 4 credits $391
History of a century of American immigration. Considers migration patterns, ethnic communities and conflict, maintenance of ethnic cultures, immigration legislation, social mobility, and the emergence of a pluralistic America. Students will compare immigrant experiences in both urban and rural settings.

American Indian History 1850 to the Present
University of Minnesota
MINN#AMIN3112 **Undergraduate 4 credits $391**
Completes American Indian history from pre-contact to the present. Stresses general themes in Native American history and focuses on the efforts of Native American nations to control their cultural destiny against the efforts of the U.S. government to forcibly assimilate them into European culture. Discusses the ways change is incorporated within the belief systems of Native American cultures from the perspective of members of those cultures, connects U.S. Indian policy to national and international events, and explores the tension between cultural persistence and incorporation of change within both Native American and European American cultures.

American Indian History I (15th Century to 1850)
University of Minnesota
MINN#AMIN3111 **Undergraduate 4 credits $391**
Explores the history of Native North American nations and groups from the pre-European-contact period to the end of the removal period. Addresses central themes relating to various Native American cultures, as well as their interactions with various European invaders. Brief case studies highlight the complexity and diversity of Native American groups. Stresses the integrity and viability of Native American societies, the dynamism of their largely self-directed culture change in response to contact with other Native American groups and European invaders, and the duality of the culture change--European invaders were also profoundly changed by the clash of cultures.

American Labor History
Indiana University
INDI#L101 **Undergraduate 3 credits $268**
A survey of the origin and development of unions and the labor movement from colonial times to the present. The struggle of working people to achieve a measure of dignity and security is examined from social, economic, and political perspectives.

American Literary Masterpieces
University of Missouri
MOCE#LI17 **Undergraduate 3 credits $387**
An introduction to major themes and works in American literature emphasizing the nineteenth century to the present, this course studies literary pieces from Hawthorne, Twain, Faulkner, O'Connor, and others.

American Literature
University of Missouri
MOCE#LI175 **Undergraduate 3 credits $387**
A survey of major American writers from colonial days to the present, this course provides an overall view of the development of American literature.

American Literature
Strayer University
STRA#ENG220 **Undergraduate 4.5 credits $665**
Provides a critical survey of the development of American literature from its origins to the present. Covers major authors and works critical to an understanding of major literary genres. Discusses the relationship between society and the rise of specific literary movements.

American Literature Before 1860
Rio Salado College
RISA#ENH241 **Undergraduate 3 credits $186***
Includes literature written prior to 1860 in the United States.
* AZ residents pay $37 per credit.

American Literature I
Brevard Community College
BREV#AML2012 **Undergraduate 3 credits $435**
A critical survey and study of American literature from the early period to 1865. Students are required to rent course related films locally. Prerequisite: appropriate placement test scores in reading and writing.

American Literature II
Fayetteville Technical Community College
FAYE#ENG232 **Undergraduate 3 credits $489***
This course covers selected works in American literature from 1865 to the present. Emphasis is placed on historical background, cultural context, and literary analysis of selected prose, poetry, and drama. Upon completion, students should be able to interpret, analyze, and respond to literary works in their historical and cultural contexts. This course has been approved to satisfy the Comprehensive Articulation Agreement general education core requirement in humanities/fine arts. Prerequisites: ENG112, ENG113, or ENG114.
* NC residents pay $20 per credit.

American Literature since 1914
Indiana University
INDI#L354 **Undergraduate 3 credits $268**
American writers since 1914: Toomer, Hemingway, Faulkner, Fitzgerald, O'Neill, Eliot, and Frost.

American Music - Rock and Roll
University of Iowa
IOWA#045075 **Undergraduate 3 credits $240**
Rock and roll is more than just music. It is a socially defined art movement which began in the early 1950's with its own language, style, and value system. Rock and roll is a continually developing subculture, and while its forms of expression may vary, one element has remained constant. It is always in rebellion against the hegemony of the predominant forms of expression and the ethos which they endorse. While it was easy to distinguish between Chuck Berry and Perry Como in 1955, it has become much harder to perceive the differences between rock and roll and popular music in the 1980's.

American Poetry - A Survey
University of Missouri
MOCE#LI101A   Undergraduate   3 credits $387
In this course, students read and evaluate works by ten poets, dating from the mid-19th century to the 1960s.

American Politics through Film and Fiction
Indiana University
INDI#Y373   Undergraduate   3 credits $268
The recurrent theme of power in politics is explored in depth by means of five novels and five films. From a list of selected works, students must choose and locate the novels and videos, many of which may be borrowed from libraries. Film choices include El Norte, Reds, Citizen Kane, The Candidate, Mr. Smith Goes to Washington, All the King's Men, JFK, Apocalypse Now, Absence of Malice, And Justice for All, Roger and Me, Do the Right Thing, Norma Rae, Network, Fahrenheit 451, The Last Hurrah, and China Syndrome.

American Short Story
University of Minnesota
MINN#ENGL3455   Undergraduate   4 credits $391
Historical developments of the literary forms of the short story in American culture. Students read the works of Irving, Poe, Melville, Crane, Cather, Hemingway, Updike, Cheever, and others.

American Social History, 1865 to Present
Indiana University
INDI#A317   Undergraduate   3 credits $268
America's transformation from being a predominantly rural to a predominantly urban nation; and how that transformation impacted our social groups, institutions, and values.

American Women's History
Eastern Oregon University
EAOR#HIST410A   Undergraduate   5 credits $415
Traces change over time related to American women. Deals with group subjugation wherein gender analyses is informed by consideration of race and class.

An Introduction to Film
Indiana University
INDI#C190   Undergraduate   3 credits $268
Nature of film technique and film language; analysis of specific films and introduction to major critical approaches in film studies.

Ancient Greek Philosophy
Indiana University
INDI#P201   Undergraduate   3 credits $268
Selective survey of ancient Greek philosophy (pre-Socratics, Plato, Aristotle). Recommended: 3 credit hours of philosophy.

Ancient Mayan Art
California State University - Dominguez Hills
CADO#HUX576   Undergraduate   3 credits $405
An examination of the art and architecture of the Mayan civilization in Mesoamerica in the context of its history, mythology and archaeology. Prerequisite: HUX501 and HUX504 are recommended.

Andersen and the Scandinavian Fairy Tale
University of Minnesota
MINN#SCAN3602   Undergraduate   4 credits $391
An exploration of Hans Christian Andersen's stories and tales (in English).

Anthropology of Religion
Western Illinois University
WEIL#ANT324   Undergraduate   3 credits $795*
Is a comparative study of people's beliefs. This course is concerned with how people's beliefs and religious practices influence their lives. Topics include the concepts and approaches to studying religion and an examination of two belief systems--one African, one Korean.
* IL residents tuition: $88 per credit.

Archetypal Criticism in Literature
California State University - Dominguez Hills
CADO#HUX573   Undergraduate   3 credits $405
Exploration of a 20th century movement in literature, archetypal criticism, which focuses on recurrent patterns in literature and their analogies in folk tales, dream, ritual and myth.

Art & Culture II
Pima Community College
PIMA#ART131   Undergraduate   3 credits $165*
This is a survey of western civilization's major contributions to the development of sculpture, painting, and architecture from the Late Gothic period into the Contemporary World. students will explore computer generated images on web sites relevant to textbook reading assignments, link into current art historical research, and participate in on-line discussions based on weekly assignments. Student testing will take place both on-line and a Pima Community College approved testing centers.
* AZ residents, $32/credit hour.

Art & Lit of Harlem Renaissance
California State University - Dominguez Hills
CADO#HUX531   Undergraduate   3 credits $405
An exploration of the literary and visual art of the Harlem Renaissance within the political and philosophical framework of the movement. The course will focus on the radicalism of the period and its influence on art and literature. The self-help ideology of Marcus Garvey, the philosophies of Alain Locke and W.E.B. DuBois, and the historical significance of the migration of rural southern blacks to New York City will serve as a basis for study of the material.

Art Aesthetics and Theory
California State University - Dominguez Hills
CADO#HUX504   Undergraduate   2 credits $270
Advanced study of key concepts in art by focusing on aesthetics and art theory.

Art Appreciation
Fayetteville Technical Community College
FAYE#ART111   Undergraduate   3 credits $489*
This course introduces the origins and historical development of art. Emphasis is placed on the relationship of design principles to various art forms including but not limited to sculpture, painting, and architecture. Upon completion, students should be able to identify and analyze a variety of artistic styles, periods, and media. This course has been approved to satisfy the Comprehensive Articulation Agreement general education core requirement in humanities/fine arts.
* North Carolina residents and non-resident US military personnel stationed within the state tuition: $60; NC senior citizens: free.

Art History & Appreciation
Barstow Community College
BARS#ARTS2   Undergraduate   3 credits $???
Understanding of the resources and value of the arts and the significance of taste and style. History of painting, sculpture and architecture from Gothic Art to the present.

Art History I, Prehistoric-Middle Ages
Yavapai Community College
YAVA#ART200   Undergraduate   ?? credits $???
(Course description not available at press time.)

Art History II - 1400-1850
Rogers State University
ROGE#ART2723   Undergraduate   3 credits $495*
The study in chronological sequence of major art styles and movements from 1400 to 1850 AD. Video: Art History 1400-1850 (Lectures 1-28).
* OK residents $315.

Art History Seminar - Women Artists
University of Northern Colorado
CONO#ART680   Graduate   4 credits $320
Survey of women artists working in Western tradition from the Middle Ages to the Twentieth Century, including women artists of color. Uses videotapes, readings, Website, e-mail. 8 discussions, one research paper, final exam/studio project. Student must have Internet address.

Art History Survey
Mercy College
MERC#AR107   Undergraduate   3 credits $900
A one-semester survey of the history of art from cave-painting to the modern era: the understanding and appreciation of style; the social, religious, political, and literary conditions influencing artistic trends. Lectures, discussions, films, slides.

Art Nouveau
New School for Social Research
NEWS#4013   Undergraduate   3 credits $1092
At the end of the 19th century, architects and designers spread fantasy and invention throughout Europe while searching for an original expression for the new century. Explore the Art Nouveau movement and its various styles from the sensuous, exuberant style of Victor Horta, Hector Guimard, Emile Galle, and L'Ecole de Nancy, to the restrained, linear style of C.R. Mackintosh, Josef Hoffman and the Vienna Secession. Examine the architecture, furniture and decorative objects of these designers and many others who captured the essence of the fin-de-siecle.

Art of Being Human
Brevard Community College
BREV#HUM2390   Undergraduate   3 credits $485
An interdisciplinary introduction to the humanities. Each unit represents a major theme, problem or aspect of human existence explored through art, music, literature, philosophy, drama and religion. Prerequisite: appropriate test scores in reading and writing.

Asian-American Literature
University of Minnesota
MINN#GC1836   Undergraduate   4 credits $356
The challenges presented to Asian immigrants and their children are examined in this course, with special attention to the clash between ethnic identity and the American situation. Students will analyze historical and contemporary works by Carlos Bulosan, Louis Chu, Joy Kogawa, Amy Tan, and others.

Baroque Music
California State University - Dominguez Hills
CADO#HUX571   Undergraduate   3 credits $405
An examination of Baroque music and the period in Western Europe (1600-1750) during which it evolved. The ability to read music is not required, though helpful.

Baroque through Modern Arts
New Hampshire College
NEHA#HUM202   Undergraduate   3 credits $1656
This course introduces visual arts, music, literature, and ideas in various cultural environments, including the Baroque, Enlightenment, Romanticism, post-Romanticism and Modernism. May be taken independently of HUM201.

Baseball History
Texas Technical University
TETE#HIST3339   Undergraduate   3 credits $???
This course examines the history of the national pastime with an eye to how the sport has reflected and influenced American society since the late 19th century.

Basic Graphic Design
State University of New York
SUNY#GC111   Undergraduate   3 credits $540*
This course is an introduction to the elements and principles of design. Emphasis is placed on technical proficiency in the handling of tools and materials, and the mastery of a visual language via basic problem-solving. Prerequisites: Students must have successfully completed, or be concurrently enrolled in GC131 Studio Procedures. Special Requirements: Students must have access to a scanner to post sketches for critiques.
* NY residents tuition: $90 per credit.

Basic Photography
New School for Social Research
NEWS#2514   Undergraduate   3 credits $360
For people who manage to get film into their cameras but often find themselves disappointed after it has been processed. The class is open to photographers at various levels who want to create a unified body of work. Students can work in color or black & white. The course begins with a matching of your camera and subject matter with film that will enable you to get the most accurate exposure every time you take a picture. You learn to make photographs that appeal to an audience beyond your family and friends.

Basic Photography
State University of New York
SUNY#GC126   Undergraduate   3 credits $540*
Students will be introduced to photography and the photograph as a medium of the graphic communicator. The course will include basic photographic principles and procedures. The student will learn how to operate a 35 mm adjustable camera, develop black/white film, make contact prints and enlargements. The aesthetics of the photograph and its use as a medium of graphic communications will be emphasized.
* NY residents tuition: $90 per credit.

Basic Problems of Philosophy
Pennsylvania State University
PENN#PHIL001   Undergraduate   3 credits $345
Issues such as the foundations of knowledge, the existence of God, the problem of freedom, and the nature of reality.

Beethoven
California State University - Dominguez Hills
CADO#HUX551   Undergraduate   3 credits $405
An examination of the life and music of Ludwig Van Beethoven. The ability to read music is not required, though helpful.

Beginning & Advanced Screenwriting
Marylhurst College
MARY#WR327   Undergraduate   3 credits $651
These screenwriting workshops are designed to provide students a solid foundation for their screenplay. Students will plot, research, prepare, and write the first act of their script. The advanced workshop allows students to continue their work.

British History II for the Internet
University of Nevada-Reno
NERE#C394   Undergraduate   3 credits $210
Covers the political, social, and economic history of England and her Empire.

British Literature I
Fayetteville Technical Community College
FAYE#ENG241   Undergraduate   3 credits $489*
This course covers selected works in British literature from its beginnings to the Romantic Period. Emphasis is placed on historical background, cultural context, and literary analysis of selected prose, poetry, and drama. Upon completion, students should be able to interpret, analyze, and respond to literary works in their historical and cultural contexts. This course has been approved to satisfy the Comprehensive Articulation Agreement general education core requirement in humanities/fine arts. Prerequisites: ENG112, ENG113, or ENG114.
* NC residents pay $20 per credit.

Broadcast News Writing
State University of New York
SUNY#BRC326   Undergraduate   3 credits $1038*
Students will gather, write, and edit broadcast news. Some distinction will be made on the nature of the presentation for local and network operations and the various news agencies (such as the Associated Press). Because local radio news is the building block of all broadcast news, it shall be given special attention. Tips for those seeking entry level radio newscasting opportunities will also be included.
* NY residents tuition: $137 per credit

Broadcast Script and News Writing
City University
CITY#COM403   Undergraduate   5 qu. credits $785
This course presents the techniques of scriptwriting for video and audio productions for broadcast purposes. Students write a variety of scripts according to appropriate formats, emphasizing production language, writing styles, audio-visual elements, target audiences, conceptualization of themes, storyboards and research. Study focuses on news gathering, broadcast news writing, electronic news gathering (ENG), production techniques, news sources, and interviewing concepts. Prerequisite: Strongly Recommended: BSK210 or its equivalent.

Buddhist Influences in American Literature
New School for Social Research
NEWS#0686   Undergraduate   3 credits $1638*
How is it that Jack Kerouac came to write a life of the Buddha? We explore the fruitful encounter of American literature with Asian religion--a bumping of cultural heads that has influenced writers as different as Ralph Waldo Emerson, Jack Kerouac, Sam Hamill, and Jane Hirschfield. We read Kerouac's Dharma Bums as well as shorter works by Kerouac, Allen Ginsburg, Gary Snyder, and other Beat writers, Hamill's Destination: Zero, selections from Hirschfield's works, and even Kerouac's Beat biography of the Shakyamuni Buddha himself!.
* Non-credit option, tuition: $365.

Building Visual Collections
Marylhurst College
MARY#HUM449 Undergraduate 3 credits $651
Open to both librarians and non-librarians. This class deals with the nature and aesthetics of visual information such as video/film, scientific visualization, maps and map making, satellite resources, and visual resources on the Internet. The class offers an opportunity to examine the way representation changes information. Among those studied will be the works of Edward Tufte, Diane Ackerman, Clement Monk, and Richard Saul Murman.

California History
California State University - San Marcos
CASA#HIST347 Undergraduate 3 credits $345*
This is an upper division survey course. We will not focus on any one aspect of California history (such as social history, political history, economic history, or environmental history), or any one period, but rather will study the ways in which many elements have interacted to shape California as we now know it.
* CA residents pay $13 per credit.

Carnegie, Rockefeller and Ford
California State University - Dominguez Hills
CADO#HUX554 Undergraduate 3 credits $405
The rise of American industrial capitalism, viewed through the activities of three business giants, and the course of American economic history to the present, with special emphasis on World War I and the Great Depression.

Cartography I
Eastern Oregon University
EAOR#GEOG201 Undergraduate 3 credits $240
A survey of the physical properties and uses of maps and geodesy. Special emphasis is placed on the identification, analysis and interpretation of landscape elements utilized by geographers and planners. Lecture and laboratory. Prerequisite: GEOG105, GEOG106.

Cartography II
Eastern Oregon University
EAOR#GEOG306 Undergraduate 5 credits $410
This course is an introduction to thematic map construction, including map design, compilation of data, lettering techniques, generalization and symbolization. Prerequisite: GEOG201.

Children Literature
State University of New York
SUNY#3551202 Graduate 3 credits $1038*
Children's Literature is an area with many possibilities. It can be used as a basis for teaching reading, it can be the main theme in a unit, it can be illustrative of writing techniques. The possibilities are endless. This course is designed to provide the participant with the knowledge base to evaluate children's literature and to determine a wide range of uses for it. It is also aimed at giving the participants the opportunity to discuss the relevancy of children's literature and to examine the various strengths and concerns found in children's literature.
* NY residents tuition: $137 per credit

Children's Literature
University of Colorado-Boulder
COBO#EDUC4161 Undergraduate 3 credits $240
Reading and evaluation of books, children's interests, authors and illustrators, folk literature, multicultural literature, modern fanciful tales and trends.

Children's Literature
Indiana University
INDI#L390 Undergraduate 3 credits $268
Historical and modern children's books and selections from books; designed to assist future teachers, parents, librarians, or others in selecting the best in children's literature for each period of the child's life.

Civil War and Reconstruction
University of Minnesota
MINN#HIST3812 Undergraduate 4 credits $391
Integrates scholarly readings with the award-winning PBS video series, The Civil War. The course covers politics and society from 1848 to 1877. Topics: sectional differences and the causes of the war; the military aspects of the conflict; slavery, emancipation, and how the slaves helped transform the war into a revolutionary struggle; and Reconstruction politics.

Civil War and Reconstruction
Western Illinois University
WEIL#HIS415G Undergraduate 3 credits $795*
Is an examination of the major developments in U.S. History from the mid 1840s to the mid 1870s. Major issues to be investigated include: What caused the Civil War? Was Union victory in the Civil War inevitable? Was Reconstruction a misguided policy doomed to fail? Students will get to know the key personalities of the period such as Stephen A. Douglas, Zachary Taylor, Abraham Lincoln, Jefferson Davis, Robert E. Lee, U.S. Grant, Andrew Johnson, and Frederick Douglass.
* IL residents tuition: $88 per credit.

Civil War Literature
Northwest College
NOCO#GE261 Undergraduate 3 credits $???
Examining the literature of the United States during the period of the Civil War, readings include slave-narrations, war memoirs, short stories, poetry and a novel. Prerequisite: GE180.

Classical Mythology
Indiana University
INDI#C205 Undergraduate 3 credits $268
Introduction to Greek and Roman myths, legends, and tales, especially those that have an important place in the Western cultural tradition.

Collage with Digital Techniques
Yavapai Community College
YAVA#ART165 Undergraduate 3 credits $???
Exploration of collage techniques with computer application, the history of collage, collage applications, and compositional methods. Application of design principles.

Color and Design
State University of New York
SUNY#GC125   Undergraduate   3 credits $540*
This course is a study of the application and importance of color to graphic design. Emphasis is placed on the symbolic, aesthetic and psychological aspects of color. Experimentation and flexibility of approach are stressed, as are both two-dimensional and three-dimensional applications. Color theory, subtractive color mixing, and additive color mixing will be explored.
* NY residents tuition: $90 per credit.

Columbus and the Age of Encounter
University of Minnesota
MINN#HIST3700   Undergraduate   4 credits $391
This course places the familiar figure of Columbus in the context of the world of the late 15th century. Through the course readings, students will examine Europe and the rest of the known world, the New World of the Western Hemisphere, the motives and means through which Europeans expanded their interests around the globe, and the far-reaching consequences of Columbus's voyages.

Commentary on Art
Pennsylvania State University
PENN#ART122W   Undergraduate   3 credits $345
An introduction to verbal commentary, both oral and written, about art. The development of critical and expressive skills is given emphasis.

Communication and Society
University of Colorado-Boulder
COBO#COMM2400   Undergraduate 3 credits $270
Seeks to increase students' awareness of the ways in which gender, dialect (ethnic, regional, and social class), and cultural background influence communication behavior and its consequences. Deepens understanding of communication as a social process, making students more sophisticated observers and participants in their own and other cultures.

Comparative Philosophical Concepts
Strayer University
STRA#HUM205   Undergraduate   4.5 credits $665
Studies perennial philosophical issues and concepts facing man. Examines epistemological, political, religious, and socioeconomic questions.

Composition
Charter Oak State College
CHOA#ENG101   Undergraduate   3 credits $390*
This course will deal with short and long expository papers and the elements of style which articulate well organized writing. All students will learn research techniques and will write a research paper.
* CT residents pay $95 per credit.

Composition
College of DuPage
DUPA#EN101   Undergraduate   3 qu. credits $90
These three English writing courses make up the traditional 1-year freshman composition sequence. They are designed to introduce the student college level writing as a process of developing and supporting a thesis in organized essay. The emphasis is on using diction and language, reading and responding to the writing of others and observing the conventions of standard written English. The second course has more of an emphasis on reading, thinking and writing critically including the ability to analyze and evaluate the ideas of others and integrate them into their own writings.

Composition - Exposition
University of Washington
WASH#ENGLC131   Undergraduate ?? credits $370
Study and practice of good writing: topics derived from a variety of personal, academic and public subjects. By the end of this course, students will be able to read and evaluate complex material; revise essays and discuss essays of other students in terms of responsiveness, thesis, support, development, unity and presentation; and revise their own writing at both the macro level (i.e., content and organization issues) and the micro level (i.e., paragraph- and sentence-level issues). Instructor: Linda Avraamides, doctoral candidate, comparative literature.

Composition I
Roane State Community College
ROAN#ENG101   Undergraduate   3 credits $459*
Narrative, descriptive, expository, and argumentative writing as applicable to major fields of study and societal issues. Research paper required.
* Tennessee residents tuition: $48 per semester hour.

Computers in the Humanities
Dakota State University
DAKO#CHUM650   Undergraduate   4 credits $550
A study of computer applications in the humanities such as analysis of texts, arranging data from research, and formatting for printing and desktop publishing. Prerequisite: Be able to execute DOS and Windows and to download files from Web sites.

Concert Music
California State University - Dominguez Hills
CADO#HUX522   Undergraduate   3 credits $405
Attendance and analysis of several concerts representing the general categories of symphonic, vocal and chamber music. Critical reviews required for each of six musical encounters.

Contemporary Art
California State University - Dominguez Hills
CADO#HUX570   Undergraduate   3 credits $405
Exploration of the complex cultural development known as modern art by investigation of six major artistic movements: Cubism, Expressionism, Dada/Surrealism, Pop Art, Conceptual Art and Technological Art.

Contemporary Cinema
Rio Salado College
RISA#HUM210 Undergraduate 3 credits $186*
A study of contemporary films, directors and critics with emphasis on evaluating film as an art form.
* AZ residents $37 per credit.

Contemporary Ethics
Thomas Edison State College
THED#OLPHI286 Undergraduate 3 credits $397*
Examines contemporary ethical conflicts and provides a grounding in the language, concepts, and traditions of ethics. At the core of the course, experts from government, the press, medicine, law, business and the military grapple with moral concerns that arise in both personal and professional life. Following a case study approach, the course provides students with the intellectual tools to analyze moral dilemmas in the fields they choose to pursue - and in the society in which all of us live.
* NJ residents tuition: $33 per credit.

Contemporary Moral Problems
MiraCosta College
MIRA#PHIL02 Undergraduate 3 credits $357
In this course we will be studying why, how, and to what extent one should care about the environment. There are obvious prudential (self-interested) answers to these questions -- we should care about the natural environment because its destruction and degradation decreases longevity and happiness for us and our families. The moral answers to these questions are much less obvious, yet these are the focus of this course. Prerequisite: The Environmental Ethics and Policy Book, 2d ed.; Donald VanDeVeer and Christine Pierce Ishmael, by Daniel Quinn.

Contemporary World
New York Institute of Technology
NYIT#SS2540 Undergraduate 3 credits $???
The transformation of Europe as a consequence of the First and Second World Ward; the polarity of the postwar world; the impotence of the superpowers; the impact of science and technology; the image of contemporary man in literature and visual arts; and the search for meaning in the twentieth century.

Core Composition I
University of Colorado
CUON#ENGL1020 Undergraduate 3 credits $1953*
Core Composition I develops the writing of long, well-structured, and graceful essays. Writers passing this course will enrich their writing with strong material, organization, and focus; and they will write with excellent sentence structure, grammar, and mechanics.
* CO residents tuition: $136 per credit.

Core Composition II
University of Colorado
CUON#ENGL2030 Undergraduate 3 credits $1953*
Emphasis on the documented essay, structure of argument, and the research paper in a workshop setting. Prerequisite: ENGL1020.
* CO residents tuition: $136 per credit.

Creating Culture
Marylhurst College
MARY#HUM355 Undergraduate 3 credits $651
We make sense of our lives and our identities within the realm of our own selective experiences. This course examines definitions of identity, culture, and the way we move through everyday life, and offers skills and insights to move more successfully through the saturation of late 20th-century media.

Creative Typography
State University of New York
SUNY#GC210 Undergraduate 3 credits $540*
This course is an introduction to creative applications of typography. Students will build upon the vocabulary they have already learned by mastering a series of visual problems typographically. Historic and contemporary applications will be demonstrated. In executing their graphic solutions, students will work in both traditional and digital media. Prerequisites: GC125 Color and Design, and GC141 Digital Illustration.
* NY residents tuition: $90 per credit.

Creative Writing
Barstow Community College
BARS#ENGL7 Undergraduate 3 credits $???
An introductory course to the creative writing process in which students produce a body of creative fiction: poetry, short story and drama. Word processing as a creative wring and editing device. May be taken twice for credit.

Creative Writing
Northwest College
NOCO#GE279 Undergraduate 3 credits $???
Students practice writing creatively by using both hemispheres of the brain: left-brain-oriented expository writing (e.g., letters-to-the-editor and persuasive arguments), as well as right-brain-oriented fiction and poetry. Prerequisite: GE180.

Creative Writing
Rogers State University
ROGE#ENGL2023 Undergraduate 3 credits $495*
This course covers devices and techniques necessary to write and publish, particularly fiction. It includes an introduction to publishing markets and proper manuscript submission. This course challenges students to regain their eloquence with the written word and with each other. It encourages you to rediscover your unique voice and to take pride in your own words and experiences. The course focuses on the practical aspects of writing, introducing students to revision and editing techniques. For those interested in publishing, the course outlines standard submission techniques and strategies.
* OK residents $315.

Creative Writing - Fiction
University of Missouri
MOCE#WR50 Undergraduate 3 credits $387
This course introduces basic writing narrative techniques, including writing original stories.

Creative Writing - Getting Started
Kennesaw State University
KENN#FMV203 Undergraduate 3 credits $149
This online Creative Writing workshop is ideal for people looking for writing ideas and inspiration and/or those who want to overcome writer's block. After an introduction to the creative writing process (research, creation, editing), three writing exercises (freefall, clustering, modeling) will be used to get you writing. The material you develop as you write will be used as the basis for producing fiction, non-fiction and poetry.

Creative Writing - Poetry
University of Missouri
MOCE#EN70 Undergraduate 3 credits $387
This course introduces different poetic forms and basic elements of poetry, including sound, rhyme, meter, and figurative language. Students will learn to apply these elements to their own poetry.

Creative Writing I
Fayetteville Technical Community College
FAYE#ENG125 Undergraduate 3 credits $489*
This course is designed to provide students with the opportunity to practice the art of creative writing. Emphasis is placed on writing, fiction, poetry, and sketches. Upon completion, students should be able to craft and critique their own writing and critique the writing of others.
  * North Carolina residents and non-resident US military personnel stationed within the state tuition: $60; NC senior citizens: free.

Creative Writing I
Front Range Community College
FRCC#ENG221 Undergraduate 3 credits $790
This course teaches the techniques of creative writing. Students explore imaginative uses of language by writing short stories, drama, poetry, and creative nonfiction. 45 Contact Hours. Prerequisite: Permission of instructor.

Crime and Punishment
New School for Social Research
NEWS#9998 Undergraduate 3 credits $1638*
What do the dynamics of murder trials have to do with Greek tragedy? Where does the law depart from its goal of "reasoned moral judgment" and take up with irrational (emotional/religious) forces? How has the balance of emotion and reason in our idea of "justice" shifted over time? We study and discuss murder trials in literature and in real life: the dueling trials in the courtroom, the community, and the media, and their different ways of representing "justice," the performance of guilt and innocence, the function of punishment, and the meaning of death.
* Non-credit option, tuition: $365.

Critical Thinking
Christopher Newport University
CHNE#PHIL101 Undergraduate 3 credits $993
Designed to impact the basic skills of logical reasoning in natural languages: analyzing statements for consistency, implications, contradictions; distinguishing fact from opinion and evaluating testimony; identifying, analyzing, and evaluating arguments; recognizing fallacies of equivocation and relevance; understanding necessary and sufficient conditions and the logic of conditional statements.

Critical Thinking
Charter Oak State College
CHOA#IDS110 Undergraduate 3 credits $390*
A set of tools to help students recognize the structure of arguments, analyze those arguments for soundness and validity, and build effective and persuasive arguments of their own. Particular attention is given to connecting evidence to a thesis in college writing.
* CT residents pay $95 per credit.

Critical Thinking and Argument
Pennsylvania State University
PENN#PHIL010 Undergraduate 3 credits $345
Principles of correct thinking; deductive and inductive inference; use and misuse of language in reasoning.

Cultural Pluralism in American History
University of Minnesota
MINN#HIST1305 Undergraduate 4 credits $356
This course provides a survey of the development of American society focusing on the roles of African Americans, Native Americans, Asian Americans, and Hispanic Americans. The issues of cultural pluralism, empowerment, racism, and intergroup relations are explored within a comparative historical framework.

Culture from Reformation to Present
New Jersey Institute of Technology
NJIT#HUM231 Undergraduate 3 credits $1143*
People's changing view of themselves and their world as seen in the history, literature, arts and philosophy of past eras, from the 17th century through the contemporary world. An interdisciplinary approach. Prerequisites: NJIT#ENG111, Culture and History I. Optional: 26 video lessons of 30 minutes each.
* NJ residents: $184/semester hour.

Current Children's Literature
The Heritage Institute
HEON#HU402V Undergraduate 3 qu. credits $215
Take this opportunity to review and read new children's literature and learn how to integrate it into your current curriculum. You'll read recently published books and critical reviews, including literature illustrating cultural diversity. You'll become familiar with trends in picture books, modern realism, mystery, historical fiction, biography and non-fiction. Learn ways to teach students reflective and critical thinking skills through literature. This course is appropriate for K-6, media specialists and reading consultants.

CyberCinema - Introduction to Film
MiraCosta College
MIRA#FILM101   Undergraduate   3 credits $357
An introduction to the study of film as an art form.

D. H. Lawrence and Freud
University of Minnesota
MINN#ENGL3910B   Undergraduate 4 credits $391
An intensive reading of the prose fiction and poetry of D. H. Lawrence alongside key texts by Freud. The course examines modern culture and its discontents as interpreted by these two writers.

D.H. Lawrence and the Language of Love
New School for Social Research
NEWS#0666   Undergraduate   3 credits $1638*
In a letter about his novel Lady Chatterley's Lover, D.H. Lawrence wrote, "But you know it's not really improper--I always labour at the same thing, to make the sex relation valid and precious, instead of shameful.... To me it is beautiful and tender and frail as the naked self is." Contrary to Lawrence's own claims of nobly freeing sexual behavior from perverse inhibitions, Kate Millett sees him as an "evangelist of quite another cause--'phallic consciousness,'" and labels him "the most talented and fervid of sexual politicians." Against a backdrop of Millett's Sexual Politics, we attempt to reexamine Lawrence and form our own conclusions of the differing kinds of love he depicts in Sons and Lovers, The Rainbow, Women in Love, and Lady Chatterley's Lover.
* Non-credit option, tuition: $365.

Deviance in U.S. Society
University of Colorado-Boulder
COBO#SOCY1004   Undergraduate 3 credits $240
Examines deviant groups in the United States, emphasizing existing theory and research about such issues as deviant careers, deviant lifestyles and behavior, and the processes of social control.

Drama
Strayer University
STRA#ENG305   Undergraduate   4.5 credits $665
Traces the development of drama from its inception to the present day. Presents representative plays of major dramatists throughout the world, including Sophocles, Shakespeare, Moliere, Ibsen, Shaw, and Williams. Provides opportunity to attend plays at local theaters.

Dramatica Screenplay Writing
Kennesaw State University
KENN#FMV208   Undergraduate   3 credits $149
Dramatica is a unique way of looking at the structure and dynamics of story which provides writers with powerful practical tools for creating stories that effectively communicate a message to an audience. Based on the notion that every complete story is a model of the mind's problem-solving processes, this exciting new theory is being used by aspiring and practicing authors alike to write and improve their screenplays, novels, plays, short stories, documentaries, etc.

Dying and Death in Contemporary Society
University of Minnesota
MINN#PUBH5040   Undergraduate 3 credits $300
Provides basic information on concepts, attitudes, ethics, and lifestyle management in relation to dying, death, grief, and bereavement. Emphasis placed on the educational aspects of these topics for community health and helping professionals and educators.

Eastern Religions
Thomas Edison State College
THED#OLREL406   Undergraduate   3 credits $397*
Emphasis is on specific forms of religious expression and practice, rather than the more abstract or theological aspects. Religions covered by the course are those of the majority of humankind and living traditions in today's world: Hinduism, Buddhism, religions of China and Japan, Judaism, Christianity, Islam, and several African primal religions. One section deals with alternatives to religion, such as Marxism and scientific humanism.
* NJ residents tuition: $33 per credit.

Eastern Religious Traditions
State University of New York
SUNY#HIS305   Undergraduate   3 credits $1038*
An examination of the religious traditions of Asia showing the historical interaction of folk religion with the developing concepts and institutions of Hinduism, Buddhism, Confucianism, Taoism, and Shinto. The impact of unique cultural environments on religious thought and practice is a principle focus. Prerequisite: An upper division standing.
* NY residents tuition: $137 per credit

Elements of Arts Administration
Golden Gate University
GOLD#AA300   Undergraduate   3 credits $960
Presents an intensive survey of the field of arts administration. Examines the major functions and processed involved in the operation of both non-profit arts organizations and arts businesses. Includes overview of organizational development issues such as strategic and long-range planning, principles and techniques of management for boards, staff and volunteers, advocacy, gramming and presenting. Note: AA300A to be taken as the first three units in the Advanced Program.

English Composition
Barstow Community College
BARS#ENGL1A   Undergraduate   3 credits $???
English composition and reading using descriptive, narrative, expository, argumentative, essay and research techniques.

English Composition
Dakota State University
DAKO#ENGL101 Undergraduate 3 credits $447
An introduction to and practice in the skills that are needed for effective written communication in the academic community. Using computer technology for rhetoric usage, research skills, MLA style and critical thinking, students complete short researched compositions. Prerequisite: Passing score on the English placement exam or grade of "C" or better in ENGL019.

English Composition
Great Basin College
GRBA#ENG101 Undergraduate 3 credits $186*
(Course description not available at press time.)
* NV residents tuition: $43 per credit.

English Composition
Northwest College
NOCO#GE180 Undergraduate 5 credits $???
The aim of this course is to help students learn to write competently at the college level. Emphasis is placed on organization and development of ideas. Some essays are typed and revised on the microcomputer. Outside lab time is required. Prerequisite: GE174, TY139 or equivalents.

English Composition
Shawnee Community College
SHAW#ENG0112 Undergraduate 3 credits $114
This course stresses further development of writing skills and explores a variety of compositional forms. Students will continue to develop awareness of the writing process and become competent in inventional, organizational and editorial strategies. This course emphasizes critical skills in reading, thinking and writing and includes production of documented, multi-source writing. Prerequisite: English Composition - ENG-0111 with a minimum grade of C. .

English Composition
Shawnee Community College
SHAW#ENG111 Undergraduate 3 credits $114
This is a course designed to introduce you to a variety of writing strategies. It will teach you about organization, style, focus, mechanics, and development. The course is designed for you to complete in asynchronous fashion. It includes a series of lessons and a bulletin board. To complete this course you will need access to an internet-based computer, Microsoft Word, and an e-mail address.

English Composition - Logic and Style
Chemeketa Community College
CHEM#WR122 Undergraduate 3 credits $123
The second-term college-level English Composition course teaching logical, effective, argumentative prose, awareness of stylistic elements, and critical reading. Prerequisite: WR121 or consent of instructor.

English Composition - Research Writing
Chemeketa Community College
CHEM#WR123 Undergraduate 3 credits $123
The third-term college-level English Composition course teaches the acquisition and evaluation of evidence, integration of opinion, and the appropriate process and forms for developing the research paper. Prerequisite: WR121 and WR122.

English Composition Exposition
Chemeketa Community College
CHEM#WR121 Undergraduate 3 credits $123
The first-term college-level English composition course emphasizes clear, detailed informative writing, clear thinking, and active reading. Prerequisite: Ability to organize thoughts and competency in standard written English, as demonstrated by (a) standard placement test or (b) completion of WR115.

English Composition I
Darton College
DART#ENG101 Undergraduate 5 qu. credits $605**
This course emphasizes the development of thought and expression through personal, descriptive, and expository essays. Involves substantial reading and analysis of ideas in preparation for the written assignments. Promotes the development of the language based process of reading, speaking, listening, critical thinking, and problem solving. Includes study of grammar and punctuation. Exit requirements: C average on course work and completion of the Mock Regents' Test.
* GA residents tuition: $160.

English Composition I
Front Range Community College
FRCC#ENG121 Undergraduate 3 credits $790
Emphasizes the planning, writing, and revising of compositions, including the development of critical and logical thinking skills. Includes a minimum of five compositions that stress analytical, evaluative, and persuasive/argumentative writing. 45 Contact Hours.

English Composition I
Rogers State University
ROGE#ENGL1113 Undergraduate 3 credits $495*
Practical writing experience emphasizing basic sentence structure, vocabulary, spelling and other mechanics. The focus is on student-written essays and improving self-expression. Prerequisite: ACT score of 19 or equivalent SAT score.
* OK residents $315.

English Composition I
Yavapai Community College
YAVA#ENG101 Undergraduate ?? credits $???
(Course description not available at press time.)

English Composition II
Front Range Community College
FRCC#ENG122 Undergraduate 3 credits $790
Expands and refines the objectives of English Composition I. Emphasizes critical/logical thinking and reading, problem definition, research strategies, and writing analytical, evaluative, and/or persuasive papers that incorporate research. 45 Contact Hours. Prerequisite: ENG121.

English Composition II
Rogers State University
ROGE#ENGL1213 Undergraduate 3 credits $495*
English composition is a dry, boring course about grammar and commas. NOT! This course will benefit you as a student, a professional, and a person. You're already a writer. Now you can become a better writer. Learn to better express the self you are - in writing. Learn about the relationship that you already have with literature. Take a leap into the pool of the writer's experience - yours, and others'!.
* OK residents $315.

English Composition II
State University of New York
SUNY#ENG102 Undergraduate 3 credits $545*
A continuation of English Composition I with further study of the resources of the language through a critical analysis of imaginative forms of writing. Well organized written composition, factually supported conclusions, and awareness of language variety are emphasized, along with effectiveness of expression and validity of judgement in the student's writing. Genre reading will include fiction, poetry, and drama. Prerequisite: English Composition I with a grade of 'C' or better.
* NY residents tuition: $278

English Literature from 1600 to 1800
Indiana University
INDI#L298 Undergraduate 3 credits $268
Representative selections, with emphasis on major writers from Donne to Johnson and on their cultural context.

English Literature I
University of Missouri
MOCE#LI131 Undergraduate 3 credits $387
This course follows the development of English literature from the Middle Ages through the eighteenth century; students will read and analyze representative works of selected major writers. Perquisites-English 20 or equivalent.

Enjoying Jazz
University of Alaska - Fairbanks
ALFA#MUS125 Undergraduate 2 credits $142
Overview of the jazz idiom. Study of performers, styles, and music through records, CDs, cassettes, and videotapes. Course is listening-intensive. Requires VCR and CD Player.

Ethics
Lake Superior College
LASU#PHIL1130 Undergraduate 3 credits $210
You know what its like to be in an ethical dilemma. (If you don't, then this is not the course for you.) But what is it that makes a choice an ethical choice - or a difficult ethical choice? And how can you know - or at least think through - what the right choice is? What makes some acts good and other acts bad? These are much harder questions that have and always will challenge those who live reflectively. In this course you will read and discuss, some of the world's most influential theories of right and wrong and apply them to the choices of everyday living.

Ethics
Northwest College
NOCO#GE281 Undergraduate 3 credits $???
The purpose of the course is to examine the principles of ethics involved in many areas of life. The course will explore the moral impact of acts not only on the individual but on the community as a whole. Prerequisite: GE180.

Ethics
State University of New York
SUNY#HUM13042S Undergraduate 3 credits $399*
This course is a study of various historical and contemporary value systems with emphasis upon alternative criteria for making decisions in the contemporary conflict of moral values, and is designed to help students develop their own value system and basis for ethical decision.
* NY residents tuition: $90 per credit.

Ethics
Waukesha County Technical College
WAUK#809158007 Undergraduate 3 credits $192*
This course is designed to provide a basic understanding of the foundations of ethics, and to encourage personal assessment of same. It will provide opportunity to analyze and compare life issues from an ethical perspective and to apply a systematic decision-making process in evaluation of situations at the personal, occupational and societal levels.
* WI residents pay $54 per credit.

Ethics & Social Responsibility
The Graduate School of America
TGSA#OM821W Graduate 4 credits $795
This course analyzes, from both conceptual and applied points of view, the interaction between business and society. Through an examination of basic assumptions, attitudes and values, learners build an ethical foundation for understanding and reacting to issues and policies of their companies.

Ethics and Social Issues
Pennsylvania State University
PENN#PHIL103W Undergraduate 3 credits $345
Ethical issues such as war, privacy, crime and punishment, racism and sexism, civil liberties, affirmative action, abortion, and euthanasia.

Ethics and Social Philosophy
New York Institute of Technology
NYIT#SS1530 Undergraduate 3 credits $???
An examination of some of the most critical issues of moral and social philosophy. These include subjects such as the linguistic analysis of terms such as "good", "evil", "duty", "right", and others. The basis of different moral systems will be studied, and selections from ethical and social philosophers will be read.

Ethics and Social Responsibility
Western Illinois University
WEIL#MAN481 Undergraduate 3 credits $795*
Is a contemporary study of relationships between the business institution and government. This course deals with social responsibility of business, societal forces exerted, external environmental factors, and the individual company as a part of the economic system. Prerequisite: Management 349.
* IL residents tuition: $88 per credit.

Ethics and Stakeholder Management
University of Minnesota
MINN#BGS3002 Undergraduate 4 credits $400
Basic economic and social goals, and various attempts to meet them. Emphasis on American society. Business as an institution; its relationships to other institutions and society; ethical and practical conflicts in the role of the firm and the manager are examined in the context of the public policy process. Current social issues and their impact on business.

Ethics and Standards of Professional Practice
Walden University
WALD#PSYC8260 Graduate 5 credits $1500
Ethical principles and professional standards and legal responsibilities of psychologists will be discussed. The course will focus on the interpretation of ethics and laws as they pertain to the practice of psychology and research.

Ethics and the Family
New School for Social Research
NEWS#0333 Undergraduate 3 credits $1638*
Family, Paul West tells us in The Nation, is "this thing that we curse and yet prize [and] is really the main stuff of life, the source of endurance and mutation, the irreducible focus and context, the dimension in which all things happen ... and happy or unhappy, is the team version of the existential pain." Against a backdrop of readings from Anne Roiphe's Fruitful and John Cleese's discussion with his former therapist Robin Skynner in Families and How to Survive Them, we examine both traditional and non-traditional family arrangements.
* Non-credit option, tuition: $365.

Ethics and the Professions
University of Missouri
MOCE#HU135 Undergraduate 3 credits $387
This course examines ethical issues confronted by individuals in professions such as medicine, law, business, journalism, and engineering. Perquisites: sophomore standing.

Ethics in Government and Politics
Christopher Newport University
CHNE#GOVT355 Undergraduate 3 credits $993
An examination of the process of generating criteria derived from democratic theory for making ethical judgments. The application of criteria to political situations as depicted in selected case studies. A review of ethical principles and their application, misleading assumptions, and false distinctions that may obstruct effective ethical decision-making about political actions.

Europe - Napoleon to the Present
Indiana University
INDI#H104 Undergraduate 3 credits $268
The development of European society from the downfall of Napoleon in 1815 to the present; the impact of the industrial revolution; the rise of the middle class; liberalism, Marxism, and mass politics; nationalism and imperialism; international communism and fascism.

Europe - Renaissance to Napoleon
Indiana University
INDI#H103 Undergraduate 3 credits $268
Major developments in European thought during Renaissance, Reformation, scientific revolution, and Enlightenment; traditional politics, economy, and society and their transformation by enlightened despotism, the French Revolution, and Napoleon.

Europe in the Twentieth Century II
Indiana University
INDI#B362 Undergraduate 3 credits $268
Economic, social, political, and military-diplomatic developments, 1930-present: depression politics, crisis of democracy; German national socialism. World War II; Cold War; postwar reconstruction and recovery.

European Civilization 1715-Present
University of Missouri
MOCE#HI32 Undergraduate 3 credits $387
This course studies modern western civilization from the 17th century to the present, with special emphasis on the philosophical, political, social, and economic backgrounds of modern society.

European Folktales
University of Minnesota
MINN#CLIT5414 Undergraduate 4 credits $391
This course explores the folktales of Germany, Scandinavia, France, Russia, and England. Discusses the structure, message for adults and children, and origins of folktales as a genre, compares the tales of different nations, and analyzes them within the broader context of oral literature and folklore.

European Heritage - Rome
University of Minnesota
MINN#HUM1113 Undergraduate 4 credits $391
This course deals with the major texts of Roman culture and the early development of Christianity. The course reading assignments include works by Plutarch, Vergil, the Stoics, Lucretius, St. Augustine, and the New Testament.

European History to 1500
Mercy College
MERC#HI101 Undergraduate 3 credits $900
This is a survey history course with two major themes. First, students will receive an introduction to more than 2,000 years of history in fifteen weeks! Second, students will be learning about the techniques that historians use to deal with sources and create the narrative history that is read in textbooks.

Ever-present Past in Spanish and Portuguese Culture
University of Minnesota
MINN#SPAN3970 Undergraduate 4 credits $391
Investigates how the concept of "regenerationism" has retained and exerted cultural force in the Iberian nations, forming a part of their cultural systems--and how it continues to exert that force today. Course materials chronologically structured around the development of the notion that, in Spain and Portugal, there are no beginnings--only "re-beginnings." Selections from literature, philosophy, and social commentary illustrate this sense of a lost past of imperial greatness and the need to re-create it. Begins with the Portuguese poet Luis de Camões' epic poem of 1578 and ends with documents about Spanish "nationalities" of the post-Franco era. Prerequisite: Spanish major.

Evolution of Jazz
Pennsylvania State University
PENN#MUSIC007 Undergraduate 3 credits $345
Study of origins and development of jazz as an art form.

Experiencing American Cultures in the Contemporary Novel
University of Missouri
MOCE#LI101B Undergraduate 3 credits $387
This multicultural literature course features novels and memoirs by contemporary Native American, African-American, Mexican-American, and Chinese-American writers. Audiocassettes containing selected readings and interviews with the writers are also included.

Expository Composition
Bakersfield College
BAKE#ENGLB1A Undergraduate 4 credits $460*
Expository writing and reading. Emphasizes the organization and development of expository essays, study of style, application of critical reading and thinking skills, and preparation of a research paper. Prerequisite: ENGL1 or ESL1 with a grade of C or English Level 1 required.
* CA residents pay $40 per credit.

Expository Composition
Cerro Coso Community College
CECO#ENGL1A Undergraduate 3 credits $345*
A composition course for transfer to four-year institutions. Seven to nine expository and argumentative essays, mostly out of class, and a 2,000-word reference paper (total 7,000 words). Investigation of writing strategies; analysis and evaluation of expository and argumentative prose; study of a novel and critical essays.
* California resident tuition: $13 per credit.

Expository Prose Writing
Eastern Oregon University
EAOR#WR121 Undergraduate 4 credits $320
College-level review of writing skills using both student's experiences, observations, and readings keyed to the modes and theories of discourse. Prerequisites: TSWE of 41-49 or completion of WR115 and a composition of a diagnostic essay demonstrating the capability of producing college-level written work.

Expository Writing
Fayetteville Technical Community College
FAYE#ENG111 Undergraduate 3 credits $489*
This course is the required first course in a series of two designed to develop the ability to produce clear expository prose. Emphasis is placed on the writing process including audience analysis, topic selection, thesis support and development, editing, and revision. Upon completion, students should be able to produce unified, coherent, well-developed essays using standard written English. This course has been approved to satisfy the Comprehensive Articulation Agreement general education core requirement in English composition.
* North Carolina residents and non-resident US military personnel stationed within the state tuition: $60; NC senior citizens: free.

Expository Writing
Golden Gate University
GOLD#ENGL1A Undergraduate 3 credits $960
Introduces the comprehensive skills of expository writing and critical reading. You will learn to critically analyze various types of reading material and will strengthen your writing skills in a variety of genres. These skills will support your academic work and prepare you to meet the reading and writing demands of professional activities. Prerequisites: Satisfactory score on the English Placement Exam or a grade of "C" or better in ENGL10B. (CAN ENGL2).

Expressionist Film in Scandinavia - Ingmar Bergman
University of Minnesota
MINN#SCAN3606 Undergraduate 4 credits $391
This multimedia course focuses on the films of Ingmar Bergman. Students view videos of eight films (including such classics as Seventh Seal, Wild Strawberries, and Cries and Whispers) and listen to audiotape commentary on the films. An introduction to film theory will help students develop a framework for their critical analysis of Bergman's films.

Fantasy Literature
University of Colorado
CUON#ENGL4770 Undergraduate 3 credits $1953*
This course introduces the lively history of fantastic literature, providing an in-depth study of representative texts. Beginning with myths, legends, and fairy tales, we will explore some major types of fantasy, including heroic fantasy, horror fiction, speculative fiction, and magic realism. These different forms of fantasy will guide us through a study of several thematic issues: the creation of alternate realities; the role of nostalgia in imagining utopias; the nature of good and evil, chaos and order; the depiction of altered states of consciousness; and an inquiry into human desires, wishes, and fears.
* CO residents tuition: $136 per credit.

Female Coming of Age in World Lit.
California State University - Dominguez Hills
CADO#HUX578 Undergraduate 3 credits $405
An examination of 20th century world literature by female authors writing on the theme of "coming of age." Through fiction and autobiography from diverse world cultures including France, China, South Africa, Vietnam and the U.S., a study of the influence of ethnic background and cultural traditions on the coming of age experience. Examines modern definitions of women and their survival and growth strategies. Critical analysis in a comparative literature and cultures framework with feminist perspectives. Prerequisite: HUX502 is recommended.

Feminine and Masculine in Native America
New School for Social Research
NEWS#0498 Undergraduate 3 credits $1638*
Traditional Native American cultures celebrate the importance of difference and interconnectedness between males and females. Their views on male and female principles, identities, responsibilities, and roles differ greatly from those in Western cultures. Drawing on examples from such Southwestern peoples as Pueblo, Hopi, Navajo, and Apache, and from other diverse Native peoples, this course explores a wide variety of issues related to gender roles. Topics include: How do traditional male/female roles manifest themselves in daily life? How are they learned? How do people court, marry, and establish families?.
* Non-credit option, tuition: $365.

Fiction Fundamentals
UCLA
UCLA#X450E Undergraduate 3 credits $450
It has been said that all of us have locked inside at least one good story to tell. This course is designed to tap into that story--and others. Students learn the fundamental elements of fiction writing through a combination of written exercises, extensive online group discussions, and instructor feedback. Through this process, students learn the fundamentals of fiction writing, including plot, point-of-view, setting, description, dialogue, tension, rewriting, and submission strategies.

Fiction Writing
Trinidad State Junior College
TRIN#ENG255 Undergraduate ?? credits $???
If you've already written some, maybe published a story or two, this course can help you take your fiction to greater heights. If you're new to writing but have a real desire to learn, this course may also be for you. For fifteen weeks you will read, write, and correspond with the instructor one-on-one. You will learn theory and techniques from a text and from critical analysis of published work.

Fiction Writing - Memory, Imagination, Desires
New School for Social Research
NEWS#1695 Undergraduate 3 credits $1638*
Fiction, though we write it to share with the world, comes from a place within us that is a private, interior alembic in which memory and imagination, heated by desire, mix. We help students discover this special place and the voices that rise from it, and learn how to draw these voices into a well-written story. We ponder the essential mystery by which we put words on paper--how to discover material, conquer initial confusion or lack of confidence, and proceed with discipline.
* Non-credit option, tuition: $365.

Film & International Culture
Marylhurst College
MARY#HUM322 Undergraduate 3 credits $651
This course will look at contemporary cinema from India, China, Japan, Canada, Mexico, Macedonia, Germany, Australia, Russia, and Iran. This multicultural selection will introduce various filmaking traditions that have developed independently from Hollywood.

Film and Literature
Northwest College
NOCO#GE280 Undergraduate 3 credits $???
This course presents the relationships between film and literature. Attention will be given to problems involved in adapting literature to another art form. Prerequisite: GE180.

Film and Society
Strayer University
STRA#ENG310A Undergraduate 4.5 credits $665
Involves a sociological-historical study of the development of film and film-making from its beginnings in the early twentieth century to the present. Included viewing of classic films of representative film-makers with emphasis on content and technique.

Film and TV Criticism
University of Alaska - Fairbanks
ALFA#JB308   Undergraduate   3 credits $237
Theoretical approaches to viewing, analyzing, and evaluating film and television program content.

Film Criticism
Marylhurst College
MARY#HUM323 Undergraduate   3 credits $651
A practical course in film criticism, involving attending selected films, reading published reviews, and writing reviews for posting to the class. Students hone their writing skills while gaining greater understanding of the art-historical context of motion pictures and of how they are received by the critical community.

Film Encounter
California State University - Dominguez Hills
CADO#HUX524 Undergraduate   3 credits $405
Watching and analyzing several movies with special focus on the techniques and content of the medium. Requires extensive notebook of descriptions and analyses of eight different film experiences.

Film Studies
Trinidad State Junior College
TRIN#LIT103   Undergraduate   ?? credits $???
This course is intended to introduce students to some basic concepts in regard to film history and film theory, and to introduce them to various film genres.

Finance & Budgeting in Arts Admin
Golden Gate University
GOLD#AA303   Undergraduate   3 credits $1059
Focuses on special events, corporate gifts, grants, major gifts and endowments with special. Attention paid to integrating fund-raising into the arts program. Incorporates the responsibility of arts organizations for public service to the greater community. Requires case study preparation of a nonprofit arts organization. Prerequisite: AA300A.

First Year Reading and Composition
Humboldt State University
HUMB#ENGL100 Undergraduate   3 credits $345
The on-line version of English 100 relies upon an interactive web site where students find a syllabus, schedule, and assignments; a synchronous conferencing interface; the on-line reader of model texts and links to many web-based composition and research resources. Students must "attend" weekly electronic conferences with the instructor and with their peer response group. Mandatory class meetings, May 18 and 19, 1200-1450, FH 202. Prerequisite: English Code 40.

First-Year Composition
Rio Salado College
RISA#ENG101 Undergraduate   3 credits $186*
Standard English writing skills. Emphasis on expository composition. Prerequisites: Appropriate English placement test score or "C", or better, in ENG071.
* AZ residents $37 per credit.

First-Year Composition
Rio Salado College
RISA#ENG102 Undergraduate   3 credits $186*
Continued development of standard English writing skills. Introduction to research, note taking, organization, and documentation in the preparation and writing of a research paper. Prerequisites: ENG101 with a grade of "C" or better.
* AZ residents $37 per credit.

For All Practical Purposes I
Eastern Oregon University
EAOR#MATH110A Undergraduate 4 credits $320
Designed for the non-specialist to demonstrate the usefulness and ongoing nature of mathematics and develop skills in logical thinking and critical reading. Topics covered include graph theory methods used in planning and scheduling, linear programming methods in optimization, and statistical methods for estimation and inference. Prerequisite: MATH095 or equivalent.

For All Practical Purposes II
Eastern Oregon University
EAOR#MATH110B Undergraduate 4 credits $320
Continuation of MATH110 For All Practical Purposes I including election theory, weighted voting, games of conflict, scale/form, populations, conic sections and measurement. Prerequisite: MATH095 or equivalent.

Forbidden Literature
New School for Social Research
NEWS#0675 Undergraduate   3 credits $1638*
Book burning, death threats, denunciations. ... What was all the fuss about? The reasons for suppressing books-- political, social, cultural, sexual, and religious--are as varied as the cultures that gave birth to such works as D.H. Lawrence's Lady Chatterley's Lover; Bulgakov's comic masterpiece of early Soviet life, Heart of a Dog; Ngugi's denunciation of post-colonial Kenya in the drama I Will Marry When I Want; or Duong Thu Huong's look at Vietnam through the exploration of a young woman's family history in Paradise of the Blind.
* Non-credit option, tuition: $365.

Formal Logic
University of Missouri
MOCE#LO160 Undergraduate   3 credits $387
This course presents an introductory study of logical truth and deductive inference, with emphasis on the development and mastery of a formal system. Perquisites- grade of C- or better in Math 10 or equivalent.

Foundations of Visual Literacy
Eastern Oregon University
EAOR#ART101 Undergraduate   5 credits $400
This course is designed to increase visual literacy through explorations of aesthetic, trends in the visual arts of historical and critical importance. Field experience is a component of this course. This class will require a field trip to an art museum and the submission of artistic creations.

Foundations of Western Culture
University of Nevada-Reno
NERE#C201   Undergraduate   3 credits $210
An introduction to the Greek, Roman, and Judeo-Christian roots of Western Civilization and to the early development of the West during the Middle Ages. The goals of the course are to present to students the great ideas and issues that have persisted throughout the ages (love, freedom, happiness, justice, etc.) and the books in which they are contained; to gain knowledge and understanding of the Western Tradition, how it originated, how it developed, and how it relates to other cultures and civilizations; to improve writing through written assignments and essay examinations.

Four American Classics
New School for Social Research
NEWS#0641   Undergraduate   3 credits $1638*
We read four classics of American fiction: Portrait of a Lady by Henry James, Herland by Charlotte Perkins Gilman, Death Comes for the Archbishop by Willa Cather, and Invisible Man by Ralph Ellison. These works, chosen not only for their intrinsic merit but for their capacity to inspire animated discussion, are examined closely in terms of style, psychological resonance, and historical context. Since we are doing only four books, this is an opportunity to take a leisurely look at "large" books by major authors that may incarnate our ideas of literary possibility.
* Non-credit option, tuition: $365.

Four European Classics
New School for Social Research
NEWS#0643   Undergraduate   3 credits $1638*
This class reads four classic works of modern European literature and discusses their relationship to social and political issues of the 20th century that concern us to this day. We also examine how each writer depicts such timeless topics as the mysteries of identity, youth and age, love and death, freedom and authority, good and evil, and the search for happiness. Readings: The Lady from the Sea, Henrik Ibsen's mysterious play set in the Norwegian fjords; Death in Venice, Thomas Mann's novella of crisis in the German soul; et al.
* Non-credit option, tuition: $365.

Frank Lloyd Wright
California State University - Dominguez Hills
CADO#HUX550   Undergraduate   3 credits $405
Intensive study of the major buildings and architectural influence of Frank Lloyd Wright.

Freshman Composition
Lake Superior College
LASU#ENGL1106   Undergraduate 3 credits $210
Need a course which will help you get through college? Want a promotion in your current job? Freshman Composition is the writing course which will teach you the skills to write papers and answer essay questions in college classes, to improve your written communication at home and at work, and to read and write critically and effectively. For this Internet course, you will need either Corel WordPerfect (6.1 or newer, preferably 7.0) or Microsoft Word (6.0 or newer, preferably the 97 version). Prerequisite: College level reading and writing ability.

Freshman Composition I and II
Trinidad State Junior College
TRIN#ENG121   Graduate   3 qu. credits $???
This two-semester freshman composition sequence is required of all students at the college. Each course is available for 3 credits, and both are part of the core requirements for graduation from the college. In ENG121, students write a variety of basic essays designed to get them back into the swing of writing again, since many students at the college are non-traditional and may have been out of school for quite awhile.

From Con Man to Death of a Salesman
Marylhurst College
MARY#LIT385   Undergraduate   3 credits $651
Look at how U.S. writers and society see the world of business as a cultural center, an enemy of culture, a gendered activity, and one influenced by race and class. The main focus will be on works of fiction, but in your own writing, you will consider how your experience in the business world has influenced their cultural perceptions.

From Silence to Poem
New School for Social Research
NEWS#1645   Undergraduate   3 credits $1638*
Beginning and advanced writers work on dismantling silences in their lives and generating poems from personal experience. We work in a safe, functional community to open hidden, unsaid places within ourselves. The heretical Gospel according to Thomas says, "If you do not bring forth that which is within you, that which is within you will destroy you. If you bring forth that which is within you, that which is within you will save you." This notion informs one aspect of our work together, enabling the writer to follow the poem's impulse in order to break old habits and write something challenging and difficult.
* Non-credit option, tuition: $365.

Fund Raising in Arts Administration
Golden Gate University
GOLD#AA304   Undergraduate   3 credits $1059
Surveys to various kinds of legal problems and issues faced by administrators of arts organizations in their dealings with unions, artists and other employees, and with artistic property. Prerequisite: AA300A.

Fundamentals of Music
University of Minnesota
MINN#MUS1001   Undergraduate   4 credits $356
Explores topics in musical pitch and rhythm, and skills such as singing, playing the piano, clapping rhythms, and discriminative listening. Recommended for students who have an avocational interest in music or who will use basic music skills in their careers.

Fundamentals of Music II
University of Minnesota
MINN#MUS1002   Undergraduate   4 credits $356
Basic procedures for harmonizing melodies, including chord construction and succession, voice-leading, and stylistic considerations. Development of basic listening and sight-singing skills. Rigorous review of music fundamentals. Prerequisite: MUS1001 or ability to read music in the treble and bass clefs and a thorough knowledge of intervals, scales, and chord qualities.

Goddesses in World Mythology
Humboldt State University
HUMB#RS390   Undergraduate   3 credits $345
A survey based on Graham's forthcoming book from Abbeville. Topics: Life & Death, Love & Sex, Health & Healing, War and Victory, Knowledge & Wisdom. The textbooks are Gadon, Once & Future Goddess and Graham, Goddess.

Gothic Fiction
University of Missouri
MOCE#LI101C   Undergraduate   3 credits $387
A survey of English and American Gothic fiction from the 18th century to the present, this course examines major novels and short stories that define the Gothic tradition in literature.

Graphics and Layout in Print Media
New Hampshire College
NEHA#COM330   Undergraduate   3 credits $1656
In this course students practice the art and craft of graphic design and layout, including copy fitting, font selection, and other aspects of the printing process. Students produce a variety of pieces during the semester including brochures, flyers, and pamphlets. Prerequisite: ENG121.

Great Writers
Salve Regina University
SALV#HUM503   Grad   3 credits $???
Students read and discuss classic works of major significance in world literature. Emphasis is given to the writer's depiction of universal themes that are met in every culture and to how this seminal literature can enrich our cross-cultural experience.

Greece through Renaissance
New Hampshire College
NEHA#HUM201   Undergraduate   3 credits $1656
Assuming little or no previous exposure to its content, this course offers vocabulary, understanding, and appreciation of the visual arts, music, literature, and ideas in the context of changing cultural environments, including ancient Greece and Rome, the Medieval Period, and the Renaissance. May be taken independently of HUM202.

Greek and Roman History
Edmonds Community College
EDMO#HIST111   Undergraduate   5 credits $260
(Course description not available at press time.)

Greek and Roman Mythology
University of Minnesota
MINN#CLAS1042   Undergraduate   4 credits $356
The heroes, gods, and goddesses of ancient Greece and Rome are investigated, as are the myths and the stories behind them.

Greek Mythology
Edmonds Community College
EDMO#HUM109   Undergraduate   5 credits $260
Our myths are "classical" in the sense that we have already been exposed to them. Thus, this course will help the student to understand the code of allusion, symbol and metaphor that are part of the western literary tradition. This course will contribute to the student's cultural literacy in English.

Harlem Renaissance
Mercy College
MERC#HU224   Undergraduate   3 credits $900
This course critically examines the period between 1917-31, commonly called the Harlem Renaissance. This period is filled with ambiguities. It produced an important body of art, music and literature and did establish the "New Negro" who broke from slavery and raised his/her political consciousness. But the movement died in the 1930s and did not take root because it was not truly grounded in its community. One of its shining lights, Jean Tommer, remained on the periphery of the Harlem community and even denied his ethnicity. The course will weigh the achievements and consider its failures.

Harlem Writers Guild On-Line Fiction Workshop
New School for Social Research
NEWS#1706   Undergraduate   3 credits $1638*
This creative writing workshop features on-line participation by several distinguished members of the 45-year-old Harlem Writers Guild. In a unique cyberspace roundtable, students post short stories or chapters from longer works for comment and critique by their peers, the coordinator, and guest authors. Participating Guild members: Walter Mosley, writer of best-selling mysteries; Grace Edwards Yearwood, novelist and mystery writer; Rosemary Bray, former associate editor of the New York Times Book Review; and John Henrik Clarke, co-founder of the Harlem Writers Guild.
* Non-credit option, tuition: $365.

Hemingway
University of Minnesota
MINN#ENGL3940B   Undergraduate 4 credits $391
The course covers Hemingway's writing career from 1921 to 1929, when he developed the most influential prose style in the history of American literature and produced the body of work that earned him recognition as one of the greatest fiction writers of 20th-century literature. Students will read two novels--The Sun Also Rises and A Farewell to Arms--and many short stories. Particular attention is paid to the dominant themes and conflicts of Hemingway's fiction, the evolution of his style, and the unusually illuminating interrelationships between his life and his fiction.

Hemingway and Faulkner
California State University - Dominguez Hills
CADO#HUX553   Undergraduate   3 credits $405
An examination of the major works and influence of two modern American authors, Ernest Hemingway and William Faulkner.

Hinduism
Ohio University
OHIO#PHIL370 Undergraduate 4 credits $256
Vedic religion, Hinduism, Jainism. Note: A VHS videotape is an optional supplement to the course.

History
California State University - Dominguez Hills
CADO#HUX501 Undergraduate 2 credits $270
Advanced study of the nature of history through examination of historical method and its application to a history book of the student's choice.

History
California State University - Dominguez Hills
CADO#HUX523 Undergraduate 3 credits $405
Exploring the historical roots of one's own community. Requires papers (including photographs) involving descriptions and analyses of five different historical sites.

History of 20th Century Fashion
New School for Social Research
NEWS#4008 Undergraduate 2 credits $1092
As the 20th century draws to a close, it is particularly important to understand the meaning of fashion in an era of unprecedented economic, social and cultural changes. Trace the development of 20th century fashion in the context of the history of modern art, design and popular culture.

History of Africa II
Indiana University
INDI#E432 Undergraduate 3 credits $268
1750 to present. Slave trade, European imperialism, impact of Islam and Christianity, new state formations, reassertion of African culture and identity. Some map study.

History of Alaska
University of Alaska - Fairbanks
ALFA#HIST461 Undergraduate 3 credits $237
Alaska from prehistoric times to the present, including major themes such as Native Alaska, colonial Alaska, military Alaska, statehood, Alaska Native Claims Settlement Act of 1971, and the Alaska National Interest Lands Act of 1980. Prerequisite: Jr. standing.

History of Ancient Philosophy
Christopher Newport University
CHNE#PHIL201G Undergraduate 3 credits $993
An historical study of the development of philosophical thought of the European, Middle-Eastern, and Far Eastern cultures from ancient times to 1500 A.D. Readings from original sources will include topics such as early Greek explanations of the physical world, Plato's theory of abstract forms and his account of political obligation, Aristotle's theory of the soul, Epicurean and Stoic accounts of the highest moral good, Medieval arguments for God's existence, Confucian and Taoist concepts of the individual and society, Buddhist and Hindu views of self and world and the significance of meditative techniques and practices.

History of Education in the United States
Pennsylvania State University
PENN#EDTHP430 Undergraduate 3 credits $345
American educational ideas and practice, critically examined in terms of their historical development and contemporary significance. Note: 400-level courses are available only to students with junior or senior standing.

History of Film
University of Colorado
CUON#ENGL3065 Undergraduate 3 credits $1953*
Surveys the history of film form its beginnings until 1941, and examines how the essential techniques of film (script writing, editing, acting, laboratory work, and sound production) were mastered. Films of merit and interest by Melies, Griffith, Chaplin, Keaton, Eisenstein, Pudovkin, Murnau, Lang, Dreyer, Flaherty, Welles, and others will be studied.
* CO residents tuition: $136 per credit.

History of Journalism
University of Minnesota
MINN#JOUR5601 Undergraduate 4 credits $391
From scratches in wet clay to messages bounced by satellite and now the information highway, communication has a fascinating history. This course covers First Amendment rights, press credibility and governments seeking cover from "sunshine" laws, muckraking, infomationals and advertorials, fictionalized documentaries, video newspapers, 500 cable choices, and other influences that keep reshaping journalism and the events and trends it records. Attention is given to improving writing skills and identifying job opportunities.

History of Missouri
University of Missouri
MOCE#HI107 Undergraduate 3 credits $387
This course surveys Missouri's political, social, economic, and cultural development, from the beginning of settlement to the present. Perquisites-History 175 or 176.

History of Modern Europe
University of Missouri
MOCE#HI2 Undergraduate 3 credits $387
This course covers selected major themes in European history from the French Revolution to recent times. Topics include the breakdown of traditional institutions and ideas; political and social revolution; industrialization, nationalism, imperialism, and world wars; democratic and totalitarian ideologies and movements; the quest for national order; and European unity.

History of Modern Philosophy
Christopher Newport University
CHNE#PHIL202G Undergraduate 3 credits $993
An historical study of the development of philosophical thought of the European, Middle-Eastern, and Far Eastern cultures from 1500 A.D. to the present. Readings from original sources will include topics such as Descartes' theory of mind and body, Hobbes' social contract theory, Berkeley's denial of the material world, Hume's attack on miracles, Kant's theory of the phenomenal and noumenal worlds, logical positivists' criticism of ethics and metaphysics, Sartre's theory of human existence, Neo-Confucian conceptions of the Tao, and Zen Buddhism's view of knowledge and enlightenment.

History of Science
University of Missouri
MOCE#SC275 Undergraduate 3 credits $387
This course surveys science from ancient times to the 20th century, focusing on the leading conceptual developments within science, the scientific revolution, and science's role in society. Perquisites: History 111 or 112 or 175 or 176.

History of Texas
Texas Technical University
TETE#HIST3310 Undergraduate 3 credits $???
This course surveys Texas history beginning with the Native American occupation and traces the major social, political, and economic developments of the state into the modern era.

History of the American West
Eastern Oregon University
EAOR#HIST410B Undergraduate 5 credits $415
Considers political, economic, social, and cultural forces in terms of change over time from the sixteenth to twentieth centuries in the region of the American West.

History of the Arab World
California State University - Dominguez Hills
CADO#HUX579 Undergraduate 3 credits $405
Political and cultural history of the Arab World from the 7th century to the present. Consideration of historiographic problems such as the "Great Man," cycles, and the influence of ideas on events. Prerequisite: HUX501 is recommended.

History of the Cinema
University of Alaska - Fairbanks
ALFA#JB105 Undergraduate 3 credits $210
History and development of the medium of film in the United States and abroad during the last 100 years.

History of the Old South
University of Missouri
MOCE#HI254 Undergraduate 3 credits $387
This course studies the history of the American South to 1860. Perquisites-History 175.

History of the Pacific Northwest
Eastern Oregon University
EAOR#HIST410C Undergraduate 5 credits $415
An advanced survey of Pacific Northwest history beginning in the 18th century with the maritime trade and extending into the contemporary era of the late twentieth century. Political, economic, social cultural and environmental history are presented with analyses of class, race, and gender.

History of the United States to 1877
Texas Technical University
TETE#HIST2300 Undergraduate 3 credits $???
HIST 2300 and HIST 2301 satisfy the legislative history requirement. This course combines political, military, constitutional, and social history.

History of the US
Cerro Coso Community College
CECO#HIST17A Undergraduate 3 credits $345*
Social, political, economic, and cultural history of the United States from colonial times through the Civil War. Selected topics, including American institutions and Constitutional development, will be stressed.
* California resident tuition: $13 per credit.

History of the US I
University of Alaska - Fairbanks
ALFA#HIST131 Undergraduate 3 credits $213
Discovery of America to 1865, colonial period, revolution, formation of constitution, western expansion, Civil War.

History of the US I
University of Alaska - Fairbanks
ALFA#HIST132 Undergraduate 3 credits $213
History of the US from reconstruction to the present.

History of the US II
Cerro Coso Community College
CECO#HISTC17B Undergraduate 3 credits $345*
Social, political, economic, and cultural history of the United States from the Reconstruction to the present. Selected topics, including American institutions and Constitutional development, will be stressed. Prerequisite: Level 1 reading, level 2 writing classification recommended.
* CA residents pay $13 per credit.

History of the US Since 1877
Texas Technical University
TETE#HIST2301 Undergraduate 3 credits $???
This course is a continuation of HIST 2300.

History of US Mass Communications
City University
CITY#COM402 Undergraduate   5 qu. credits $785
Traces the historical role of the American media in discovering and interpreting news, offering intelligent opinion, and entertaining the mass audience. Helps students evaluate the relationship between information flow and subsequent public opinion. Students will assess the means, as well as the various media, by which news, opinion and information reach the public during the various technical stages of news processing. Prerequisite: Strongly recommended: BSK 210 or its equivalent.

History of Washington/Pacific NW
Edmonds Community College
EDMO#HIST204 Undergraduate   5 credits $260
(Course description not available at press time.)

History of Women in the United States
Indiana University
INDI#H260 Undergraduate   3 credits $268
How have women's lives changed from the colonial period to the twentieth century? This introductory survey focuses on women's historical roles in the work place, the family, and politics. Material will be drawn from legal, constitutional, political, social, demographic, economic, and religious history. National award winner.

History of World Civilization
Chemeketa Community College
CHEM#HST110 Undergraduate   3 credits $123
A survey of human cultural, social, economic, and political development of the world's civilizations. The course will cover from ancient times to 1500 C.E.

How and Why My Family Came to This Country
New School for Social Research
NEWS#1743 Undergraduate   3 credits $1638*
Where did your ancestors come from? Why did they leave their homeland? How did they travel? How was their journey? Students trace their families' journeys by conducting interviews with family members and friends and religious and ethnic associates; some may visit museums, cultural centers, genealogical centers, libraries, or national archives (located in lower Manhattan); some may search the Internet and create family Web pages. Students research the social, economic, and political events that drove or carried their ancestors from their homeland and the expectations their ancestors held for the New World.
* Non-credit option, tuition: $365.

How to Write Television Soap Opera
Kennesaw State University
KENN#FMV209 Undergraduate   3 credits $149
Writing a Soap Opera can be a lot of fun and at the same time a challenge of time and resources. It takes a great deal of thought to make all your creative energies to come together. The objective of this course is not to write a full length script, but rather to focus in on a scene. If trained properly, a scriptwriter will be able to expand beyond the scene to use the same techniques to write a full length version.

Humanities I
Rogers State University
ROGE#HUM2113 Undergraduate   3 credits $495*
Humanities is the study of culture ... a study which encompasses all of the arts as well as philosophy and religion. Although this course is taught chronologically, history will be a frame and not the focus. We will note the WHY of human achievements in the context of the WHAT, WHEN, and WHERE.
* OK residents $315.

Humanities II
Brevard Community College
BREV#HUM2230 Undergraduate   3 credits $485
An integral course designed to increase the student's understanding and appreciation of the creative process in western culture through the study of representative materials in art, music, literature, and philosophy from the Renaissance through the 19th century. Prerequisite: Appropriate test scores in reading and writing.

Humanities II
Rogers State University
ROGE#HUM2223 Undergraduate   3 credits $495*
This is a course about people and their creativity . . . about achievements and values . . . about how you can learn about yourself and the world you live in by studying worlds and people no longer in existence. Learn what you have in common with Tutankhamen, Mozart, and me! The focus of this course - which has a strong and engaging video series as its core - is seven of the major art forms: film, drama, music, literature, painting, sculpture, and architecture.
* OK residents $315.

Humanities in the Modern West II
University of Minnesota
MINN#HUM1002 Undergraduate   4 credits $356
Industrial Revolution, Romanticism, socialism, individualism. Selected documents of economic and socialist theory and the Romantic movement; representative works by Zola, Ibsen, Dostoevsky, and Tolstoy.

Humanities in the Modern West III
University of Minnesota
MINN#HUM1003 Undergraduate   4 credits $356
Focuses on the late 19th century. The topics examined in this course include evolution (Darwinism) and the beginnings of existentialism. The authors students will study are Kierkegaard, Nietzsche, Turgenev, Thomas Mann, and Chekhov.

Independent Studies in Humanities
Pima Community College
PIMA#HUM130 Undergraduate   3 credits $165*
Reading and research projects to be arranged with the instructor. Of course this class will make extensive use of humanities resources located on the Internet. Students will complete a significant research project as part of this course.
* AZ residents, $32/credit hour.

Intercultural Communications Skills
University of Massachusetts - Dartmouth
MADA#PRD22481 Undergraduate 0 credits $135
An introductory course for anyone needing to communicate with culturally-different others socially, at work, or while living or travelling abroad. The course seeks to increase students' understanding of their own cultural patterns and values and how culture influences the communication patterns of others. In addition to readings, the course will include experiential activities such as: opportunities to seek out intercultural encounters on the Web; role-plays; simulations; and case studies.

Intermediate Exposition
University of Alaska - Fairbanks
ALFA#ENGL213 Undergraduate 3 credits $213
Instruction in writing through close analysis of expository prose from the social and natural sciences. Research paper required. Prerequisite: Sophomore standing and completion of ENGL111 or equivalent.

Intermediate Expository Writing
University of Washington
WASH#ENGLC281 Undergraduate 5 qu. credits $370
Writing papers communicating information and opinion to develop accurate, competent and effective expression. Recommended: sophomore standing.

Intermediate Photography
New School for Social Research
NEWS#2516 Undergraduate 3 credits $360
Building on Basic Photography, this class focuses on student work, with in-depth discussions of the aesthetic and technical merits of the images. There are "field trips" to World Wide Web sites with photography exhibitions and resources. There are also discussions of how to sell your photographic work. Students should be prepared to present ten photographs by the second week of class. Prerequisite: Basic Photography: Critique and Response or B&W Photography 1 or equivalent experience.

Intermediate Poetry Writing
University of Minnesota
MINN#ENGW3103 Undergraduate 4 credits $391
This course offers students a variety of exercises and readings to help them develop an awareness of the way they use language to describe the worlds of experience and imagination. Substantial reading in contemporary poetry will help students focus on image, diction, voice, tone, and structure in their own poems. Some previous experience with writing poetry is expected. Prerequisite: ENGW1101 or 1103.

Interrelation of Art, Drama, and Music
University of Alaska - Fairbanks
ALFA#ART200 Undergraduate 3 credits $213
Understanding and appreciation of art, drama, and music through an exploration of their relationship. Topics include the creative process, structure, cultural application and diversity, the role of the artist in society, and popular movements and trends.

Intro to World Women's Poetry
Kennesaw State University
KENN#FMV211 Undergraduate 3 credits $149
Women from every corner of the globe have found themselves unstoppably drawn to poetry as a means of expression. In this introductory course, we explore the poetry and lives of accomplished poets such as Edith Sodergran (Finland), Yu Hsuan-chi (China), Claribel Alegria (El Salvador), and Nina Cassian (Romania). The poets cover politics, social conditions, nature, mortality, love, art universal topics discussed from their time-and-place-specific point of view. Class members are required to keep response journals and to do a final project, which involves reporting to the class on a woman poet of their choosing.

Introduction to African Literature
University of Minnesota
MINN#AFRO3601 Undergraduate 4 credits $391
A survey of 19th- and 20th-century African literature, including oral narratives, written poetry, short stories, novels, plays. All readings in English.

Introduction to American Literature
Chemeketa Community College
CHEM#ENG253 Undergraduate 3 credits $123
What a student might gain from the study of American literature Beginnings-1800: Deeper awareness of the American experience, American psyche, American identity through its body of literature. (What does it mean to be American? What are the roots of that identity? Where do I place myself in this context? How does literature help us to explore these questions?).

Introduction to American Literature
University of Minnesota
MINN#ENGL1016 Undergraduate 4 credits $356
Introduction to some major themes and writers in American literature. Readings from Faulkner, Malamud, Melville, Fitzgerald, Chopin, Ellison, Henry James, and Dickey are complemented by audio programs by Professor Edward Griffin. Emphasizes the American experience, myths of the American wilderness, dreams of innocence, freedom, and social responsibility among the peoples of the New World.

Introduction to Art
Cerro Coso Community College
CECO#ART10 Undergraduate 3 credits $345*
Exploring the meaning of art through an investigation of historical and contemporary principles. Accompanied by individual explorations in various studio media.
* California resident tuition: $13 per credit.

Introduction to Art
University of Colorado
CUON#FA1001 Undergraduate 3 credits $1953*
An introduction to art, both in our everyday lives and in the more formal appreciation of the art world in general.
* CO residents tuition: $136 per credit.

Introduction to Art
Rio Salado College
RISA#ARH100 Undergraduate 3 credits $186*
Understanding and enjoyment of art through study of painting, sculpture, architecture and design.
* AZ residents $37 per credit.

Introduction to Art, Music and Literature
Strayer University
STRA#HUM100 Undergraduate 4.5 credits $665
Focuses on the interplay between art, music, and literature. Shows how different epochs exhibit unique cultural values and life-styles which are mirrored in the various art forms. Critically examines representative art throughout the world and history from cultural, social, and esthetic perspectives.

Introduction to Audio Concepts
Fayetteville Technical Community College
FAYE#MIT120 Undergraduate 3 credits $489*
This course provides an opportunity to gain a basic level of competence in the integration of digital and analog audio. Emphasis is placed on understanding integration of audio resources such as MIDI, WAV, Real-audio, and Redbook Resources. Upon completion, students should be able to demonstrate familiarity with basic audio integration techniques and applications for stand-alone personal computers, networks, and integrated room systems.
* NC residents pay $20 per credit.

Introduction to Composition
Chemeketa Community College
CHEM#WR115 Undergraduate 3 credits $123
This course, which is introductory to WR121, focuses on writing at the paragraph level. It teaches students to write well-developed, unified, coherent paragraphs, and to formulate and develop a main idea in the composing of short, expository essays. The course explores techniques for generating and controlling topic sentences, selecting and incorporating supporting details, and creating coherence within and between paragraphs. Students are also taught writing a.,; a recursive process to generate and shape essays. Reading selections are used to model effective writing, enhance vocabulary, and develop the ability to read for information and understanding.

Introduction to Creative Writing
University of Colorado
CUON#ENGL2154 Undergraduate 3 credits $1953*
Reading, discussing, and writing short fiction and poetry in a workshop setting.
* CO residents tuition: $136 per credit.

Introduction to Creative Writing
Pennsylvania State University
PENN#ENGL050 Undergraduate 3 credits $345
Practice and criticism in the reading, analysis, and composition of fiction, nonfiction, and poetry writing.

Introduction to Expository Writing
Eastern Oregon University
EAOR#WR115 Undergraduate 4 credits $320
Intensive college-level practice in writing for students with pre-college skills. Students extend and enhance control of composing and rhetorical processes. Basic mastery of keyboarding skills is expected. Prerequisites: TSWE of 31-40 or satisfactory completion of WR040, satisfactory in-class diagnostic essay.

Introduction to Fiction
Chemeketa Community College
CHEM#ENG104 Undergraduate 3 credits $123
Features analysis of fiction through the reading of works in English and in translation. This course introduces the short story, novel, and/or novella, basic literary concepts (which may include a thematic or chronological or stylistic approach, etc.), and terminology.

Introduction to Fiction
Indiana University
INDI#L204 Undergraduate 3 credits $268
Representative works of fiction; structural techniques in the novel. Novels and short stories from several ages and countries.

Introduction to Film Studies
Auburn University
AUBU#RTF235 Undergraduate 3 credits $126
An introduction to film analysis, modes of film practice and critical approaches to the study of cinema.

Introduction to Folklore
Indiana University
INDI#F101 Undergraduate 3 credits $268
A view of the main forms and varieties of folklore and folk expression in tales, ballads, gestures, beliefs, games, proverbs, riddles, and traditional arts and crafts. The role of folklore in the life of human beings. A cassette tape recorder and blank tape are required for field work. This course includes two optional borrowed videotapes. National award winner.

Introduction to Folklore
University of Missouri
MOCE#FO184 Undergraduate 3 credits $387
This course introduces the study of folklore, including the methodology, approaches and genres of folklore.

Introduction to Folklore
University of Missouri
MOCE#FO185 Undergraduate 3 credits $387
This course introduces the study of folklore, including the methodology, approaches and genres of folklore. Prerequisite: English 20 or equivalent.

Introduction to Folklore in the US
Indiana University
INDI#F131 Undergraduate 3 credits $268
Folklore and traditional expressive behavior in the United States. Traditional arts, ideas, and practices of folk groups in the United States, including ethnic, occupational, regional and religious groups. Uses videotapes.

Introduction to Interior Design
New School for Social Research
NEWS#4014 Undergraduate   3 credits $368
A multi-sided overview of technical and aesthetic principles of interior design. Topics include drafting, color theory, scale and proportion, proper space allocation, visualizing room layouts, floor and wall coverings, furniture arrangement, aesthetics and conceiving a design philosophy, client psychology and business practices. You are expected to complete a term project involving conceptualization, execution and presentation of design. Prerequisites: basic drafting or equivalent experience.

Introduction to Judaism
University of Minnesota
MINN#JWST3034 Undergraduate 4 credits $391
Concepts, movements, and institutions in the development of classical Judaism, as manifested in the literature and festivals of the Jewish people from Second Commonwealth times to the present.

Introduction to Literature
Barstow Community College
BARS#ENGL1B Undergraduate   3 credits $???
Critical reading and written analysis of standard literary works: poetry, short story, novel and drama.

Introduction to Literature
Dakota State University
DAKO#ENGL210 Undergraduate   3 credits $447
A survey of the types (poetry, fiction, and drama), themes, and values of literature. Prerequisite: ENGL101 or consent of instructor.

Introduction to Literature
Eastern Oregon University
EAOR#ENGL104 Undergraduate   4 credits $320
Study of the basic forms of literary expression: fiction, drama, poetry. Emphasis on careful reading and guided analysis of representative works ranging from classic to contemporary. Prerequisite: College-level reading and writing skills.

Introduction to Literature
Rio Salado College
RISA#ENH110 Undergraduate   3 credits $186*
Introduces students to literature through various forms of literary expression; e.g., poetry, drama, essay, biography, autobiography, short story, and novel.
* AZ residents $37 per credit.

Introduction to Literature
Trinidad State Junior College
TRIN#LIT115 Undergraduate   3 credits $???
This course is designed to be a basic introduction to literature, and is often taken by students who have never studied literature before. Emphasis is placed on basic terms and concepts related to reading and understanding short stories, poetry, and drama.

Introduction to Literature I
Front Range Community College
FRCC#LIT115 Undergraduate   3 credits $790
Introduces students to fiction, poetry, and drama. Emphasizes active and responsive reading. 45 Contact Hours.

Introduction to Modern Drama
University of Minnesota
MINN#ENGL1019 Undergraduate 4 credits $356
A study of modern drama, including plays by Ibsen, Strindberg, Chekhov, Synge, Shaw, O'Neill, Pirandello, Brecht, Williams, Miller, Ionesco, and Beckett. Prerequisite: COMP1011 or equivalent.

Introduction to Modern Poetry
University of Minnesota
MINN#ENGL1017 Undergraduate 4 credits $356
A study of modern British and American poetry organized around themes (war, the city, nature, death, love) and including such writers as Yeats, Thomas, Auden, Eliot, Cummings, Frost, and Stevens. Audiocassette programs by Lynette Reini-Grandell complement this course.

Introduction To Music
Dakota State University
DAKO#MUS100 Undergraduate   3 credits $447
This course provides the listener with the understandings about music today, including rock, pop, jazz, aleatoric, electronic, symphonic and other styles. Changes in the basic elements of music are studied to provide a perspective about the music performed and heard in the US.

Introduction to Music Appreciation
University of Nevada-Reno
NERE#C121 Undergraduate   3 credits $210
The purpose of this course is to increase your understanding, appreciation, enjoyment, and love of music. With this in mind, upon successful completion of the course, you should be able to do the following: identify and understand the elements of music; listen critically and comment intelligently on all styles of music; attend and enjoy concerts of all kinds, feeling comfortable in many musical situations; identify representative composers/performers of different musical eras; identify representative compositions of different musical eras; and understand a bit about the process of making music.

Introduction to Music Theory
Pima Community College
PIMA#MUS102 Undergraduate   3 credits $165*
Introduction to the fundamentals of music designed to develop basic literacy in music for non-majors. Includes the study of notation, melody, harmony, rhythm, and musical terminology. Prerequisites: It is recommended that students who are thinking of pursuing music as a major take MUS027 and MUS102 concurrently.
* AZ residents pay $32 per credit.

Introduction to Philosophical Problems
Cerro Coso Community College
CECO#PHILC1 Undergraduate 3 credits $345*
A survey of the nature of human interactions within the self, with other persons, with society, with one's surroundings, and in relation to ultimate beliefs, with the goal of increased awareness of the limitations of human certainty. Prerequisite: Level 1 reading, level 2 writing classification recommended.
* CA residents pay $13 per credit.

Introduction to Philosophy
City University
CITY#HUM200 Undergraduate 5 qu. credits $785
An overview of classical, ethical theories and moral responsibility; sources of morality, free will versus determinism, and debates centering on truth, knowledge & justice.

Introduction to Philosophy
University of Minnesota
MINN#PHIL1002 Undergraduate 5 credits $445
For much of its history, Western philosophy has been largely a matter of attempting to provide an unshakable foundation for either morals or the natural sciences. Most Western philosophers have spent their intellectual careers trying to define what knowledge and certainty are for the benefit of these two areas of knowledge. Course traces the history of that endeavor by looking at philosophers who are usually cited as pillars of the Western theory of knowledge and metaphysics: Plato, Descartes, Hume, Kant, Wittgenstein, and Kuhn.

Introduction to Philosophy
New Hampshire College
NEHA#PHL110 Undergraduate 3 credits $1656
This course provides a general introduction to philosophy beginning with issues raised by contemporary problems. Traditional problems and approaches in philosophy are examined in relation to the present.

Introduction to Philosophy
Rio Salado College
RISA#PHI101 Undergraduate 3 credits $186*
General consideration of human nature and the nature of the universe. Knowledge, perception, freedom and determinism, and the existence of God.
* AZ residents $37 per credit.

Introduction to Poetry
Indiana University
INDI#L205 Undergraduate 3 credits $268
Kinds, conventions, and elements of poetry in a selection of poems from several historical periods.

Introduction to Radio and Television
State University of New York
SUNY#13116 Undergraduate 3 credits $1038*
This course is a survey of American radio and television, including historical and technological development and the effects of broadcasting and corresponding technologies on society. Programming concepts and industry structure, ethical considerations in broadcasting, current and future directions in broadcast technology, and the changing nature of this industry are also considered. Prerequisites: Students need to communicate at an English I level.
* NY residents tuition: $137 per credit.

Introduction to Religion
Mercy College
MERC#RE109 Undergraduate 3 credits $900
An introduction to some fundamental questions underlying the study of all religions. Where does religion come from? Were the religions of early civilizations "primitive"? Are there reasons for religious beliefs or is religions simply a matter of subjective feeling? How would one try to distinguish between religion and magic?.

Introduction to Screenwriting I
UCLA
UCLA#X451D Undergraduate 3 credits $450
This course involves practical analysis of screenplays, emphasizing story structure, scenes, dialogue, and characterization. Students download and transmit writing assignments electronically, then receive feedback from their electronic "classmates" and individual notes from the instructor. Assignments are tailored to help students master the basics of screenwriting as well as conceptualize and begin to shape their own script. The course goal is to complete an outline or treatment and be ready to begin writing a screenplay.

Introduction to Screenwriting II
UCLA
UCLA#X451E Undergraduate 3 credits $450
For students familiar with the fundamental elements of film and television screenplays, this online course devotes special attention to shaping and refining the story-the all important building block of successful screenplays that is often vastly underestimated by beginning writers. Students work on projects at their own pace as well as receive weekly transmissions giving extensive feedback on their work.

Introduction to Shakespeare
Indiana University
INDI#L220 Undergraduate 3 credits $268
Study of Shakespeare's major plays and poems.

Introduction to The Music Business
University of Colorado
CUON#MUS2700 Undergraduate 3 credits $1953*
An overview of the Music and Entertainment Industries, with emphasis on the function and interaction of the music industry "system," including artists, songwriters, publishers, record labels, trade associations, performing rights societies, producers, managers and myriad others. The current market for music and entertainment will be discussed, as well as exposure to the possibilities brought about through technological and global developments.
* CO residents tuition: $136 per credit.

Introduction to the Religions of South Asia
University of Minnesota
MINN#RELS1031 Undergraduate 4 credits $356
Introduction to Hinduism, Buddhism, and Jainism.

Introduction to the Theatre
University of Minnesota
MINN#TH1101 Undergraduate 4 credits $356
An eclectic overview of Western drama from Aeschylus to August Wilson, from Shakespeare to Sam Shepard. This course focuses on the plays, playwrights, and players that have shaped today's theatre, film, and television. Students are required to attend theatre performances and to enhance their critical skills and understanding of the processes and forms of drama and of production.

Introduction to the Visual Arts
University of Minnesota
MINN#ARTH1001 Undergraduate 4 credits $356
Considers the basic issues of art. Examples of painting and sculpture are analyzed to illustrate the roles of art in society. Problems of design, materials, and technique are presented topically rather than chronologically.

Introduction to Theatre
Northern State University
NOST#THE100 Undergraduate 3 credits $248
A historical survey of all elements of the theatre designed to create an appreciation and understanding. This course fulfills three semester hours of the Fine Arts requirements for general education.

Introduction to World Religions
Christopher Newport University
CHNE#RSTD211 Undergraduate 3 credits $993
Involves a consideration of the external history and the inner dynamics of diverse religious traditions. Prehistoric and primal religions will be considered alongside such traditions as Judaism, Christianity, Islam, Hinduism, Buddhism, Confucianism, Taoism, and Shinto. Questions regarding the general nature of religious belief and practice will also be discussed. What is religion? What is a myth? What is the relation of religion and society?.

Introduction World Religions
Thomas Edison State College
THED#OLREL405 Undergraduate 3 credits $397*
Emphasis is on specific forms of religious expression and practice, rather than the more abstract or theological aspects. Religions covered are those of the majority of humankind and living traditions in today's world: Hinduism, Buddhism, religions of China and Japan, Judaism, Christianity, Islam, and several African primal religions. A section deals with alternatives to religion, such as Marxism and scientific humanism.
* NJ residents tuition: $33 per credit.

Islam
Ohio University
OHIO#PHIL372 Undergraduate 4 credits $256
Introduction to basic ideas, history, and background. Note: A VHS videotape is an optional supplement to the course. Prereq: jr rank.

Issues in Ethics & Leadership
Marylhurst College
MARY#MGT418 Undergraduate 6 credits $1,302
Are you a transformational leader or a transactional leader? How do ethical considerations become incorporated into decision processes? How do you prefer to use power in organizational settings? These issues and many others are explored in this course. With the completion of this course of study, you will have gained new insights into yourself as a manager, as a leader, and as decision maker as we prepare to enter the second millenium. Prerequisite: MGT303, MGT338.

James Joyce
University of Minnesota
MINN#ENGL5363 Undergraduate 4 credits $391
An introduction to the life and works of Joyce, including the epiphanies, the poems, the short story collection Dubliners, and the novels Portrait of the Artist as a Young Man and Ulysses and bits of Finnegans Wake.

Journal and Memoir Writing
University of Minnesota
MINN#ENGW5201 Undergraduate 4 credits $391
Students read selected journals and memoirs, as well as complete exercises based on the readings. The journal writing process--informal and fragmentary--is the basis of all writing suggestions; students are encouraged to work from memory and personal experience. The course project is to write a memoir or autobiographical work. Students are encouraged to submit more polished memoir or autobiography and not the originating journal exercises.

Journal and Memoir Writing II
University of Minnesota
MINN#ENGW5202 Undergraduate 4 credits $391
Using the process of writing from brainstorming to drafting to revision, this course guides students to involve memory in writing several genres: poems, traditional memoir essays, and fiction. The range of genres allows students to consider which genre best suits them or a particular subject. The course also looks at how cultures shape memory differently, suggesting work from Native American, Hispanic, Asian American, and African American writers.

Journaling into Fiction
University of Minnesota
MINN#ENGW3110 Undergraduate 4 credits $391
An exploration of the links between private and public writing. Students build on the strengths and skills already present in their private writing as they move more fully into the world of the imagination to create fiction, poems, or song. Writing assignments illustrate the ways private journaling may be turned into fiction, using techniques such as dreams, prose poems, stream of consciousness, found art, and other. Prerequisites: ENGW1101, 1102, 1103, or equivalent.

King Lear Online
University of Wisconsin
WISC#ENGL0290 Undergraduate 1 credits $???
Students spend the semester in an on-line discussion of "King Lear," one of Shakespeare's greatest tragedies, with side glances at the play's sources and critical approaches to it through the years. Students may choose between a traditional term paper and an on-line project.

Knowledge and Reality
MiraCosta College
MIRA#PHIL101 Undergraduate 3 credits $357
In this course we will be studying the nature of philosophy, in general, and several of the major issues in philosophy: the existence of an essential self or mind, personal identity, the nature of belief, the possibility of knowledge, the nature of reality, and the varieties of religious belief. Through readings from a variety of cultural and philosophical traditions we will be looking at several methodologies for finding answers to fundamental questions, and examine them for similarities and differences. We will also be honing our abilities to think and write philosophically. Prerequisite: Traversing Philosophical Boundaries, Max O. Hallman Do Androids Dream of Electric Sheep, Phillip K. Dick.

Late Plays of Shakespeare
Indiana University
INDI#L314 Undergraduate 3 credits $268
Close reading of eight of Shakespeare's later plays.

Latin American Culture and Civilization I
Indiana University
INDI#H211 Undergraduate 3 credits $268
1492-1850. African, Indian, Spanish, Portuguese heritage. Discovery and conquest. Clash of cultures. Spanish empire. Society, culture, economics, politics. Bourbon reform, independence, new republics.

Latin American History 1929 to Present
University of Minnesota
MINN#HIST3403 Undergraduate 4 credits $391
Provides students with an understanding of 20th-century Latin American social, economic, and political history, focusing on the struggles staged by the popular classes. Particular attention is given to the activities of peasants and workers as well as to the movements for national liberation and civil rights.

Latin American History Colonial Period to 1800
University of Minnesota
MINN#HIST3401 Undergraduate 4 credits $391
An examination of the pre-Hispanic and colonial period to 1800, with emphasis on social, cultural, and economic aspects. Also considers the settlement of the Americas by Europeans and Africans, the exploitation of the Americas, and the responses of dominated people in the Americas.

Latin Poetry - Cicero
University of Minnesota
MINN#LAT3105 Undergraduate 5 credits $489
The complete speech "Pro Rabirio." Prerequisite: LAT1103 or equivalent.

Latin Poetry - Vergil's Aeneid
University of Minnesota
MINN#LAT3106 Undergraduate 5 credits $489
Readings of selections from Books I-II; background material about Roman life and thought is included in the text. Prerequisite: LAT1103, 3105, or equivalent.

Latin Prose and Poetry - Caesar and Others
University of Minnesota
MINN#LAT1104 Undergraduate 5 credits $445
Selections from Cicero, Livy, and Ovid are read. In addition to the review of Latin grammar incorporated in the readings, the readings familiarize students with the legends of Rome's founding and early heroes, the defeat of its army by Hannibal at Cannae, the first important speech of its most brilliant orator, Cicero, his correspondence after the assassination of Julius Caesar, and Ovid's poetic interpretation of several Greek myths. Literary and historical background material is provided in English. Prerequisite: LAT1103 or equivalent.

Legal Aspects of Arts Administration
Golden Gate University
GOLD#AA302 Undergraduate 3 credits $1059
Applies accounting and budgeting principles to management situation of non-profit and for-profit arts organizations. Incorporates techniques and processes of financial planning and control. Prerequisites: ACCTG 201 (or ACCTG 1A), and AA300A.

Literature of Alaska & Yukon Territory
University of Alaska - Fairbanks
ALFA#ENGL350 Undergraduate 3 credits $237
Study of representative works of fiction, verse, and non-fiction which deal with Alaska and the Yukon Territory. Prerequisite: ENGL111 or permission of instructor.

Literary Aspects of Journalism
University of Minnesota
MINN#JOUR5606 Undergraduate 4 credits $391
A study of the literary aspects of journalism as exemplified in, and influenced by, works of English and U.S. writers, past and present--John Hersey, Lillian Ross, Joan Didion, Truman Capote, Tom Wolfe, and others. Explores the relationship between journalism and literature and how this relationship has figured in the development of U.S. journalism. Written assignments focus on analysis of readings; also, students may opt to write a piece of their own literary journalism.

Literary Types
University of Missouri
MOCE#LI12 Undergraduate 3 credits $387
This course introduces the student to various literary types, including poetry, drama, and the short story.

Literature
California State University - Dominguez Hills
CADO#HUX502 Undergraduate 2 credits $270
Advanced study of the nature of literature by examination of images of self in selected poems and novels.

Literature and Ideas II
Christopher Newport University
CHNE#ENGL208G Undergraduate 3 credits $993
A thematic study of novels, stories, plays, and poems written by the best of writers world-wide. Readings introduce Asian, African, and South American traditions, as well as North American and Europe. Designed for non-English majors for humanities requirement and elective credit. Prerequisite: Six-hour freshman English sequence.

Literature and Society of the Middle East
University of Colorado
CUON#ENGL3300 Undergraduate 3 credits $1953*
This course is a study of the contemporary literatures of the Middle East through exposure to representative samples of Turkish, Persian, Arabic, and Hebrew novels, short stories, plays, and poetry in English translation. At the same time, diverse approaches to social and literary interpretation and evaluation will be discussed as warranted. Although the course is not intended to follow a rigid thematic approach, the works have been selected with a view toward a greater understanding of important interrelated issues in these literatures.
* CO residents tuition: $136 per credit.

Literature of American Minorities
University of Minnesota
MINN#ENGL1591 Undergraduate 4 credits $356
Fiction, autobiography, and poetry by award-winning African American, American Indian, Asian American, and Chicano/Chicana writers. Introduction to social and literary issues affecting minority group identity and individual writers. Offers perspectives on American minorities through the lens of modern and contemporary literature.

Literature of the Americas
Western Illinois University
WEIL#ENG400A Undergraduate 6 credits $1590*
Deepen your understanding of what constitutes American literature through an exploration of Spanish-American, African-American, and French- and English-Canadian fiction. The novels and short stories illuminate the themes common to all four cultures--the nature of myth and history, the dilemma of the intellectual, the clash of cultures, the war of the sexes--all dramatized in very different ways.
* IL residents tuition: $88 per credit.

Literature of the New Testament
University of Missouri
MOCE#LI124 Undergraduate 3 credits $387
This course presents a comprehensive understanding of the New Testament: its literary background and its significance for Western Civilization.

Literature of the Old Testament
University of Missouri
MOCE#LI125 Undergraduate 3 credits $387
This course analyzes representative stories, themes, and concepts of the Old Testament by examining nineteen of its books from a literary perspective.

Literature Seminar
New York Institute of Technology
NYIT#EN1100 Undergraduate 3 credits $???
An advanced course which explores in depth each semester one major literary figure, one historical period, one movement, one literary type, one work, or the writing of literature in the areas of fiction, nonfiction, poetry, or drama. The subject will vary from offering to offering. A student may repeat the seminar but not any one given course content.

Literature-Based Research
Fayetteville Technical Community College
FAYE#ENG113 Undergraduate 3 credits $489*
This course, the second in a series of two, expands the concepts developed in ENG 111 by focusing on writing that involves literature-based research and documentation. Emphasis is placed on critical reading and thinking and the analysis and interpretation of prose, poetry, and drama: plot, characterization, theme, cultural context, etc.
* North Carolina residents and non-resident US military personnel stationed within the state tuition: $60; NC senior citizens: free.

Literatures of the United States
University of Minnesota
MINN#GC1365 Undergraduate 4 credits $356
A historic survey and analysis of nearly 30 giants of American fiction. Students examine the development of the form of the short story in America to enhance their understanding and appreciation of a wide range of writers, from Irving's early sketches to Barthelme's and Coover's present-day experiments.

Living Myths
Humboldt State University
HUMB#RS300 Undergraduate 3 credits $345
Myths, "sacred stories," as reservoirs of people's articulate thought about themselves and their condition. How myths convey a culture's meanings and values.

Logic
Strayer University
STRA#HUM200 Undergraduate 4.5 credits $665
Enables students to develop analytical, inductive and deductive reasoning through the study of syllogistic, symbolic, and informal logic. Provides methods of constructing arguments, evaluating statements, and recognizing fallacies in theory as well as in practice.

Logic and Language
University of Missouri
MOCE#LO60 Undergraduate 3 credits $387
This course studies the basic rules of informal and symbolic logic; it includes discussion on the types of argumentation; methods of reasoning; valid reasoning; and inductive and deductive reasoning as used in the sciences and in communication. Perquisites-sophomore standing.

Logic and Scientific Method
New York Institute of Technology
NYIT#SS515 Undergraduate 3 credits $???
An introduction to the valid forms of reasoning and the methods of inquiry practiced by the natural, social and behavioral sciences.

Loss Prevention - Internship
Fox Valley Technical College
FOVA#504-102 Undergraduate 3 credits $200
This course allows the student to gain experience in the loss prevention field through actual on-the-job activities. These experiences will relate most directly to the areas of interest to the student. Possible experiences could include retail theft investigation, internal theft investigation, industrial/commercial security patrol, private detective shadowing, CCTV monitoring and alarm installation work. Students will also participate in a security survey of a business in their community. The intern experience would integrate the classroom knowledge previously gained. Prerequisite: 50 credit minimum program completion.

Madness and Deviant Behavior in Ancient Greece and Rome
University of Minnesota
MINN#CLAS5005 Undergraduate 4 credits $391
Definitions of madness in Greece and Rome and theories of its etiology; assessment of predisposing factors in Greece and Rome. Examples of madness from mythology, legend, and history; cross-cultural comparison with contemporary United States.

Magic, Witchcraft, and the Occult in Greece and Rome
University of Minnesota
MINN#CLAS1019 Undergraduate 4 credits $356
Magic and witchcraft in classical literature and mythology as observed from papyri, epigraphical and literary evidence. Beliefs and practices concerning prophecy and the interpretation of dreams. Explores the changing role of witchcraft and divine possession from early to later antiquity, and the relation of these phenomena to changes in economic and social conditions.

Major American Writers - Fitzgerald and Hemingway
University of Minnesota
MINN#ENGL3410 Undergraduate 4 credits $391
An examination of the short stories of two contemporary early 20th-century writers--F. Scott Fitzgerald and Ernest Hemingway--in the context of Jazz Age literary, cultural, and artistic developments.

Major American Writers I
Eastern Oregon University
EAOR#ENGL253 Undergraduate 4 credits $330
A survey of major American authors from the Colonial period through the Civil War. Prerequisite: WR121 or WR131 and any 100-level English course.

Major American Writers II
Eastern Oregon University
EAOR#ENGL254 Undergraduate 4 credits $320
A survey of major American authors from reconstruction to the present. Prerequisite: WR121 or WR131 and any 100-level English course.

Major Philosophers - Socrates-Sartre
Thomas Edison State College
THED#OLPHI376 Undergraduate 3 credits $397*
An introductory course in philosophy. The course examines six major philosophers of Western Civilization: Plato, Descartes, Hume, Hegel, Marx and Sartre. Each will be shown developing his own position as a response to the real problems which define his particular time. Each philosopher's distinctive treatment of these problems conditioned the way in which later thinkers dealt with similar problems, and raised new problems which became the subject matter for future thought and investigation.
* NJ residents tuition: $33 per credit.

Major Questions in Philosophy
University of Missouri
MOCE#PH50 Undergraduate   3 credits $387
This course presents an introduction to traditional philosophical problems and methods of philosophical inquiry. Consideration is given to different philosophical theories on reality, man, nature, God, knowledge and how it is acquired, values, and social issues. Perquisites-sophomore standing or consent of instructor.

Making of Modern Britain
University of Missouri
MOCE#HI220 Undergraduate   3 credits $387
This course surveys modern Britain from the era of the Restoration and Glorious Revolution (1660-1689) to the present. Major themes include the social, intellectual, cultural, political, and economic aspects of modern and contemporary Britain. Perquisites: History 112.

Marketing & PR in Arts Administration
Golden Gate University
GOLD#AA301 Undergraduate   3 credits $1059
Introduces the principle and practices of marketing and public relations in arts administration. You will study the formulation and implementation of marketing and PR strategies including box office procedures, pricing, season ticket campaigns, telemarketing, direct mail, special events, design and printing of brochures, community outreach and marketing aspects of touring and booking of arts group. Prerequisite: AA300A.

Mass Communication
New Hampshire College
NEHA#COM226 Undergraduate   3 credits $1656
This is a survey course that covers the nature of mass media communication, its development, and its effect upon modern forms of communication. The course focuses on how and why the media operate as they do, as well as on how media performance might be improved.

Masterpieces of Western Literature Since the Renaissance
Pennsylvania State University
PENN#CMLIT002 Undergraduate   3 credits $345
Universal themes and cultural values by such writers as Voltaire, Goethe, Ibsen, Flaubert, Doestoevsky, Dickinson, Mann, Duras, Borges, and Rich. Note: 400-level courses are available only to students with junior or senior standing.

Masterpieces of World Literature I & II
Trinidad State Junior College
TRIN#LIT201 Undergraduate   6 credits $???
This two-semester sequence of courses focuses on introducing students to masterpieces of world literature, with LIT201 focusing on the Greek classics up until about the time of Shakespeare, and LIT202 covering material from the Enlightenment to the present.

Memorializing Vietnam
New School for Social Research
NEWS#0699 Undergraduate   3 credits $1638*
"Vietnam, Vietnam, Vietnam," wrote the war correspondent Michael Herr, "say [it] again, until the word lost all its old loads of pain, pleasure, horror, guilt, nostalgia." But the memory of Vietnam still weighs heavily upon America's conscience. We focus upon the genre of modern American war literature and students are asked to view several Vietnam War films. In particular, we explore the innovations and conventions found in the novels, memoirs, and short stories dealing with the Vietnam War.
* Non-credit option, tuition: $365.

Methods of Written Communication
University of Alaska - Fairbanks
ALFA#ENGL111 Undergraduate   3 credits $213
Instruction in writing expository prose, including generating topics as part of the writing process. Practice in developing, organizing, revising, and editing essays. Prerequisite: Placement exam or DEVE070.

Middle Ages-Dostoevsky in Translation
University of Minnesota
MINN#RUSS3421 Undergraduate 4 credits $391
The history of Russian literature from its beginning (about A.D. 1000) to the middle of the 19th century. Covers Pushkin, Gogol, and Dostoevsky. Students read both literary works (in English) and scholarly materials (historical, biographical, critical commentary), and complete essay writing assignments.

Modern Authors
New Hampshire College
NEHA#ENG334 Undergraduate   3 credits $1656
This course will focus entirely on the short story, and since the short story has had its most extraordinary flowering in the 20th- century, we will deal primarily with the modern short story. We will read not only many by great English and American writers, but also stories from other cultures written originally in other languages. We will begin with works from the late 19th-century and work our way up to contemporary masterpieces. Prerequisite: any 200-level literature course or permission of the instructor.

Modern Drama
Western Illinois University
WEIL#ENG360 Undergraduate   3 credits $795*
Is a survey of drama beginning with the plays of August Strindberg and Henrik Ibsen. The course traces various elements of theatre through the works of several established playwrights, including Oscar Wilde, Anton Chekhov, John Synge, George Bernard Shaw, and Tennessee Williams. In addition to reading several dramas, you have the opportunity to view and listen to a play.
* IL residents tuition: $88 per credit.

Modern Drama since 1920
University of Minnesota
MINN#ENGL5175 Undergraduate 4 credits $391
This course provides an introduction to the themes and techniques of modern drama since the 1920s. The topics explored include the nature of the theatrical play, the "modernism" in modern drama, and 13 important plays written from 1920 to 1960 by 10 major playwrights--Pirandello, Anouilh, Giradoux, O'Neill, Miller, Lorca, Williams, Brecht, Beckett, and Pinter.

Modern Women Writers
University of Minnesota
MINN#ENGL3920 Undergraduate 4 credits $391
Fiction and poetry by British and American women writers from 1900 to the present--Kate Chopin, Edith Wharton, Virginia Woolf, Doris Lessing, Eudora Welty, Sylvia Plath, Anne Sexton, Toni Morrison, Audre Lorde, and Adrienne Rich. Emphasizes how these writers perceived themselves as women and as artists, their analyses of the roles of women in modern society, and the literary qualities of their works.

Modes of Literature
University of Alaska - Fairbanks
ALFA#ENGL211 Undergraduate 3 credits $213
Instruction in writing through close analysis of literature. Research paper required. Prerequisite: Sophomore standing and completion of ENGL111 or equivalent.

Moral Philosophy
Western Illinois University
WEIL#PHI330 Undergraduate 3 credits $795*
Presents a broad treatment of the central problems of moral philosophy. The course is organized around major topics such as the nature of morality, theories of values, varieties of egoism, theories of obligation, and views about rights and justice. The contributions of classical philosophers such as Plato and Aristotle are studied, along with the views of contemporary thinkers. The practical implications of various theories are explored.
* IL residents tuition: $88 per credit.

Morality in 20th Century Thought
California State University - Dominguez Hills
CADO#HUX548 Undergraduate 3 credits $405
An examination of values and morality in modern culture against a backdrop of seemingly amoral scientific and technological progress.

Multigenre Writing From Multicultural Roots
New School for Social Research
NEWS#1804 Undergraduate 3 credits $1638*
As Cornel West has written, our postmodern, postcolonial texts "reject the abstract, general, and universal in light of the concrete, specific, and particular; [instead they] historicize, contextualize, and pluralize by highlighting the contingent, provisional, variable, tentative, shifting, and changing." While the text cites oppression or inequality, it also digs into the past to create critical perspectives of the present, and ultimately to question categories that fix superficial identities. Workshop participants select from genealogy, etymology, memoirs, interviews, history, and interdisciplinary research to write a holistic manuscript. The sum of the parts may be autobiography, novel, personal essay, or narrative poem.
* Non-credit option, tuition: $365.

Music
California State University - Dominguez Hills
CADO#HUX503 Undergraduate 2 credits $270
Advanced study of music, focusing on concepts of meaning and form in music at a philosophical rather than theoretical level. The ability to read music is not required.

Music Appreciation
Cerro Coso Community College
CECO#MUSC22 Undergraduate 3 credits $345*
Understanding music as a listener. Study of ingredients found in music (melody, harmony, rhythm and form, etc.), choral and instrumental mediums (oratories, symphonies, etc.), and the various styles and historical periods of music. Some concert attendance is required.
* California resident tuition: $13 per credit.

Music Appreciation
University of Colorado
CUON#PMUS1001 Undergraduate 3 credits $1953*
For non-music majors who want to learn how to listen to music with greater understanding and pleasure. Explores the style of music in the major compositional periods, including contemporary pops music. No degree credit for music majors.
* CO residents tuition: $136 per credit.

Music Appreciation
Mercy College
MERC#MU107 Undergraduate 3 credits $900
Characteristics of the periods of music history; important composers; significant musical/stylistic elements; the organization of musical ideas and sounds; musical terms and vocabulary. Directed listening; lectures; films; readings.

Music Appreciation
University of Missouri
MOCE#MU120 Undergraduate 3 credits $387
Designed for students with little or no music background, this course emphasizes the basic elements of music and the historical and stylistic periods, which are illustrated by examples of different genres. Perquisites: Course cannot be used toward a music degree.

Music Appreciation
Roane State Community College
ROAN#MUS130   Undergraduate   3 credits $459*
Open to all students who desire a better understanding of music. In this one-semester course, traditional art music will be explored. Listening assignments are included.
* Tennessee residents tuition: $48 per semester hour.

Music Fundamentals
University of Alaska - Fairbanks
ALFA#MUS103   Undergraduate   3 credits $213
An introductory study of the language of music. Includes basic notation, melodic and rhythmic writing, scales, bass and treble clefs, and basic harmony.

Music Fundamentals
University of Colorado
CUON#PMUS1010   Undergraduate 3 credits $1953*
An introduction to the rudiments of music notation, basic ear training, and reading of music. Intended for the student with little or no musical background. No degree credit for music majors.
* CO residents tuition: $136 per credit.

Narrative Art of Alaska Native Peoples
University of Alaska - Fairbanks
ALFA#ENGLF349   Undergraduate 3 credits $237
The course is divided into six units, with the first five covering material from different community and cultural groupings. The sixth unit consists of a consideration of a collection of material from all of the groups we will have covered. Each of the lessons will start with a reading or listening assignment. Questions have been included to assist you in your consideration of the text material. Additionally, journal suggestions have been made to assist you in starting this course requirement. Finally, discussion questions and writing assignments are identified.

Native American Literature
Yavapai Community College
YAVA#ENG239E   Undergraduate   3 credits $???
The landscape in the Southwest is diverse, dramatic and wondrous. It's very close to the large population of native peoples who come from varied, vital and rich cultures, peoples who have lived with this land in harmony and balance for thousands of years. "We are the land," writes Paula Gunn Allen from Laguna Pueblo. "The Earth is, in a very real sense, the same as ourselves, and it is the primary point that's made in the fiction and poetry of Native American writers of the Southwest." In recent years there has been a literary explosion in the Southwest, often cited as a Native American Renaissance. This course explores this immense and exciting body of literature - oral and written, ancient and contemporary.

Natural History of Alaska
University of Alaska - Fairbanks
ALFA#BIOL104   Undergraduate   3 credits $213
Aspects of the physical environment peculiar to the north and important in determining the biological setting; major ecosystem concepts to develop an appreciation for land use and wildlife management problems in both terrestrial and aquatic situations.

Nature Writing
UCLA
UCLA#X445   Undergraduate   3 credits $450
Primarily directed toward aspiring nature and outdoors writers, this online course focuses on basic and specific exercises in writing about nature, guiding participants to explore, observe, and record what they see outdoors to capture memories about the role nature has played in their life. Lectures cover the practical information about the physical realities of nature writing, techniques for writing in the wild, capturing thoughts in a notebook, finding a market for nonfiction articles and essays with an outdoor focus, and developing the writer's voice and style.

News in Historical Perspective
State University of New York
SUNY#243504   Undergraduate   4 credits $586*
Become more informed about contemporary issues, problems, controversies, questions, and topics of national and international significance. Gain an appreciation of the deep connections with the past the historical perspective. Although The New York Times will serve as the main vehicle for monitoring the news, read other publications and follow radio and television broadcast news. This writing and research course requires ready access to library resources, in person and/or by computer and modem. Prerequisite: Six credits in college level history courses.
* NY residents tuition: $515

Nineteenth-Century British Fiction
Indiana University
INDI#L348   Undergraduate   3 credits $268
Forms, techniques, and theories of fiction as exemplified by such writers as Thackeray, Dickens, Eliot, and Hardy.

North America in the New World
Salve Regina University
SALV#INR550   Grad   3 credits $???
Topics studied include the postwar "revolution" in North American foreign policy and the effects of rapid change and economic ecological crisis on that policy.

Novel Writing I
UCLA
UCLA#X450G   Undergraduate   3 credits $450
That novel is inside you waiting to emerge, but deciding where and how to begin and organizing yourself to handle the demands of writing the manuscript seems daunting. It need not be. This limited-enrollment workshop focuses on identifying obstacles to writing a novel and eliminating them, as well as establishing an intimacy with your characters and creating a solid outline to guide you through your story.

Online Book Club
Waukesha County Technical College
WAUK#801645001   Undergraduate .25 credits $48
The purpose of our club is to have fun and to learn by reading, discussing, and recommending books. We will read a book each month and meet in our chat room on the Internet. If we choose, we can step up our pace of reading and chatting. Except for the first selection, club members, as a group, will decide the reading list. Members are encouraged to make proposals and book recommendations and to correspond regularly with each other by e-mail. Members may decide to have additional meetings either on or off campus.

Online Drawing Workshop for Beginners
New School for Social Research
NEWS#2305   Undergraduate   2 credits $1092
We experiment, investigate, and experience drawing as a unique process of expression. This class allows for continuous discussion, instruction, and slide presentations, while taking you through a progressive series of drawing exercises that develop an understanding of a wide range of drawing principles from line and form to transformation and memory. The course takes advantage of both the private experience of this activity and the new technology, which allows 24-hour access to an exchange of information and inquiry, and gives us a non-judgmental space within which to explore drawing.

Online Fiction Workshop
State University of New York
SUNY#ENG329001   Undergraduate 3 credits $540*
In this course, the student will be asked to read and write, and to share their stories with the class in workshops. They will cover the fundamentals of narrative technique, point of view, characterization, and voice. The slightly unusual thing about this course is that it is not taught in the "traditional" classroom. This means that the students will not be sitting in desks, staring at a teacher who will be verbalizing for an hour and a half.
* NY residents tuition: $90 per credit

Online Fiction Workshop
Syracuse University
SYRA#ETS200   Undergraduate   3 credits $960
This is an intensive workshop in the art and craft of writing fiction, primarily the short story. You read the work of other writers in this cyberspace class, as well as the work of more established contemporary writers. Course work is distributed and discussed via E-mail. Students write two or three short stories, with extensive revisions. Limited enrollment.

Oral Tradition and Folklore
University of Alaska - Fairbanks
ALFA#ANTH230   Undergraduate   3 credits $213
Study and collection of folklore and oral history and importance in communication; advantages, disadvantages of their recording and study. Sociocultural anthropology and anthropological linguistics related to oral traditions. Methods of folklorists and historians. Prerequisite: ANTH104.

Parent-Child Relationships
University of Iowa
IOWA#07E114   Undergraduate   3 credits $240
Most people have experienced a parent-child relationship either by growing up in a family or being a parent themselves. A variety of surveys indicate that most people feel that a satisfactory family life is one of the most important things that one can accomplish in life. However, relatively few people take the opportunity to seriously consider the choices possible in being a parent. Perhaps because family life is so common, it is assumed that living in a family is all the preparation that is needed.

Personal Nonfiction
Western Illinois University
WEIL#ENG400B   Undergraduate   3 credits $795*
These literary forms reflect the writer's self directly, often with surprising insight and remarkable poignancy. You may select six books you wish to read from a list of 32 titles by Jane Addams, Maya Angelou, Frederick Douglass, Loren Eiseley, Anne Frank, Thomas Merton, Anais Nin, Henry David Thoreau, and many other writers.
* IL residents tuition: $88 per credit.

Perspectives on American Culture
Marylhurst College
MARY#HUM357   Undergraduate   3 credits $651
This course considers contrasting images of the US as represented in history, fiction and visual media. Students examine and create a reconciled view of differences reflected in seeing America as cradle of democracy, as imperialist nation, capitalist nation, cultural desert, as well as apex of civilization.

Perspectives on Death and Dying
State University of New York
SUNY#HMS240Y01   Undergraduate   3 credits $570*
We face many losses throughout the course of our lifetimes. Through the understanding of the different components of loss, the grief process and interventions to assist individuals and families who experience loss, the care giver can be instrumental in assisting clients to recovery.
* NY residents tuition: $90 per credit

Philosophical Problems -Metaphysics
Chemeketa Community College
CHEM#PHL201   Undergraduate   3 credits $123
This course is designed to give the student a general survey of one of the major areas of philosophy: Metaphysics (the study of the ultimate nature of reality). The emphasis of the course will be on the understanding of metaphysical terms and on the analysis of metaphysical theories and arguments. The course will prepare the student for other classes in Philosophy, such as logic, theory of knowledge, and ethics.

Philosophy
California State University - Dominguez Hills
CADO#HUX505   Undergraduate   2 credits $270
Advanced study of key concepts of Philosophy by focusing on contemporary issues and conflicts and their analogies in traditional philosophical readings.

Philosophy and History of Religion
New York Institute of Technology
NYIT#SS1525   Undergraduate   3 credits $???
This course acquaints the student with major elements associated with the development of religion as examined by psychologists, anthropologists, sociologists, and historians, as well as selected theologians. Special attention is paid to the philosophical analysis of religious analysis of religious phenomena, clarifying issues, such as the existence of God and gods, the nature of religious experiences, the belief in the soul, and other typically religious subjects.

Philosophy of Religion
Marylhurst College
MARY#PHL327   Undergraduate   3 credits $651
An introduction to some of the classical and contemporary issues in the philosophy of religion, including the arguments for the existence of God, the status of religious experience, and the relationship of faith and reason. Through reading and discussion of primary and secondary sources students will be encouraged to bring these issues to bear on their own beliefs. Prerequisite: introductory course or readings in philosophy.

Philosophy, Religion, and Ethics
Strayer University
STRA#HUM400   Undergraduate   4.5 credits $665
Offers an integrative approach to philosophical and religious world views in relation to such questions as the origin of all things, the limits of knowledge, and the role and responsibilities of the individual. Also examines the philosophical and religious views of the great thinkers throughout history.

Playwriting
New School for Social Research
NEWS#1786   Undergraduate   3 credits $1638*
An introduction to the basics of drama, including story, character, conflict, scene construction, and overall plotting. Students also consider issues such as drama as metaphor, realities of staging, and production problems. The course is geared to the theatrical experience of each individual student, with readings and writing exercises suggested when appropriate. Feedback from classmates approximates an audience experience, and the instructor provides detailed responses to all work submitted. Students should expect to complete at least twenty pages of script by the end of the course.
* Non-credit option, tuition: $365.

Playwriting I
University of Minnesota
MINN#TH5115   Undergraduate   4 credits $391
Designed to introduce the craft of writing for the theatre to students who have no experience in playwriting. This course provides a forum in which students complete their first one-act play, and emphasizes the technical elements, vocabulary of playwriting, the nature of the writing experience--from germinal idea to completed script--and strategies for taking a new play to market.

Poetry Workshop
UCLA
UCLA#X450F   Undergraduate   3 credits $450
What is a poem and how does it differ from prose? What sources can you, the beginning poet, look to for ideas and inspiration? How can you encourage a raw unfinished poem to become a thing of consummate power and beauty? This course presents a series of enjoyable and illuminating exercises to expand the imagination and introduce the complex issues of craft and revision in an accessible way.

Polish Culture and Civilization
Pennsylvania State University
PENN#POL100   Undergraduate   3 credits $345
Survey of Polish culture and civilization from 966 to the present.

Post Modernism in Theory and Practice
University of Central Florida
FLCE#LIT4932   Graduate   3 credits $1305*
This course will investigate postmodernism not merely as an aesthetic movement within the narrow bounds of contemporary literature, but as a much more broad-based occurrence in culture. We will investigate various definitions of what constitutes postmodernism including such matters as: the aesthetics of kitsch, the rise of multiculturalism, visions of 'late' capitalism, the end of Enlightenment metanarratives and of humanism, the status of simulation as opposed to representation, whether postmodernism is a chronological period or a recurrent historical moment and the effect of the increasing proliferation of digital technology.
* FL residents pay $129 per credit.

Preparatory College English
University of Alaska - Fairbanks
ALFA#DEVE070   Undergraduate   3 credits $213
Instruction in writing to improve students' fluency and accuracy and communication skills. Covers writing paragraphs to short essays. Preparation for ENGL111.

Preparatory Writing
New School for Social Research
NEWS#1612   Undergraduate   3 credits $1638*
A workshop for the new, rusty, or uncertain writer. Focus is on nonfiction, defined as writing that describes, explains, or argues. Students review grammar, punctuation, and usage. They work on assignments ranging from autobiographical sketches to persuasive essays, with the goal of producing clear and well-organized writing and developing their own voices and styles. A stylebook and reader are required texts. Since the ability to read critically is essential to the writing process, selected essays are assigned for class discussion.
* Non-credit option, tuition: $365.

Preparatory Writing for Grad School
UCLA
UCLA#X340D Undergraduate   2 credits $390
This online course reviews and clarifies the tools necessary for good writing a grasp of conventional English grammar and usage, an ability to vary sentence structure, and a sense of connotation for tone and style. Embedded in these skills are contextual vocabulary development and recognition of graduate audience expectations. Students experience both peer review and instructor feedback on a regular basis.

Problems of Philosophy
New York Institute of Technology
NYIT#SS1510 Undergraduate   3 credits $???
An introduction to philosophy by way of selected problems from various areas of philosophy. Topics include: the nature of prior knowledge and of scientific explanation, the existence of God, whether or not there can be moral knowledge, and the problem of free will. The course objective is to acquaint students with these philosophical issues, and through detailed discussion, to teach them how to analyze ideas critically.

Professional & Scientific Ethics
The Graduate School of America
TGSA#HS815W Graduate   4 credits $795
This course examines the historical origins of professional ethics, including issues affecting education, psychotherapy, law and institutional guidelines for protecting human subjects in research. Attention will be given to identifying effective methods for addressing ethical dilemmas and to current ethical issues in the human services.

Professional Novel Writing
UCLA
UCLA#X450C Undergraduate   3 credits $450
For those students with a novel-in-progress, this online workshop focuses on the necessary craft and vision of the novel-particularly character, structure, and emotional content-so that the work receives careful consideration from agents and editors. To accomplish this, the instructor reviews each student's project individually as well as promotes constructive feedback from other students. The student's goal is to produce a work of professional caliber toward the completion of a final draft.

Publication Design
State University of New York
SUNY#GC215 Undergraduate   3 credits $540*
This course is an exploration of visual problem-solving as it relates to the area of publication design. Students test their knowledge of the basic principles of design by applying those principles to magazine cover design, brochure design and annual reports. Experimentation in several areas of publication design is encouraged. Prerequisites: Digital Typography, Desktop Publishing for Windows or Mac and Digital Illustration.
* NY residents tuition: $90 per credit.

Reading Poetry
Pennsylvania State University
PENN#ENGL263 Undergraduate   3 credits $345
Elements of poetry, including meter, rhyme, image, diction, and poetic forms in British, American, and other English-language traditions. Prerequisite: ENGL015 or ENGL030.

Readings in Swedish Literary Texts
University of Minnesota
MINN#SWED3670 Undergraduate 4 credits $391
Swedish immigrants and a discussion of Swedes in America will be used to develop reading and writing skills. Samples from taped interviews are available on audiocassette. Prerequisite: SWED1106 or equivalent.

Regions and Nations of the World I
University of Missouri
MOCE#GE1 Undergraduate   3 credits $387
This introductory course studies regional character; spatial relationships; and major problems of Europe, Anglo-America (United States and Canada), and Latin America. It is organized around basic geographic concepts.

Regions and Nations of the World II
University of Missouri
MOCE#GE2 Undergraduate   3 credits $387
This introductory course studies regional character; spatial relationships; and major problems of the Commonwealth of Independent States, the Middle East, the Orient, Africa, and the Pacific world. It is organized around basic geographic concepts.

Religion and Human Culture
Southwest Missouri State University
MOSW#REL580 Graduate   3 credits $???
Employees in businesses, the military, government agencies, and those interested in learning about different faiths will benefit from a deeper understanding of the significance of religion in culture formation. This course will examine the role of religion in the human experience. As such, it introduces the student not only to the five major world religions (Hinduism, Buddhism, Judaism, Islam, and Christianity), but also to the scholarly study of religion and the role that religion plays in ethics. No prior study of religion is required.

Religion and Society
Indiana University
INDI#S313 Undergraduate   3 credits $268
The nature, consequences, and theoretical origins of religion, as evident in social construction and functional perspectives; the social origins and problems of religious organizations; and the relationships between religion and morality, science, magic, social class, minority status, economic development, and politics. Prerequisite: 3 credit hours of sociology or consent of instructor.

Religion in America
Western Illinois University
WEIL#PHI301 Undergraduate 3 credits $795*
This WIU teleclass investigates American religions from a historical perspective, from pre-colonial Native American cultures to the present. Particular attention is given to the impact of religion on the development of the culture core of the United States, the relationship between religion and politics in American social experience, popular religion, and the great religious Awakenings that helped American citizens redefine the identity and purpose of the nation in the face of cultural changes and challenges.
* IL residents tuition: $88 per credit.

Religion in American Life
Great Basin College
GRBA#PHIL145 Undergraduate 3 credits $186*
This course covers the history and organization of religious groups in America, with special attention being given to the relationships between religious convictions and social issues such as racial issues, sexual mores, and political affiliation.
* NV residents tuition: $43 per credit.

Religions of East Asia
University of Minnesota
MINN#EAS1032 Undergraduate 4 credits $356
A survey of the religious traditions of China and Japan, exploring beliefs and practices from antiquity to modern times. Course covers the elements of Confucianism, Taoism, Buddhism, and Shintoism, and examines the general role of religion in East Asian society. Readings include both primary and secondary materials.

Religions of the World
Northwest College
NOCO#GE270 Undergraduate 3 credits $???
This course is a survey of the major world religions, examining their beliefs and values. Current issues in religion will also be discussed. Prerequisite: GE180.

Research
Christopher Newport University
CHNE#GOVT492 Undergraduate 3 credits $993
Recommended for Government and Public Affairs majors and minors only. This course is designed to permit seniors an opportunity to explore their major and specialty fields through an applied or theoretical research effort. Prerequisite: GOVT201-202, or GOVT103G-104G and senior standing; or consent or instructor.

Research Seminar
Salve Regina University
SALV#HUM500 Grad 3 credits $???
In this course, students explore various research techniques and apply that knowledge not only in critically analyzing existing research but also in designing and implementing their own research project. Concepts addressed in the course include preparation of a literature review, qualitative and quantitative approaches, triangulation methods, research designs and their inherent threats to internal and external validity, sampling techniques, data collection methods, and ethical considerations. Note: this course must be taken in the first year of the program.

Reviewing and Criticism
Western Illinois University
WEIL#ENG405 Undergraduate 3 credits $795*
Provides practice in reviewing for the mass media, with a special emphasis on motion pictures. Focusing on American film genres, you will review seven films (seen in theatres, on videotape, or on television) for this course. Prerequisite: 2 years of English.
* IL residents tuition: $88 per credit.

Revolutionary America, 1754-1789
University of Missouri
MOCE#HI342 Undergraduate 3 credits $387
This course studies the causes and consequences of the American Revolution. Emphasis is placed upon the social conditions in America that contributed both to the Revolution and to the writing of the 1787 Constitution. Perquisites: History 175.

Rewriting the Screenplay
UCLA
UCLA#X451 Undergraduate 3 credits $450
For students who have completed a rough draft and are ready to tackle a major rewrite, this intensive six-week workshop devotes special attention to rewriting a rough draft screenplay. Students analyze their drafts during the first two weeks and rewrite 30 pages per week over the following four weeks. Weekly topics are presented to help the student throughout the writing process. The instructor closely monitors each student's progress, providing weekly feedback.

Rhetoric and Composition
Pennsylvania State University
PENN#ENGL015 Undergraduate 3 credits $345
Instruction and practice in writing expository prose that shows sensitivity to audience and purpose. Prerequisite: ENGL004 or satisfactory performance on the English placement examination.

Rock Music Style and Development
State University of New York
SUNY#MUS11571 Undergraduate 3 credits $1038*
This course explores rock music in terms of historical development, musical style and societal influence. The course discusses the pre-existing styles (pop, country and western, rhythm and blues, jazz, folk, gospel, and classical music) that have impacted on the evolution of rock music. The development of music listening skills is emphasized. Directed listenings reinforce the concept of musical style as a synthesis of musical elements (rhythm, pitch, dynamics, timbre, and form). The role of rock music as a social, cultural, economic and political force is examined.
* NY residents tuition: $137 per credit.

Rousseau
California State University - Dominguez Hills
CADO#HUX552 Undergraduate 3 credits $405
An examination of the life, thought, and influence of Rousseau, focusing on several recurrent themes: self-other, rational/non-rational, classic-romantic, dependence-independence, democracy-totalitarianism.

Science Fiction
Great Basin College
GRBA#ENG190 Undergraduate 3 credits $186*
An introduction to literary study through representative works of science fiction. Readings include Mary Shelly's Frankenstein, representative works by 20th century writers (such as Cordwainer Smith, Frederik Pohl, Samuel R. Delaney, James Tiptree Jr., Ursula K. Le Guin, Marion Zimmer Bradley, and Kim Stanley Robinson), and other works available on the Web.
* NV residents tuition: $43 per credit.

Science Fiction
Indiana University
INDI#L230B Undergraduate 3 credits $268
Study of the kinds, conventions, and theories of science fiction. Includes predominantly British and American literature.

Science Fiction and Fantasy
University of Minnesota
MINN#ENGL1020 Undergraduate 4 credits $356
The evolution of science fiction and fantasy from their 19th-century roots to the popular literature and mass media phenomena they are today. Considers such major themes as religion, sexuality, and the future of technology in the works of Ursula K. LeGuin, Frank Herbert, and Robert Heinlein, among others, and the contributions of such eminent and diverse fantasists as J. R. R. Tolkien, George Lucas, and Stephen King.

Scientific and Technical Literature
New York Institute of Technology
NYIT#EN1056 Undergraduate 3 credits $???
An intermediate-level course in which the art of prose writing is explored in depth. This course focuses on style and rhetoric and covers the development of scientific and technical literature. This course may be chosen to fulfill the Group A requirement. Prerequisite: EN1020.

Screenwriters, Playwrights & Fiction
UCLA
UCLA#X450H Undergraduate 3 credits $450
Scenes aren't just a lot of talk, they're the moving parts of a script. So writers beware: a static scene can grind a work to a dead halt. In this course, the various layers and levels of scene writing are explored to provide tools for creating dynamic scenes--i.e., scenes that move the story and characters along to the inevitable climax. Various tensions in the scene--between what is said and what is unspoken, between the upfront reason-to-be and the background motives--are investigated.

Screenwriting 1 - Fundamentals
New School for Social Research
NEWS#2816 Undergraduate 3 credits $455
This course for the beginning screenwriter introduces and demonstrates the tools, vocabulary, and techniques used to tell a screen story and take an original idea to outline form. Assignments illustrate basic three-act structure, the economic use of dialogue, visual storytelling elements, the development of complex characters, the revelation of background information, and the effective use of dramatic tension. Students become familiar with screenwriting terminology as scenes from well-known films are analyzed on video to reveal structural elements in the writing.

Screenwriting 2 - Facing the Blank Page
New School for Social Research
NEWS#2823 Undergraduate 3 credits $455
This course focuses on taking existing story elements and outline, developing them to the next level, and beginning to write the script. We concentrate on refining the script's core elements to avoid the stumbling blocks of inadequate development. By creating in-depth character studies and examining underlying structural components such as unity, tension, obstacles, exposition, and foreshadowing, students are able to further detail their scene-by-scene outline. The first act is then written in proper format and style and individually critiqued by the instructor.

Screenwriting Fundamentals
Eastern Oregon University
EAOR#WR310 Undergraduate 4 credits $320
This course introduces students to the process of conceiving, pitching, developing and writing stories (screen plays) appropriate for marketing in the contemporary Hollywood film environment. (Web Based).

Secrets of the South
New School for Social Research
NEWS#0679 Undergraduate 3 credits $1638*
We journey down to the land of moonlight and magnolias and immerse ourselves in a stunning selection of 20th-century novels, short stories, and autobiographies written by Southern authors. We trace some of the intriguing threads that run through the distinctly American body of work that has come to be called "Southern Literature." Race, gender, family, and the legacy of the Civil War (the "Lost Cause") are among the topics negotiated by each of the writers.
* Non-credit option, tuition: $365.

Selected Topics in Writing
Eastern Oregon University
EAOR#WR210 Undergraduate 2 credits $160
Prepares students for writing and writing-intensive courses beyond freshman composition and/or to attempt to pass the WPE.

Selections from Latin Literature
University of Minnesota
MINN#LAT1103 Undergraduate 5 credits $445
A review of the elements of LAT1101 and LAT1102, with a shift of emphasis to longer passages of continuous reading in 38 Latin Stories. A considerable amount of historical and literary background is presented in English to orient the student to the material. Prerequisite: LAT1102 or equivalent.

Seminar in Advanced Writing
New Hampshire College
NEHA#ENG330 Undergraduate 3 credits $1656
ENG330 is a course of study for students seeking experiences in writing beyond freshman composition. Various models of writing are studied and practiced. Prerequisite: B grades in ENG102 and ENG103 or permission of instructor.

Seven Visionary Poets
New School for Social Research
NEWS#0655 Undergraduate 3 credits $1638*
Wordsworth called it "seeing into the life of things": seeing beyond the commonplace, beyond the veil of the mundane, to witness the primal material. Rimbaud wrote that in order to do this, to be a visionary, a poet needed to go through a long, systematic disordering of the senses, exhausting all of life's poisons and preserving their quintessences. (And if the human being is ruined in the process, at least the visions remain.)
* Non-credit option, tuition: $365.

Shakespeare
University of Missouri
MOCE#LI135 Undergraduate 3 credits $387
This course studies Shakespeare's life and includes a reading of 13 of his major plays — histories, comedies, and tragedies — that represent all phases of his development. Students will read Hamlet, Romeo and Juliet, King Lear, Macbeth, and other Shakespearean plays. Perquisites: English 20 or equivalent.

Shakespeare
New York Institute of Technology
NYIT#EN1083 Undergraduate 3 credits $???
An advanced course which selected texts and critiques from Shakespearean literature are examined intensively.

Shakespeare
Western Illinois University
WEIL#ENG412 Undergraduate 3 credits $795*
This IUC video course surveys the works of the greatest and most influential writer in English literature. The course covers eight representative plays that span the length of Shakespeare's career--from one of his early works, A Midsummer Night's Dream, to one of his last plays, The Tempest. During the course you view video versions of five plays and listen to audiotapes of others. Although you discover some of the infinite variety in Shakespeare's plays, you also focus on key issues that tend to unify his plays.
* IL residents tuition: $88 per credit.

Shakespeare I
University of Minnesota
MINN#ENGL3241 Undergraduate 4 credits $391
Study of Shakespeare's early and middle comedies, tragedies, and history plays (Romeo and Juliet, A Midsummer Night's Dream, Henry IV Part 1, Henry V, Much Ado about Nothing, Julius Caesar, and Hamlet). Guided reading questions provided. Special attention is given to ways of reading the plays to help students imagine theatrical performance. Students may begin with either Shakespeare I or II; both courses contain introductory materials. The plays read in Shakespeare I or II should be the student's basis for choice. The same audiocassettes are used for both courses.

Shakespeare II
University of Minnesota
MINN#ENGL3242 Undergraduate 4 credits $391
Study of Shakespeare's middle comedies and tragedies and late romances with attention to history, literary values, and theater performance. Special attention is given to ways of reading the plays that will help students imagine theatrical performance. Students read As You Like It, Macbeth, King Lear, Antony and Cleopatra, Coriolanus, The Winter's Tale, and The Tempest.

Shakespeare Online
Emporia State University
EMPO#EN540 Undergrad/Grad 3 credits $228
Focusing on the second half of Shakespeare's career as a dramatist, this course will cover Hamlet, Othello, King Lear, Macbeth, Twelfth Night, The Winter's Tale, and The Tempest. Lectures covering the historical and cultural backgrounds will be available on line via ESU's World Wide Web site; students will submit responses to lectures, questions , and contributions to virtual discussions through that site (or email) as well. Students may begin the course at any time but should attempt to complete all of the requirements within the regular 16-week semester.

Short Stories
Northwest College
NOCO#GE278 Undergraduate 3 credits $???
This course has two objectives: to introduce students to the short story genre and its techniques and to provide the opportunity to become careful, aware readers. The study begins briefly with the earliest types of stories--legends, fables and allegories--and extends through modern-day writings. Prerequisite: GE180.

Short Story
Strayer University
STRA#ENG300 Undergraduate 4.5 credits $665
Provides a survey of the development of short fiction from beginnings to the present. Discusses critical aspects of the genre as exemplified in major authors from representative countries throughout the world. Clarifies the relationship between theme and technique within the genre of short fiction.

Short Story
Texas Technical University
TETE#ENGL3331 Undergraduate 3 credits $???
Students read and write about short stories from around the world. Prerequisites: ENGL1301 and ENGL1302 or equivalent.

Short Story
Western Illinois University
WEIL#ENG300 Undergraduate 3 credits $795*
Studies the short story from its beginnings in the early 19th century to the present. Students will read about 30 stories written by such masters as Poe, Maupassant, Twain, Chopin, Joyce, Hemingway, Ellison, and Barthelme. Nearly all assignments include writing short essays assigned by the instructor. One assignment is a full-length interpretive essay. Some attention is given to the form and technique of the short story.
* IL residents tuition: $88 per credit.

Six African-American Women Writers
New School for Social Research
NEWS#0658 Undergraduate 3 credits $1638*
Are race relations a necessary concern of feminist thought? Should Blacks concerned about racial rights also concern themselves with sexism and homophobia? The works of African-American women writers during this century constitute a rich identifiable literary tradition. Within that tradition some of the keenest insights into gender and race relations are voiced. Through an analysis of the writings, we discuss the impact of race and gender in these writers' lives and works. Thematic, structural, and character similarities/contrasts between writing styles are discussed.
* Non-credit option, tuition: $365.

Social and Political Philosophy
Pennsylvania State University
PENN#PHIL108 Undergraduate 3 credits $345
Philosophical analysis of political and communal order; theories of individual and group action within the structure of social obligation.

Social Ethics
Rogers State University
ROGE#PHILO2213 Undergraduate 3 credits $495*
An introduction to the historical approach to social ethics. The course focuses on the ethical and religious values of society as they serve as a basis for social, legal and political decisions. The style of this course emphasizes interactive discussion among participants -- a course which will engage both your mind and your emotions.
* OK residents $315.

Society, Ethics and the Professions
University of Colorado-Boulder
COBO#CSCI2830 Undergraduate 1 credits $80
Issues in Computer Science An introduction to the larger social context in which the discipline of computing exists, with an emphasis on how the discipline interacts with and serves the interests of society. Social and ethical responsibilities of the computing professional are emphasized. Includes a survey of the kinds of risks that can accompany a computing application. Discussion of losses and questions of liability. Identification of the main forms of intellectual property, protection, and penalties for violation.

Sociology of Religion
University of Southern Colorado
COSO#SOC491A Undergraduate 3 credits $210
Students will study the effects of religion on society through history and across cultures as a way to increase understanding of how religion shapes their own lives.

Special Topics in History
Northwest College
NOCO#GE260 Undergraduate 3 credits $???
Selected topics in history will be available some quarters. Course descriptions will be posted when offered. Prerequisite: GE180.

Sports and Recreation in the U.S.
Texas Technical University
TETE#HIST3338 Undergraduate 3 credits $???
This course covers the development and role of sports and recreation in American social history with an emphasis on organized amateur and professional sports.

Sports in History
Indiana University
INDI#H233 Undergraduate 3 credits $268
Examines the historical conditions in which sports have developed from ancient to contemporary times, with particular emphasis on modern American society and sport.

Stalin
California State University - Dominguez Hills
CADO#HUX555 Undergraduate 3 credits $405
Stalin was arguably the most powerful and effective leader in history, whose influence will be felt for ages to come. Examines Stalin the person through a biography; his effect upon the people, through a novel; and his place in history as interpreted today. Prerequisite: HUX501 is recommended.

Studies in American Drama
Western Illinois University
WEIL#ENG341 Undergraduate 3 credits $795*
Traces the development of American drama away from romanticism and melodrama, resulting in brilliant achievements in realism and other dramatic modes. You will read plays by Eugene O'Neill, Arthur Miller, Tennessee Williams, and others.
* IL residents tuition: $88 per credit.

Studies in American Poetry - Voices and Visions
Western Illinois University
WEIL#ENG335 Undergraduate 3 credits $795*
Explores the lives and works of America's greatest poets: Walt Whitman, Emily Dickinson, Robert Frost, Marianne Moore, Hart Crane, Wallace Stevens, Langston Hughes, T.S. Eliot, Ezra Pound, Robert Lowell, Elizabeth Bishop, Sylvia Plath, and William Carlos Williams. This PBS telecourse will show you how to read poetry with more comprehension, sensitivity, and appreciation; recognize the qualities that define the art of poetry--its concentrated imagery, patterns of sound, and complex forms; gain insight into major poets' visions of the world; and assimilate each poet's views on the theory and practice of verse.
* IL residents tuition: $88 per credit.

Studies in Modern World Literature
California State University - Dominguez Hills
CADO#HUX556 Undergraduate 3 credits $405
An examination of representative major works by recent Nobel Laureates whose art epitomizes diverse cultural, literary, and social viewpoints. Authors include Mann, Pirandello, Camus, Kawabata, Solzhenitsyn, Neruda, and Bellow.

Studio Procedures
State University of New York
SUNY#GC131 Undergraduate 2 credits $360*
Students will learn to master the tools necessary for professional execution of studio procedures. Tools include pencil, triangle, T-square, cutting devices, proportion wheel, graphics ruler and others. Techniques using these tools will be demonstrated and practiced. Students will be presented with a basic grounding in design and illustration fundamentals.
* NY residents tuition: $90 per credit.

Survey of American Literature I
New Hampshire College
NEHA#ENG213 Undergraduate 3 credits $1656
English 213 is a survey of American writers from 1620 through the Civil War. Authors of Colonial, Enlightenment, and Romantic periods in American literature are considered with the emphasis on their historical backgrounds. Prerequisite: Eng102.

Survey of American Literature II
New Hampshire College
NEHA#ENG214 Undergraduate 3 credits $1656
English 214 is a survey of major American writers from the 1870s through the contemporary age. Emphasis in this course is on the role of the individual and the artist in an increasingly industrialized and technological culture. Prerequisite: ENG102.

Survey of American Literature to 1850
University of Minnesota
MINN#ENGL3411 Undergraduate 4 credits $391
The development of American literature and thought from pre-Columbian days through the early American Renaissance. Authors studied include Native American and African American writers from the colonial and early national periods, together with such major white writers as Poe, Emerson, and Hawthorne.

Survey of American Literature, 1850-1900
University of Minnesota
MINN#ENGL3412 Undergraduate 4 credits $391
Literature and thought from the American Renaissance through the 19th century. Authors studied include Whitman and Dickinson as poetic giants, Twain and Chopin as experimental novelists.

Survey of American Literature, 1900-1945
University of Minnesota
MINN#ENGL3413 Undergraduate 4 credits $391
American literature during the break-up of social and literary norms caused by two world wars, feminism, and the emergence of the civil rights movement. Authors studied include Frost and Eliot, Fitzgerald, Hurston and Hughes, Wright, Olsen, and Rich.

Survey of British Literature I and II
Trinidad State Junior College
TRIN#LIT221 Undergraduate 6 credits $???
This is a two-semester course sequence which specifically focuses on British literature. LIT221 begins with Beowulf and Old English and ends with literature from the Restoration time period. LIT222 begins with the Romantic period and ends with modern and contemporary British literature.

Survey of Civilizations in Ancient Asia
University of Minnesota
MINN#HIST1451 Undergraduate 4 credits $391
Ancient societies, political systems, religions and cultures in East, South, and West Asia.

Survey of English Literature I
University of Minnesota
MINN#ENGL3111 Undergraduate 4 credits $391
A historical survey of major figures, movements, and trends in English literature and culture during the Middle Ages and the Renaissance. Chaucer, Shakespeare, Marlowe, and the metaphysical poets, along with topics such as attitudes toward women and generic development of the sonnet and drama, are featured. Optional use of course Web site for class discussion.

Survey of English Literature I
New Hampshire College
NEHA#ENG223 Undergraduate 3 credits $1656
This is a survey of English literature including Beowulf and the works of Chaucer, Shakespeare, Milton, Swift, Pope, and Johnson. This course examines the history and evolution of English literature as well as a variety of literary types. Prerequisite: ENG102.

Survey of English Literature II
University of Minnesota
MINN#ENGL3112 Undergraduate 4 credits $391
This course focuses on the literature of the Restoration and the 18th century (Age of Reason), especially Milton, Johnson, Swift, Austen, and Pope. Optional use of course Web site for class discussion. Read a detailed description of ENGL3112.

Survey of English Literature II
New Hampshire College
NEHA#ENG224 Undergraduate 3 credits $1656
This course covers the Romantic, Victorian and Modern literary periods. It examines the works of the Romantic poets, Victorian novelists and Modern literary artists including Shaw, Joyce and Eliot. Prerequisite: ENG102.

Survey of U.S. History
Barstow Community College
BARS#HIST2A Undergraduate 3 credits $???
Development of the United States from the founding of the colonies through the Reconstruction Period.

Survey of Western Art I
Pennsylvania State University
PENN#ART111 Undergraduate 3 credits $345
Survey of the major monuments and trends in the history of art from prehistory through the late Gothic period.

Survey of World Literature in Translation
New Hampshire College
NEHA#ENG202 Undergraduate 3 credits $1656
This course is a survey covering major works of world literature in translation, excluding the American and British traditions. Will include African, Asain, European, Latin American, and Middle Eastern literature, with an emphasis on the European. Begins with the late 17th century and continues to the present day. Prerequisite: ENG120.

Symbols, Themes and Traditions in Mythology
Humboldt State University
HUMB#RS399 Undergraduate 2 credits $230
Popular or Esoteric topics you may wish to study in depth include: Joseph Campbell's Vision of Mythology, Angels, Androgynes, Alchemy, Halos and Auras, Eros and the Mythology of Love, the Double-Serpent, the Goddess, the Mandala, Myths and Mystery, Religions of Greece, the Sacred Marriage Ritual, and Shamanism. You select the topic, read the books, see the videotapes and write the essays.

Techniques of Literary Study
University of Minnesota
MINN#ENGL3008 Undergraduate 4 credits $391
Training and practice in the analysis of various literary forms, with a special emphasis on poetry. Use of argument, evidence, and documentation in literary papers; introduction to major developments in contemporary criticism. This course is a required foundation course for all English majors and minors.

Telling Tales - Narrative Art in Literature and Film
University of Colorado
CUON#ENGL1601 Undergraduate 3 credits $1953*
"Telling Tales" asks students to explore how stories determine who we are. Everything people do fits into a narrative pattern, from TV news to memory to daily schedules. We tell ourselves stories about ourselves and others--how do these stories reshape who we are as cultural beings?.
* CO residents tuition: $136 per credit.

The 1920s - The Emergence of Modern America
New School for Social Research
NEWS#0307 Undergraduate 3 credits $1638*
This course is a comprehensive look at the period usually called "the Roaring Twenties" or the "Jazz Age"--images that evoke a carefree, sensual, experimental period. We associate the 20s with Scott and Zelda Fitzgerald cavorting in the Plaza fountain, flappers with boyish figures and long chains of pearls, college boys with hipflasks filled with booze, O'Neill introducing a Freudian psychodrama to the theater, the Harlem Renaissance--Langston Hughes, the Cotton Club, Louis Armstrong, and the like--and the stockmarket booming as fortunes were made.
* Non-credit option, tuition: $365.

The Age of Revolution
California State University - Dominguez Hills
CADO#HUX574 Undergraduate 3 credits $405
An examination of the French Revolution of 1789-1815 through the eyes of an historian and a novelist.

The Alaska Native Land Settlement
University of Alaska - Fairbanks
ALFA#ANS310 Undergraduate 3 credits $237
Native corporation goals and methods as they implement the Alaska Native Claims Settlement Act and establish themselves within the larger political economy. Prerequisite: ANTH242 or PS263 or HIST100; ECON101, ECON137; or permission.

The American Revolution and the New Nation
Western Illinois University
WEIL#HIS413G   Undergraduate   3 credits $795*
Covers the causes of the American Revolution, the nature of the War of Independence, the consequences of the conflict, and the issues of the Constitutional Convention of 1787. Emphasis is also given to the administrations of Washington and Adams. Prerequisite: History 105 or consent of instructor.
* IL residents tuition: $88 per credit.

The American West
Western Illinois University
WEIL#HIS308   Undergraduate   3 credits $795*
Follows the westward movement in U.S. history. It is less concerned with who went where and when than with the process of settling the West and its impact upon American culture. Attention is given to the Native Americans as people, not merely as impediments to Anglo- American expansion. Differing interpretations of the "significance of the frontier" are considered, and the "real West" is compared to the West of legend and pop culture. Prerequisite: History 105 and 106 or consent of instructor.
* IL residents tuition: $88 per credit.

The Ancient World
Edmonds Community College
EDMO#ENGL140   Undergraduate   3 credits $220
This is an on-line course that deals with Greek and Roman literature in translation. Communication between instructor and students shall be via the Internet, and thus shall require a computer, a modem, and service access to the Internet.

The Art of Drama
New York Institute of Technology
NYIT#EN1053   Undergraduate   3 credits $???
An intermediate-level course in which selected works of fiction are examined in an effort to understand its ritualistic origins, historical role, and current significance. Prerequisite: EN1020.

The Art of Fiction
New York Institute of Technology
NYIT#EN1054   Undergraduate   3 credits $???
An intermediate-level course in which selected works of fiction are examined in an effort to understand the approaches, strategies, and techniques of artists in this compelling medium. This course may be chosen to fulfill the Group A requirement. Prerequisite: EN1020.

The Avant-Garde
University of Minnesota
MINN#MUS3045   Undergraduate   4 credits $391
You do not need to read music or have any prior experience in music to enjoy this stimulating introduction to recent music. The course centers on composers of the American musical avant-garde, ca. 1950-1970, including John Cage and Pauline Oliveros, in their sonic and social contexts. Attention is given to the recent impact on music from non-Western culture. Assignments (reading, listening, journal writing, original composition, and performance) are designed to be achievable by people with no prior musical training.

The Biblical Movement
California State University - Dominguez Hills
CADO#HUX572   Undergraduate   3 credits $405
An examination of modern scholarship on the Bible and it impact on Christianity; analysis of three types of Bible interpretation: fundamentalism, liberalism, and humanism.

The Celtic World
University of Minnesota
MINN#ENGL3910   Undergraduate   4 credits $391
A wide-ranging introductory survey of the history, music, folk ways, and traditional oral culture of the six Celtic countries (Brittany, Cornwall, Ireland, Isle of Man, Scotland, and Wales). The topics explored include ancient culture; tribal society; saints, druids, bards, poets; age of King Arthur; languages; and the future of Celtic culture.

The Elements of Fiction Writing
New York University
NEYO#X329354   Undergraduate   4 credits $450
This on-line fiction class explores the craft of fiction. Lectures on different aspects of craft are posted each week: plot, point-of-view, narrative distance, dialogue, setting, character, time, as well as other issues involved in writing both short stories and novels. Exercises are assigned with each lecture. Students e-mail their stories and critiques of stories to the class on a weekly basis. In addition, there is a discussion area where students can post their ideas and exchange information and concerns about fiction writing.

The Historic Country Houses of England
New School for Social Research
NEWS#4012   Undergraduate   2 credits $1092
To study the history of the English country houses is to discover a centuries-old world of elegant masterpieces in which architecture, decor, furniture and gardens are vivid statements of the taste and vision of outstanding architects, innovative designers and powerful owners. Ranging from medieval Hever Castle in Kent and the extravagant 16th century Hardwick Hall to the important early 18th century Chiswick House and the William Morris designs at Standen in Sussex, this illustrated course examines many influences.

The Holocaust
University of Massachusetts - Dartmouth
MADA#HST356   Undergraduate   3 credits $408
This course will cover the ideas and events leading up to the Holocaust (the Nazi war against the Jews, 1933-1945), as well as a chronology of the Holocaust itself. Be prepared for a course carrying significant intellectual and emotional weight. The Internet/Web will be used to "visit" relevant libraries, museums, and databases all over the world.

The Lesbian Literary Tradition
New School for Social Research
NEWS#0711 Undergraduate 3 credits $1638*
We study literature in which relationships between women are central, in which concepts of gender and sexual difference define identity, and in which meaning derives from understanding these concepts of difference within a cultural and historical framework. We read representative works, primarily by 20th-century women, including Radclyffe Hall, Gertrude Stein, Isabel Miller, Audre Lorde, Dorothy Allison, Rita Mae Brown, Leslea Newman, Jane Rule, and Judy Grahn. We observe how lesbian literature shapes and is shaped by cultural beliefs about sexualities; how these sexualities are represented, symbolized, and characterized in literature.
* Non-credit option, tuition: $365.

The Life and Times of Peter the Great
University of Minnesota
MINN#HIST3700B Undergraduate 4 credits $391
A study of tsar Peter the Great and his impact on both his country and Europe as a whole. In looking at Peter's 43-year reign, two major themes are explored--his efforts to westernize Russia and his constant wars against his neighbors, especially Sweden. The topics examined in this course include Peter's early years; various wars, battles, and peace treaties; and the reforms he introduced into Russian life.

The Living Theatre
California State University - Dominguez Hills
CADO#HUX521 Undergraduate 3 credits $405
How to recognize, appreciate and evaluate a variety of dramatic experiences. Requires extensive notebook of descriptions and analyses of eight different types of theatrical performances.

The Media in American History and Law
University of Minnesota
MINN#JOUR3007 Undergraduate 4 credits $391
Using a case-study approach, this course focuses on ethical and legal issues, examining the media in the cultural, socioeconomic, political, and technological context of a specific historical period: the Vietnam War. The audiocassettes include interviews with war correspondents.

The Middle and Far East, The Mediterranean, Medieval Europe
Eastern Oregon University
EAOR#HIST101 Undergraduate 5 credits $410
Course will cover the history of the development of civilizations in the middle and far East, the Mediterranean, and Europe, through the time of the Reformation.

The Modern World
University of Nevada-Reno
NERE#C202 Undergraduate 3 credits $210
Covers from the Renaissance to the twentieth century. During this period, western Civilization matured and reached a high level of development that allowed it to have a major role in global affairs. The goals of the course are to present to students the great ideas, events, and issues that have persisted throughout the ages (love, freedom, happiness, justice, peace, war, etc.) and the books in which they are discussed. Students will also gain knowledge and understanding of Western Civilization, how it developed and how it relates to other cultures and civilizations.

The Mother/Daughter Theme in Literature
New School for Social Research
NEWS#0715 Undergraduate 3 credits $1638*
"But what mother and daughter understand each other, or even have the sympathy for each other's lack of understanding?"--Maya Angelou, I Know Why the Caged Bird Sings. Our purpose here is to assess the mother/daughter theme from the perspective of the daughter, the mother, and several generations of women in multicultural works of fiction. We find that, except for the myth of Demeter and Persephone and a few peripheral references in 19th-century fiction, the mother/daughter relationship has been conspicuously absent from world literature until the mid-20th century.
* Non-credit option, tuition: $365.

The Nature Writers
New Hampshire College
NEHA#ENG332 Undergraduate 3 credits $1656
This course introduces students to the prose and poetry by major British and American writers and naturalists who observe nature vividly and who write about a human's relationship to the natural environment. Prerequisite: One 200-level literature survey course.

The Occult in Western Civilization
Indiana University
INDI#X207 Undergraduate 3 credits $268
Critical and historical evaluation of a wide range of occult topics: superstitions, magic, witchcraft, astrology, the Cabala, alchemy, psychic phenomena (mesmerism, spiritualism, ESP), and UFOs. Course includes a borrowed videotape. National award winner.

The Origins of Western Culture
Strayer University
STRA#HUM310 Undergraduate 4.5 credits $665
Studies civilizations and cultures such as ancient Egypt, Crete, Greece, and Rome which have given root to Western culture. Analyzes the artistic, intellectual, religious, political, and socioeconomic aspects of each culture and traces their development in Western civilization.

The Pacific Century
New School for Social Research
NEWS#0302 Undergraduate   3 credits $1638*
Since the U.S. conquest of the Philippines in 1898, the United States has been expanding its presence in the Pacific Rim, engaging its neighbors from Mexico to Japan and from China to Vietnam in a host of complicated colonial, military, and economic conflicts. At the same time, the United States has been increasingly influenced by cultural exchanges and immigration from Asia and Latin America. This course explores the interactions between the United States, Asia, and Latin America during the 20th century, as well as the far-reaching effects of diplomacy, trade, and cultural exchange.
* Non-credit option, tuition: $365.

The Para-Rational Perspective
California State University - Dominguez Hills
CADO#HUX542 Undergraduate   3 credits $405
Interdisciplinary exploration of non-rational alternatives in modern culture, focusing on the non-logical, the visionary, and the religious/mystical.

The Philosophy of Cultures & Nations
City University
CITY#PHI407 Undergraduate   5 qu. credits $785
A philosophical approach to the evolution of nations, examining their social and historical roots and focusing on their premodern ethnic foundations. The course investigates the process by which historical forces lead to differing national identities and cultural values and explores the social and political consequences of these differences. Prerequisite: Strongly recommended: HUM200 or its equivalent.

The Rational Perspective
California State University - Dominguez Hills
CADO#HUX541 Undergraduate   3 credits $405
The meaning of rationality from the perspectives of philosophy, history, literature, music and art. Special emphasis on the possible differences between scientific and humanistic rationality.

The Short Story
University of Minnesota
MINN#ENGW3102 Undergraduate 4 credits $391
The short story form provides a challenge to beginning and intermediate writers. Its compressed form occupies a position closer to poetry than the novel. Its variety and flexibility demand a close study of craft and a willingness to take risks. In this course, students will explore the craft of writing the short story by writing, reading, and listening. The course audiocassettes contain a discussion of craft and content with several writers. Prerequisite: ENGW1102.

The Twilight of the Sioux
University of Missouri
MOCE#LI101D Undergraduate   3 credits $387
This course is designed to give students a better understanding of the novel and the epic poem through examination of Sioux culture, legends, myths, and understanding of the world. The student will learn how to read literature and draw inferences about its implied thematic concerns, and how to express those interpretations in a clear, unified, and coherent written form.

The United States in the 20th Century 1932-60
University of Minnesota
MINN#HIST3822 Undergraduate 4 credits $391
The Great Depression and the New Deal; the challenge of fascism and the coming of World War II; the origins of the cold war; the great red scare; the politics and culture of the Eisenhower era; the origins of the civil rights movement; and labor relations are examined. Students view videos (available from video rental outlets).

The United States, 1917-1945
Indiana University
INDI#A314 Undergraduate   3 credits $268
Political, demographic, economic and intellectual transformation 1917-1945; World War I, the twenties, the Great Depression, New Deal.

The War in Vietnam and the U.S.
University of Missouri
MOCE#HI101 Undergraduate   3 credits $387
This course provides an understanding of the political experience and the lessons and legacies of the Vietnam War both in Vietnam and in the United States.

The War in Vietnam and the U.S.
University of Missouri
MOCE#HI161 Undergraduate   3 credits $387
This course provides an understanding of the political experience and the lessons and legacies of the Vietnam War both in Vietnam and the United States.

The War in Vietnam and the U.S.
University of Missouri
MOCE#HI380F Undergraduate   3 credits $387
This course provides an understanding of the political experience and the lessons and legacies of the Vietnam War in both Vietnam and the United States.

The Woman Writer in 19th-Century Fiction
University of Minnesota
MINN#ENGL3940 Undergraduate 4 credits $391
Short stories and novels by 19th-century women writers-- Jane Austen, Elizabeth Gaskell, Charlotte Brontë, Harriet Beecher Stowe, George Eliot, Sarah Orne Jewett, Mary E. Wilkins Freeman, and Charlotte Perkins Gilman. Emphasizes the ways women writers' professional roles evolved during the 19th century, the conflicts they faced as their careers developed, the extent to which their writing satisfied the requirements of their audiences, and the literary qualities of their works.

Theatre History
University of South Florida
FLSO#THE3100 Undergraduate 3 credits $???
The purpose of this course is to study the development of theatrical production in its cultural context from ancient times to the contemporary stage. The assigned readings (textbook, plays and other sources) provide the foundation for our collaborative learning experience. Lectures, video viewing, group projects and class discussions will supplement the reading and clarify key ideas. As we explore the material together, the student is encouraged to develop a basic understanding of the dramatic experience and become familiar with the known elements of theatrical practice in a wide variety of cultures throughout the ages.

Themes and Forms in Literature - Shakespeare
University of Missouri
MOCE#LI225 Undergraduate 3 credits $387
This course is designed to give students a better understanding of Shakespearean drama in performance. Using the BBC-TV video series, this course examines the following plays: A Midsummer Night's Dream, Richard III, Romeo and Juliet, The Merchant of Venice, Julius Caesar, Hamlet, Othello, King Lear, Measure for Measure, and The Winter's Tale. The video productions play a central role in the course. In assignments and examinations, students are asked to consider various aspects of these productions: director's interpretations; actors' realizations of major roles; and the effect of camera work and lighting.

Topics in Art History
State University of New York
SUNY#GC244 Undergraduate 3 credits $540*
This course is a discussion and exposition of the history of graphic design. Students will be presented with information regarding the social and cultural impact, artistic value, and historical significance of major movements of the late nineteenth and twentieth centuries. Each student will select a movement and gather information and a collection of illustrations from the selected style. The course emphasizes the integration of graphic design into world culture and specific societies. Prerequisite: English 1: Composition or permission of Instructor.
* NY residents tuition: $90 per credit.

Topics in Writing - Culture
University of Colorado-Boulder
COBO#UWRP3020 Undergraduate 3 credits $423
Students choose an essay, abstract its argument, analyze it, and agree or disagree with the author. They thus learn the principal modes of academic rhetoric: description, analysis, and argument.

Travel the Lewis and Clark Trail
Syracuse University
SYRA#HSC0021 Undergraduate 0 credits $120
Come and join a virtual expedition along the Lewis and Clark trail from Mandan, North Dakota to Fort Clatsop, Oregon, on the Pacific Coast. During the summer of 1998, the instructor will retrace Lewis and Clark's route along the Upper Missouri, across the Continental Divide, through the Rocky Mountains and down the Columbia River. His travels, together with extensive background information, will provide the foundation for this course. Still photos depicting the route, maps, video panoramas and audio pieces, including narration from some of Lewis and Clark's actual journals, will supplement textual material.

Twentieth Century Europe
Western Illinois University
WEIL#HIS429G Undergraduate 3 credits $795*
Introduces you to the major historical themes in Europe from the pre-World War I period to the contemporary period. Both Western Europe (including Great Britain) and Eastern Europe (including the Soviet Union) are covered in the course. Major topics include an overview of Europe before World War I, causes and consequences of World War I, the Russian Revolution, the search for stability in the 1920s, the Great Depression, the rise of Fascism, the causes and consequences of World War II, postwar reconstruction and revival, etc.
* IL residents tuition: $88 per credit.

Twentieth-Century American Music
University of Minnesota
MINN#MUS5702 Undergraduate 4 credits $391
Analysis of American music during this century: folk, popular, classical, black, Chicano, opera and symphony, contemporary. Background knowledge of musical terms necessary.

Typography
State University of New York
SUNY#0930702 Undergraduate 3 credits $1038*
Writing without a pen. Covers technical, formal and expressive aspects of type, the designer's primary vehicle for visual communications. Prerequisite: The Visible Word (09306) and permission of Instructor.
* NY residents tuition: $137 per credit

U. S. in the 20th Century, 1890-1917
University of Minnesota
MINN#HIST3821 Undergraduate 4 credits $391
Based on the CD-ROM Who Built America?, the course describes the formation of modern America from 1876 to 1914: its transportation network, its basic industries, many of its familiar brand-name products, its multiethnic society, and the beginnings of its popular culture.

U.S. History I
Front Range Community College
FRCC#HIS201 Undergraduate 3 credits $790
Examines the major political, economic, social, diplomatic/military, cultural and intellectual events in American History from the first inhabitants through the Civil War/Reconstruction. 45 Contact Hours.

U.S. History - 1870-Present
Northwest College
NOCO#GE285 Undergraduate 3 credits $???
A survey of the history of the United States from 1870 to the present with a view toward the rise to world prominence of the U.S., the course will include an examination of both World War I and II, plus the "roaring" twenties, "depressionary" thirties, and "crises" of the sixties, seventies and eighties, focusing upon the social and political effects of each area. Prerequisite: GE180.

U.S. History II
Front Range Community College
FRCC#HIS202 Undergraduate 3 credits $790
Examines the major political, economic, social, diplomatic/military, cultural and intellectual events in American History from Reconstruction to the present. 45 Contact Hours.

U.S. History Since 1876
University of Colorado
CUON#HIST1362 Undergraduate 3 credits $1953*
Provides an introduction to the major forces, events, and individuals that shaped the historical development of American society from the Civil War to the present.
* CO residents tuition: $136 per credit.

U.S. Military History
Western Illinois University
WEIL#HIS304 Undergraduate 3 credits $795*
Surveys the military policies and engagements that had significance in America's independence and expansion. This knowledge provides insight into how our national character, political leadership, economic development, and national boundaries have been affected by our military operations. Prerequisite: History 105 and 106 or consent of instructor.
* IL residents tuition: $88 per credit.

United States History I
Brevard Community College
BREV#AMH2010 Undergraduate 3 credits $485
A survey of the social, political, economic, geographic, and cultural development of the American people through the Civil War and Reconstruction. Emphasis on enabling students to understand and appreciate their heritage.

United States History I, 1607-1865
New Hampshire College
NEHA#HIS113 Undergraduate 3 credits $1656
The first half of the U.S. survey, covering the period from the founding of Jamestown to the end of the Civil War. The development of regionalism and its effect on the coming of the Civil War provides a framework for investigation.

United States History II
Brevard Community College
BREV#AMH2020 Undergraduate 3 credits $485
American history from 1865. Emphasis on some of the social, political, and economic factors instrumental in the rise of the United States to a position of world leadership. Enables student to better understand some of the problems of the present.

United States in the Modern Age
University of North Alabama
NOAL#HIST202 Undergraduate 3 credits $258
This course is the second in a two-semester sequence dealing with the history of the United States, from the end of the Civil War to about as close to the present as we dare to get. During this period America underwent rapid and profound changes, the full consequences of which we are still trying to fathom.

United States, 1829-1865 II
Indiana University
INDI#A304 Undergraduate 3 credits $268
A continuation of A303. May be taken without A303.

US History 1865 to present
MiraCosta College
MIRA#HIST111 Undergraduate 3 credits $357
By the end of the course, students will have demonstrated the ability to: analyze primary documents and investigate historical questions; explain the development of modern American history in terms of society, economics, politics, geography, and ideas; explain the role of concepts such as populism, imperialism, democracy, immigration, isolationism and progressivism; clarify the role of cultural diversity in modern American history; and analyze the role of popular culture in expressing the values and concerns of modern Americans.

Uses and Abuses of Ethics
City University
CITY#BC306 Undergraduate 5 qu. credits $785
Examination of ethical dilemmas confronting the mass media, political arena, political advertising and marketing, and teledemocracy.

Using Child & Adolescent Literature
New Jersey City University
NJCU#LTED642 Graduate 3 credits $635
This course will focus on the many uses of children's and adolescent literature in the classroom, and the ways in which this literature can be linked to the curriculum. We will use the wealth of children's and adolescent literature materials available on the World Wide Web.

Vietnam at War
Pennsylvania State University
PENN#HIST173 Undergraduate 3 credits $345
Rise of nationalism and communism; origin of conflict; United States involvement; impact on postwar regional and international politics; contemporary Vietnam.

Visual/Photo Communication
City University
CITY#COM304 Undergraduate   5 qu. credits $785
Study of the basic elements of visual representation of news through photography and captioning. Presents the fundamentals of still photography, composition and lighting and its relationship to computerized production of today's printing process.

Western Civilization 1 - Antiquity to 1600
University of Colorado-Boulder
COBO#HIST1010 Undergraduate 3 credits $240
Survey course on the development of Western civilization from its beginnings in the ancient Near East through the Reformation of the sixteenth century.

Western Civilization 2 - 1500s to Present
University of Colorado-Boulder
COBO#HIST1020 Undergraduate 3 credits $240
Survey course dealing with political, economic, social, and intellectual development in European history from the sixteenth century to the present. Similarities and contrasts between European states are underscored, as is Europe's changing role in world history.

Western Civilization I
University of Alaska - Fairbanks
ALFA#HIST101 Undergraduate   3 credits $213
The origins and major political, economic, social, and intellectual developments of western civilization to 1500.

Western Civilization I
Brevard Community College
BREV#EUH1000 Undergraduate   3 credits $435
A survey of the political, economic, social and cultural beginnings of civilization and the diffusion and accumulation of culture through 1648; ancient Near East, Greece, Rome, Medieval Age, Renaissance and the Reformation.

Western Civilization I
Edmonds Community College
EDMO#HIST104 Undergraduate   5 credits $260
History 104 is a survey from prehistoric time to the late Middle Ages of the cultural, political and economic aspects of the civilizations that comprise the mosaic of the western tradition. This is an experimental course in which our goal is your percept ion of the main themes and values in the cultural interaction of Greece, Rome, Christianity, The Germanic Peoples, Islam, and Byzantium.

Western Civilization I
Front Range Community College
FRCC#HIS101 Undergraduate   3 credits $790
This course explores the major political, social, diplomatic, military, cultural, intellectual and economic aspects of European history from prehistory to the seventeenth century. 45 Contact Hours.

Western Civilization I
Texas Technical University
TETE#HIST1300 Undergraduate 3 credits $???
Students examine Western civilization from its dawn to the 17th century. Culture and the arts are stressed alongside politics.

Western Civilization I - Prehistory to 1648
New Hampshire College
NEHA#HIS109 Undergraduate   3 credits $1656
An overview of the major developments in western history from antiquity to the Peace of Westphalia in 1648. The course examines the civilizations of Mesopotamia, Egypt, Greece, Rome, and Western Europe in detail.

Western Civilization II
Front Range Community College
FRCC#HIS102 Undergraduate   3 credits $790
Explores the major political, social, diplomatic, military, cultural, intellectual and economic aspects of European history from 1650 to the present day. 45 Contact Hours.

Western Civilization II
Texas Technical University
TETE#HIST1301 Undergraduate 3 credits $???
This course covers the revolutionary transformations of European civilization in the 17th, 18th, and 19th centuries; the world wars; and intellectual and cultural developments.

Western Civilization II -1648 to Present
New Hampshire College
NEHA#HIS110 Undergraduate   3 credits $1656
This course traces the growth of Western history from the rise of nation-state in the seventeenth century to the present. The ideologies and political developments which produced modern Western Europe receive careful study.

Western Civilization III
Edmonds Community College
EDMO#HST106 Undergraduate   3 credits $220
Welcome to Western Civilization III, 1815 to the present, History 106 at Edmonds Community College. I am Dr. Eileen Soldwedel, your instructor. I wish to acknowledge the inspiration and example of Dr. James O'Donnell of the Department of Classical Studies, University of Pennsylvania, a pioneer in instruction on the internet who has generously shared his experience.

Western Civilization to 1689
Greenville Technical College
GRTE#HIS101 Undergraduate   3 credits $381*
A survey of western civilization from ancient times to 1689, including the major political, social, economic and intellectual factors shaping western cultural tradition. This course examines the history of Western Civilization (that is European) from ancient times to 1689 in a thematic and chronological approach.
* NC residents pay $48 per credit.

Western Culture and History I
New Jersey Institute of Technology
NJIT#HUM112 Undergraduate 3 credits $1143*
People's changing view of themselves and their world as seen in the history, literature, arts, and philosophy of past eras, from ancient time through the Renaissance. This is an interdisciplinary approach. Prerequisite: English 111. Optional: 26 video lessons of 30 minutes each.
* NJ residents: $184/semester hour.

Western Religions
Thomas Edison State College
THED#OLREL407 Undergraduate 3 credits $397*
Emphasis is on specific forms of religious expression and practice, rather than the more abstract or theological aspects. Religions covered by the course are those of the majority of humankind and living traditions in today's world: Hinduism, Buddhism, religions of China and Japan, Judaism, Christianity, Islam, and several African primal religions. One section deals with alternatives to religion, such as Marxism and scientific humanism.
* NJ residents tuition: $33 per credit.

Western World Literature
Charter Oak State College
CHOA#ENG252 Undergraduate 3 credits $390*
This course is designed to introduce students to western literature from the Age of Reason through the Modern Period and (for purposes of comparison) to introduce students to a variety of so-called "noncanonical" texts from writers who, until very recently, were not studied in college classrooms. Students will examine the poetic and narrative strategies of writers from a variety of classes and cultures.
* CT residents pay $95 per credit.

William Blake
New School for Social Research
NEWS#0629 Undergraduate 3 credits $1638*
William Blake is arguably one of the best-known and - loved poets of the English language. Even to an experienced reader, however, his work comes across as challenging, elusive, and often maddeningly opaque. In this course, we explore this most compelling of writers by examining a selection of Blake's early productions (texts and images both) in their historical contexts. We see him respond to the American and French Revolutions, Mary Wollstonecraft's feminist thought, slavery in the New World, conformity on the London art scene, and the radical religious movements of his time.
* Non-credit option, tuition: $365.

Women and Literature
Northwest College
NOCO#GE290 Undergraduate 3 credits $???
The objectives of the course are to read several novels by women authors, with women as main characters, and explore themes dealing with women's issues, including the search for independence and the question of roles in society. Prerequisite: GE180.

Women in Religion
Western Illinois University
WEIL#PHI303 Undergraduate 3 credits $795*
Investigates the powerful presence of women in the shaping of the world's religious consciousness. Part one of the WIU teleclass attempts to reconstruct the global shift in human religious perception from nonviolent, earth-centered, egalitarian matrilocal societies to violent, sky-god, hierarchical patriarchal cultures. Part two examines the basic facts and ideological issues concerning the position of women in the major religious traditions of humanity: Buddhism, Christianity, Confucianism, Hinduism, Islam, Judaism, Taoism, and tribal religions. Part three looks at current feminist thinking on topics such as religion, spirituality, patriarchal culture, and the environment.
* IL residents tuition: $88 per credit.

Women's & Family History in America
State University of New York
SUNY#243254 Undergraduate 4 credits $586*
Discover the history of women and the family in the United States. Examine differences in the way historical events have affected men and women. Study the effects of historical circumstances on the structure of relationships between men and women and within families. Investigate the diversity of women's experiences, including differences in cultural background and socioeconomic status. Develop an appreciation of the impact of historical ideals, perspectives and events on modern American women and families. Prerequisite: Previous study in American History and/or politics.
* NY residents tuition: $515

Women's Autobiographical Writing
New School for Social Research
NEWS#0645 Undergraduate 3 credits $1638*
Women have always put pen to paper. They have written about their own lives in the form of journals, letters, travel writings, and more recently as official autobiographies. Often their work had to be hidden from a society that frowned on literary women. Many women had difficulty affording the pen and paper. These records of the famous and the not-so-famous are a window through which we can see how someone else lived and how she viewed the world around her.
* Non-credit option, tuition: $365.

Women's Experiences in Modern Fiction
University of Missouri
MOCE#LI101E Undergraduate 3 credits $387
A survey of modern fiction by and about women, this course includes related essays, many of which are written by the women whose fiction is studied.

Women's Experiences in Modern Fiction
University of Missouri
MOCE#LI101F Undergraduate 3 credits $387
A survey of modern fiction by and about women, this course includes related essays, many of which were written by the women whose fiction is studied. Perquisites: sophomore standing.

World Art
Strayer University
STRA#HUM103 Undergraduate 4.5 credits $665
Analysis of works of painting and sculpture from Africa, Asia, and Latin America, as well as from other parts of the world, are studied in context of the history and values of the specific cultures out of which they arise.

World Civilization
Honolulu Community College
HONO#HIST151 Undergraduate 3 credits $714*
The World Civilization course is intended to give the student a sense of the scope and diversity of human culture and historical experience. Through a brief overview of the prominent civilizations and key events of this period, students will better understand the historical context of contemporary issues, as well as gain an appreciation for the contributions of different cultures.
* Hawaiian residents tuition: $39 per credit.

World Civilization Since 1500
Eastern Oregon University
EAOR#HIST102 Undergraduate 5 credits $400
The development of the autonomous nation state, the interdependent urban societies, the diplomatic and military conflicts which have shaped the modern world.

World History 1
State University of New York
SUNY#242104 Undergraduate 4 credits $586*
World History 1 covers the period from the earliest times through c. 1600 AD. Examine the factors that contributed to the rise of early civilizations. Compare and contrast the world's first major civilization in Mesopotamia, China, India, and Egypt. Focus on civilizations which reached maturity through military superiority, great and extensive political power, or culture, such as China. Examine the special characteristics of Greek and Roman civilization and the impact of Judaism, Christianity, Islam, and Buddhism in shaping civilization. Explore the transitional period of 1000 - 1400.
* NY residents tuition: $515

World History since 1500
University of Colorado
CUON#HIST1026 Undergraduate 3 credits $1953*
Surveys the interactions of the world's civilizations in modern times. The emphasis is on understanding the concept of modernization within a global context.
* CO residents tuition: $136 per credit.

World Literature
Strayer University
STRA#ENG225 Undergraduate 4.5 credits $665
Surveys world literature through representative literary masterpieces of major writers,. Relates developments within genres to their historical, sociological, and literary contexts. Emphasizes nineteenth and twentieth century writers, including Chekhov, Ibsen, Shaw, Yeats, Lawrence, Achebe, and Sartre.

World Literature
Strayer University
STRA#HUM104 Undergraduate 4.5 credits $665
Surveys world literature through representative literary masterpieces of major writers. Relates developments within genres to their historical, sociological, and literary contexts. Emphasizes nineteenth and twentieth century writers, include Chekhov, Ibsen, Shaw, Yeats, Lawrence, Achebe, and Sarte.

World Literature - Ancient World Through The Renaissance
State University of New York
SUNY#11203 Undergraduate 3 credits $528*
A survey of world masterpieces from the ancient world through the Renaissance, presenting literature as a reflection of time, place, and thought. Major works are examined in depth. Prerequisite: Freshman English I and Freshman English II.
* NY residents tuition: $88 per credit.

World Literature I
Fayetteville Technical Community College
FAYE#ENG261 Undergraduate 3 credits $489*
This course introduces selected works from the Pacific, Asia, Africa, Europe, and the Americas from their literary beginnings through the seventeenth century. Emphasis is placed on historical background, cultural context, and literary analysis of selected prose, poetry, and drama. Upon completion, students should be able to interpret, analyze, and respond to selected works. This course has been approved to satisfy the Comprehensive Articulation Agreement general education core requirement in humanities/fine arts. Prerequisites: ENG112, ENG113 or ENG114.
* NC residents pay $20 per credit.

World Philosophies I
Lansing Community College
LANS#PHIL211 Undergraduate 4 credits $420
This course surveys major developments in theories of knowledge, reality, ethics, and society, and their historical role in shaping cultures and human identity. It covers Chinese, Indian, Greek, Roman, Christian, Islamic, and European thought from mythic beginnings to the period of early scientific reasoning.

World Religious Perspectives
California State University - Dominguez Hills
CADO#HUX547 Undergraduate 3 credits $405
Survey of ancient and modern religious systems, focusing upon an exploration of the general characteristics of religious beliefs.

Writing
Lansing Community College
LANS#WRIT121 Undergraduate   4 credits $420
The study and practice of expository and argumentative discourse to help students write more effectively. Emphasizes content development, organization, and style, and includes instruction in basic library skills. Students will read and write expository and argumentative essays. Some sections use word processing and networked computer classrooms.

Writing about Literature
University of Minnesota
MINN#ENGC3011 Undergraduate 4 credits $391
Developing a critical argument about literary texts (novels, poems, plays, short stories) with attention to use of secondary sources. Examination and use of different modes of explication and criticism. Prerequisite: Writing Practice requirement.

Writing Comedy for Film and TV
UCLA
UCLA#X451B Undergraduate   3 credits $450
A detailed overview of the many specialized techniques essential for successful comedy writing for television and film, such as creating characters, setting and mood, developing storylines, constructing scenes, and marketing your work. Students complete weekly writing assignments and share thoughts on each other's work, as well as discuss current films and television shows.

Writing Creative Nonfiction
New School for Social Research
NEWS#1732 Undergraduate   3 credits $1638*
Creative nonfiction (personal reminiscence, reflective essays, reportage) treats the real world with the imaginative richness more often associated with fiction. This workshop, built around structured exercises, allows students to experiment while focusing on specifics: choosing a subject, finding a "hook," developing a sense of structure, tone, style, and personal voice. Students are encouraged to work with material from their own lives and emphasis is placed on the process of writing. We look at student work in class, remembering that the best writer is first a responsive reader. Pertinent examples from professional writers are also discussed.
* Non-credit option, tuition: $365.

Writing Experimental Fiction
New School for Social Research
NEWS#1702 Undergraduate   3 credits $1638*
Cut-ups, collage, use of dream images, and heightened language are often the provenance of poetry; in this class, experimentation with words and text is applied to the writing of fiction. Building upon pre-existing narratives, stories, or characters--or creating them through assignments and in-class writings--writers produce an exploded prose that opens new avenues for further creation and interpretation. Model readings such as Woolf's Mrs. Dalloway, Bataille's The Impossible, and Cisneros' House on Mango Street are paired with writing assignments.
* Non-credit option, tuition: $365.

Writing Fiction
Marylhurst College
MARY#WR341 Undergraduate   3 credits $651
Through guided discussion, writing, and structured readings, you'll learn both the conventions of writing fiction and techniques for breaking those conventions. Begin mastering the craft of fiction and plan on completing the class with real work in hand.

Writing for Episodic Television
UCLA
UCLA#X451C Undergraduate   3 credits $450
In television, the art of writing and the business of producing are inextricably linked. In this nuts-and-bolts workshop, students are given a detailed look at the process of creating a script for a typical dramatic series and learn the professional skills that win assignments. Students learn to analyze the unique style of a show, develop saleable stories, and effectively capture series characters. Students are expected to write a one-hour-long script for an existing series of their choice.

Writing for Interactive Media
University of Massachusetts - Lowell
MALO#42221 Undergraduate   3 credits $395
An introduction to writing for interactive multimedia. Material presented includes: the role of the interactive writer, thinking interactively, interactive structure, script format, flowcharts, and the special challenges of presenting information and stories interactively. Software useful to the interactive writer will also be introduced. Sample programs and scripts will be studied, including multimedia for training, education, museums, games, the interactive movie, advertising, and online networks. Students will write interactive scripts, design flowcharts, and critique each other's writing in workshop sessions.

Writing For Quality Results
Rio Salado College
RISA#TQM105 Undergraduate   2 credits $124*
Theory and practice of writing business correspondence in a quality-oriented organization. Includes the orientation of the writer to the internal/external customer's needs and writing in positive, negative and persuasive settings. Prerequisites: Appropriate English placement test score in ENG101, or "C" or better in ENG071. OAS108 and TQM101 or TQM101AA and TQM101AB are recommended.
* AZ residents pay $37 per credit.

Writing for the Arts
University of Minnesota
MINN#COMP3013 Undergraduate 4 credits $391
Descriptions of painting, film, music, architecture, and other types of art (other than literature) as the basis for analysis. Initial emphasis is on developing concise and unambiguous descriptions of art objects or performances. The chief emphasis is on how descriptions and organization of content serve as the basis for more complicated writing assignments, such as formal analyses, reviews, and review-based research. Prerequisite: Writing Practice requirement or equivalent.

Writing Fundamentals
Pima Community College
PIMA#WRT100 Undergraduate 3 credits $165*
Review of sentence structure, mechanics and usage. Includes paragraph development and short essay organization. Prerequisites: WRT070 or satisfactory score on writing assessment test.
* AZ residents pay $32 per credit.

Writing I
Pima Community College
PIMA#WRT101 Undergraduate 4 credits $220*
This course covers the principles of good writing with emphasis on the technique and practice of description, explanation, and argumentation. Prerequisites: WRT100 or satisfactory score on writing placement exam.
* AZ residents, $32/credit hour.

Writing II
Pima Community College
PIMA#WRT102 Undergraduate 4 credits $220*
Practice in writing analytical compositions, including a research paper or annotated papers. Includes readings in fiction, poetry, drama or non-fiction as a basis for writing. Prerequisite: WRT101 or satisfactory score on writing placement exam.
* AZ residents, $32/credit hour.

Writing in the Humanities and Social Sciences
Western Illinois University
WEIL#ENG380 Undergraduate 3 credits $795*
Is a course for people interested in developing their ability in popular or scholarly writing as it relates to one or more of the humanistic fields, such as history, literature, sociology, education, religion, and art. However, it is equally useful for those who want to write about sciences, the business world, or current events from a humanistic perspective. The course improves your investigative and analytical abilities, develops familiarity with various modes and techniques, and increases the clarity and effectiveness of your writing. Prerequisite: Freshman composition or consent of instructor.
* IL residents tuition: $88 per credit.

Writing Nonfiction for Publication
UCLA
UCLA#X450B Undergraduate 3 credits $450
This course covers the craft, marketing, and business of nonfiction writing step-by-step. Students explore the basics of writing articles, essays, reviews, columns, and books, with the emphasis on finding their natural writing "voice" and developing professional techniques. Through course notes, class assignments, "group editing" via e-mail, and individual revision, participants learn how to write and polish magazine and newspaper pieces that are creatively satisfying and commercially appealing to editors and readers.

Writing Practice I
University of Minnesota
MINN#ENGC1011 Undergraduate 5 credits $445
The novice, rusty, or insecure writer learns 22 'don'ts'--common errors of the beginning writer--and gains a clear, confident, college-level approach to writing. Each unit introduces several blunders, such as the passive voice and the apathetic title, and presents strategies for recognizing and overcoming them. Because writing is a learned skill and not a mysterious talent, much emphasis is on pre-writing, from choosing an appropriate topic to considering the audience.

Writing Skills Review
Lansing Community College
LANS#WRIT119 Undergraduate 1 credits $105
This course is designed to help WRIT121-122 composition students, and others, improve their basic sentence and mechanics skills by providing intensive writing and editing practice in an on-line workshop setting.

Writing through Childhood
Kennesaw State University
KENN#FMV210 Undergraduate 3 credits $149
Childhood is a gold mine of writing ideas. This online Writing Through Childhood workshop will help you dig deep and find writing ideas that reside in memories. After an introduction to the creative writing process (research, creation, editing), five recollection exercises will be used to help you dig through the rubble of childhood and unearth memories and emotions. The material you find will then be used as the basis for reminiscences, poetry and fiction.

Writing Workshop - Poetry
University of Colorado
CUON#ENGL3020 Undergraduate 3 credits $1953*
This course is both a creative and an academic course. Students will be writing their own poetry and critiquing the poetry of their peers in class. They will learn the "craft" of poetry and studying and writing about the work of past and contemporary poets. Students will be able to talk intelligently about the poetry of other writers using the appropriate critical terms.
* CO residents tuition: $136 per credit.

Written Communications
Northwest College
NOCO#BU271 Undergraduate   3 credits $???
Students are shown the correct way to write and format letters, memos and short reports. Correct grammar, punctuation and spelling are emphasized. Prerequisites or Corequisites: GE174 and GE180 (as applicable).

Written Communications
Waukesha County Technical College
WAUK#801195019 Undergraduate 3 credits $193
In this online course, you will learn the fundamentals of effective writing for use in everyday life and in business and professional environments. In addition, you will learn online communication skills that are extremely beneficial in today's marketplace. We will use a class listserv, e-mail directly to me and between your peers, and our class home page to conduct this online, workshop-oriented writing class. This course is designed as a workshop because learning, thinking, and writing are all social, collaborative processes.

Written English and Literary Studies I
Mercy College
MERC#EN111 Undergraduate   3 credits $900
The writing of expository prose, particularly in the analysis of literature. students read and analyze representative plays and write essays on assigned topics. Introduction to critical essays and research methods. There is a uniform exit examination.

Business

Accounting

Communications

Finance

General Management

Human Resources

International Business

Labor Relations

MIS

Marketing

Organizational Behavior

Other

Production

Quantitative Methods

Small Business

Accounting
Heriot-Watt University
HERI#01 Graduate   4 credits $???
Accounting is often described as the language of business. It is concerned with the gathering, ordering, checking, presenting and communication of financial data so that informed decisions can be made. Decision makers are positioned both outside and inside an organization. Outsiders include shareholders who want information to help them decide whether to buy or sell shares, tax authorities who require information on profits as a basis for taxation, and creditors who need to assess the organization's ability to pay its debts.

Accounting and Business
Pennsylvania State University
PENN#ACCTG211 Undergraduate 4 credits $345
Introduction to the role of accounting numbers in the process of managing a business and in investor decision making.

Accounting and Finance for Managers
University of Minnesota
MINN#ABUS3101 Undergraduate 4 credits $400
Accounting and Finance for Managers emphasizes practical decision making using accounting and finance data. The course is divided into three parts. The first concentrates on financial statement analysis, cash flow analysis, and how firms decide on appropriate financial strategies. The second covers capital investment analysis, the makeup of interest rates and how they affect financial decision making, and the tradeoff between risk and rates of return. The final section includes a study of cost and differential analysis, standard costs, activity-based costing, and product and service pricing.

Accounting and Financial Management
The Graduate School of America
TGSA#OM815W Graduate   4 credits $795
This course addresses accounting and financial concepts and their applications to the management of an organization, and presents a framework for financial decisions in organizations.

Accounting and Information Systems
Bellevue University
BELL#MBA541 Graduate   3 credits $825
This course provides students with an overall understanding of the manner in which business gathers, processes, and uses information.

Accounting and Information Systems
Bellevue University
BELL#MBA642 Graduate   3 credits $825
Provides an understanding of management information systems used in decision-making processes.

Accounting for Decision Making, Concepts and Theory
State University of New York
SUNY#ACC19571 Undergraduate 3 credits $1038*
This course introduces the student to financial accounting. Emphasis is on the analysis and interpretation of financial information. Generally accepted accounting principles will be discussed throughout the course. The standard reports of financial accounting will be studied as well as the process of identifying, measuring, recording and reporting financial information. The accounting information system and bookkeeping procedures will be introduced. Internal control procedures, corporate assets, liabilities, and shareholders equity will also be studied as well as reporting concerns of international companies.
* NY residents tuition: $137 per credit.

Accounting for Non-Accountants
UCLA
UCLA#X429 Undergraduate   4 credits $500
This online course is designed for non-accounting managers and personnel in organizations of all sizes who must work with and understand internal accounting/financial data--without overemphasizing the detailed mechanics and technical language of accounting. It also is appropriate for entrepreneurs and business owners who desire a greater understanding of what your accounting and financial information systems can and should be supplying you.

Accounting Fundamentals
Edmonds Community College
EDMO#OTA121 Undergraduate   5 credits $260
This is a beginning accounting course with emphasis on journalizing, posting, financial statements, adjustments, worksheets, cash funds, and payroll entries. Group critical thinking outcomes are included. Computer applications are used.

Accounting Fundamentals I
University of Minnesota
MINN#GC1540 Undergraduate   4 credits $356
The first of a two-part course in college accounting, designed for both business and nonbusiness students. This course considers balance sheet and income statement methodology, the accounting cycle for both service and merchandising businesses, and an examination of special journals, inventories, receivables, and accounting for plant assets.

Accounting Fundamentals II
University of Minnesota
MINN#GC1542 Undergraduate   4 credits $356
Continuation of GC1540. The topics examined include: handling dividends, retained earnings and treasury stock, debt, investments, financial reporting, and sources and uses of working capital. Also examines financial statements, accounting for manufacturing operations, and cost analysis problems. Prerequisite: GC1540.

Accounting I
University of Missouri
MOCE#AC130 Undergraduate   3 credits $387
This course uses the problem approach to cover accounting principles in relation to business papers, journals, ledgers, balance sheets, income statements, trial balances, and worksheets.

Accounting I
University of Missouri
MOCE#AC36 Undergraduate   3 credits $387
An introduction to the field of accounting, this course covers the fundamentals of financial accounting. Perquisites: sophomore standing.

Accounting I
Northwest College
NOCO#AC100 Undergraduate   5 credits $???
Students receive a basic knowledge in double-entry accounting theory. Instruction will be given in posting accounts, periodic adjustments, report preparation, special journals and financial statement analysis. Prerequisite: DP105 and MH165.

Accounting I
New York Institute of Technology
NYIT#BUS3511 Undergraduate   3 credits $???
A study of accounting fundamentals. Topics include the accounting cycle, statement preparation, systems, asset valuations, accounting concepts, and principles for the sole proprietorship.

Accounting I
Strayer University
STRA#ACC101 Undergraduate   4.5 credits $665
Covers analysis and recording of business transactions; accounting for sales, purchases, cash disbursements, and receivable; includes end-of-fiscal period work, adjustments, financial statements, and closing procedures.

Accounting I
State University of New York
SUNY#BUS1404S Undergraduate 4 credits $532*
This course covers basic principles and purposes of financial accounting as applied to business organizations. Topics include the preparation and use of financial statements, analysis and recording of business transactions, the accounting cycle for service and merchandising enterprises, the worksheet, accrued and deferred items, valuation of assets, and payroll and payroll taxes. Students will explore both the theoretical and practical aspects of accounting.
* NY residents tuition: $90 per credit.

Accounting II
University of Missouri
MOCE#AC37 Undergraduate   3 credits $387
This course covers the fundamentals of managerial accounting and additional topics in financial accounting. Perquisites: Accounting 36 and sophomore standing.

Accounting II
Northwest College
NOCO#AC101 Undergraduate   5 credits $???
The study of accounting principles continues with more specific processes explained. Students will be exposed to partnerships and corporations and how they are formed, financed and operated. Prerequisite: AC100.

Accounting II
New York Institute of Technology
NYIT#BUS3521 Undergraduate   3 credits $???
Continues the study of accounting fundamentals. Topics include partnership, corporations, liabilities, manufacturing, accounting, and statement analysis. Prerequisite: BUS3511.

Accounting II
Strayer University
STRA#ACC105 Undergraduate   4.5 credits $665
Provides an understanding of accounting concepts, assumptions, and principles. Progresses to evaluation of accounting data for merchandise inventory, deferrals and accruals, plant assets, intangibles, payables and payroll. Introduces accounting for corporations as related to stocks, bonds, and corporate earnings. Introduces partnership accounting and, in addition, introduces the statement of cash flows. Prerequisite: ACC100.

Accounting II - Managerial
Rogers State University
ROGE#ACCT2203 Undergraduate 3 credits $495*
Managerial accounting is what you, the manager, will use to run the daily operations of a business and make decisions about its future. Managerial accounting uses past data and future predictions as information for decision-making about such practical matters as pricing the items to be sold, purchasing and maintaining inventories, and ensuring profitability.
* OK residents $315.

Accounting Information Systems
Golden Gate University
GOLD#ACCTG319A Graduate   3 credits $1404
Examines accounting systems as integral components of management information systems. Course work will provide you with an understanding of general systems theory, information theory, data bases and systems analysis. You will focus on detailed examination of specific accounting applications. Prerequisite: ACCTG100A, CIS10.

Accounting Information Systems
Strayer University
STRA#ACC564 Undergraduate   4.5 credits $665
Introduces the student to systems analysis and application of information systems concepts to the accounting process and accounting models, both manual and automated. prereq: CIS500.

Accounting Policy
Strayer University
STRA#ACC566 Undergraduate   4.5 credits $665
Provides for the analysis of accounting information and comprehension of its value, uses and limitations. Upgrades the knowledge, nature, and source of accounting information necessary to analyze accounting data for decision making. Helps the accountant work more intelligently with the financial executive to maximize the usefulness of the accounting information received and to recognize whether the accounting function is providing all the relevant accounting information necessary for sound decision making. prereq: ACC305 or equivalent.

Accounting Principles I
National American University
NAAM#AC105D Undergraduate   4.5 credits $900
This is an introductory courses to the world of accounting. The student will learn basic accounting principles and terminology to classify and record transactions, prepare adjusting and closing entries, and prepare financial statements. This course also presents accounting principles and concepts applicable to inventories and long term assets and liabilities.

Accounting Theory
Strayer University
STRA#ACC415 Undergraduate   4.5 credits $665
Examines the basic concepts that underlie accounting principles and procedures associated with placement grouping and terminology used in statement preparation and analysis. Included numerous publications of the AICPA, AAA, FASB and the SEC which highlight these basic concepts. Gives special attention to working capital, depreciable assets, intangible assets, deferred credits and liabilities, owners' equity, the income statement, earning per share, pension costs, leases, and income tax allocations. prereq: ACC305.

Advanced Accounting
City University
CITY#AC405 Undergraduate   5 qu. credits $785
Preparation and analysis of consolidated financial statements, mergers, restatement of financial statements to reflect international monetary differences; governmental and non-profit accounting and review of trusts and estates.

Advanced Accounting I
Strayer University
STRA#ACC401 Undergraduate   4.5 credits $665
Covers accounting for home office and branches, business combinations and consolidations. Provides continuation of the preparation for the CPS examination as well as various techniques for solving some of the more complex problems in the business environment. prereq: ACC305.

Advanced Accounting II
Strayer University
STRA#ACC402 Undergraduate   4.5 credits $665
Continues coverage of business combinations and corporate consolidation concepts and procedures, including FASB, SEC and AICPA pronouncements. Provides continuation of the preparation for the CPA examination as well as various techniques for solving some of the more complex problems found in the business environment. Covers accounting for multinational companies, estate trusts and bankruptcy. prereq: ACC401.

Advanced Accounting Theory
Strayer University
STRA#ACC563 Undergraduate   4.5 credits $665
Provides a frame of reference for advanced accounting theories. Emphasizes income, liability, and asset valuation based on inductive, deductive, and capital markets approaches. Also surveys price level changes, monetary and non-monetary factors, problems of ownership equities and the disclosure of relevant information to investors and creditors. prereq: ACC305 or equivalent.

Advanced Auditing
Strayer University
STRA#ACC562 Undergraduate   4.5 credits $665
Surveys in-depth analysis of current auditing issues, including professional standards and ethics, internal control gathering and documentation of evidences, and statistical sampling. focuses on detailed analysis of audit programs and EDP as well as concepts concerning the financial condition of operation of commercial enterprises. prereq: ACC403 or equivalent.

Advanced Financial Accounting Theory
State University of New York
SUNY#ACC68535 Graduate   3 credits $1038*
An examination and analysis of Generally Accepted Accounting Principles. The course reviews Financial Accounting Standards in detail and include a critical review of the research that is at the theoretical foundation of GAAP. In addition, the process by which the Financial Accounting Standards Board promulgates new FAS will also be analyzed. Prerequisite: Intermediate Accounting II (ACC386) or equivalent.
* NY residents tuition: $137 per credit

Advanced Human Resource Management
Bellevue University
BELL#LDR661 Graduate   4 credits $1100
This class focuses on the trends and issues of human resource management challenging today's leaders. Participants are exposed to several major workforce trends and their implications for leaders and their followers in military and non-military environments. Participants also explore research on employment relations in a global employment marketplace, and examine the implications of such research for world leaders. What followers and those external to organizations expect from a leader is important in terms of how effective that organization and its mission are perceived to be.

Advanced Managerial Accounting
Strayer University
STRA#ACC561 Undergraduate 4.5 credits $665
Investigates advanced topics in managerial accounting and expands upon topics covered in ACC560. Topics include; cost projections, analysis and interpretation, analysis under uncertainty, capital budgeting, linear programming, and decentralized operations. Prerequisite: ACC560.

Advanced Marketing Management
The Graduate School of America
TGSA#OM853W Graduate 4 credits $795
This course examines the application of the marketing concept in the development of a product or service from conception to launch. Topics treat the subject of marketing from producer or provider to consumer, with emphasis given to the planning required for the efficient use of marketing methodology.

Advanced Organizational Behavior
Western Illinois University
WEIL#MAN350 Undergraduate 3 credits $795*
Increases your understanding of fundamental concepts of human behavior by reviewing what has been learned in the behavioral and social sciences regarding people's behavior at work. The course focuses on the interrelationships of peoples, the work they perform, and the organizations where they work. The role of management in employee need satisfaction and organizational effectiveness is also studied. Prerequisite: Management 349.
* IL residents tuition: $88 per credit.

Advanced Professional Communication
New Jersey Institute of Technology
NJIT#ENG601 Undergraduate 3 credits $1143*
This course provides the foundation for all Professional and Technical Communication coursework. Using principles of modeling and cognitive apprenticeship, faculty from both academic and corporate communities show the cognitive and metacognitive processes that comprise their expertise as they solve communication problems. Optional: 35 video lessons of 30 minutes each.
* NJ residents: $184/semester hour.

Advertising
City University
CITY#MK390 Undergraduate 5 qu. credits $785
This course investigates various promotional tools used in the communication-mix/promotion-mix, i.e. advertising, sales promotion, and publicity. Concepts include: advertising planning process; determining advertising and promotional goals and objectives; control and evaluation of advertising and promotional programs; ethical and regulatory issues.

Advertising
Northwest College
NOCO#MT120 Undergraduate 3 credits $???
Students will study advertising concepts and the proper use of advertising in business, how to design ads and the different types of advertising media available.

Advertising 101
New School for Social Research
NEWS#4010 Undergraduate 3 credits $1092
You've studied graphic design, but can you imagine art directing an advertising campaign? In this introduction to advertising, put together the advertising for a product or service of your choice. Create print ads, TV storyboards, posters and various promotional items, where the only creative limitations are the ones you set for yourself. Discover the process of getting illustrations and running a photo shoot. You'll learn to choose the right headlines and best type to get your message across.

Advertising Concepts
Ohio University
OHIO#BMT270 Undergraduate 4 credits $256
General course in advertising that emphasizes psychology, advertising agency, media research, brands, and labels.

Advertising Copywriting
UCLA
UCLA#X401B Undergraduate 3 credits $450
From soft drinks to software, florists to fashion consultants, products and services are sold largely on the strength of their ads. This beginning course for aspiring copywriters covers all aspects of creating ads for a portfolio, including headline writing, body copy, theme lines, and campaigns for magazines, newspapers, billboards, and other print media. The concept behind the ad is emphasized through weekly assignments, a customized course workbook, sharing and analyzing sample portfolios, and online discussions.

American Labor and Unions
Eastern Oregon University
EAOR#ECON481 Undergraduate 5 credits $400
Economic analysis of the formation, growth, operation, and effects of unions in the U.S. economy; determination of wages and working conditions; human capital theory and the education and training of workers; discrimination and other sources of wage differentials; unemployment and public policy toward labor markets.

Applied Business Economics
The Graduate School of America
TGSA#OM854W Graduate 4 credits $795
A survey of macroeconomics and microeconomics. Current developments in the economy, inflation, unemployment, resource allocation, market structures and competition, and the relationship of economic policy to business are examined.

Auditing
City University
CITY#AC411 Undergraduate 5 qu. credits $785
The establishment and evaluation of management controls, and the conduct of operational and internal financial audits as they relate to both profit and non-profit organizations; auditing standards and accounting principles; independence and the code of professional ethics; legal liability; internal control, types of evidence, the auditing environment and auditing objectives. Prerequisite: AC302 or its equivalent.

Auditing I
Strayer University
STRA#ACC403 Undergraduate 4.5 credits $665
Covers theory of auditing, including the educational and moral qualifications for auditor, as well as the role of the auditor in the American economy. Emphasizes professional standards, professional ethics, and the legal liability of auditors. Comprehensively covers planning and designing the audit program, gathering and summarizing evidence, and internal control. Prerequisite: ACC401.

Auditing II
Strayer University
STRA#ACC405 Undergraduate 4.5 credits $665
Introduces the audit working papers and examination of the general records. Covers auditing of cash and marketable securities, accounts and notes receivable, and sales transactions; inventories and cost of sales, fixed assets, depreciation and depletion; prepaid expenses, deferred and intangible assets; current and long-term liabilities, owners' equity, and opinions concerning the financial condition and operation of the financial enterprise. Prerequisite: ACC403.

Automotive Aftermarket Management
Northwest College
NOCO#MA215 Undergraduate 5 credits $???
This course discusses procedures and relationships involving all aspects of the automotive/vehicle aftermarket - from manufacturer to consumer. Those areas covered are marketing, sales, advertising, budgeting, and professional activities.

Basic Accounting Skills
Indiana University
INDI#A100 Undergraduate 1 credits $89
The course covers the process of capturing and recording economic events that underlie accounting reports. Particular emphasis is placed on the process of generating financial reports: source documents, original entries, special journals, ledgers, adjusting entries, closing entries, and financial statement preparation. The course provides students with the foundation necessary for higher-level accounting courses.

Basic Functions and Calculus for Business
Bakersfield College
BAKE#MATHB2 Undergraduate 4 credits $460*
Modern concepts in mathematics including functions, matrix algebra and sequences; the basic concepts of differential calculus with an introduction to integral calculus involving numerous applications to business.
* CA residents pay $40 per credit.

Basics of Budgeting
UCLA
UCLA#X430 Undergraduate 4 credits $500
Budgets represent an organization's formal expression of management plans and objectives. Consequently, the budget often serves as the most powerful tool for developing an overall strategy and communicating that strategy to employees and the public. This course provides tips, techniques, and tools designed to enable students to develop a budget that serves as a strong management tool. It also examines how effective budgets boost organization profits and lead employees to higher levels of performance and success. Topics include budget planning; cost behavior; capital, production, sales, and cash budgeting; analyzing financial statements; and overall budget administration.

Bed & Breakfast Management
Chemeketa Community College
CHEM#HTM112 Undergraduate 3 credits $123
This is an overview course designed to explore the subject of the bed and breakfast and innkeeping industry. Course discusses the realities of purchasing, owning and operating a successful inn. Topics will explore design, financing, operations, food service and sanitation, marketing and governmental regulations.

Behavioral Science & Management
Thomas Edison State College
THED#OLMAN352 Undergraduate 3 credits $397*
This course covers the management of individuals and groups in organizations. Topics covered are individuals at work; group dynamics; the organizational goals, structure and technology; information; and organizational quality and productivity. It presents the organization in practice and explores the core functions and issues involved in managing. The challenges, opportunities, and satisfactions of managing are stressed.
* NJ residents tuition: $33 per credit.

Behavioral Science in Marketing
New York Institute of Technology
NYIT#BES2451 Undergraduate 3 credits $???
An investigation of the behavioral sciences disciplines as they affect marketing decisions. Consideration of such fields as psychology, sociology, and anthropology as the basis for studying consumer motivation and behavior. Prerequisite: BES2401.

Bureaucracy and Formal Organization
Western Illinois University
WEIL#SOC330 Undergraduate 3 credits $795*
Explores the ways in which membership in an organization affects the lives of its participants. This WIU teleclass evaluates the general impact of bureaucracy on contemporary society as a whole. While the course does not attempt to teach specific administrative skills or practical management techniques, it does take an analytical approach by presenting a series of different perspectives on how to view modern organizations. In some cases, these perspectives are critical of bureaucracy and skeptical of many modern management practices.
* IL residents tuition: $88 per credit.

Business & Computer Curriculum
Emporia State University
EMPO#BE882 Graduate 3 credits $315
A study of the growth, development and present status of business education. Evaluation of present curricular practices and trends. Principles and practices involved in curriculum construction as applied to the secondary and post-secondary schools.

Business & Professional Communication
Indiana University
INDI#S223 Undergraduate 3 credits $268
Examines organizational communication, with emphasis on skills acquisition. Developed skills include interviewing, group discussion, parliamentary procedure, and public speaking. Cassette tapes are utilized in this course. Prerequisite: S121.

Business and Its Environment
Ohio University
OHIO#BA101 Undergraduate 4 credits $256
Nature of business and of economic, social, and political environments of business firm. Emphasis on ways in which such surroundings affect business policies and operations.

Business Communication
Eastern Oregon University
EAOR#OADM225 Undergraduate 3 credits $240
Written communication in the business environment to include correspondence in sales, collections, bad news, promotion letters and memos. Also, basic concepts of successful business writing skills and styles.

Business Communication
New Hampshire College
NEHA#ENG220 Undergraduate 3 credits $1656
A practical introduction to the preparation of business correspondence, employment applications and resumes, and formal research reports. Emphasis is placed on written communication skills. Prerequisite: ENG121.

Business Communication
Rio Salado College
RISA#GBS233 Undergraduate 3 credits $186*
Internal and external business communications, including verbal and nonverbal techniques. Prerequisite: ENG102 with grade of "C" or better, or permission of department/division.
* AZ residents $37 per credit.

Business Communication
Strayer University
STRA#ENG105 Undergraduate 4.5 credits $665
Focuses on written and oral discussions of ideas as integral aspects of a general education. Emphasizes data collection, organization, interpretation and presentation of results within both oral and written formats of increasing length and complexity; stresses determination of purpose and audience as part of this process. Prerequisite: ENG102.

Business Communications
Barstow Community College
BARS#BUSI75 Undergraduate 3 credits $???
A survey of the principles and techniques of business communications as a tool for business decision making. Focus is on effective oral and written business communications. Methods of investigating, organizing and presenting business data and ideas are developed through practical involvement. Ethical and legal implications as well as other critical thinking techniques are emphasized.

Business Communications
Brevard Community College
BREV#OST2335B Undergraduate 3 credits $485
To develop the ability to write effective business letters, memorandums, and reports; and to develop effective techniques for oral communications with emphasis on promoting and maintaining good human relations in business.

Business Communications
Indiana University
INDI#X204 Undergraduate 3 credits $268
Theory and practice of written communication in business; use of correct, forceful English in preparation of letters, memoranda, and reports.

Business Communications
Lansing Community College
LANS#WRIT127 Undergraduate 3 credits $315
Writing 127 concentrates on the real-world applications of business communications. Audience viewpoint is emphasized, with problem-solving correspondence as the primary focus of the course. Formats include memoranda, letters, proposals, reports, and an interview portfolio.

Business Communications
Strayer University
STRA#BUS490A Undergraduate 4.5 credits $665
Introduces the importance of communication in the workplace. Focuses on the meaningful exchange of information through messages both outside and inside the organization. Applies business communication theory directly to simulated work-place situations.

Business Communications
State University of New York
SUNY#BAUD101 Undergraduate 3 credits $1038*
Business Communications introduces fundamental concepts and techniques of effective communications in business with emphasis on writing business letters, memoranda, and reports. Consideration is given to collecting data and organizing materials for the presentation of a business report. The importance of the psychological approach to modern business communications is stressed. Prerequisite: English 101.
* NY residents tuition: $137 per credit.

Business Computer Programming
UCLA
UCLA#X41420 Undergraduate   4 credits $500
This is a comprehensive course which introduces students to, and builds proficiency in, computer programming for business. The Pascal programming language is used to illustrate concepts common to most high-level programming languages. Topics include top-down modular program design; user interface design; elements of algorithms, coding, and data structures; procedures; flow of control, including loops and conditionals; structured and unstructured files and record processing; and program testing, debugging, and documentation. Examples and assignments illustrate typical business applications. Weekly programming assignments required. Prerequisite: X414.10 Introduction to Computing for Business or consent of instructor.

Business Correspondence
Cerro Coso Community College
CECO#BSADC55 Undergraduate 3 credits $345*
Discussion, critique, and practice of business writing techniques, emphasizing the psychology of effective writing. Prerequisite: Level 1 reading classification recommended.
* CA residents pay $13 per credit.

Business Correspondence
Cerro Coso Community College
CECO#ENGLC55 Undergraduate 3 credits $345*
Discussion, critique, and practice of business writing techniques, emphasizing the psychology of effective writing. Prerequisite: Level 1 writing classification recommended.
* CA residents pay $13 per credit.

Business Correspondence
College of DuPage
DUPA#OFC150 Undergraduate   4 qu. credits $120
Basic instruction and practice in developing the vital employment skill of planning, writing and formatting effective business communication including sentences, paragraphs, memos, letters, email and employment communications. Business spelling, punctuation and grammar skills will be reviewed.

Business English
Edmonds Community College
EDMO#OTA107 Undergraduate   5 credits $260
Designed to provide students with comprehensive, up-to-date, and relevant instruction in the correct use of the English language. Language practices vary among business leaders. Some people continue to use outdated or ungrammatical constructions, but it is wise for the current students of business to know the language most acceptable to those in their field. It is the purpose of this course to concentrate on rules and recommendations that have direct application to the business community today.

Business Ethics
City University
CITY#PHI404 Undergraduate   5 qu. credits $785
A survey of the fundamental concepts and problems of business ethics, based on ethical systems from traditional to postmodern. The course examines how philosophies have shaped social relationships in business and uses of goods. The course applies its findings, through readings and cases, to current social, economic, and environmental situations. Prerequisite: HUM200 or its equivalent.

Business Ethics
New Hampshire College
NEHA#PHL216 Undergraduate   3 credits $1656
Business Ethics examines a philosophical study of moral issues in business. Topics include such issues as corporate responsibility, conflicts of interest, morality in advertising, preferential hiring (e.g., minorities and women), personal morality vs. loyalty to employer, as well as theoretical issues such as capitalism vs. socialism.

Business Ethics
Strayer University
STRA#BUS290 Undergraduate   4.5 credits $665
Deepens awareness of ethical principles through the consideration of problems encountered by the business person. Analyzes the need for honesty in contracts, budgeting, developing products, promotions, pricing, distribution strategies, and customer service. Prerequisite: BUS200.

Business Finance
Fayetteville Technical Community College
FAYE#BUS225 Undergraduate   3 credits $489*
This course provides an overview of business financial management. Emphasis is placed on financial statement analysis, time value of money, management of cash flow, risk and return, and sources of financing. Upon completion, students should be able to interpret and apply the principles of financial management. Prerequisites: ACC120.
* NC residents pay $20 per credit.

Business Information Systems
Bellevue University
BELL#MGTC310 Undergraduate 3 credits $750
The what and why of information systems, beginning with the business need. Hands-on use of the Internet and also application packages for word processing, spreadsheet, and data base with basic computer skills.

Business Internet Access and Usage
Golden Gate University
GOLD#TM396F Graduate   3 credits $1404
Examines the Internet from a managers perspective. Seminar format, with some hands-on experience and demonstrations. Focuses on the application and strategic value of the Internet to the business community. Covers the fundamentals of access and use of the Internet and its configurations and components. Includes a survey of the present business applications and a discussion of future business use as the Internet continues to evolve. You will create a personal or business web page.

Business Logistics Management
Pennsylvania State University
PENN#BLOG301 Undergraduate 3 credits $345
Management of logistics function in firm, including physical supply and distribution activities such as transportation, storage facility location, and materials handling. Prerequisite: third-semester standing.

Business Math
Northwest College
NOCO#MH169A Undergraduate 5 credits $???
Problems in real business situations are studied. Business applications such as bank records, payroll, inventory, statistics and merchandising are studied. This course also studies percentages and their applications to a variety of business and consumer loans. Prerequisite: MH165 or proficiency exam credit.

Business Mathematics
Brevard Community College
BREV#MTB1103 Undergraduate 3 credits $435
To develop the ability to apply the fundamentals of mathematics to inventory, depreciation, turnover, overhead, taxes, insurance, and other business operations.

Business Organization & Management
Rio Salado College
RISA#MGT175 Undergraduate 3 credits $186*
Covers basic principles of managing quality and performance in organizations. Covers management functions: planning, organizing, leading, and controlling. Emphasizes continual improvement, ethics, and social responsibility.
* AZ residents $37 per credit.

Business Organization and Admin.
New York Institute of Technology
NYIT#BUS3900 Undergraduate 3 credits $???
A study of organizations and of the activities of the manager in an organization. The course follows a functional approach, analyzing such management concepts as organizing decentralization, use of staff, human relations, conflict, decision making, planning, supervision, communication, and financial and production control systems such as budgeting and PERT. To enable the student to develop skills in analysis and judgment, the case method is used as an integral part of this course. Prerequisite: BUS3906.

Business Organizations
Brevard Community College
BREV#PLA2433 Undergraduate 3 credits $485
Course provides student with procedurals information on such topics as corporations, partnerships, proprietorships and other business vehicles. A survey of the fundamentals principles of the law applicable to each area.

Business Organizations
City University
CITY#PL203 Undergraduate 5 qu. credits $785
Legal concepts and principles which routinely impact business organizations and commercial transactions, including contracts, agency, employment relationships, corporations, property, negotiable instruments, secured transaction, and consumer protection laws.

Business Plan for New Media Venture
UCLA
UCLA#X402 Undergraduate 4 credits $550
An effective and persuasive business plan is crucial to obtaining financing for entertainment or new media ventures, but benchmark data for entertainment ventures is often hard to come by and data for new media ventures is sometimes nonexistent. Therefore, an entrepreneur who wants to gain financing for a project may find it difficult to support the potential of the venture without a business plan. Writing a business plan of this type requires a specialized search for data, as well as a creative and diligent presentation of the project's potential.

Business Policy
Strayer University
STRA#BUS490B Undergraduate 4.5 credits $665
Provides the opportunities for students to integrate management principles, techniques, and theories by applying previously acquired knowledge of accounting, law, personnel, economics, and statistics. Utilizes cases from the federal government and private industry with emphasis on problem identification, analysis, and decision-making within the organization. Prerequisite: All major core courses, with the exception of BUS499, must be completed.

Business Policy
State University of New York
SUNY#214814 Undergraduate 4 credits $586*
Formulate, implement and evaluate organizational strategy and policy in a complex business environment. Topics include objectives and strategic management of the business portfolio; analysis and diagnosis of the organization's external opportunities and threats, and the internal competitive advantages or weaknesses related to its marketing, production, personnel and financial areas; strategy alternatives and choice (including acquisitions, mergers and divestments); and implications of strategy for organizational structure and change. Prerequisites: Course work or equivalent knowledge in the following subjects: Management Principles, Marketing Principles, Human Resource Management, and Corporate Finance.
* NY residents tuition: $515

Business Policy and Strategy
Golden Gate University
GOLD#MGT362   Graduate   3 credits $1404
Studies the functions of senior management using advanced case analysis, focusing on general management and decision making. Topic include setting objectives; implementing, supporting and controlling organization-wide policies; developing strategies to achieve objectives; setting standards for measuring performance; evaluating and reformulating policies in response to change. Stresses leadership responsibilities toward customers, investors, employees, suppliers and the community, governmental relations and international management. Prerequisite: Satisfactory completion of MGT300; MGT362 must be taken as part of the final six units in the advanced program.

Business Policy Seminar
New York Institute of Technology
NYIT#BUS3909   Undergraduate   3 credits $???
This is a capstone senior-year course in which the disciplines of business and economics will be focused on the solution of specific business problems. Case studies and a computer-based management game will be employed in this course. Prerequisite: Upper senior standing.

Business Process Innovation
New Jersey Institute of Technology
NJIT#CIS684   Undergraduate   3 credits $1143*
The notion of a process architecture activity structure will be introduced as the basic framework for managing change. A spiral BPI implementation methodology will be introduced in detail, interwoven with many case studies. Finally, a software process engineering support environment will be discussed. This course is part of the Graduate Certificate in Object-Oriented Design. Optional: 26 video lessons of 60 minutes each. Prerequisite: NJIT#CIS610 Data Structures; NJIT#CIS673 Software Engineering; knowledge of C programming.
* NJ residents: $184/semester hour.

Business Processes and Functions
Bellevue University
BELL#MBA501   Graduate   3 credits $825
Provides participants with conceptual and experiential familiarity with aspects of administrative processes and basic functions of an organization.

Business Statistics
Northwest College
NOCO#MH267   Undergraduate   3 credits $???
Statistics is the science of collecting, organizing, presenting and interpreting numerical data for the purpose of making better decisions in the face of uncertainty. This course presents the students with the basic material necessary to understand statistics, probability and statistical inference. Prerequisite: MH169.

Business Statistics
Rio Salado College
RISA#GBS221   Undergraduate   3 credits $186*
Business applications of descriptive and inferential statistics, measurement of relationships, and statistical process management. Prerequisite: Grade of "C" or better in GBS220, or MAT172, and MAT212.
* AZ residents $37 per credit.

Business Statistics
State University of New York
SUNY#BSAD221   Undergraduate   3 credits $1038*
Principles and methods of the theory and methodology of elementary statistics with the development of an understanding of the role of statistics in business and practical affairs. Emphasis on the use of statistical methods as an analytical tool. Sources of basic data, tabular and graphic presentation, frequency distributions, averages, measures of dispersion, index numbers, sampling methods, quality control, probability, regression and correlation, and hypothesis testing. Focus is on computerized calculations and case studies.
* NY residents tuition: $137 per credit

Business Statistics I
National American University
NAAM#MA210D   Undergraduate   4.5 credits $900
Topics studied include presentation and interpretation of numerical data; measures of central tendency, dispersion, probability, and continuous and discreet probability distributions.

Business Statistics II
National American University
NAAM#MA220D   Undergraduate   4.5 credits $900
This course is a continuation of MA210D. Topics include continuous probability distributions, estimation and testing of hypothesis, regression and correlation, and quality control.

Business Systems Analysis and Design
Rio Salado College
RISA#CIS225   Undergraduate   3 credits $186*
Investigation, analysis, design, implementation and evaluation of business computer systems. Prerequisite: CIS158 or BPC117 (any module) or CIS117 (any module) or permission of instructor.
* AZ residents $37 per credit.

Business Writing
University of Colorado
CUON#ENGL3170   Undergraduate 3 credits $1953*
This course introduces the study of writing for business. The emphasis will be on style, structure, memoranda, letters, resumes, and short reports. Prerequisite: ENGL1020.
* CO residents tuition: $136 per credit.

Business Writing
Golden Gate University
GOLD#ENGL120 Undergraduate 3 credits $960
Helps you develop the skills necessary for effective business writing. You will write, edit and format letters, memos, reports and a research paper. You will critically analyze business articles and other professionally-oriented material. Prerequisite: ENGL1A; ENGL1B or consent of the Department Chair; students must complete ENGL1B with a grade of C or better.

Business Writing
University of Massachusetts - Lowell
MALO#42224 Undergraduate 3 credits $395
This course in Business Writing places an emphasis on the development of writing for businesses. Office automation and information technology will be utilized to help focus the need to approach writing as a process of making deliberate decisions about purpose and audience. Overall, the course is designed to develop accurate, concise writing skills and to improve the student's powers of effective communication.

Business Writing
Marylhurst College
MARY#WR214 Undergraduate 3 credits $651
This course develops business communication skills with an emphasis on writing. It focuses on the styles and formats of business correspondence, memos, letters, resumes, and business reports. This is a required course for Business and Management majors.

Business Writing
New York Institute of Technology
NYIT#EN1042 Undergraduate 3 credits $???
An intermediate-level writing course for students in business. Instruction and practice in all phases of business communications, such as reports, memoranda and correspondence, as well as in-depth study of research methods. Required of all business and management majors. Coursework includes a computer lab component. Prerequisite: EN1020.

Business Writing (ESL)
New School for Social Research
NEWS#1492 Undergraduate 0 credits $370
Permission required. Coursework is based on common problems for non-native business writers, including correct form and American business usage appropriate for memos, letters, and reports. American idioms, avoiding embarrassing mistakes, and the common errors are covered. Call (212) 229-5372 for required placement advising.

Business, Grant and Report Writing
University of Alaska - Fairbanks
ALFA#ENGLF212 Undergraduate 3 credits $213
Many distance delivery courses create a package of lessons to be completed one right after the other. This seven-section course is arranged with flexibility. Each section may be worked on independently and in the order that feels most comfortable. The instructor will suggest a certain order of completion. Although the course title lists business and report writing, components of this course emphasize constructing a grant proposal as a project. Students can select a local agency project in their community or create proposals from my files.

Business, Grant, and Report Writing
University of Alaska - Fairbanks
ALFA#ENGL212 Undergraduate 3 credits $213
Forms and techniques of business, grant, and report writing. Does not fulfill the second half of the baccalaureate requirements in written communication. Prerequisite: ENGL111.

Calculus with Business Applications
State University of New York
SUNY#MAT125 Undergraduate 3 credits $545*
A survey of the basic concepts and operations of calculus with business and management applications. Designed for students in a business administration program and not to be taken by mathematics and science majors. Prerequisite: High School Intermediate Algebra with a grade of 85 or better, or MAT110 with a grade of 'C' or better.
* NY residents tuition: $278

Client and Relationship Management
University of Denver, University College
DEUC#TELE4804 Undergraduate 3 qtr. hrs. $885
With the emergence of competition in the telecommunications market, understanding and serving the customer has never been more important. Students in this course will learn to research and identify customer needs, measure customer satisfaction, and evaluate competition in the market. Students will also examine effective systems for managing customer service and methods of relationship management. Prerequisite: Principles of Telecommunications or equivalent experience.

Collective Bargaining
Indiana University
INDI#L250 Undergraduate 3 credits $268
The development and organization of collective bargaining in the United States, including union preparation for negotiations; bargaining patterns and practices; strategy and tactics; economic and legal considerations.

Collective Bargaining
New York Institute of Technology
NYIT#BUS3902 Undergraduate 3 credits $???
This course is designed to meet two objectives: to introduce the student to the background and relationships between economies, public policy, unionism, and business management-labor relations; to provide a basic orientation to the framework, processes, and strategies involved in collective bargaining and the resolution of labor grievances and the arbitration in management labor relations. Prerequisite: BUS3917.

Collective Bargaining and Labor Relations
University of Minnesota
MINN#IR3007 Undergraduate 4 credits $400
An introduction to collective bargaining and labor-management relations. Students examine the historical evolution of trade unions in the United States, the structure and administration of trade unions, and the processes of collective bargaining and contract administration. The coursework incorporates case exercises that provide students with insights into the real-world nature of labor-management relations and that develop negotiation skills transferable to business and personal situations.

Commercial Security
Fox Valley Technical College
FOVA#504-104 Undergraduate 3 credits $200
In this course, students will study security problems that affect retail business. The course deals with specific problems such as burglary, robbery, shoplifting, check fraud, credit card fraud, business safe selection, and confidence schemes.

Commodity Markets and Futures Trading
Western Illinois University
WEIL#AGR447G Undergraduate 3 credits $795*
Studies multiple hedging and speculation. An introduction to the institutions and jargon of the futures market is followed by the study of technical analysis to identify trading signals: bar chart, point-and-figure, moving averages, volume and open interest, momentum, HI/LO, %R, RSI, stochastics, and DMI.
* IL residents tuition: $88 per credit.

Communication and Public Relations
City University
CITY#COM303 Undergraduate 5 qu. credits $785
Introduces the fundamental theories and practical applications of Public Relations, its functions in organizations, and its role in society. Stresses three critical aspects of public relations work: communication, writing and problem solving. Traces the professional development of the field and anticipated concepts and theories related to public relations management in the future. Prerequisite: BSK210 or its equivalent.

Compensation and Benefit Administration
New Hampshire College
NEHA#ADB325 Undergraduate 3 credits $1656
The course covers the development and administration of compensation and benefit programs for organizations. Wage theory, principles and practices, unemployment security, worker income security, group insurance, and disability and pension plans are investigated. Emphasis on objectives, policies, organizations, implementation and revision of compensation and benefit systems are studied. Prerequisites: ADB211 and junior standing.

Complete Manager
State University of New York
SUNY#FSD24571 Undergraduate 3 credits $1038*
An in-depth look at the various roles food retail managers play throughout their careers. The student is introduced to all areas of management including communication, interviewing and conflict resolution, planning and problem solving. This courses examines how the qualities of the professional manager can be used in such areas as training, delegating, goal setting, and performance evaluation.
* NY residents tuition: $137 per credit.

Computer Graphics for Managers
Nova Southeastern University
NOVA#MMIS625 Graduate 3 credits $1,110
Presents computer graphics as an aid to information managers who need a clear means of presenting the analysis of information. Topics include basic graphic techniques (e.g. histograms, bar charts, pie charts), the theory of graphic presentation of information, desktop publishing software, presentation software, graphics monitors (EGA, CGA, VGA, RGB, composite), laser printers, computer screen projection systems, and standards.

Computer Information Systems
Lansing Community College
LANS#CISB100 Undergraduate 3 credits $315
This course provides an introduction to computers, their role in managing business information systems, their influence on society, and their use in personal productivity. It includes a hands on introduction to three major microcomputer tools: word processors, spreadsheets, and database management systems.

Computer Integrated Manufacturing
Nova Southeastern University
NOVA#MMIS624 Graduate 3 credits $1,110
Provides a framework for understanding how functional organization structure impacts the design of a management information system in a manufacturing setting. Special emphasis will be on marketing, manufacturing, and financial information systems. Topics covered include the product life cycle; production scheduling and capacity requirements planning; techniques for using MIS in inventory management decisions, quality control, internal accounting, and funds management. Planning strategies for forecasting services, developing requirements and specifications, writing requests for proposals, and project management will be examined within the context of functional information systems.

Computer Systems Management
New Jersey Institute of Technology
NJIT#CIS455   Undergraduate   3 credits $1143*
An overview of computing centers and their organization for accomplishing specific objectives. Includes a classification of systems, analysis of cost and size, layout of equipment, methods of accessing computer facilities, equipment selection, and facilities evaluation. Prerequisite: completion of a 100-level GUR course in CIS. Optional: 26 video lessons of 60 minutes each.
* NJ residents: $184/semester hour.

Computer Systems Performance Analysis
University of Minnesota
MINN#CSCI5863   Undergraduate   4 credits $400
Teaches computer designers and users the basic performance measurement and simulation techniques necessary for experimental computer science and engineering. Concentrates on hands-on performance evaluation techniques using both simulations and measurements of existing systems. Students will develop an understanding of how to use measured data to compare computer systems and how much a new architectural feature improves systems performance.

Computer Systems Performance Analysis
University of Minnesota
MINN#EE5863   Undergraduate   4 credits $400
Teaches computer designers and users the basic performance measurement and simulation techniques necessary for experimental computer science and engineering. Concentrates on hands-on performance evaluation techniques using both simulations and measurements of existing systems. Students will develop an understanding of how to use measured data to compare computer systems and how much a new architectural feature improves systems performance.

Computer Techniques for MIS
New Jersey Institute of Technology
NJIT#CIS465   Undergraduate   3 credits $1143*
Design and programming concepts are presented for automation of management information systems. Includes the organization of files and techniques for processing information based upon organizational requirements and available hardware and software. Some case studies are presented. Prerequisites: NJIT#CIS431 (Database System Design and Management) or equivalent. Optional: 26 video lessons of 60 minutes each.
* NJ residents: $184/semester hour.

Computer-Assisted Management
Northwest College
NOCO#MA127   Undergraduate   5 credits $???
Students should acquire basic knowledge of the automotive management field, encompassing the use of the microcomputer in parts ordering and handling, inventory control and system pricing. Instruction will include service management, covering such areas as manager, writer and advisor. Students will be exposed to the evaluation of technicians, including time study proficiency as well as the use of the microcomputer in assisting with management operations. Prerequisite: DP105.

Computerized Accounting
Eastern Oregon University
EAOR#OADM210A   Undergraduate 3 credits $240
Principles of accounting applied to a computerized environment using accounting software and the personal computer.

Computerized Accounting
Rio Salado College
RISA#ACC115   Undergraduate   2 credits $???
Mastery of a microcomputer accounting system including the general ledger, accounts receivable, accounts payable and payroll. Prerequisite: ACC107, or higher level accounting course, or permission of instructor.

Computerized Accounting
Strayer University
STRA#ACC208   Undergraduate   4.5 credits $665
Integrates knowledge acquired in separate accounting and computer courses as applied to bookkeeping and other financial and managerial accounting procedures. Topics covered include preparation of the computer system; double-entry bookkeeping of transactions, adjustments and closing; statement generation' financial analysis; and budgeting. Based on commercially-used spreadsheet and accounting computer packages. Prerequisite: ACC110 and CIS107.

Computing Concepts for Managers
New Jersey Institute of Technology
NJIT#MIS620   Undergraduate   3 credits $1143*
For students of management who wish to specialize in information systems or who plan to use the computer as a tool in auditing. Includes: operating systems and compilers, networking and telecommunications, principles of database management, and personal computer or workstation database software packages. This course is part of graduate certificate in MIS &AMP Health Care. Optional: video lessons.
* NJ residents: $184/semester hour.

Concepts and Analysis of Communication in Organizations
Southwest Missouri State University
MOSW#COM638   Graduate   3 credits $362
Advanced study of communication in organizations. Application of traditional and contemporary theories of communication and organizations in current research and practice. Particular attention is given to the symbolic nature of organizing and to the analysis of organizational culture.

Concepts of Leadership and Power
Bellevue University
BELL#LDR601 Graduate   4 credits $1100
LDR 601 explores concepts of leadership within diverse organizational and situational contexts. Participants review major leadership themes that articulate with objectives specially designed for military and corporate environments. Biographies and writings of historical and current leaders, and leader philosophies and practices within corporate and military cultures are examined. Styles of leadership, leadership roles and leader behaviors as they relate to different organizational configurations are applied to case study.

Concepts of Marketing
Ohio University
OHIO#BMT140 Undergraduate   4 credits $256
Introduction to problems of manufacturers, wholesalers, and retailers as they relate to modern marketing, market, and product.

Consulting Practice
The Graduate School of America
TGSA#OM879W Graduate   4 credits $795
This course examines the roles of a consultant (the consultant-client relationship, how to discover client needs and how to sell consulting services), preparing proposals, costing and pricing, and the ongoing consulting process.

Consumer Behavior
Bellevue University
BELL#BA656 Graduate   3 credits $825
Review of the classical areas of perceptions, cognition, attitudinal formation, and cultural influences that affect individual and group purchasing behaviors.

Consumer Behavior
New Hampshire College
NEHA#MKT345 Undergraduate   3 credits $1656
This course explores the behavior that consumers display in searching, purchasing, using, evaluating, and disposing of products. Prerequisites: MKT113, PSY108, or SOC112.

Consumer Behavior
Western Illinois University
WEIL#FIN333 Undergraduate   3 credits $795*
Analyzes the sociocultural and psychological foundations of consumer market behavior. Included are a survey of the various theoretical positions taken as a basis for model development and relevant concepts from the areas of motivation, perception, personality, attitudes, culture, social class, and reference groups. Prerequisite: Marketing 327.
* IL residents tuition: $88 per credit.

Consumer Psychology
City University
CITY#PSY307 Undergraduate   5 qu. credits $785
Consumer information processing and buying behavior. Types of communicating behaviors in progressively more complex situations with emphasis upon the influence of the media. Prerequisite: Strongly recommended: SSC205 or equivalent.

Contemporary Business
Waukesha County Technical College
WAUK#102100 Undergraduate   3 credits $315
Contemporary Business was developed on the idea that everyone should know and have a basic understanding of some of the principles and terminology employed in the business world. Contemporary Business will give you the opportunity to learn these basics principles and vocabulary. It will also provide you with insight into some of the specific fields of business such as marketing, business management, data processing and accounting.

Contemporary Labor Problems
Indiana University
INDI#L105 Undergraduate   3 credits $268
An examination of some of the major problems confronting society, workers, and the labor movement. Topics cover labor-management participation (or cooperation) programs; plant closures, union avoidance and union destruction by employers; and economic development efforts and labor/community coalitions.

Contemporary Marketing
Rogers State University
ROGE#BMA2143 Undergraduate 3 credits $495*
Introduction to basic marketing concepts with emphasis on practical application and relationship to contemporary living. Includes evaluation of environmental factors which influence marketing decisions and how a marketing manager interacts with diverse areas of business. Covers fundamental principles of product strategy, promotion, pricing and distribution and the interrelationships between them. Video: Marketing (revised) from Coast Community College.
* OK residents $315.

Contract Administration and Management
Strayer University
STRA#BUS330 Undergraduate   4.5 credits $665
Emphasizes the general policies and procedures for contract administration functions and applies accounting and management principles. Uses extensive case studies to discuss the structure and responsibilities of contract administration including pre-and-post-award activities, contract oversight, quality assurance, compliance, financing, cost controls, documentation, termination and disputes, and subcontract management. Discusses coordination with procurement activities and audit agencies.

Contract and Purchasing Negotiation Techniques
Strayer University
STRA#BUS340 Undergraduate   4.5 credits $665
Covers theory, strategies, techniques and tactics for negotiating contracts, and principles and practices of negotiations for corporate or institutional procurements. Includes preparation and conduct of negotiations and emphasizes interactions prior to/during negotiations and methods of dealing with situations under different types of negotiations. Utilizes role playing techniques and methodologies.

Corporate Finance
New York Institute of Technology
NYIT#BUS3630 Undergraduate   3 credits $???
An overview of the financial management function in modern business, emphasizing the time value of money and financial analysis. The financial and economic environment and capital markets and securities are covered. Prerequisite: BUS2072 and BUS3511, MA3010.

Corporate Finance
State University of New York
SUNY#213514 Undergraduate   4 credits $586*
Focuses on the dynamic economic environment in which corporate financial decisions are made, the role of the financial manager within the firm and the empirical aspects of corporate finance. Topics include the financial environment, techniques of financial analysis and planning, management of working capital; fixed assets and capital budgeting cost off capital; dividend policies and sources of long-term financing. Prerequisites: Students should have completed Introduction to Accounting, Economics/Macro (112014), or Economics/Micro (112214), or their equivalents.
* NY residents tuition: $515

Cost Accounting
City University
CITY#AC312 Undergraduate   5 qu. credits $785
Accounting for material and labor, overhead classifications and budgets; analysis and application of overhead rates; process costs, job costs, standard costs, distribution costs, analysis of cost variations; break-even analysis, decision-making, direct costing and activity based costing. Prerequisite: AC301, AC302 and AC303 or their equivalents.

Cost Accounting
Fayetteville Technical Community College
FAYE#ACC225 Undergraduate   3 credits $489*
This course introduces the nature and purposes of cost accounting as an information system for planning and control. Topics include direct materials, direct labor, factory overhead, process, job order, and standard cost systems. Upon completion, students should be able to demonstrate an understanding of the principles involved and display an analytical problem-solving ability for the topics covered.
* North Carolina residents and non-resident US military personnel stationed within the state tuition: $60; NC senior citizens: free.

Cost Accounting I
New Hampshire College
NEHA#ACC207 Undergraduate   3 credits $1656
These courses examine in-depth the account concepts and practices used in recording, classifying and reporting of cost data. An analysis is made of the behavior of costs, and their use to management in the planning and control process. Budgeting, standard cost, job order, and process are examined, along with special problems in cost accounting. Prerequisites: For ACC102.

Cost Accounting I
Strayer University
STRA#ACC225 Undergraduate   4.5 credits $665
Introduces accounting procedures and financial reporting identified with a job-order cost system. Emphasizes the concepts of cost control in the accounting for materials, labor, and factory overhead as well as procedures for maximizing conversion costs. Introduces variance analysis. Prerequisite: ACC110.

Cost Accounting II
New Hampshire College
NEHA#ACC208 Undergraduate   3 credits $1656
Continuation of ACC207. Prerequisites: ACC207.

Cost Accounting II
Strayer University
STRA#ACC325 Undergraduate   4.5 credits $665
Covers accounting procedures relating to the process cost system, the estimated cost system, and the standard cost system. Examines the accounting for by-products. Includes comprehensive coverage of budgeting for all areas of the business enterprise--sales, production, commercial expenses, capital investment, and forecasting. Prerequisite: ACC225.

Cost and Price Analysis
Strayer University
STRA#FIN230 Undergraduate   4.5 credits $665
covers establishment and administration of equitable pricing arrangements for goods and/or services. Analyzes the total price (cost plus profit) and the individual elements of cost (labor, materials, indirect costs, and profit). Emphasizes techniques for determining proper prices and estimating. Discusses methods of pricing research and development, and the selection of hardware and services.

Cost Estimating for Capital Projects
New Jersey Institute of Technology
NJIT#EM691 Undergraduate   3 credits $1143*
Cost estimating techniques and procedures for budgeting used in evaluation, planning, and control of capital investments. Emphasis on updating for change, escalation, and statistical and computer methods. Optional: 12 video lessons of 180 minutes each.
* NJ residents: $184/semester hour.

Cost Management 2
University of Colorado-Boulder
COBO#ACCT3320 Undergraduate 3 credits $240
Cost analysis for purposes of control and decision making. Analysis of activities, cost behavior, role of accounting in planning and control, and managerial uses of cost accounting data. Prerequisite: BCOR2100 and junior standing.

Creating Messages that Get Results
Kennesaw State University
KENN#FMV202 Undergraduate 3 credits $149
Topics include, the study of persuasion, persuasion theory, source credibility, logical supports of persuasion, audience psychology, message construction, handling difficult communicative situations, persuasion as a tool of motivation and goodwill, and writing persuasive communication for business. A persuasive communication campaign is developed over the term of the course.

Creative Basics for Direct Marketing
Mercy College
MERC#MK322 Undergraduate 3 credits $900
The course covers the process of selecting a product or service based on market research. Topics include generating direct marketing instruments (e.g., direct mail packages, solos, catalogs, coops, card decks, PIPs), developing the sales promotion mix (e.g., tokens, coupons, sweepstakes, contests), and scheduling production with computer service bureaus, printers, and letter shops. Prerequisites: DM301 Introduction to Direct Marketing.

Critical Reading and Writing for Management
University of Minnesota
MINN#COMP3022 Undergraduate 4 credits $391
Develops general strategies for engaging texts critically, both as a reader and as a writer. Three major assignments-- abstract, critique, and synthesis--gradually teach the skills needed for precise understanding, critical analyses, and sophisticated use of texts. Prerequisite: Writing Practice requirement or equivalent; management or pre-management student.

Cultural Heritage Tourism
Chemeketa Community College
CHEM#HTM111 Undergraduate 3 credits $123
This is an overview course designed to explore the subject of cultural heritage tourism and the value of this niche market.

Culture and Politics of International Business
New Hampshire College
NEHA#INT316 Undergraduate 3 credits $1656
The course introduces the student to primary cultural factors -- religion, language, values, technology, social organization and political environment -- that affect U.S. firms doing business outside of the United States. Students learn the significance of identifying and assessing the importance of these factors so they can more effectively manage in the international environment. A variety of international environments will be studied. The course uses text, cases, and exercises. Prerequisite: ADB125.

Current Topics in Accounting
Strayer University
STRA#ACC291299 Undergraduate 4.5 credits $665
Offers current topics from the area of accounting.

Current Topics in Business Administration
Strayer University
STRA#BUS291299 Undergraduate 4.5 credits $665
Offers current topics from the area of business administration. (The exact topic will be announced in the schedule of classes.)

Customhouse Brokers License Preparation
Pace University
PACE#OL705 Undergraduate 4 credits $750
A "cram" course to prepare students to take the Customhouse Brokers Examination. Test answers will be reviewed each week. Topics to be covered include: types of entries; entry requirements and procedures; bonds; currency conversion; power of attorney; classification; appraisement; examination of merchandise; prohibited and restricted merchandise; temporary importation under bond; marking of imported merchandise; in-bond entries and procedures; mail importation; items exported and returned; drawbacks; protests; and licensing of Customhouse brokers.

Data Modeling and Analysis
UCLA
UCLA#X418H Undergraduate 4 credits $575
This course provides a strategy for optimizing the implementation of business process re-engineering, information management, and hardware/software technology. Concepts and techniques for building logical and physical information models are presented. Students are shown how an Enterprise Information Model, when encapsulated within a four-to-six-month Rapid and Joint Applications Development (RAD/JAD) iteration cycle, can be used to design and build database applications that are extensive and integrable with the rest of the enterprise.

Decision Making Under Risk & Uncertainty
The Graduate School of America
TGSA#OM836W Graduate 4 credits $795
All managers are decision makers. Management decision making typically occurs in situations where information is incomplete or ambiguous, and where there are substantial organizational risks and rewards. By reviewing practical case materials from real business situations in the light of systematic analytic strategies, you will develop your skill in organizing available information and using that information to reduce uncertainty. In addition, you will gain access to a managerial tool kit that will help you apply qualitative and quantitative decision rules to making appropriate alternative choices.

Decision Modeling and Analysis
City University
CITY#BSC400 Undergraduate   5 qu. credits $785
An examination of the analytical tools used to make optimal business decisions. Topics covered include: forecasting; transportation decisions; waiting line models; project management; and linear programming. Prerequisite: BC303 and BSK200 or their equivalents.

Decision Support Systems
New Jersey Institute of Technology
NJIT#MIS648 Undergraduate   3 credits $1143*
Use of decision support systems to support management decision-making in a real world environment. Topics include: establishing and measuring decision support systems success criteria, software tools, model management, elements of artificial intelligence, and statistics. Justification, design, and use of decision support systems. Students will develop examples from actual use. This course is part of graduate certificate in MIS &AMP Health Care. Prerequisites: NJIT#MIS545, NJIT#MIS645. Optional: video lessons.
* NJ residents: $184/semester hour.

Decision Support Systems
Nova Southeastern University
NOVA#MCIS671 Graduate   3 credits $1,110
Examines concepts of decision support in both non-automated and automated environments. Emphasis on structures, modeling, and the application of various decision support systems in today's corporate environment. Additional emphasis is placed on the use of executive information and expert system applications. Case studies examine applications of each of these types of technology.

Decision Support Systems
Nova Southeastern University
NOVA#MMIS671 Graduate   3 credits $1,110
Examines concepts of decision support in both non-automated and automated environments. Emphasis will be placed on structures, modeling, and the application of various decision support systems in today's corporate environment. Additional emphasis will be placed on the use of executive information and expert system applications. Case studies will be used to look at existent applications of each of these types of technology.

Decision-Making Techniques
Heriot-Watt University
HERI#08 Graduate   4 credits $???
The fundamentals of good decision-making are, first, a clear understanding of the decision itself and, second, the availability of properly focused information to support the decision. Decision-making techniques help with both of these problems. Their value has been greatly increased in recent years through micro-computers which have made the power of the techniques available to general managers. However, the techniques should be thought of as aids to decision-making and not substitutes for it.

Deming Quality Management Philosophy
Roane State Community College
ROAN#BUS210 Undergraduate   3 credits $459*
An introduction to the concepts and applications of quality management through the lens of Dr. W. Edwards Deming's System of Profound Knowledge and his 14 Points for the Transformation of Management.
* Tennessee residents tuition: $48 per semester hour.

Develop Your Own Business Plan
Waukesha County Technical College
WAUK#145465 Undergraduate   3 credits $315*
In this course, students will research their business ideas and then develop a complete business plan. Some work outside of class may be required. At the end of the course, students will have the opportunity, if they desire, to present their business plan to a panel of experts for evaluation. Text required.
* WI residents pay $54 per credit.

Developing a Business Plan
UCLA
UCLA#X497B Undergraduate   2 credits $425
Those interested in a new or growing business must possess a comprehensive business plan if they hope to compete effectively in the marketplace. A comprehensive business plan is necessary to attract sources of financing and evaluate the viability of a venture; it also is a requirement for companies that want to be considered for joint ventures with larger corporations or those that are transitioning from entrepreneurial to professional management. This online course focuses on all facets of business plan development, including assessing the competitive environment, developing venture concept and growth strategies, etc.

Developing Management Skills
Bellevue University
BELL#MGTC340 Undergraduate   3 credits $750
Personal, interpersonal and group skills needed for good management practice. Preparation for handling such real-world situations as staff meetings, customers, discussions with employees, and performance evaluations. Use of a personal planner and keeping a daily journal.

Direct Marketing
State University of New York
SUNY#DMR110Y01 Undergraduate 3 credits $570*
This course is a specialty within the field of theoretical marketing, and focuses on the specific components unique to Direct Marketing: Channels of Distribution and Promotion, and the Development of Databases, as a means of product and service delivery to specifically identified consumers. The course concentrates on the interactive system of direct marketing that uses one or more advertising media to effect a measurable response at a specified location. Prerequisite: Marketing Principles or permission of the Instructor.
* NY residents tuition: $90 per credit

Diversity in the Workplace
State University of New York
SUNY#213164 Undergraduate 4 credits $586*
Gain an understanding of diversity issues encountered in the workplace. Examine the impact of a multi-cultural society on organizations, including multi-nationals. Incorporating both theory and practice, students analyze critical issues from multiple perspectives including historical, legal, economic and sociological frameworks. Students are expected to integrate these perspectives in their assignments. Course is applicable to profit, non-profit and government organizations. Prerequisites: At least one introductory course in one of the following subjects: economics, sociology, history, management principles, public administration/policy.
* NY residents tuition: $515

Effective Business Management
Kennesaw State University
KENN#FMV221 Undergraduate 3 credits $149
This 6 week course will provide participants with an overview of The Deming System of Profound Knowledge (tm) as a system needed to provide for the transformation of individuals and organizations. Dr. Deming stated that without an aim, there is no system. In this context, this course is a system and therefore requires an aim. The AIM of this course is to initiate the individual transformation process in participants via the appreciation for, understanding of, and application of The Deming System of Profound Knowledge (SoPK).

Effective Org Communications
City University
CITY#BSM304 Undergraduate 5 qu. credits $785
A study of effective communication in the contemporary, evolving organization. Decreased numbers of supervisory personnel in the workplace make effective interpersonal communication on the peer level far more important. Other topics include the prevention of communication breakdowns; the effective use of communications technology; small group dynamics; and interviewing and listening skills.

Effective Writing for Public Presentations
Marylhurst College
MARY#CM431 Undergraduate 3 credits $651
For those who design their own speeches or assist in preparing messages to be presented by others, this course shows how to take a speech beyond the realm of the ordinary. Topics include writing for the spoken word; using rhetorical devices to command attention and make for more literary, musical, and polished speech; and creating a personalized speaker's resource collection of effective anecdotes, jokes, quips, and quotes.

EHS Project Management
Rochester Institute of Technology
ROCH#63075090 Undergraduate 4 credits $923
This course focuses on and introduces unique factors in environmental, health and safety management.

Elementary Accounting I
New Hampshire College
NEHA#ACC101 Undergraduate 3 credits $1656
Elementary Accounting is a two-class course designed to introduce the student to the need for accounting in business and its relevance to society; develop an understanding of the basic financial statements used by business; develop an understanding of the composition of basic asset, liability, equity, and income determining accounts, in accordance with current accounting concepts and principles.

Elementary Accounting II
New Hampshire College
NEHA#ACC102 Undergraduate 3 credits $1656
Continuation of ACC101. Prerequisite: ACC101.

Elementary Ethics
Roane State Community College
ROAN#PHL121 Undergraduate 3 credits $459*
Critical analysis of the principle ethical theories and their applications to the problems of life.
* Tennessee residents tuition: $48 per semester hour.

Elements of Business Writing
New School for Social Research
NEWS#1518 Undergraduate 2 credits $1092
Limited to 20. Clarity of purpose, conciseness, style, organization, tone ... these are some of the important elements of good business writing. In this course, you learn the principles of good business writing and apply them to your own memos, letters, reports, and other correspondence. You also learn how to make your writing process more effective and less time-consuming. You get individual feedback from the instructor on five different pieces of business writing that you submit over the course of the semester. Call (212) 229-5372 for suggested placement advising. (2 credits).

Elements of Supervision
Barstow Community College
BARS#MGMT50 Undergraduate 3 credits $???
Basic responsibilities of a supervisor in business and industry, organizational duties, human relations, grievances, training, rating promotions quality control, and management-employee relations.

Elements of Supervision
Ohio University
OHIO#BMT150 Undergraduate 4 credits $256
Concepts of modern-day supervision. Emphasis on supervisor's major functions and development of sensitivity to human facets in management, using behavioral science findings.

Employee Skills Assessment
Edmonds Community College
EDMO#JOBDV105 Undergraduate 3 credits $220
This class takes you through the first step of a successful job search -- clarifying and clearly describing what you can do for an employer. During this course you'll identify your Dependable Strengths , those things that you do extremely well. You will verify these talents by giving specific examples of situations when you have demonstrated them.

Enterprise Networking
City University
CITY#CS494 Undergraduate 5 qu. credits $785
Identification of organization-wide network requirements to provide an integrated company-wide network strategy. Integrating business systems among dissimilar computing systems and protocols. Building a network that is a corporate asset and gives business a competitive edge. Examination of the integration of network hardware, software, network management systems and applications.

Entrepreneurial Businesses Marketing
UCLA
UCLA#X497 Undergraduate 4 credits $500
This online course provides practical ideas and applications of marketing, advertising, and sales promotion techniques for managers, owners, and marketing personnel of small-to-medium-size businesses. Topics include marketing, planning, and budgeting; company positioning; networking; personal selling; improving the company image; public relations and product/service publicity; designing and creating advertising and brochures; selecting, organizing, and motivating sales representative and dealer/distribution organizations; marketing on the Internet; market research; and selecting and using the right advertising medium-- trade shows, direct mail, yellow pages and local print ads, telemarketing, sales promotion, etc.

Entrepreneurship
New Hampshire College
NEHA#ADB320 Undergraduate 3 credits $1656
The course focuses on the factors contributing to the personal success of entrepreneurs and on the major factors that affect successful entrepreneurship. Entrepreneurship itself is also studied. Case studies, contemporary readings, and simulations are used. International considerations are included. Prerequisite: ADB110.

Entrepreneurship
The Graduate School of America
TGSA#OM876W Graduate 4 credits $795
This course provides an overview of fundamental management and marketing practices essential to successful entrepreneurial development.

Entrepreneurship and the Smaller Enterprise
University of Minnesota
MINN#MGMT3008 Undergraduate 4 credits $400
Assessment of opportunities and constraints in establishing and managing one's own firm; structuring a new venture, buying into an existing enterprise, owning an enterprise versus becoming a principal employee in a new venture. Case method. Designed to accommodate both undergraduate students who want course credit and nondegree-seeking entrepreneurs who want information/planning guidelines to help them start and manage their own small business. Prerequisite: completion of business core courses or instructor permission.

Essentials of Management
Bellevue University
BELL#MGTC350 Undergraduate 3 credits $750
The process of achieving desired results through efficient utilization of human and material resources. Planning, directing, organizing, staffing and leading. Conducting an in-depth personal interview.

Essentials of Marketing
Bellevue University
BELL#MGTC420 Undergraduate 3 credits $750
The techniques and skills needed to sell products and services. Market segmentation and targeting, product positioning, advertising and promotion, and distribution decisions. Ethical issues in marketing and developing marketing plans.

Ethical Issues in Marketing
New Hampshire College
NEHA#MKT350 Undergraduate 3 credits $1656
This course explores current ethical issues and problems in marketing. The emphasis is on identifying crucial issues, exploring all possible viewpoints, and examining remedies in order to facilitate the development of students' own positions on those issues. Prerequisite: MKT113.

Evolving Technical Communication
Kennesaw State University
KENN#FMV235 Undergraduate 3 credits $149
Your potential is limitless as a technical communicator. An user documentation is just one area in which to specialize. But it you're tired of writing user documentation, explore another genre in which to showcase your writing talent. In this course, you'll identify and hone skills you already have and discover how to transfer those skills to other types of writing, specifically marcomóor "marketing communications." Participate in a hands-on distance learning experience. Develop a plan to market yourself in a new genre, while learning how to turn technical writing skills into marcom writing assignments.

Export/Import Letters of Credit
Pace University
PACE#OL706 Undergraduate 3 credits $500
This course reviews Uniform Customs and practices for Documentary Credits, including the latest changes and terms of sale and delivery (INCOTERMS). Additional topics include: letters of credit - basic types (including amendments and partial shipments); back-to-back, revolving, red clause, food and drug, standby performance; transfers under letters of credit; assignment of proceeds under letters of credit Documentary examination (examination of specimen set of documents); resolving discrepancies and refusals; methods of payment and reimbursement; and bankers' acceptances.

Fashion Business Practices
State University of New York
SUNY#FM116 Undergraduate   3 credits $1038*
A comprehensive introduction of the modern fashion business environment. The structures, financing, management, organization, and ethical responsibilities of fashion enterprises are examined in a global context.
* NY residents tuition: $137 per credit.

Fashion Merchandising Principles and Techniques
State University of New York
SUNY#FM122 Undergraduate   3 credits $1038*
Analyzes the buying function and the differences of buyers' responsibilities in various types of merchandising organizations. Studies the principles, procedures, and techniques practiced by merchandisers of fashion goods in determining what assortments to buy and which resources to select.
* NY residents tuition: $137 per credit.

Finance
Heriot-Watt University
HERI#03 Graduate   4 credits $???
The course captures the most important modern ideas in corporate finance, and has been structured as a logical progression of ideas starting at a rudimentary level and progressing to an advanced level of financial sophistication. Finance is a theoretical subject with important applications to decision-making. It establishes the link between company decision-making and the operation of capital markets. The course starts with a description of the participants in financial markets, the decisions they must take and the basic processes which are common to all financial decisions.

Finance
The Graduate School of America
TGSA#OM720W Graduate   4 credits $795
This course emphasizes and develops an understanding of financial concepts and major decision areas related to the financial management of business including valuation of the firm, projects, securities and financial implications of new policies. In support of this goal, participants master tools and concepts in the structure of global capital markets, cost of capital, capital allocation and budgeting, financial analysis, resource allocation, dividend policy, long-term debt policy, and the uses of funds during restructuring and conditions of changing financial markets.

Finance Fundamentals
University of Minnesota
MINN#BFIN3000 Undergraduate   4 credits $400
A comprehensive, analytical introduction to the principal concepts of finance. All major business financial decisions are discussed--balance-sheet and income- statement management, the general business environment, valuation theory, financial management decision concerning uses and sources of funds, and a survey of the nation's financial markets. A-F grading only. Prerequisites: ACCT1050 or 1025 and at least 90 credits completed or in progress.

Finance I
National American University
NAAM#FN201D Undergraduate   4.5 credits $900
This course is an examination of the role of financial management in business. Topics studied include: analysis, forecasting, mathematics, working capital management, cash and marketing securities management, accounts receivable, inventory management, and short term financing.

Financial Accounting
Bakersfield College
BAKE#BSADB1A Undergraduate   4 credits $460*
Introduction to accounting theory and practice. First semester presents the recording, analyzing, and summarizing procedures used in preparing balance sheets and income statements. Prerequisite: Reading Level 1 , English Level 2 recommended.
* CA residents pay $40 per credit.

Financial Accounting
Brevard Community College
BREV#ACG2021 Undergraduate   3 credits $435
Financial accounting for service and merchandising enterprises organized as sole proprietorships, partnerships, and corporations. Emphasis on the accounting cycle, financial statements, receivables/payables, inventory costing, depreciation and disposal of plant assets, corporate stock and bond issues.

Financial Accounting
Rogers State University
ROGE#ACCT2103 Undergraduate   3 credits $495*
Everyone who manages in business - whether a mom and pop store or a huge multinational corporation - needs to understand and speak the language of accounting. This course introduces you to the language and concepts of accounting. The course takes you through basic accounting theory, classified financial statement preparation, accounting systems design, and corporate stocks and bonds, as well as other subjects.
* OK residents $315.

Financial Accounting I
Chemeketa Community College
CHEM#BA211 Undergraduate   4 credits $159
The complete accounting cycle for service and merchandising firm including recording transactions, adjustments, financial statements, worksheets, closing entries, cash and accounts receivable, notes and interest, and accounting for inventories. For students enrolled in the accounting program and/or students transferring to four-year institutions. Prerequisite: MTH062 or higher math or concurrent enrollment in MTH062.

Financial Accounting I
City University
CITY#AC210 Undergraduate 5 qu. credits $785
Introduction to basic accounting concepts and techniques; fundamentals of the accounting process and preparation of basic financial statements; uses and interpretation of accounting data derived from the operation of an organization.

Financial Accounting I
Edmonds Community College
EDMO#ACCT201 Undergraduate 5 credits $260
Financial Accounting I (ACCT 201) is designed for students who have successfully completed an introductory accounting class in high school or at a community college, or have on-the-job experience in accounting. This class represents an alternative method of teaching and learning Financial Accounting. Successful completion of an introductory accounting or bookkeeping course, or work experience in accounting is a prerequisite.

Financial Accounting II
City University
CITY#AC220 Undergraduate 5 qu. credits $785
Accounting principles involved in the measurement and reporting of assets and liabilities; elements of consolidated statements and statement of cash flows; using and interpreting financial statements for decision making. Prerequisite: AC210 or its equivalent.

Financial Accounting II
Edmonds Community College
EDMO#ACCT202 Undergraduate 5 credits $260
This course represents a continuation of the development of Financial Accounting concepts, procedures and practices introduced in ACCT 201. The course is designed for students who have successfully completed an initial course in Financial Accounting. We will emphasize the development and interpretation of accounting information for decision-making purposes As a comprehensive review of the course, students will use basic tools of financial analysis to evaluate the current condition and financial performance of a publicly traded corporation.

Financial Analysis for Management
Golden Gate University
GOLD#FI203 Undergraduate 3 credits $???
Introduces financial analysis and serves as a foundation for the more advanced business courses. Topics include time value of money, fundamental security evaluation models, cost of capital, capital budgeting, investment analysis and financial statement analysis. Prerequisites: ACCTG201 (or ACCTG1A and ACCTG1B) and MATH200 (or MATH30).

Financial Management
University of Colorado
CUON#BUSN6640 Undergraduate 3 credits $1953*
(Course description not available at press time.)
* CO residents tuition: $136 per credit.

Financial Management
Golden Gate University
GOLD#FI100 Undergraduate 3 credits $???
Introduces financial analysis and management in terms of its most important functions: raising funds at minimum cost and risk, and allocating those funds among competing short and long term users. Topics include working capital management, capital budgeting, long-term capital structure, securities valuation and dividend policy. Prerequisites: ACCTG1A, ACCTG1B, ECON1 and MATH30.

Financial Management
Strayer University
STRA#BUS534 Undergraduate 4.5 credits $665
Involves in-depth discussions of working capital management, capital budgeting, the cost of capital, debt and equity financing, and financial statements. Analyzes the effects of multinational operations, multiple currencies, international tax laws, money and capital markets, and political risk environments. Prerequisite: ACC560.

Financial Management
Strayer University
STRA#FIN300 Undergraduate 4.5 credits $665
Studies the financial management of the business firm, primarily corporations. Topics covered include: the financial goals of the firm, its economic and legal context, valuation of financial securities, analysis of financial statements, and the efficient management of capital resources and investments within the risk-return trade-off. topics are explored in theory, using analytical techniques, and through financial markets and institutions. Prerequisite: ECO100 and ACC100.

Financial Management
State University of New York
SUNY#BFIN5257172 Graduate 3 credits $1038*
The fundamental principles of modern financial economics. Demonstrates the most common applications of these ideas in the realm of corporate and individual financial decisions. The organization of the material follows the traditional lines of analysis in corporate finance and includes current notions of market behavior and efficiency. Prerequisites: Courses in the following: Accounting, Economics, Statistics, and knowledge of spreadsheets (Excel is preferred).
* NY residents tuition: $137 per credit

Financial Management of Practice Groups
New School for Social Research
NEWS#8563 Undergraduate 3 credits $622
This course explores in depth the concepts of cost accounting, systems of expense management, reporting functions and physician bill mechanisms. The principals of managerial finance within a healthcare setting are discussed, including risk, return and valuation in relation to the decision process of allocation of resources in changing financial markets. In addition, students will examine national standards for expense management, capitation and prospective payment systems.

Financial Risk Management
Heriot-Watt University
HERI#09 Graduate   4 credits $???
Risk is a prevalent in the human condition. Everything we do in our lives has a degree of risk attached to it. In living with risk, however, certain potential high risk or potential events require us to take corrective action, for instance insuring our life, home, and other possessions. Risk management is the process of monitoring risks and taking steps to minimize their impact. Financial risk management is the task of monitoring financial risks and managing their impact.

Financial Strategy
Bellevue University
BELL#MBA612 Graduate   3 credits $825
Analysis of the financial aspects of a corporation, using theory and application.

Financing for Entrepreneurs
UCLA
UCLA#X897 Undergraduate   3.6 CEU $500
This online course explores the financing options available to start-ups, rapidly growing enterprises, and established small businesses. Surveys new, emerging, and traditional sources of debt and equity; joint ventures; venture capital; commercial bank and institutional financing; informal or alternative sources for capital; and government-guaranteed financing options. Examines the costs/benefits of various investment and loan structures and the potential rewards of pursuing strategic alliances, joint ventures, partnerships, "angels," and intrapreneurships. Designed for owners, managers, and aspiring entrepreneurs who need access to capital to have their businesses grow, thrive, or simply survive.

Financing Organizations
City University
CITY#BSC402 Undergraduate   5 qu. credits $785
An examination of the analytical tools used to manage and control finances. Concepts studied include: The acquisition and oversight of working capital; intermediate and long-term financing; and the cost of capital and capital budgeting. Prerequisite: Strongly recommended: BSC400 and BSC401 or their equivalents.

Fiscal Management
Bellevue University
BELL#MGTC410 Undergraduate 3 credits $750
The "dollars and cents" language of business. Reading and interpreting balance sheets, financial statements, and annual reports. Getting numbers a manager can trust. Conducting a financial analysis of a company.

Food and Beverage Management
UCLA
UCLA#X407 Undergraduate   4 credits $500
This course covers operational components for effective management of food and beverage. Topics include purchasing, inventory analysis, portion control techniques, accrued cost control analysis, weekly period-to-date and its effect on annual costing, systems development in both manual and computerized environments, kitchen organization, and receiving and storage.

Fundamentals of Management
University of Minnesota
MINN#MGMT3001 Undergraduate 4 credits $400
Leadership and management functions such as those required to establish goals, policies, procedures, and plans. Motivation, planning, and control systems, and concepts of organizational structure and behavior.

Fundamentals of Management
University of Missouri
MOCE#MA202 Undergraduate   3 credits $387
This organizational course introduces the basic concepts of management and their application to operations and human resource management. Perquisites: junior standing.

Fundamentals of Marketing
National American University
NAAM#MG105D Undergraduate   4.5 credits $900
This is an introductory course in marketing for both business and non profit organizations. The student will explore how activities revolving around the marketing mix of product, price, place and promotion create value for customers. Additional topics include: international marketing and marketing ethics.

Fundamentals of Public Relations
UCLA
UCLA#X422 Undergraduate   3 credits $450
This online course is an introduction to the public relations practice and profession. Study focuses on real-life examples that exemplify the basic theories, principles, and methods of public relations practice. Discusses research, planning, and evaluation, as well as communication tools and techniques. Emphasizes problem solving and exposure to various aspects of public relations through guest lecturers.

General Management Perspectives
The Graduate School of America
TGSA#OM871W Graduate   4 credits $795
Explores the dynamics of management in the context of the individual, the group, and the organization. Topics covered include motivation, leadership, managing the Generation X workforce, communication, power and politics, work teams, organizational culture, and work design as they relate to being a manager. Learners will be challenged to assess the qualities that are required to be a successful manager in the '90s.

Global Financial Management
The Graduate School of America
TGSA#OM721W   Graduate   4 credits $795
This course covers topics related to the treasury function of a global business with an emphasis on an understanding of foreign exchange and its impact on firm decisions. It develops the framework for understanding the exchange rate impact and either mitigating it or managing in the face of it by considering such issues as transfer pricing, performance evaluation, capital structure, working capital management, and valuation. Additional topics will be included as current events dictate.

Global Issues of Quality Management
Bellevue University
BELL#IBMC340   Undergraduate   3 credits $750
A course designed to provide a study of quality management concepts and methods developed with ISO 9000.

Global Management
Bellevue University
BELL#BA637   Graduate   3 credits $825
Focus on international management concepts and procedures.

Global Purchasing
Bellevue University
BELL#IBMC410   Undergraduate   3 credits $750
A course designed to provide the skills necessary to facilitate global sourcing of raw materials, products or services.

Global Quality Imperative
Roane State Community College
ROAN#BUS213   Undergraduate   3 credits $459*
An examination of the factors and competitive challenges of the global economy and the necessary steps organizational leaders and participants must take to remain competitive. Topics include the new global market place, understanding the quality culture, what changes are needed and how to make them, and what the future of quality looks like.
* Tennessee residents tuition: $48 per semester hour.

Global Sourcing
Pennsylvania State University
PENN#BLOG297B   Undergraduate   3 credits $345
This course explores the issues of transporting foreign sourced materials and products into the United States, the entry of goods into commerce through customs, and the use of intermediaries. Emphasis is placed on the management of process complexity, developing, maintaining, and simplifying global supplies relationships. It is a logical sequel to BLOG297A. Prerequisite: BLOG301 is strongly recommended.

Global Workplace and Employers, Workers & Organizations
State University of New York
SUNY#263724   Undergraduate   4 credits $586*
The workplace of the future is now shaped by the forces of economic globalization and competition. New technologies have characterized economic development for the last twenty-five years, leading us toward new relationships to work and to one another. Explore the interrelationships among global economic competition, technological change, and resulting structures of corporate and workplace arrangements, innovations in labor-management relations and programs of worker participation. Consider both the promise and the problems which economic forces represent for corporations, labor, work, and society.
* NY residents tuition: $515

Golf Course Management
State University of New York
SUNY#GLF130   Undergraduate   3 credits $630*
The course is designed to provide the student with an understanding of the maintenance operations of golf courses and with an understanding of the equipment needed to operate a golf course.
* NY residents tuition: $105 per credit.

Golf Shop Operation
State University of New York
SUNY#GLF118   Undergraduate   3 credits $630*
This course is designed to provide the student with an overview for the development of a golf shop operation's manual, an understanding of the methods used to merchandise equipment used by the players of the game, and prepare them for planning and conducting competitive golf events.
* NY residents tuition: $105 per credit.

Government, Industry & Privatisation
Heriot-Watt University
HERI#10   Graduate   4 credits $???
The objective is to make you aware of the important influence exercised by government on the actions of companies. The course is designed to explain what happens when a government deliberately and systematically tries to alter the behavior of companies. It performs this task by using a framework derived from economic analysis in which the government is the "principal" and the companies are its "agents." The principal has certain policy aims and tries to induce the agents to conform to these aims.

Graduate Research Project
Embry-Riddle Aeronautical University
EMRI#MAS690   Graduate   3 credits $840
A written document on an aviation/aerospace topic which exposes the student to the technical aspects of writing. This course is included in the MAScurriculum to provide the student with the opportunity to pursue a project of special interest, but not to the level of a thesis. This is a required course for those students who choose not to write a thesis.

Grant & Proposal Writing
Marylhurst College
MARY#WR305 Undergraduate 3 credits $651
Learn the procedures and process for writing successful grant proposals. Explore diverse funding opportunities related to specific areas of interest. You will review and evaluate a sample of proposals as well as developing one in your interest area.

Grant and Report Writing
Dakota State University
DAKO#ENGL305 Undergraduate 3 credits $447
This intensive writing course covers researching of granting organizations as well as the writing of grants and reports on the use of grant money and similar and related documents. The course includes appropriate persuasive assignments, cover letter, and resume. Prerequisite: ENGL101 and CSC105 or consent of instructor.

Grant Proposals
UCLA
UCLA#X480 Undergraduate 3 credits $450
In this online course, participants learn how to maximize their efforts in such areas as effective program planning, searching for data and resources, writing and packaging a proposal, submitting a proposal to a funder, and follow-up--all with an emphasis on foundations and the corporate sector. Essential grant writing focuses on structure, attention to funding guidelines, concise persuasive writing, and developing a reasonable budget. In addition, participants learn the basic World Wide Web techniques necessary to identify appropriate funders, etc.

Grant Writing for Non-Profits
University of Colorado
CUON#PSC5830 Undergraduate 3 credits $1953*
Designed to help current and future professionals in the non-profit sector understand the social, political, and economic context and mechanics of pursuing grants, government contracts, and other funding for non-profit organizations.
* CO residents tuition: $136 per credit.

Grant Writing for Technology
The Heritage Institute
HEON#BU400F Undergraduate 3 qu. credits $200
Money flows to good ideas, and this course will help you develop your ideas for technology or any other project into winning grants. You'll learn a standard grant format, terminology to get your ideas across and hundreds of on-line as well in-print listings of potential funding agencies for all kinds of grants, including those in technology. You'll complete the course with a ready-to-go proposal in a fundable format and will benefit from the instructor's experience as a grants manager and Assistant Superintendent.

Grantsmanship
University of Southern Colorado
COSO#SOC491B Undergraduate 3 credits $210
In the late 1990s, funding from state and federal sources has diminished, making support from corporations and foundations vitally important to the life of small businesses. As part of this course, students will have the opportunity to write a grant to be funded for any project desired.

Grievance Arbitration
Indiana University
INDI#L320 Undergraduate 3 credits $268
Recommended only after L220 or with consent of instructor. The legal and practical context of grievance arbitration, and its limitations and advantages in resolving workplace problems. Varieties of arbitration clauses and the status of awards. Students analyze a cassette tape of a mock arbitration hearing.

Grievance Representation
Indiana University
INDI#L220B Undergraduate 3 credits $268
Union representation in the workplace. The use of grievance procedures to address problems and administer the collective bargaining agreement. Identification, research, presentation, and writing of grievance cases. Analysis of relevant labor law and the logic applied by arbitrators to grievance decisions.

Historical Perspectives and Contemporary Business Challenges
University of Minnesota
MINN#ABUS3011 Undergraduate 4 credits $400
An overview of the major challenges faced by contemporary business organizations against the background of evolving management practices. The history of business and management and the impact it has on organizations today and in the future are explored. By understanding the changing roles and career patterns of business in a historical context, students will be able to criticize and evaluate the opportunities and possibilities they will face in the evolving world of global business.

Horse Production
University of Missouri
MOCE#HO325 Undergraduate 3 credits $387
This course covers horse production; students learn proper ways to breed, feed, and manage horses. Perquisites: Animal Science 202, 213, and 304.

Hospitality Management
Brevard Community College
BREV#HFT1000 Undergraduate 3 credits $485
Growth, development, and career opportunities in the major segments of the hospitality, travel and tourism industry: food service, hotels, motels, resorts, clubs, amusements, theme parks, agencies.

How to Delegate Effectively
Chemeketa Community College
CHEM#BA062H Undergraduate 1 credits $140
How to Delegate Effectively focuses on methods to become more effective in the delegation process. Designed for managers and supervisors in business, industry and Government.

How to Write a Business Plan and Financial Proposal
University of Minnesota
MINN#ABUS3501 Undergraduate 4 credits $400
This course systematically leads students through preliminary exercises and drafts to produce a completed business plan and accompanying financial plan or management summary. Students learn how to articulate the mission, goals, and objectives of their business; conduct market and competitive analyses; formulate marketing strategies; determine staffing and organizational structures; conduct strategic planning; and project growth and expansion. The optional software allows students to produce and submit their work entirely on disk.

Human Behavior and the Organization
State University of New York
SUNY#HMS250Y02 Undergraduate 3 credits $570*
A basic course in the study of human service organizations. Students learn about the basic concepts and propositions that provide insight into the organizational dynamics that confront members of all types of human service organizations such as perception of roles, norms, communication, power, leadership, and other issues. In addition, students will gain a heightened understanding of human organizational culture issues that are specific to human and health care services in the context of their changing economic, political, and ecological environments. The new organizational forms, strategies, and innovations made by human and health care services.
* NY residents tuition: $90 per credit

Human Relations in Administration
New Hampshire College
NEHA#ADB125 Undergraduate 3 credits $1656
Human relations skills needed by managers to develop effective interaction skills which contribute directly to effective resource management and development of higher productivity are studied. Skill areas include leadership, motivation, communications, group dynamics, organizational development, management by objectives, stress and time management. Students learn techniques for becoming more effective managers, subordinates, peers and persons. Students are introduced to the international aspects of human relations.

Human Relations in Business
Cerro Coso Community College
CECO#BSADC40 Undergraduate 3 credits $345*
A behavioral approach to the business environment; self-improvement through self-understanding, elements of job applications and job advancement; motivation, people-to-people relationships and techniques of leadership on the job. Prerequisite: BSGN C10. Level 1 reading, level 2 writing classification recommended.
* CA residents pay $13 per credit.

Human Relations in Business
Rio Salado College
RISA#MGT251 Undergraduate 3 credits $186*
Analysis of motivation, leadership, communications, and other human factors. Cultural differences that may create conflict and affect morale individually and within organizations. Prerequisites: MGT101 or MGT175 or MGT229 suggested, but not required.
* AZ residents pay $37 per credit.

Human Resource Management
Fayetteville Technical Community College
FAYE#BUS153 Undergraduate 3 credits $489*
This course introduces the functions of personnel/human resource management within an organization. Topics include equal opportunity and the legal environment, recruitment and selection, performance appraisal, employee development, compensation planning, and employee relations. Upon completion, students should be able to anticipate and resolve human resource concerns.
* NC residents pay $20 per credit.

Human Resource Management
University of Missouri
MOCE#MG310 Undergraduate 3 credits $387
Topics in this course include workforce policies and procedures of the business enterprise. Perquisites: Mgt. 202 or instructor's consent.

Human Resource Management
New Hampshire College
NEHA#ADB211 Undergraduate 3 credits $1656
This course examines the fundamentals of policies and administration. Major tasks of procedures, developing, maintaining and utilizing an effective team are studied. Students are introduced to international human resource management. Prerequisite: Sophomore standing.

Human Resource Management
Strayer University
STRA#BUS310 Undergraduate 4.5 credits $665
Analyzes the major personnel management problems in organizations. Emphasizes recruitment, selection, wages and salary administration, manpower planning, time management, performance appraisal programs, and disciplinary actions. Prerequisite: BUS100.

Human Resource Management
Strayer University
STRA#BUS530 Undergraduate 4.5 credits $665
Examines the concepts and techniques of manpower planning, job evaluation, incentive and performance standards, and the impact of labor organizations on management. Creates a problem-solving environment to integrate knowledge in various functional areas of business and to provide direct management experience.

Human Resource Management
State University of New York
SUNY#213504 Undergraduate 4 credits $586*
Surveys the Personnel/Human Resource Management (P/HRM) function and related activities. Focuses on effective management and utilization of human resources in an organization or enterprise setting. Understand the role of the human resource department in modern day organizations. Address the motivational-performance issue and develop sensible views of current social policy. Emphasizes the theory and issues associated with the forecasting, recruiting, selecting, developing, motivating, compensating and retaining employees. Also covers current issues such as equal employment, occupational safety and health, work restructuring, and employee involvement. Prerequisite: Management Principles or equivalent.
* NY residents tuition: $515

Human Resource Management
Western Illinois University
WEIL#MAN353 Undergraduate 3 credits $795*
Examines the principles of personnel management as they relate to the function of personnel administration. Such topics as employee development, personnel recruitment, wage and salary administration, union-management relations, and performance evaluations are examined. Prerequisite: Management 349.
* IL residents tuition: $88 per credit.

Human Resource Management and Development
New Hampshire College
NEHA#ADB442 Undergraduate 3 credits $1656
This capstone course, which must be taken as the final course in the human resource management concentration of the business studies major, examines contemporary issues in human resource management resulting from new and changing legislation, demands of the work place, and emerging quality of work and life trends. Emphasis is place on software applications. The international aspects of human resource management are also studied. Prerequisite: ADB211.

Human Resources Management
Northwest College
NOCO#MA226 Undergraduate 3 credits $???
This course is to aid human resource managers in the methods used to implement the human resource program in business. Emphasis is placed in the areas of planning, staffing, compensation, representation and employee protection. Prerequisite: MA121.

Human Resources Management
New York Institute of Technology
NYIT#BUS3917 Undergraduate 3 credits $???
An introduction to the management of human resources for the effective support and achievement of an organization's strategies and goals. The major functions of planning and staffing, employee development and involvement, compensation and reward and employee relations are examined. Decision making skills in these areas are developed through class assignments. Prerequisites: BUS3900.

Human Resources Management
UCLA
UCLA#X450J Undergraduate 4 credits $500
This online course provides an overview of and an introduction to the basic human resources management (HRM) functions: employment, employee relations, training and development, compensation, benefits, and human resources information systems (HRIS). Topics include the various aspects of designing and structuring an HR/personnel department, the history and future of HRM, the changing nature of work, the relationship of HR functions, the current legal environment in which HR operates, sources for obtaining answers to most operational HR problems, and an exploration of HR as a career.

Human Resources Management
The Graduate School of America
TGSA#OM845W Graduate 4 credits $795
This course is designed to broaden managers' understanding of the role and importance of human resources, and assist them in maximizing the effectiveness of employees within their organizations. It focuses on such topics as human resource planning, recruitment and selection, evaluation, equal employment, job design, training and development and compensation.

Human-Computer Interaction
Nova Southeastern University
NOVA#MCIS680 Graduate 3 credits $1,110
Focuses on the dynamics of human-computer interaction (HCI). Provides a broad overview of HCI as a sub-area of computer science and explores user-centered design approaches in information systems applications. Addresses the user interface and software design strategies, user experience levels, interaction styles, usability engineering, and collaborative systems technology. Students will perform formal software evaluations and usability tests.

Human-Computer Interaction
Nova Southeastern University
NOVA#MCTE680 Graduate 3 credits $1,110
Explores the emerging field of human-computer interaction. Emphasis is placed on how software design practices are integrated with human factors principles and methods. Other issues covered include user experience levels, interaction styles, usability engineering, interaction devices and strategies, user-centered design, human information processing, social aspects of computing, and computer-supported cooperative work.

Humanities I
Brevard Community College
BREV#HUM2210 Undergraduate 3 credits $485
An integral course designed to increase the student's understanding and appreciation of the creative process in western culture through the study of representative materials in art, music, literature, and philosophy from prehistory through the 14th century. Prerequisite: Appropriate test scores in reading and writing.

Import Regulations and Documentation
Pace University
PACE#OL702 Undergraduate   3 credits $500
This popular course includes: types of entries; purpose, preparation and use of documents required Bill of lading, its value and endorsement; delivery order; classification of invoices; dutiable and non-dutiable charges; examination of merchandise (on dock, at public stores) Basis of value determination and collection of duties Cartage; transportation in bond; re-export; restricted or prohibited items; Department of Health, Education and Welfare forms and procedures, etc.

Import Transportation Management
Pace University
PACE#OL708 Undergraduate   3 credits $500
A hands-on, decision-making approach to total import transportation: via land, sea, air, purchase orders, landed cost quotations, routing, rating, customs clearance, inland U.S. transport, containerization, how to avoid legal liability/disputes/claims, understanding the relationship between international/national shipping laws and cargo owner/common carrier rights and responsibilities Common carrier claims, marine insurance quotation/underwriting techniques, claims collection, and important aspects of transportation of "in bond" cargo.

Importing Techniques
Pace University
PACE#OL707 Undergraduate   3 credits $500
Types of import activity (direct, commission house, broker or factor, agency); raw materials; finished products; terms and definition; contracts; placing of order, cables and codes, delivery specifications; packing, marking, invoicing; import duties; Customs regulations; miscellaneous cost (inland freight, cartage, ocean transportation, warehousing, packing, consular fees, loading charges, export duties, stamps, etc.); documents; types of service available through banks, forwarders, carriers, customs brokers, insurance companies; consignments; samples; special licenses; and methods of finance.

Improvement Using Gemba Kaizen
Roane State Community College
ROAN#BUS214 Undergraduate   3 credits $459*
The Aim of this course of study focuses on the results-boosting techniques of Kaizen on the place where they will do the most good, the Gemba. Gemba is defined as the "real place" where real action occurs in an organization. For manufacturing, this is the plant floor; and for service industries, this is the customer contact point.
* Tennessee residents tuition: $48 per semester hour.

Independent Record Production
University of Colorado
CUON#MUS3740 Undergraduate   3 credits $1953*
Setting up an independent record label has never been easier, whether you are a single artist looking to put out your own music or an entrepreneur wanting to market talented artists or license out-of-date recordings. This course tells you how to; set up the business plan, start a business, evaluate recording and manufacturing options, work with producers and engineers, choose studios, maximize your recording budget, protect your copyrights, and market and promote your recordings.
* CO residents tuition: $136 per credit.

Industrial Management
New Jersey Institute of Technology
NJIT#EM501 Undergraduate   3 credits $1143*
Operational aspects of management techniques: organization, product design and development, distribution logistics, marketing, plant location and layout, ,materials handling, production planning and control, inventory control, quality control, work analysis, and incentive plans. Optional: video lessons.
* NJ residents: $184/semester hour.

Industrial Psychology
University of Missouri
MOCE#PS212 Undergraduate   3 credits $387
This course examines the principles involved as employees interact with the social and physical events in their industrial work environment. Perquisites: Psych. 50.

Industrial Quality Control
New Jersey Institute of Technology
NJIT#IE672 Undergraduate   3 credits $1143*
The management of quality assurance: operational and statistical principles of acceptance sampling and process control; quality problems in production lines, and introduction to total quality management concepts. This course is part of the graduate certificate in Continuous Process Improvement. Prerequisite: Engineering Statistics. Optional: 14 video lessons of 120 minutes each.
* NJ residents: $184/semester hour.

Industrial Security
Fox Valley Technical College
FOVA#504-147 Undergraduate   3 credits $200
Industrial security topical areas include a study of protective lighting, physical barriers, Crime Prevention Through Environmental Design (CPTED), cargo transportation security, bomb search procedures and identification, electronic access control, closed circuit television, and locking devices and key control.

Industry Structure, Roles and Change
The Graduate School of America
TGSA#OM889W Graduate   4 credits $795
Issues related to the structure of telecommunications as a changing industry are examined. Partnerships and competition are considered. Topics related to manufacturers of equipment and software, vendors, global change and telecommunication investments are included.

Information in an Era of Overload
Marylhurst College
MARY#CLL373C Undergraduate 3 credits $651
The ability to find and manage information is an essential skill for all educated people. Students will learn how to define and focus their information needs in any subject area, how to access needed information, how to evaluate information, and how to transform information into a body of knowledge and a basis for informed action through the use of critical thinking.

Information Industry Finance
University of Denver, University College
DEUC#TELE4822 Undergraduate 3 qtr. hrs. $885
This course will focus on financial principles as specifically related to information technology industries, providing students with an overall vision of the financial factors which drive those industries. Students will apply financial analysis to decision-making and problem-solving in business scenarios. Topics to be covered include time value of money, internal rate of return on investments, analysis of capital acquisitions, capital budgeting, rate setting, lease versus purchase decision-making and technological departmental budget management. (Prerequisite: Principles of Telecommunications or equivalent experience.)

Information Processing
Greenville Technical College
GRTE#EET145B Undergraduate 3 credits $381*
Designed to provide a basic understanding of microcomputer concepts and literacy with emphasis on an office environment. It includes a hands-on application of the DOS operating system and a simulation of electronic mail. This course also is designed to refine written communication skills. Pre-requisite: English Skills.
* NC residents pay $48 per credit.

Information System Principles
New Jersey Institute of Technology
NJIT#CIS677 Undergraduate 3 credits $1143*
Reviews the role of information systems in organizations and how they relate to organizational objectives and organizational structure. Identifies basic concepts such as the systems point of view, the organization of a system, the nature of information flows, the impact of systems upon management and organizations, human information processing and related cognitive concepts Prerequisites: Familiarity with the organization of a computer system and knowledge of at least one higher-level language. Optional: 12 video lessons of 150 minutes each.
* NJ residents: $184/semester hour.

Information Systems
City University
CITY#MG416 Undergraduate 5 qu. credits $785
An overview of the concepts, tools, and organizational structures required for the effective management of the firm's information resources; emphasis on understanding the managerial issues associated with acquiring, organizing, and controlling information and information processing resources and anticipated impacts of future developments in information systems technology.

Information Systems and Analysis
UCLA
UCLA#X418 Undergraduate 4 credits $575
Covers tools and techniques used in systems analysis, design, and project management, such as the preparation of systems specifications, detail systems designs, GANTT, PERT charts, and data-flow diagrams. Includes practical discussions of alternative forms of input, output, processing, storage, and telecommunications, as well as a methodology for analyzing business needs, designing appropriate solutions, and managing their implementations.

Information Systems Applications
Marylhurst College
MARY#CIS345 Undergraduate 3 credits $651
Information technology plays a key role in the business environment of the 90s, and successful managers are those who understand how to use these critical resources effectively. This is a basic appreciation course in telecommunications, data processing, electronic search, and office automation applications from a non-technical standpoint. Students will become acquainted with applications theory. Prerequisite: CIS 211.

Information Systems Concepts
New Hampshire College
NEHA#CIS200 Undergraduate 3 credits $1656
This course identifies managerial and organizational needs and describes the role of information systems including current professional practices and methodologies in management. It also includes a presentation of systems theory, decision theory, organization models, types of information systems, information systems planning, and information systems development. Prerequisite: CIS100.

Information Systems Planning
Bellevue University
BELL#MISC340 Undergraduate 6 credits $1500
This course takes students through the process of developing and implementing information systems plans at both the strategic and tactical (project) levels.

Information Systems Problem Solving
Lansing Community College
LANS#CISB200 Undergraduate 3 credits $315
Fundamental changes have occurred in organizations with the application of computer technology. This course chronicles the source of that technology in science, explores the limitations of computer technology, examines the impact of the technology in business organizations and society, and develops problem solving techniques for use in conjunction with computers. TQM techniques will be used with team projects.

Information Systems Projects
Nova Southeastern University
NOVA#MCIS621 Graduate   3 credits $1,110
Life-cycle models/paradigms. Project planning and risk analysis. Project control including work breakdown structures, project scheduling, activities and milestones. Software cost estimation techniques/models. Software quality assurance and metrics for software productivity and quality. Inspections, walkthroughs, and reviews. Approaches to team organization. Configuration management. Automated project management tools. Software maintenance. Information system security. Procurement of software services and systems. Management of operational systems. Legal/ethical issues associated with CIS and software.

Information Systems Projects
Nova Southeastern University
NOVA#MMIS621 Graduate   3 credits $1,110
Practical examination of how projects can be managed from start to finish. Life-cycle models and paradigms. Life-cycle phases. Project planning and risk analysis. Project control including work breakdown structures, project scheduling, activities and milestones. Software cost estimations techniques/models. Software quality assurance and metrics for software productivity and quality. Inspections, walkthroughs, and reviews. Approaches to team organization. Documentation and configuration management. Automated project management tools. Software maintenance. Procurement of software services and systems.

Information Systems Strategies
Marylhurst College
MARY#CIS445B Undergraduate   3 credits $651
Learn to communicate more effectively with information systems professionals. Explore concepts and methods of systems analysis, planning, design, implementation, and evaluation. The focus is on the use of these methods to support the modern organization in decision-making and problem-solving. Prerequisite: CIS345.

Integrative Management Project
The Graduate School of America
TGSA#RM810W Graduate   4 credits $795
This capstone requirement for the M.S. degree requires a demonstration of breadth and depth of knowledge through the development of an instructional design project, course or curriculum.

Intermediate Accounting I
City University
CITY#AC301 Undergraduate   5 qu. credits $785
An in-depth examination of the theory and practice in financial accounting, including the environment and underlying conceptual framework. Detailed study of the four major financial statements: cash, receivables, inventories, and applications of time value of money concepts. Prerequisite: AC210 and AC220 or their equivalents.

Intermediate Accounting I
Fayetteville Technical Community College
FAYE#ACC220 Undergraduate   4 credits $652*
This course is a continuation of the study of accounting principles with in-depth coverage of theoretical concepts and financial statements. Topics include generally accepted accounting principles and statements and extensive analyses of balance sheet components. Upon completion, students should be able to demonstrate competence in the conceptual framework underlying financial accounting, including the application of financial standards.
* North Carolina residents and non-resident US military personnel stationed within the state tuition: $80; NC senior citizens free.

Intermediate Accounting I
New Hampshire College
NEHA#ACC203 Undergraduate   3 credits $1656
These courses cover an intensive examination and analysis of the accounting theory for assets, liabilities and stockholders' equity essential for the development and understanding of financial statements. The underlying concepts of matching revenue and expenses for the determination of net income are stressed. Particular emphasis is placed on the study and application of APB opinions and FASB opinions along with problem solving. Prerequisite: ACC102.

Intermediate Accounting I
Strayer University
STRA#ACC200 Undergraduate   4.5 credits $665
Provides and in-depth study of accounting theory and a review of the accounting cycle. Concentrates on the preparation of financial statements, the valuation of cash and temporary investments, receivable and accounting for inventories. Refers to pronouncements of the American Institute of Certified Public Accountants (AICPA). Prerequisite: ACC110 or equivalent.

Intermediate Accounting II
City University
CITY#AC302 Undergraduate   5 qu. credits $785
Continuation of the theory and practice of financial accounting. Detailed study of acquisition and deposition of property, depreciation, intangible assets, liabilities, stockholder's equity, investments and earnings per share. Prerequisite: AC301 or its equivalent.

Intermediate Accounting II
New Hampshire College
NEHA#ACC204 Undergraduate   3 credits $1656
Continuation of ACC203. Prerequisite: ACC203.

Intermediate Accounting II
Strayer University
STRA#ACC205 Undergraduate   4.5 credits $665
Covers accounting for current and non-current liabilities; accounting for tangible assets, stockholders' equity and dilutive securities. Provides an evaluation of various investment securities. Refers to pronouncements of the AICPA. Prerequisite: ACC200.

Intermediate Accounting III
City University
CITY#AC303 Undergraduate   5 qu. credits $785
Final class in the intermediate series. Detailed study of statement of cash flows, financial statement analysis, full disclosure, accounting changes, leases, accounting for income tax, post retirement benefits and revenue recognition. Prerequisite: AC302 or its equivalent.

Intermediate Accounting III
Strayer University
STRA#ACC305 Undergraduate   4.5 credits $665
Covers accounting for income taxes, pension costs, and leases. Considers special problems related to income determination, preparation of financial position statement, and accounting for reporting general price-level change. Prerequisite: ACC205.

International Business
Bellevue University
BELL#IBMC350 Undergraduate   3 credits $750
A course designed to provide a study of the major problems related to international business organization production, finance, marketing and economics.

International Business
City University
CITY#BSM404 Undergraduate   5 qu. credits $785
An evaluation of forces currently encouraging businesses to globalize their operations and the rules which govern such activities. Topics include: the legal, business, and cultural environments of Asia, Eastern, and Western Europe; international business contracts; the resolution of trade and contract disputes; import and export regulations; and international forces affecting the uses of labor, competition and the environment.

International Business
Mercy College
MERC#IB250 Undergraduate   3 credits $900
An introduction to international business. Topics include the international environment, international trade, foreign direct investment, foreign exchange, regional economic integration, the role of the multinational corporation, and business strategies. Prepares students for a changing world.

International Business
University of Minnesota
MINN#BGS3004 Undergraduate   4 credits $400
An exploration of world business, with emphasis on international concepts, comparative cultures and environments, global business strategies, multinational corporations, and management operations in the global scene. International constraints in the multinational corporation are examined. This course is in preparation; please inquire before enrolling.

International Business
State University of New York
SUNY#213314 Undergraduate   4 credits $586*
Acquire an understanding of the theories and practices involved in international business. Students follow a learning plan and acquire knowledge in areas such as the nature and patterns of international business; role of international organizations; economic, socio-cultural, political, legal and labor issues, and operational and strategic management issues related to business with foreign nations, including topics on international human resource development. Special components on NAFTA and GATT are included to deliberate on their significance for North American business establishments. Prerequisite: At least one course in Economics.
* NY residents tuition: $515

International Business
Waukesha County Technical College
WAUK#138150003 Undergraduate 3 credits $192*
A broad introductory course on the fundamentals of international trade. An overview of business in the international setting, including marketing of products, exporting and importing principles, financial considerations in the international marketplace, and trade regulations that affect international operations. Basic terminology of international business is of primary importance.
* WI residents pay $54 per credit.

International Business
Western Illinois University
WEIL#FIN317 Undergraduate   3 credits $795*
International marketing requires adaptation to the cultural, legal, political, economic, and often religious norms of other societies. The achievement of business objectives by U.S. multinational corporations rests on the awareness that international competition is not the only obstacle. In many cases, the uncontrollable foreign cultural environment decides the success or failure of the international marketing plan. Examine the ethical value systems of foreign markets and their impact on the business culture of U.S. corporations.
* IL residents tuition: $88 per credit.

International Business
The Graduate School of America
TGSA#OM838W Graduate   4 credits $795
This course provides an overview of managing a business in an international environment.

International Business Environment
Strayer University
STRA#BUS250 Undergraduate   4.5 credits $665
Introduces the student to international business. Covers international trade theory, government influence on world trade patterns, the international monetary system, the effects of cultural differences in world trade and the various forms of international business organizations. Discusses the methods used to trade, such as exporting, direct investment, joint ventures, and trade finance. Includes the special problems of East-West trade and the political and economic impact of the multinational enterprise.

International Business I
Northwest College
NOCO#BU240 Undergraduate 5 credits $???
This course is designed to provide students with knowledge of worldwide aspects of different business functions. Emphasis will be on the nature of international business, international government and foreign environment. Prerequisites or Corequisites: MA121 and MT220.

International Business Management
Golden Gate University
GOLD#MGT304 3 Graduate 3 credits $1404
Examines theory of foreign direct investment; role of multinationals in the global economy; legal, cultural and financial environments facing multinational corporations; host/home country relationships with multinationals; policy, strategy and management challenges in marketing, finance, production and personnel faced by multinational corporations.

International Business Management
New School for Social Research
NEWS#8635 Undergraduate 3 credits $622
Introduces problems created by operating a business in more than one country. Difficulties for multinational firms caused by differing laws, economic, social and cultural environments; and keveks if education and technology are studied. Students analyze the impact of these factors on operations and decision making with particular focus on their organizational and control implications.

International Environment of Financial Management
Strayer University
STRA#ECO410 Undergraduate 4.5 credits $665
Introduces the cultural and human environments of international finance and management. Emphasizes political and social dimensions and consequences of capital management and budgeting, debt and equity financing, international and domestic tax laws and other financial issues facing the MNC's in the Third World countries.

International Finance
Bellevue University
BELL#IBMC420 Undergraduate 3 credits $750
A course designed to provide an examination and analysis of international financial decision-making.

International Human Resources
UCLA
UCLA#X450D Undergraduate 4 credits $500
This online course introduces the human resources practitioner and international line manager to the legal, practical, and successful human resources strategies used by international companies in today's global economy. Topics include employment and staffing; compensation; benefits; labor laws; employment-related taxation; leadership, management, and supervisory practices among international corporations; immigration; permanent resident and temporary work visa status; and expatriate and repatriation policies and practices.

International Management
New Hampshire College
NEHA#INT315 Undergraduate 3 credits $1656
This course introduces the student to the management of global operations. It covers the major functional areas of management as they are practiced in a multinational corporation. This includes: participation, organization, financial management, production/souring, and marketing strategies, as well as human resource development, communications and control, and the formation of strategic alliances. The course uses texts, simulations and cases. Prerequisite: ADB215.

International Marketing
Bellevue University
BELL#IBMC450 Undergraduate 3 credits $750
A course designed to provide a managerial approach to international marketing with an emphasis on comparative systems and controllable key variables.

International Marketing
City University
CITY#MK388 Undergraduate 5 qu. credits $785
This course introduces students to the challenges and possibilities of marketing and exporting internationally. Environmental and cultural considerations are examined as they impact various elements of the marketing plan.

International Marketing
Waukesha County Technical College
WAUK#138155 Undergraduate 3 credits $192*
This is a comprehensive look at the manner in which commodities and industrial products are marketed at the international level. Distribution channels, trade patterns, and competition, product planning and life cycle, advertising and promotion, marketing research and the adaptation of the marketing mix to foreign environments are analyzed. Distributor relationships, agency and licensing will also be analyzed. Some background in marketing is recommended.
* WI residents pay $54 per credit.

International Marketing
Western Illinois University
WEIL#FIN417 Undergraduate 3 credits $795*
Examines the cultural, political, economic, and other important factors affecting the international marketer and international marketing operations. The emphasis is on marketing planning and strategies in the global environment.
* IL residents tuition: $88 per credit.

International Marketing Management
The Graduate School of America
TGSA#OM867W Graduate 4 credits $795
This course focuses on the application of marketing management principles and practices to international markets.

International Perspectives of Human Resources
University of Nebraska
NEBR#FCS865 Undergraduate   3 credits $467
A study of cultures from a political, economic, physical, and psychosocial perspective.

International Tourism
Western Illinois University
WEIL#REC462 Undergraduate   3 credits $795*
Looks at the organization of the world tourism industry as it has evolved by the end of the twentieth century. Marketers, facilitators, and suppliers are described. The course is necessarily geographic in scope. It emphasizes existing and emerging national markets where travel services are demanded, and conducts a world region-by-region analysis of current and emerging visitor attractions. The course includes additional information on industry trends and market behavior.
* IL residents tuition: $88 per credit.

International Trade & Finance
Heriot-Watt University
HERI#11 Graduate   4 credits $???
International economic influences are becoming increasingly important to companies in all countries. Obviously companies involved in exporting and importing goods and services operate within the international marketplace. However, companies attempting to raise finance or undertake investment decisions are also exposed to international influences. The course combines technical and descriptive material with analysis of managerial decision-making problems. The course explores in detail the main elements in the bargaining relationship. Competence in Economics is required for this elective.

International Trade - Inside the Global Economy
Western Illinois University
WEIL#ECO470 Undergraduate   3 credits $795*
Examines the theoretical and institutional aspects of international trade. Topics include the effect of trade and factor movements on economic welfare, balance of payments, problems of international disequilibrium, process of balance of payments adjustments, barriers to trade, and the search for economic stability and growth through international cooperation. Prerequisite: Economics 232.
* IL residents tuition: $88 per credit.

International Trade Policy
Bellevue University
BELL#IBMC440 Undergraduate   3 credits $750
A course designed to discuss the implications of international trade policy. Differentiation of the functions of free trade and fair trade.

International Travel and Tourism
Auburn University
AUBU#GY320 Undergraduate   1.8 credits $76
Environmental and Cultural Patterns related to tourism, with specific country examples. This course is designed to be viewed via multimedia CD-ROM.

Internet Marketing
New Mexico Highlands University
NMHI#8523A Undergrad/Grad   3 credits $297
Internet Marketing is emerging as a major aspect of Electronic Commerce. This course provides an introduction to Internet Marketing. The course will focus on the place of Internet Marketing in an integrated marketing strategy, consumer behavior on the Internet, current Internet marketing practices, and its future evolution.

Interpersonal Communications
Northwest College
NOCO#GE179 Undergraduate   3 credits $???
Nonverbal communications, small-group dynamics and public speaking are introduced. Emphasis will be placed on building skills in interpersonal relations.

Interpretation of Financial Accounting
City University
CITY#BSC401 Undergraduate   5 qu. credits $785
An overview of financial accounting statements from a user perspective. The interpretation of financial data for decision analysis will be emphasized. The impact of current accounting recommendations on organizational decision making will be evaluated. Prerequisite: Strongly recommended: BSC400 or its equivalent.

Into Technical Writing for Industry
Kennesaw State University
KENN#FMV233 Undergraduate   3 credits $149
A recent survey of employers in a variety of fields indicated that most well-paying jobs require clear, effective writing on an everyday basis. Furthermore, a rising number of employees at all levels realize that having effective writing skills contributes to their success and advances their careers. This course will focus on developing the technical writing skills that are most needed in the workplace: how to write appropriately for particular readers, how to write clearly and concisely, how to use headings, lists, and other formatting to make your writing more readable, etc.

Intro to International Business
New York Institute of Technology
NYIT#BUS3907 Undergraduate   3 credits $???
Techniques for analyzing and understanding the world of international business. Students will examine the challenges posed by the multinational firm and the dynamic nature of international business. Case studies and discussions will complement lectures. Prerequisite: SS2010 or SS2011.

Intro to International Business
UCLA
UCLA#X460 Undergraduate   4 credits $500
This online course introduces a framework for the analysis of international business operations, including basic characteristics and concepts of international business, the growth and magnitude of international business, and international economic and political institutions. Topics include multinational business and the national interest of host countries, investments and monetary relations with special emphasis on issues of trade restrictions, and direct foreign investment and balance-of-payments. Includes and overview of the particulars of international business functions: personnel, marketing, finance, and production.

Intro to MIS
UCLA
UCLA#X418D Undergraduate   4 credits $500
This online course surveys the elements of typical business systems and how they combine into an operational system. It covers major considerations in analyzing, planning, designing, documenting, presenting, implementing, and auditing systems. The course also discusses techniques for presenting results of a systems study, and synthesizes and summarizes subjects covered in the Management Information Systems curriculum. Students work on projects related to their own fields of concern.

Introduction to Marketing
New York Institute of Technology
NYIT#BUS3400 Undergraduate   3 credits $???
Study of the process by which consumers needs and wants are analyzed and satisfied within the context of a modern marketing system. Investigation of current developments in the external environment affecting the marketing process. The role of marketing institutions in facilitating the flow of goods and services from producers to consumers is analyzed.

Introduction to Accounting
Rogers State University
ROGE#ACCT1113 Undergraduate   3 credits $495*
Everyone who manages in business - whether a mom and pop store or a huge multinational corporation - needs to understand and speak the language of accounting. This course introduces you to the language and concepts of accounting. Emphasis is on record-keeping, double entry method, and financial reports. May be used as a preparatory course for Accounting 2103 (transferability should be checked with the intended college). Principles are reinforced through the use of computerized practice sets. No previous computer experience is required.
* OK residents $315.

Introduction to Airline Reservations Systems-SABRE
State University of New York
SUNY#TVL210 Undergraduate   3 credits $630*
An introduction to American Airline's SABRE computer reservation and ticketing system. Course uses simulated SABRE. Programmed lessons are used to acquire proficiency in SABRE formats.
* NY residents tuition: $105 per credit.

Introduction to Automotive Industry
Northwest College
NOCO#MA130 Undergraduate   5 credits $???
This course is designed to provide an overview of the automotive/vehicle industry, including the history, terminology, and trends.

Introduction to Business
University of Alaska - Fairbanks
ALFA#BA151 Undergraduate   3 credits $213
Business organization, nature of major business functions such as management, finance, accounting, marketing, personal administration. Opportunities and requirements for professional business careers.

Introduction to Business
Barstow Community College
BARS#BADM5 Undergraduate   3 credits $???
Survey of functions, objectives, organization, and structure of business within the American free enterprise system.

Introduction to Business
College of DuPage
DUPA#BUS100 Undergraduate   5 qu. credits $150
An introduction to the environment and functions of business. Functions studies include marketing, production management, retailing, wholesaling, advertising, risk, pricing, personnel and business environments. Part of a certificate program in Supervision when completed with Management 100 and Management 210 course.

Introduction to Business
Edmonds Community College
EDMO#BUS100 Undergraduate   5 credits $260
(Course description not available at press time.)

Introduction to Business
Fayetteville Technical Community College
FAYE#BUS110 Undergraduate   3 credits $489*
This course provides a survey of the business world. Topics include the basic principles and practices of contemporary business. Upon completion, students should be able to demonstrate an understanding of business concepts as a foundation for studying other business subjects.
* NC residents pay $20 per credit.

Introduction to Business
Front Range Community College
FRCC#BUS115 Undergraduate   3 credits $790
This course surveys the operation of the American business system: fundamentals of the economy, careers and opportunities, marketing, management, production, governmental regulations, tools of business, and social responsibility. 45 Contact Hours.

Introduction to Business
New Hampshire College
NEHA#ADB110　Undergraduate　3 credits　$1656
Introduces basic business functions and how businesses are owned, managed and controlled. Elements of a business are integrated to reflect how each interacts with the other to provide the concept of a systems background. A broad background in business practices, principles, and economic concepts is discussed and provides the basis for use in more advanced courses. Includes an introduction to international business.

Introduction to Business
Northwest College
NOCO#BU120A　Undergraduate　3 credits　$???
Students receive an understanding of the broad area of activity known as business. A vocabulary of business terms, the varied careers available in the business world and an understanding of the methods and procedures used by business in decision making will be discussed.

Introduction to Business
New York Institute of Technology
NYIT#BUS3906　Undergraduate　3 credits　$???
Broad overview of functions, institutions, principles and practices of business; provides basic foundation for the student who will specialize in some aspect of business in college and emphasize dynamic nature of business and the role of change as evidenced by current events.

Introduction to Business
Rio Salado College
RISA#GBS151　Undergraduate　3 credits　$186*
Characteristics and activities of current local, national, and international business. An overview of economics, marketing, management and finance.
* AZ residents $37 per credit.

Introduction to Business
Rogers State University
ROGE#BMA1203　Undergraduate　3 credits　$495*
This course is for everyone who wants to expand their understanding of business. It provides a comprehensive view of the contemporary business environment from the internal functions of a business to the challenges of business on an international scale. After completing this course you should have a better understanding of several areas of business and have a foundation to build on in related business courses. One area is heavily emphasized -- the global marketplace.
* OK residents $315.

Introduction to Business
Strayer University
STRA#BUS100　Undergraduate　4.5 credits　$665
Provides a basic approach to business life through a survey of major functions. Offers an overview of business, organizations, finance, milepost budgeting, management, and marketing.

Introduction to Business
Strayer University
STRA#BUS532　Undergraduate　4.5 credits　$665
Discusses business strategies in the changing environment of today's highly competitive world. Explains the impact of technology, government policy, and world economics/political forces on executive decision-making. Analytical, integrative, and decision-making skills are stressed. Case problems, films and research projects are used to sharpen skills in fact-finding and decision-making. Prerequisite: BUS533.

Introduction to Business and Society
University of Minnesota
MINN#GC1511　Undergraduate　4 credits　$356
Intended for both business and general education, this course provides an overview of the economic environment in which business operates. Major functions of a business organization are surveyed, including production, finance, personnel, and marketing. A useful introductory course for students planning to do more work in business, but also recommended for those who want only to survey the field.

Introduction to Business Computing
Edmonds Community College
EDMO#CIS100　Undergraduate　3 credits　$220
This course is designed for the computer beginner. It you've never used a computer before, the only computer skill you need to take this class is to be able to access the Internet site.

Introduction to Business Finance
New Hampshire College
NEHA#FIN320　Undergraduate　3 credits　$1656
This course is designed to survey the corporate finance discipline, examine the financial management of corporations, develop skills necessary for financial decision-making, such as financing, investments and dividends, and acquaint students with money and capital markets and institutions. Prerequisites: ECO 201, ECO 202 and MAT 120.

Introduction to Business Management
New School for Social Research
NEWS#2862　Undergraduate　3 credits　$1638*
A skill-building, introductory course for people whose job responsibilities or career interests require knowledge of basic management principles. The class studies concepts of business organization, communication, decision-making, planning, motivating, cont. rolling, group dynamics, leadership, and change. Examples of common day-to-day management and supervisory problems provide realistic case studies.
* Non-credit option, tuition: $365.

Introduction to Computer Information Systems
Bakersfield College
BAKE#COMSB2 Undergraduate 3 credits $345*
Introduction to the concept of electronic data processing and the use of the computer systems as problem-solving tools in business, economics, mathematics, and the sciences. Includes the history of data processing, computer systems components, and sequential and direct-access processing. Database management systems, teleprocessing, and distributed processing are covered. An overview of personal computer applications software (word processing, electronic spreadsheets, and personal database management systems) are also included. Prerequisite: One year of high school Algebra or Math A; Reading Level 1 recommended.
* CA residents pay $40 per credit.

Introduction to Computer Information Systems
Strayer University
STRA#CIS105 Undergraduate 4.5 credits $665
Provides a basic knowledge of computer systems software and hardware. Surveys data processing as applied to business applications, and emphasized information system concepts and organization. Offers a hands-on introduction to basic MS-DOS commands and MS Windows usage.

Introduction to Computing for Business
UCLA
UCLA#X414 Undergraduate 4 credits $575
This online course presents an overview of computer applications and programming in the business world, including desktop publishing, financial analysis and accounting, and data management. It examines how a computer does what it does; computer hardware and software; concepts of microcomputers, minicomputers, mainframes, and computer networks; systems design; programming concepts and languages; office automation; and the impact of computers in business and society.

Introduction to Direct Marketing
Mercy College
MERC#MK321 Undergraduate 3 credits $900
Students are introduced to the basic principles and practices of direct marketing in the course. Topics include direct marketing's history and development, who uses it and the leading players (i.e., mailers, brokers, etc.) in the field. The course also covers the products and services that sell best through direct marketing, the development and techniques of database marketing, how to sell through direct marketing, and its measurability.

Introduction to Ecotourism Planning & Management
Humboldt State University
HUMB#NRPI218 Undergraduate 3 credits $350
The course will be internet-based, focusing on eight distinct modules linked together in a sequence. Course material will introduce the student to the history, concepts and principles behind the phenomenon of ecological tourism, knowledge of the tourism market and marketing to tourists, and practical applications for planning and managing ecotourism development activities that conserve natural resources and provide community economic benefits. This course is part of the Certificate Program in Ecotourism. For a brochure about this program, contact The Office of Extended Education.

Introduction to EDP in Business
New York Institute of Technology
NYIT#BUS3801 Undergraduate 3 credits $???
The role of computers in business organizations will be explored. There will be an emphasis on the use of such software packages as spreadsheets, database and word processing.

Introduction to Fashion Industry
State University of New York
SUNY#FM114 Undergraduate 3 credits $1038*
This survey covers the history, characteristics, and global interrelationships of all segments in the fashion industry. The course explores how fiber, textile, and apparel producers, retailers, and home furnishing companies merchandise and market their products within the industry and to the ultimate consumer.
* NY residents tuition: $137 per credit.

Introduction to Finance
Pennsylvania State University
PENN#FIN100 Undergraduate 3 credits $345
The nature, scope, and interdependence of the institutional and individual participants in the financial system. Prerequisite: third-semester standing.

Introduction to Finance
Western Illinois University
WEIL#FIN311 Undergraduate 3 credits $795*
Is an introductory course in finance intended for the non-finance major. The focus is on the study of money and its management. The course is divided into three sections that encompass the major areas of finance: financial institutions, investments, and business finance. Prerequisites: Accounting 200 or 241; Economics 231, or 232.
* IL residents tuition: $88 per credit.

Introduction to Financial Accounting
Strayer University
STRA#ACC104 Undergraduate 4.5 credits $665
Provides basic knowledge of financial accounting concepts and standards essential to decision-making for investments and for the management of business and government organizations. Topics include the structure of accounting, accounting for assets and liabilities, accounting for partnerships and corporate transactions, and the analysis of accounting information.

Introduction to Financial Planning
Waukesha County Technical College
WAUK#114105004 Undergraduate 3 credits $193
Emphasizes how to develop and implement long-range plans to achieve financial objectives. This approach requires not a single plan, but a coordinated series of plans covering various parts of a person's overall financial affairs. Such financial planning is customized, because it takes into consideration all financial aspects as an individual or family moves through life, making adjustments as they become appropriate, planning for changing financial needs in life, and dealing with each new situation as it occurs.

Introduction to Hospitality Industry
State University of New York
SUNY#HRMG100 Undergraduate 3 credits $1038*
This course studies the growth and development of the hospitality industry, its present status, and future trends, including an introduction to the various areas of specialization. Areas covered include hotels, restaurants, resorts, casinos, and travel and tourism. Personal and professional qualifications for different career options will be discussed.
* NY residents tuition: $137 per credit.

Introduction to International Business
New Hampshire College
NEHA#INT113 Undergraduate   3 credits $1656
Introduction to International Business is designed to provide students with an initial examination of the differences between business within the domestic context and business in the international context. It will also include some exposure to those basic concepts deemed important to an understanding of how inter- national business works. These concepts include: (1) importing (2) exporting (3) political, cultural, and social environment considerations, (4) trade theory (5) government influence on trade, and (6) global management strategy. Freshmen and sophomores only.

Introduction to Leisure Studies
University of Missouri
MOCE#HE327A Undergraduate   3 credits $387
This course examines the history of recreation and the leisure movement; the theories and philosophies of play, recreation, and leisure; and the developmental stages of leisure services to their contemporary status.

Introduction to Management Accounting
Mercy College
MERC#AC121 Undergraduate   3 credits $900
The contribution of accounting to management planning and control; cost behavior patterns; absorption and variable costing; cost-profit-volume analysis; short-range planning and budget preparation; responsibility accounting; performance reporting for cost, profit and investment centers; accounting approaches to special decision making; the use of accounting information in financial statement analysis; and career opportunities in accounting. Prerequisite: AC120.

Introduction to Management Accounting
University of Minnesota
MINN#ACCT3001 Undergraduate 4 credits $400
A broad overview of management accounting as the main information collection and analysis technology of an organization. Topics include analysis of cost-volume-profit relationships, budgeting and analysis of variances from budgeted performance, and issues relating to decentralized organizational design. Prerequisite: ACCT1050.

Introduction to Marketing
Indiana University
INDI#M300 Undergraduate   3 credits $268
An examination of the market economy and marketing institutions in the U.S. Decision making and planning from the manager's point of view; impact of marketing actions from the consumer's point of view. No credit given toward a degree in business. Prerequisite: A200 or A201 and A202.

Introduction to Marketing
University of Minnesota
MINN#GC1551 Undergraduate   4 credits $356
Emphasizes application of the fundamentals of marketing through case study and decision making. Topics: target markets, segmentation analysis, marketing mix, and strategic marketing. Students are placed in various marketing roles (e.g., assistant to the marketing director) and make decisions about pricing, promotion, targeting, international approaches, etc. Answers to the marketing challenges are provided by experts in the field. Emphasis on marketing ethics is maintained throughout the course. Students must indicate whether they want to take the course with the optional videocassette.

Introduction to Marketing
New Hampshire College
NEHA#MKT113 Undergraduate   3 credits $1656
The course examines the basic functions involved in the exchange process designed to meet customer's needs. Such functions include marketing research, product design, promotional activities, distribution, and pricing.

Introduction to Marketing
Thomas Edison State College
THED#OLMAR301 Undergraduate 3 credits $397*
This course presents an introduction to marketing as it relates to contemporary living and society's changing needs. The course examines how a marketing manager interacts with diverse areas of business, as well as basic marketing principles, including product promotion, pricing, distribution and their inter-relationships. Course topics include consumer markets, planning and forecasting, product adoption, wholesaling, retailing, advertising and publicity, pricing strategies, selling and international marketing.
* NJ residents tuition: $33 per credit.

Introduction to MIS
New York Institute of Technology
NYIT#BUS3811 Undergraduate 3 credits $???
The concept of management information systems is introduced and examined. The focus of the course is on the application of spreadsheet and database management systems, as decision support tools, in various functional areas of business. The necessary concepts, such as forecasting, capital budgeting, management reports, etc. will be taught in the context of the case studies. Prerequisites: BUS3801 or CS5645 (except MIS majors).

Introduction to Operations Management
New Hampshire College
NEHA#ADB331 Undergraduate 3 credits $1656
This introductory course in operations and production management considers the evolution of the modern operations function, design of the system supervision scheduling, materials management and the provision of services. Prerequisites: ECO201, ACC102, and MAT220.

Introduction to Retail Merchandising
University of Minnesota
MINN#DHA1211 Undergraduate 4 credits $356
General aspects of retailing, including types of retailers, market research, management, buying, promotion, and trends. Focuses on aspects of retailing careers within the structure of existing retail firms. Students will develop a retail portfolio that will assist them in networking, including opportunities to conduct interviews with practitioners in the field.

Introduction to the Hospitality Industry
Chemeketa Community College
CHEM#HTM100 Undergraduate 3 credits $123
This course is designed to introduce the student to the hospitality industry. It defines the hospitality industry as a single, interrelated industry composed of food and beverage, travel and tourism, lodging, meeting and planning, leisure, and recreation, recreational entertainment, eco and heritage tourism. Emphasis on understanding industry components and their current issues and future trends. Course assess the impact of North America's rapidly changing demographics and lifestyle changes. Economic impact of the hospitality industry discussed. Career opportunities and the service ethics are discussed.

Introduction to the Leisure and Recreation Industry
Chemeketa Community College
CHEM#HTM108 Undergraduate 3 credits $123
An overview of the role of leisure in America. Examines factors influencing leisure; the relationship of leisure to demographics, personality development, health, and the changing lifestyles in American society. Course will examine how leisure plays a central role in how we define who we are, but is often thought of as unimportant. Students will learn how the leisure industries play a critical role in our economy. Discussion of how the development of young children, the success of marriages, the maintenance of intellectual capacity among older people are all critically linked to play.

Introduction to the Supermarket Industry
Rio Salado College
RISA#SPM101 Undergraduate 3 credits $186*
Overview of the supermarket industry from its historical origins to the present. Provides a detailed examination of supermarket economics and reviews basic departmental, merchandising, and advertising operations. Identifies current trends and career opportunities within the industry.
* AZ residents pay $37 per credit.

Introduction to the Travel and Tourism Industry
State University of New York
SUNY#TT130 Undergraduate 3 credits $435*
An introduction to the size and scope of the Travel and Tourism Industry. This course provides a comprehensive overview of the many components that comprise this exciting field. Career options within the worldwide travel and tourism industry will also be explored.
* NY residents tuition: $80 per credit.

Introduction to World Trade
Pace University
PACE#OL701 Undergraduate 3 credits $350
This course focuses on fundamental principles of global trade and is designed for newcomers to this field of study. It briefly reviews theory of world trade and present global trends. It views world trade from a high level taking into perspective the macro environmental factors impacting it: economics, politics, technology, cultural/social, demographics, and physiological. It provides a survey and analysis of international business terms and procedures.

Introductory Accounting 1
State University of New York
SUNY#212054 Undergraduate 4 credits $586*
This course is divided into four modules: Module 1: Provides an introduction to the language of accounting. Introduces the student to forms of business organizations, financial reporting, financial statements, journals, ledgers and the accounting cycle, including year end activities. Module 2: Examines accounting for merchandising activities, including inventory systems. Provides in-depth examination of sole proprietorships, partnerships and corporations. Students also study accounting systems, internal control and audits. Module 3: Examines accounting for assets and liabilities. Module 4: Examines financial statement analysis and the statement of cash flows.
* NY residents tuition: $515

Introductory Accounting 2
State University of New York
SUNY#212064 Undergraduate 4 credits $586*
This course is a continuation of Introductory Accounting 1 (212054) which covers Modules 1-4: Module 5: Examines financial reporting issues, including corporate organizations and stockholders' equity, reporting unusual events and special equity transactions, and special types of liabilities. Module 6: Focuses on managerial accounting topics including accounting for manufacturing operations, measuring unit costs, and cost control. Module 7: Examines cost-volume-profit analysis and increment analysis in decision-making. Module 8: Focuses on three topics: income taxes and their effect on business decisions, operational budgeting, and capital budgeting. Prerequisite: Introductory Accounting 1 or equivalent.
* NY residents tuition: $515

Introductory Accounting Lab
Rio Salado College
RISA#ACC250 Undergraduate 1 credits $62*
Procedural details of accounting for the accumulation of information and generation of reports for internal and external users.
* AZ residents pay $37 per credit.

Issues in International Advertising
The Graduate School of America
TGSA#OM872W Graduate 4 credits $795
The purpose of this course is to provide a comprehensive framework for understanding international advertising. In addition to covering basic principles of international marketing and advertising, the course will focus on the issues involved in advertising across cultures and on the social and ethical issues related to advertising in the developing countries.

Labor and the Economy
Indiana University
INDI#L230 Undergraduate 3 credits $268
Analysis of the political economy of labor and the role of organized labor within it. Emphasis on the effect on workers, unions, and collective bargaining of unemployment, investment policy and changes in technology and corporate structure. Patterns of union political and bargaining responses.

Labor Relations
Strayer University
STRA#BUS405 Undergraduate 4.5 credits $665
Presents the principles of labor-management relations with emphasis on the role of the Federal Labor Relations Authority, the Federal mediation and Conciliation Service, and other third parties under the Civil Service Reform Act of 1978. Compares federal, state, local, and private sector labor laws. Includes the topics of union representation rights and obligations, employee rights, organizing, and election procedures, unfair labor practice, collective bargaining negotiations, mediation impasses, grievances, and arbitration.

Labor Relations and Arbitration
New Hampshire College
NEHA#ADB318 Undergraduate 3 credits $1656
The course examines union-management relationships. Elements of a good union-management contract, the law, and the role of the arbitrator are emphasized.

Leadership and Management Principles
University of Central Florida
FLCE#NUR4932OE91 Graduate 3 credits $1305*
This course stresses scientific theories and principles of leadership and management needed to function in leadership, management, and teaching roles in professional nursing. Application of decision-making process is also covered.
* FL residents pay $129 per credit.

Leadership and Organizational Change
Bellevue University
BELL#LDR651 Graduate 4 credits $1100
This course examines the critical role a leader has in realizing change within complex organizations. Participants are exposed to ideas about how to carry out and manage planned change in complex military, non-profit and corporate organizations and in ambiguous situations. Participants examine models of organizational and situational change and develop a basis from which to analyze, diagnose and act within rapidly changing climates. Planned change also takes place during times of relative tranquillity and must be dealt with through strategic long-term planning tied to organizational objectives.

Leadership and the Process of Change
Walden University
WALD#PSYC8530 Graduate 5 credits $1500
The course will identify and study the prevailing theories of leadership and how they impact on organizations in process of change and transition. The student will review and develop an understanding of the definition of leadership, models of leadership, its impact on the organization, how it is measured and how it might be further developed.

Leadership for Entrepreneurs
Kennesaw State University
KENN#FMV213A Undergraduate 3 credits $149
If you are a mover and shaker, you will benefit from the topics discussed in this workshop. Learn the differences between leadership and managership, how the mentoring process works, tips to succeed as a leader, and workable plans developed by you to become a more effective leader. Learn more about yourself through a Leadership Profile and use this information to develop the skills you already have or will need to move yourself to the top of an organization.

Leadership for Front-Line Employees
Rio Salado College
RISA#TQM200 Undergraduate 2 credits $124*
Methods of traditional management concepts and their application to a quality oriented environment for the front-line employee. Covers planning, goal-setting, problem-solving, motivation, time management, adaptability, flexibility and dependability in a quality setting. Prerequisites: TQM101 or TQM101AA and TQM101AB are recommended.
* AZ residents pay $37 per credit.

Leadership in Formal Organizationals
Bellevue University
BELL#LDR611 Graduate 4 credits $1100
Provides participants an opportunity to explore a variety of effective formal organizational structures and to examine subsystems of power within differing sectors. The essential roles leaders play in directing, empowering, developing and helping commit organizational constituents to mission and vision are examined. Actions of leaders that involve directive and collaborative strategic planning in order to achieve organizational targets are discussed.

Leadership in Public Organizations
Christopher Newport University
CHNE#GOVT401 Undergraduate 3 credits $993
A study of modern management strategies and their applicability to the public and non-profit sectors. The course covers such topics as planned change, organization development, management by objectives, democratic management, interpersonal interaction, and reinventing and restructuring government. Prerequisite: GOVT371 recommended.

Leadership Models for Organizations
Bellevue University
BELL#LDR641 Graduate 4 credits $1100
The focus of this course is to explore leadership behavior models that exist in organizations today and to look at emerging models of leadership in light of the rapid change occurring in the structure of organizations heading toward the millennium. This course starts with what is "out there" today in industrial, military and non-profit sectors, and outlines leadership in the context of behavioral and organizational models evolving for the future. The course takes a dual perspective: first, what leadership is from an individual perspective and second, what impact those behaviors have on organizations as a whole.

Leadership Strategy and Policy
Bellevue University
BELL#LDR671 Graduate 4 credits $1100
This course describes leader roles in the creation and maintenance of business, military and non-profit organizational strategy and policy in organizations. Major strategic planning tools are discussed and their use by global leaders and commanders are examined. Emphasis is placed on global aspects of strategy and policy, including cross-cultural issues, global competitiveness, partnerships and threats, and strategic alliances. Emerging themes in strategy and policy are considered.

Leadership Tools for Successful Project Management
The Graduate School of America
TGSA#OM885W Graduate 4 credits $795
Effective project management is a key activity for achieving organizational goals on time and within budget. Allocating and scheduling tasks and resources so that projects move reliably toward completion are critical management skills. Using readings, online discussions and practical exercises, you will gain in this course a command of systematic processes supported by computer-based tools that will enhance your skills in managing projects effectively.

Leadership/Human Relations
Barstow Community College
BARS#BADM53 Undergraduate .5 credits $???
Leadership and human relations programs which emphasize common basic life values. Examination of different forms of leadership related to problems identified by participants. May be taken four times for credit.

Leading the High Performance Organization
The Graduate School of America
TGSA#OM844W Graduate 4 credits $795
Leadership effectiveness is a critical determinant of both the individual performance of the manager and the performance of the organization. This course provides the knowledge and skills necessary to create and lead a high performance organization. You will be encouraged to assess your own leadership style and to develop a leadership action plan.

Learning Organizations in Practice
Marylhurst College
MARY#MGT564 Undergraduate 3 credits $651
Any time you learn a new skill, it takes time and practice. the learning challenge is to become aware of your current skills, while experimenting with alternative ones. This course takes up where MGT 463/563 left off -- building in support from others, deepening your knowledge of learning organization concepts, and providing a forum for practicing your new skills. Work in facilitated groups to apply mental model skills to each other's case studies, and learn how to tackle the tough problems as they really emerge in organizations. Prerequisite: MGT463/563.

Legal & Ethical Issues in Management
Bellevue University
BELL#MGTC450 Undergraduate 3 credits $750
Management's responsibility to customers, employees and society at large. How successful managers maintain awareness of key issues in business legislation, regulation and ethical standards. EEO/AA, staffing, T&D, labor unions, consumer protection, and environmental issues. Planning, presenting and developing an executive report.

Legal, Ethical, and Regulatory Issues in Business
Rio Salado College
RISA#GBS205 Undergraduate 3 credits $186*
Legal theories, ethical issues and regulatory climate affecting business policies and decisions.
* AZ residents pay $37 per credit.

Loan Servicing
Waukesha County Technical College
WAUK#115101001 Undergraduate 3 credits $193
This specialized course examines how mortgage lenders handle mortgage loans from the time a loan is closed until the final payment is made. The course focuses on legal aspects and actual procedures used in the daily operations of the loan servicing function.

Logistic Support Analysis
Brevard Community College
BREV#ETI2203 Undergraduate 3 credits $435
LSA principles and techniques: engineering process interfaces including reliability, maintainability, system support, requirements determination, trade-off analyses, level of repair analysis, reliability-centered maintenance, life-cycle cost and tailoring procedures are discussed.

Making Managerial Decisions
New York Institute of Technology
NYIT#BUS3803 Undergraduate 3 credits $???
Quantitative techniques for managerial decisions will be covered. These techniques include decision theory, linear programming, and inventory models. Prerequisites: MATH3019, BUS3802.

Management
State University of New York
SUNY#BADM249 Undergraduate 3 credits $1038*
A second-year level course designed for students with a special interest in management. The course assimilates previous learning and presents more advanced techniques, examines the most modern and advanced managerial and administrative principles and theories, and applies these to solutions of incidents, case studies, and actual business situations. Prerequisite: BADM or permission of the department.
* NY residents tuition: $137 per credit

Management (Internal) Auditing
Strayer University
STRA#ACC420 Undergraduate 4.5 credits $665
Examines the efforts of the internal auditor to assist management in effective use of available resources to achieve stated goals. Covers the foundation of internal auditing and areas of operational auditing. Reviews financial statements and administration of the internal auditing department. Prerequisite: MAT 300 or equivalent.

Management Across Cultures
National American University
NAAM#MT430D Undergraduate 4.5 credits $900
This course gives the student a sense of the diversity of cultures and business practices throughout the world. The students will study: stages of adjustment experience during exposure to other cultures, international workplace issues, global management across cultures.

Management and Analysis of Quantity Food
Pennsylvania State University
PENN#DSM260 Undergraduate 4 credits $460
Principles of management applied to menu planning, purchasing, food and labor costing, and analysis for the institutional food service setting. Prerequisite: DSM250; approval by a Dietetic program adviser.

Management and Leadership I
Rio Salado College
RISA#MGT229 Undergraduate 3 credits $186*
Covers management concepts and applications for business, industry, and government organizations.
* AZ residents $37 per credit.

Management and Organizational Behavior
Western Illinois University
WEIL#MAN349 Undergraduate 3 credits $795*
Is a comprehensive and integrated introduction to the principles of management. The course emphasizes the management functions of planning, organizing, and control as well as such behavioral processes as communication, leadership, and motivation. A major objective is to provide you with the necessary information to enhance your ability to perform effectively in a managerial position.
* IL residents tuition: $88 per credit.

Management and Supervision
State University of New York
SUNY#PT404 Undergraduate 2 credits $692*
Problem-solving exercises and case studies, including management concepts relative to administration within the health-care system. Prerequisite: PT senior or permission of Instructor.
* NY residents tuition: $137 per credit

Management Communication
Strayer University
STRA#BUS531 Undergraduate 4.5 credits $665
Analyzes the nature of effective and dysfunctional forms of communication within an organizational environment. Covers interpersonal, group and presentation methods.

Management Essentials
Bellevue University
BELL#MISC300 Undergraduate 5 credits $1250
This course provides students with a foundation for managing themselves and others. In addition to personal productivity and effectiveness, the course covers the five functions necessary for managing others: planning, directing, organizing, staffing and leading.

Management Foundations
Marylhurst College
MARY#MGT500B Undergraduate 3 credits $651
This course provides students with an overview of the following areas: Strategic Planning, Marketing, Operations, Human Resources, and Finance and Accounting. An emphasis will be placed on developing an integrated view of these functions, i.e., how they fit together in achieving the overall goals of the organization.

Management Information Systems
Golden Gate University
GOLD#CIS125 Undergraduate 3 credits $1164
Studies the managerial aspects of Information Systems in business organizations. Emphasis is placed on the planning, implementation, evaluation, budgeting and management of information systems. Emerging technological trends will be explored. Prerequisite: CIS1 or CIS10 or CIS100A-G or consent of the Department Chair.

Management Information Systems
Golden Gate University
GOLD#CIS301 Graduate 3 credits $1404
Provides a broad survey of information technology in current business conditions. Gives you a basic understanding of the most relevant aspects of information technology. You will also gain an understanding of the differences between a data processing system, a management information system, a decision support system, office automation and an expert system. This course may be substituted for another 300-level Information Systems course for students majoring in Information Systems or related fields with the consent of the Department Chair.

Management Information Systems
Southwest Missouri State University
MOSW#CIS661 Graduate 3 credits $???
This course will be part of the core requirements for an online Master of Science in Administrative Studies currently under development. It presents an overview of managerial applications of information technology to increase organizational effectiveness. Students will discuss the use of information technology to enhance organizational intelligence, cooperative work, organizational competitive advantage, inter-organizational computing, and the role of technology in the transforming industries. Case methods will be used to illustrate information management and planning approaches in a variety of industries.

Management Information Systems
New Jersey Institute of Technology
NJIT#MIS545 Undergraduate 3 credits $1143*
Tools and techniques of management information systems and how they can be used to improve the quality of management decisions. Includes computer-based solutions to management problems in office automation, budgeting, communications, and decision support, major features of hardware and software computer system components and how to design a system, and technical tools ranging from flowchart and decision tables to automated design. Optional: 15 video lessons of 60 minutes each.
* NJ residents: $184/semester hour.

Management Information Systems
Nova Southeastern University
NOVA#MMIS620 Graduate 3 credits $1,110
The application of information system concepts to the collection, retention, and dissemination of information for management planning and decision-making. Issues such as personnel selection, budgeting, policy development, and organizational interfacing are discussed. Conceptual foundations and planning and development of management information systems. The role of MIS in an organization and the fit between the system and the organization.

Management Information Systems
Nova Southeastern University
NOVA#MMIS691 Graduate 3 credits $1,110
This seminar will focus on the professor's current research interests. Prerequisite: prior consent of instructor and program director.

Management Information Systems
State University of New York
SUNY#273654 Undergraduate 4 credits $586*
Explore the impact of advances in Information Technology in the context of organizational decision-making and the potential of an effective management information system to contribute to organizational learning, to be a source of competitive advantage, and to assist an organization in a global arena. This course focuses on understanding the use and management of information as an organizational resource. Prerequisites: An understanding of computer information systems and of basic management principles either through prior study or experience, and be prepared for upper-level course work.
* NY residents tuition: $515

Management of Information Technology
New Hampshire College
NEHA#CIS430 Undergraduate 3 credits $1656
The course focuses on demonstrating a comprehension of the principles and concepts involved in the management of organizational information systems resources. It includes CIO functions, information systems planning, legal and professional issues, and strategic impact of information systems. Prerequisite: CIS415.

Management of Promotion
New York Institute of Technology
NYIT#BUS3405 Undergraduate   3 credits $???
A firm's promotional efforts focus on developing and managing marketing communications. This course studies the planning and implementation of demand stimulating promotion, i.e., advertising, personal selling, sales promotion and publicity/public relations. Promotion is seen as a key element of the marketing mix which contributes to an organization's cohesive marketing strategy. Prerequisite: BUS3400.

Management Science
Eastern Oregon University
EAOR#BA366 Undergraduate   5 credits $400
Management decision processes utilizing mathematical models and computer software. Models include mathematical programming, decision theory, simulation and others. Prerequisites: MATH241, STAT315, STAT316.

Management Science
New Jersey Institute of Technology
NJIT#EM602 Undergraduate   3 credits $1143*
Linear programming: formulation, methodology, and application, the transportation problem; the assignment problem; Markov chains and their applications in decision making; queuing systems; deterministic and stochastic inventory models. Optional: 13 video lessons of 180 minutes in length. Prerequisites: undergraduate calculus and probability and statistics.
* NJ residents: $184/semester hour.

Management Theory
Strayer University
STRA#BUS541 Undergraduate   4.5 credits $665
Discusses the modern theory and practice of coordinating an organization's resources in order to accomplish organizational goals. Examines management by categorizing functions performed, roles assigned, and skills required. Incorporates topics such as creative leadership and proven quality management theories.

Management Theory & Applications
Golden Gate University
GOLD#MGT310 Graduate   3 credits $1404
Reviews the basic functions of management planning, organizing, staffing, leading and controlling and applies them to the executive level. Gives a management perspective to management theory, decision processes, conflict management, risk-taking and problem-solving in the internal and external environment. Instruction includes guest lecturers, case studies, historic and contemporary management readings, a research paper and presentation. Full discussion expected. Recommended proficiency: MGT205 (or MGT140).

Managerial Accounting
Brevard Community College
BREV#ACG2071 Undergraduate 3 credits $435
Accounting as it applies to managerial theory and practice; cost accounting concepts and relationships; forecasting and budgeting; business information requirements. (The accounting courses meet A.S. requirements and/or A.A. Degree elective courses. Many upper division Business Administration colleges recommend that these courses be completed at the community college level.) Prerequisite: Financial Accounting.

Managerial Accounting
Edmonds Community College
EDMO#ACCT203 Undergraduate 5 credits $260
Managerial Accounting (ACCT 203) represents an introduction to managerial accounting procedures and concepts. The course is designed for students who have successfully completed an initial course in Financial Accounting. Prerequisite: Successful completion of the first quarter of Financial Accounting.

Managerial Accounting
New York Institute of Technology
NYIT#BUS3501 Undergraduate   3 credits $???
Special emphasis is placed on the collection and interpretation of data for managerial decision-making purposes. A study is made of cost concepts used in planning and control, cost-profit-volume analysis, and budgeting. This course carries no credit for the public accounting major. Prerequisite: BUS3511.

Managerial Accounting
Strayer University
STRA#ACC560 Undergraduate   4.5 credits $665
Covers the creation, use, and interpretation of internal accounting data and information. Emphasizes the managerial functions of cost control reporting, budgeting, profit planning, and projections used in decision-making. Prerequisite: ACC100 or equivalent.

Managerial Accounting
The Graduate School of America
TGSA#OM868W Graduate   4 credits $795
This course examines management accounting as part of a company's quantitative information system. Emphasis is placed on the role of accounting in decision making. Importance is also placed on the business planning and control from the managerial point of view.

Managerial Accounting & Control Systems
Marylhurst College
MARY#FIN510 Undergraduate   6 credits $651
This course will provide a fundamental understanding of an accounting and financial information system and how such a system interfaces with and supports financial and economic planning within the company. Prerequisite: MGT500.

Managerial Accounting (Accounting III)
Strayer University
STRA#ACC110 Undergraduate 4.5 credits $665
Covers corporation long-term and investments; departmental and branch accounting; accounting for manufacturing costs, budgetary control and standard cost systems, income taxes and their effect on business decisions; the statements and analysis; and financial statement analysis. Prerequisite: ACC105.

Managerial Communication
The Graduate School of America
TGSA#OM827W Graduate 4 credits $795
This course emphasizes the role of communication in effective management. Skills in counseling, interviewing, conducting meetings, and using groupware and presentation software will be included.

Managerial Communications
Golden Gate University
GOLD#MGT300 Graduate 3 credits $1404
Develops skills needed for individual effectiveness as a manager, including clear and persuasive written and oral communication, interpersonal skills, and business problem-solving and analysis. Stresses the importance of your presentation skills — both written and oral. Case material with examples drawn from a wide variety of business settings. Prerequisites: ACCTG201 (or ACCTG1A and ACCTG1B), ECON202 (or ECON1 and ECON2) and FI203 (or FI100). (An MBA core course to be taken at the beginning of the Advanced Program).

Managerial Economics
New Jersey Institute of Technology
NJIT#ECON565 Undergraduate 3 credits $1143*
Managerial economics combines traditional economic analysis with the tools and techniques of statistical analyses and decision sciences. Optional: 14 video lessons of 60 minutes in length plus additional 60 minute recitations.
* NJ residents: $184/semester hour.

Managerial Economics
Western Illinois University
WEIL#ECO332 Undergraduate 3 credits $795*
Focuses on the application of economic principles that business firm managers use for making decisions. This course covers topics such as demand, revenue, production, costs, supply, pricing, and competition. You will learn how decisions affect profits and will study the tools and concepts necessary to maximize those profits. Prerequisite: Economics 232.
* IL residents tuition: $88 per credit.

Managerial Finance
Marylhurst College
MARY#FIN420B Undergraduate 3 credits $651
This course provides an overview of the financial processes of organizations. Topics include preparing operating cash and capital budges, interpreting financial statements and understanding appropriate types and uses of financing. Prerequisites: ACT 211/212/213 or equivalent.

Managerial Finance and Accounting
Bellevue University
BELL#MISC360 Undergraduate 4 credits $1000
This course explores the key elements of finance and accounting used by managers to support long- and short-term decision, including balancing sheets, income statements, cash flow, budgeting, activity-based costing, performance measures and compensation issues.

Managerial Issues in Hazardous Materials
Western Illinois University
WEIL#SAF478 Undergraduate 3 credits $795*
Examines regulatory issues, hazard analysis, multi-agency contingency planning, response personnel, multi-agency response resources, agency policies, procedures and implementation, public education and emergency information systems, health and safety, command post dynamics, strategic and tactical considerations, recovery and termination procedures, and program evaluation.
* IL residents tuition: $88 per credit.

Managerial Leadership
State University of New York
SUNY#214624 Undergraduate 4 credits $586*
Learn about the nature of leadership, particularly the issue of leadership effectiveness. Review theory as well as guidelines and recommendations for improving managerial leadership effectiveness. Topics include the nature of managing and leading, behavioral indicators of leadership ability and effectiveness, theories of leadership, and sources of power and influence. Students will have the opportunity to integrate previous learning about management, administration, leadership and organizations. Prerequisite: Organizational Behavior (114614) or equivalent. Students should also have a general knowledge of how organizations are structured and of the significant issues impacting organizations today.
* NY residents tuition: $515

Managing and Motivating Generation 'X'
The Graduate School of America
TGSA#OM831W Graduate 4 credits $795
This course provides a clear understanding of who 'Generation X'ers' are and why their dominance in the entry-level workforce today has created a major management challenge. The Generation X work ethic, expectations and values will be explored and compared to that of the Baby Boomers and other previous generations. A practical five-point model for managing and motivating Generation X will then be proposed and depicted through case examples in leading companies. Learners will be asked to assess the quality and consistency of this model's application in real organizations using standard gaps analysis techniques.

Managing in Organizations
Western Illinois University
WEIL#MAN420 Undergraduate 6 credits $1590*
Studies the systems approach as a way of understanding and managing complex organizations. A central theme of this IUC course is that organizational processes--rather than offices, groups, and functions--are the proper primary focus. The systems approach treats interdependence among process inputs as a given and recognizes this interdependence as a major source of organizational complexity. Recognition of these interdependencies is emphasized in the two written assignments for the course. These assignments require you to integrate course material while answering questions about organizations.
* IL residents tuition: $88 per credit.

Managing in the Wired Organization
Marylhurst College
MARY#MGT454 Undergraduate 3 credits $651
How does contemporary information technology affect the structure, role, scope and tasks of management? What ripple effects does the organization experience with the integration of technology and how does this change the manager's role and focus in the organization? This course looks at the dual challenge of successfully living with the changes technology brings.

Managing Information and Communications Technology
The Graduate School of America
TGSA#OM843W Graduate 4 credits $795
Today's most powerful business resource is information. Managers need to be able to make knowledgeable decisions about technologies. Through readings, online discussions and the analysis of business scenarios, you will gain hands-on experience and skill in evaluating, planning and implementing technology projects. This course is intended for those who are not technology experts.

Managing Organizational Change
New Hampshire College
NEHA#ADB322 Undergraduate 3 credits $1656
This course focuses on the effective management of human resources during the process of change. It emphasizes change management as a tool for survival, growth, increasing productivity and conflict management in the complex and volatile business environment of today and in the future. Change in an international environment is included. Prerequisites: ADB215.

Managing Process Technology
University of Colorado-Boulder
COBO#MBAT6450 Undergraduate 3 credits $240
Examines the critical role of technological process innovation in the global competitiveness of the firm. Provides students with tools and techniques for managing process technology.

Managing Security Systems
State University of New York
SUNY#CRJ302002 Undergraduate 3 credits $1038*
The course introduces students to loss control theory with an analysis of threat models to develop comprehensive protection plans for organizations. This course provides the theoretical foundation for the more advanced segments of the Security Systems program with a study of the theory, design, programming, management, and operations of security systems. The computer as an integrating technology is emphasized to achieve effectiveness as well as efficiency of protection performance. Prerequisites: Criminal Investigation or equivalent and Criminal Law or equivalent.
* NY residents tuition: $137 per credit

Market Research
New Hampshire College
NEHA#MKT630 Undergraduate 3 credits $1656
Addresses identification of the value of research as well as identification of the problem to be resolved. Numerous mathematical analysis techniques will be incorporated into the course as well as research design issues. Prerequisite: MKT500 (Marketing Strategies) and MBA510 (Quantitative Analysis for Decision Making).

Marketing
Heriot-Watt University
HERI#04 Graduate 4 credits $???
In recent years marketing has become an increasingly important force in the strategic and operational life of an organization. As a result, marketing management has become intimately linked to strategic decisions made at higher organizational levels and with the operational decisions taken in other departments. These internal linkages, together with direct links to the external market and the competitive environment, make marketing an important field of study.

Marketing
Kansas City Kansas Community College
KACI#BU113 Undergraduate 3 credits $324*
Students will learn how marketing managers develop strategy and make decisions concerning pricing, distribution, promotion, and products. Concepts are presented by tapping internet, CD-ROM, and multimedia resources. The student will watch and assess video programs which present basic marketing concepts by utilizing real-world case studies.
* KS residents pay $40 per credit.

Marketing
Marylhurst College
MARY#MKT438B Undergraduate 6 credits $1301
Explore the foundation of classical marketing paradigms, the dynamic tensions between real-world constraints and marketing theory, as well as contemporary developments in the art and craft of marketing. Case studies and practical problem solving for today's marketing manager will be featured.

Marketing Grain and Livestock Products
Western Illinois University
WEIL#AGR442G Undergraduate 3 credits $795*
Examines the trading of futures contracts as a basis hedge. Introductory material includes basic jargon, the use of hedging by agribusiness, and a pricing-strategy decision framework. A comparison of basis hedging and multiple hedging is considered in the context of business objectives, evaluation criteria, market risk, and profit potential.
* IL residents tuition: $88 per credit.

Marketing Hospitality Services
UCLA
UCLA#X491B Undergraduate 4 credits $500
With an emphasis on strategic use of advertising, promotion, merchandising, pricing, and public relations to increase the hospitality industry's market share, this online course covers such specific issues as the intangibility of services and the seasonality of business; development of marketing plans, complete with mission statement, objectives, and tactics to achieve objectives; the structure of the lodging industry; analysis of demand; development of sales and action plans to reach corporate decision makers.

Marketing I
Northwest College
NOCO#MH169B Undergraduate 5 credits $???
The philosophy of marketing is introduced. The marketing environment, consumer and business markets, demographics and marketing research are covered. Special attention is given to the product: development, product-mix strategies, brands, packaging and other product features.

Marketing II
Northwest College
NOCO#MT230 Undergraduate 5 credits $???
Topics covered relate to the marketing mix: price, distribution, product and promotion. Emphasis will be on pricing strategies, channels of distribution and the promotional programs. Wholesaling, retailing, personal selling, advertising and public relations are covered. Prerequisite: MT220.

Marketing Management
Golden Gate University
GOLD#MKT300 Graduate 3 credits $1404
Focuses on marketing management and problem-solving. You will learn methods for managing product positioning, pricing, distribution and external communications. You will learn about customer behavior, demand determination and marketing research. Emphasis is on developing fully integrated marketing programs. The case method is used.

Marketing Management
Northwest College
NOCO#MT232 Undergraduate 3 credits $???
Decision making in marketing is discussed. Each case studied is designed to bring an important and difficult marketing concept to life. Students will observe the marketplace and reflect on their own past experiences as consumers to make decisions. Prerequisite: MT230 and MT231.

Marketing Principles
State University of New York
SUNY#212414 Undergraduate 4 credits $586*
Develop a strong, conceptual framework for the understanding and application of the principles of marketing in this introductory survey. Marketing is viewed as a complete system of action in the complex field of business and the socio-economic system. Topics include modern marketing, markets, products, price systems, distribution structures, promotional activities, marketing arithmetic, and planning and evaluating the marketing effort. Using a case study approach, apply readings to real world marketing problems.
* NY residents tuition: $515

Marketing Principles
Western Illinois University
WEIL#FIN327 Undergraduate 3 credits $795*
Studies the activities, people, and institutions involved in getting goods from producer to consumer. Course objectives include developing your ability in problem-solving concepts, using models in the marketing field, and evaluating decision-making techniques in marketing management and planning. From the study of the basic marketing mix elements through current marketing and social trends, this course enables you to realize your objectives.
* IL residents tuition: $88 per credit.

Marketing Research
City University
CITY#MK386 Undergraduate 5 qu. credits $785
An introduction to research methods utilized in marketing environments with an emphasis on the managerial design, application and interpretation of marketing research.

Marketing Research
Northwest College
NOCO#MT231 Undergraduate 3 credits $???
This course emphasizes the problem-oriented nature of marketing research and investigates how marketing research activities are implemented. Students will study sampling theory, questionnaire design and an overview of acquiring data. Prerequisite: MH267 and MT230.

Marketing Research
New York Institute of Technology
NYIT#BUS3406 Undergraduate 3 credits $???
Research activity in the field of marketing, methods of data collection and analysis thereof, quantitative techniques in marketing, the role of the computer in marketing research, control and evaluation of the marketing function. Prerequisite: BUS3400 (or HT4860; not offered online).

Marketing Research
State University of New York
SUNY#214924 Undergraduate 4 credits $586*
Develop a conceptual framework for the understanding and application of the principles, skills and techniques used in marketing research. Topics include marketing problem identification, sources of secondary data, marketing decision-making and research planning, sampling, experimentation, measurement concepts, data collection, analysis and report preparation. Case study analysis enables students to apply the various research concepts in a marketing arena. Investigate data analysis opportunities. Develop a marketing research proposal for a real life situation or problem. Prerequisites: Statistics (112134) and Marketing Principles (112414) or equivalents.
* NY residents tuition: $515

Marketing Research & Communication
Bellevue University
BELL#IBMC330 Undergraduate 3 credits $750
A course that provides instruction in assessing typical marketing problems and problem-solving, as well as oral and written presentation of research results.

Marketing Strategies
New Hampshire College
NEHA#MKT500 Undergraduate 3 credits $1656
A study of the process of searching for, and identifying, prospective opportunities for establishing effective relationships with markets, and of the techniques of marketing. Background preparation: three credit hours in marketing, or equivalent.

Marketing Strategy
Bellevue University
BELL#MBA652 Graduate 3 credits $825
Examines the development of marketing strategy from a practical managerial perspective.

Marketing Strategy
City University
CITY#MK400 Undergraduate 5 qu. credits $785
This course investigates a structured approach to strategic market planning and toward developing sustainable competitive advantages. Models are developed, principles are applied to actual companies, and to the investment decision-making process.

Marketing Strategy and Practice
The Graduate School of America
TGSA#OM814W Graduate 4 credits $795
Marketing is a core business process that all managers must understand. The objective of this course is to provide a broad, practical understanding of marketing strategy and practice. As part of the course, you will be have the opportunity to develop a marketing plan for your organization.

Material Management II
Brevard Community College
BREV#ETI2228 Undergraduate 3 credits $435
Continues principles and methods of inventory management and material management and the introduction of supplier management, stores and receiving, general material and professional standards; and government purchasing. Prerequisite: ETI2227.

Materials Management I
Brevard Community College
BREV#ETI2227 Undergraduate 3 credits $435
Principles and methods related to purchasing operation, inventory control and materials management from inbound raw materials to outbound finished goods. Covers role of purchasing and materials management, operating procedures, make-or-buy-decision and supply sources.

Math for Business
Lansing Community College
LANS#MATH117 Undergraduate 4 credits $420
This course surveys math applications in business. Applications representing management, marketing, finance, accounting, and statistics are used. Analysis of situations in business and correct use of business theory is emphasized in addition to accuracy in math. In this class you will use the math related to stocks and bonds, loans, payroll, prices, and credit. You will also use technology, including the Internet for up-to-the-minute information, and computer spreadsheets for calculations.

Mathematical Concepts and Techniques for Business
New Hampshire College
NEHA#MAT121 Undergraduate 3 credits $1656
An anthology for business majors, this course enriches and augments the techniques developed in MAT120. Special attention is given to developing the topics using business examples and employing calculators and computer packages wherever possible. Topics covered will include matrices and their application, introduction to linear programming, the summation notation, introduction to calculus applied to polynomials. Prerequisite: MAT120 or MAT150.

Media Ethics
New School for Social Research
NEWS#3939 Undergraduate 3 credits $455
Has media ethics become an oxymoron? This course will examine the key ethical issues confronting journalists, new media professionals and others working in today's media industry. To provide background and context, the class will first examine the traditional rights and obligations the media has had in this country as conferred by the First Amendment. We'll also discuss the specific duties journalists have been expected to carry out as part of a functioning democracy. We will then spend time focusing on three major ethical problem areas.

Media Management and Leadership
New School for Social Research
NEWS#3938   Undergraduate   3 credits $455
Dramatic changes in technology and in the media's role in converging technologies require new management and leadership techniques and paradigms. This course aims to give students a survey of some of the latest management and leadership theories, including those encouraging a new sense of social responsibility. It also gives students the opportunity to apply these theories to a number of different competitive, structural, motivational, strategic, and organizational issues in the media world, by writing original case studies and solving problems in existing case studies.

Meeting and Conference Management
New York University
NEYO#X659560   Undergraduate   3.5 CEU $550
This survey course provides a solid understanding of the numerous tasks that go into making a meeting successful. In this course, you learn the importance of clear meeting objectives, how to apply principles of adult learning to program development, and how the program impacts your selection of a site. Assignments clarify each step of the planning process. Topics include: creating meeting goals/objectives; setting timelines; selecting and contracting for sites, food and beverage, transportation, and a variety of other suppliers; registering participants; and managing on-site tasks.

Meeting and Convention Management
Chemeketa Community College
CHEM#HTM126   Undergraduate   3 credits $123
This course covers the management and operations of the convention and meetings market of the hospitality and tourism industry. Includes an introduction to the meetings industry, promotional activities, negotiations for meeting services, convention market salesmanship, customer service, and convention servicing. Facilities, technology and media are discussed.

Merchandise Planning and Control
State University of New York
SUNY#FM121   Undergraduate   3 credits $1038*
Provides an understanding of the concepts and calculations necessary in successful merchandising, and familiarizes students with the terminology in operating statements, retail method of inventory, planning seasonal purchases, methods of figuring markups, turnover, stock-sales ratios, open-to-buy, markdowns, and terms of sale.
* NY residents tuition: $137 per credit.

Microcomputer Accounting Systems
Great Basin College
GRBA#ACC220   Undergraduate   3 credits $186*
This course is an introduction to actual computerized accounting systems used in the business world. Emphasis is on the application of basic accounting principles using a case-study approach. ACCPAC Simply Accounting, a commercial software package, is used for the course. After loading the software on their own computer, students work on their own, turning in hard copies of assigned problems each week. The course is a hands-on application of accounting principles learned in other courses.
* NV residents tuition: $43 per credit.

Microcomputer Applications in Business I
Strayer University
STRA#CIS107   Undergraduate   4.5 credits $665
Explores various types of software available for more efficient business and personal management. Covers the use of word-processing software and hardware, and incorporates specific applications. Covers the principles of the electronic spreadsheet, specific applications of spreadsheet models, and the practical applications of spreadsheet use.

Microcomputer Applications in Business II
Strayer University
STRA#CIS108   Undergraduate   4.5 credits $665
Covers the formulation, preparation, execution and presentation of graphic software to enhance business communications and presentations. Introduces the Internet and the World Wide Web. Topics covered include navigating, searching, and exploring the Web. Prerequisite: CIS105.

Microcomputer Business Software
Kansas City Kansas Community College
KACI#BU111   Undergraduate   3 credits $324*
This course covers the concepts, design and implementation of five Microsoft software packages on the microcomputer. Windows 95 will be explored in detail. Word Processing will be introduced as a part of the course. The student will also learn how to develop a variety of management and financial models using the electronic spreadsheet. The value of the electronic spreadsheet in performing "what if" analysis will also be explored. The student will learn about and create databases.
* KS residents pay $40 per credit.

MIS for Planning and Control
UCLA
UCLA#X418G   Undergraduate   4 credits $500
This online course covers conceptual approaches to the development and implementation of computer-based information systems for managerial planning and control in private and government organizations. It examines business, managerial, and organizational factors; technical and design considerations, trends, and approaches; and types of applications in use.

MIS Operations & Planning
New Jersey Institute of Technology
NJIT#MIS645   Undergraduate   3 credits $1143*
The management of information processing resources, including: role of information processing, estimates of personnel resources and budgets, integration of corporate and MIS plans, organizational alternatives for MIS departments and support staffs, management of computer operations, equipment and general software acquisitions, integration of personal computers, minicomputers, and mainframes, and security and controls. This course is part of graduate certificate in MIS and Health Care. Prerequisite: NJIT#MIS545. Optional: 14 video lessons of 120 minutes each.
* NJ residents: $184/semester hour.

Multinational Corporate Finance
New Hampshire College
NEHA#INT336 Undergraduate 3 credits $1656
This course emphasizes aspects of financial planning for corporations with overseas operations. The sources and uses of corporate funds abroad are evaluated including an analysis of the criteria for choices among alternative foreign investments. The effects of international corporate financial planning are examined including such factors as the characteristics of foreign money and capital markets, international financial institutions, exchange rate changes, currency restrictions, tax regulations and accounting practices. Prerequisite: FIN320.

Negotiation
Heriot-Watt University
HERI#12 Graduate 4 credits $???
Management requires negotiating skills. Suppliers, customers and colleagues are unlikely to forego their own interest merely because someone else thinks that they ought to. Nor are important decisions likely to be agreed upon without some form of negotiation between those able to influence the shape of the decisions or their impact. Negotiation is one of several means available to managers to assist in the making of decisions.

New Information Technologies
New York University
NEYO#Y26607401 Undergraduate 4 credits $450
This course reviews the older technologies of radio and TV and covers newer ones such as satellites, interactivity, computer-generated information sources, video-texts, slow-scan telecommunicating, fiber optics, and points ahead to new developments on the horizon. Students gain familiarity with these new technologies and their capabilities for communications in the present and future.

New Product Management
New York Institute of Technology
NYIT#BUS3904 Undergraduate 3 credits $???
Techniques and practices applied to conceiving, developing, launching, and management of new products. An in-depth evaluation of the life cycle concept will analyze various stages and how careful planning and management can extend it. The product management concept and its effectiveness as a management tool will also be studied. Prerequisite: BUS3400.

Non-Profit Accounting
Eastern Oregon University
EAOR#BA420 Undergraduate 3 credits $240
This course is an in-depth examination of the principles, procedures, and theory applicable to accounting for not-for-profit organizations. Types of organizations covered include state and local governments, hospitals, colleges, health-welfare and other non-profit organizations.

Non-profit/Municipal Accounting
Strayer University
STRA#ACC410 Undergraduate 4.5 credits $665
Analyzes accounting procedures peculiar to non-profit organizations and municipalities. Illustrates statements commonly prepared for each type of fund and account group. Encompasses recent reporting changes as a result of Federal and State revenue sharing. Discusses recent GASB and GAAP rulings as they relate to non-profit and governmental accounting. Prerequisite: ACC305.

Office Automation Concepts
Rio Salado College
RISA#OAS250 Undergraduate 3 credits $186*
Basic concepts of word/information processing; understanding systems approach to communication; measurement and control; future dimensions of word processing.
* AZ residents $37 per credit.

Office Automation Systems
Nova Southeastern University
NOVA#MMIS622 Graduate 3 credits $1,110
This course focuses on strategies for utilizing technology to handle the information used in the office to improve the quantity, content, and format of work performed. Topics include the design and implementation of an office automation system; strategies for successful end-user computing; OA applications including electronic mail and voice mail; windowing; multitasking; computer conferencing; computer supported cooperative work; project management software; and decision support programs. The impact of ISDN on the office environment.

Office Communications
Greenville Technical College
GRTE#OST234 Undergraduate 3 credits $381*
This course integrates composition skills and grammar skills which are necessary in the preparation of business correspondence and report writing. Pre-requisite: OST134 or ENG165 or ENG101.
* NC residents pay $48 per credit.

Office Procedures I
Eastern Oregon University
EAOR#OADM261 Undergraduate 5 credits $400
Study and application of the principles, procedures, and tools necessary to establish and utilize administrative and office services with emphasis on the professional requirements, personnel, office equipment and other office procedures. Prerequisite: OADM121 (Keyboarding).

Office Procedures I
Greenville Technical College
GRTE#OST141 Undergraduate 3 credits $381*
This is an introductory course to a variety of office procedures and tasks using business equipment, systems, and procedures. Pre-requisite: OST105 (Keyboarding) and OST134 (Office Communications).
* NC residents pay $48 per credit.

Office Procedures II
Eastern Oregon University
EAOR#OADM262 Undergraduate 5 credits $400
Study and application of administrative support services with emphasis on travel and conference responsibilities, organizing business data, financial and legal reports. Prerequisite: OADM261.

Operations Management
Bellevue University
BELL#MGTC440 Undergraduate 3 credits $750
This course expands upon the basic managerial functions, integrating them to modern operations management. Students study production design for goods and services, process design including process flow and plant layout, planning and scheduling to include facilities decisions, and workforce management to include work measurement and job design.

Operations Management
City University
CITY#BSM405 Undergraduate 5 qu. credits $785
Production management in the manufacturing and service environments. Planning and controlling systems as well as continuous improvement of existing systems will be examined. Special emphasis will be given to the use of cost accounting information to improve efficiency and product quality. Specific topics covered include: total quality management; activity-based management; materials resource planning; and cost-volume profit. Prerequisite: Strongly recommended: BSC400, BSC401 and BSC402 or equivalents.

Operations Management
State University of New York
SUNY#214204 Undergraduate 4 credits $586*
Study those activities and processes which combine to produce goods and services. Students bring to bear a number of analytical tools to resolve challenges faced by managers as they plan, organize and control the operations of the firm. In the context of this course, the word 'operations' refers to the output of the firm, be it physical goods or a variety of services. Prerequisite: An understanding of management principles and statistics through prior study or experience.
* NY residents tuition: $515

Operations Management
The Graduate School of America
TGSA#OM855W Graduate 4 credits $795
This course addresses select topics in operation management for product or service firms.

Operations Management
Western Illinois University
WEIL#MAN352 Undergraduate 3 credits $795*
Analyzes the supply side of both goods and service-type operations. The course provides an appreciation of the current problems and issues as well as the analytical tools used to resolve operation/production problems in the modern organization. Topics include quality control, inventory planning and control, scheduling and capacity planning, designing facilities, job design, and work measurement.
* IL residents tuition: $88 per credit.

Operations Management Methods
Bellevue University
BELL#MISC400 Undergraduate 6 credits $1500
This course looks at how to structure/manage work to maximize the efficiency of their internal operations.

Operations of International Enterprises
Indiana University
INDI#D302A Undergraduate 3 credits $268
The administration of international aspects of business organizations through an examination of their policy formulation, forms of foreign operations, methods of organization and control, and functional adjustments. Prerequisite: D301.

Operations of Markets
Bellevue University
BELL#MISC420 Undergraduate 4 credits $1000
This course integrates key concepts of macroeconomics and focuses on marketing factors including strategy, product and place, target markets, promotion, distribution systems, and marketing information and research.

Organizational and Group Dynamics
The Graduate School of America
TGSA#OD501W Graduate 4 credits $795
Managers achieve their objectives through skillful interaction with other people acting individually and in groups. Through readings, case material, and online discussion, this course will improve your ability to understand organizational behavior and culture, leadership styles, group processes and individual interactions. This understanding will improve your ability to develop management strategies, policies and procedures which facilitate employee commitment and productivity.

Organizational Behavior
Bellevue University
BELL#MBA633 Graduate 3 credits $825
This course is designed to encourage the application of diverse conceptual and theoretical perspectives to the analysis and control of behavior in organizations.

Organizational Behavior
Heriot-Watt University
HERI#05 Graduate 4 credits $???
The Organizational Behavior course brings together the most recent developments in the understanding of human behavior in organizations. The modules are designed to combine theoretical knowledge and practical managerial prescriptions. The objective of the course is to provide students with an understanding of the importance of individual differences; work attitudes and their antecedents and consequences; and the role of process and content theories of employee motivation and performance. These are the fundamental aspects of human behavior in work settings.

Organizational Behavior
New Hampshire College
NEHA#ADB342 Undergraduate   3 credits $1656
This course focuses on the primary factors which influence behavior in organizations to include: leadership, group dynamics, intergroup dynamics, organizational structure and design, change, culture, power and politics, environment and technology, as well as organizational behavior in an international context. Prerequisite: ADB125 and junior standing. Writing intensive course.

Organizational Behavior
New School for Social Research
NEWS#8643 Undergraduate   3 credits $622
Designed to give students an appreciation of organizational behavior and its emergence as a field of practice and research, as well as some understanding of major theoretical and methodological approaches to the study of organizational behavior, including the decision-making process.

Organizational Behavior
New York University
NEYO#Y10130101 Undergraduate   4 credits $450
Human behavior and behavioral issues in organizations are studied from two perspectives, that of the individual member and that of the manager. Topics include: individual and group behavior motivation; leadership; performance appraisal; communication; power and conflict; career dynamics; and organizational change. Extensive use is made of experiential learning and case studies, with group work.

Organizational Behavior
New Jersey Institute of Technology
NJIT#HRM301 Undergraduate   3 credits $1143*
Process such as perception, motivation and leadership are examined with a focus on issues central to technology based organizations (innovation, creativity, managing technical professionals) Prerequisites: upper division standing. A foundation course in individual and group behavior in organizations. Optional: video lessons.
* NJ residents: $184/semester hour.

Organizational Behavior
New York Institute of Technology
NYIT#BUS3903 Undergraduate   3 credits $???
An introduction to the fundamental concepts of human behavior within organizations. Topics covered include: motivation, group dynamics, informal organizational design, leadership, performance measurement, organizational changes, conflict management and organizational behavior. Prerequisites: BUS3906 or BUS3900.

Organizational Behavior
Strayer University
STRA#BUS520 Undergraduate   4.5 credits $665
Analyzes the elements of organizational behavior. Topics include human behavior and problems; methods for dealing with personnel problems; motivation, formal and informal behavior, communications, and ethics; stress management, conflict resolution, workforce diversity and managing change. Prerequisite: BUS100.

Organizational Behavior and Systems Theory
Walden University
WALD#EDUC6140 Undergraduate 4 credits $920
Examination of organizational behavior as it relates to educational structure, process and human factors. Study of systems theory as a perspective on learning organizations.

Organizational Communication
University of Colorado-Boulder
COBO#COMM4600 Undergraduate 3 credits $240
Reviews current research and theory on topics such as communication and organizational decision making, organizational culture, communication and power in organizations. Prerequisite: COMM2600 recommended.

Organizational Communication
Front Range Community College
FRCC#SPE225 Undergraduate   3 credits $790
This course studies the systems and patterns in business and organizational communication. It explores leadership strategies, effective managerial communication skills with peers, superiors, and subordinates, and organizational communication environments, networks, and goals. 45 Contact Hours.

Organizational Communication
Southwest Missouri State University
MOSW#COM638 Graduate   3 credits $315
This course will be part of the core requirements for an online Master of Science in Administrative Studies currently under development. It will cover topics such as: the socialization of new employees; the role of communication in power, motivation, conflict, and leadership; communication and gender; communication and new technologies in organizations; and identifying and managing barriers to effective communication in organizations. Instruction will rely heavily upon written and video case studies.

Organizational Communication
Rochester Institute of Technology
ROCH#53541590 Undergraduate 4 credits $923
This course examines both interpersonal and small group communication in organizational settings.

Organizational Leadership
New Hampshire College
NEHA#ADB328 Undergraduate   3 credits $1656
This course examines leadership, as an interpersonal and intraorganizational phenomenon with an emphasis on student leadership development. It includes leadership assessment, leadership development, the leadership process, the contagious nature of leadership, leadership and productivity, and motivation, effective leadership styles and theories. An international perspective is included. Current readings, research, simulations and exercises are used. Prerequisites: ADB125.

Organizational Psychology
Walden University
WALD#PSYC8480 Graduate   5 credits $1500
The course focuses on the application of psychological principles to the workplace. It considers multiple theories involving individual, group, and organizational behavior.

Organizational Theory
Bellevue University
BELL#MBA634 Graduate   3 credits $825
Application of diverse conceptual and theoretical perspectives to the design of organizations and successful functioning within them.

Organizational Theory
University of Missouri
MOCE#OR330 Undergraduate   3 credits $387
This course examines what an organization is and how it functions. Course topics include theories and practical information about organizations; models for decision making; and environmental factors and their effects on organizations. Perquisites: Mgt. 202 or instructor's consent.

Organizationals & Gender
Marylhurst College
MARY#MGT508 Undergraduate   3 credits $651
This course asks students to examine the connection between communication and the composition of gender. A variety of interdisciplinary perspectives lead students through alternative understandings of the social process of gender constitution and its practical implications. Theories of gender are applied to the everyday world to discover the ways in which communication is used to establish and maintain gendered relationships in organizational settings.

Organizations, Paradigms, and Change
Rio Salado College
RISA#MGT172 Undergraduate   1 credits $62*
Examines the nature of organizations, paradigms, and change as organizations manage for excellence. Focuses on current practices and future trends in total quality management. Includes ethics and the future of organizations in a global economy.
* AZ residents pay $37 per credit.

Parts & Service Management
Northwest College
NOCO#MA210 Undergraduate   5 credits $???
This course covers the activities involved in managing parts and service departments in an automotive/vehicle business - organization, equipment, and operations.

Performance Management
The Graduate School of America
TGSA#OM869W Graduate   4 credits $795
Focuses on the changing role of the traditional "training" function in most organizations to that of "performance management," thus creating a more direct link between job behaviors and the bottom line. Topics covered include the role of the performance consultant, defining business needs in operational terms, doing performance assessments, and contracting for performance implementation. Learners will create a strategic plan for transition to a performance management consulting model as the result of their research on the practices of real companies.

Personnel Administration
The Graduate School of America
TGSA#ED857W Graduate   4 credits $795
This course will address staffing, assignment, policy making, salary negotiation, grievance procedures, records, supervision and evaluation of professional and non-professional employees.

Personnel Management
State University of New York
SUNY#MBA538 Graduate   3 credits $1038*
This course is built around a model managing personnel systems and programs. The course will include the specific type of activities undertaken to influence personnel effectiveness, as well as general strategy for implementing these activities. The extended factors which impact on employees effectiveness will also be studied in depth. Prerequisite: Admission to program or permission of department.
* NY residents tuition: $137 per credit

Philosophy of Corporations
City University
CITY#PHI409 Undergraduate   5 qu. credits $785
An investigation of the historical and cultural background of the nature and evolution of corporations. The course shows how corporate structures and economic philosophies have shaped attitudes towards, and uses of, goods in human societies, with varying degrees of failure and success. Prerequisite: Strongly recommended: HUM200 or its equivalent.

Position Management and Classification
Strayer University
STRA#BUS215 Undergraduate   4.5 credits $665
Introduces and analyzes the basic concepts of compensation administration in organizations. Provides an intensive study of the coordinated federal wage system, factor evaluation system, job engineering, methods of job evaluation, wage and salary structures, and the legal constraints on compensation programs.

Practical Accounting
Edmonds Community College
EDMO#ACCT101 Undergraduate   5 credits $260
This is a beginning accounting course with emphasis on journalizing, posting, financial statements, adjustments, worksheets, cash funds, and payroll entries. Group critical thinking outcomes are included. Computer applications are used.

Preprofessional Writing for Business
University of Minnesota
MINN#ENGC3032 Undergraduate   4 credits $391
Focus on content, form, and style of business writing in reports, job-search materials, and correspondence. Case studies and practical examples. Prerequisite: Writing Practice requirement or equivalent.

Principles of Advertising
New Hampshire College
NEHA#MKT329 Undergraduate   3 credits $1656
This course is designed to give students and understanding of advertising, and of the role the media play in advertising strategy. This course focuses on the planning, research, and creative skills needed to reach promotion objectives. Prerequisites: MKT113 and ENG103.

Principles of Accounting
New York University
NEYO#Y10014203 Undergraduate   4 credits $450
The principles of double-entry systems, control accounts, and subsidiary records are reviewed and detailed. Emphasis is on worksheets and variations of systems as well as accounting procedures involved with partnership and corporation capital accounts. End results of the accounting process, such as costs, financial relationships, financial analysis, taxes, and budgeting are investigated as a beginning to a managerial accounting approach. Prerequisite: One semester of college algebra or placement testing.

Principles of Accounting
UCLA
UCLA#X1A Undergraduate   4 credits $500
An introduction to accounting theory, principles, and practice, covering the uses, communication, and processing of accounting information, as well as the recording, analyzing, and summarizing procedures used in preparing balance sheets and income statements. Other topics include accounting for purchases and sales, receivables and payables, cash and inventories, plant and equipment, depreciation and natural resources, intangible assets, and payrolls. Also examines sole proprietorships and partnerships.

Principles of Accounting 1B
UCLA
UCLA#X1B Undergraduate   4 credits $500
This course covers partnerships and corporations, analysis and interpretation of financial statements, and statements of changes in financial positions. Accounting for operations of departments, branches, and manufacturing also is examined.

Principles Of Accounting I
Fayetteville Technical Community College
FAYE#ACC120 Undergraduate   4 credits $652*
This course introduces the basic principles and procedures of accounting. Emphasis is placed on collecting, summarizing, analyzing, and reporting financial information. Upon completion, students should be able to analyze data and prepare journal entries and reports as they relate to the accounting cycle.
* NC residents pay $20 per credit.

Principles of Accounting I
Lansing Community College
LANS#ACCG210 Undergraduate   4 credits $420
Accounting is the language of business. To excel in business you must speak the language. The focus is on financial accounting and reporting. By the end of the course the student more easily can decipher the financial statements of a business and start using them as a decision-making tool.

Principles of Accounting I
State University of New York
SUNY#ACCT101 Undergraduate   3 credits $1038*
An introduction to accounting theory and principles as applied to business enterprise. Principles and procedure as applied to the accumulation, processing and reporting of financial information resulting from business transactions. Manual and electronic media for the preparation of journals, ledgers, financial statements. Inventories, receivables, payables, plant assets and payroll accounting. Prerequisite: Minimum of MATH 102, which can be taken concurrently.
* NY residents tuition: $137 per credit

Principles of Advertising
University of Alaska - Fairbanks
ALFA#BA326 Undergraduate   3 credits $237
Advertising including strategy, media use, creation and production of advertisements, and measurement of advertising effectiveness. Prerequisite: Junior standing.

Principles of Advertising
University of Alaska - Fairbanks
ALFA#JB326 Undergraduate   3 credits $237
Advertising including strategy, media use, creation and production of ads, and measurement of advertising effectiveness. Prerequisite: Junior standing.

Principles of Business Finance
Mercy College
MERC#FI320 Undergraduate   3 credits $900
Students study the functions of business finance in this course. Topics include financial statement analysis; funds flow and breakeven concepts; tax and other organizational considerations in forming businesses; current and long-term asset management; types of instruments of corporate finance; stock and bond markets and their regulation; investment banking; and, short and long-term financing decisions. Prerequisites: Six credits in Accounting.

Principles of Finance
Eastern Oregon University
EAOR#BA313 Undergraduate   5 credits $400
This is an introductory course to the field of managerial finance. As such it covers basic topics such as financial analysis, time value of money, risk/return analysis, capital budgeting, cost of capital, and capital structure. Prerequisite: BA213, ECON202, STAT315.

Principles of Finance
Strayer University
STRA#FIN100 Undergraduate 4.5 credits $665
Serves as a foundation course in business finance. Provides a conceptual framework for the financial decision-making process and introduces tools and techniques of finance including financial mathematics, capital budgeting, sources of funds and financial analysis. Topics include acquisition and use of short-term and long-term capital; financial markets, institutions and instruments; financial control; time value of money; cash, operation and long-range budgeting; and cost of capital.

Principles of Investment
Strayer University
STRA#ECO150 Undergraduate 4.5 credits $665
Analyzes operation of the securities markets, basic concepts in security valuation with emphasis analysis, valuations in convertible securities, bonds, and preferred stocks.

Principles of Loss Prevention
Fox Valley Technical College
FOVA#504-148 Undergraduate 3 credits $200
Topics in this course include internal theft, white collar theft, computer security, workplace violence, business travel security, emergency/disaster planning. This course is designed to detect and reduce the incidence of losses associated with potential 'hidden' losses in a company.

Principles of Management
College of DuPage
DUPA#MGT210 Undergraduate 5 qu. credits $150
Provides the student with the working knowledge of the essential principles and concepts of management theory and practice. It is structured to develop a concise framework interrelating to major business disciplines and a comprehensive perspective to organize additional study in management. Practical applications of the manager's role in planning, organizing, staffing, directing and controlling are demonstrated and explored. Part of a certificate program in Supervision when completed with Management 100 and Business 100 course.

Principles of Management
Fayetteville Technical Community College
FAYE#BUS137 Undergraduate 3 credits $489*
This course is designed to be an overview of the major functions of management. Emphasis is placed on planning, organizing, controlling, directing, and communicating. Upon completion, students should be able to work as contributing members of a team utilizing these functions of management.
* North Carolina residents and non-resident US military personnel stationed within the state tuition: $60; NC senior citizens: free.

Principles of Management
Mercy College
MERC#MG120 Undergraduate 3 credits $900
The managerial principles and techniques underlying the 'successful' organization are examined. Emphasis is placed on the basic functions of planning for future organizational growth, organizing and staffing for efficient operation. Effective leadership and motivational techniques, and practical methods of control. This course forms the base for all management course offerings.

Principles of Management
New Hampshire College
NEHA#ADB215 Undergraduate 3 credits $1656
This course is designed to examine the fundamentals and principles of management in any formal organization. Special attention is paid to planning and decision-making. International management is also covered. Prerequisite: Sophomore standing. Writing intensive course.

Principles of Management
New Jersey Institute of Technology
NJIT#MGMT390 Undergraduate 3 credits $1143*
Course organization is based on the major functions of management-planning, organizing, staffing, directing, and controlling. Topics of such current importance as the cultural and social diversity of the workforce. Total Quality Management (TQM), social responsiveness and ethics, and multinational markets and competition are woven throughout the course. Optional: 26 video lessons of 30 minutes each.
* NJ residents: $184/semester hour.

Principles of Management
Northwest College
NOCO#MA121 Undergraduate 5 credits $???
This course combines the analysis of the familiar management principles and the newer systems concept of management. The planning, organization, leadership and control functions of management are analyzed in detail.

Principles of Management
Rogers State University
ROGE#BMA2013 Undergraduate 3 credits $495*
Introduction to practical management with an emphasis on the role of the manager/supervisor within the organization. Includes communication, leadership, motivation, organizational structure, the effects of organizational change, and decision-making as applied to management systems, organizations, interpersonal relationships, and production. Suggested for all students who may supervise on their jobs, regardless of major. Video: Modern Management.
* OK residents $315.

Principles of Management
Strayer University
STRA#BUS200 Undergraduate 4.5 credits $665
Emphasis is on aspects of the planning process, such as organizing for action, concepts of control, the communication system, and motivating employees.

Principles of Management
Thomas Edison State College
THED#OLMAN301 Undergraduate 3 credits $397*
Introductory course in management. Includes essential skills in planning and organizing, staffing and directing, controlling decision making, motivation, communication, and the application of management principles to the business organization.
* NJ residents tuition: $33 per credit.

Principles of Management of Marketing
University of Minnesota
MINN#GC1553 Undergraduate 4 credits $356
Emphasis on application of the principles of management. Topics: the environment in which managers operate, including the ethical environment and social responsibility, planning, decision making, organizing, controlling, motivation, leadership, communications, group dynamics, and total quality management. Several exercises provide students with insight into personal managerial behavior. Students have an opportunity to make managerial decisions and be assessed on the soundness of those decisions. Critical thinking is a major component of this course. Prerequisite: GC1551 or permission.

Principles of Marketing
University of Alaska - Fairbanks
ALFA#BA343 Postgrad 3 credits $237
Managing of a firm's marketing effort focusing on products, distribution, pricing, and promotion to targeted consumers. Practices appropriate to domestic or international, small or large, goods or services, and for-profit or non-profit organizations included. Prerequisite: Upper division standing.

Principles of Marketing
Fayetteville Technical Community College
FAYE#MKR120 Undergraduate 3 credits $489*
This course introduces principles and problems of marketing goods and services. Topics include promotion, placement, and pricing strategies for products. Upon completion, students should be able to apply marketing principles in organizational decision making.
* North Carolina residents and non-resident US military personnel stationed within the state tuition: $60; NC senior citizens: free.

Principles of Marketing
Mercy College
MERC#MK220 Undergraduate 3 credits $900
(Course description not available at press time.)

Principles of Marketing
University of Minnesota
MINN#MKTG3000 Undergraduate 4 credits $400
Focuses on marketing as a process of managing exchanges. Students learn the environmental factors that impact the strategic marketing process and explore interrelationships between strategic and tactical marketing issues concerning product/service, price, promotion, and distribution decisions.

Principles of Marketing
University of Missouri
MOCE#MA204 Undergraduate 3 credits $387
This course studies institutions, processes, and problems involved in transferring goods from producer to consumer; emphasis is on the economic and social aspects of the transfer. Perquisites: Econ. 4 and 5; or 14; or 51; and junior standing.

Principles of Marketing
New Jersey Institute of Technology
NJIT#MRKT330 Undergraduate 3 credits $1143*
This course examines the factors relating to the marketing process within the organizations and its environments. The nature and significance of consumer and organization buying behavior, competition, government regulations, consumerism, and social responsibility are analyzed. The methods of decision making in the areas of marketing research, product development, pricing, etc. Optional: 26 video lessons of 30 minutes each.
* NJ residents: $184/semester hour.

Principles of Organizational Behavior
Strayer University
STRA#BUS105 Undergraduate 4.5 credits $665
Emphasizes the fundamental concepts of organizational behavior. Emphasizes the human problems and behaviors in organizations and methods of dealing with these problems. Focuses on motivation, informal groups, power and politics, communication, ethics, conflict resolution, employment laws, technology and people, and managing change.

Principles of Public Relations
New Hampshire College
NEHA#COM335 Undergraduate 3 credits $1656
This course introduces students to the theory and practice of public relations in the United States. Students study the major figures in this field as well as organizations, their behavior, and the relationships between organizations and their publics. Prerequisite: ENG103.

Principles of Retailing
New Hampshire College
NEHA#MKT222 Undergraduate 3 credits $1656
This course studies the basics of retailing with emphasis on the development of retail institutions, merchandising, pricing, and contemporary problems of retailers in today's business environment. Prerequisite: MKT113.

Principles of Retailing and Business
State University of New York
SUNY#RET101 Undergraduate 3 credits $630*
Provides an understanding of the overall world of business and how individuals fit into it. The role of retailing in the structure of our economic system. Consideration given to the relative importance of factors such as physical plant, staffing concepts, merchandising methods, customer services, wrap and sales promotion and the role of sales.
* NY residents tuition: $105 per credit.

Principles of Supervision
Fayetteville Technical Community College
FAYE#BUS135 Undergraduate   3 credits $489*
This course introduces the basic responsibilities and duties of the supervisor and his/her relationship to higher-level supervisors, subordinates, and associates. Emphasis is placed on effective utilization of the work force and understanding the role of the supervisor. Upon completion, students should be able to apply supervisory principles in the work place.
* North Carolina residents and non-resident US military personnel stationed within the state tuition: $60; NC senior citizens: free.

Principles of Supervision
Front Range Community College
FRCC#MAN116 Undergraduate   3 credits $790
This course presents the principles and techniques of managing and motivating people, from a behavioral viewpoint, for the student who is interested in supervising others or for those presently in supervisory positions. Class discussions focus on the human interaction within the work environment. 45 Contact Hours.

Principles of Supervision
National American University
NAAM#MT330D Undergraduate   4.5 credits $900
This course focuses on the art of empowering and developing people. It provides a thorough review of the supervisory/management functions of planning, organizing, leading and control while addressing such contemporary issues as the quest for quality, teambuilding, coaching, group dynamics, facilitation skills, and managing human resources and diversity.

Problem Solving in Security
Fox Valley Technical College
FOVA#504-140 Undergraduate   2 credits $150
In this course, students will learn and practice interactive as well as individualized problem-solving skills involving the security and loss prevention industry. The concept of using a scientific method for quality improvement is introduced.

Problems of Small Business
Pennsylvania State University
PENN#BA250 Undergraduate   3 credits $345
Analysis of problems of the small firm, particularly for the student who wishes to venture into business. Prerequisite: 3 credits in economics.

Process Management for Improved Performance
The Graduate School of America
TGSA#OM842W Graduate   4 credits $795
Leading edge management is increasingly focused on improving core business processes as a key factor in creating sustainable competitive advantage. Process Management involves the systematic planning and control of functions that permit successful execution of the organization's mission. Through readings, case analysis and online discussions, you will develop critical process management and process improvement skills.

Production & Operation Management
New York Institute of Technology
NYIT#BUS3916 Undergraduate   3 credits $???
Operations Management deals with activities required in the process of production of products and delivery of services. Background of concepts, processes and institutions in the production of goods and services will be covered. Computer applications are an integral part of this course. Prerequisites: BUS3906 and BUS3801.

Production and Operations Management
Bellevue University
BELL#MBA626 Graduate   3 credits $825
This course will examine the operations component of the organization.

Production and Operations Management
Strayer University
STRA#BUS540 Undergraduate   4.5 credits $665
Focuses on techniques for planning, organizing and controlling the conversion process for manufacturing and service operations in a dynamic environment. Discusses product and system improvement methods. Incorporates quantitative and qualitative tools to support the decision-making process. Prerequisite: MAT540.

Professional and Technical Writing
Lake Superior College
LASU#ENGL1107 Undergraduate   3 credits $210
This course is designed to strengthen skills in various areas of professional communications. It emphasizes skills of problem solving and analysis as well as proficiency in using traditional formats for writing memos, letters, and reports. Upon completion of the course, students will be more confident communicators having been introduced to professional workplace situations and issues. For this Internet course, you will need either Corel WordPerfect (6.1 or newer, preferably 7.0) or Microsoft Word (6.0 or newer, preferably the '97 version). Prerequisite: Freshman Composition or the equivalent.

Professional Leadership Project
Bellevue University
BELL#LDR681 Graduate   1 credits $275
The professional leadership project requires that participants become fully involved in the process of research and in the application of strategic models for change within military, corporate and other organizational environments. Review of secondary research and the use of data analysis are key components of this course. Conclusions drawn during development and presentation phases of the project are based on a synthesis of concepts presented throughout leadership, management, etc.

Professional Selling
Northwest College
NOCO#BU111B Undergraduate   3 credits $???
Numerous aspects of the sales profession are explored. The concepts and applications of adaptive selling and the selling process as a series of interrelated activities will be included.

Project Control
New Jersey Institute of Technology
NJIT#EM637 Undergraduate 3 credits $1143*

This course is designed to give students knowledge in the following areas: project control, estimating; planning and scheduling; presenting; value prediction and control; and management. Computer programs for scheduling will also be discussed. Optional: 12 video lessons of 120 minutes each.

* NJ residents: $184/semester hour.

Project in Information Systems
Nova Southeastern University
NOVA#MCIS682 Graduate 3 credits $1,110

Students pursue a project, research study, or implementation under the supervision of a faculty member.

Project in MIS
Nova Southeastern University
NOVA#MMIS682 Graduate 3 credits $1,110

Students are assigned a project that involves part or all of the system development cycle and gain experience in analyzing, designing, implementing, and evaluating information systems. Prerequisite: prior consent of instructor.

Project Management
Marylhurst College
MARY#MGT303B Undergraduate 3 credits $651

Learn the basic concepts and techniques of project management, including the principles of defining, planning, reporting and visually representing the elements of a project, as well as understanding enhanced project team performance. The instructor is an experienced consultant who has managed projects in the last year with combined construction value in excess of $30 million. His work in training and teaching in the online environment includes the design and implementation of an intranet instructional program at the Kennedy Space Center.

Project Management
New Jersey Institute of Technology
NJIT#EM636 Undergraduate 3 credits $1143*

Introduction to concepts of project management and techniques for planning and controlling of resources to accomplish specific project goals. Prerequisites: Graduate course in behavioral organization in engineering organization (NJIT#IE603) and undergraduate course in engineering management or equivalent knowledge. Optional: 14 video lessons of 120 minutes each.

* NJ residents: $184/semester hour.

Project Management
Rochester Institute of Technology
ROCH#63049090 Undergraduate 4 credits $923

Covers planning, design and implementation.

Promotional Concepts
Western Illinois University
WEIL#FIN331 Undergraduate 3 credits $795*

Examines marketing communication as a vital component of our free enterprise system. You can gain insight into the importance of communication, advertising, and promotion to the life of a firm, business, or institution as a going concern. Learn to define, use, and apply the theories and concepts of advertising, promotion, professional selling, sales promotion, and direct marketing as well as to visualize how public relations and publicity relate to promotion. Prerequisite: Marketing 327.

* IL residents tuition: $88 per credit.

Proposal Writing
New Jersey Institute of Technology
NJIT#ENG620 Undergraduate 3 credits $1143*

Provides an understanding of and practice in proposal writing for corporations, foundations, and government agencies. Builds skills to create a range of persuasive documents including proposals for research grants, responses to requests for proposal, and government proposals.

* NJ residents: $184/semester hour.

Psychology in the Workplace
Walden University
WALD#PSYC8520 Graduate 5 credits $1500

The objective of this course is to enable the student to learn to use and apply psychological theories in work and employment settings. Current, actual work situations and on-the-job problems provide the basic focus for this course in industrial/organizational psychology.

Psychology of Advertising
State University of New York
SUNY#PSY240Y01 Undergraduate 3 credits $570*

This course emphasizes the psychological dimensions of advertising as a basis for attracting and retaining consumer awareness of products, companies and services. Various aspects of psychology and communication theories, as they pertain to the diffusion of media advertising messages, are examined and analyzed utilizing television, radio, print, and Internet media. Prerequisite: General Psychology or permission of Instructor.

* NY residents tuition: $90 per credit

Public Relations
Strayer University
STRA#BUS300 Undergraduate 4.5 credits $665

Surveys the history and practice of public relations in business, non-profit organizations, and governmental institutions. Examines the major forms of media used in public relations: news releases, broadcast publicity, public service announcements, and institutional advertising.

Public Relations
State University of New York
SUNY#BU221 Undergraduate   3 credits $435*
Principles and practices of building good public relations between industry and employees, stock-holders, consumers and suppliers. Emphasis on modern media and the growth and development of public relations as a managerial function.
* NY residents tuition: $80 per credit.

Purchasing and Materials Management
Strayer University
STRA#BUS230 Undergraduate   4.5 credits $665
Examines integral aspects of purchasing and materials management including function, organization, quality and quantity considerations, pricing policies, supplier selection, and ethical and legal implications. Reviews purchasing procedures, value analysis, inventory control, warehousing and traffic, capital equipment, make-or-buy decision making, automation, budgets and institutional and governmental purchasing practices.

Purchasing Management
Pennsylvania State University
PENN#BLOG297A Undergraduate   3 credits $345
This course explores the entire process of purchasing, beginning with the development of need or demand through, to, and including, evaluation of the source of supply and the method employed for the transaction. The student will gain both an understanding and an appreciation for the various tools employed by successful purchasers, as well as those variable measures.

Quality Customer Service
Rio Salado College
RISA#TQM101 Undergraduate   3 credits $186*
Examines the nature of quality customer service and the attitudes, knowledge, and skill needed to work effectively in a quality customer service environment. Foundation skills for quality customer services are taught, applied, and practiced.
* AZ residents $37 per credit.

Quality Management Methods
Marylhurst College
MARY#MGT532 Undergraduate   3 credits $651
This course presents quality management, past, present, future, with application in competitive global markets. Methods employed over the past thirty years are summarized including a detailed examination of the "quality management revolution" that has occurred within the last ten years.

Quality Systems Development
Roane State Community College
ROAN#BUS217 Undergraduate   3 credits $459*
Using the Malcolm Baldrige criteria, participants learn to both develop and assess integrated quality systems within organizations. Participants complete a Level II Quality Award (15 page version of the 75 page Baldrige application process) application and/or assessment. This course stresses the systems and interdependencies of quality management processes in organizations.
* Tennessee residents tuition: $48 per semester hour.

Quantitative Analysis for Management
Golden Gate University
GOLD#MATH106 Undergraduate   3 credits $960
Examines the applications of quantitative analysis to the formulation and solution of managerial problems. You will study decision theory, linear programming, inventory theory, network diagramming, queuing analysis, simulation, and computer applications. Prerequisites: MATH30 and MATH40.

Quantitative Methods
Bellevue University
BELL#BA623 Graduate   3 credits $825
This course covers advanced topics in management science and quantitative analysis.

Quantitative Methods
Heriot-Watt University
HERI#06 Graduate   4 credits $???
In order to make decisions it is necessary to have access to information. In the world of business, that information will often be in numerical form. To make good decisions it is essential to be able to organize and understand numbers. This is what statistics is about, and why it is important to have some knowledge of the subject. Statistics can be divided into two parts. The first part, "descriptive statistics," handles the problem of sorting a large amount of collected data in ways which enable its main features to be seen immediately.

Quantitative Methods
Nova Southeastern University
NOVA#MMIS615 Graduate   3 credits $1,110
An introduction to the basic quantitative tools needed to support problem solving and decision-making in the information systems environment. Heavy emphasis is placed on the application of these tools in a case-based, real world environment.

Quantitative Methods in Business
New York Institute of Technology
NYIT#MA3019 Undergraduate   3 credits $???
Applications of calculus to business and social science. Intuitive use of limits and continuity. Derivatives, extrema, concavity, and applications such as marginal analysis, business models, optimization of tax revenue, and minimization of storage cost. The exponential and logarithm functions. Antiderivatives and the definite integral. Areas and consumer's surplus. Some concepts of probability extended to discrete and continuous sample spaces. Prerequisite: MA3010 or MA3014.

Real Estate Finance
Waukesha County Technical College
WAUK#194184003 Undergraduate   3 credits $193
An applied study of money markets, interest roles and financing of real estate. Actual cases are used for illustrations. Lending policies, problems, and rules involved in financing real property are explored. Prerequisites: 194-180 Real Estate Fundamentals or consent of instructor.

Real Estate Finance and Investment
Western Illinois University
WEIL#FIN421 Undergraduate   3 credits $795*
Learn how to finance your home and other real estate investments, how the savings and loan debacle has cost taxpayers hundreds of billions of dollars and changed the real estate industry forever, and how sweet "Ginnie Mae" securities really are. This course examines the various financing techniques and innovations associated with real estate. While home financing is surveyed, the primary focus of the course is on the secondary mortgage market and commercial financing and investment.
* IL residents tuition: $88 per credit.

Real Estate Fundamentals
Waukesha County Technical College
WAUK#194180006 Undergraduate   3 credits $193
Fundamentals of Real Estate provides a foundation for those pursuing Real Estate as a career and also basic information for owners and/or sellers or residential and investment property.

Real Estate Principles
UCLA
UCLA#X475 Undergraduate   5 credits $500
A practical study of the basic principles, economic aspects, and fundamental laws of real estate, this online course is designed to acquaint the student with the basic information needed for a real estate license and/or better management of the individual's personal investments. Topics include legal descriptions and estates, encumbrances, liens and homesteads, agencies, contracts, mathematics, financing, lenders, appraisal, escrow, title insurance, leases, landlords and tenants, urban economics and planning, taxation, and careers in real estate.

Recent Developments in Textiles
University of Nebraska
NEBR#TXCD811 Masters   3 credits $467
Recent Developments in Textiles is designed to increase knowledge about textiles, enhance skills in analyzing and evaluating textile projects and predicting their performance, and provide an update on the many and varied recent developments which have launched new fibers and enhanced the performance of traditional fibers and fabrics. Emphasis will be on developments occurring during the past five to seven years.

Records Management and Filing
Brevard Community College
BREV#OST2335A Undergraduate   3 credits $435
Principles, procedures, and systems of filing are presented. Records management covers the creation, storage, protection, control, use and disposition of records. Basic considerations for selection of equipment and supplies is studied.

Recruitment and Placement
Strayer University
STRA#BUS220 Undergraduate   4.5 credits $665
Introduces the fundamental policies, procedures and regulations of the staffing function. Extensive use is made of work groups and practical exercises to understand the importance of staff planning and utilization, budgeting, qualification standards, recruitment, examining, testing, and selecting, promotion and other placement actions, and special interest in employment areas.

Recruitment, Interviewing, Selection
UCLA
UCLA#X450 Undergraduate   4 credits $500
A high-quality workforce is essential to the success of businesses today. This online course provides the strategies, concepts, and practices essential to the effective selection of personnel to accomplish a business objective. Emphasis is placed on recruiting, promoting, and retraining employees. The course also covers budget development, job descriptions, interviewing techniques, assessment, testing, background investigations, legal requirements, reporting of results to management, employee orientation, outplacement, and ethnic diversity issues.

Redefining the Workplace
The Graduate School of America
TGSA#OM874W Graduate   4 credits $795
The traditional workplace and the concept of work as we know it are rapidly changing. This course will explore the advent of the virtual office, changing workforce demographics and socio-economic trends which all drastically transform our notions of "job", "work", and "organizations".

Report Writing
Eastern Oregon University
EAOR#BA225 Undergraduate   4 credits $320
Analysis of methods of investigating, collecting, organizing, and presenting data for formal and informal business reports.

Report Writing
New York Institute of Technology
NYIT#EN1044 Undergraduate   3 credits $???
An intermediate-level course for students of the behavioral and social sciences. Methods and procedures of research; emphasis on reports and advanced research papers and strategies for effective business communication including resume writing. Recommended for all major in the behavioral sciences, political science, and economics. Coursework includes a computer lab component. Prerequisite: EN1020.

Research and Business Applications
City University
CITY#CS445 Undergraduate   5 qu. credits $785
A case-based exploration of internetworking and its applications in various settings. Systems will be analyzed, applications will be discussed and then designed to meet client, corporate and educational needs. Database and resource management issues, in conjunction with web-based application, will be reviewed and developed.

Research and Discovery in Communication
Marylhurst College
MARY#CM400 Undergraduate   **3 credits**   **$???**
Effective research is an essential component in developing and writing about concepts related to human communication. This course examines various research methods, strategies for selecting research topics, and appropriate documentation.

Retail Management
Indiana University
INDI#M419 Undergraduate   **3 credits**   **$268**
Major management problems in retail institutions. Treatment of retail/marketing strategy design and problems related to financial requirements, buying, inventory, pricing, promotion, merchandising, physical facilities, location, and personnel. Prerequisite: M300 and A202.

Retail Management
Northwest College
NOCO#MA225 Undergraduate   **5 credits**   **$???**
All phases of the retailing trade are thoroughly covered in this course, which include such topics as selling, buying, pricing, display, stock control, store organization, advertising and government regulations. Prerequisite: MA121.

Retailing Management
Eastern Oregon University
EAOR#BA350 Undergraduate   **3 credits**   **$240**
Operations of retailing firms; coordination of retailing practice; planning for retail operations. Prerequisite: BA312, BA321.

Retailing Management
Western Illinois University
WEIL#FIN343 Undergraduate   **3 credits**   **$795***
Studies all facets of retailing management--retailing career opportunities, store location and layout, organization, buying, selling, sales promotion, and control. Prerequisite: Marketing 327.
* IL residents tuition: $88 per credit.

Risk and Insurance
Strayer University
STRA#BUS305 Undergraduate   **4.5 credits**   **$665**
Offers practical knowledge of the types of risks encountered both as an individual and as a business person. Emphasizes selecting the appropriate types of insurance to cope with the risks.

Risk Management and Insurance
Western Illinois University
WEIL#FIN351 Undergraduate   **3 credits**   **$795***
Provides valuable information to the potential consumer of insurance. The course also covers the operation of insurance companies and the role of insurance in an overall personal investment scheme. Some specific contracts to be analyzed include individual life, health, homeowners, and automobile policies. Prerequisite: FIN 311 or 331 or permission of instructor.
* IL residents tuition: $88 per credit.

Rooms Division Management
State University of New York
SUNY#HRMG103 Undergraduate   **3 credits**   **$1038***
Basic procedures for front desk operations, housekeeping, and properties management will be covered in this course. The duties of the front office manager, the executive housekeeper, and maintenance engineer will be discussed. Included will be a study of basic hotel engineering involving heating, lighting, air conditioning, refrigeration, energy usage, and equipment maintenance.
* NY residents tuition: $137 per credit.

Sales and Persuasion
New Hampshire College
NEHA#MKT335 Undergraduate   **3 credits**   **$1656**
This course develops for the student and understanding of, and practical ability to use intelligent, ethical techniques of information presentation and persuasion. although focused upon the sales function, learned persuasive techniques will have value in many other areas of social and professional life. Prerequisite: MKT113.

Sales Management
New Hampshire College
NEHA#MKT320 Undergraduate   **3 credits**   **$1656**
This course analyzes the sales function in modern business. The course consists of a study of management of field sales forces with special emphasis on structural planning as well as on operational control over recruiting, retention, supervision, motivation, and compensation of sales personnel. Prerequisite: MKT113, junior standing or permission of instructor. Writing intensive course.

Sales Management
New York Institute of Technology
NYIT#BUS3401 Undergraduate   **3 credits**   **$???**
Planning, supervising and evaluation of sales force efforts within the guidelines set by strategic marketing planning are the principal responsibilities of sales managers. This course examines both the theory and practices which are encompassed within the role of sales manager. Prerequisite: BUS3400.

Sanitation Practices in Food Service Operations
Pennsylvania State University
PENN#DSM101 Undergraduate   **3 credits**   **$345**
Practical applications related to the management of the sanitation subsystem within a food service operation. This course will not meet the prescribed requirements for the HR&IM major in any option. Note: All students must be approved by a Dietetic program adviser.

Scenarios & Information Planning
Emporia State University
EMPO#LI863 Graduate   2 credits $210
This course will offer an examination of scenarios and their role as a management tool for planning and future forecasting. Scenarios have become increasingly powerful tools for developing strategic visions within information organizations. As a planning tool, scenarios have many advantages including: 1) providing a way to embody information, so it can be communicated effectively and efficiently, 2) opening people to multiple perspectives, 3) providing a psychological impact that graphs and equations lack, and 4) providing a means of summarizing both information and the surrounding context in an incomparable way.

Scenarios & Information Planning
Marylhurst College
MARY#MGT516 Undergraduate   3 credits $651
This course offers an examination of scenarios and their role as a management tool for planning and future forecasting. Scenarios have become increasingly powerful tools for planning and developing strategic vision within organizations. Scenarios are stories that give meaning to events. They provide a tool for ordering one's perceptions about alternative future environments in which one's decisions might be played out. As a planning tool, scenarios have many advantages.

Security for Investment Environment
Bellevue University
BELL#BA616 Graduate   3 credits $825
Introduction to the realities of the capital environment.

Security Markets
Pennsylvania State University
PENN#FIN204 Undergraduate   3 credits $345
Analysis of the organization and operation of stock and bond markets; security speculation, brokerage houses; exchange relations with other institutions; security price behavior; exchange regulation. Prerequisite: fifth-semester standing.

Selling
Marylhurst College
MARY#MKT425 Undergraduate   3 credits $651
Great ideas and great products don't necessarily mean booming business. Sales are the key determining factor in the long-term success of a new organization. Learn to overcome the obstacles to successful sales and ensure the longevity of your company or product.

Seminar in Aviation Labor Relations
Embry-Riddle Aeronautical University
EMRI#BA632 Graduate   3 credits $840
A study of union movement, labor legislation, representation elections, the collective bargaining process, contract administration, and conflict resolution. The focus of the course will be on current issues in labor relations, and the evolution of private and public sector bargaining practices in the aviation industry. The impact on human resource management is analyzed.

Seminar in International Business
Bellevue University
BELL#IBMC460 Undergraduate   3 credits $750
Participants will demonstrate their knowledge about the basic concepts of International Business.

Senior Seminar in Business Administration
Strayer University
STRA#BUS499 Undergraduate   4.5 credits $665
An in-depth seminar focusing on contemporary issues in business administration. Analysis of selected topics may include management, business policy, administrative situation, international business environment, and business ethics. Each student conducts an investigation of a current topic in business administration. Prerequisite: To be taken as last or next to last course in major.

Services Marketing
City University
CITY#MK389 Undergraduate   5 qu. credits $785
This course examines the marketing and management of services. The interdisciplinary nature of the field, development of services marketing mix and implementation strategies are studied.

Site Search, Inspection, and Selection
New York University
NEYO#X659513 Undergraduate   3.5 CEU $345
This survey course provides a solid understanding of the numerous tasks that go into making a meeting successful. In this course, you learn the importance of clear meeting objectives, how to apply principles of adult learning to program development, and how the program impacts your selection of a site. Assignments clarify each step of the planning process. Topics include: creating meeting goals/objectives; setting timelines; selecting and contracting for sites, food and beverage, transportation, and a variety of other suppliers; registering participants; and managing on-site tasks.

Small Business Fundamentals
University of Minnesota
MINN#GC1513 Undergraduate   4 credits $356
The importance of small business in the United States, and the challenges, pitfalls, and procedures related to starting and operating a small business are examined. This course emphasizes the analysis of the economic environment, strategic planning, internal analysis of a potential firm's strengths and weaknesses versus the competition, and writing a business plan. It also considers accounting, finance, marketing, management. There are distinct assignments for those who want to learn about small business and those who plan to start a small business.

Small Business Management
Edmonds Community College
EDMO#MGMT260 Undergraduate   5 credits $260
(Course description not available at press time.)

Small Business Management
New Hampshire College
NEHA#ADB317 Undergraduate 3 credits $1656
The problems involved in starting and operating a successful small business, selecting the location, determining how to borrow money, budgeting, and credit are discussed. Emphasis is on developing a comprehensive business plan. Prerequisites: ACC102, MKT113, and ADB215.

Small Business Management
Northwest College
NOCO#BU120B Undergraduate 3 credits $???
Primarily, this course is designed to provide a complete coverage of small business operations with a proper balance between business functions, including purchasing, production, sales and finance, and the management functions of planning, organizing, actuating and controlling. Prerequisite: MA121.

Small Business Management
New York Institute of Technology
NYIT#BUS3905 Undergraduate 3 credits $???
An examination of required skills, resources, and techniques which transform an idea into a viable business. Entrepreneurial decision making will be stressed and the role it plays in idea generation, conception, opportunity analysis, marshaling of resources, implementation of plans, management of ongoing operations, and providing for growth will be stressed. Prerequisite: BBUS3906, BUS3400, BUS3511.

Small Business Management
Strayer University
STRA#BUS205 Undergraduate 4.5 credits $665
Provides the basic principles of operating and managing a small business. Topics include buying, merchandising, pricing, promotions, inventory management, customer service and location decisions. Field trips to retail establishments, guest speakers, and development of a plan for a new retail store are some of the major areas of focus. Prerequisite: BUS100.

Small Business Operation
Rio Salado College
RISA#MGT253 Undergraduate 3 credits $186*
Starting, organizing, and operating a small business, including location, finance management processes, advertisement and promotion, credit, inventory control and ethics.
* AZ residents $37 per credit.

Small Group Communication
Marylhurst College
MARY#CM321 Undergraduate 3 credits $651
In our complex and interdependent society, communicating effectively in groups is a necessity. Decision making, problem-solving, conflict resolution, and presentation all demand special skills in group settings. Drawing on current research in communication, this course explores the concepts and teaches the skills necessary for improved leadership and membership in groups.

Small Group Communication Lab
University of Wisconsin
WISC#COMM380 Undergraduate 3 credits $312
Tired of "can't"? Do you feel like you are "stuck in a rut"? Want to "break out of the paradigm"? This course introduces you to structured approaches to determining the cause of a problem, developing creative solutions, making better decisions, and establishing a strategy for implementing solutions. Approaches to problem solving will be presented at the lectures, and applications of these problem solving methods will be conducted on-line. You will acquire problem solving skills that you will find applicable for a life time - in a personal, as well as professional context.

Social and Psychological Aspects of Apparel
Western Illinois University
WEIL#HEA313 Undergraduate 3 credits $795*
Throughout history, clothing has been recognized as one of the primary needs of all peoples in various parts of the world. Manner of dress reflects the times and serves as an expression of an era's culture. The course examines the social, psychological, emotional, and utilitarian roles clothing plays in people's lives.
* IL residents tuition: $88 per credit.

Social, Legal, and Ethical Environment of Business
Pennsylvania State University
PENN#BA243 Undergraduate 4 credits $460
Explores the ethical, political, social, legal and regulatory, technological, and demographic diversity environment of business.

Special Topics in Information Systems
Nova Southeastern University
NOVA#MCIS691 Graduate 3 credits $1,110
This seminar focuses on the professor's current research interests. Requires consent of instructor and program director.

Specification & Design of Info Systems
Rochester Institute of Technology
ROCH#60282190 Undergraduate 4 credits $923
Current methods and techniques used in the specification and design of information systems.

Sports Management
State University of New York
SUNY#PPE215 Undergraduate 3 credits $630*
Survey course addressing the role of administration specific to fitness, athletic, recreational and physical education facilities. It will present general administrative principles as well as those specific to the field.
* NY residents tuition: $105 per credit.

Statistical Decision Making
University of Nebraska
NEBR#BIOM896 Masters   3 credits $467
Statistical Decision Making is a one semester course that presents statistical procedures useful for making practical decisions in every day life. Objectives are to acquaint beginning graduate students with: 1. Basic statistical terminology, 2. Sufficient background in probability to understand risks associated with decisions based on experimental data, 3. Basic methods of statistical analysis to draw experimental data, 4. Fundamental considerations on the design of experiments from which useful and valid statistical decisions can be obtained, 5. Elementary tools with which to read and evaluate critically, research articles having statistically derived conclusions.

Statistical Process Control
Roane State Community College
ROAN#BUS290 Undergraduate   3 credits $459*
An introduction to the application of statistical process control for the identify and eliminate wasteful variation in processes and systems. Variable and attribute control charts are addressed. Participants complete a project including control plan development, control chart selection, control chart development and interpretation, and capability study and analysis.
* Tennessee residents tuition: $48 per semester hour.

Statistical Quality Control II
Rochester Institute of Technology
ROCH#30773190 Undergraduate   3 credits $693
The investigation of modern acceptance sampling techniques with an emphasis on industrial applications is the focus of this course.

Strategic Business Writing
UCLA
UCLA#X409 Undergraduate   1.95 credits $425
This online tutorial is for individuals who have a need to write critical business reports, proposals, and customer letters. It is designed to help participants achieve the ability to effectively examine business issues in writing. Students can develop skills which will allow them to make a positive impact, capture the main idea, and reduce writing time.

Strategic Communication Leadership
Bellevue University
BELL#LDR621 Graduate   4 credits $1100
The focus of this course is strategic leadership communication as it relates to organizational constituents in corporate, military and non-profit sectors. Emphasis is on the unique skills, knowledge and abilities requisite of leaders, including those needed for effective interpersonal and group communication, networking and problem solving. This course demonstrates the complexity involved in communication with others, and value-added components of listener-orientation and effective feedback and response modes.

Strategic Information Systems
Heriot-Watt University
HERI#13 Graduate   4 credits $???
The course examines what general managers require to know about Information Systems, both to help exploit potential opportunities and to avoid potential disasters. This is a management and not a technical course. It will show managers how the exploitation of Information Systems is now an important managerial role in order to achieve a wide range of business benefits. However, it will also show technical Information Systems managers how their roles must expand to incorporate strategic business issues.

Strategic Management
Bellevue University
BELL#MBA639 Graduate   3 credits $825
Students will develop an understanding of strategic management and the 'why' and 'how' strategic decisions are made.

Strategic Management
Bellevue University
BELL#MGTC411 Undergraduate   3 credits $750
Effective application of strategic planning in organizations and the role of the manager. Corporate mission and goals, external and internal analysis, business and corporate-level strategies, portfolio analysis and entry/exit strategies, organizational structure and controls, and matching strategy, structure and control.

Strategic Management
New Hampshire College
NEHA#MBA700 Undergraduate   3 credits $1656
An application of learned skills, and a testing, distillation, and integration of insights gained from preceding courses and other sources. Prerequisite: Successful completion of at least ten graduate courses (eight if a full time day student). In addition, all background prerequisites must be satisfied as well as the following courses: MBA500, HRM500, ACC500, FIN500, MBA510, and CIS500.

Strategic Media Planning for Direct Marketing
Mercy College
MERC#MK323 Undergraduate   3 credits $900
The course focuses on the media used in direct marketing. Students will examine the functions of list brokers, list managers, media buyers, and alternative media brokers as well as the different types of mail lists. The course presents various criteria and techniques for list selection (e.g., geo/demo/psychographics, house file/rental files, segmentation, CPM, testing, interfacing with database segmentation and modeling capabilities). Merge/purge criteria and processing are also covered. Prerequisites: DM 301 Introduction to Direct Marketing.

Strategic Planning
The Graduate School of America
TGSA#OM816W Graduate   4 credits $795
This course examines practices, methodology and theories of business strategy. It reviews decision making models and the development of plans for assessing company capabilities.

Strategies for Change
Heriot-Watt University
HERI#14   Graduate   4 credits $???
To survive in a dynamic and competitive business world, companies have to be aware of the need for self-renewal. Old work practices and procedures have to be replaced by new management ideas and fresh business strategies. In the post-entrepreneurial environment this renewal process will have to be more than a cosmetic exercise. What will be required is a paradigm shift in the way managers approach strategic decision making.

Supervision
College of DuPage
DUPA#MGT100   Undergraduate   3 qu. credits $90
Sets forth the supervisor's responsibilities, problems, challenges and opportunities from the management perspective. Built around the major needs of the supervisor: management mindedness, leadership and job knowledge. Part of a certificate program in Supervision when completed with Business 100 and Management 210 courses.

Supervisory Principles
The Graduate School of America
TGSA#ED856W   Graduate   4 credits $795
This course focuses on analysis of various methods of supervision. The skills, aptitudes and attitudes required for pre-conferencing, observation, analysis and diagnosis, post-conferencing and follow-up are studied.

Survey of Energy Industries
University of Alaska - Fairbanks
ALFA#PETE103   Undergraduate   1 credits $71
Overview of global energy supply and demand, alternate energy options, and petroleum production technology.

Survey of the Environment of Business
Bellevue University
BELL#MBA565   Graduate   3 credits $825
This course introduces the prospective manager to the legal system.

Survey of Unions and Collective Bargaining
Indiana University
INDI#L100   Undergraduate   3 credits $268
A survey of labor unions in the United States, focusing on their organization and their representational, economic, and political activities. Includes coverage of historical development, labor law basics, and contemporary issues. Learning guide may be sent via e-mail if requested.

System Planning and Design
The Graduate School of America
TGSA#OM886W   Graduate   4 credits $795
System analysis and design, and vendor service analysis and equipment selection are considered. Students develop presentation and sales skills and learn to write and respond to an RFP.

Systems & Management
Thomas Edison State College
THED#OLMAN351   Undergraduate   3 credits $397*
This course includes discussion on the approaches to understanding complex organizations. Included are lessons on the systems approach, the contingency approach, the behavioral view and the management practice and process view. The purpose of the course is to give students a conceptual framework for making sense of complex organizations in practice and for identifying opportunities for quality improvement.
* NJ residents tuition: $33 per credit.

Tao, Zen & Baseball - Asian Influences on Management Thought
Eastern Oregon University
EAOR#BA407   Undergraduate   5 credits $400
A cultural and managerial study of selected Chinese, Japanese, and other Asian philosophies and their applicability in the American economy. Course requires the preparation of five papers and the quiet exploration of four books. (Students will communicate among themselves and with the instructor using the Web, e-mail, a listserv discussion group, and a course-related newsgroup. Papers and exams will be submitted and reviewed electronically.)

Team and Group Dynamics
Bellevue University
BELL#LDR631   Graduate   4 credits $1100
This course examines the leader's role in facilitating teams, and groups in command, within divergent organizational climates. LDR 631 explores the process and content issues of team building and maintenance, interpersonal and group relations, and use of effective problem solving and decision making skills within teams and groups in military, corporate and non-profit cultures. Emphasis is placed on the interaction of group members with personnel located in other organizational subsystems, in a way that enhances.

Team Building Skills
Rio Salado College
RISA#HCC100AF   Undergraduate   3 credits $186*
(Course description not available at press time.)
* AZ residents pay $37 per credit.

Teaming and Group Dynamics
Roane State Community College
ROAN#BUS230   Undergraduate   3 credits $459*
Participants utilize experiential learning to understand and learn the effective psychological factors, group dynamics, behaviors and skills needed for successful project, continuous improvement, and work teams in organizations.
* Tennessee residents tuition: $48 per semester hour.

Teamwork Dynamics
Rio Salado College
RISA#TQM230 Undergraduate   2 credits $124*
Theory and practice of how team members and team leaders use listening, negotiating and interpersonal skills for the enhancement of team process. Included are concepts of team development and team problem-solving techniques. Prerequisites: TQM201 is recommended.
* AZ residents pay $37 per credit.

Technical and Business Writing
University of Massachusetts - Dartmouth
MADA#ENL600 Undergraduate   3 credits $483
This graduate-level course introduces students to the many purposes, audiences, forms, and formats of technical documents written for lay audiences. Since this is an on-line course, most assignments will focus on writing and formatting technical information for Internet and World Wide Web audiences or for audiences who want to learn about these resources.

Technical Support Functions I
Pitt Community College
PITT#CIS170 Undergraduate   3 credits $???
This course introduces a variety of diagnostic and instructional tools that are used to evaluate the performance of technical support technologies. Emphasis is placed on technical support management techniques and support technologies. Upon completion, students should be able to determine the best technologies to support and solve actual technical support problems. At PCC, lab will introduce students to help desk support principles using telecommunications and networking tools. Prerequisites: CIS115.

Technology and Leadership
University of Wisconsin
WISC#COMM303 Undergraduate   3 credits $312
Teachers, administrators, managers or executives who wish to creatively address technology issues will benefit from this course. Today's society confronts the most turbulent era of change in human history. Technology is one of the primary forces driving that change. Changes in technology present both dangers and opportunities. This course explores the organizational issues raised by technology and the vital behaviors critical to successfully guiding change with a focus on leadership communication strategies.

The Effective Organization
City University
CITY#BSC407 Undergraduate   5 qu. credits $785
An investigation of dilemmas which routinely plague organizations as well as possible solutions to these dilemmas. Topics include diversity within the organization; conflict and negotiation; motivation; leadership roles throughout the organization; team building; and organizational change and development.

The Grammar of Business Writing
New School for Social Research
NEWS#1512 Undergraduate   2 credits $1092
Limited to 20. Correct grammar is essential if your business writing is to be clear, concise, and effective. In this course, you learn the most up-to-date rules of English grammar, punctuation, and business usage and apply them to your own memos, letters, reports, and other business correspondence. Classwork focuses on problems commonly found in business writing today, and you get individual feedback from the instructor on five different pieces of business writing you do over the course of the semester. Call (212) 229-5372 for suggested placement advising.

The International Business Environment
Indiana University
INDI#D301 Undergraduate   3 credits $268
The national and international environmental aspects of international business. Examines the cultural, political, economic, systemic, legal-regulatory, trade, and financial environments and how they affect the international business activities of firms in the U.S. and in selected other countries.

The International Business Environment
Indiana University
INDI#D301A Undergraduate   3 credits $268
The national and international environmental aspects of international business. Examines the cultural, political, economic, systemic, legal-regulatory, trade, and financial environments and how they affect the international business activities of firms in the U.S. and in selected other countries. Prerequisite: Junior standing.

The Leadership Challenge
The Graduate School of America
TGSA#OM896W Graduate   4 credits $795
This course is designed to provide a thorough and very applied treatment of the study of leadership as it applies to organizational management. The texts are written by the most renowned authors on the subject, and provide diverse approaches to addressing the topic of leadership, e.g., case study, "best of" compendium of articles, and workbook-style field guide. Learners enrolled in this course will gain a well-rounded, cutting-edge foundation that will enhance their awareness and application of leadership to business and personal growth.

The Marketing Process
Strayer University
STRA#BUS533 Undergraduate   4.5 credits $665
Focuses on the major controllable marketing variables of product, price, promotion and distribution. Explains key marketing concepts such as consumer decision-making processes, market segmentation and development strategies and their significance in domestic and international activities of organizations and individuals in a social context.

The Power of Macroeconomics
University of California-Irvine
CAIR#ACC1   Undergraduate   3 credits $395

Understand how today's business and political headlines affect you in your personal and professional life. Through a self-paced, multimedia CD-ROM with concise audio lectures and animated graphic presentation, the course provides a basic understanding of macroeconomics on a business and professional level. It applies concepts that can help you answer questions such as: How much should I manufacture this month? And how much inventory should I maintain? Should I invest in new plant and equipment? Expand to foreign markets? Or downsize my firm?.

Theory and Research in Audience Analysis
University of Minnesota
MINN#RHET8110 Undergraduate   4 credits $944

This course provides students with a review of research on human learning and understanding. Students will explore theories of audience analysis and the preparation of written messages to reach defined audiences. They will also learn applications to problem-solving strategies in technical communication.

Theory, Structure and Design of Organizations
The Graduate School of America
TGSA#OM846W Graduate   4 credits $795

This course examines various types of organizational structures and processes with emphasis on those which enhance productivity and innovation. Special emphasis is given to the practical process of designing efficient organizations, and the concepts and techniques that can be applied in organization renewal and planned change.

Topics in Management
Thomas Edison State College
THED#OLMAN353 Undergraduate   3 credits $397*

The topics of this course cover organizational ethics and culture, future prospects, and career opportunities in management. The latter topics covers some of the more recent developments in the field and helps students plan their futures as managers.
* NJ residents tuition: $33 per credit.

Total Customer Management
The Graduate School of America
TGSA#OM851W Graduate   4 credits $795

Providing superior customer value is the single most important determinant of organizational success. Customer-focused management requires the integration of customer-driven marketing approaches into a comprehensive management framework. Through the course readings, case studies and online class discussions, you will gain the knowledge and skills needed to lead your organization toward achievement of distinctive customer value.

Total Quality Management
New Hampshire College
NEHA#ADB324 Undergraduate   3 credits $1656

Total Quality Management (TQM), crucial to efficient resource allocation and effective human resource management, is studied. Major factors affecting quality and strategies for effective total quality management are covered through the use of contemporary texts, reading, cases, exercises, and simulations. International considerations are also studied. Prerequisites: ADB125 and junior standing.

Total Quality Management
New Jersey Institute of Technology
NJIT#IE673 Undergraduate   3 credits $1143*

This course develops a general framework to understand all facets of Total Quality Management (TQM) and to gain familiarity with specific techniques, tools and approaches. It fosters sufficient analytical and objective thinking about the role of TQM in business and government to allow intelligent selection of appropriate approaches and techniques in a given situation. This course is part of the graduate certificate in Continuous Process Improvement. Prerequisite: Engineering Statistics. Optional: 13 video lessons of 180 minutes each.
* NJ residents: $184/semester hour.

Total Quality Management
University of Massachusetts - Lowell
MALO#69275 Undergraduate   3 credits $395

American industry is at the start of a new industrial revolution, where management and labor roles must be redefined. As part of this revolution, new emphasis is being placed on quality. Quality is becoming part of every manager's job. Historically, the greatest emphasis in American industry has been placed on quantity of production rather than quality of production. Due to increased competition, especially from Japan, American industry is starting to embrace the philosophies of Deming, Juran, and Ishikawa to name a few.

Tourism
Western Illinois University
WEIL#REC362 Undergraduate   3 credits $795*

Introduces the travel phenomenon and tourism business for both the interested traveler and the individual planning a career in commercial leisure services or the travel industry. Topics include components of the travel industry, modes of travel (air, train, ship, car, motorcoach), travel agents, reasons for tourist travel, economic and social impact of tourism, travel destination area development, travel market research, and weather and health in travel.
* IL residents tuition: $88 per credit.

Tourism Principles and Practice
University of Alaska - Fairbanks
ALFA#BA160 Undergraduate   3 credits $213

Forces which influence the international and domestic hospitality, leisure, travel, and recreation industries. Socioeconomic models and measure of regional impact, demand, supply.

U. S. Destinations & Domestic Ticketing
State University of New York
SUNY#TT131　Undergraduate　　3 credits　　$435*
A study of United States geography and an introduction to domestic airline ticketing.
* NY residents tuition: $80 per credit.

Union Government and Organization
Indiana University
INDI#L270　Undergraduate　　3 credits　　$268
An analysis of the growth, composition, structure, behavior, and governmental processes of U.S. labor organizations, from the local to the national federation level. Consideration is given to the influence on unions of industrial and political environments; to organizational behavior in different types of unions; and to problems in union democracy.

Voice Communications
New York Institute of Technology
NYIT#TN4703　Undergraduate　　3 credits　　$???
This course discusses telephones, PBX systems, key systems, and network design. Review of acoustics of voice generation. Bandwidth requirements for successful information carriage and interfacing. Digital and analog voice signal processing. Prerequisite: TN4701.

Working with Boards and Volunteers
UCLA
UCLA#X413　Undergraduate　　3 credits　　$425
An online opportunity to develop skills and strategies for successful development. Case studies and exercises supplement instructor presentations to explain how effective boards and committees are selected, maintained, and motivated over time and distance. Covers leadership skills for envisioning the future, keeping an organization on track, and helping volunteers build and articulate a case for support.

Workplace Leadership and Influence
UCLA
UCLA#X491　Undergraduate　　4 credits　　$500
All great individuals have one trait in common: the ability to influence and persuade. This online course introduces the powerful ideas of cognitive psychology and discusses the collective wisdom used by salespeople. It also covers both logical and emotional arguments, persuasive patterns, means of recognizing fallacious arguments, and how to enhance relationships and create positive first impressions. Responses to arguments and the importance of different types of nonverbal factors are also addressed.

Workplace Resolution and Negotiation Strategies
Rio Salado College
RISA#CPD127　Undergraduate　　1 credits　　$62*
Basic workplace conflict resolution and negotiation strategies. Includes establishing and maintaining effective working relationships as well as options and alternatives to conflict resolution.
* AZ residents pay $37 per credit.

Workplace Violence
Waukesha County Technical College
WAUK#001　Undergraduate　　3 credits　　$192*
This course presents the perspective and terminology of the phenomenon of workplace violence. Students will learn about the nature of violence in the workplace, its causes and contributing factors. It will enable us to understand the methods for minimizing its occurrence.
* WI residents pay $54 per credit.

Worldwide Special Event Tourism
Golden Gate University
GOLD#HRTM138　Undergraduate　　3 credits　　$1059
Introduces you to the components of the special events industry and their domestic and worldwide economic impact. Particular emphasis will be placed on development, marketing and planning special events.

Writing Effective Proposals
UCLA
UCLA#X439C　Undergraduate　　1.8 credits　　$375
Proposals play a pivotal role in business development for today's high-technology companies. This course helps writers recognize the steps essential to proposal development, the key elements of government and commercial proposals, and the voice and formulas that give proposals the winning edge. The course begins with an overview of the business development process, then reviews various proposal types, such as solicited/unsolicited proposals, grants, and SF 254/255s.

Writing for Management Success
Chemeketa Community College
CHEM#BA062M　Undergraduate　　1 credits　　$140
Writing for Management Success focuses on methods to improve writing and grammar skills. Emphasis will be on writing, letter writing, memos, and reports. Designed for managers and supervisors in business, industry, and government.

Writing for Public Relations
UCLA
UCLA#X439D　Undergraduate　　3 credits　　$450
This online course is an overview of all the key types of writing that a public relations practitioner uses and how to target the appropriate audience. Students practice writing new product press releases, pitch letters, media alerts, and new business proposals. Students should be generally adept in nonfiction writing.

Writing SBIR Proposals
Dakota State University
DAKO#ENGL670　Postgrad　　3 credits　　$447
Study of and practice in the process of developing and writing a research grant. Emphasis is placed on the Small Business Innovation Research (SBIR) proposals. The course is designed for graduate students who are interested in further researching and developing a grant proposal for an innovation or concept in their major field of study. The course involves several case studies and the development of a complete Phase I SBIR proposal. Prerequisite: Completion of a baccalaureate degree or consent of the instructor.

Writing Tools for Consultants
Kennesaw State University
KENN#FMV205 Undergraduate   3 credits $149

This course will focus on several key written documents that are critical for independent consultants as well as people in the workplace in general: instructions, recommendation reports, proposals, and business plans. Included in our studies will be a focus on headings, lists, notices, tables, and emphasis, important techniques for producing professional documents as well as good clear writing style. You'll send your writing projects by e-mail to the instructor; we'll use e-mail and chat rooms to discuss; and learning materials will be available on the World Wide Web.

Writing Tools for Independent Consultants
Kennesaw State University
KENN#FMV234 Undergraduate   3 credits $149

Do you want to succeed as a technical writer in the 21st century? Then there are three online communication skills that you need to master to meet the demands of this increasingly complex field. This course provides an overview of the three major skills, including authoring online help systems, authoring online reference systems, and authoring technical content for the Web. The primary focus will be on authoring skills in a Windows environment. Required skills and access: Access to e-mail and a Web browser, ability to successfully attach document files to email.

Written Business Communications
Northwest Technical College
NOTE#ADMS1342 Undergraduate   3 credits $240*

(Course description not available at press time.)
* Residents rates may apply.

Written Communications for Business
The Graduate School of America
TGSA#OM895W Graduate   4 credits $795

This course provides opportunities to develop practical, useful writing skills to plan, draft, and edit business communications. The student will gain experience in writing memos, letters, and reports that serve as strategic tools to gain results.

Computers

Applications

Hardware

Internet

Languages

Media

Networks

Operating Systems

Other

Programming

A Virtual Tour of The Internet
Kennesaw State University
KENN#FMV218   **Undergraduate**   **3 credits**   **$149**
This course is designed to give students who are relatively new to the Internet a tour of the most informative, helpful, educational, entertaining, and downright fun sites around. We will begin by explaining basic terminology. Then we'll explore the best sites in a variety of categories. Along the way, we'll learn to: find what we want effectively, protect sensitive information (such as credit card numbers), find bargains and be '''smart" consumers, block specific types of content, download free software, and prevent viruses.

Access/Windows
Edmonds Community College
EDMO#PCAPP118   **Undergraduate**   **3 credits**   **$220**
Microsoft Access for Windows 95 Step by Step.

Adobe Illustrator Level 1 (Macintosh)
New School for Social Research
NEWS#3226   **Undergraduate**   **0 credits**   **$580**
Limited to 14. Illustrators, designers, and desktop publishers use this powerful software program to create high-quality, finely detailed line and continuous-tone art in black & white and color. With its outstanding type manipulation and graphing capabilities, Illustrator is excellent for such diverse applications as illustrations, maps, logos, package designs, flyers, and forms. Prerequisite: Using the Macintosh or equivalent experience.

Adobe Illustrator Level 2 (Macintosh)
New School for Social Research
NEWS#3234   **Undergraduate**   **0 credits**   **$580**
Limited to 14. This course builds on experience gained in Level 1 with emphasis on precision drawing, advanced use of filters, patterns and masking, using Streamline, and pre-press considerations such as trapping and using Separator. Prerequisite: Illustrator Level 1 or the equivalent; students must be proficient in use of the Macintosh and the Pen tool.

Advanced Access '97
Shawnee Community College
SHAW#COM273   **Undergraduate**   **3 credits**   **$114**
Advanced form features such as customizing form controls, multiple page forms, subforms along with grouped reports producing subtotals and totals. Introduction to macro creation and multitasking with Access using a Switchboard form.

Advanced Access Applications
Strayer University
STRA#CIS113   **Undergraduate**   **4.5 credits**   **$665**
Concentrates on the development of applications using the Access database. Topics include design, reports and queries, subforms, multiple table queries, macros, and implementation of applications. prereq: CIS111.

Advanced Access Office '97 for Win95
Rio Salado College
RISA#BPC217AM   **Undergraduate**   **3 credits**   **$186***
Basic database concepts including database design, primary and secondary key selection and relationships between tables. Queries, subforms, macros, events, Visual Basic modules and Access '97 Internet features also covered. Prerequisites: BPC/CIS117 or instructor approval.
* AZ residents pay $37 per credit.

Advanced Administration, Installation & Configuration
Strayer University
STRA#CIS280   **Undergraduate**   **4.5 credits**   **$665**
Covers the advance network administration concepts. Focuses on the file server, NetWare directory services, netWare management, workstations, security and auditing. NetWare server, installation, and configuration. prereq: CIS180 or equivalent.

Advanced Data Structures
New Jersey Institute of Technology
NJIT#CIS435   **Undergraduate**   **3 credits**   **$1143***
Advanced topics in data structures and algorithms, including mathematical induction, analysis and complexity of algorithms, and algorithms involving sequences, sets, and graphs such as searching, sorting, order statistics, sequence comparisons, graph traversals, etc. Optional topics include geometric, algebraic, and numeric algorithms. Prerequisites: NJIT#CIS114 or NJIT#CIS335. Optional: 27 video lessons of 60 minutes each.
* NJ residents: $184/semester hour.

Advanced DOS
Rio Salado College
RISA#CIS221   **Undergraduate**   **2 credits**   **$124***
Advanced DOS commands, concepts, and usage. Emphasis on batch file programming, configuration and optimization of the DOS environment, various commercial utilities, security and disaster planning, and legal considerations. Prerequisites: CIS121AB or (BPC102AA and BPC102BA) or permission of instructor.
* AZ residents $37 per credit.

Advanced Excel '97
Shawnee Community College
SHAW#COM271   **Undergraduate**   **3 credits**   **$114**
Manipulation of lengthy worksheet by freezing panes, adjusting print settings along with headers/footers, and grouping related sheets for more efficient data entry. Extensive experience with managerial "what-if" analysis tools such as solver, scenario maker and the goal seek.

Advanced Instructional Delivery
Nova Southeastern University
NOVA#MCTE661   Graduate   3 credits $1,110

An investigation of the expansion and applications of instructional delivery systems such as electronic delivery via telecommunications (e-mail, electronic bulletin boards, conferencing systems), electronic classrooms or electronic whiteboards, audioconferencing, compressed video, World Wide Web (including HTML interfaces), group support systems, computer-aided instruction, broadcast via satellite, and multimedia. Comparative evaluation of instructional delivery systems.

Advanced Internet
Barstow Community College
BARS#COMP101   Undergraduate   1 credits $???

This course will cover downloading and installing files from the Internet, subscribing/unsubscribing to listservs, subscribing/posting to news groups, creating web pages, and the advanced Netscape features of bookmark management and configuration options.

Advanced Internet for Business and Ed
Lansing Community College
LANS#CISB202   Undergraduate   2 credits $210

This course works with advanced features of common e-mail and World Wide Web programs, allowing students to compare and contrast different programs. Hands on assignments to be completed on the WWW, via e-mail and using other Internet applications will allow the student to experience using the Internet in a wide variety of ways. Students will use additional types of Internet software, plan for future changes, and develop advanced strategies involving multiple mediums for using the Internet and Intranets as business and research tools. The course attempts to stay current with the rapidly changing world of the Internet.

Advanced Internet Publishing and Web Design
City University
CITY#CS350   Undergraduate   5 qu. credits $785

This course is the continuation of CS340. Students will continue to develop their knowledge of Internet programming and design. Topics include the evaluation of Internet standards and specifications, HTML, SGML, CGI, and VRML features, characteristics of current HTML authoring tools, advanced features of web publishing, tools needed for graphic creation and editing, image mapping, basic multimedia application and adding search parameters to Web pages.

Advanced Microcomputer Applications
New School for Social Research
NEWS#8592   Undergraduate   3 credits $622

This course is designed for students with microcomputer experience. Students are introduced to advanced features of several software packages and design, implementation, testing and documentation of individual applications. Students demonstrate mastery through the application of computer techniques to actual management and policy problems.

Advanced Programming Environments
New Jersey Institute of Technology
NJIT#CIS786   Undergraduate   3 credits $1143*

This course examines in depth the special interest area of software quality assurance including software process definition and measurement, data analysis and control, model and improvement, and applications to selective processes. This course is part of the graduate certificate in Programming Environment Tools. Prerequisites: Familiarity with the organization of a computer system and knowledge of at least one higher-level language. Optional: 14 video lessons of 160 minutes each.
* NJ residents: $184/semester hour.

Advanced RPG on the AS/400
Lansing Community College
LANS#CISB275   Undergraduate   4 credits $420

This course is a continuation of CISB175 and continues the development of RPG skills including problem definitions, file procedures, control-level processing, physical and logical file processing, subfile processing, printer files and fundamentals of interactive programming on the AS/400. Advanced topics such as Application Programming Interfaces, CL programming and commands, and RPG IV will also be covered.

Advanced Structured COBOL
Strayer University
STRA#CIS249   Undergraduate   4.5 credits $665

Covers advanced structured programming techniques involved in business applications, including editing/updating, sequential, and indexed sequential. Prerequisite: CIS248.

Advanced Visual Basic
Pitt Community College
PITT#CSC239   Undergraduate   3 credits $???

This course is a continuation of CSC 139 using Visual BASIC with structured programming principles. Emphasis is placed on advanced arrays, tables, file management/processing techniques, data structures, subprograms, interactive processing, sort/merge routines and libraries. Upon completion, students should be able to design, code, test, debug, and document programming solutions. Prerequisite: CSC139 Visual Basic.

Advanced Web Design
Kennesaw State University
KENN#FMV227   Undergraduate   3 credits $149

This workshop is designed to show the student how to plan, design and produce effective and attention getting web page. The workshop focuses on design principles and how it applies to the design of web pages. Topics covered includes Bandwidth usage, multimedia, content planning and Interface Design. This student will also learn how to use CSS (cascading style sheets) DHTML (Dynamic HTML) CGI, and JavaScript to produce a truly interactive web site. Web tips and tricks will also be covered. Student must have prior knowledge in web page creation and HTML.

Advanced Web Technology
New Hampshire College
NEHA#CIS271 Undergraduate   3 credits $1656
Applications are becoming increasingly diversed and advanced on the World Wide Web. This course will start with a quick review of HTML, such as frames, tables, and image maps. An examination of Web application architectures will then be provided, looking at options for server and client functionality. Examples, such as corporate intranets will be covered. Each student will design and implement a set of Web pages for personal or business use. On overview of Java and an introduction to emerging development tools. Prerequisites: CIS270 or equivalent with a B or higher required.

Advanced WebCraft Workshop
University of Massachusetts - Dartmouth
MADA#CMP310 Undergraduate   0 credits $135
This is a course where you pull it all together, applying what you've learned in previous web related courses. You'll study and apply advanced concepts for effective design of large Web sites. This online workshop will include a seven-step process of Web design, analysis of the good, the bad, and the ugly in Web design and creation of your own complex Web site and/or a team project (your choice).

Advanced Windows Appl. Development
City University
CITY#CS464 Undergraduate   5 qu. credits $785
Students continue to develop their knowledge of C, Visual C++, and Object-Oriented programming in a Windows environment. Extensive use of the Software Development Kit (SDK) applied to user interface input validation, providing user help, printer control, managing mouse events, DDE, OLE, and DLL. Prerequisite: Advanced C and OOP or C++ and Windows programming experience.

Advanced Word '97
Shawnee Community College
SHAW#COM263 Undergraduate   3 credits $114
A continuation of word processing concepts consisting of macros, templates and styles. Creation of long reports with table of contents and indexes.

Advanced Word for Windows
Rio Salado College
RISA#BPC235DK Undergraduate   2 credits $124*
Using Word word processing software features such as math, columns, macros, styles, graphics, sort, outlines, and table of contents. Prerequisites: BPC/OAS135DK or permission of instructor.
* AZ residents $37 per credit.

Application Design and Implementation
New Hampshire College
NEHA#CIS310 Undergraduate   3 credits $1656
The use of information systems techniques to solve managerial and organizational problems of limited complexity is the focus of this course. CASE tools, quality assurance and testing, and interactive systems are emphasized. Supervised structured laboratory exercises are included. Prerequisite: CIS210.

Application Development
New Hampshire College
NEHA#CIS210 Undergraduate   3 credits $1656
Students in this course use information systems techniques to solve managerial and organizational problems of limited complexity. In addition students learn to solve formal analytical problems and implement solutions using information systems development techniques with a procedural language. Supervised structured laboratory exercises are included. Prerequisites: CIS100.

Applications of the Internet
Nova Southeastern University
NOVA#MCIS654 Graduate   3 credits $1,110
Enterprises thrive on information, and telecommunications is now viewed as an efficient and effective means of disseminating and receiving information. The Internet has emerged as the dominant server for national and international data communications between commercial, government, military, and academic organizations and network hosts. This course will study the structure, organization, and use of the Internet. Internet technologies and their potential application are examined including electronic commerce, database connectivity, and security. An emphasis will be placed on evaluating, organizing, and developing efficient models of electronic transactions.

Applications to Commercial Problems
New Jersey Institute of Technology
NJIT#CIS365 Undergraduate   3 credits $1143*
The design and implementation of commercially oriented computer systems. Emphasis is placed on modern computers as a tool for solving business problems. The COBOL programming language will be extensively studied and utilized in developing techniques for the solution of these problems. Prerequisites: NJIT#CIS113 or NJIT#CIS231 or completion of 100 level GUR in NJIT#CIS plus C++. Optional: 26 video lessons of 60 minutes each.
* NJ residents: $184/semester hour.

Artificial Intelligence
Mercy College
MERC#CS339 Undergraduate   3 credits $900
The course studies how computers can emulate the processes by which humans use logic and knowledge to solve problems. Topics include expert systems, intelligent databases, robotics, philosophical foundations, game-playing programs and formal proofs. Recent literature on artificial intelligence also will be discussed. Prerequisites: CS 231 - Foundations of Computing II.

Artificial Intelligence
Nova Southeastern University
NOVA#CISC670 Graduate   3 credits $1,110
Basic principles and techniques of artificial intelligence will be covered. Concepts of knowledge representation including formalized symbolic logic, inconsistency and uncertainty, probabilistic reasoning, and structured knowledge will be presented. Other areas are (1) knowledge organization and manipulation including search and control strategies, matching techniques, and knowledge management, (2) perception and communication including natural language processing and pattern recognition, and (3) the architecture of expert systems.

Artificial Intelligence
Nova Southeastern University
NOVA#MMIS670 Graduate   3 credits $1,110
This course will include an introduction to artificial intelligence as well as historical and current trends and characterization of knowledge-based systems. Search, logic and deduction, knowledge representation, production systems, and expert systems will be examined. Additional areas include architecture of expert systems and criteria for selecting expert system shells, such as end-user interface, developer interface, system interface, inference engine, knowledge base, and data interface. The student will use a commercial shell to build a working expert system.

Artificial Intelligence, Expert Systems
Nova Southeastern University
NOVA#MCIS670 Graduate   3 credits $1,110
Includes an introduction to artificial intelligence as well as historical and current trends and characterization of knowledge-based systems. Search, logic and deduction, knowledge representation, production systems, and expert systems will be examined. Additional areas include architecture of expert systems and criteria for selecting expert system shells, such as end-user interface, developer interface, system interface, inference engine, knowledge base, and data interface. The student will use a commercial shell to build a working expert system.

Authoring Systems Design
Nova Southeastern University
NOVA#MCTE626 Graduate   3 credits $1,110
Functionality and characteristics of PC and Macintosh authoring systems, frame-based, multimedia, and hypertext are explored in this course. Instructional systems design methodology in conjunction with authoring tools is examined and critiqued.

Basic PC Literacy
Fayetteville Technical Community College
FAYE#CIS111 Undergraduate   2 credits $326*
This course provides a brief overview of computer concepts. Emphasis is placed on the use of personal computers and software applications for personal and workplace use. Upon completion, students should be able to demonstrate basic personal computer skills.
* NC residents pay $20 per credit.

Basic Programming
Dakota State University
DAKO#CSC130 Undergraduate   3 credits $447
Hands-on introduction to programming using Visual Basic for Windows. Students will learn sequence, selection and repetition routines. Application and use of files, arrays, sound, graphics and event-driven programming concepts. Visual Basic software is included with the text. Prerequisite: CSC105.

Beginning Database
Cerro Coso Community College
CECO#CSCI52A Undergraduate   1 credits $115*
Hands-on microcomputer course designed to provide a basic understanding of database programs. Database design, creation and revision, and report formatting and printing are covered.
* California resident tuition: $13 per credit.

Beginning Internet
Barstow Community College
BARS#COMP100 Undergraduate   1 credits $???
Introduction to Internet and software used to access it. Principles associated with Internet to include FTP, telnet, Gopher, World Wide Web, and email. Non Degree Applicable.

Beginning Keyboarding
Northwest College
NOCO#TY139 Undergraduate   2 credits $???
Students are provided with a knowledge of the keyboard. Emphasis is placed on accuracy, speed and proofreading. A speed of 25 net words per minute must be attained.

Beginning RPG on the AS/400
Lansing Community College
LANS#CISB175 Undergraduate   3 credits $315
This Course Develops competence in RPG programming. It includes problem definitions, file procedures, control-level processing, physical and logical file processing, and fundamentals of interactive programming. An AS/400 computer will be used and RPG/400 topics covered. In this course the student will use a web browser or Telnet application to access the AS/400 and perform the tasks a RPG programmer typically performs when directly attached to an AS/400. In addition, the student will learn enough about the AS/400 environment to be able to program in a typical AS/400 shop.

Beginning Spreadsheets
Cerro Coso Community College
CECO#CSCI51A Undergraduate   1 credits $115*
Hands-on microcomputer course designed to provide a basic understanding of spreadsheets. Spreadsheet design, creation, revision, formatting, and printing are covered.
* California resident tuition: $13 per credit.

Beginning Word Processing
Cerro Coso Community College
CECO#CSCI50A Undergraduate   1 credits $115*
Hands-on microcomputer course designed to provide a basic understanding of word processing. Document creation, editing, formatting, printing and filing are covered.
* California resident tuition: $13 per credit.

Beginning WordPerfect Windows
Rio Salado College
RISA#BPC235DD Undergraduate   2 credits $124*
Using WordPerfect word processing software features such as math, columns, macros, styles, graphics, sort, outlines, and table of contents. Prerequisites: BPC/OAS135DD or permission of instructor.
* AZ residents $37 per credit.

Beyond HTML
University of Massachusetts - Dartmouth
MADA#CMP308   Undergraduate   0 credits $135
The Web has moved beyond the confines of HTML. With the advent of scripting languages, CGI, Java, Macromedia's Shockwave, Adobe's Acrobat, and the growing use of databases to serve both legacy data and Web pages, there are many ways to enhance a web site. This is an advanced course in the Online Communications Skills Program and should be taken after the WebCraft course, or its equivalent.

Building and Using Graphic-Based Virtual Environments
East Carolina University
EACA#EDTC6242   Undergraduate   3 credits $927*
Graphics-based virtual reality for education: environment design, building, application, and evaluation. Prerequisite: EDTC 6240 or consent of departmental chairperson.
* NC resident tuition $135.

Building and Using Text-Based Virtual Reality Environments
East Carolina University
EACA#EDTC6244   Undergraduate   3 credits $927*
Text-based virtual reality for education: environment design, building, applications, and evaluation. Prerequisite: EDTC 6240 or consent of departmental chairperson.
* NC resident tuition $135.

Building Web Pages
Great Basin College
GRBA#COT207B   Undergraduate   3 credits $186*
The course starts with the basics of the HyperText Markup Language and continues on, covering such topics as titles, headlines, paragraphs, font styles, special characters, links to other documents, links within the same document, unordered and ordered lists, definition lists, backgrounds, images, tables, frames, and basic forms. New assignments will be posted each week, due the following week. Some of the assignments will involve downloading files from various sites.
* NV residents tuition: $43 per credit.

Business and Society in the Information Age
State University of New York
SUNY#213254   Undergraduate   4 credits $586*
Examine the international trends and the nature of socio-technological change over the past 25 years. Develop the skills necessary to forecast current and future trends in business, trade, capital and labor flows, human rights issues and politics. Prerequisite: Three (3) courses in business, economics, history and/or social sciences.
* NY residents tuition: $515

Business Computer Programming
UCLA
UCLA#X414B   Undergraduate   4 credits $500
This is a comprehensive course which introduces students to, and builds proficiency in, computer programming for business. The Pascal programming language is used to illustrate concepts common to most high-level programming languages. Topics include top-down modular program design; user interface design; elements of algorithms, coding, and data structures; procedures; flow of control, including loops and conditionals; structured and unstructured files and record processing; and program testing, debugging, and documentation. Examples and assignments illustrate typical business applications. Weekly programming assignments required.

C Advanced Programming Language
New Hampshire College
NEHA#CIS231   Undergraduate   3 credits $1656
Advanced "C" Programming continues where the Introduction to "C" Programming course finishes. A brief review of arrays, pointer manipulation, structures, and functions will set the foundation for advanced programming techniques in "C". Advanced topics include scanners and parsers, data structures and algorithims, recursion, optimization techniques, memory management, bit operations and interrupts, and managing large scale "C" projects. Principles of good program design will also be covered. Prerequisites: CIS230.

C Language Programming
Front Range Community College
FRCC#CSC230   Undergraduate   4 credits $1052
Students are introduced to the C programming language, which is a "mid-level" language whose economy of expression and data manipulation features allow a programmer to deal with the computer at a "low-level." 60 Contact Hours. Prerequisites: MAT121 and either CSC150 or CSC160 or permission of instructor.

C Language Programming
New School for Social Research
NEWS#3127   Undergraduate   0 credits $580
C is a system programming language that combines the flexibility and complexity of Assembly Language with the programming ease and readability of high-level languages like ADA. C is the only high-level language used successfully in constructing operating systems. This course uses Borland C, covering all its language constructs, data structures, and operators. Standard input/output routines and the C Preprocessor (for macros) are discussed, as are differences among various compilers for small computers and C's relation to the UNIX operating system. Prerequisite: familiarity with at least one other programming language.

C Programming
University of Massachusetts - Lowell
MALO#92267   Undergraduate   3 credits $395

Introduces students to the techniques of programming in C. The language syntax, semantics, its applications and the portable library are covered. This course is not an introductory course in programming. However, it will teach some of the basics in the first few weeks. Students should have a working knowledge of at least one high-level programming language (Pascal-92265, Fortran-92263, or equivalent experience).

C Programming
New Hampshire College
NEHA#CIS230   Undergraduate   3 credits $1656

This course is designed to introduce the students to block structure thereby reinforcing the structure programming techniques learned in COBOL. This language is a cross between a high level and an assembly level language and is heavily dependent on the use of functions. Students will be involved in writing programs of increasing complexity throughout the course. Prerequisite: CIS100.

C Programming
New Jersey Institute of Technology
NJIT#CIS105C   Undergraduate   1 credits $381*

This course covers the fundamentals of "C" programming including all basic structures of the language. It deals with datatypes, functions, arrays, structures, pointers, formatted input/output and recursion. Optional: 18 video lessons of 60 minutes each.

* NJ residents: $184/semester hour.

C Programming
Rogers State University
ROGE#CS2223   Undergraduate   3 credits $495*

This course is a must for serious computer professionals and anyone who wants a degree in computer science. You will learn to write, debug, and run programs in C -- the increasingly popular UNIX-related, intermediate-level software development language. The course covers operators, variables, loops, functions, pointers, input-output, data types, structures, and file operations. The instructor is Julie Luscomb, an experienced distance-learning instructors in the Advanced Technologies Division at Rogers University.

* OK residents $315.

C Programming - Advanced C++
Brevard Community College
BREV#COP1002   Undergraduate   3 credits $435

Introduction to advanced "C" data structures such as as-link lists, stacks and queues using structures. The preprocessor is presented as an integrator of modules and enhancer of program portability.

C Programming I
Rio Salado College
RISA#CIS162AB   Undergraduate   3 credits $186*

Beginning C programming. Includes features needed to construct programs, functions, pointers, input and output options, data types, structures, and unions, and disk file operations. Prerequisites: CIS152, or CIS155, or CIS156, or CIS157, or CIS158, or CSC100 or permission of instructor.

* AZ residents $37 per credit.

C Programming Language I
Strayer University
STRA#CIS240   Undergraduate   4.5 credits $665

Involves practical applications in coding, compiling, and executing. Provides a structured approach to the development of functions, which are the building blocks of concise C programs. Prerequisite: CIS110 or equiv.

C Programming Language II
Strayer University
STRA#CIS241   Undergraduate   4.5 credits $665

Extends the structured programming approach to the integrated handling of pointers, strings, file input/output, and the derived data types of arrays, structures, and unions. Includes consideration for storage classes, the C Preprocessor, and the techniques for manipulating bits. Students write and test short C programs to strengthen their retention of syntax requirements and programming development. Prerequisite: CIS240.

C++ Computer Programming
Rogers State University
ROGE#CS2323   Undergraduate   3 credits $495*

C++ is an object-oriented extension of the C computer language. Object-oriented approaches to creation of software are covered in this course using C++ for illustration.

* OK residents $315.

C++ in Embedded Systems
University of Minnesota
MINN#IDLS0001   Undergraduate   0 credits $149

This noncredit short course gives C++ programmers practical, hands-on information about using C++ in embedded systems. The online study guide discusses operating issues such as memory management and virtual functions; programming exercises help illustrate what works and what doesn't when using C++. An optional online video clip supplements information in the online study guide. Prerequisites: one year of programming experience in C++; access to a computer with a C++ compiler and profiler.

C++ Programming
Cerro Coso Community College
CECO#CSCIC28A   Undergraduate   3 credits $345*

Introduces techniques and principles of problem solving using computer systems with C++ language. Appropriate for liberal arts and business students as well as for technically-oriented students. Laboratory projects are submitted. Prerequisite: CSCIC15 and MATHC72 or equivalent.

* CA residents pay $13 per credit.

C++ Programming
Delaware County Community College
DECO#DPR226   Undergraduate   3 credits $???

This course develops Object Oriented programs in a Windows environment using C++ programming language. Students learn the fundamentals of C++ by designing, developing and testing programs. This is not an introductory programming course.

C++ Programming
University of Massachusetts - Lowell
MALO#92268 Undergraduate 3 credits $395
This course will cover the C++ language and show the student how to use the language. We will cover class construction, operator overloading, virtual functions, templates, and introduce the student to the IO streams. Inheritance and its use in creating extendable libraries will be presented. Object oriented concepts will be presented in the context of the C++ language and its support for object oriented programming. Programming examples will be presented during the course.

C++ Programming
New Jersey Institute of Technology
NJIT#CIS105E Undergraduate 1 credits $381*
This course covers the fundamentals of object-oriented programming. It introduces object-oriented concepts, such as data abstractions, encapsulation, inheritance, dynamic binding, and polymorphism, and uses C++ as the vehicle for illustrating and implementing these concepts. Prerequisites: Knowledge of at least one programming language; knowledge of C language helpful. "C" compiler required. Optional: 15 video lessons of 60 minutes each.
* NJ residents: $184/semester hour.

C++ Programming Language
Nova Southeastern University
NOVA#MCIS501 Graduate 3 credits $1,110
An in-depth study of the C++ programming language. Principles of the object-oriented paradigm. Object-oriented programming theory and practice.

C++ Windows Programming 1
Red Wing Technical College
REWI#CC2521 Undergraduate 3 credits $120*
Description: This course introduces Windows programming concepts using the C++ language. Topics include application and window classes, windows program startup and shutdown tasks, creating and using menus, resource identifiers and response tables, dialog boxes and controls (pushbuttons, radio buttons, checkboxes, list boxes, etc.), and control objects. Prerequisites: CC2512 (may be taken concurrently) or instructor's permission.
* Resident rate $215; contact the provider for more info.

CAD Fundamentals
Rogers State University
ROGE#CAD2114 Undergraduate 3 credits $495*
This course is an introduction to AutoCAD Release 12, an industry standard in computer aided drafting. The student will receive a solid foundation in basic 2D CAD concepts such as object selection, object snap, symbol creation, coordinates key-in, object editing, external reference, model space/paper space, and object dimensioning. More advanced 3D concepts will not be covered. Prerequisite: Microcomputer Applications or knowledge of DOS 5.5 or higher and Windows 3.11.
* OK residents $315.

Capstone Project in IS Technology
Bellevue University
BELL#MISC460 Undergraduate 4 credits $1000
Students will act as a new information systems manager in analyzing their company's mission, critical success factors, information systems infrastructure, and at least one of the following: financial position, marketing strategy, production operations, or anticipated changes resulting from new technology, competition, or regulation. Students will present a tactical two-year information systems plan that addresses issues and supports the goals of the company.

Careers in Cyberspace
Kennesaw State University
KENN#FMV223 Undergraduate 3 credits $149
This course is designed to help students explore the world of work and choose careers compatible with one's strengths and interests. It teaches students how to use career resources, computerized career programs and the internet to investigate specific career choices, including job responsibilities, desired employee characteristics, training requirements, salary ranges and employment trends.

ClarisWorks
International Society for Technology in Education
ISTE#EDUC508K Grad 4 qu. credits $540*
This eight-lesson course provides a significant introduction to ClarisWorks. The course is offered for either IBM or Macintosh. Students will learn to use the word-processing, drawing, painting, database, and spreadsheet components. Assignments enable students to demonstrate mastery of the new features introduced in each lesson. Students read background articles on using ClarisWorks in the classroom. The final lesson involves a major project that integrates many ClarisWorks components.
* Non-credit option, tuition: $460.

Client-Server Computing
Nova Southeastern University
NOVA#CISC665 Graduate 3 credits $1,110
Topics include the components of client/server architecture, security, networking aspects, interprocess communication (RPC), role of the GUI and front-end development tools (from screen scrapers to ICASE), middleware (2-tier and 3 tier) and back-end concerns. The role of standards in client/server development is discussed including DCE, CORBA, ODBC, COM, and OLE, along with object-oriented aspects of client/server and distributed computing. Also included are the various relationships between client/server computing and business process reengineering, workflow automation, and groupware. Migration from legacy systems is considered along with concerns for meeting customer requirements (TQM, QFD, etc.)

Client-Server Distributed Computing
Nova Southeastern University
NOVA#MMIS626 Graduate   3 credits $1,110
Included in this course are a wide range of issues, methods, techniques, and case examples for developing and managing client/server and distributed systems. These include client/server development using RAD methodologies, transaction process monitors, types of aboveware and middleware, middleware standards (DCE, RPC, and CORBA), managing client/server environments, software installation and distribution, electronic mail architectures in C/S systems, evaluation of vendor strategies, issues in selecting C/S products, legacy system migration issues, interoperability, scalability, network and security concerns, the emerging desktop standards, the role of network computers and thin clients, etc.

Client/Server Architecture
New Jersey Institute of Technology
NJIT#CIS785P Undergraduate   3 credits $1143*
This course examines in depth the special interest area of client/server architecture including UNIX systems and networking, open systems, local area network technology concept, TCP/IP networking, NFS, client/server concept, managing client-server migration and internetworking and interoperability. This course is part of the graduate certificate in Programming Environment Tools. Prerequisites: Familiarity with the organization of a computer system and knowledge of at least one higher-level language. Optional: video lessons.
* NJ residents: $184/semester hour.

COBOL I
Dakota State University
DAKO#CSC221 Undergraduate   3 credits $447
Introduction to structured COBOL programming: Input, output, and reformatting; arithmetic programming design; report writing; control breaks; program maintenance, conditional names; validity checking one,-two-, and three-dimensional tables; table look-up, and interactive programming. Prerequisite: CSC150.

Communication Protocols and Internet Architectures
Harvard University
HARV#CSCIE131B Graduate   4 credits $1,200*
Networks are now too large, complex, and diverse to be built on an ad hoc basis. This course provides a structured approach to the design, analysis, and implementation of networks and protocols. We will study various protocols, including TCP/IP, WWW/HTTP, ATM, e-mail protocols, client/server protocols, and the IEEE 802 LAN protocol suite. In each case, the protocol's functions and the underlying reference model will be discussed. LAN architecture and design, internetworking using bridges and routers, and the implementation of ATM and frame relay networks will be presented. The course also will discuss new areas of work, including enterprise network management and broad-band/gigabit networks. Prerequisite(s): programming or computer architecture experience and a basic understanding of the principles of communication.
* Noncredit option: $950.

Communication Skills for MIS
Bellevue University
BELL#MISC320 Undergraduate   3 credits $750
This course covers forms, styles and methods used in business communication. Includes practice of oral communication and listening skills, as well as written correspondence.

Communication Software Update
Strayer University
STRA#CIS304 Undergraduate   4.5 credits $665
Compares and contrasts the new communications software for LANS and WANS to prior releases. Topics covered include administration, advanced administration, support, and advantages and disadvantages. Prerequisite: CIS175.

Comp Concepts & Software Systems
Rochester Institute of Technology
ROCH#60241090 Undergraduate   4 credits $923
An introduction to the overall organization of digital computers and operating systems for nonmajors.

Compiler Implementation C
Nova Southeastern University
NOVA#ISC632 Graduate   3 credits $1,110
Design, implementation, and testing of a compiler for a high-level language. The project will utilize state-of-the-art compiler generation tools, including parser generators and code generator generators. Prerequisite: CISC630.

Computer Applications
University of Alabama
ALAB#BCT300 Undergraduate   3 credits $250
This course features an examination of advanced applications of current and emerging instructional technologies in a variety of settings and in the context of various fields of study and job environments. Cognitive, product and skill competencies are included. Cognitive competencies are integrated into product & skills evaluations.

Computer Configuration and Enhancement
Rio Salado College
RISA#PC225 Undergraduate   1 credits $62*
Configuration and enhancement of a computer. Emphasis on configuration of hardware and software to optimize computer performance. Includes memory configuration and the identification and troubleshooting of configuration problems. Prerequisites: BPC125 or permission of instructor.
* AZ residents pay $37 per credit.

Computer Graphics for Information Managers
Nova Southeastern University
NOVA#MCIS625 Graduate   3 credits $1,110
Presents computer graphics as an aid to information managers who need a clear means of presenting the analysis of information. Topics include basic graphic techniques (e.g. histograms, bar charts, pie charts), the theory of graphic presentation of information, desktop publishing software, presentation software, graphics monitors (EGA, CGA, VGA, RGB, composite), laser printers, computer screen projection systems, and standards.

Computer Networks
Nova Southeastern University
NOVA#MCTE650 Graduate   3 credits $1,110
This course is focused on the following areas: fundamental concepts of computer network architecture and topologies, open system interconnection models and standards, analysis of transport protocol specification, network program interface, network management, and emerging computer network applications. An area that is covered in detail includes network standards that determine how data are transferred: Ethernet, token ring, and Fiber Distributed Data Interface. Attention will also be directed toward issues affecting operating peripherals, including CD-ROM drives and printers.

Computer Networks & Internets
Emporia State University
EMPO#CS410 Undergraduate   3 credits $228
This course answers the basic question "how do computer networks and internets operate?" in the broadest sense. The course provides a comprehensive, self-contained tour through all of networking from the lowest levels of data transmission and wiring to the highest levels of application software.

Computer Networks I
University of Denver, University College
DEUC#CIS4815 Undergraduate   3 qtr. hrs. $885
This course provides end to end coverage of the computer networking environment in significant detail from both the technical and business-case points of view. It will enable students to apply network concepts in the solution of operational hardware and software problems, and to assist others in understanding network architectures, communications concepts, protocols, facilities/media and their application. Topics also include internetworking, middleware, and network traffic loading. (Prerequisite: College Algebra; Introduction to Computer Networks).

Computer Operating Systems
Nova Southeastern University
NOVA#MCIS615 Graduate   3 credits $1,110
Objectives of managing computer system resources. Memory management, process management, file system management, scheduling, synchronization, interrupt processing, distributed processing, and parallel systems. An analysis of the role of operating systems in computer information systems development, operation, and evolution.

Computer Programming Design
Strayer University
STRA#CIS110 Undergraduate   4.5 credits $665
Involves extensive work in the solution of problems on a digital computer. Covers structured programming concepts, proper documentation techniques, coding, debugging, and running programs using I/O files, subroutines, arrays, searching and sorting. Prerequisite: CIS105.

Computer Programming II
State University of New York
SUNY#CISY2133 Undergraduate   3 credits $1038*
A continuation of CIS Y1113. Emphasis will be on advanced algorithms and the top down design of program development, data types and construction, control structures, recursion files. A high level language will be used to implement these solutions on a computer. Students will write, debug and execute programs in the business or scientific areas. Prerequisite: CIS Y1113.
* NY residents tuition: $137 per credit

Computer Programming Languages
New Jersey Institute of Technology
NJIT#CIS635 Undergraduate   3 credits $1143*
The theory and design of computer language systems; the formal theory of syntax and language classification; a survey of procedure and problem-oriented computer programming languages, their syntax rules, data structures, and operations; control structures and the appropriate environments and methods of their use; a survey of translator types. Prerequisites: Course in programming data structures and algorithms and course in assembly language programming and principles. Optional: 13 video lessons of 120 minutes each.
* NJ residents: $184/semester hour.

Computer Security
Nova Southeastern University
NOVA#MCIS652 Graduate   3 credits $1,110
Provides a foundation for understanding computer and communications security issues and a framework for creating and implementing a viable security program. Topics include hardware, software, and network security; the regulatory environment; personnel considerations; cryptography; protective controls against potential threats including hackers, disgruntled insiders, and software viruses; and techniques for responding to security breaches.

Computer Security
Nova Southeastern University
NOVA#MMIS652 Graduate   3 credits $1,110
Provides a foundation for understanding computer and communications security issues and a framework for creating and implementing a viable security program. Topics include hardware, software, and network security; the regulatory environment; personnel considerations; cryptography; protective controls against potential threats including hackers, disgruntled insiders, and software viruses; and techniques for responding to security breaches.

Computer Structures and COBOL
Nova Southeastern University
NOVA#MMIS611 Graduate   3 credits $1,110
Data and file structure concepts, data record format and file organization, sequential vs. random file access methods, tree-based file structure and search techniques, indexing and data clustering, multiway sort/merge and sort algorithms, input/output blocking and buffering. The student will design and implement programs in COBOL.

Computer Survival - Applications
University of Missouri
MOCE#CO100 Undergraduate   3 credits $387
Course is not applicable to computer science major requirements. Students must have Internet access to complete this course. This course covers essential computer skills and concepts. The emphasis is on using the computer as a tool to enhance productivity. Students will learn how to create word processing, spreadsheet, database, and presentation documents using the Microsoft Office suite of applications. Perquisites: Basic math skills, including fractions and percentages.

Computer Text Analysis
Dakota State University
DAKO#ENGL350 Undergraduate   3 credits $447
Applications of computers to writing and analysis of texts. Prerequisite: ENGL320 or INFS320 or CSC130 or consent of instructor.

Computer Usage and Applications
Rio Salado College
RISA#BPC110 Undergraduate   3 credits $186*
Exploration of computer operations and uses. Specific applications to business-personal computers.
* AZ residents $37 per credit.

Computer-Aided Software Engineering
Nova Southeastern University
NOVA#MMIS672 Graduate   3 credits $1,110
Computer-Aided Software Engineering (CASE) is a technique in which the path between initial systems analysis and the final coding of programs can be at least partly automated. Topics include a critical comparison between CASE and 4GLs (Fourth-Generation Languages), upper CASE (analysis/design), lower CASE (code generation and testing), tool kits, workbenches, methodology companions, platforms, completeness and consistency checking.

Computers and Programming
Greenville Technical College
GRTE#CPT114 Undergraduate   3 credits $381*
This course introduces computer concepts and programming. Topics include basic concepts of computer architecture, files, memory, and input/output devices. Programming is done in a modern high-level procedural language. You must have access to a copy of QBasic, which is included with most IBM-compatible computers' operating systems. This is the programming language which will be used in this course.
* NC residents pay $48 per credit.

Computers and Society I
Thomas Edison State College
THED#OLCOS161 Undergraduate   3 credits $397*
To develop a working vocabulary, know how a computer works, compare the functions of various devices, use problem-solving approaches, describe specific capabilities and limitations of BASIC and Logo, describe system analysis and design use application programs successfully, discuss ethical and social concerns raised by computer applications, evaluate appropriateness and probable effectiveness of using computers for given applications.
* NJ residents tuition: $33 per credit.

Creating Your Own Web Pages
University of Massachusetts - Dartmouth
MADA#CMP300 Undergraduate   0 credits $135
This seven-week, non-credit course will introduce the beginner to HTML, as well as basic issues of style and communications related to creating effective Web pages. Topics covered will include related software tools for Macintosh and Windows; the basics of HTML through to the more advanced features of Netscape and HTML 3.0; as well as an introduction to the fundamentals of Web style.

Critical Survey of Technology
Walden University
WALD#EDUC6150 Undergraduate   4 credits $920
Survey of innovative technologies including microcomputers, information systems, communication technologies, productivity tools, CD-ROM, courseware authoring systems, videodisc, interactive video, multimedia, and home based technologies. Critical evaluation related to effectiveness in improving the educational process.

Current Office Software - Database
Chemeketa Community College
CHEM#CS118C Undergraduate   1 credits $51
A hands-on introduction to software that is currently being used in business and industry. The brands of software in this class may change as industry standards evolve. Database Software: MS Access 7.0 for Windows. Includes database basics for forms design, data entry, queries, and reports.

Current Office Software - Worksheets
Chemeketa Community College
CHEM#CA118B Undergraduate   1 credits $51
A hands-on introduction to software that is currently being used in business and industry. The brands of software in this class may change as industry standards evolve. Spreadsheet Software: Microsoft Excel 7.0 for Windows. Includes worksheet basics and an introduction to charting.

Current Topics in Computer Information Systems
Strayer University
STRA#CIS291-299 Undergraduate   4.5 credits $665
Offers current topics from the area of computer information systems. Prerequisite: Permission of a Campus Dean.

Current Topics in Computing
Rio Salado College
RISA#CIS280 Undergraduate   3 credits $186*
Critical inquiry of current topics in computing. Application of industry trends to solve problems and/or investigate issues. Prerequisites: Permission of instructor.
* AZ residents pay $37 per credit.

Cutting-Edge Documentation
UCLA
UCLA#X860 Undergraduate   2.4 CEU $425
Documentation is the number-one reason organizations fail ISO 9000 and other quality and personnel systems audits. Too much, too little, or the wrong kind of documentation also wastes financial and human resources. This eight-week online course is designed for those who need to design, develop, or write policies and procedures, forms, memos, or other business documentation. Not a course in grammar, this practical workshop presents techniques for producing clear, concise, and accessible documentation.

Data and Computer Communications I
Nova Southeastern University
NOVA#CISC650 Graduate   3 credits $1,110
A course on the fundamentals of data communications and data communication networking. Topics include data transmission and encoding, digital data communication techniques, data link control, multiplexing, switched communications networks, circuit-switched networks, packet-switching techniques and systems (ARPANET/DDN, TYMNET, SNA, X.25 standard), local area networks, metropolitan area networks, optical fiber bus and ring topologies, the Fiber Distributed Data Interface (FDDI) standard, and LAN/MAN standards such as IEEE 802.

Data and Computer Communications I
Nova Southeastern University
NOVA#MCIS650 Graduate   3 credits $1,110
The fundamentals of data communications and data communication networking. Topics include data transmission and encoding, digital data communication techniques, data link control, multiplexing, switched communications networks, circuit-switched networks, packet-switching techniques and systems (ARPANET/DDN, TYMNET, SNA, X.25 standard), local area networks, metropolitan area networks, optical fiber bus and ring topologies, the Fiber Distributed Data Interface (FDDI) standard, and LAN/MAN standards such as IEEE 802.

Data and Computer Communications II
Nova Southeastern University
NOVA#CISC651 Graduate   3 credits $1,110
Communications protocol concepts, the open systems interconnection (OSI) model, the TCP/IP protocol suite, systems network architecture (SNA), internetworking, transport protocols, ISO transport standards, XTP transfer protocol, OSI session services and protocol, presentation concepts, Abstract Syntax Notation One (ASN.1), encryption, virtual terminal protocols, distributed applications including network management (SNMPv2), file transfer (FTAM), and electronic mail (X.400). The integrated services digital network (ISDN) architecture and services, broadband ISDN, and the impact of frame relay and cell relay technologies on network design. Prerequisite: CISC650.

Data and Computer Communications II
Nova Southeastern University
NOVA#MCIS651 Graduate   3 credits $1,110
Communications protocol concepts, the open systems interconnection (OSI) model, the TCP/IP protocol suite, systems network architecture (SNA), internetworking, transport protocols, ISO transport standards, XTP transfer protocol, OSI session services and protocol, presentation concepts, Abstract Syntax Notation One (ASN.1), encryption, virtual terminal protocols, distributed applications including network management (SNMPv2), file transfer (FTAM), and electronic mail (X.400). The integrated services digital network (ISDN) architecture and services, broadband ISDN, and the impact of frame relay and cell relay technologies on network design. Prerequisite: MCIS650.

Data and File Structures
Nova Southeastern University
NOVA#MCIS610 Graduate   3 credits $1,110
Data and file structure concepts, data record format and file organization, sequential vs. random file access methods, tree-based file structure and search techniques, indexing and data clustering, multiway sort/merge and sort algorithms, input/output blocking and buffering, and advanced secondary storage technology for multimedia binary large objects.

Data Base Systems
State University of New York
SUNY#CS532 Graduate   3 credits $1038*
Associations between data elements and data models: entity-relationship, relational, and object oriented. Relational data base techniques. Formal and commercial query languages. Introduction to query processing, transaction management, and currency control. Prerequisite: CS333, Algorithms.
* NY residents tuition: $137 per credit

Data Center Management
Nova Southeastern University
NOVA#MMIS683 Graduate   3 credits $1,110
Information center methods for building systems. The traditional life-cycle development will be reviewed. The role and services of the information center will be discussed within the context of these issues: user support, goals in terms of user education and training, promoting systems support and development services, and promulgating and monitoring use of standards for software and for protection of data resources. Other topics include principles of application generators, prototyping, user and provider roles in an information center. Students will learn to identify strengths and limitations of the information center approach.

Data Comm & Comp Networks
Rochester Institute of Technology
ROCH#60241190 Undergraduate   4 credits $923
An introduction to data communications hardware and software and use of these components in computer networks.

Data Communication
Strayer University
STRA#CIS185 Undergraduate 4.5 credits $665
Provides students with a technical foundation in networking technologies. Covers the technical aspects of networking connectivity, network management, media protocols and network services. Prerequisite: CIS175 or equiv.

Data Communications
City University
CITY#TM304 Undergraduate 5 qu. credits $785
Examination of the basic hardware and software components of data communications systems including the transmission media, encoding schemes, data-link and physical link protocols and interfaces. Included are sections on network security and management, and design methodologies used to build data communications systems.

Data Communications
University of Colorado
CUON#ISMG6120 Undergraduate 3 credits $1953*
Students will study basic concepts of data transmission, principles governing the design and administration of both wide and local area networks, and specific issues pertaining to client server computing and open system interconnection. Prerequisite: ISMG6020 or knowledge of business programming.
* CO residents tuition: $136 per credit.

Data Communications
Lansing Community College
LANS#CISB130 Undergraduate 3 credits $315
This course provides a comprehensive introduction to data communications systems: the major components, how they are integrated, and the differences between the various networks and network carriers. Successful students will learn the terminology and major protocols to a depth adequate to design application programs and discuss data communication topics with other professionals.

Data Communications
New York University
NEYO#X529028 Undergraduate 3.5 CEU $895
This course provides students with an in-depth study of data communications and local area network systems. Topics include: fundamental concepts of data communication; communication standards including communication codes, protocols, and network architecture; bridges, routers, and gateways; and computer environments.

Data Communications
New York Institute of Technology
NYIT#TN4704 Undergraduate 3 credits $???
Data concepts and terminology, transmission, networks, packet and other protocols, modulation techniques. Analog and digital data transmission. Prerequisite: TN4701.

Data Communications
Shawnee Community College
SHAW#COM0230 Undergraduate 3 credits $114
This is an introductory course dealing with the different areas in data communications. Topics include different topology design, protocols, networking hardware and software setup, and debugging network problems. Prerequisite: Business Computer Systems (COM-0111) or consent of instructor.

Data Communications Concepts, Security and Management
State University of New York
SUNY#273304 Undergraduate 4 credits $586*
Provides an overview of data communications concepts, security and management as they pertain to today's corporate environments. Topics covered include: network applications, data transmission and hardware, local, wide and metropolitan area network topologies and management, backbone networks, network design and implementation, and network security. This is an upper level study for those in telecommunications management or those who will deal with data communications in their future or current work environment.
* NY residents tuition: $515

Data Management System Design
New Jersey Institute of Technology
NJIT#CIS631 Undergraduate 3 credits $1143*
Covers the principles of database management systems design. Topics include: introduction to data models, E-R model, DBTG and hierarchical model, relational model, relational algebra, relational calculus, relational query languages; relational database design theory, query optimization; database protection, database recovery, concurrent operations on database systems. Prerequisite: NJIT#CIS610. Optional: 34 video lessons of 60 minutes each.
* NJ residents: $184/semester hour.

Data Networking and Network Architectures
Harvard University
HARV#CSCIE132 Graduate 4 credits $1,200*
This course provides in-depth exploration of a number of topics important in the design and operation of modern data networks. It is intended for people who will be involved in the details of data network planning, design, or support. Topics will include TCP/IP, IPv6 (the next generation of IP), SNMP, network architectures, quality of service, network security, performance testing of network devices, routing theory and practice, and the architecture and operation of routers, frame switches, and ATM switches. Prerequisite(s): a good understanding of data networks or CSCI E-131B.
* Noncredit option: $950.

Data Structures
City University
CITY#CS366 Undergraduate 5 qu. credits $785
Efficient use of data structures in programming. Structures studied include strings, pointers, objects, lists, queues, stacks, and trees. Application of structures to the analysis of problems associated with searching and sorting and study of the security, complexity and storage requirements of algorithms. Prerequisite: CS362, proficiency in C.

Data Structures and Algorithms for CIS
Nova Southeastern University
NOVA#MCIS503 Graduate 3 credits $1,110
Sorting and searching, algorithms for tree structures, advanced data structures, graph algorithms, complexity, dynamic programming, optimization problems. Prerequisite: MCIS501 or equivalent.

Data Warehousing
Nova Southeastern University
NOVA#MMIS642 Graduate 3 credits $1,110
This course includes the various factors involved in developing data warehouses and data marts: planning, design, implementation, and evaluation; review of vendor data warehouse products; cases involving contemporary implementations in business, government, and industry; techniques for maximizing effectiveness through OLAP and data mining.

Data-based Instruction
California State University - San Marcos
CASA#EDUC596 Post-bac 3 credits $315
This class will help special education teachers meet two standards. Standard 13 (Data-Based Decision Making): "Each candidate demonstrates the ability to continually analyze assessment and performance data to determine whether to maintain, modify, or change specific instructional strategies, curricular content or adaptations, behavioral supports and/or daily schedules to facilitate skill acquisition and successful participation for each student.".

Database Applications
Pitt Community College
PITT#CIC153 Undergraduate 6 credits $???
(Course description not available at press time.)

Database Management
City University
CITY#CS416 Undergraduate 5 qu. credits $785
Course focuses on effective, efficient use of data resources. Topics include configuration/change control, security, input validation, searching and sorting, database design, administration and management, data integrity and redundancy, data dictionary, the relational model, distributed processing, distributed data, disaster recovery planning, k back-up and recovery, client/serve systems, file servers, legal requirements, and Etherics. Database technologies will include Access, Paradox, SQL, and dBase IV. Prerequisite: CS090.

Database Management Systems
Golden Gate University
GOLD#CIS315 Graduate 3 credits $1404
Explains and compares the techniques and methodologies of data-base management systems; limitations and applications of the various data-base management systems; application of cost and benefits methodology in system selection; and management of databases. Uses ORACLE. Recommended prerequisite: CIS301.

Database Management Systems
Nova Southeastern University
NOVA#CISC660 Graduate 3 credits $1,110
The principles of database management systems are presented. Topics include concepts of database architectures such as three schema architectures, logical and physical data organizations, data models for database systems (network model, hierarchical model, relational model and object-oriented model), relational algebra and calculus, query languages, design theory for relational databases, functional dependencies and normal forms, null values and partial information, semantic data modeling, transaction management and concurrency control, index schema, file structures and access methods, query systems and query optimization, view management, client/server database architectures, distributed databases, etc.

Database Management Systems Practicum
Nova Southeastern University
NOVA#CISC661 Graduate 3 credits $1,110
Techniques of database management will be applied to practical projects. Prerequisite: CISC660.

Database Systems
Nova Southeastern University
NOVA#MCIS630 Graduate 3 credits $1,110
Methodologies and principles of database analysis and design are presented. Conceptual modeling and specifications of databases, database design process and tools, functional analysis and methodologies for database design, entity relationship model and advanced semantic modeling methods. Auxiliary concepts and theories of database systems including the architectures of database systems, logical and physical database organizations, data models for database systems (network, hierarchical, relational and object-oriented model), relational algebra and calculus, query languages, normal forms, null values and partial information, relational database design utilizing dependencies, view design and integration, concurrency control, etc.

Database Systems
Nova Southeastern University
NOVA#MCTE630 Graduate 3 credits $1,110
This course covers fundamentals of database architecture, database management systems, and database systems. Principles and methodologies of database design, and techniques for database application development.

Database Systems Practicum
Nova Southeastern University
NOVA#MCIS631 Graduate 3 credits $1,110
The techniques of database management systems are applied to practical projects. Prerequisite: MCIS630.

Databases in MIS
Nova Southeastern University
NOVA#MMIS630 Graduate 3 credits $1,110
The application of database concepts to management information systems. Design objectives, methods, costs, and benefits associated with the use of a database management system. Tools and techniques for the management of large amounts of data. Database design, performance and administration. File organization and access methods. The architectures of database systems, data models for database systems (network, hierarchical, relational and object oriented model), client/server database applications, distributed databases, and object-oriented databases.

Databases in MIS Practicum
Nova Southeastern University
NOVA#MMIS631 Graduate 3 credits $1,110
The techniques of database management systems will be applied to practical projects. Prerequisite: MMIS630.

Design and Analysis of Algorithms
Nova Southeastern University
NOVA#CISC615 Graduate 3 credits $1,110
Topics include sorting, algorithms for tree structures, dynamic programming, greedy methods, advanced data structures, divide and conquer, graph algorithms, arithmetic operations, algorithms for parallel computers, matrix operations, string/pattern matching, network problems, approximation algorithms, and NP-completeness.

Design and Implementation and TCP/IP
Strayer University
STRA#CIS300 Undergraduate 4.5 credits $665
Covers the design and implementation process for establishing networks. Focuses on planning the NetWare directory services tree and network access, advanced NetWare directory services design and implementation, TCP/IP and NetWare, configuration TCP/IP on a NetWare server, internet working IP LANS and troubleshooting IP LANS. Prerequisite: CIS285 or equivalent.

Design and Production of Multimedia
University of Colorado
CUON#MUME2000 Undergraduate 3 credits $1953*
This course is designed to give a comprehensive introduction to the issues that surround the design, production, and delivery of interactive multimedia presentations. It will be taught on-line and will use, where possible, computer generated teaching modules for instruction.
* CO residents tuition: $136 per credit.

Design Of Interactive Systems
New Jersey Institute of Technology
NJIT#CIS732 Undergraduate 3 credits $1143*
State-of-the-art guidelines and procedures for designing interactive systems. Emphasis will be placed on the design of systems with high cognitive variability: management information systems, decision support systems, computer mediated communication systems. Course will focus on current issues and research in this field. Prerequisites: Evaluation of Information Systems course or graduate course in development and use of information systems. Optional: 14 video lessons of 180 minutes each.
* NJ residents: $184/semester hour.

Desktop Publishing
Mercy College
MERC#CS240 Undergraduate 3 credits $900
(Course description not available at press time.)

Desktop Publishing
New Hampshire College
NEHA#COM331 Undergraduate 3 credits $1656
This course is a hands-on introduction to desktop publishing utilizing Adobe Pagemaker software. In this course students learn the purposes, advantages, and disadvantages of desktop publishing. They also learn how to create internal and external publications, logos, resumes, visual aids, and how to choose hardware and software. Students will need a copy of Pagemaker 6.5, which can be purchased at an educational discount at the NHC bookstore. Prerequisite: COM330.

Desktop Publishing
Rio Salado College
RISA#BPC128AC Undergraduate 1 credits $62*
Presents basic concepts of commercially prepared software used to do desktop publishing. Incorporates a combination of narrative and pictorial/graphic creation and presentation, including set up, text entry, graphic generation, text and graphic merging, and other computer-based functions.
* AZ residents $37 per credit.

Desktop Publishing - Word 7.0
Rio Salado College
RISA#BPC128AE Undergraduate 1 credits $62*
Presents basic concepts of commercially prepared software used to do desktop publishing. Incorporates a combination of narrative and pictorial/graphic creation and presentation, including set up, text entry, graphic generation, text and graphic merging, and other computer-based functions.
* AZ residents pay $37 per credit.

Desktop Publishing 1
Pitt Community College
PITT#CIS165 Undergraduate ?? credits $???
An introduction to desktop publishing software capabilities. Topics will include design principles and utilization of these principles given design specifications. Upon completion the student will be able to demonstrate desktop publishing proficiency by creating a letterhead, brochure, factsheet, menu, newsletter, advertisement and electronic publications.

Desktop Publishing Applications
Eastern Oregon University
EAOR#OADM210E Undergraduate   3 credits $240
This course is designed to help participants develop basic desktop publishing skills and general layout and design techniques. Students will use basic and intermediate PageMaker features to create a variety of projects. It is designed to give students practical experience using Adobe PageMaker and become familiar with desktop publishing techniques. Requ.: Adobe PageMaker.

Desktop Publishing I - Pagemaker
Chemeketa Community College
CHEM#CA205 Undergraduate   3 credits $123
A hands-on microcomputer desktop publishing course using Aldus PageMaker. Includes microcomputer use, an overview of the printing process, typography and basic design, and the use of PageMaker software. Prerequisite: Touch typing ability, 25 wpm minimum. Previous computer experience required.

Developing a C Application
University of Washington
WASH#C900 Undergraduate   4 CEUs $359
Students work one-on-one with the instructor to develop a C or C++ application which demonstrates their knowledge and skills. Those taking this noncredit course prepare a proposal for an application project and develop a schedule for the project. They develop general source code, debug, improve and enhance the program, and prepare appropriate documentation to design a significant application in C or C++ in the areas of graphics, database or statistics.

Developing a Web Page Using HTML
Cerro Coso Community College
CECO#CSCIC56C Undergraduate   2 credits $230*
Students will learn the basic skills necessary to author a Web Page through the use of HyperTextMarkup Language (HTML); and will learn to integrate text, graphics and hypertext links. Students will complete lessons, which will result in the development of their own personal home page. The skills learned during these lessons are basic to Web development. All home pages completed during this class will be placed on the college server to be viewed over the World Wide Web. Prerequisite: CSCIC56A.
* CA residents pay $13 per credit.

Developing a Web Page With HTML2
Cerro Coso Community College
CECO#ART56C Undergraduate   2 credits $230*
Students will learn the basic skills necessary to author a Web Page through the use of HyperTextMarkup Language (HTML); and will learn to integrate text, graphics and hypertext links. Students will complete lessons which will result in the development of their own personal home page. The skills learned during these lessons are basic to Web development.
* California resident tuition: $13 per credit.

Digital Illustration
State University of New York
SUNY#GC141 Undergraduate   3 credits $540*
This course is an introduction to computer graphics and digital illustration. Although there are no prerequisite design courses, a basic course is suggested. Students will use desktop computers, video interfacing equipment, desktop scanners and other devices to generate and output computer graphic images. The course is lab-oriented, as well as being task oriented. Studio time is augmented by lecture.
* NY residents tuition: $90 per credit.

Digital Imaging
State University of New York
SUNY#GC142 Undergraduate   3 credits $540*
This course introduces the student to digital imaging technologies impacting graphic communication. Students will explore the potential of imaging software, scanners, dye sublimation printers and other technologies. The use of digital media and the creation of computer-based imagery will be emphasized. The course is balanced between aesthetic potential and technological mastery. Students will learn how to input image and text, and how to combine and manipulate those visual elements.
* NY residents tuition: $90 per credit.

Digital Typography
State University of New York
SUNY#GC121 Undergraduate   3 credits $540*
This course will cover the fundamentals of typesetting and typography. Students will study the development of type designs, typesetting methods, type measurement, and page layout. During the course, the student will use desktop computers to prepare one color mechanicals and become familiar with one or more software programs appropriate for typesetting. Special Requirements: Students must have their own computer with QuarkXpress software.
* NY residents tuition: $90 per credit.

Distributed Computing Systems
Nova Southeastern University
NOVA#CISC646 Graduate   3 credits $1,110
Concepts and design of distributed computing systems and the state of the art of distributed computing application programming. Included are the basic concepts of distributed systems: transparency, heterogeneity, network process communication, distributed client-server and other distributed computer system models, network file systems (NFS), communication protocols (TCP/IP), synchronization, naming, and process and resource management. The state-of the-art portion concentrates on developing distributed applications by both low-level and high-level remote procedure (RPC) programming, socket-based interprocess communication and implementation. Network programming projects will be on the UNIX-based platforms. Prerequisites: C Programming Language, Data Structures, Operating Systems and UNIX. Prerequisite: CISC650.

Distributed Database Management
Nova Southeastern University
NOVA#MCIS632 Graduate   3 credits $1,110
Information storage and retrieval in a distributed environment. Distributed processing networks; degrees of distribution; approaches to distribution in multiple unduplicated/duplicated and centralization/decentralization issues; management concerns and criteria; and technical developments in office systems (digital voice communications, LANS, electronic mail, decision support systems, etc.) Alternatives to distributed processing. Prerequisite: MCIS630.

Distributed Database Management
Nova Southeastern University
NOVA#MMIS632 Graduate   3 credits $1,110
Students will study information storage and retrieval in a distributed environment. Topics include distributed processing networks; degrees of distribution; approaches to distribution and multiple unduplicated/duplicated and centralization/decentralization issues; management concerns and criteria; and technical developments in office systems (digital voice communications, LANS, electronic mail, decision support systems, etc.), and alternatives for distributed processing. Prerequisite: MMIS630.

Distributed Databases
Nova Southeastern University
NOVA#CISC662 Graduate   3 credits $1,110
The study of information storage and retrieval in a distributed environment and distributed processing networks. Prerequisite: CISC660.

Document Design
University of Minnesota
MINN#RHET5581 Undergraduate   4 credits $400
Designing documents to meet the user's needs, completing a draft, and evaluating effectiveness are covered in this course. It will also give students an opportunity to examine forms and software input sheets for databases, decision aids, computer-aided instruction, online programs, or visual displays. As part of the coursework, students will participate in review team assessing multimedia projects.

Document Design & Desktop Publishing
New Jersey Institute of Technology
NJIT#ENG605 Undergraduate   3 credits $1143*
Provides an understanding of and capability in the visual presentation of information. Course integrates theories of design, principles of layout and format, and technology of desktop publishing. Modules include theory and practice in design and information processing, design and visual coherence, visual aspects of documents, tools of design, and production and integration of graphics into documents.
* NJ residents: $184/semester hour.

Economy as Ecosystem
George Mason University
GEMA#LRNG592B Graduate   3 credits $???
This is a graduate course offered by George Mason University. Its topic is bionomics, an approach to economics that conceives of the economy as being like an ecosystem. The course thus focuses on evolutionary processes in the economy. It views the economy as a complex, dynamic system in which information and innovation are of the essence. Prerequisites: CD-ROM drive.

EFF Guide to the Internet
Rio Hondo College
RIHO#WWW8 Undergraduate   ?? credits $???
This course is designed to introduce the you to an "EFF's (Extended) Guide to the Internet. This course explores email, Usenet, mailing list, Telnet, FTP, Gophers, WAISs, and the World Wide Web in more detail. The major emphasis will be on: 1) Gopher search and gopher sites, 2) FTP (File Transfer Protocol) for obtaining documents, graphics, and sound, and 3) Newsgroups/Usenet - The seven traditional newsgroups; "news", "rec", "soc", "talk", "comp", "misc", and "sci".

Electronic Commerce
New Mexico Highlands University
NMHI#8552A Undergrad/Grad   3 credits $297
Teleshopping, telecommuting and online research are fast becoming routine business practices. This course provides an introduction to Electronic Commerce for business students. The course will focus on the impact of electronic commerce on business, its current state of development, successful business strategies, and its future development.

Electronic Commerce
Strayer University
STRA#BUS213 Undergraduate   4.5 credits $665
Examines business implications of evolving and new automation technologies and telecommunications systems. Demonstrates the utilization of electronic commerce tools based on Electronic Data Interchange, the Internet, and other applications. Topics include procurement process stovepipes and handoffs, business volume profile, security issues, electronic catalogs, Internet and the procurement cycle, and options for low-value/low-complexity buys. Prerequisite: CIS105.

Electronic Commerce on the Internet
Nova Southeastern University
NOVA#MMIS654 Graduate   3 credits $1,110
Enterprises thrive on information, and telecommunications is now viewed as an efficient and effective means of disseminating and receiving information. The Internet has emerged as the dominant server for national and international data communications between commercial, government, military, and academic organizations and network hosts. This course will study the structure, organization, and use of the Internet. Internet technologies and their potential application are examined including electronic commerce, database connectivity, and security. An emphasis will be placed on evaluating, organizing, and developing efficient models of electronic transactions.

Electronic Commerce via the Internet
Golden Gate University
GOLD#TM396H Graduate   3 credits $1404
Examination of the Internet as an emerging marketing medium used by innovative enterprises to maximize promotion and reduce costs. Electronic Commerce (EC) and the use of telecommunications will be discussed via practical case studies.

Electronic Communications
University of Denver, University College
DEUC#TELE4801 Undergraduate   3 qtr. hrs. $885
This course is the continuation of the technical basics of modern telecommunications systems offered in Tele 4800. An understanding of those basic technical fundamentals is vital to the success of the modern telecommunications manager. The course emphasis is on applications of basic electronic knowledge for the telecommunications professional, and is intended for those who are new to electronics and circuits.

Electronic Mail & Online Services
University of Alaska - Fairbanks
ALFA#ED293A Undergraduate   1 credits $71
Introduction to telecommunications using a personal computer and modem. Learn to use the services available through the University of Alaska Computer Network including electronic mail, SLED library services, Alaskanet, and Legislative Information Office system.

Electronic Mail & Online Services
University of Alaska - Fairbanks
ALFA#ED593A Undergraduate   1 credits $100
Introduction to telecommunications using a personal computer and modem. Learn to use the services available through the University of Alaska Computer Network including electronic mail, SLED library services, Alaskanet, and the Legislative Information Office system. Use these resources to prepare a research paper on a telecommunications topic and submit it electronically.

Ethical Issues in Information Systems
Bellevue University
BELL#MISC440 Undergraduate   4 credits $1000
This course examines human, ethical and legal issues resulting from technology and stresses the role of ethics in effective leadership.

Evaluation of Information Systems
New Jersey Institute of Technology
NJIT#CIS675 Undergraduate   3 credits $1143*
Techniques, methodologies, and approaches to evaluate information systems within the context of the user and organization environment. Emphasis on the application of these techniques in assessing information systems and their performance for users and organizations. Optional: 12 video lessons of 120 minutes each.
* NJ residents: $184/semester hour.

Excel On Line
Edmonds Community College
EDMO#PCAPP167 Undergraduate   3 credits $220
Provide an overview of the features and skills required to get maximum benefit from using this "industry standard" spreadsheet program called Excel for Windows. Using the Microsoft Step by Step textbook, students will gain hands-on knowledge and experience creating spreadsheets (entering and modifying data, creating formulas, formatting data); creating charts and graphs (entering and editing data, creating and modifying charts); printing spreadsheets and charts; managing data (workbooks, worksheets, sorting, subtotaling, database and analysis functions); sharing data; automating tasks with macros.

Excel Spreadsheet
Rio Salado College
RISA#BPC114DE Undergraduate   3 credits $186*
Computer spreadsheet skills for solving business problems using Excel, including calculations, forecasting, projections, macro programming, database searching, extraction, linking, statistics, and matrix manipulation. Production of graphs and reports. Project design using multiple, integrated spreadsheets.
* AZ residents $37 per credit.

Exploring the Internet
Great Basin College
GRBA#COT133B Undergraduate   1 credits $62*
The Internet is a vast, social establishment tied together by thousands of computers and millions of people around the world. This class is aimed at finding resources, communicating with people and enjoying this social phenomenon.
* NV residents tuition: $43 per credit.

Fundamentals in Electronic Commerce
New York University
NEYO#X529027 Undergraduate   3.5 CEU $895
This course examines the impact of emerging technologies on how we conduct business in a 3wired2 world. Topics include: ingredients of a commerce-enabled Web site from hardware and software to necessary operational processes; copyright, authentication, encryption, certification, and security; on-line payment strategies (SET, E-cash, check, and charge) and companies offering solutions; e-commerce business models, including development costs, ongoing operations, and marketing; impact of e-commerce on the traditional marketplace; and potential future commerce scenarios.

Fundamentals of Visual Basic
University of California-Irvine
CAIR#COM1 Undergraduate   3 credits $395
Learn the fundamentals of Microsoft Visual Basic (VB), an easy-to-learn programming environment for Microsoft Windows. Explore how VB can add programming power to popular Windows applications such as Word, Excel, and Access. Learn how to develop simple standalone Windows applications. Topics in this on-line course include the VB programming environment, VB program structure, programming tools, active controls, menus, dialog boxes, file manipulation, graphics, use of the mouse and keyboard, data controls, and debugging techniques. Register early, enrollment is limited.

Fundamentals of Visual C++
University of California-Irvine
CAIR#COM2 Undergraduate   3 credits $395
Learn the fundamentals of Microsoft Visual C++, a powerful programming environment for Microsoft Windows. Explore how Visual C++ can expand your programming capabilities with the Microsoft Foundation Classes (MFC) library as you learn how develop object-oriented, user interface applications. Topics in this online course include Microsoft Integrated Development Environment (IDE), ActiveX controls, classes, modules, plug-ins, file access, serialization, graphics, multi-tasking, and the development of both Single-Document Interface (SDI) and Multiple-Document Interface (MDI) applications.

Fundamentals of Visual J++
University of California-Irvine
CAIR#COM3 Undergraduate   3 credits $395
Learn the fundamentals of Java applications and applets using Microsoft Visual J++. This on-line course focuses on the Microsoft Visual J++ integrated development environment (IDE) and explores the full capabilities of this programming tool in designing applications and applets. The course covers the language's essential features including variables and expressions, control and repeat structures, arrays and files, as well as advanced Java features such as advanced GUI elements and the use of Visual J++'s interactive debugger. An introduction to HTML language is provided as well.

Geographic Information Systems
Humboldt State University
HUMB#CIS499 Undergraduate   3 credits $345
Microcomputer hardware and software developments have contributed to a dramatic proliferation of analytical resources within the area of Geographic Information Systems. This course will familiarize students with the general and specific concepts associated with GIS. Students will explore basic and advanced principles of geographic information systems theory. Students will develop an understanding , which can later be applied in a laboratory-based course.

Global Communications
University of Wisconsin
WISC#COMM302 Undergraduate   3 credits $312
This course introduces teachers and business people to the opportunities, problems, and issues of the emerging global communications system. Participants discover life on the Internet, including global technology used for education, commerce, community-building, journalism, health, politics, and the arts. The course introduces the variety of multimedia services now available via the Internet and the World Wide Web. Students learn the tools for research and publishing using Netscape and are introduced to the HTML language to create electronic documents.

Graphics-Based Virtual Environments I
East Carolina University
EACA#EDTC3242 Undergraduate   3 credits $927*
An intermediate course in the design, building, application, and evaluation of graphics-based virtual environments for specific applications. Prerequisite: EDTC2240 or consent of instructor.
* NC resident tuition $135.

Graphics-Based Virtual Environments II
East Carolina University
EACA#EDTC3243 Undergraduate   3 credits $927*
An advanced course in the design, building, applications, and evaluation of graphics-based virtual environments for specific applications. Prerequisite: EDTC2240 or consent of instructor.
* NC resident tuition $135.

Guided Design in Software Engineering
New Jersey Institute of Technology
NJIT#CIS490 Undergraduate   3 credits $1143*
This course focuses on the methodology for developing software systems. Students will prepare a proposal for a project which includes its functional specifications and preliminary design. Prerequisites: Senior standing or departmental approval. Optional: :26 video lessons of 90 minutes each.
* NJ residents: $184/semester hour.

History of Communication Technologies
New School for Social Research
NEWS#3937 Undergraduate   3 credits $455
Throughout history, new communication technologies have permanently altered the worlds that spawned them. With the luxury of historical hindsight, we trace the profound social, cultural, and political changes triggered by the invention of writing (the first communication revolution) and the development of the phonetic alphabet; the invention of the printing press and cheap paper (the basis of the second communication revolution, which has dominated all aspects of Western civilization during the last 500 years); and the discovery of television (the third communication revolution, which has revived in new ways important qualities of the preliterate world).

Home Page Design and Presentation
Yavapai Community College
YAVA#ART108 Undergraduate   ?? credits $???
An introduction to the design and construction of an Internet home page with basic Hyper Text Markup Language tags. Application of design principles.

How To Do Research Online
New School for Social Research
NEWS#2687 Undergraduate   3 credits $1638*
It seems as if everything is going on line: books, magazines, government data, and much more. What does this mean for researchers? Can you really find everything you need on the Internet, Consumer On-Line, or CD-ROM? This course identifies what is available on line, how to find what you need, and how to quickly assess what you have located for quality and reliability. Also examined are emerging trends in on-line research and the impact of new technology on libraries, newspapers, and other institutions.
* Non-credit option, tuition: $365.

HTML Tags for Page Design
Yavapai Community College
YAVA#ART109 Undergraduate   ?? credits $???
Internet research of HTML tags from a provided source list. Produce an appealing homepage with tags from the provided list.

Human-Computer Interaction
Nova Southeastern University
NOVA#CISC685 Graduate   3 credits $1,110
Focuses on the dynamics of human-computer interaction (HCI). Provides a broad overview of HCI as a sub-area of computer science and explores user-centered design approaches in information systems applications. Addresses the user interface and software design strategies, user experience levels, interaction styles, usability engineering, and collaborative systems technology. Students will perform formal software evaluations and usability tests.

Human-Computer Interaction
Nova Southeastern University
NOVA#MMIS680 Graduate   3 credits $1,110
The dynamics of human-computer interaction (HCI). Provides a broad overview and offers specific background relating to user-centered design approaches in information systems applications. Areas to be addressed include the user interface and software design strategies, user experience levels, interaction styles, usability engineering, and collaborative systems technology. Students will perform formal software evaluations and usability tests.

Imaging Processing
State University of New York
SUNY#MAT433085 Undergraduate   4 credits $1038*
Image Processing has become a familiar term in recent years due to the many technologies that rely on the manipulation and analysis of pictorial information. It is perhaps not so well known that mathematics provides much of the framework for such work. This course will explore the role of mathematics in image processing and will include hands-on programming in C. Prerequisites: Calculus I & II and an introductory course in C programming or by permission of the Instructor.
* NY residents tuition: $137 per credit

Information Literacy
State University of New York
SUNY#LIB111 Undergraduate   1 credits $178*
This course will introduce students to the organization, retrieval and evaluation of electronic and print information. Students will be provided with an overview of college library systems, networked information systems, traditional scholarly resources, evolving delivery systems, and the concepts underlying the research process. Students will gain an understanding of the importance of the Internet as a research tool and the changing nature of information resources. Students will utilize electronic databases, the World Wide Web, and print resources. Students will be able to apply principles learned in this course to research assigned in other courses.
* NY residents tuition: $89.

Information Sources on the Internet
Rio Hondo College
RIHO#PAC43036 Undergraduate   0.5 credits $???
This course is designed to introduce the student to information sources on the Internet; with an emphasis on Justice sites. Topics include; search engine, electronic libraries, and justice sites. The course will expose the student to search and retrieval of data.

Instructional Design for Multimedia
The Graduate School of America
TGSA#ED847W Graduate   4 credits $795
This course introduces an instructional design model for developing effective multimedia instruction. It discusses a variety of instructional methodologies, such as tutorials, simulations and hypermedia, and deals with the fundamental principles of good hum an-computer interface design.

Instructional Software
International Society for Technology in Education
ISTE#EDUC508B Grad   4 qu. credits $540*
In this unique course, you will be provided with access to software and current theories on evaluating and integrating software into the curriculum. Participants will design, teach, and evaluate lessons using software of potential interest. Alternately, participants may use and evaluate personal productivity software in performing teacher tasks such as creating tests or student reports. The software list includes new and well-established programs.
* Non-credit option, tuition: $460.

Intelligent Agents
University of Colorado
CUON#CSC5805 Undergraduate   3 credits $1953*
(Course description not available at press time.)
* CO residents tuition: $136 per credit.

Interactive Computer Graphics
Nova Southeastern University
NOVA#CISC681 Graduate   3 credits $1,110
Principles of interactive computer graphics. Concepts include fundamental raster operations such as scan conversion, fill methods, and anti-aliasing; transformations; graphic languages such as PHIGS and Open GL; projection; hidden surface removal methods; 3D modeling techniques; ray tracing; animation; and graphical user interfaces.

Interactive Multimedia Systems
University of Colorado
CUON#ISMG6240 Undergraduate   3 credits $1953*
Covers the theories and principles governing the analysis, design, and development of interactive multi-media information systems. Technical, legal, and security issues for distributed hypermedia are also addressed. Prerequisite: ISMG6080 or ISMG6140.
* CO residents tuition: $136 per credit.

Interactive Three-Dimensional Internet Applications
East Carolina University
EACA#EDTC4246 Undergraduate   3 credits $927*
Design and construction of interactive three-dimensional Internet applications, e.g., VRML. Prerequisites: EDTC 2240 and working knowledge of HTML, or consent of instructor.
* NC resident tuition $135.

Intermediate Business Computing
Edmonds Community College
EDMO#CIS102 Undergraduate   3 credits   **$220**
This course is a continuation of CIS100--Introduction to Business Computing. CIS100 course or an equivalent course is a prerequisite for this course. For details on the CIS100 course refer to on-line course noting the course objectives. If you are signed up for this course, I will assume that you have the skills to take this course.

Internet and Intranet Business Applications
New York University
NEYO#X529418 Undergraduate   3.5 CEU   **$895**
The Internet has grown into a pervasive, international communications network. Although the Internet is a tremendous strategic resource, it is also rapidly becoming a business necessity. To best leverage the Internet in a business environment, you must understand its unique components, capabilities, and culture. This entry-level survey course introduces the fundamental protocols, technologies, applications, and services of the Internet. Instruction includes network architecture, business issues, security, and future developments. The World Wide Web, Mosaic, and Netscape are also discussed.

Internet Client/Servers
City University
CITY#CS443 Undergraduate   5 qu. credits   **$785**
This course is a study of intranet/internet principles. A variety of system clients will be examined. Server technology and techniques, with an emphasis on Microsoft Windows NT Server will be discussed. Case studies will be used to promote an understanding of the role this technology plays in business and education.

Internet Curriculum Development
University of Washington
WASH#LIBRC498 Undergraduate   5 qu. credits   **$370**
For teachers, school library/media specialists, those in educational technology, principals and others who want to utilize the Internet for curriculum enhancement. You will learn to design and manage collaborative classroom projects through the Internet, communicate with colleagues throughout the world, analyze issues affecting educators, such as ethics of access, copyright, network structures and censorship, use the basic Internet tools such as Gopher, LISTSERVs, World Wide Web, etc., as resources for curriculum development, gather information and expand your knowledge in areas of interest, use the Internet to solve real-world problems through a constructivist model.

Internet for Educators
Texas Technical University
TETE#EDIT4000 Undergraduate   3 credits   **$159**
This course covers the basics of computer communications, e-mail, online conferencing, Internet issues, finding information on the Internet, advanced web techniques, Internet file transfer, and constructing a personal web page. Prerequisite: EDIT2318 or another course covering fundamental computer operations.

Internet for New Computer Users
Pima Community College
PIMA#CSC110 Undergraduate   1 credits   **$55***
This class will have a cable TV component! You will have the option of taking the class as a combination cable/Internet class or as a pure internet class. Since it's a one credit class, it will be offered beginning at three different five week intervals throughout the semester. The topics covered included the history, principles, and use of the Internet. Also included are the use of the following Internet services: e-mail, Telnet, FTP, WWW, Archie, Gopher, and others. Students will develop their own home page.
* AZ residents, $32/credit hour.

Internet For Office Professionals
Chemeketa Community College
CHEM#CA118D Undergraduate   1 credits   **$51**
(Course description not available at press time.)

Internet Organization, Design, and Resource Discovery
East Carolina University
EACA#EDTC6050 Undergraduate   3 credits   **$927***
An overview of the organization and design of the Internet with emphasis on the tools available for discovering useful resources for instructional and other purposes. By the end of the course, students will be able to demonstrate an understanding of the scope, development, and growth of the Internet; demonstrate an understanding of the various legal, economic, technological, political, behavioral, ethical, and access issues associated with the Internet; demonstrate an understanding of the various Internet protocols and how they operate; demonstrate an understanding of the concepts of (as well as utilize) electronic mail, remote logins, file transfers, information services, discussion groups, and name servers; create an html document.
* NC resident tuition $135.

Internet Program Development
Strayer University
STRA#CIS309 Undergraduate   4.5 credits   **$665**
Focuses on the development of programs related to the design and creation of a web. Other topics covered are the Gateway Interface Programming, the creation of Image Maps, setup of a Web Browser Prerequisite: CIS307 or equivalent.

Internet Publishing for Educators
UCLA
UCLA#X333 Undergraduate   3 credits   **$425**
Designed especially for educators, this comprehensive online hands-on study of the Internet and World Wide Web has two specific goals: First, participants learn how to access the Internet and World Wide Web's many educational resources. Through readings, demonstrations, and discussions, the course also develops a critical framework for assessing the appropriate use of the various resources available on the Internet and Web in the elementary and secondary curriculum.

Internet Research for Online Courses
UCLA
UCLA#X396B Undergraduate   4 credits $500
This course explores how to meet the information needs of business and academe through Internet tools. Applied cases are used to demonstrate the availability and accessing of various research databases, libraries, special information services, and information retrieval services on the Internet.

Internet Search Strategies
Kennesaw State University
KENN#FMV215 Undergraduate   3 credits $149
The World Wide Web is a fast growing database of information that can be useful to those who want to get at information that they can use. Unfortunately, not all information is useful nor does it serve the purposes of the searcher. In this workshop Dr. Reid helps you quickly negotiate around typical problems facing those new to online research.

Internet Security
Strayer University
STRA#CIS311 Undergraduate   4.5 credits $665
Covers the topical subjects related to information security and the Web. The security capable browsers, secure transaction techniques such as cryptography, and the use of a firewall protection are explored. Prerequisite: CIS309 or equivalent.

Internet Topics
Strayer University
STRA#CIS307 Undergraduate   4.5 credits $665
Covers the internet in terms of how it works and the services available such as electronic mail, file transfer, remote login and information browsing (GOPHER), and automated contents search (WAIS). Webs also are covered, including the design and creation of web pages using one of the commercially available Web programming languages. Prerequisite: CIS110 or equivalent.

Internet Web Publishing I
Rio Salado College
RISA#CIS233AA Undergraduate   1 credits $62*
Introduction to designing and creating pages on the Internet's World Wide Web using the hypertext markup language (HTML). Hands-on experience authoring HTML and preparing beginning web documents. Prerequisites: BPC/CIS133BA or permission of instructor.
* AZ residents pay $37 per credit.

Internet Web Publishing III
Rio Salado College
RISA#CIS233CA Undergraduate   1 credits $62*
Introduction to Web server access, security and design issues. Covers emerging issues in web publishing. Prerequisites: BPC/CIS233BA or permission of instructor.
* AZ residents pay $37 per credit.

Internetworks in International Development
University of Iowa
IOWA#047150 Undergraduate   3 credits $240
In offering this course, I hope to accomplish two main goals. First, I hope to provide you with the technical information and skills that you will need to make managerial decisions about this kind of information technology. My assumption being that you are not aiming to be a highly skilled production worker or a technical support wizard, but rather that you will be assessing these tools for their usefulness in your overall communication and research endeavors. My second goal is to examine how communications fit into the larger picture of development.

InterNIC and 15 Minute Series
Rio Hondo College
RIHO#WWW5 Undergraduate   ?? credits $???
This course is designed to introduce the you to the InterNIC. This is the organization is a cooperative activity between the National Science Foundation and AT&T. This course uses the "15 Minute Series" as additional training for users of the Internet and WWW. Topics include; Electronic Mail, Indexing and Search Services. World Wide Web, and The Basics, Technology. This is a dynamic site and topics are being added.

Intranets and Electronic Commerce
The Graduate School of America
TGSA#OM894W Graduate   4 credits $795
This course considers the potential benefits and problems resulting from the use of intranets and electronic commerce for corporate communications and business transactions. The technological requirements for intranets and electronic commerce are also included.

Intro to AltaVista Forum
Lansing Community College
LANS#CABS100 Undergraduate   0.75 credits $79
The participant in this seminar will learn how to use the interactive AltaVista Forum software in an on-line educational environment. This includes an introduction to the Forum's team concept and the basic Internet browser skills needed to be successful in the LCC Virtual College program. Additional activities covered are communication with the instructor and classmates, use of Forum to retrieve and submit homework assignments, and collaboration in team projects. On successfully completing this seminar the student will have sufficient mastery of the Forum software to allow them to be active participants in other LCC on-line courses.

Intro to C/C++ Programming
Red Wing Technical College
REWI#CC2511 Undergraduate   4 credits $155*
Description: This is the first of a series of courses on programming in the C++ language. Topics include: C++ program structure, data types, control structures, functions, parameters, input-output, arrays, and pointers. (Prerequisites: 4 credits of programming languages or permission of instructor).
* Resident rate $256; contact the provider for more info.

Intro to Client-Server Computing
UCLA
UCLA#X418C   Undergraduate   4 credits   **$575**
Today's networks are now recognized as the most important component in information processing; this has led to a new style of computing called client/server, where the power of an individual computer is only limited by the network that connects to it. This course provides an introduction to client/server computing and discusses its benefits as well as the advantages it offers over time-sharing and networked PCs. Topics include client/server model, standard middleware in client/server computing, remote procedure calls (RPC), security in a client/server model, and integration of existing environments.

Intro to Computer Info - Software Apps
Lansing Community College
LANS#CISB099   Undergraduate   0 credits   **$160**
CISB099 is the "hands-on" portion of the CISB100 course. CISB099 has 0 credits, but the points you earn within this course are given to your CISB100 instructor at course end. Half of the points that determine your grade in CISB100 come from CISB099. By having two separate courses for the two parts of CISB100, you have maximum flexibility in deciding how you want to learn more about computers and their potential role in your life.

Intro to Internet and Web Publishing
City University
CITY#CS340   Undergraduate   5 qu. credits   **$785**
This course focuses on the tools available to the users of the information superhighway. Topics include the Internet and it's history, effective and efficient use of search engines, characteristics of current web browsers, using e-mail systems and e-mail programs, using effective and efficient use of search engines, characteristics of current web browsers, using e-mail systems and e-mail programs, using Gopher, FTP, Telnet and Usenet. In addition to the above topics, students will be introduced to the concept of TCP/IP, HTML, and web publishing.

Intro to Java Programming
Front Range Community College
FRCC#CSC226   Undergraduate   4 credits   **$1052**
(Course description not available at press time.) Prerequisite: Previous programming experience.

Intro to Local Area Networks
Lansing Community College
LANS#CISB230   Undergraduate   3 credits   **$315**
This course offers an opportunity to learn how to install and maintain a local area network (LAN). It currently uses Novell IntranetWare 4.11 on an Ethernet (IEEE 802.3) network.

Intro to Spreadsheets – MS Excel 97
Great Basin College
GRBA#COT134   Undergraduate   1 credits   **$62***
Excel is a computerized spreadsheet. A spreadsheet is an important business tool that helps you analyze and evaluate information. This course acquaints you with building spreadsheets. You will study Excel Version 97 to make you proficient using a spreadsheet to solve problems and produce results in a business setting.
* NV residents tuition: $43 per credit.

Intro to UNIX Administration
Front Range Community College
FRCC#CIS178   Undergraduate   4 credits   **$1052**
(Course description not available at press time.) Prerequisite: CIS175, CIS103.

Intro to Computer Conferencing
New York Institute of Technology
NYIT#EN1006   Undergraduate   3 credits   **$???**
Students learn how a computer conferencing system is structured, how it works and how to use it. Particular attention paid to user behavior in a computer conference and to the application of computer conferencing in a distance learning environment.

Intro to Computer Programming
Rogers State University
ROGE#CS2113A   Undergraduate   3 credits   **$495***
If you're getting ready to work in computing or related fields, or want to participate more knowledgeably in our increasingly computerized world, this is the course for you! The instructor is Julie Luscomb, a Rogers University faculty member and an experienced distance-learning instructor. The course includes a review of the DOS operating environment and leads into actually writing programs in the C computer programming language. Video: Introduction to Computer Programming from Rogers University Telecourses.
* OK residents $315.

Intro to Computers & Programming
Rochester Institute of Technology
ROCH#69225090   Undergraduate   4 credits   **$923**
Basic concepts and overview of computer science.

Introduction to Application Software
Carlow College
CARL#IM101   Undergraduate   3 credits   **$345***
A hands-on introduction to computing using IBM compatible computers. Includes Windows 95, word-processing, and spreadsheet software.

Introduction to AutoCAD
New School for Social Research
NEWS#4002   Undergraduate   2 credits   **$1092**
Log on and learn AutoCAD (release 14) working and collaborating over the internet. Through simple exercises and step-by-step guidance, take a project from its initial stages to completion and full documentation. Acquire confidence in working with AutoCAD on your own or on a team to produce drawings efficiently. Prerequisite: Basic Drafting and Auto CAD (release 14) or AutoCAD LT.

Introduction to BASIC
University of Missouri
MOCE#CO71   Undergraduate   3 credits   **$387**
An introduction to Microsoft and IBM PC BASIC, this course emphasizes language syntax, structured programming, and problem solving; it is designed for teachers and persons in related occupations. Students may use any computer capable of running BASIC; however, the lessons will focus on IBM DOS.

Introduction to C Programming
UCLA
UCLA#X418B   Undergraduate   4 credits   **$500**
The C language has emerged as a primary programming language for application and systems programming in a broad range of software development environments. A program written in C can be easily ported from system to system, such as Unix, DOS, Windows, OS/2, and even mainframe systems. This online course covers data types, operators and expressions, control flow, pointers and arrays, function and program structure, storage classes, structures and unions, I/O functions and systems interfaces, macros, and other preprocessor directives. (Required course in Sequential Program in C/Unix.)

Introduction to CGI
New School for Social Research
NEWS#4005   Undergraduate   0 credits   **$600**
Advance your Web design easily with PERL as applied to CGI (Common Gateway Interface) programming. Topics covered include form parsing, cookie technology and dynamic HTML generation. Prerequisite: Web design and familiarity with HTML, or equivalent experience.

Introduction to Communication Studies
Marylhurst College
MARY#CM200   Undergraduate   3 credits   **$651**
An overview of the field of human communication; personal, social, and cultural dimensions; verbal and non-verbal elements of interaction; and basic features of common contexts: interpersonal, organizational, small group, speaker/audience-event, technology mediated, and mass communication. The relationship of communication studies to professional opportunities and employment options is explored.

Introduction to Computer Networking
Strayer University
STRA#CIS175   Undergraduate   4.5 credits   **$665**
Introduces the concepts of computer networks. Covers basic design considerations for LANS/WANS, protocols, performance issues, security, and popular commercial communication packages. Prerequisite: CIS105.

Introduction to Computer Networks
University of Denver, University College
DEUC#CIS3813   Undergraduate   3 qtr. hrs.   **$885**
To keep up with the constantly changing world of computer communications, it's necessary to understand the fundamentals of digital networking technology: data communication concepts, protocols, and facilities, LAN architectures, components, and capabilities, and the related standards. (Prerequisite: Introduction to Computer Information Systems, or equivalent experience.)

Introduction to Data Processing
Brevard Community College
BREV#CGS1000   Undergraduate   3 credits   **$435**
An introduction to the capabilities of digital computers and the methods used in software development, including exposure to systems design, flowcharting, programming languages and related subjects.

Introduction to Database Management Systems
Strayer University
STRA#CIS275   Undergraduate   4.5 credits   **$665**
Covers concepts of database systems and their impact on information systems. Studies data structure and their relationships in sets of integrated files. Surveys design concepts and available commercial database software. Prerequisite: CIS110.

Introduction to Database Systems
New Jersey Institute of Technology
NJIT#CIS431   Undergraduate   3 credits   **$1143***
Course will focus on database system architecture and the functions of a database management system (DBMS). Topics will include data-modeling using entity-relationship model; storage of databases; the hierarchical, network and relational data models, formal and commercial query languages; functional dependencies and normalization for relational database design; relation composition; concurrency control and transactions management. Prerequisites: NJIT#CIS114 or equivalent. Optional: 26 video lessons of 60 minutes each.
* NJ residents: $184/semester hour.

Introduction to Fashion Computing with Photoshop
New School for Social Research
NEWS#4004   Undergraduate   0 credits   **$750**
Use your modem to develop your apparel and textile design presentation skills and learn the basics of fashion computing using Adobe Photoshop. This course covers the procedures and techniques used in the fashion and textile design computing industry. Learn how to simulate yarn-dyes, create colorways, edit pattern repeats, and match colors. Create presentation material and embellish design illustrations. Scanning techniques and portfolio development are discussed. Some familiarity with print design helpful but not necessary. Prerequisite: Access to the internet and Photoshop.

Introduction to HTML
Kennesaw State University
KENN#FMV001   Undergraduate   3 credits   **$149**
This is a beginner class for the novice for producing documents in HTML, the markup language used by the World Wide Web. This course covers all the WC3 HTML tags including HTML 4.0 (the current version.) The course is designed to help the beginner with internet acronyms including URL, links, HTML markup tags and their uses. The student will also be able to create and publish a web page.

Introduction to Hypermedia
New Jersey City University
NJCU#EDTC642 Graduate   3 credits $635

This course will explore the historical development of hypermedia and will explain information presentation using hypermedia. Teachers will examine the way that hypermedia can be used to enhance learning in the classroom by using different learning styles through the personalization of hypermedia. Teachers will learn not only how to link the hypermedia software with other media such as laser disks, but also how to use other peripherals for video, still graphics and sound capture.

Introduction to Internet in Business
Lansing Community College
LANS#CISB102 Undergraduate   2 credits $210

This course is designed to introduce a computer user to the potential of the Internet for business and personal use. This is a novice course, meant for someone who is just beginning to use the Internet, and who wants to get a broad overview of what can be done on the Internet, and how that might be of value. It provides practice through a variety of exercises that help students become comfortable using some of the most popular Internet applications.

Introduction to Internet Resources
Honolulu Community College
HONO#CENT102 Undergraduate   3 credits $714*

This course introduces the many resources available on the Internet. Topics will include history, current issues and how the Internet works. Terminology, file formats, and naming conventions will be covered. Students will be introduced to the concept of client-server programs as they apply to the Internet. Special emphasis will be placed on the World Wide Web, where students will learn to browse through information as well as publish it. Prerequisites: ICS100, 100E, 100M, 100T or ICS101.
* Hawaiian residents tuition: $39 per credit.

Introduction to Internet Searching
Greenville Technical College
GRTE#CPT105 Undergraduate   1 credits $127*

Prepares students who are new to Online Learning by modeling and building essential skills, concepts, approaches, and strategies that will contribute to their success as online students. Focuses on basic mastery of the online learning environment including: searching, email, newsgroups, asynchronous and synchronous discussion, mastery learning habits, investigative problem solving, personalized learning, and active participation in a community of learners.
* NC residents pay $48 per credit.

Introduction to Local Area Networks
College of DuPage
DUPA#CIS151 Undergraduate   3 qu. credits $90

A survey course in network management that provides the critical foundation of the theory and design of Local Area Networks (LAN). Topics include network topologies, standards and protocols, and LANs as nodes in larger networks in micro-to-mainframe links. Students must be knowledgeable of computer systems and computer terminology.

Introduction to Local Area Networks
Rio Salado College
RISA#CIS190 Undergraduate   3 credits $186*

Overview of local area networks. Emphasis on the elements of a local area network, current issues and products, and use of a local area network. Includes terminology, hardware and software components, connectivity, resource monitoring and sharing, electronic mail and messaging, and security issues. Prerequisites: CIS105, or permission of instructor.
* AZ residents pay $37 per credit.

Introduction to Microcomputer Applications
Chemeketa Community College
CHEM#CS101 Undergraduate   3 credits $123

An introduction to the basic microcomputer hardware/software system. Covers the concept of system software and application software including word processing, spreadsheet, database, and introduction to Internet. Prerequisite: Touch typing ability and current enrollment in RD010, College Textbook Reading, or equivalent.

Introduction to Microcomputer Applications
University of Minnesota
MINN#GC1571 Undergraduate   5 credits $445

This hands-on laboratory course teaches students how to use the computer as a tool for word processing, data manipulation, and data analysis. All assignments done on computer. The course covers: basic concepts (the operating system and user interface); word processing (how to enter, edit, and format memos, letters, and reports); spreadsheets (how to enter data, do calculations, and make decisions based on data); and how to manipulate sets of data.

Introduction to Microcomputing
Northwest College
NOCO#DP105 Undergraduate   3 credits $???

This introductory course provides hands-on experience with IBM or compatible microcomputer systems through the use of popular business applications including DOS, Microsoft Windows, Microsoft Word and Access. Programming is not involved. Prerequisites or Corequisites: TY139 or TY141.

Introduction to Microprocessors with Digital Logic
State University of New York
SUNY#EGR279Y01 Undergraduate   3 credits $570*

An introduction to microprocessors with digital logic, machine and assembly language programming, serial and parallel input/output, A/D, and hardware interfacing with switches, lights, etc. Projects and simulation laboratory experiences using EWB are included as part of this course. Prerequisites: Physics II and Computer Programming experience or equivalent.
* NY residents tuition: $90 per credit

Introduction to Microsoft Access '97
Shawnee Community College
SHAW#COM173 Undergraduate 3 credits $114
This course introduces the steps of creating a relational database with multiple tables. Online form entry methods will be presented and report preparation. Query data procedures will be practiced to produce day-to-day data from the database.

Introduction to Microsoft Excel '97
Shawnee Community College
SHAW#COM171 Undergraduate 3 credits $114
This course introduces the steps of creating an electronic spreadsheet with labels, values, formulas and functions. Students will use the fill command to copy formulas with relative cell references to maximize spreadsheet calculation efficiency. Chart analysis of data will be prepared and manipulated with type, color, legends, titles and scaling. Conversion of the workbook or individual sheets to html for publication on the web will also be introduced.

Introduction to MiniCAD
New School for Social Research
NEWS#4001 Undergraduate 0 credits $600
Log on and learn how to design and draft with MiniCAD, a flexible CAD program for architects and design professionals, which integrates 2D and 3D objects into one drawing window. Use architectural drafting elements such as hybrid doors, window objects and stairs. Integrate spreadsheets, text and import elements into your presentation drawings, models and construction documents. Learn to set up resource libraries, layered files and communicate with other programs cross platform. Customize the program to fit your specific needs. Digital output and plotting techniques for truly professional CAD documents are discussed. Prerequisite: Basic drafting and MiniCAD 7.0.

Introduction to Online Courses
Barstow Community College
BARS#COMP111 Undergraduate 0.5 credits $???
This course will introduce students to the Internet software necessary to successfully complete an online course. It will teach students how to access the online course materials using an Internet browser, as well as how to effectively use word processing, e-mail and discussion group software used by the online courses.

Introduction to Online Technologies
UCLA
UCLA#X396C Undergraduate 4 credits $500
This course provides an overview of the communications technologies used in presenting online education to users in diverse locations. Asynchronous, synchronous, hybrid, and special configurations are discussed in the context of the online learning environment. The course covers technical subjects but does not require a technical background for assimilation. Recommended as the first course to be taken in the Online Teaching Program.

Introduction to Operating Systems
State University of New York
SUNY#2143101 Undergraduate 3 credits $1038*
System software organization, purpose and functions of computer operating systems, batch processing systems: translation, loading and execution, serial and parallel I/O processing, spooling, interrupt facilities, memory protection and management, file systems, multi-access and special-purpose systems, process scheduling, accounting procedures and resource management, classical and popular operating systems. Prerequisites: Computer Science courses in Computer Organization and Data Structures.
* NY residents tuition: $137 per credit

Introduction to Page Design with Quark XPress
New School for Social Research
NEWS#4000 Undergraduate 2 credits $1092
Launch your browser and gain a working knowledge of QuarkXPress, the industry standard page layout program. Cover the basics of designing with type, graphics and images. Learn to manage and format images to create exceptional page layouts. Get aquainted with the menus, control palettes, and features. Previous computer experience helpful but not necessary. You also need access to the internet and QuarkXPress.

Introduction to PASCAL
Emporia State University
EMPO#CS250 Undergraduate 3 credits $228
This course is designed to introduce students to the discipline of computer science. Major emphasis will be placed on problem solving by decomposition top-down design of algorithms, elementary control and record structures, array, string and file processing, recursion and pointer variables. Prerequisite: MA110.

Introduction to Photoshop
Kennesaw State University
KENN#FMV224 Undergraduate 3 credits $149
Learn the basics of this popular graphics program and its uses. This course takes you through a step by step overview of the tools, interface and menus in this graphics program. Learn the difference between tiff and bmp, rgb and cmyk, color palettes, layering. You will be able to unleash your creative talents in your own digital studio. Learn how to create and manipulate images in Photoshop, save images for use in Multimedia, Print and Internet.

Introduction to Power Point '97
Shawnee Community College
SHAW#COM172 Undergraduate 3 credits $114
Preparation of business on-screen presentations involving the following slide layouts: title, bulleted list, columns, organizational charts and clip art. Presentations will incorporate transitional effects for objects on slides as well as build effects for presentation of text on a slide. Insertion of video and audio clips will enhance the business presentation.

Introduction to Programming
Rochester Institute of Technology
ROCH#60220890 Undergraduate   4 credits $923
A first course in programming using C++ in writing modular, well documented programs.

Introduction to Programming and Logic
Pitt Community College
PITT#CIS115 Undergraduate   3 credits $???
This course introduces computer programming and problem solving in a programming environment, including an introduction to operating systems, text editor, and a language translator. Topics include language syntax, data types, program organization, problem solving methods, algorithm design, and logic control structures. Upon completion, students should be able to manage files with operating system commands, use top-down algorithm design, and implement algorithmic solutions in a programming language.

Introduction to QuickBooks
Great Basin College
GRBA#COT198A Undergraduate   1 credits $62*
The major purpose of this course is to introduce students to an actual computerized accounting system being used in the business world.
* NV residents tuition: $43 per credit.

Introduction to the Internet
Cerro Coso Community College
CECO#CSCIC56A Undergraduate   1 credits $115*
Hands-on introduction to the Internet including electronic mail, file transfer protocol (FTP), browser use and web page development. Prerequisite: CSCIC2 or CSCIC70 or equivalent.
* CA residents pay $13 per credit.

Introduction to the Internet
Edmonds Community College
EDMO#PCAPP256 Undergraduate   2 credits $179
By teaching this course on-line, instead of in a computer lab on campus, students are able to learn to use a dial-up connection to the Internet on their own computer and in the environment where they actually do their computing. By breaking it into six weekly lessons, students have time to practice what they are learning, which is easier than trying to cram everything into a six hour session in a computer lab. It's also a fun way to learn to use the basic Internet tools.

Introduction to the Internet
Fayetteville Technical Community College
FAYE#CIS172 Undergraduate   3 credits $489*
This course introduces the various navigational tools and services of the Internet. Topics include using Internet protocols, search engines, file compression/decompression, FTP, e-mail, listservers, and other related topics. Upon completion, students should be able to use Internet resources, retrieve/decompress files, and use e-mail, FTP, and other Internet tools.
* North Carolina residents and non-resident US military personnel stationed within the state tuition: $60; NC senior citizens: free.

Introduction to the Internet
Kennesaw State University
KENN#FMV219 Undergraduate   3 credits $149
This six week course, taught on-line, is designed to teach users how to use the Internet. The first week's lesson is mailed to students (postal) and subsequent lessons will be delivered via email. Individual support is provided throughout the course. Topics covered: getting on-line, establishing an account and using email, basic Unix, Usenet, Newsgroups, Readers, Telnet, Gopher, World Wide Web, Archie and Veronica, FTP and a final Scavenger Hunt using all resources.

Introduction to the Internet
Pitt Community College
PITT#CIS172 Undergraduate   3 credits $???
This course introduces the various navigational tools and services of the Internet. Topics include using Internet protocols, search engines, file compression/decompression, FTP, e-mail, listservs, creating web pages and other related topics. Upon completion, students should be able to use Internet resources, retrieve/decompress files, and use e-mail, FTP, and other Internet tools.

Introduction to the Internet
Pitt Community College
PITT#CSC106 Undergraduate   ?? credits $???
A study of the Internet and the World Wide Web. Topics will include: an overview of file transfer protocols, search engines and directories, the basics of email, discussion groups, Usenet, writing your own Web Pages, and legal, ethical privacy, and security issues. Prerequisites: CSC112 and CSC114, or permission of the instructor.

Introduction to the Internet I
University of Alaska - Fairbanks
ALFA#ED293B Undergraduate   1 credits $71
Accessing Internet services including USENET, a global electronic bulletin board; TELNET to log on to other computer systems; and the GOPHER and Worldwide Web menu systems. Prerequisite: ED293 - or permission of instructor.

Introduction to the Internet II
University of Alaska - Fairbanks
ALFA#ED293C Undergraduate   1 credits $71
Additional Internet resources including ARCHIE file searches, FTP file transfers, binary file uploads/downloads, and listservers. Prerequisite: ED293 or permission of instructor.

Introduction to UNIX Operating System
New Hampshire College
NEHA#CIS350 Undergraduate   3 credits $1656
This course provides an in-depth introduction to the structure and functioning of the UNIX operating system. It is designed to give students a solid foundation into the design and organization of the operating system and to familiarize them with the base set of UNIX commands.

Introduction to Visual Basic
City University
CITY#CS220 Undergraduate   5 qu. credits $785
Introduction to structures programming using Visual Basic. Students will program Windows applications while learning menu layout, programming logic, Visual Basic data types, forms design and control, structured testing and debugging, user interface, conditional logic and loops, input validation, searching and sorting, form connecting, and database front end design.

Introduction to Visual Basic
National American University
NAAM#CI202D Undergraduate   4.5 credits $900
This introductory programming course assumes no prior knowledge of computer programming and is intended for the beginner. The focus is on learning the principles of programming. These principles include, planning before writing, proper use of the three logic structures, sequence, selection and iteration, modular design, string manipulation, array handling and common business algorithms. A small portion of the complete visual basic language is used to practice these principles. Since it allows the novice programmer to create programs with a graphical user interface.

Introduction to Windows 95
Great Basin College
GRBA#COT204 Undergraduate   1 credits $62*
This one-credit course is designed for new users of Microsoft Windows 95. Students must have access to a computer with Internet/e-mail capabilities and Microsoft Windows 95. Contact with the instructor will be made via e-mail. The topics in this course include exploring the basics of Windows 95, managing files and folders, using Explorer for better file organization, and customizing Windows 95 for increased productivity. Windows 95 is loaded with accessories which will also be introduced in this course.
* NV residents tuition: $43 per credit.

Introduction to Windows NT
Cerro Coso Community College
CECO#CSCIC69NT Undergraduate   0.5 credits $58*
Introduces the Windows 3.x user to the Windows 95/NT interface. Formatting disks, copying/deleting/moving files, launching programs and managing the desktop will be addressed. The difference between Windows 3.x, Windows 95 and Windows NT 4.0 will be discussed. Prerequisite: Level 1 reading, level 2 writing classification recommended.
* CA residents pay $13 per credit.

Introduction to Word '97
Shawnee Community College
SHAW#COM163 Undergraduate   3 credits $114
An introduction to word processing concepts from creating simple text documents to the beginning techniques of mail merge. Incorporating copy/cut and paste, borders and bullets and use of the program's writing tools.

Introduction to WordPerfect 6.1 for Windows
Great Basin College
GRBA#COT198B Undergraduate   1 credits $62*
WordPerfect is one of the most popular word processing programs. This course uses a task-driven approach to present such program features as the fundamentals of creating a document; formatting and editing; using additional features such as the spell-checker, grammar checker and thesaurus; formatting multiple-page documents; merging documents and creating mailing labels; and desktop publishing.
* NV residents tuition: $43 per credit.

Introductions to Oracle
Strayer University
STRA#CIS276 Undergraduate   4.5 credits $665
Covers the concept, design and components of the Oracle Database. Involves the creation of tables, modification of tables, defining transactions, basics of SQL, basics of PL/SQL, datatypes, backup and recovery, and querying the database with SQL. Prerequisite: CIS111.

ISDN and Broadband ISDN
City University
CITY#TM490 Undergraduate   5 qu. credits $785
Examination and analysis of the technology and architecture of ISDN (Integrated Services Digital Network) and Broadband ISDN. Course covers integrated digital network (IDN), ISDN services and architecture, signaling system no. 7 (SS7), CCITT standards, and frame relay. Specific Broadband ISDN topics include ATM (Asynchronous Transfer Mode) and SONET (Synchronous Optical Network). Prerequisite: TM304 or its equivalent.

Java for C++ Programmers
New York University
NEYO#X529269 Undergraduate   3.5 CEU $895
This course, designed for the C++ programmer, provides an introduction to the Java programming language. Topics include: classes and objects, inheritance, interfaces, exception handling, applets, threads, input/output, utility classes, Java architecture, security, garbage collection, and other Java features. A major emphasis is on object-oriented design principles and techniques. Prerequisite: X52.9264 or equivalent knowledge.

JAVA Programming
City University
CITY#CS440 Undergraduate   5 qu. credits $785
This Object Oriented Programming course is designed to introduce students to JAVA programming using applets. Topics include basics of JAVA environment, control structures, methods, arrays, JAVA ADTs, classes, superclasses and subclasses, graphics, screen manipulation and other basic fundamentals of the JAVA language.

Java Programming
University of Colorado
CUON#CSC2801 Undergraduate   3 credits $1953*
This course is an introduction to the Java programming language. This course will introduce key object-oriented concepts required to use Java effectively and cover the Java programming language constructs as well as the API for the libraries that come with the language. In particular, the course will give an introduction to the core API's viz. java.lang, java.util, java.awt, java.net, and java.io. The course will cover both applet and application development.
* CO residents tuition: $136 per credit.

JAVA Programming for the Internet
Syracuse University
SYRA#CIS300 Graduate   3 credits $1960
This course serves as an introduction to the JAVA programming language, object-oriented programming concepts and windows programming. Topics include an introduction to JAVA; identifiers, variables and data types; expressions evaluation, control flow statements, and stand-alone programs; object oriented programming; inheritance, polymorphism, applet programming and the graphics class; arrays, strings and things; Java's parcel post; interfaces and threads; windows and widgets on the web; images, animation and sound; and JAVA support libraries. Prerequisite: Previous knowledge of programming in algorithmic language such as C or PASCAL.

Java Programming Fundamentals
UCLA
UCLA#X418F Undergraduate   2 credits $450
Java is the newest and most highly acclaimed programming facility of the '90s. Similar to C++, Java enables programmers to develop robust applications on the Internet; simplify object-oriented programming; and add security, portability, advanced networking, and multithreading power to applications. Designed for experienced programmers familiar with Web technology, this intensive online course allows students to acquire practical skills and immediately employ them in their computing environment.

Java Programming I
Rio Salado College
RISA#CIS163AA Undergraduate   3 credits $186*
(Course description not available at press time.)
* AZ residents pay $37 per credit.

Javascript for Educators
UCLA
UCLA#X396D Undergraduate   4 credits $500
JavaScript is a valuable tool for adding interactivity and two-way communication to previously static Web pages. With JavaScript, an inventive educator can use the Web not just to deliver content to students but to monitor students' participation and progress, to administer quizzes, to test each individual student's understanding before allowing him or her to move on to new material, and to give a student the chance to send immediate feedback to the teacher. JavaScript also can enliven Web pages, engaging students more deeply and holding their attention more thoroughly.

LAN Implementation
City University
CITY#CS394 Undergraduate   5 qu. credits $785
Hands-on installation of LAN hardware and software components. Discussion of LAN concepts and terminology including protocols, architectures, topologies, bridges, routers, and gateways. Other topics include printer sharing and problem solving.

LAN Operations and Concepts
Rio Salado College
RISA#CIS109 Undergraduate   1 credits $62*
Overview of basic local area networking concepts. Introduction to industry language, computer network hardware, LAN operating systems, and data communication basics. Prerequisites: BPC/CIS121AB, or (BPC102AA and BPC102BA), or CIS105, or BPC110, or permission of instructor.
* AZ residents $37 per credit.

Language Theory and Automata
Nova Southeastern University
NOVA#CISC631 Graduate   3 credits $1,110
Introduction to formal grammars, Backus-Naur notation. The formal theory behind the design of a computer language is studied. The corresponding types of automata which may serve as recognizers and generators for a language will be described.

Learn About the Internet on the Internet
Waukesha County Technical College
WAUK#103413 Undergraduate   3 credits $192*
This self-paced Internet class is for the person who wants to learn about the Internet in an on-line situation. Students will work on their own to develop Internet skills, such as browsing, FTP and discussion on on-line service providers.
* WI residents pay $54 per credit.

Legal and Ethical Aspects of Computing
Nova Southeastern University
NOVA#MCIS623 Graduate   3 credits $1,110
Focuses on issues that involve computer impact on society and related concerns. Transitional data flow; copyright protection; information as a source of economic power; rights to access computer systems; computer crime; data privacy; establishing national priorities in the technical and social aspects of computing; current and anticipated uses of computer prediction; and protection of personal ethical concerns. National computer policies of Japan, France, Great Britain, and the European Economic Community. The status of regulation and emerging standards.

Legal and Ethical Aspects of Computing
Nova Southeastern University
NOVA#MMIS623 Graduate   3 credits $1,110

Focuses on issues that involve computer impact and related societal concerns. Topics include transitional data flow; copyright protection; information as a source of economic power; rights to access to computer systems; computer crime; data privacy; establishing national priorities in the technical and social aspects of computing; current and anticipated uses of computer prediction; and protection of personal ethical concerns. National computer policies of Japan, France, Great Britain, and the EEC, and the status of regulation and emerging standards.

Library and Information Access Tools
UCLA
UCLA#X340C Undergraduate   1 credits $290

The professional access skills needed for success in graduate school include knowledge of computers and software - word processing, database, bibliography, and specialized thesis programs; library search and retrieval techniques; use of online databases; and more. These topics are covered in this course as well as how to cite information sources using appropriate protocols.

Library and Information Strategies
University of Alaska - Fairbanks
ALFA#LS100 Undergraduate   1 credits $71

Principles of information organization and how libraries can provide access to information and scholarly resources. Emphasis on use of a library via distance delivery methods. For students who do not have direct access to the Rasmuson Library. Prerequisite: ED293 or equivalent.

Live Picture
New School for Social Research
NEWS#3275 Undergraduate   0 credits $580

Live Picture is the most important breakthrough in digital imaging since Photoshop. It can be used as a stand-alone image manipulation and composite tool or as a companion to Photoshop. Live Picture's biggest strength is its ability to accurately manipulate high resolution images without the excessive wait encountered with Photoshop. This makes it terrific for low-memory environments. We explore the wide range of tools in Live Picture, with an emphasis on its flexibility for producing single-use images or images destined for different media at varying sizes and resolutions. Prerequisites: Using the Macintosh and working knowledge of Photoshop.

Living with the Internet
State University of New York
SUNY#CIS115 Undergraduate   3 credits $1038*

Techniques for accessing, and applications in using, the Internet in both professional and private situations, including gaining access to the Internet, accessing a variety of resources, publishing on the Internet, and legal and ethical concerns associated with use of the Internet. Current Internet access hardware and software will be utilized. Course will be taught through in-class lecture and demonstrations, supported by extensive hands-on experience.
* NY residents tuition: $137 per credit

Local Area Network Installation
Rio Salado College
RISA#CIS242 Undergraduate   1 credits $62*

Installation of a local area network (LAN). Emphasis on LAN product overview and requirements, preinstallation procedures and testing, installation, administration, use, and problem resolution of a local area network product. Includes installation scheduling, preparation and installation of hardware and network operating system, configuration of security parameters and user accounts, installation of applications software, testing of network and applications, consoleoperations, problem resolution, and use of the network. Prerequisites: CIS190 or permission of instructor.
* AZ residents pay $37 per credit.

Local Area Network Planning and Design
Rio Salado College
RISA#CIS240 Undergraduate   3 credits $186*

Analysis of the needs and requirements for a local area network (LAN). Emphasis on basic systems analysis and design for a local area network, selection of appropriate hardware and software components. Includes current and future issues, needs analysis, cost estimation, selection of connectivity and network components, and issues relating to access, security, and support. Prerequisites: CIS190 or permission of instructor.
* AZ residents pay $37 per credit.

Local Area Networks
City University
CITY#CS390 Undergraduate   5 qu. credits $785

Overview of the hardware and software components of Local Area Network (LAN) Systems, including media, topologies, access methods, LAN architectures and implementations including Ethernet. Analysis of standardization and future LAN trends, alternatives, implementation and planning strategies, and LAN Management considerations. Includes examination of LAN interconnection using bridges, routers and gateways.

Machine and Assembly Language
New Jersey Institute of Technology
NJIT#CIS231 Undergraduate   3 credits $1143*

Fundamentals of machine organization and machine language programming. Representation of computer instructions and data in machine, assembly and macro-assembly; languages together with intensive practice in formulating programming, running, and debugging programs for both numerical and logical problems. Assemblers and loaders are discussed. Prerequisites: Introduction to Computer Science I or completion of a course in higher level programming language. Optional: 25 video lessons of 60 minutes each.
* NJ residents: $184/semester hour.

Machine Transcription
Eastern Oregon University
EAOR#OADM222 Undergraduate 5 credits $400

Skill development in the use of machine transcription equipment to include transcription theories, grammar, punctuation and proofreading skills. Emphasis is on mailable standard. Prerequisite: OADM121.

MacroMedia DreamWeaver
New School for Social Research
NEWS#3347 Undergraduate 0 credits $580

DreamWeaver offers the productivity of a visual web page layout tool and the control of an HTML text editor while supporting sophisticated functions like Dynamic HTML. This course covers the tools of the software and quickly moves to topics included cascading style sheets, cross-browser DHTML generation, link checking and repair, visual table and frame design, Director-style HTML animation timeline, JavaScript behaviors, and more. DreamWeaver yields concise, readable HTML code. Prerequisite: WWW Page Design and Construction or equivalent experience.

Managing Information on the Internet
University of Minnesota
MINN#RHET3400 Undergraduate 3 credits $300

Explores the current and developing tools of Internet-based communication. The course will introduce students to various forms of asynchronous communication, including concepts of EMail, Usenet News, mailing lists, and web-based chats; synchronous communication, including MOOs (multiuser domains, object oriented) and Internet Relay Chat, with an opportunity to explore audio and video communication methods; and Internet publication, primarily through an examination of the characteristics of the World Wide Web. Emphasis is on examining the technology, assessing the information delivered by the technology, and developing criteria for disseminating information. Prerequisites: RHET1200 or equivalent; access to a computer, Netscape Navigator, and related Internet resources.

Marketing on the Internet
University of Massachusetts - Dartmouth
MADA#CMP305 Undergraduate 0 credits $135

An introduction to marketing on the Internet. Emphasis will be placed on the four controllable marketing variables(product promotion, price and distribution) and their adaptation to hypermedia-mediated environment. Students will be exposed to a variety of corporate Internet sites that illustrate these adaptation techniques.

Marketing on the Internet
Rochester Institute of Technology
ROCH#10544090 Undergraduate 4 credits $923

The purpose of his course is to make students Internet literate for the business world.

Mastering Microsoft Office
Brevard Community College
BREV#CFPX0448 Undergraduate 0 credits $155

This course covers word processing, spreadsheets, databases, and presentation software used by millions of people at work and at home. Includes a quick review of the operating system for Windows 95. Then covers techniques and problem-solving in the four elements of Microsoft Office: Word, Excel, Access and Powerpoint.

Micro Database Software - Access
Chemeketa Community College
CHEM#CS125 Undergraduate 3 credits $123

A microcomputer database software course using Microsoft Access divided into three one credit hour. Topics covered include: Part 1) Navigation through Windows and Access menus, PC relational database concepts, creation and updating of a relational database; Part 2) Simple queries, reports, and forms; Part 3) Complex queries, reporting, and forms. Prerequisite: CS101, Introduction to Microcomputer Applications or consent of instructor.

Microcomputer Applications
Brevard Community College
BREV#CGS1530 Undergraduate 3 credits $485

An introductory course in the application of commercially available software for microcomputers - topics include: word processing, electronic spreadsheets, data base management, computer graphics and key pad.

Microcomputer Applications
Greenville Technical College
GRTE#CPT270 Undergraduate 3 credits $381*

This course emphasizes the integration of popular microcomputer software packages using advanced concepts in microcomputer applications software. Prerequisites: CPT101 with a grade of C or higher, Windows 3.1 or higher.

* NC residents pay $48 per credit.

Microcomputer Applications
Rogers State University
ROGE#CS2113B Undergraduate 3 credits $495*

This course is for 'everybody' -- those who want to continue in computer science, those working toward a business degree, and those who just want to know more about computers and applications programs. The course introduces Windows and gives you hands-on experience with word processing, spreadsheets, and database management on IBM personal computers. Video: Rogers University Telecourses.

* OK residents $315.

Microcomputer Applications
State University of New York
SUNY#271454   Undergraduate   4 credits $586*

Learn to use computers effectively for business and personal applications. Includes general concepts of how the personal computer operates, the vocabulary and uses of popular application software, and hands on learning of word processing, spreadsheet, database and communications software. (Choose alternate applications such as graphics or desktop publishing with permission of the Instructor). Learn functions of several software applications using a workbook approach. Apply skills in producing projects such as resumes, budgets, and address data bases. Gain competence in learning how to learn new software packages -- a critical skill for future employment.

* NY residents tuition: $515

Microcomputer Set Up & Maintenance
Rio Salado College
RISA#BPC125   Undergraduate   1 credits $62*

How to install and maintain a microcomputer (personal computer). Steps used to set up a new or add options to a previously installed microcomputer. Installation of internal options (memory, graphics, modems, etc.), as well as external options and devices (printers, monitors, communications, etc.) Trouble shoot (identify and repair or have repaired) microcomputer problems. Prerequisites: CIS105 or BPC/CIS121 or BPC110 or permission of instructor.

* AZ residents $37 per credit.

Microcomputer Software Installation
Rio Salado College
RISA#BPC278   Undergraduate   3 credits $186*

Installing and configuring microcomputer software. Emphasis placed on the installation, configuration, upgrade, and related problem resolution of microcomputer operating system and applications software. Prerequisites: CIS105, CIS121, CIS114 (any module whose course number suffix begins with a "D"), CIS117 (any module whose course number suffix begins with a "D"), and BPC170 with grade of C or better, or permission of instructor.

* AZ residents pay $37 per credit.

Microsoft PowerPoint
New School for Social Research
NEWS#3165   Undergraduate   0 credits $340

PowerPoint is a powerful yet easy-to-use presentation graphics program from Microsoft. You start your design by typing the content directly onto a slide, or if you prefer, in an outline. Then you simply apply one of PowerPoint's more than 150 templates to turn your content into a professional-looking presentation. You can add clip art using PowerPoint's gallery, and you can create graphs from your data. You can incorporate freehand drawings into the presentation or use pre-defined shapes. Prerequisite: Using the PC & Compatibles or equivalent experience.

MS Access - Database Management
Rio Salado College
RISA#PC117DM   Undergraduate   3 credits $186*

Introduction to the basic elements, exploration of additional components and common database management problems related to the Microsoft Access program. Combines the contents of BPC/CIS117AA and BPC/CIS117BA and BPC/CIS117CA.

* AZ residents $37 per credit.

MS Word Level 2 (Windows 95)
New School for Social Research
NEWS#3179   Undergraduate   0 credits $340

Building on the concepts in MS Word Level 1, this hands-on course explores the advanced tools and functions of the software. Topics include Merges, Section Breaks, Tables (formulas), advanced Page Layout, Graphics, Templates, Ruler Bar functions, Outline Numbering, Styles, Keep Lines Together, Macros, Labels and Envelopes, and Creating a Table of Contents. Prerequisite: MS Word Level 1 or equivalent experience.

MS-DOS Advanced Desktop Publication
Rio Salado College
RISA#BPC238AA   Undergraduate   3 credits $186*

Advanced use of MS-DOS microcomputers and commercial software packages to compose and print textual and graphic materials of high quality. Includes review of fundamental desktop techniques and concepts, alternative treatment of copy, use of complex graphics programs, typographical manipulation, color separating, exploration of alternative layout programs, preparation of larger-scale and unusual publications, and additional printing alternatives. Prerequisites: BPC138AA or permission of instructor.

* AZ residents pay $37 per credit.

MS-DOS Desktop Publication
Rio Salado College
RISA#BPC138AA   Undergraduate   3 credits $186*

Use of MS-DOS microcomputers and appropriate commercial software packages to compose and print textual and graphic materials of high quality. Includes overview of micro operating system, word processing of copy, use of graphics programs, layout of design elements, and printing alternatives. Prerequisites: BPC102AA or BPC/CIS121AB or permission of instructor. Recommend concurrent enrollment in JRN133AA.

* AZ residents pay $37 per credit.

Multimedia and Emerging Technologies
Nova Southeastern University
NOVA#MCTE660   Graduate   3 credits $1,110

Recent advances and future trends in learning technology and educational computing are examined. Innovations in teacher and student workstation technology are reviewed. Emphasis is placed on an examination of audio/video and computer-based tools currently in use in schools and training centers. Special attention is given to CD-ROM technology and laser disk technology. Guidelines for selection and implementation of multimedia projects are presented.

Multimedia and Emerging Technologies
Nova Southeastern University
NOVA#MMIS681 Graduate   3 credits $1,110
Recent advances in high performance computing and computer networks and their impact on network-based applications and work-group productivity are examined. New developments in optical storage technologies, imaging systems, computer architectures, communications services, and graphical user interfaces are delineated. Trends in the development and the use of multimedia. Tools, techniques, and guidelines facilitating the planning, design, production, and implementation of multimedia products.

Multimedia Design and Development I
Delaware County Community College
DECO#MCR20151 Undergraduate   3 credits $???
The focus of this courses is to provide participants with an introduction to multimedia and its development tools, as well as its professional application in business and industry, education, research and development, marketing and entertainment. The Instructional Design Process, including a needs analysis, design goals, storyboarding, and formative and summative evaluations are incorporated into the seven week sessions.

Multimedia Design and Development II
Delaware County Community College
DECO#MCR20253 Undergraduate   3 credits $???
Continuation of DECO#MCR20151.

Multimedia Home Pages for WWW
Lansing Community College
LANS#CISB258 Undergraduate   2 credits $210
The goal of this course is to help the student recognize and apply the principles of web page design to the development of web pages that include multimedia components. Students also learn to create original sound and video clips and select and apply appropriate compression algorithms to the files for their web page's target audience.

Multimedia Systems
New Jersey Institute of Technology
NJIT#CIS658 Undergraduate   3 credits $1143*
Introduction to multimedia information systems; the nature of multimedia data types including text, image, audio, video and animation; multimedia data models and system architectures; design of multimedia systems including interfaces, storage models and structures, filtering, browsing and composing paradigms, query processing, and information retrieval. Students will develop applications in multimedia authoring environments. This course is part of the graduate certificate in Programming Environment Tools. Prerequisites: Knowledge of data structures and graphics required (equivalent to NJIT#CIS610).
* NJ residents: $184/semester hour.

Network Design
City University
CITY#CS490 Undergraduate   5 qu. credits $785
An examination of the broad scope of data and computer communications standards, architectures, hardware, software, protocols, technologies and services as they relate to designing data networks. Emphasis is placed on those technologies playing a dominant role in the 1990's, including X.25 packet switching, frame relay, SMDS, ARM, and SONET. Design methodologies will also include planning business cases, capacity planning, vendor selection and compiling requirements.

Network Management
The Graduate School of America
TGSA#OM888W Graduate   4 credits $795
This course examines the important issues in network management including outsourcing, licensing, growth planning, traffic management, configuration management, network security and virus protection.

Network Operating Systems Survey
City University
CITY#CS392 Undergraduate   5 qu. credits $785
Analysis of protocols and sub protocols supported in LAN environments such as MAC and LLC/LLC2. The features, advantages and disadvantages of client/server systems and network operation systems will be covered. An introduction to Windows NT., Novell NetWare PC systems, and other available services will be discussed. Specific LAN protocols analyzed include: IBM Token Ring related protocols (NETBIOS/SMB), Banyan VINES, AppleTalk, and Novell Netware (IPX). In addition to the above topics, the concept of Internetworking will be introduced. Topics include: Internet Architecture, Protocols for Internetworking, Client-Server interaction and TCP/IP.

Network Technology
The Graduate School of America
TGSA#OM884W Graduate   4 credits $795
This course presents an overview of network technology. Learners consider video systems, LAN/MAN/WAN, wireless systems, satellite communications, Internet and the World Wide Web, cable networks, and voice and data communications.

Networking Administration
Strayer University
STRA#CIS180 Undergraduate   4.5 credits $665
Focuses on the skills necessary to maintain and manage a NetWare network. The basic areas include NetWare directory services, connecting to the network, NetWare file system, menus, objects, security, login scripts, and network printing. Prerequisite: CIS175 or equiv.

Networking Technology
Rochester Institute of Technology
ROCH#61447790 Undergraduate   4 credits $923
Provides a practical overview of data communications environment, historical evolution, technology and applications.

Object Oriented Analysis & Design
Red Wing Technical College
REWI#CC2510 Undergraduate   2 credits $85
Description: This course covers fundamental concepts of the object model, the process and notation of object oriented analysis and design, the use of design tools, and gives strategies and patterns for applying object oriented methodologies to realistic applications. (Prerequisite: CC2513 - may be taken concurrently).

Object Oriented C++ 1
Red Wing Technical College
REWI#CC2512A Undergraduate   4 credits $155
This course introduces object oriented programming concepts using the C++ language. Topics include: class declarations, data and function members, creating and using objects, constructors and destructors, passing objects as function arguments, class inheritance, inline functions, dynamic allocation, friend functions, function and operator overloading, and object I/O. (Prerequisites: CC2511 Into to C/C++ Programming or instructor's permission).

Object Oriented C++ 2
Red Wing Technical College
REWI#CC2512B Undergraduate   4 credits $155
This is the third in a series of three courses covering the C++ programming language. Topics include: base class access control, constructors & inheritance, multiple inheritance, aggregate objects, object association, I/O formatting, file I/O, virtual functions, templates, container classes, and exception handling. (Prerequisite: CC2512).

Object Oriented Programming in C++
New Hampshire College
NEHA#CIS232 Undergraduate   3 credits $1656
This course will teach students how to design, implement, and test applications in the C++ programming language. Topics include: C++ data types, operators, functions, classes, and inheritance. The course will introduce the student to issues associated with developing real-world applications by presenting several case studies. The concepts of object-oriented design and programming will be covered. Prerequisites: CIS230.

Object-Oriented Analysis and Design
New York University
NEYO#X529267 Undergraduate   2.0 CEU $895
This course introduces the fundamental concepts of object-oriented analysis (OOA), design (OOD), and programming (OOP), and how object-oriented languages differ from procedural languages. Notation is used to teach the concepts of abstraction, encapsulation, modularity, hierarchy, and polymorphism. This course is designed for both programmers and analysts. No coding is required. However, prior experience in a modern general-purpose programming language (C, C++, Smalltalk, Ada) is expected. Prerequisite: X52.9232; X52.9264; or equivalent.

Object-Oriented Applications for CIS
Nova Southeastern University
NOVA#MCIS661 Graduate   3 credits $1,110
Principles of the object-oriented paradigm. Application of object-oriented methods in computer information systems. Object-oriented languages and design methods for class creation. Study of the use of object-oriented techniques in applications such as user interfaces, graphics, database systems, visual programming, hypermedia, office automation systems, and decision support systems. Techniques for software reuse.

Object-Oriented Applications for MIS
Nova Southeastern University
NOVA#MMIS661 Graduate   3 credits $1,110
Principles of the object-oriented paradigm. Application of object-oriented methods in management information systems. Object-oriented languages and design methods for class creation. Study of the use of object-oriented techniques in applications such as user interfaces, graphics, database systems, visual programming, hypermedia, office automation systems, and decision support systems. Techniques for software reuse.

Object-Oriented Database Systems
Nova Southeastern University
NOVA#CISC663 Graduate   3 credits $1,110
Object-oriented data models and other data models with semantic extensions such as functional data models, object oriented database query model and languages, object-oriented database schema evolution and modification, version management and control, object data storage structure (clustering and indexing), query processing and transaction management, authorization mechanism and security, integrating object-oriented programming and databases, and applications of object-oriented databases. Prerequisite: CISC660 or equivalent.

Object-Oriented Design
Nova Southeastern University
NOVA#CISC683 Graduate   3 credits $1,110
The concepts and principles of the object-oriented paradigm. Approaches to analyzing and modeling a system using object-oriented techniques. Techniques for the design of objects, classes, and modules. The use of inheritance to enhance reusability. Object-oriented analysis and object-oriented programming.

Object-Oriented Programming C++
City University
CITY#CS364 Undergraduate   5 qu. credits $785
Examine Object-Oriented concepts including abstract data types, object identity, and inheritance. The course will also cover fundamental concepts of Visual C++, comprehensive class libraries, security, MIS management, user interface, input validation, functions, integrated graphics tools, and Visual C++ source code editor, compiler/linker and class browser. Prerequisite: CS362 or proficiency in C.

Object-Oriented Programming C++
UCLA
UCLA#X418J Undergraduate   4 credits $575
The growing popularity, availability, efficiency, and portability of C++ programming language and its compatibility with C is making C++ the programming language of the '90s for the development of large-scale software projects for a variety of applications. The course also concentrates on interfaces, expert systems, real-time systems, simulation, and C++ software development environments and tools. C++ also is compared to other object-oriented programming languages.

Object-Oriented Programming I
Strayer University
STRA#CIS265 Undergraduate   4.5 credits $665
Covers the traditional C language and object-oriented extensions that are found in the C++ language. Describes concepts of objects, encapsulation, data hiding, polymorphism and inheritance as well as the C++ techniques that implement them. Prerequisite: CIS241.

Object-Oriented Programming II
Strayer University
STRA#CIS266 Undergraduate   4.5 credits $665
Develops a working knowledge of object-oriented concepts in areas of classes, friends, inheritance, and polymorphism. The C++ language is used to develop these concepts through the design, development, and implementation of C++ programs. Prerequisite: CIS265.

Object-Oriented Programming in C++
New Jersey Institute of Technology
NJIT#CIS601 Undergraduate   3 credits $1143*
This course introduces object-oriented concepts and some of the theory involved in illustration and implementation. This course is part of graduate certificates in Object-Oriented Design and Program Environment Tools. Prerequisites: Prior programming experience in "C" and "C++" languages. Optional: 24 video lessons at 60 minutes each. Requires C++ software.
* NJ residents: $184/semester hour.

Object-Oriented Software Development
New Jersey Institute of Technology
NJIT#CIS683 Undergraduate   3 credits $1143*
A study of object-oriented analysis and design, and implementation phases of software development. This course is part of the Graduate Certificate in Object-Oriented Design. Prerequisites: NJIT#CIS635 (Programming Languages) and substantial experience in software design and development or explicit approval of the instructor. Optional: 27 video lessons of 60 minutes each.
* NJ residents: $184/semester hour.

Office Microcomputer Applications
Chemeketa Community College
CHEM#CA210 Undergraduate   3 credits $123
Integrated software training using Clarisworks. Includes training in word processing, database, spreadsheet, graphics and communications on the microcomputer. Application problems will consist of using the integrated programs in business-related projects. Prerequisite: Keyboarding touch skill; OA200, Introduction to Information Processing.

Office Microcomputer Applications - Windows
Chemeketa Community College
CHEM#CA210W Undergraduate   3 credits $123
Integrated software training using Microsoft Works. Includes training in word processing, database, spreadsheet, graphics, and communications on the microcomputer. Application problems will consist of using the integrated program in business-related projects. Prerequisite: Keyboarding touch skill; CS101, Introduction to Microcomputer Applications.

Office Spreadsheet Applications
Greenville Technical College
GRTE#OST261 Undergraduate   3 credits $381*
An introductory course to the concepts of spreadsheets in an office environment. ASSEST numerical skills score (45 or greater) or related studies math level (53).
* NC residents pay $48 per credit.

On Line Internet Basics
Edmonds Community College
EDMO#PCAPP155G Undergraduate   1.5 credits $125
(Course description not available at press time.)

Online Global Business Presence
UCLA
UCLA#X898 Undergraduate   3.6 CEU $500
Designed for entrepreneurs, small business managers, corporations, and nonprofit organizations looking to develop an online business presence, this online course examines how to utilize e-mail, USENET, World Wide Web, Telnet, and other sources to reach both new and established customers and clients. Using online exercises, participants compose and edit advertising and marketing materials designed to be integrated into Web sites and home pages and examines the tools designed for developing guest books, order forms, product/service information forms, and online surveys. Covers online research techniques.

Online Interpersonal Communications
University of Massachusetts - Dartmouth
MADA#CMP302 Undergraduate   0 credits $135
The Internet now offers a fascinating (and bewildering) variety of interpersonal communications tools ranging from Email to the exciting new collaborative environments using phone, whiteboards, and interactive video. In this course we will examine these choices, as well as the effect they have on the quality of the interaction that takes place. This is a basic course in the Online Communications Skills Program and should be taken before, at the same time, or right after the WebCraft course.

Open Systems Networking
New Jersey Institute of Technology
NJIT#CIS456 Undergraduate 3 credits $1143*
An introduction to Internet working, including an in-depth study of the architecture of network interconnections, the Internet services, and the protocols needed to provide these services. Prerequisite: NJIT#CIS451. Optional: 26 video lessons of 90 minutes each.
* NJ residents: $184/semester hour.

Operating Systems
City University
CITY#CS470 Undergraduate 5 qu. credits $785
Analytical view of the evolution, function, features, uses, advantages/disadvantages, management and networking of modern operating systems. Students focus on MS-DOS., Windows, Macintosh, UNIX, and OS/2 and evaluate operating systems in terms of security, MIS Management, feasibility studies, user interface, system architecture, and memory allocation.

Operating Systems
Rogers State University
ROGE#CS2153 Undergraduate 3 credits $495*
What's the most popular operating system in the world? If you thought MS-DOS, you'd be wrong. It's UNIX, and that's the system that's covered in great detail in this course. You'll study the components, functions, and relationships of computer operating systems and their interactions with user programs. You'll become familiar with popular operating systems other than UNIX. Prerequisite: course in C programming (RU course CS2223).
* OK residents $315.

Operating Systems
State University of New York
SUNY#CS552 Graduate 3 credits $1038*
Advanced topics in operating systems. Process synchronization, linguistic support for concurrency, virtual memory, deadlock theory, robustness, security, mathematical models, and correctness of concurrent programs. Treatment of selected topics in distributed and multiprocessor operating systems. Prerequisite: CS350, Operating Systems.
* NY residents tuition: $137 per credit

Operating Systems Fundamentals
Greenville Technical College
GRTE#CPT255 Undergraduate 3 credits $381*
This course examines popular operating systems of several different types of computers. Topics include command languages, utility programs and screen design. Pre-requisite: Completion of CPT101 with a grade of C or higher, Windows 3.1 or higher.
* NC residents pay $48 per credit.

Operating Systems Implementation
Nova Southeastern University
NOVA#CISC644 Graduate 3 credits $1,110
Implementation and testing of operating system designs. Prerequisite: CISC640.

Operating Systems Theory and Design
Nova Southeastern University
NOVA#CISC640 Graduate 3 credits $1,110
Analysis of computer operating systems with emphasis on structured design. Multiprogramming and multiprocessing, real time, time-sharing, networks, job control, scheduling, synchronization, and other forms of resource management, I/O programming, and memory and file system management.

Oracle and PL/SQL
Strayer University
STRA#CIS305 Undergraduate 4.5 credits $665
Covers the use and programming of the Oracle Database. Topics covered include PL/SQL fundamentals, SQL statements, records in PL/SQL, loops, variables and program data, tables, built in functions, using packages, and PL/SQL debugging. Prerequisite: CIS276 or equivalent.

Paradigms of Programming Languages
State University of New York
SUNY#2132101 Undergraduate 3 credits $1038*
A brief history of programming languages, language design issues, syntax and translation, data types, sequence control, data control, procedural paradigm, object oriented paradigm, functional paradigm, logical paradigm. Prerequisite: Computer Science II.
* NY residents tuition: $137 per credit

PC Operating Systems - DOS 6.22
Pitt Community College
PITT#CSC147 Undergraduate ?? credits $???
A study of DOS 6.22 on a personal computer. Topics will include: a solid overview of computer hardware, DOS, and it's operations. Upon completion, the student will be able to use a personal computer utilizing DOS to manage files on hard drives and floppy drives. This includes: creating and removing directories; creating, copying, renaming, deleting, and backing up files; and creating simple batch files in DOS. Prerequisites: CSC112 and CSC114, or permission of the instructor.

Photoshop 4.0 Level 1 (Macintosh)
New School for Social Research
NEWS#3248 Undergraduate 0 credits $580
Adobe Photoshop is a retouching and image-editing program. Working with Version 4.0, this course introduces Photoshop's extensive toolbox and covers scanning, image transformation and conversion, using filters, making color corrections, and preparing files for export and printing. Prerequisite: Using the Macintosh Computer and any software application.

Photoshop for Artists
New School for Social Research
NEWS#2287 Undergraduate 2 credits $1092
The computer may soon become as common in artists' studios as canvas, paint, and brushes. Students learn to use the imaging software, Photoshop, to explore the computer's unique capabilities to spur and enhance their creative process. Photoshop presents multiple ways for an artist to work, from drawing directly in the program to scanning and manipulating photographs. Artists can create collages, easily combine text and image, or explore variations of their own paintings, drawings, or photographs.

Photoshop for the Photographer
New School for Social Research
NEWS#2526 Undergraduate   3 credits $360
Adobe Photoshop, the powerful imaging software that is transforming the field of photography, has tremendous potential for both commercial and fine art photographers. This course teaches students how to use Photoshop as a tool to enhance traditional photographic practices. With Photoshop it is possible to retouch, crop, lighten, darken, add or remove color, make collages, create images with text, and much more. Critiques of students' work and individual guidance are supplemented with "field trips" on the Internet to sites with photography shows and technical data pertinent to Photoshop users.

Photoshop Fundamentals
University of Massachusetts - Dartmouth
MADA#001 Undergraduate   0 credits $135
A beginning course in Adobe Photoshop and its fundamental techniques. Emphasis on imaging tools, along with resolution, masking, painting and photo manipulation, filters and the exporting of images for use in page layout programs. This course will be taught with version 4.0 in mind, but version 3.0 is also acceptable. Both Macintosh and Window environments will also be covered throughout the course. Prerequisite: Adobe Photoshop 3.0 or 4.0 software (Mac or PC). Basic HTML knowledge is a plus if you are interested in personalizing your Virtual Portfolio.

Powerpoint
Rio Salado College
RISA#BPC120AE Undergraduate   1 credits $62*
Provides students with the capability to use IBM Powerpoint graphics software on a microcomputer. Includes business charts and graphs, abstract art, graphics design, color graphics and plotting math equations.
* AZ residents $37 per credit.

Powerpoint 7 Beginning Workshop
Kennesaw State University
KENN#FMV225 Undergraduate   3 credits $149
Learn the basics of this popular graphics program and its uses. This course takes you through a step by step overview of the tools, interface and menus in this graphics program. Learn the difference between tiff and bmp, rgb and cmyk, color palettes, layering. You will be able to unleash your creative talents in your own digital studio. Learn how to create and manipulate images in Photoshop, save images for use in Multimedia, Print and Internet.

PowerPoint for Microsoft Office 95
Great Basin College
GRBA#COT136B Undergraduate   1 credits $62*
This one-credit course is designed for new users of Microsoft PowerPoint for Office 95, which is PowerPoint version 7. Students must have access to a computer with Internet/e-mail capabilities and PowerPoint. Contact with the instructor will be made via e-mail. This course will explore the basics of PowerPoint including choosing templates and slide layouts; creating slides with text, clip art, tables, graphs, and organizational charts; distinguishing among PowerPoint views; running customized "slide shows;" using master slides; and drawing graphically on slides.
* NV residents tuition: $43 per credit.

Powerpoint On Line
Edmonds Community College
EDMO#PCAPP194 Undergraduate   3 credits $220
Provides an overview of the features and skills required to get maximum benefit from using this "industry standard" presentation program called PowerPoint for Windows. Using the Microsoft Step by Step textbook, students will gain hands-on knowledge and experience creating, modifying, and printing presentations; applying templates, color schemes, and clipart, to presentations; drawing and modifying pictures (objects); creating and editing graphs and organization charts; producing a slide show; creating a multimedia presentation; conferencing a presentation.

Preparing Images for the Web
University of Massachusetts - Dartmouth
MADA#CMO303 Undergraduate   0 credits $135
This course will move beyond the basics of GIFs and JPEGs to explore methods for optimizing all types of online images. Special attention will be paid to usability, download times, and avoiding cross-platform pitfalls. Students will gain a working knowledge of the 216 color browser-safe palette--how and when to use it, and how to know when it's not the best choice. This is an advanced course in the Online Communications Skills Program and should be taken after the WebCraft course, or its equivalent. Prerequisite: Knowledge of basic HTML, access to and basic understanding of a sophisticated raster graphics program such as Adobe Photoshop (recommended), Corel Photopaint (version 6 or later preferred), or JASC Paint Shop Pro.

Presentation Software
Cerro Coso Community College
CECO#CSCIC53 Undergraduate   1 credits $115*
Hands-on microcomputer course designed to provide a basic understanding of a presentation program. Slide show planning, creating, editing, viewing, and printing are covered. Prerequisite: CSCI C2 or CSCI C70 or equivalent.
* CA residents pay $13 per credit.

Principles of Operating Systems
New Jersey Institute of Technology
NJIT#CIS332 Undergraduate   3 credits $1143*
This course covers the organization of operating systems including structure, process management and scheduling; interaction of concurrent processes: interrupts, I/O, device handling; memory and virtual memory management and file management. Laboratory work will require that students have access to a computer. Prerequisites: A course in machine and assembly programming or equivalent. Optional: 26 video lessons of 60 minutes each.
* NJ residents: $184/semester hour.

Principles of Programming
Dakota State University
DAKO#CSC150 Undergraduate   3 credits $447
An introduction to computer programming. Emphasis on maintaining programs and on logical design, structured programming techniques, flowcharting and pseudocode.

Program Design in C
City University
CITY#CS362 Undergraduate 5 qu. credits $785
Students learn to develop modular software using C. Topics include problem solving, programming logic, data types, user interface, input validation, security, software documentation, testing and debugging, conditional logic and loops, functions, pointers, memory allocation, searching and sorting, input/output, and preprocessing. Prerequisite: CS241 or proficiency in a programming language.

Programming and Problem Solving
New Jersey Institute of Technology
NJIT#CIS101 Undergraduate 2 credits $762*
Covers computer science and FORTRAN programming and its use in solving engineering and scientific problems. The emphasis is on logical analysis of a problem and the formulation of a computer program leading to its solution.. Optional: 32 video lessons of 30 minutes each.
* NJ residents: $184/semester hour.

Programming Design & Validation
Rochester Institute of Technology
ROCH#60221090 Undergraduate 4 credits $923
A second course in programming and data structures where students use C++ to implement moderately large programs.

Programming for GUI
Dakota State University
DAKO#CSC403 Undergraduate 3 credits $447
A course dealing with the issues of programming in a graphical user interface environment. In-depth programming will be done in a graphical operating system environment. Issues such as design of user interfaces, object-oriented programming and networking will be covered along with examples of other environments. Prerequisite: CSC310 and CSC346.

Programming Language Concepts
New Jersey Institute of Technology
NJIT#CIS280 Undergraduate 3 credits $1143*
Conceptual study of programming language syntax, semantics and implementation. Course covers language definition structure, data types and structures, control structures and data flow, run-time consideration, and interpretative languages. Prerequisites: Introduction to Computer Science II (NJIT#CIS114) or equivalent. Optional: 27 video lessons of 60 minutes each.
* NJ residents: $184/semester hour.

Programming Language Survey
City University
CITY#CS423 Undergraduate 5 qu. credits $785
A comparative study of the development and use of several major programming languages. Topics include syntax and grammatical structure, MIS management, programming logic, feasibility studies, system integration, software maintenance, security, Object-Oriented programming, and the effect of run time environment. The student gains limited experience with Visual Basic, C, Visual C++, Pascal, COBOL, Prolog, and Fortran. Prerequisite: CS241 or proficiency in a programming language.

Programming Languages
Nova Southeastern University
NOVA#CISC610 Graduate 3 credits $1,110
Formal languages and language hierarchies, syntactic and semantic specification, abstract machines and corresponding languages, context-free languages, abstraction, modularity, and program structure. Fundamental programming language concepts. Analysis of imperative, object-oriented, and declarative language paradigms. Several programming languages will be analyzed.

Programming Languages
State University of New York
SUNY#CS571 Graduate 3 credits $1038*
Selected topics in programming languages and alternative programming paradigms. Functional and imperative languages. Logic programming and object-oriented programming paradigms. Languages for concurrent computation. Semantics of programming languages. Prerequisite: CS471, Programming Languages or equivalent.
* NY residents tuition: $137 per credit

Programming Principles
Lake Superior College
LASU#CIS1415 Undergraduate 3 credits $210
This course highlights the difference between heuristic and logical problem-solving methods. Students will learn to use analytical methods to gather detailed information in order to solve problems with a computer.

Publishing on WWW with HTML
Delaware County Community College
DECO#DPR999 Undergraduate 3 credits $???
This course introduces the student to publishing on the World Wide Web using HyperText Mark-up Language (HTML) and other Web development tools. Students will acquire hands-on experience in creating web pages that include text, images and animations. Concepts and features of the World Wide Web will also be studied and analyzed. Prerequisite: Introduction to Computers (DPR 100) or permission from instructor.

QuarkXPress Level 1 (Macintosh)
New School for Social Research
NEWS#3208 Undergraduate 0 credits $580
XPress is one of the most popular desktop publishing packages and the program of choice for many professional applications. This course covers basic document construction, typography, manipulation of text and graphics, etc. Students acquire experience by laying out flyers, brochures, newsletters, and single- and multi-page ads. Prerequisite: Using the Macintosh or equivalent experience.

Real World Math via the Internet
The Heritage Institute
HEON#ED408P Undergraduate   3 qu. credits $215
Traditional math teaching has often been skill-based, lacking in relevance and hard or uninteresting for many students. Yet, the teaching of math can be dynamic when we consider how much material from real life involves mathematical knowledge. In this course we'll learn how to make math at all levels K-12 come alive with real world problems and data that will support an interdisciplinary teaching of such areas as science, social studies, history and business.

Requirements Analysis
New Jersey Institute of Technology
NJIT#CIS390 Undergraduate   3 credits $1143*
Theories, methodologies and strategies for information requirements, including the assessment of transactions and decisions, fact-finding methodologies, structured analysis development tools, strategies of prototype development, and an overview of computer-aided software engineering (CASE) tools. Theory, methodologies and strategies for systems design, including the design of user-interfaces, particularly menu-driven and keyword dialogue strategies, and issues in the proper design of computer output. Prerequisites: NJIT#CIS114 or equivalent knowledge. Optional: 39 video lessons of 30 minutes each.
* NJ residents: $184/semester hour.

Reusable Software Design
Rochester Institute of Technology
ROCH#60272590 Undergraduate   4 credits $923
Further study of the principles and techniques of designing and implementing large software systems, focusing on software reuse.

Riding Information Super Highway
California State University - San Marcos
CASA#HTM423 Undergraduate   2 credits $210
Study of the Information Superhighway with an emphasis on hands-on usage of the Internet, and the personal, business, technical, and social implications of the Superhighway.

Script Writing
State University of New York
SUNY#ENGL200 Undergraduate   3 credits $1038*
This course is designed to introduce students to the fundamentals of developing and writing screenplays for film and television. The course emphasizes story, plot, characterization, dialogue, structure, script format and the process of developing and writing a screenplay. Other topics include agents, pitching, story conferences, script evaluation and screenwriting resources. Prerequisite: English 101 by permission of Instructor.
* NY residents tuition: $137 per credit.

Search Bank Remote Access
Cerro Coso Community College
CECO#INST89SB Undergraduate   0.5 credits $58*
Ability to remotely access Cerro Coso library's subscription to SearchBank, an online periodical database.
* California resident tuition: $13 per credit.

Semiconductor Device Packaging
State University of New York
SUNY#EE577 Graduate   3 credits $1038*
Electrical, thermal, and mechanical design aspects of packaging. Devices and printed circuit boards, wire-bonding, die attachment, hybrids, electrical interconnections, materials, adhesion, reliability. Prerequisite: EE332, Semiconductor Devices or equivalent.
* NY residents tuition: $137 per credit

Seminar on Virtual Reality
East Carolina University
EACA#EDTC4900 Undergraduate   3 credits $927*
An exploration of problems and issues affecting the building, use, and evaluation of virtual environments. Prerequisite: 16 semester hours in virtual reality, or consent of department chair.
* NC resident tuition $135.

Seminar on Virtual Reality and Education
East Carolina University
EACA#EDTC6848 Undergraduate   3 credits $927*
An exploration of problems and issues affecting the building, use, and evaluation of virtual reality environments in educational settings. Prerequisites: EDTC 6242, 6244; or consent of chairperson.
* NC resident tuition $135.

Service and Support
Strayer University
STRA#CIS285 Undergraduate   4.5 credits $665
Provides the skills necessary to troubleshoot the network. Focuses on network problems, network connections, storage devices, troubleshooting the DOS workstation, printing systems, network optimization, and disaster recovery. Prerequisite: CIS280 or equivalent.

Small Business Marketing on Internet
Kennesaw State University
KENN#FMV220 Undergraduate   3 credits $149
This course is designed to introduce students to marketing in the new, international marketplace that exists on the Internet the World Wide Web. The course will examine marketing research, promotional strategy (including free promotional methods), and payment security issues. We will also discuss Internet Service Providers and the Do's and Don'ts of commercial site design. The course will emphasize techniques that are especially applicable to small businesses with limited resources.

Sociology of the Internet
Syracuse University
SYRA#SOC4005 Undergraduate   3 credits $960*
The course examines the sociological implications of the Internet and also provides hands-on training in constructing web-pages. The Internet is a major communication source for anyone who has access to a computer and a modem. Who uses this communication resource? How do they use it? What are the implications for understanding social processes, social interactions, social inequalities, cultural values, and more. Students will construct their own web pages and do original research on topics such as censorship, pornography, under-represented voices, chat rooms, advertising, social movements, hate groups, or other topics.
* Graduate level course tuition: $1587.

Software Design and Production
New Jersey Institute of Technology
NJIT#CIS673 Undergraduate   3 credits $1143*
Modern techniques and methods employed in the development of large software systems, including a study of each of the major activities occurring during the lifetime of a software system. From conception to obsolescence and replacement. This course is part of the graduate certificate in Object-Oriented Design. Prerequisites: Courses in operating system design, data management system design and computer programming languages (NJIT#CIS630, 631 and 635). Optional: 26 video lessons of 60 minutes each.
* NJ residents: $184/semester hour.

Software Engineering
Nova Southeastern University
NOVA#CISC680 Graduate   3 credits $1,110
The development of software-intensive systems; software quality factors; software engineering principles; system life cycle models and paradigms; requirements definition and analysis; behavioral specification; software design; implementation; software testing techniques; verification and validation; system evolution; software project management.

Software Engineering Implementation
Nova Southeastern University
NOVA#CISC682 Graduate   3 credits $1,110
Techniques of software engineering will be applied in projects. Prerequisite: CISC680.

Software for the Office - Evaluation and Use
Mercy College
MERC#CS353 Undergraduate   3 credits $900
The course covers an evaluation and use of information management software designed for the office environment, including word processing, spreadsheet, database, desktop publishing, graphics, communication and utility software. Topics also include the determination of the suitability of software; assimilation of software into existing business systems; and, transfer of documents between different software packages and computer systems. Prerequisites: CS120 Introduction to Computers and Application Software and MG120 Principles of Management or CS220 Introduction to Programming using Application Software.

Software Project Management
City University
CITY#CS480 Undergraduate   5 qu. credits $785
Apply planning and management to the system development life cycle including configuration management, financial management of computer system resources, feasibility studies, security, software documentation, software maintenance, strategic planning. Students learn to organize, staff and control software projects and develop a project plan using MS Project for Windows. Prerequisite: At least 4 of CS322, CS390, CS416, CS420, CS450 and CS470 or their equivalents.

Software Project Management
University of Colorado
CUON#ISMG6260 Undergraduate   3 credits $1953*
Provides an in-depth coverage of software metrics and their use in software project management. Students will study quantitative models for estimating software costs, quality, and schedules. Methods for ensuring software production quality are also covered. Prerequisite: ISMG6060 or ISMG6140.
* CO residents tuition: $136 per credit.

Spreadsheet Applications
Northwest College
NOCO#DP150 Undergraduate   3 credits $???
This introductory course exposes students to a wide variety of fundamental electronic spreadsheet operations and functions through business-related applications.

Spreadsheet, Database, and Graphing Applications
Nova Southeastern University
NOVA#MCTE645 Graduate   3 credits $1,110
This course provides experience with the multiple roles of electronic spreadsheets, databases, and graphs in teaching, learning, and the management of instruction. Using an integrated software package, these tools will be used to develop and reinforce skills in organizing, problem solving, generalizing, predicting, decision-making, and hypothesizing.

Spreadsheets I
Fayetteville Technical Community College
FAYE#CIS120 Undergraduate   3 credits $489*
This course introduces basic spreadsheet design and development. Topics include writing formulas, using functions, enhancing spreadsheets, creating charts, and printing. Upon completion, students should be able to design and print basic spreadsheets and charts. Prerequisites: CIS110 or CIS111.
* NC residents pay $20 per credit.

Spreadsheets in the Workplace
Great Basin College
GRBA#COT132B Undergraduate 3 credits $186*
Spreadsheets in the Workplace will concentrate on three of the most important computer skills needed in the business world. Spreadsheets are the most often needed software. Windows and File Management skills allow you to work with the many data files on today's large disks and hard drives. The class will introduce these subjects to the student and provide practice utilizing them.
* NV residents tuition: $43 per credit.

Streaming Internet Technologies
Humboldt State University
HUMB#CIS180 Undergraduate 3 credits $365
This course in multimedia concepts will explore advanced concepts and applications of multimedia production and design for delivery on the WWW. The course concentrates on the computing aspects of multimedia (i.e. how to make the computer do what you want it to) with an emphasis on the emerging field of streaming internet media types. You may view the instructor's web page at www.humboldt.edu/~jds1 Prerequisite: access to Adobe Photoshop and Premiere.

Structured COBOL
Strayer University
STRA#CIS248 Undergraduate 4.5 credits $665
Involves extensive work in the solution of business applications in structured COBOL language. Emphasizes the fundamentals of structured program design, development, testing implementation, and documentation. Diverse techniques involved in business applications, including control break, table handling, and sorting. Prerequisite: CIS110.

Supporting Systems Management Servers
Strayer University
STRA#CIS302 Undergraduate 4.5 credits $665
Covers the concepts to set up a Microsoft Systems Management Server. Topics include introduction to the management server, setting up a primary site, providing remote help-desk support, administrating, inventory collection, managing jobs, distributing software, managing network applications, setting up multiple sites, communicating between sites, planning a systems management site, and troubleshooting. Prerequisite: CIS282 or equivalent.

Supporting Windows '95
Strayer University
STRA#CIS182 Undergraduate 4.5 credits $665
Focuses on the skills necessary to install and manage a windows environment. The basic areas covered include installation and configuration, architectural overview, user interface, memory management, file I/O, network administration, communications and printing, disk utilities, troubleshooting, and multimedia. Prerequisite: CIS175.

Supporting Windows NT
Strayer University
STRA#CIS187 Undergraduate 4.5 credits $665
Provides students with a foundation on the Windows NT workstation and fundamentals. Topics include the Windows NT environment, workstation, printing, remote access, troubleshooting, configuration, installation, managing accounts and user rights, securing directory and file resources, securing the system, networking environment and communication, networking browsing and booting Windows NT, and supporting applications. Prerequisite: CIS175.

Survey of Computer Languages
Nova Southeastern University
NOVA#MMIS610 Graduate 3 credits $1,110
A study of high-level languages, fourth-generation languages, and command languages used in the development of software for management information systems. The logical and physical structure of programs and data. Concepts of structured programming. Data structures, file management, and their use in problem solving. Students will complete a variety of high-level language computer programs.

Survey of Courseware
Nova Southeastern University
NOVA#MCTE625 Graduate 3 credits $1,110
State-of-the-art, content-rich courseware, across the grades, subjects, and platforms, will be explored and evaluated for educational value. Methods for integrating these programs into the curriculum will be discussed. Tutorials, drill and practice, instructional games, simulations, tests, and reference programs are included.

Survey of Microcomputer Uses
Pima Community College
PIMA#CSC105 Undergraduate 3 credits $165*
Study of microcomputer application packages. Includes Windows 95 operating system, Office 95: the Microsoft Word word processor, the Excel spreadsheet, and the Access database program. It would be best if the student has his/her own computer containing the Office program suite. However, project work may be completed at any of the campuses open - access microcomputer labs.
* AZ residents pay $32 per credit.

Survey of Operating Systems
Pitt Community College
PITT#CIS130 Undergraduate 3 credits $???
This course covers operating system concepts which are necessary for maintaining and using computer systems. Topics include disk management, file management, and directory structures; installation and setup; resource allocation, optimization, and configuration; system security; and other related topics. Upon completion, students should be able to install and configure operating systems and optimize performance.

Survey of Programming Languages
Nova Southeastern University
NOVA#MCIS611 Graduate   3 credits $1,110
Organization and types of programming languages. Analysis of imperative, object-oriented, and declarative language paradigms. Higher-level languages. Comparative analysis of programming languages used in the development of computer information systems.

System Development in Visual Basic
City University
CITY#CS322 Undergraduate   5 qu. credits $785
Develop structured software using Visual Basic. Students learn the systems development life cycle, problem solving, user interface, input validation, security, providing user help, software documentation, managing mouse events, Dynamic Data and Exchange (DDE), Object Linking and Embedding (OLE), Dynamic Link Libraries (DLL), accessing Windows Clipboard, and error trapping. Prerequisite: CS220 or knowledge of Visual Basic.

Systems Administration for SQL Server
Strayer University
STRA#CIS289 Undergraduate   4.5 credits $665
Provides the skills necessary to plan, install and administer a Microsoft SQL server. Topics include Microsoft TCP/IP addressing, subnet addressing, implementing IP routing, dynamic host configuration, managing databases and devices, managing user accounts, managing login security, assigning user permissions, backup and recovery, importing, exporting, and distributing data, scheduling, tasks, monitoring, and tuning, and setting up and configuration replication. Prerequisite: CIS282 or equivalent.

Taming the Electronic Frontier
George Mason University
GEMA#LRNG572 Undergraduate   3 credits $851
Taming the Electronic Frontier is a 15 week distributed learning community that uses several technologies, including television, telephones, telecomputing, videotapes and face to face meetings, to deliver experiential and interactive learning experiences to students in homes and offices. Lectures are broadcast on local cable TV. Lectures are also available on videotapes in the GMU library or you can arrange for Virtual School to deliver tapes to your home or office.

TCP/IP for Windows NT
Strayer University
STRA#CIS287 Undergraduate   4.5 credits $665
Focuses on Internet working Microsoft TCP/IP using Microsoft Windows NT. Topics include Microsoft TCP/IP addressing, subnet addressing, implementing IP routing, dynamic host configuration protocol, IP address resolution, NetBIOS name resolution, Windows Internet name service, host name resolution, connectivity, SNMP, and troubleshooting. Prerequisite: CIS282 or equivalent.

Text-Based Virtual Environments
East Carolina University
EACA#EDTC3245 Undergraduate   3 credits $927*
The design, building, application, and evaluation of applications of text-based virtual environments. Prerequisite: EDTC2240 or consent of instructor.
* NC resident tuition $135.

The Internet
Nova Southeastern University
NOVA#MCTE615 Graduate   3 credits $1,110
The Internet and other online information systems associated with the evolving information superhighway will soon have a dominant role in how information is organized and retrieved. This course emphasizes the development of effective online skills so that bibliographic, full-text, graphical, and numerical information can be accessed in an efficient manner. It also addresses skills and approaches required to teach the Internet.

The Internet
Rio Salado College
RISA#BPC133DA Undergraduate   3 credits $186*
Overview of the Internet and its resources. Hands-on experience with various Internet communication, resource discovery, and information retrieval tools.
* AZ residents $37 per credit.

The Internet - Level I
Rio Salado College
RISA#BPC133AA Undergraduate   1 credits $62*
Overview of the Internet and its resources. Hands-on experience with various Internet communication tools.
* AZ residents $37 per credit.

The Internet - Level II
Rio Salado College
RISA#BPC133BA Undergraduate   1 credits $62*
Exploration of additional Internet resources. Hands-on experience with a variety of resource discovery and information retrieval tools. Prerequisites: BPC/CIS133AA.
* AZ residents $37 per credit.

The Internet - Level III
Rio Salado College
RISA#BPC133CA Undergraduate   1 credits $62*
Independent exploration of the Internet. Prerequisites: BPC/CIS133BA or permission of instructor.
* AZ residents $37 per credit.

The Internet Web Publishing II
Rio Salado College
RISA#CIS233BA Undergraduate   1 credits $62*
Advanced hypertext markup language (HTML), including tables, forms, image maps, gateway scripts, and multimedia. Hands-on experience designing advanced Web presentations. Prerequisites: BPC/CIS233AA or permission of instructor.
* AZ residents pay $37 per credit.

The Interpersonal Internet
University of Wisconsin
WISC#COMM385 Undergraduate 3 credits $312

Remember the phrase, "I like to work with people"? How often do you come home from work or school completely stressed by your work with people, by frustrations in communication and interactions? Recent web-based tools such as e-mail, on-line information retrieval systems, real-time discussion rooms, etc., provide some creative options for enhancing working with others. This course will help you understand different interpersonal roles people play in groups, stages of group development, the difference between a group and a team, and different types of teams within today's organizations (cross-functional teams, self-directed teams. short-term project teams).

The Politics of the Information Revolution
Syracuse University
SYRA#PSC3001 Undergraduate 3 credits $960

This course examines a range of political, economic, and social questions related to the emergence of the information revolution. The topics are dynamic and cover issues that are being debated by policymakers around the world today. As the first W in World Wide Web indicates, the issues discussed here are global in nature, but they also have very local impacts. Consequently we will blend the domestic and the international perspectives in exploring these issues. While the focus will primarily be on the Internet and related on-line technologies, it will also examine other information issues.

Topics in Computers & Society Information Superhighway
State University of New York
SUNY#272154 Undergraduate 4 credits $586*

What is the Information Superhighway' How much information should be made available, to whom' What are the appropriate roles for government in the growth and development of this infrastructure' Explore the history, culture, and social impact of the Internet and changing telecommunications technologies. Gain the skills and knowledge necessary to begin exploring the Internet/World Wide Web and use it as a source of information.
* NY residents tuition: $515

Troubleshooting Web Graphics
New School for Social Research
NEWS#3341 Undergraduate 0 credits $385

This course is for anyone who creates or wants to create web pages. Are you disappointed with loss of detail? Color shifts? Blotchy images? Understanding the constraints inherent with graphics and images on the World Wide Web is critical to successful web design. This course covers scanning, color palettes, dithering, file formats, planning for cross-platform and cross-browser display, resolution, and more. The class also explores the many software applications available to create and process images for on-line display such as Adobe Photoshop, Illustrator, DeBabalizer, and many shareware applications. An understanding of website design and Photoshop is assumed.

Understanding and Using the Internet
Rio Hondo College
RIHO#WWW6 Undergraduate ?? credits $???

This course is designed to introduce the you to the Internet using the PBS online series as the teaching tool. This course is divided into two major sections: Starting Out (Overview, Subject Indexes and Search Tools, and Netiquett) and Applications (Email, WWW, FTP, Usenet, IRC, Gopher, Telnet, and other topics). The series is available on video tape and at the completion of the course the student can receive a certificate by taking an online quiz.

UNIX
Front Range Community College
FRCC#CIS175 Undergraduate 4 credits $1052

This course is an introduction to the Unix operating system. It includes an introduction to the Unix file system and utilities, shell programming, Sed and Awk, and an overview of Unix system administration. 60 Contact Hours. Prerequisite: CIS115 and one programming language or permission of instructor.

UNIX Operating System
University of Massachusetts - Lowell
MALO#92311 Undergraduate 3 credits $395

This course provides students with an introduction to the UNIX" Operating System. The course addresses manipulating and maintaining files within the UNIX file system; creating and editing text files using the vi and ed editors; using pipes, redirection, and filters; using advanced text processing utilities; using electronic mail; writing and debugging shell scripts; submitting and executing processes.

UNIX Operating System
University of Massachusetts - Lowell
MALO#92312 Undergraduate 3 credits $395

This course teaches students the concepts, features, and functions of the Bourne Shell. The course covers the building blocks necessary to programming the shell. Shell scripts are developed which can be used as new utilities. The instructor will post weekly lecture notes, readings and a range of assignments geared to illustrate the students command of UNIX. Students can complete assignments on most UNIX host machines and are eligible for TELNET accounts on the University's UNIX system. Prerequisites: 92311. Other programming experience may be applied to the prerequisite for non-matriculated students.

UNIX Operating System
New School for Social Research
NEWS#3123 Undergraduate 0 credits $580

A foundation lecture course in UNIX, probably the most powerful and easy-to-use operating system for all types of computers, micro to mainframe. Students learn about multiprocessing, file structure, and real-time computing. All standard features of any UNIX system are covered: common file commands, file filters, shell programming, text editors/formatters, and communications; a UNIX PC is available for lab practice. Prerequisite: familiarity with another computer operating system--DOS, VMS, or JCL.

UNIX Operating System
Strayer University
STRA#CIS155 Undergraduate   4.5 credits $665
Covers the development and execution of structured shell programs including scripts, menus, I/O redirection, pipes, variables, and other UNIX commands. UNIX administration techniques also are covered including electronic mail, editors, on-line help, and file and directory techniques. Prerequisite: CIS110 or equiv.

UNIX Operating System and Internet
Syracuse University
SYRA#CIS333 Undergraduate   3 credits $960
This course explores the UNIX operating system: commands, hierarchical file systems, editors, windowing, networking, security, administration. Emphasis on shell programming, awk scripts, sed, e-mail, newsgroups, Internet, telnet/ftp, search tools (Archie, Gopher, WAID, Mosaic).

UNIX Operating Systems
Rio Salado College
RISA#CIS122AC Undergraduate   1 credits $62*
The use of the UNIX operating system on a midrange or mainframe computer; basic concepts, commands, file organization and management, and task management.
* AZ residents pay $37 per credit.

UNIX Systems Programming
Harvard University
HARV#CSCIE215 Graduate   4 credits $1,200*
An introduction to the fundamental structure and services of the UNIX operating system. The course combines theory with programming at the system call level. Topics include files and directories, device control, terminal handling, processes and threads, signals, pipes, and sockets. Examples and exercises include directory management utilities, a shell, and an internet database client. Prerequisite(s): solid knowledge of C or C++, a data structures course such as CSCI E-119, some experience using UNIX helpful.
* Noncredit option: $950.

Using and Programming Access
Strayer University
STRA#CIS111 Undergraduate   4.5 credits $665
Covers the use and programming of the Access Database. Topics covered include creating tables, maintaining tables, querying tables, designing forms, and creating reports. Prerequisite: CIS105 or equiv.

Using the Internet
University of Alaska - Fairbanks
ALFA#ED593B Undergraduate   1 credits $100
Accessing Internet services including USENET, a global electronic bulletin board; TELNET to log on to other computer systems; GOPHER and Worldwide Web menu systems; ARCHIE file searches; FTP file transfers; binary uploads/downloads; and listservers. Prerequisite: ED593 or permission of instructor.

Using the Internet in Education
New Jersey City University
NJCU#EDTC621 Graduate   3 credits $635
This course will introduce teachers and other educators to methods for finding and using educational resources on the Internet. Basic tools of the Internet will be used to develop educational activities such as: problem-solving, collaborative projects, interpersonal and global exchanges, and media literacy analyses. In this course, students will use web editors to create documents in HTML and will be required to develop their own home pages.

Using the World Wide Web
Emporia State University
EMPO#SP370 Undergrad/Grad   2 credits $152
Introduces search strategies and professional applications for resources available on the Web including: Internet applications helpful to career and personal activities, use of the WWW as a primary access to the Internet; and hypertext navigation of the WWW using Netscape.

Virtual Reality - Introduction and Basic Applications
East Carolina University
EACA#EDTC2240 Undergraduate   3 credits $927*
Introduction to virtual reality, emphasizing basic applications in education and other fields. Students select special projects according to their interests.
* NC resident tuition $135.

Virtual Reality - Principles and Applications
East Carolina University
EACA#EDTC6240 Undergraduate   3 credits $927*
An overview of the basic principles of virtual reality with an emphasis on applications in education and other fields. Students select special projects according to their interests, and build a virtual environment.
* NC resident tuition $135.

Virtual Reality Hardware and Software
East Carolina University
EACA#EDTC3903 Undergraduate   3 credits $927*
An in-depth look at VR hardware and software, evaluation techniques, and applications. Prerequisite: EDTC2240 or consent of instructor.
* NC resident tuition $135.

Visual Basic
Delaware County Community College
DECO#DPR222 Undergraduate   3 credits $???
This course covers the fundamentals of object-oriented programming for Windows-based applications.

Visual Basic
University of Massachusetts - Lowell
MALO#92220 Undergraduate 3 credits $395
Client/Server programming is catching up the industry very fast. Visual Basic is assuming a very important role in providing graphical client environment using MS Windows. Everyday new client applications are being developed using this most popular tool. On the face VB. looks very simple to generate an appealing graphical interface using simple objects of different classes, however it gets challenging to meet the project specifications in a real business world.

Visual Basic
New Hampshire College
NEHA#CIS125 Undergraduate 3 credits $1656
(Course description not available at press time.)

Visual Basic
New Hampshire College
NEHA#CIS260 Undergraduate 3 credits $1656
The design of algorithms, manipulation of string arrays, multidimensional tables, and sequential file building and updating are major course components. Students will be involved in writing programs of increasing complexity throughout the year. Prerequisite: CIS100.

Visual Basic
Pitt Community College
PITT#CSC139 Undergraduate 3 credits $???
This course is designed to lead you step-by-step into the world of Visual Basic. You should be able to write simple applications and have an overview of objects and how they behave by the end of the course. Students who are most successful in Internet courses are those who are disciplined, can work on their own, are able to deal with uncertainty and don't let outside distractions interfere with their work. If you don't know how to use the Internet, take an Internet course before you take Visual Basic.

Visual Basic
Red Wing Technical College
REWI#CC1812 Undergraduate 4 credits $155
This course introduces programming concepts using Microsoft's Visual Basic language. Visual Basic enables programmers to create full featured Windows applications with a minimum of effort. Course includes: form layout, event-driven Windows programming concepts, variables and data types, variable and control initialization, operators, objects and properties, control structures (procedures, if-else). No previous programming experience is required.

Visual Basic
Rogers State University
ROGE#CS1133 Undergraduate 3 credits $495*
Course covers programming in Visual Basic.
* OK residents $315.

Visual Basic for Windows
UCLA
UCLA#X418E Undergraduate 4 credits $500
Visual Basic is an easy-to-learn-and-use programming environment for Windows. Basic-based languages are part of such major Windows applications as Excel, Access, and Word for Windows. Understanding Visual Basic programming is a major step toward utilizing the macro language of Windows applications and integrating their capabilities. Topics covered in this online course include an overview of the Visual Basic environment, structure of a Visual Basic program, programming tools, forms, module, controls, menus, dialog boxes, message boxes, files, graphics, mouse, keyboard, data control, procedures and functions, debugging, and error handling.

Visual Basic Programming I
Rio Salado College
RISA#CIS159 Undergraduate 3 credits $186*
Use of the Visual Basic programming language to solve problems using suitable examples from business or other disciplines. Prerequisites: CIS105 and [BPC/CIS123AA or (BPC102AD and BPC102BD)].
* AZ residents $37 per credit.

Visual Programming
Strayer University
STRA#CIS267 Undergraduate 4.5 credits $665
Covers the development and execution of windows, supporting user interface components for main windows, dialogs, menus, controls, colors, and animation. Also covers the applications framework and strategies for applications. Prerequisite: CIS110 or equivalent.

Web Design / Production
New School for Social Research
NEWS#3940 Undergraduate 3 credits $455
What is Web design? What does a Web designer do? This introductory course addresses these questions with though-provoking as well as practical exercises. The concept that Web design is a multi-faceted new medium bridging the gap between technology and art is stressed. Topics surveyed include: history of the Web, non-linear environments and human thinking, tools of the trade, organization, content preparation and storyboarding, HTML (Hypertext Markup Language), Web graphic design, and emerging Web technologies. Students will survey practical techniques as well as write assignments including a Surf Journal.

Web Design for Architects & Designers
New School for Social Research
NEWS#4003 Undergraduate   3 credits $1050
Build your knowledge of Web through lecture and directed exercise. Make your searches more efficient, and get the information you need. Learn to translate presentation materials and CAD documents into Web graphics, animation, and image maps. Optimize images using GIF, transparent GIF and JPEG formats. Understand the proper syntax of HTML, and manipulate text and graphics at your command. Design a Website with effective mapping, navigation, hypertext linking, and tables. Prerequisite: Proficiency with graphic applications. You also need access to a text editor. Other software may be downloaded from the Web.

Web Graphics
Chemeketa Community College
CHEM#VC137 Undergraduate   1 credits $51
(Course description not available at press time.)

Web Page Design-HTML
Edmonds Community College
EDMO#PCAPP155 Undergraduate   2 credits $179
On-line Basic Web Design is a six-week course in the basics of Web page design (HTML) offered over the Internet. Using a comprehensive text book along with Web-based lessons/assignments and Web site examples, participants will learn to create Web pages. Working together as a class, participants will create pages and evaluate each other's work.

Web Page with Java Applets and CGI
Kennesaw State University
KENN#FMV226 Undergraduate   3 credits $149
This workshop is designed to teach the student how to improve web pages with the use of CGI and Java. The workshop also teaches the basics of CGI scripts and Java applets for Internet use. The workshop focuses on creating web pages with media objects like Java applets and functional elements such as forms processing using CGI scripts. Student will also have hands on exercises in creating Java applets with software program and run applets on web servers. Prerequisite: Student must have prior knowledge in creating web page and HTML.

Web Photography
Chemeketa Community College
CHEM#VC199P Undergraduate   2 credits $87
Combines traditional photographic skills with digitizing, manipulating, and displaying images on the Internet.

Web Programming in Perl
Harvard University
HARV#CSCIE13 Graduate   4 credits $1200
This course gives a thorough grounding in the Perl scripting language and CGI programming, which is a major part of large web servers. Students will create web applications based on real world examples. Applications will include forms processing, database access, HTML file manipulation, authentication, and web clients. Prerequisite(s): CSCI E-50b or equivalent experience in a programming language such as C or Pascal, solid understanding of HTML (such as CSCI E-12), experience with UNIX helpful.

Web Publishing
Chemeketa Community College
CHEM#0615W Undergraduate   0 credits $83
Use HTML (Hypertext Markup Language), the basic language used to design and develop documents on the World Wide Web.

Web Site Management
Lansing Community College
LANS#CISB204 Undergraduate   2 credits $210
This course covers detailed step-by-step procedures that guide the web administrator through the process of selection of web server software and hardware. Students will learn to install and configure a server and administer the server on an ongoing basis. Topics include: security and access controls, creating professional sites, UNIX sites, and NT servers. The orientation of the course is toward people who expect to be primarily responsible for the design, creation, marketing and maintenance of a WWW site, either on their own or a commercial server.

Webmaster
New School for Social Research
NEWS#3332 Undergraduate   0 credits $385
This workshop explores the most important issues involved in creating a website, including hardware, software, telecommunications, service providers, security, access, and usability. The advantages and disadvantages of using a service provider versus building an on-site server are compared and discussed, including cabling, routers, firewalls, LAN connectivity, and data collection. Other topics include HTML, Javascript, and CGI programming.

Windows 95
Edmonds Community College
EDMO#PCAPP157 Undergraduate   3 credits $220
Provide an overview of the features and skills required to get maximum benefit from using this "industry standard" PC operating system called Windows 95. Using the Microsoft Step by Step textbook, students will gain hands-on knowledge and experience using and customizing windows; working with windows based programs, DOS based programs, wordpad and paint; organizing, storing, and managing folders and files; sharing information between computers; and connecting computers through telephone lines.

Windows NT Server Enterprise
Strayer University
STRA#CIS283 Undergraduate   4.5 credits $665
Focuses on supporting Windows NT Server in an organization's wide area network. Topics include implementing, administering and troubleshooting a heterogeneous wide area network environment. Prerequisite: CIS282 or equivalent.

Windows Operating System I
Rio Salado College
RISA#BPC121AE Undergraduate   1 credits $62*
Specific topics include booting and shutting down the computer, navigating the desktop, start button features, taskbar status, and receiving on-line help support. Exploring and managing folders and files, running programs, and learning about Wordpad and Paint application programs.
* AZ residents $37 per credit.

Windows Operating System II
Rio Salado College
RISA#CIS122AE Undergraduate   1 credits $62*
Additional capabilities of the Windows '95 program that configure devices and customize the presentation of the operating system. System tools, control panel utilities, the My Computer, Network Neighborhood, and Microsoft Exchange desktop icons. Other helpful utilities presented. Prerequisites: BPC/CIS121AE or permission of instructor.
* AZ residents $37 per credit.

Word 7.0 On Line
Edmonds Community College
EDMO#PCAPP185 Undergraduate   3 credits $220
Provide an overview of the features and skills required to get maximum benefit from using this "industry standard" word processing program called Word for Windows. Using the Microsoft Step by Step textbook, students will gain hands-on knowledge and experience creating, formatting, and printing documents; creating and applying styles and templates; creating tables, charts, columns, and outlines; and working with mail merge documents, and forms.

Word for Windows
Rio Salado College
RISA#BPC135DK Undergraduate   2 credits $124*
Using Word word processing software to create and name files, edit text, format, and print a variety of documents. Prerequisites: The ability to use a keyboard at a minimum of 24 wpm or permission of instructor.
* AZ residents $37 per credit.

Word Processing - Executive
Eastern Oregon University
EAOR#OADM210B Undergraduate   5 credits $400
This course is designed to expose you to the daily activities that executive and administrative secretaries in any type of organization might be expected to perform. A transcriber may be rented from DEP (students supply own headphone). Prerequisite: OADM121, OADM123, & OADM222 or consent of instructor.

Word Processing - Legal
Eastern Oregon University
EAOR#OADM210C Undergraduate   5 credits $400
This course is intended to give you knowledge and understanding of approximately 800 terms commonly used in the legal profession. You will learn to define the terms and to use them in legal context. A transcriber may be rented from DEP (students supply own headphone). Prerequisite: OADM121,OADM123, &OADM222 or consent of instructor.

Word Processing - Medical
Eastern Oregon University
EAOR#OADM210D Undergraduate   5 credits $400
This course is designed to teach you the language of medicine to prepare you for medical office work. A transcriber may be rented from DEP (students supply own headphone). Prerequisite: OADM121, OADM123, & OADM222 or consent of instructor.

Word Processing I
Eastern Oregon University
EAOR#OADM123 Undergraduate   2 credits $160
Introduction and application of word processing software using WordPerfect. Emphasis on beginning and intermediate aspects of word processing software and formats of business communications. Prerequisite: OADM121.

Word Processing II
Eastern Oregon University
EAOR#OADM124 Undergraduate   2 credits $160
Advanced topics of word processing including merging, math functions, desktop publishing, etc. Prerequisite: OADM121, OADM123 or instructor consent.

Word Processing Procedures I - Word for Windows
Chemeketa Community College
CHEM#CA201D Undergraduate   3 credits $123
Basic to intermediate word processing training in Microsoft Word for Windows, using IBM compatible computers. Prerequisite: Touch typing ability - 35 wpm.

WordPerfect for Windows
Rio Salado College
RISA#BPC135DD Undergraduate   2 credits $124*
Using WordPerfect word processing software to create and
name files, edit text, format, and print a variety of documents.
Prerequisites: The ability to use a keyboard at a minimum of
24 wpm or permission of instructor.
* AZ residents $37 per credit.

World Wide Web Page Design and Construction
New School for Social Research
NEWS#3312 Undergraduate   0 credits $580
This course introduces HTML (Hypertext language) on the
Internet and demonstrates techniques and tips for creating
high-impact home pages on the World Wide Web. The class
explores graphic production, text formatting, image maps, and
general design and development considerations, using low-
budget and free tools found on the Internet. Use of
commercial software is also possible but not required.
Prerequisite: Using the Macintosh, Using the PC &
Compatibles, or equivalent experience.

World-Wide Web Technology
New Hampshire College
NEHA#CIS270 Undergraduate   3 credits $1656
This course will briefly examine the evolution of the Internet
and Web and its many applications. An examination of the
TCP/IP protocol and Internet architecture will provide a
technical basis for understanding the Internet and Web. The
course will also cover the Hypertext Markup Language
(HTML), the language used for creating Web pages. Through
assignments and lab exercises, each student will create Web
pages for personal or business use. Prerequisite: CIS100 with
grade of B or higher.

WWW Interactive Programming
Lansing Community College
LANS#CISB253 Undergraduate   4 credits $420
This course provides instruction in programming the World
Wide Web (WWW) to make it interactive. The fundamentals
and techniques of Common Gateway Interface programming
are presented as step-by-step instructions. Students progress to
more advanced topics to design interactive Web pages.
Complete instructions are given on implementing JavaScript,
VBScript, C, and Perl.

WWW Page Construction
The Heritage Institute
HEON#CM400H Undergraduate   3 qu. credits $200
The research, analysis, design and publishing of WWW pages
will motivate student learning in ways not possible with
previous school technology. The opportunity to explore
educationally relevant subjects, to publish authentic student art
or writing or to conduct research surveys via on-line forms is
one of the reasons that schools with web pages increased over
1000% in 1995, according to statistics from Web 66.

WWW-Enhanced Student Writing
The Heritage Institute
HEON#ED408N Undergraduate   3 qu. credits $200
K-12 teachers with Internet and World Wide Web access
will learn to use these resources to motivate student
writing. You'll work collaboratively with other teachers
using specific WWW and other internet sites to develop
lesson plans that enhance student writing. Help your
students learn to write, illustrate, assemble and bind their
own books and even find journals, magazines, contests
or their own newsletter for publishing and showcasing
their work.

Education

Administration

Counseling

Curriculum

Evaluation

Other

Society

Teaching

Technology

Advanced Techniques in HPER
Emporia State University
EMPO#PE700B Graduate   3 credits $315
This course is designed to provide students with knowledge, skills, and tools to effectively implement technology in health, sport, and movement science. This course will examine exercise, physical fitness testing, media, and computer technology. Students will have the opportunity for practical applications of technological skills in health, sport, and movement science.

Advances in Vocational Education
University of Central Florida
FLCE#EVT4368 Undergraduate   3 credits $1305*
Study, practice and achievement of techniques including cooperative learning, simulation, instructional modeling, and evaluation of instructional effectiveness.
* FL residents pay $129 per credit.

Approaches to Grammar
Eastern Oregon University
EAOR#ENGL316 Undergraduate   4 credits $320
Study of various traditional and nontraditional approaches to grammar with specific applications to and illustrations from the field of composition. Special consideration will be given to the linguistic and rhetorical theories that inform the study of grammar. Prerequisite: Upper division standing and consent of instructor.

Art Activities in the Elementary School
University of Missouri
MOCE#T230 Undergraduate   2 credits $258
This course studies the vital role of art activities and creative experiences in the growth and development of children. Perquisites: professional standing.

Books & Other Media for Children and Young Adults
East Carolina University
EACA#LIBS6135 Undergraduate   3 credits $927*
At the completion of the course, students will be able to describe the genres of literature for children and young adults and the standards by which they are evaluated; plan programs to introduce children to the various literary genres; plan booktalk programs to motivate children and young adults to read; guide children and young adults in their choice of books and other
* NC resident tuition $135.

Changing Patterns of the Educational Process
The Graduate School of America
TGSA#ED813W Graduate   4 credits $795
This course covers the evolution of the teacher as sole authority in the educational process in contrast to contemporary theories of collaborative learning, experiential learning and individualization.

Cognition and Technological Instruction
Walden University
WALD#EDUC6400 Undergraduate   4 credits $920
Exploration of the connection between education psychology and the pedagogy of effective instruction. Instructional interventions, and their potential improvement through the application of technology.

Collaborative Nature of Adult Education
The Graduate School of America
TGSA#ED836W Graduate   4 credits $795
The successful education of adults is a collaborative effort between the learner and the facilitator. This course explores such areas as the theoretical and practical changes necessary to place adult education in a collaborative mode, a partnership of learning between colleagues and the development of facilitation skills.

College Survival
Lake Superior College
LASU#STKS1010 Undergraduate   2 credits $140
Are the responsibilities of college life getting you down? College Survival will introduce you to many strategies that will help you to become a more successful person in many areas of your life. Prerequisites: A score of 23 or above on LSC's ASAP reading assessment test, or completion of Reading 0450 with a grade of "C" or better.

Computer Enhancement of Classroom
The Heritage Institute
HEON#CM400 Undergraduate   3 qu. credits $215
Students need more than keyboarding classes to learn the computer, which is why integrating the computer into regular classroom curricula and other activities is so valuable. In this course you'll receive over 100 sample lessons involving the computer to enhance student learning and self-esteem. We'll also discuss district/school technology planning, how you can get information on what's available in your district, how to order free software, and how you can prepare for the next step in technology.

Computers in Education
East Carolina University
EACA#EDTC5010 Undergraduate   3 credits $927*
(Course description not available at press time.)
* NC resident tuition $135.

Computers in Math Education
International Society for Technology in Education
ISTE#EDUC510A Grad   4 qu. credits $540*
This Distance Education course is specifically designed for K-12 mathematics educators. The emergence of calculators and computers as useful mathematical tools has caused mathematics educators to carefully consider the role technology should play in school mathematics education. In this course, students consider unique classroom applications of technology, teaching strategies, and questions about the future of mathematics education. Teachers review software, apply problem solving models, and design and evaluate lessons for their students.
* Non-credit option, tuition: $460.

Computing in Education I
State University of New York
SUNY#ETAP5265024 Graduate 3 credits $1038*
This course explores pedagogically sound uses of computing technologies to enhance teaching and learning. Students read and discuss scholarly articles, develop practical computing skills, and complete educationally oriented projects in four areas: telecommunications, computer-based instruction, tools packages and programming/authoring. All work is collected into a portfolio to be submitted for assessment, and becomes an individualized text/reference. Prerequisite: Must have a bachelor's degree or higher. Priority enrollment in this course is given to graduate students enrolled in a University at Albany degree program.
* NY residents tuition: $137 per credit

Computing Technology in Education
Nova Southeastern University
NOVA#MCTE691 Graduate 3 credits $1,110
This course is the capstone of the program. Each student will develop a comprehensive technology-based project using an environment of choice. Its purpose is to allow students the opportunity to further pursue topics or areas in which they have considerable interest. Each project will be closely mentored by faculty.

Computing Technology in Education
Nova Southeastern University
NOVA#MCTE695 Graduate 3 credits $1,110
This seminar will focus on the professor's current research interests. Prerequisite: prior consent of instructor and program director.

Connecting With At-Risk Students
The Heritage Institute
HEON#ED411S Undergraduate 3 qu. credits $215
Build greater confidence and skills with those difficult or disruptive students who are a drain on class time and your energy. In this distance course, you'll learn a four part, proactive model to achieve step-by-step success with troubling students, beginning by a look at your own attitudes and how they can hinder your effectiveness. We'll address the importance of establishing a positive, empathic connection with each student as a basis for trust-building and problem-solving.

Cooperative Education
Front Range Community College
FRCC#LST297 Undergraduate 3 credits $790
(Course description not available at press time.)

Cooperative Education in Accounting
Strayer University
STRA#ACC399 Undergraduate 4.5 credits $665
Allows students to enrich their learning in their chosen career area and enhance their career development. Provides a three-way partnership among student, employer, and Strayer University with each sharing responsibility through a part-time or full-time supervised work experience. Prerequisite: Permission of a Campus Dean.

Cooperative Education in Business Administration
Strayer University
STRA#BUS399 Undergraduate 4.5 credits $665
Allows students to enrich their learning in their chosen career area and enhance their career development. Provides a three-way partnership among student, employer, and Strayer University with each sharing responsibility through a part-time or full-time supervised work experience. Prerequisite: Permission of a Campus Dean.

Creating Social Studies Curriculum Materials
University of Minnesota
MINN#EDUC5666 Undergraduate 3 credits $300
Using historic sites and related materials to create new social studies curricula. Implementing and evaluating living history learning experiences in the classroom.

Cultural Diversity in the Classroom
UCLA
UCLA#X325H Undergraduate 4 credits $455
An intensive consideration of culture and diversity, their impact on instruction, and issues related to demographics, migrations, and immigration. Focuses on the nature and manifestations of culture and methods and strategies for learning about cultural differences and similarities. Also examines issues of racism. Participants evaluate their personal attitudes toward people of different cultural, linguistic, racial, ethnic, and socioeconomic backgrounds and individuals with disabilities.

Cultural Values in Education
Rio Salado College
RISA#EDU230 Undergraduate 3 credits $186*
Examination of the relationship of cultural values to the formation of the child's self-concept and learning styles. Examination of the role of prejudice, stereotyping and cultural incompatibilities in education. Emphasis on preparing future teachers to offer an equal educational opportunity to children of all cultural groups.
* AZ residents $37 per credit.

Curriculum and Emerging Instructional Technologies
University of Alabama
ALAB#BCT100 Undergraduate 3 credits $250
This course features the use of advanced applications of emerging instructional technologies.

Curriculum Development
University of Alabama
ALAB#BCT400 Undergraduate 3 credits $250
This course features the application of current and emerging instructional technologies to product development embedded in the context of discipline-specific projects. Cognitive, product and skill competencies are included. Cognitive competencies are integrated into product & skills evaluations. Products are required to reflect some competencies, while skills competencies are either observed directly or inferred from the products. Prerequisite: BCT300 and grade of "C" or above in CS110 or BCT100.

Curriculum Development
The Graduate School of America
TGSA#ED825W Graduate   4 credits $795
This course explores implementation and assessment of curricula based on historical and theoretical perspectives. Learners may examine curricula from any educational setting.

Curriculum Theory and Design
Walden University
WALD#EDUC6120 Undergraduate   4 credits $920
Exploration of curriculum theory and topics related to planning, design, inter-disciplinary and multi-disciplinary models, effective instruction, and main-streaming for gifted and at risk students.

Developing Online Curriculum
UCLA
UCLA#X396F Undergraduate   4 credits $500
This course explores the special requirements of online curriculum development and provides tools and processes for meeting these requirements. In addition, individual facilitator syllabi are discussed and practiced in real use situations.

Distance Learning Assessment Theory
UCLA
UCLA#X396G Undergraduate   2 credits $425
This course includes in-depth modules which present various assessment formats that can be used for evaluating students in online courses, programs, seminars, and other virtual classroom scenarios. Standard models and hybrids are explored in order to determine the strengths and weaknesses of each. Module topics include models of assessment theory, the application of assessment theory to online education, online assessment as a learning experience, and the necessary adjustments when evaluating students in distance learning.

Economics of Education In a Time of Change
Walden University
WALD#EDUC6340 Undergraduate   4 credits $920
Examination of key economic and financial issues facing educational innovators, schools and other learning organizations as they respond to changing needs of a global, information-based society. Budget development as a basis for issue analysis.

Education and Cultural Processes
University of Alaska - Fairbanks
ALFA#ED610 Undergraduate   3 credits $474
Advanced study of the function of education as a cultural process and its relation to other aspects of a cultural system. Students will prepare a study examining some aspect of education in a particular cultural context.

Education and Cultural Processes
University of Alaska - Fairbanks
ALFA#EDF610 Undergraduate   3 credits $474
The course will focus on the advanced study of cultural processes associated with education, and the relationship of schooling to other aspects of a cultural system. Students will be required to prepare a paper in which they examine some aspect of education in a particular cultural context.

Education and the Law
The Graduate School of America
TGSA#ED823W Graduate   4 credits $795
This course explores constitutional, statutory and case law as related to school settings. Both federal and state legislation are examined.

Educational Measurement
University of Missouri
MOCE#A280 Undergraduate   2 credits $258
This course studies the basic concepts of standardized testing, evaluation techniques, and interpretation of test scores, and it addresses ways that these concepts can improve the instructional process. Perquisites: Psych. 1 or 2.

Educational Structures and Decision Making Processes
Walden University
WALD#EDUC6230 Undergraduate   4 credits $920
Examination of organizational and operational systems in education and the influence which unions, pressure groups, legislatures and management practices exert. Focus on organizational development and decision making processes.

Educational Uses of the Information Highway
State University of New York
SUNY#EST572 Graduate   3 credits $1038*
This is a practical, hands-on course designed for teachers interested in exploring the Information Highway. The information highway is a term used to describe an abundance of rich resources for students, teachers, and administrators. This course prepares teachers to 'mine' these resources and create learning opportunities for their students. The following topics are included: Integration of web resources into curriculum, development of on-line projects, web page creation, video conferencing, e-mail, Newsgroups, FTP, server and client based applications, evaluation of on-line materials, censorship, pornography and on-line service providers.
* NY residents tuition: $137 per credit

Elementary School Administration
The Graduate School of America
TGSA#ED853W Graduate   4 credits $795
This course considers current theories, principles, and practices relative to the organization, administration, and operation of elementary schools.

Email Learning Across Curriculum
The Heritage Institute
HEON#CM400L Undergraduate   3 qu. credits $200
Learn to use email to empower your current teaching in all disciplines: science, math, social studies and language arts. In this course, you'll learn strategies to enhance student thinking and writing skills by managing email correspondences with subject matter experts or other online students. We'll explore several free educational listservs and online projects, including Kidlink's KIDPROJ and the Electronic Emissary Project (EEP), coordinated by Judi Harris and the University of Texas, Austin.

Emerging Models of Assessment
The Heritage Institute
HEON#ED412L Undergraduate 3 qu. credits $325

Educators must understand how to accurately assess student learning in order to be effective in teaching toward the essential academic learning requirements. Designed to help teachers of all disciplines to address state requirements to assess and validate student learning, this course offers self-contained modules which cover all aspects of assessment. This course provides many tools which will help you to use assessments to improve student learning. For teachers of grade levels 6-12 in all subject areas.

Ethics and Social Responsibility in Distance Education
The Graduate School of America
TGSA#ED852W Graduate 4 credits $795

This course analyzes, from both conceptual and applied points of view, the interaction between education and society. Through an examination of basic assumptions, attitudes and values, learners build an ethical foundation for understanding and reacting to issues and policies related to distance education.

Evaluating the Effectiveness of the Educational Process
The Graduate School of America
TGSA#ED814W Graduate 4 credits $795

This course explores a variety of evaluation techniques to examine individual educational programs or entire educational systems. It also provides theoretical frameworks upon which evaluations are based.

Exceptional Children in the Schools
University of Central Florida
FLCE#EEX5051 Graduate 3 credits $1305*

Definition, characteristics, theories, current trends, and controversies in the various categories of exceptional children. This course is designed to introduce you to the various categories of exceptional education. Terminology, definitions, characteristics, theories, current trends, and controversies in special education will be presented. The course will examine educational problems and appropriate educational programs for exceptional individuals.
* FL residents pay $129 per credit.

Experiential Learning Portfolio I
Brevard Community College
BREV#SLS1371 Undergraduate 2 credits $155

Perquisite: Recommendation of assessment counselor. Persons with significant learning from prior experience are assisted in assembling portfolio(s) for evaluation for one (1) to ten (10) hours of college credit.

Facilitative Tools for Online Teaching
UCLA
UCLA#X396H Undergraduate 4 credits $500

This course develops skills in the teaching of courses in the online environment. Technological tools are demonstrated and used in practice situations to facilitate learning in this environment. Real-life situations are used as cases for diagnosis and developing solutions.

Family and Societal Factors in Education
Walden University
WALD#EDUC6210 Undergraduate 4 credits $920

Examination of family settings, demographic and societal factors as they relate to education and the workplace. Exploration of the role of education in relation to social issues, including socioeconomic conditions, resource enriched environments, multi-ethnic, multi-racial, and multi-language cultures.

Foundations of Library & Information Studies
East Carolina University
EACA#LIBS6010 Undergraduate 3 credits $927*

Examines the development and functions of libraries and information centers, professional practice and ethics, and current issues and trends. Serves as orientation to library and information science.
* NC resident tuition $135.

Freshman Seminar
State University of New York
SUNY#FS100 Undergraduate 1 credits $435*

A seminar is required of all new, full-time students at Herkimer County Community College. Many other institutions have a similar course requirement. The seminar is designed to help students to be successful in their classes and in adjusting to the many challenges of college life.
* NY residents tuition: $80 per credit.

Fundamentals of Extension Teaching of Adults
University of Missouri
MOCE#ED406 Graduate 3 credits $489

This course examines the special needs of adult students in extension education, including a study of classroom techniques. It is recommended for students who have work experience in extension or any other informal adult education agency in the United States. Perquisites: instructor's consent.

Fundamentals of Graduate Research
University of Central Florida
FLCE#EDF6481 Graduate 3 credits $1305*

Course Objectives: 1) To understand and correctly use the language of research. 2) To understand and correctly use basic statistical concepts used in research. 3) To know how to find and correctly use research materials. 4) To be able to identify types, evaluate, critique, and synthesize research. 5) To know how to correctly use computer research Tools (e.g. Internet and SPSS) 6) To increase students' ability to think critically within their own vocational research context. 7) To enable students to perform small scale research in their vocational context.
* FL residents pay $129 per credit.

Fundamentals of Library and Information Science
State University of New York
SUNY#CEL59130 Graduate   3 credits $1038*
This historical introduction to the profession of librarianship and information science will look at professional literature, role and structure of libraries and information agencies in the conservation and dissemination of knowledge, and the nature of research in library and information science. Prerequisite: Must have a Bachelor's degree.
* NY residents tuition: $137 per credit

Funding of Educational Institutions
The Graduate School of America
TGSA#ED822W Graduate   4 credits $795
This course examines the many issues surrounding the funding of public education. The focus is on present and future funding patterns.

General Methods in Vocational Ed.
University of Central Florida
FLCE#EVT3365 Undergraduate   3 credits $786*
Techniques specific to vocational education and industry training.

Geometric Concepts for Teachers
University of Missouri
MOCE#MA68 Undergraduate   3 credits $387
This course includes points, lines, angles, congruence, similarity, constructions, and an introduction to proof. It also covers right triangles, circles, polygons, and other solids. Transformations and trigonometry are introduced. Perquisites: Math 10 or equivalent.

High School Journalism
University of Missouri
MOCE#JO380 Undergraduate   2 credits $258
This course provides a basic background in journalism and guidelines on how to teach it at the secondary level. An analysis of problems facing scholastic journalism is included.

Higher Education Administration
The Graduate School of America
TGSA#ED855W Graduate   4 credits $795
Analysis of theory, policies and procedures involved in administering institutions of higher education.

History and Principles of Phys. Ed.
Auburn University
AUBU#HHP201 Undergraduate   1.8 credits $76
A brief overview of significant ideas and events in the development of health education, physical education and recreation.

Human Learning
University of Missouri
MOCE#ED212 Undergraduate   3 credits $387
This course studies the principles of learning and forgetting and the factors that affect human learning and retention. Perquisites: Psych. 1.

Hypermedia in the Classroom
International Society for Technology in Education
ISTE#EDUC508T Grad   4 qu. credits $540*
This eight-lesson course provides a significant introduction to HyperCard. Students first learn to create HyperCard stacks using the program's menus. They will then learn to program in the HyperTalk language built into HyperCard. Students also will read about hypermedia history, issues, and current research in education; videotaped examples will be shown.
* Non-credit option, tuition: $460.

Instructing Special Needs Students
California State University - San Marcos
CASA#EDUC501 Post-bac   2 credits $315
The class is for prospective teachers and elementary or high school teachers interested in adapting and accommodating their instruction to meet the needs of mainstreamed students with special needs. The course includes information on the current legislation policies, terminology, and trends in educating students with special needs. Characteristics of exceptional individuals and the implications for classroom teaching are featured.

Instructional Applications of Internet
Pima Community College
PIMA#CSC103 Undergraduate   1 credits $55*
Integrating Internet services into the instructional process. Includes Internet technical overview, sociological/pedagogical implications, instructional design, and use of software tools for Internet course production. Students will complete a significant curriculum development project based upon their own interests.
* AZ residents, $32/credit hour.

Instructional Design
Emporia State University
EMPO#IT841 Graduate   3 credits $315
Presents a systematic method for the planning and development of instructional programs. In addition to examining the research supporting contemporary methods of instructional design, students will apply instructional design principles to the development of an instructional program.

Instructional Design for Distance Education
The Graduate School of America
TGSA#ED846W Graduate   4 credits $795
This course introduces learners to the increasing societal demands to deliver education in new and innovative ways. The course will enable learners to design instructional applications in a distance education setting.

Instructional Strategies for Distance Learning
East Carolina University
EACA#EDTC6250 Undergraduate   3 credits $927*
This course is for practitioners and will present and model principles and theories of distance learning, including design, delivery and evaluation, and will illustrate examples of distance learning throughout the country. At the end of this course, participants will be able to describe various technologies and methods used in distance delivery; describe various uses in distance learning; give an overview of the history and theories of distance learning; describe steps for designing and developing distance learning programs; list steps for designing simple graphics for distance learning programs; evaluate one or more distance learning systems or modules.
* NC resident tuition $135.

Instructional Technology
UCLA
UCLA#X332 Undergraduate   3 credits $425
Designed to familiarize the participant with the potential of employing instructional technology in classes for adult learners. Topics include using the computer as an effective classroom tool, exposure to a variety of current technologies and their applications in classroom and total educational settings, awareness and understanding of Urban Distance Learning as related to adult education, and strategies for overcoming technophobia on the part of teachers and adult learners.

Integrated Software Across Curriculum
New Jersey City University
NJCU#EDTC625 Graduate   3 credits $635
An integrated software package integrates word processing, data base management, paint, draw, spreadsheet and presentation capabilities into one package. The package will be the starting point for a resource-based curriculum. New types of learning and assignments across the curriculum will be explored. Examples of Integrated Software programs include: Claris Works, Microsoft Office, and Microsoft Works. If you are using another program, please check with NJCU.

Integrating Art in the Curriculum
The Heritage Institute
HEON#HU403D Undergraduate   3 qu. credits $215
Take this opportunity to integrate a variety of art media into many subject areas using Crayola products and their program of art projects for schools. Keep students interested with various media such as clay dough, watercolors, special crayons and chalk using art as a tool to enhance student learning across the curriculum. Resource guides on art materials, story books, tips on how to manage art projects plus many other activities will help teachers bring art to everyday learning in such diverse subjects as geography, science, social studies and health.

Integrating Technology
East Carolina University
EACA#EDTC6035 Undergraduate   3 credits $927*
In-depth study of the NC K-12 Computer Skills curriculum with emphasis on developing strategies, materials, and staff development to integrate the technology in the communications skills, information skills, and social studies curriculums.
* NC resident tuition $135.

Integrating Technology in Math and Science Curricula
East Carolina University
EACA#EDTC6037 Undergraduate   3 credits $927*
In-depth study of the NC K-12 Computer Skills curriculum with emphasis on developing strategies, materials, and staff development to integrate technology into the mathematics, science, and health curriculums. By the end of the course, students will review three curriculum software programs, develop three units to integrate the NC K-12 Computer Skills Curriculum, research and write an acceptable use policy for a school or LEA, develop practice sheets in preparation for the Computer Skills Proficiency Test sections on spreadsheet use.
* NC resident tuition $135.

Integration of Technology into the Curriculum
Walden University
WALD#EDUC6420 Undergraduate   5 credits $1150
Creation of curriculum materials and courses that integrate technology allowing for access to new information, development of new learning skills and the empowerment students. Learning styles and the student as the center of learning. Exploration of the role of technology and its incorporation within the learning curriculum for students and teachers.

Internet for Educators
International Society for Technology in Education
ISTE#EDUC508M Grad   4 qu. credits $540*
This six lesson course covers a variety of topics from the world of the Internet. The course includes a brief discussion of the history of the Internet and issues to consider before one connects to the network. The curriculum covers vocabulary, software and hardware considerations, e-mail, listservs, bulletin boards, FTP, and using the Internet for educational purposes. This course is suitable for K-12 educators who have minimal telecommunications experience.
* Non-credit option, tuition: $460.

Internet for Educators
UCLA
UCLA#X333B Undergraduate   3 credits $425
An online introductory course for educators who want to learn more about the Internet and the resources available through it. Participants become acquainted with software applications for accessing the net, utilizing Netscape Navigator or Microsoft Internet Explorer; creating a list of network resources; developing an implementation plan while detailing how the net can be utilized in their curriculum design and developing their own Web page online; and becoming knowledgeable about the various political, social, economic, and technological implications of using the Internet in the classroom.

Internet for Math Educators
Emporia State University
EMPO#IT743 Undergrad/Grad   3 credits $228
This course is an opportunity to investigate resources on the World Wide Web that can enhance mathematics teaching/learning. Each assignment has options for response -- whether you are a novice on the WWW or a proficient surfer or somewhere in between.

Internet Resources & Tools for Educators
Emporia State University
EMPO#IT744 Undergrad/Grad   2-3 credits $152
Focuses on using the information superhighway (Internet) in education. Lessons include finding and subscribing to listservs in education, using ERIC online, accessing and employing Web search engines, locating and downloading files, handling files with email, and analyzing the implication of the Internet for lifelong learning in education. Prerequisites: computer literacy, and access to the World Wide Web and email.

Introduction to Distance Learning
Fayetteville Technical Community College
FAYE#MIT110 Undergraduate   3 credits $489*
This course covers the principles of distance learning, including an introduction to using an interactive distance learning classroom. Emphasis is placed on the different technologies utilized to provide distance learning events (NCIH, telecourses, Internet, etc.) Upon completion, students should be able to demonstrate an understanding of distance learning principles and the technologies that are used to implement distance learning events.
* NC residents pay $20 per credit.

Introduction to Educating the Gifted
University of Missouri
MOCE#ED489V Graduate   3 credits $489
This course surveys the history and philosophy of gifted education, and it examines characteristics of gifted learners and teachers of the gifted. Program models and curricular/instructional designs are also discussed.

Introduction to Educational Statistics
University of Missouri
MOCE#A354 Undergraduate   3 credits $387
This course introduces statistical techniques employed in education: descriptive statistics, correlation, simple regression, and hypothesis testing. Perquisites: Psych. 1 or 2, and a beginning course in statistics.

Introduction to Multimedia and Web-Based Instruction
The Graduate School of America
TGSA#ED720W Graduate   4 credits $795
This course lays the groundwork for designing and implementing online training and education via CD-ROM, intranets, and the World Wide Web. This course provides a solid foundation for understanding all the components necessary for completing a successful project. Topics include: effective uses of multimedia; hardware and software systems; elements of multimedia text, graphics, video and sound; designing and producing a multimedia title; and project management.

Introduction to Special Education for Regular Educators
University of Missouri
MOCE#L312 Undergraduate   3 credits $387
This course is designed to provide an overview of special education today. Current trends in special education are emphasized, and specific areas such as emotional/behavioral disorders, communication disorders, sensory impairments, and gifted education are discussed. Perquisites: Students majoring in special education should enroll in L311; all others may enroll in either L311 or L312.

Issues and Trends in Reading Instruction
University of Missouri
MOCE#T420 Graduate   3 credits $489
This course provides intensive study of significant issues and current trends in reading on all instructional levels. Perquisites: Curr. and Instr. T315, T316, or equivalent, or instructor's consent.

Issues in Teaching & Learning with Technology
Mercy College
MERC#ED675 Undergraduate   3 credits $900
(Course description not available at press time.)

Learner Assessment
New School for Social Research
NEWS#1318 Undergraduate   1 credits $546
Permission required; call (212) 229-5372. A vital part of teaching ESL/EFL and adult literacy is developing and implementing valid tools to assess the levels, needs, goals, and achievements of one's students. In this course, we examine traditional forms of testing and learn to design alternative forms of assessment, for example, conferencing, profiles, journals, portfolios, and questionnaires.

Learning and Instruction
University of Missouri
MOCE#A205 Undergraduate   2 credits $258
This course examines the nature of human learning processes and includes implications for instruction; emphasis is on the basis of learning, readiness for learning, types of learning, memory, and other related topics. Perquisites: Psych. 1 or 2.

Learning from an Interdisciplinary Perspective
The Graduate School of America
TGSA#ED827W Graduate   4 credits $795
This course focuses on developing more meaningful learning experiences from an interdisciplinary perspective. Emphasis will be on integrating subject matter to create more dynamic learning environments for students from middle school through college.

Learning Theories, Motivation, and Relationship to Technology
Walden University
WALD#EDUC6100   Undergraduate   4 credits $920
Survey of principle theories of human learning including behaviorism, cognitive information processing, and constructivism. Emphasis given to alternative educational approaches, methods, strategies, and technologies that increase learning effectiveness.

Learning Theory
New York Institute of Technology
NYIT#BES2413   Undergraduate   3 credits $???
Learning theory is a fundamental science course. The student is asked to trace the emergence of modern cognitive learning theory (neo-behaviorism) from the original works of Pavlov, Thorndike, and Watson through the "blackbox" Skinnerian school of thought. The course emphasizes theoretical rather than methodological issues and, as such, is designed to give the student a firm grasp of the conditions under which permanent behavior change occurs. Prerequisite: BES2401.

Learning Theory and Computers
Nova Southeastern University
NOVA#MCTE670   Graduate   3 credits $1,110
Students will explore learning theories and how learning is achieved when instruction is presented from a computer-based paradigm. The course will emphasize the computer as a learning device that can be used in an effective manner to model learning theories associated with behaviorism, cognitivism, and human information processing.

Library Materials for Children and Youth
University of Missouri
MOCE#ED321   Undergraduate   3 credits $387
This course studies the background of library materials for children; the psychology of children; the characteristics of print, nonprint material; and current publishing trends. Other course topics include readers' guidance, book talks, and storytelling resources.

Management of Technology for Education
Walden University
WALD#EDUC6440   Undergraduate   5 credits $1150
Identifies educators as leaders in the process of integrating technology. Focus on strategic planning and management, human resource management including faculty and staff development, and the management of information systems and technological innovation.

Measurement & Evaluation in Education
University of Central Florida
FLCE#EDF6432   Graduate   3 credits $1305*
Concepts of measurement and evaluation, classroom test construction, creation and use of derived scores, selection and use of published measurement instruments, alternative assessment, and current issues.
* FL residents pay $129 per credit.

Media in Teaching and Learning
State University of New York
SUNY#ETAP5236741   Graduate   3 credits $1038*
This course explores the unique characteristics of non-print media' graphical, audio, video, computing, multimedia, and telecommunications, and how these might be used to enhance teaching and learning. Prerequisite: Must have a bachelor's degree or higher. Priority enrollment in this course is given to graduate students enrolled in a University at Albany degree program. Others will be taken on a space available basis beginning 10 days prior to the start of semester.
* NY residents tuition: $137 per credit

Meeting Affective Needs of Gifted Individuals
University of Missouri
MOCE#ED589JM   Graduate   3 credits $489
This course provides practical tools, concepts, and techniques for counselors, teachers, and parents who have no specific training in dealing with the social, emotional, ethical, and valuing side of being gifted. It addresses the problems gifted individuals face, such as motivation, discipline, stress management, relationships, feelings of difference, and depression. It also deals with gender issues (particularly those faced by female students) and issues facing the "special" gifted, such as learning disabled, behaviorally disordered, minority, attention deficit, and exceptionally able individuals.

Methods & Techniques of Teaching ESL/EFL 1
New School for Social Research
NEWS#1333   Undergraduate   3 credits $645
Permission required; call (212) 229-5372. This is the first part of a two-semester course in ESL/EFL methodology. It is for anyone interested in or currently teaching English as a Second or Foreign Language. Participants learn the basics of student-centered teaching for beginning-level ESL/EFL students. They learn to plan lessons that integrate contextualized grammar instruction with the teaching of vocabulary and all four language skills. They also learn about error correction and classroom management. Emphasis is on communicative, contextualized learning.

Models for Online Courses
UCLA
UCLA#X396   Undergraduate   4 credits $500
This course explores a plethora of models that can be used as the structure for online courses, programs, seminars, and other virtual classroom needs. Standard models and hybrids are explored and the strengths and weaknesses of several are determined. The UCLA Extension model is featured and defined in the context of the virtual classroom, the teaching role, and the curriculum development processes.

Multimedia Across the Curriculum
The Heritage Institute
HEON#CM400K Undergraduate 3 qu. credits $200
What better way to promote higher-order thinking skills and more complete comprehension of new ideas than having students use multimedia which provides multisensory learning by combining video, sound, text, graphics-all made possible with the computer. In this course, you'll learn about the software and hardware components for multimedia production, plus multimedia design and authoring techniques and their effective integration into the existing curriculum.

Multimedia in Education
Walden University
WALD#EDUC6250 Undergraduate 4 credits $920
Examination of emerging computer-based multimedia technologies including text applications, animation, audio, and full-motion video. Review and analysis for effective application. Survey of software, courseware, playback hardware (VCRs, CD-ROMs, Videodisc), presentation devices, video and graphics devices, audio products, output and mass storage devices.

Museums in the Classroom
The Heritage Institute
HEON#ED406M Undergraduate 5 qu. credits $325
Children early-on show our very human attraction to collecting, sorting and showing off objects, starting with shells, coins, sports cards, and in time, more sophisticated collections. Educators in this course will learn how to tap the collector's curiosity in their students by providing a framework to construct their own classroom museum projects. Participants will visit museums on-line.

Nevada School Law and Nevada Constitution for Educators
University of Nevada-Reno
NERE#C791 Undergraduate 1 credits $90
This course is designed specifically to meet the Nevada Teacher Licensure requirements in Nevada School Law and Nevada Constitution. It offers an overview of current Nevada School Law statutes along with federal court decisions, congressional acts and regulations governing the operation of public schools within the state. The course follows the study guide for the Nevada Teacher Licensure Examinations, Nevada School Law for Teachers, and is supplemented with video-taped lecture segments that sequentially follow the study guide, providing practical examples of the laws' application.

Online Projects for Schools
The Heritage Institute
HEON#CM400I Undergraduate 2 qu. credits $140
What are on-line projects, and would you like to know how to join one that includes lots of other schools? This course will help teachers make sense out of the myriad projects already on-line and ways to access them that are available to educators through the Internet. Discover on-line projects in many disciplines (Mayaquest, The Jason Project, Global Lab and Global Learn) and how to evaluate them for content, process, classroom management issues and suitability to your teaching assignment.

Organization of Materials - Classification
East Carolina University
EACA#LIBS6024 Undergraduate 3 credits $927*
An introduction to the principles of classification and subject analysis; application of the Dewey Decimal Classification Scheme and subject heading authority lists. At the end of LIBS6024, the student will be able to describe the basic processes of subject cataloging and identify the functions of standard tools that are used; demonstrate a mastery of the basic principles and concepts; apply the Dewey Decimal Classification system to classify a variety of materials; apply the concepts of subject headings in cataloging a variety of materials; and describe how classification systems and subject heading authority lists are used as information retrieval resources.
* NC resident tuition $135.

Organizational Analysis in Adult Education
University of Missouri
MOCE#K420 Undergraduate 3 credits $387
This course analyzes the organizational characteristics and principles in higher and continuing education. Topics include: organizational theories and models, organizational culture, communication, innovation, planning, leadership, power and influence, and external environmental influences.

Organizations of Continual Learning
Marylhurst College
MARY#MGT463 Undergraduate 3 credits $651
Explore the characteristics of learning organizations, using focused case studies of innovative efforts in changing systems. Learn to implement mental model skills, use system maps to describe complex organizational behavior, and increase knowledge of learning organization theory.

Overview of Distance Education
The Graduate School of America
TGSA#ED845W Graduate 4 credits $795
This course provides an overview of the issues influencing distance education. It introduces a variety of paradigms and technologies by which distance education is provided, such as correspondence, video teleconferencing, World Wide Web, and multimedia. It deals with the organizational and instructional issues encountered when providing instruction at a distance.

Overview of the Community Colleges
Rio Salado College
RISA#EDU250 Undergraduate 3 credits $186*
The history, functions, organization and current issues in the community/junior college with emphasis on the Arizona community colleges. Meets Arizona community college course requirement for certification.
* AZ residents $37 per credit.

Photography for Teachers
University of Missouri
MOCE#T373 Undergraduate 3 credits $387
Course topics include basic 35mm photography techniques and processes, photo publications, and basic slide/tape productions as they apply to educational settings. Students need access to the following photographic equipment: 35mm single-lens reflex (SLR) camera, flash, tripod, and filters.

Planning Technology in Schools
International Society for Technology in Education
ISTE#EDUC507B Grad   4 qu. credits $540*
This course provides school leaders with information and guidelines for long-range strategic planning for integrating technology in schools. Given that computers will continue to have a major effect on our schools, how can we direct their impact on the curriculum? Planning for Technology in Schools addresses how we can best move our schools into the information age. Each participant completes a substantial part of a long-range plan for integrating technology into the school., a school unit, or a classroom.
* Non-credit option, tuition: $460.

Portfolio Assessment
The Heritage Institute
HEON#ED407Y Undergraduate   3 qu. credits $215
Increasing our assessment options and promoting student self-reflection are some of the reasons why increasing numbers of educators are using portfolios for assessment. Appropriate for the beginner or those with limited portfolio experience, this course will explore the many strategies and issues associated with effective portfolio use. We'll cover: What a portfolio is, how to use and maintain portfolios through the year, how they can be assessed and how to communicate about portfolio design, a portfolio review instrument, and a design for a student-led parent conference in which portfolios are used.

Practicum in Online Teaching
UCLA
UCLA#X396E Undergraduate   4 credits $500
The practicum is the capstone of the Online Teaching Program, providing an opportunity to monitor online classes in progress, demonstrate skills in preparing lessons, and developing a portfolio of work samples that demonstrate your mastery of online concepts.

Prevention in School Psychology
Walden University
WALD#PSYC8590 Graduate   5 credits $1500
This course provides an opportunity to inquire into prevention and intervention programs for school-age children and their families. We consider cultural, social, psychological, family, political factors bearing on the social, emotional, and spiritual development of school-age children.

Principles of Career/Technical Education
Emporia State University
EMPO#E581 Undergrad/Grad   2 credits $152
Deals with the foundations, goals, and operations of vocational education in secondary, post-secondary, area vocational technical, and other institutions. It is concerned with the place and function of career preparation and advancement in education today. It is designed to meet Kansas certification requirements for vocational education.

Principles of Educational Administration
The Graduate School of America
TGSA#ED820W Graduate   4 credits $795
This course offers an examination of the basic principles of administrative theory and practice. Models of administration from business and public administration, as well as theoretical constructs from various disciplines are explored.

Principles of Instructional Design
East Carolina University
EACA#EDTC6020 Undergraduate   3 credits $927*
(Course description not available at press time.)
* NC resident tuition $135.

Principles of Language Learning and Teaching
New School for Social Research
NEWS#1345 Undergraduate   3 credits $1092
Permission required; call (212) 229-5372. A teacher needs a personal philosophy of how language is acquired and how people learn. This course looks at different theories of second language acquisition and how the application of these can affect methodology and learning style.

Principles of Learning and Instructional Design
The Graduate School of America
TGSA#ED851W Graduate   4 credits $795
This course provides an overview of instructional design strategies and tactics for the development of instructive environments which foster the acquisition of skills and knowledge.

Principles of Vocational Education
University of Central Florida
FLCE#EVT4065 Graduate   3 credits $1305*
This course is for individuals seeking a degree or teacher certification in Vocational Education and Industry Training in Industrial/Technical Occupations and who wish to teach their specialization in secondary or post-secondary school. This course is also for individuals who are or who plan to be trainers in business or industry settings. Prerequisites are EVT3365 or consent of the instructor.
* FL residents pay $129 per credit.

Program Evaluation and Assessment
Walden University
WALD#EDUC6130 Undergraduate   4 credits $920
Measurement and evaluation of student learning outcomes and educational programs. Development of competency standards and expectations, alternative approaches and practical guidelines for conducting program evaluations and other forms of applied research.

Psychology of Learning
Walden University
WALD#PSYC8070 Graduate   5 credits $1500
This courses focuses attention on the complex process of human learning with special regard given to the impact of culture on psychological models of learning. Origins, contributions and limitations of the computer as a metaphor for understanding human learning are analyzed with special reference to information processing, memory operation, decision making, and motivational concepts.

Published ESL/EFL Materials
New School for Social Research
NEWS#9997 Undergraduate   1 credits $546
Permission required; call (212) 229-5372. Students examine a large variety of ESL/EFL texts, discuss different criteria for evaluating textbooks, and explore ways of using texts effectively in the ESL classroom.

Publishing, Production, and Theory
University of Alaska - Fairbanks
ALFA#JB685   Undergraduate   3 credits $474
Writing, editing, and production techniques for high school publications including short courses on desktop publishing, basic and electronic photography, advertising, management, and legal liabilities. The value of First Amendment rights to our form of government. Access to UA computer network provides network with other teachers. Prerequisite: Certified teacher or permission of instructor.

Reading Comprehension
UCLA
UCLA#X340B   Undergraduate   3 credits $455
In this online course, based on the generative learning model, students learn how to effect both increased comprehension and enhance memory as they are faced with difficult reading material. Making material one's own, remembering the connections among theories and strands, effectively using what one has read these and other skills form the basis of this course.

Recreation Activities and Leadership
Indiana University
INDI#R272   Undergraduate   3 credits $268
Analysis of recreation program activities, objectives, determinants, and group dynamics involved in the leadership process. Assessment and evaluation of programs and leadership techniques. Prerequisite: R160 Course.

Research in the Classroom
The Heritage Institute
HEON#ED409V   Undergraduate   3 qu. credits $215
Inquiry, conceptual design, goal-setting, evaluation - aren't these the kinds of skills parents and reform-minded educators want for students? That's exactly what you and your students will accomplish in this hands-on research course that can be integrated within many curricular areas. This course is appropriate for teachers at all grade levels.

Resource Development for Educators
Walden University
WALD#EDUC6240   Undergraduate   4 credits $920
Resource development and strategies for educators including overview of philanthropy and development, volunteers and development, development planning, grant source research, soliciting foundations, grant-writing, development and its relationship to technology.

Science Study on the WWW
The Heritage Institute
HEON#SC404J   Undergraduate   3 qu. credits $200
Enhance your present science curriculum by connecting your students through the resources of the WWW to information that is only accessible on-line. Up-to-the-minute data on geophysical events, current weather conditions, the latest earthquake tremors, solar activity or ocean surface temperature are just some of the many student learning possibilities as the WWW expands the walls of your classroom to explore science on a global scale.

Secondary School Administration
The Graduate School of America
TGSA#ED854W   Graduate   4 credits $795
This course considers current theories, principles, and practices relative to the organization, administration, and operation of secondary schools.

Seminar in Curriculum and Instruction
University of Missouri
MOCE#T410   Graduate   3 credits $489
This course reviews the most current research on reading comprehension. Particular emphasis is given to classroom applications and the role of the teacher. Specific techniques for improving reading comprehension are discussed and illustrated in the context of the typical classroom setting. While designed primarily for elementary teachers, the concepts and techniques taught in this course also can be applied to middle- and senior-high level reading programs.

Skills for College
Northwest College
NOCO#GE070   Undergraduate   1 credits $???
Students receive information on curricula, the grading system, note taking, study habits, methods of taking tests and previewing textbooks.

Small Schools Curriculum Design
University of Alaska - Fairbanks
ALFA#ED631   Undergraduate   3 credits $474
Salient issues involved with the development of educationally sound and culturally appropriate programs of instruction in small schools, including foundational design, conceptual models, organizational strategies, technical skills, current issues and trends, and their implications and application to the environment of rural Alaska.

Sociology of Education
City University
CITY#SOC401   Undergraduate   5 qu. credits $785
This course evaluates the process of socialization, stratification as a result of educational attainment, constraints on educational systems, and various strategies for changing education. Specific topics include: retraining, organizational innovation, community development, public policy, and institutional alternatives.

Special Needs of Vocational Students
University of Central Florida
FLCE#EVT3502   Undergraduate   3 credits $786*
This course is also for individuals who are or who plan to be trainers in business or industry settings. The course involves achievement of teacher competency in meeting the special needs of the disabled, culturally different, slower learner, those with basic skill deficiencies, and those in non-traditional programs. Prerequisites are EVT3365 or consent of the instructor.

Special Topics - Education
Front Range Community College
FRCC#LST290   Undergraduate   3 credits $790
(Course description not available at press time.)

Supervision of School Publications
Indiana University
INDI#J425   Undergraduate   3 credits $268
Examination of techniques and problems in supervising school publications. Topics covered include impact on scholastic journalism of changes in educational philosophy, law, financial support, management and technology. At the conclusion of J425, students should have both an understanding of and the competencies to advise secondary school newspapers, yearbooks and other media. Learning packet includes learning guide, videos and audio lecture tape.

Survey of Educational Reform Initiatives
Walden University
WALD#EDUC6220   Undergraduate   4 credits $920
Survey of school reform efforts from 1980

Survey of Telecommunications for Teaching and Learning
Mercy College
MERC#ED575   Graduate   3 credits $900
This course develops basic telecommunication skills that can be used for teaching and learning purposes. Students will acquire an appreciation for the confluence of the telephone and personal computing systems. Students will explore how computers send and receive information from each other and from information utilities. Students will investigate information retrieval, search strategies, file transfer protocols, conferencing and networks.

Teachers in Context
State University of New York
SUNY#ETAP5125022   Graduate   3 credits $1038*
This course explores the school level education systems of the United States and selected countries of the world from the perspective of the social, political, economic, and historical places of teachers in the system. The course is appropriate for educators, educational policy makers, parents, and community members interested in coming to understand efforts aimed at strengthening K-12 education.
* NY residents tuition: $137 per credit

Teaching and Learning with Diverse Populations
The Graduate School of America
TGSA#ED838W   Graduate   4 credits $795
This course explores teaching and learning principles and practices as applied to diverse, multicultural populations.

Teaching English Language Development
UCLA
UCLA#X325G   Undergraduate   4 credits $455
Considers the theories and methods of bilingual and English language development instruction. Focuses on such approaches to English language development as the total physical response as well as the natural, communicative, and sheltered approaches. Also covers the development and design of assessment methods and strategies appropriate for formative and summative evaluations of LEP students, state diagnoses and program placement requirements, and the relevance of standardized tests.

Teaching ESL Writing On Line
New School for Social Research
NEWS#1363   Undergraduate   0 credits $235
Designed for teachers of ESL writing at all levels who would like to learn how to teach their course on line. Teachers learn how to adapt their materials on a list-server and on the Web. Emphasis is on syllabus design and techniques for correcting grammar and assignments on line.

Teaching Exceptional Learners
UCLA
UCLA#X328   Undergraduate   3 credits $425
Introduction to students with special needs. Addresses the implications of sensory, motor, cognitive, language, and behavior problems for children with disabilities. Explores giftedness and cultural diversity as potential risk factors in the classroom. Discusses strategies for integrating and including children with disabilities into the typical classroom.

Teaching Labor Relations in the Schools
University of Minnesota
MINN#IR3000   Undergraduate   4 credits $400
This course enables elementary and secondary schoolteachers to incorporate the study of labor unions and collective bargaining into their lesson plans. It also assists teachers to discuss labor issues with their students when national and local developments demand a response. The course provides knowledge of the labor relations process as it affects the teaching profession.

Teaching of Reading
University of Missouri
MOCE#T315   Undergraduate   3 credits $387
This course studies the materials and methods used in teaching reading in elementary grades. Perquisites: junior standing.

Teaching On Line
Edmonds Community College
EDMO#PCAPP257   Undergraduate   3 credits $220
This course will introduce technologies used in on-line delivery, discuss the differences and similarities between on and off- line curriculum design, help participants develop tools for "classroom" management and the flow of electronic information, provide information about testing and assessment, present community building practices such as setting up study groups and editing partners and will explore Web sites and other resources that will help develop a conceptual framework for teaching on-line courses.

Teaching Online
Kennesaw State University
KENN#FMV217 Undergraduate   3 credits $149
This class is for college, high school or other instructors who want to teach courses that are fully "on- line" or that have on-line components. Taught over the Internet, this course will introduce technologies used in on-line delivery, discuss the differences and similarities between on and off-line curriculum design, help participants develop tools for "classroom" management and the flow of electronic information, provide information about testing and assessment, etc.

Teaching Reading in the Content Areas
University of Missouri
MOCE#T316 Undergraduate   2 credits $258
This course addresses specific ways teachers can help students improve skills at reading in content areas. Perquisites: junior standing.

Teaching Secondary School Reading
Indiana University
INDI#L517 Graduate   3 credits $531
Examines research and instructional approaches to improve the literacy of adolescents and adults when reading materials from various content areas. Special focus on understanding the reading process as it relates to the various content areas, dealing with a wide range of student literacy abilities, identifying and modifying materials, and using reading/writing/thinking activities in instruction.

Teaching the Sound System of English
New School for Social Research
NEWS#1348 Undergraduate   1 credits $546
Permission required; call (212) 229-5372. The sound system of English is studied with special attention given to those characteristics that learners of English as a foreign language often find difficult. Participants learn to develop contextualized pronunciation exercises and incorporate them into an ESL syllabus.

Teaching Writing
New School for Social Research
NEWS#1352 Undergraduate   1 credits $546
Permission required; call (212) 229-5372. Study in detail several methods for helping ESL students improve their writing in English. Emphasis is on teaching organizational and editing skills and developing effective techniques for correcting errors.

Teaching Writing Online
The Heritage Institute
HEON#ED409Q Undergraduate   3 qu. credits $215
Computers and networks have fulfilled the promise of the writing process movement begun in the 1960's, and by providing the writer an almost unlimited chance to share ideas, drafts, revisions and proofreading, technology has forever changed the nature of writing instruction. In this course for all levels K-12, teachers whose schools have local area networks or Internet access will explore the opportunities to enhance student writing, teaming and critical thinking skills by learning to write on-line.

Technologies for Library Services
East Carolina University
EACA#LIBS6042 Undergraduate   3 credits $927*
Survey of the use of technology in providing effective programs for library services including the evaluative criteria of hardware and software and methods of integrating technology into the instructional process. By the end of the course, students will be able to list a variety of variety of technologies, their characteristics, and their use in library services; identify and apply evaluative criteria in the selection of equipment, materials, and vendors; develop instructional units using technology and applying the teaching/learning process integrating media and computer skills into the curriculum or library program; produce a variety of educational materials for use with the technology.
* NC resident tuition $135.

Technology in K-12 Curriculum
UCLA
UCLA#X333C Undergraduate   3 credits $425
Educators across the country are struggling with the challenge to successfully integrate technology into the curriculum. This online course explores practical strategies for using technology as a tool to enhance and support your existing curriculum. Participants learn how to modify current thematic units and lesson plans to include a technology component that will help students practice and reinforce the skills and content they are being taught. Technology assessment models are also explored.

The Climate and Structure of the Learning Environment
The Graduate School of America
TGSA#ED824W Graduate   4 credits $795
This course examines theories and practices of the structure and climate of the learning environment, as well as policies and procedures of personnel management and supervision. Topics may include open classrooms, competency-based curricula, and mainstreaming learning disabled and physically challenged learners.

The College Library
MiraCosta College
MIRA#LIBR101 Undergraduate   3 credits $357

This tutorial will introduce you to the use of a college library. This course is designed to acquaint you with the use of the facilities and resources available to you in a typical college library or learning resources center. It has been written specifically for MiraCosta College, but the skills and knowledge acquired in this course will be useful in any library.

The Community College in America
University of Central Florida
FLCE#EDH6053 Graduate   3 credits $1305*

A study of the history, philosophy, goals, and mission of the community college from the 19th century to the present. Included are the functions, policies, and practices used by the contemporary community college to address local, state, and national needs. Trends are analyzed relative to the future mission of the community college. Details are provided on the Florida Community College System.
* FL residents pay $129 per credit.

The Exceptional Learner
University of Alaska - Fairbanks
ALFA#ED375 Undergraduate   3 credits $237

Foundation for understanding, identifying and serving the exceptional learner in rural and urban settings. A special emphasis is placed on working with exceptional learners in the regular classroom. The unique needs of exceptional students in rural settings from bilingual/multicultural backgrounds are covered. Prerequisite: ED201, PSY240.

The Future of Educational Institutions
The Graduate School of America
TGSA#ED815W Graduate   4 credits $795

Based on an examination of the formative ideas that have shaped educational institutions, this course explores both the theory and practice of changing educational institutions to meet future needs. Specifically, participants will gain an understanding of the impact of distance education and technology on educational institutions.

The Politics of Higher Education
The Graduate School of America
TGSA#ED840W Graduate   4 credits $795

This course involves an examination of the differing and changing perceptions of the role of higher education in America. The politics of competition for resources, the expectations of consumers and providers, and the role of state and local government are examined.

The Secondary School Curriculum
University of Missouri
MOCE#T445 Graduate   3 credits $489

For secondary school principals, teachers, and superintendents, this course presents trends in curricular change and methods of curricular investigation.

Theoretical Foundations of Reading & Literacy
State University of New York
SUNY#3479301 Undergraduate   3 credits $1038*

All instruction is based on the theoretical knowledge and beliefs of the teacher. This graduate level course, which fulfills the theoretical foundations component for the state certification as a Reading Specialist, K-12, covers the wide array of theories and research that inform reading/literacy instruction. Since the theories in the field of Reading/Literacy are the sources of great debate, this course is suited to the highly interactive online format. Expect to engage in questioning and lively discussion and debate in this class.
* NY residents tuition: $137 per credit

Theory and Methods of Educating Adults
The Graduate School of America
TGSA#ED829W Graduate   4 credits $795

The purpose of this course is to help learners gain an understanding of adult development through the lifespan and its relationship to adult learning; to develop an understanding of the role of the "facilitator" in adult education; and to become skillful in the selection and use of appropriate methods, techniques and materials for achieving particular learning objectives.

Transition to College
Edmonds Community College
EDMO#BR111 Undergraduate   3 credits $220

Using case study, journaling and self-assessment as well as contributing to discussion, you will apply a problem-solving approach to typical study and resource problems. The overall goal of this class is to help you develop an internal locus of control, a feeling that you are in control of your scheduling, information about yourself as a learner and about the resources that can help you be successful in a college environment, especially an online environment.

Using Instructional Media & Technology
Indiana University
INDI#R503 Graduate   3 credits $531

Surveys the pedagogical applications of widely used types of audiovisual media (e.g. bulletin boards, slides, video), computer-based media (e.g. presentation software and computer-assisted instruction) and process technologies (e.g. programmed tutoring and simulation/gaming). During this course students will learn about guidelines for selection of media and methods as well as develop media presentation skills.

Using News Media Across Curriculum
The Heritage Institute
HEON#ED410S Undergraduate   3 qu. credits $215
News and magazine media are an engaging way to
enhance student skills in reading comprehension and
writing, and can enliven your social studies curriculum
with real world stories and issues for student discussion.
This independent study will help teachers with some or no
experience in using media to explore the uses of magazine
and local news media across all curricular areas, from
history, language arts, and business to health, politics,
science and more.

Using the World Wide Web for Research
East Carolina University
EACA#EDTC6060 Undergraduate   3 credits $927*
This course covers the identification and evaluation of
resources available on the World Wide Web, and includes
an introduction to basic reference sources available.
Course participants locate and evaluate web sites and
materials on the World Wide Web on their chosen topics.
At the end of this course, participants will be familiar with
methods of locating resources, both sites and materials, on
the World Wide Web; able to evaluate resources, both web
sites and electronically published materials, on the World
Wide Web; and able to locate and evaluate materials on a
specific topic on the World Wide Web.
* NC resident tuition $135.

Virtual Reality in Education
East Carolina University
EACA#EDTC3244 Undergraduate   3 credits $927*
The role of virtual reality as an instructional tool. Types,
applications, and hardware and software. Prerequisite:
EDTC2240 or consent of instructor.
* NC resident tuition $135.

Web Teaching - Design and Development
East Carolina University
EACA#EDTC7320 Undergraduate   3 credits $927*
Principles of Internet (web-based) instruction. Topics will
include using Internet tools (e-mail, ftp, chat, listserv, and
online conferencing) for instruction, instructional design
components, and designing web pages for delivery of
instruction. Upon completion, learners will have
developed web-based course instruction ready for
implementation.
* NC resident tuition $135.

Engineering

Aeronautical

Architecture

Chemical

Civil

Computer

Electrical

Materials

Mechanical

Other

AC Circuits
Northwest Technical College
NOTE#ELTR1804 Undergraduate   3 credits $240*

This course covers the fundamentals of alternating current electricity progressing through a lecture/lab sequence of passive resistive and reactive components in series, parallel and series-parallel. Various alternating current circuit theorems relevant to circuit analysis and troubleshooting are covered. This course not available to users with Macintosh platform.
* Residents rates may apply.

Adaptive Computer Technology
University of Washington
WASH#REHABC496 Undergraduate   3 qu. credits $222

Rehabilitation counselors, physical therapists, occupational therapists, teachers in K-12 and post-secondary education, librarians, and educational technologists will learn as part of a group. You will learn to understand the benefits of adaptive computer technology, to identify the costs of adaptation and funding sources, to understand the federal laws related to disability accommodation, and to design a physical environment.

Advanced AC Circuits
Northwest Technical College
NOTE#ELTR1806 Undergraduate   3 credits $240*

This course covers the fundamentals of complex reactive circuits using imaginary numbers, series and parallel resonance, filter circuits and characteristics of antennas and transmission lines. Lab procedures verify concepts, laws and relationships learned in theory. Measured data is recorded and interpreted and conclusions drawn. This course not available to users with Macintosh platform. Prerequisites: ELTR1804.
* Residents rates may apply.

Advanced Aviation/Aero Planning
Embry-Riddle Aeronautical University
EMRI#MAS636 Graduate   3 credits $840

Planning and decision-making techniques and strategies used in the aviation industry are emphasized. The types and sources of data needed for decisions about route development and expansion, fleet modernization, and new markets are examined. The methods of collecting, analyzing, and applying the data through computer applications, modeling, heuristic, value theory, and payoff tables are studied. The limitations and problems associated with strategic planning are discussed.

Air Carrier Operations
Embry-Riddle Aeronautical University
EMRI#MAS620 Graduate   3 credits $840

A study of air carrier flight operations systems from the viewpoints of the ground-based dispatcher, operations specialists, managers, and the cockpit flight crew. Topics include advanced flight planning, aircraft performance and loading considerations, impact of weather conditions, and routing priorities.

Aircraft and Spacecraft Development
Embry-Riddle Aeronautical University
EMRI#MAS603 Graduate   3 credits $840

This course is an overview of aircraft and spacecraft development. Included are vehicle mission, the requirements directed by economics, military and defense considerations, and research and developmental processes needed to meet vehicle requirements. Aviation and aerospace manufacturing organizations and techniques are addressed to include planning, scheduling, production, procurement, supply, and distribution systems. The course studies the aviation and aerospace maintenance systems from the built-in test equipment to the latest product support activities.

Airport Operations and Management
Embry-Riddle Aeronautical University
EMRI#BA645 Graduate   3 credits $840

A study of the management and operation of public use airports. Specifically, traffic forecasting, sources of revenues and expenses, management of passenger and cargo terminal buildings, ground handling of passengers and baggage, ground access systems, and the U.S. Federal Aviation Administration Regulations dealing with airport operations. Current problems with environmental impact, land-use planning and control, airport capacity and delay, public relations, airport finance, airport privatization, liability, and economic impact will be covered.

Airport Operations Safety
Embry-Riddle Aeronautical University
EMRI#MAS613 Graduate   3 credits $840

A study of Airport Operations Safety as applied to day-to-day operations. A review and analysis of all Federal Regulations applicable to operations and safety is conducted. Prerequisite: Demonstrated knowledge of principles of airport/airline operations management or related field.

Alarm Systems
Fox Valley Technical College
FOVA#504-145 Undergraduate   3 credits $200

This course focuses specifically on electronic intrusion alarm detectors. Different sensors are analyzed for their method of operation and effectiveness in varying environments. False alarm causes and solutions are discussed. Detector defeat methods are explored to identify better design factors. Components are examined via textbook diagrams and actual photos of sensors scanned into web pages.

Analytical Mechanics I
University of Colorado
CUON#CE2121 Undergraduate   3 credits $1953*

A vector treatment of force systems and their resultants; equilibrium of trusses, beams, frames, and machines, including internal forces and three-dimensional configurations; static friction; properties of areas; distributed loads; hydrostatics.
* CO residents tuition: $136 per credit.

Assembly Language and Architecture
Nova Southeastern University
NOVA#MCIS500 Graduate   3 credits $1,110
A comprehensive examination of the fundamental concepts and architectural structures of contemporary computers. Complex instruction set architectures (CISC) and reduced instruction set architectures (RISC) will be studied from programming and structural viewpoints.

Aviation/Aero Accident & Safety
Embry-Riddle Aeronautical University
EMRI#MAS608 Graduate   3 credits $840
A critical analysis of selected aircraft accidents and an evaluation of causal factors. Particular emphasis is placed on the study of human factors connected with flight and support crew activities in aviation operations. Identification and implementation of accident prevention measures are stressed as integral parts of the development of a complete safety program.

Aviation/Aerospace Communications
Embry-Riddle Aeronautical University
EMRI#MAS606 Graduate   3 credits $840
A detailed analysis of current and future developments and trends in the control of air traffic that includes the evolution of current national policies, plans and their objectives. The most recent planned improvements for each major component of the ATC system are examined individually and as part of the system as a whole.

Aviation/Aerospace Distribution
Embry-Riddle Aeronautical University
EMRI#MAS640 Graduate   3 credits $840
A study of the elements of physical distribution that includes the structure of supply organizations, priority systems, cost categories, inventory control, and the applications of electronic data processing. Case studies are employed to present issues, problems, and analyses of supply systems in terms of customer satisfaction relative to costs incurred.

Aviation/Aerospace Industrial Safety
Embry-Riddle Aeronautical University
EMRI#MAS612 Graduate   3 credits $840
Aviation/Aerospace Industrial Safety Management examines the modern work setting from an aviation and aerospace safety and health point of view. Examination of the history of industrial safety leads the student to an understanding of why and how aviation/aerospace industrial safety management evolved into an advanced discipline. The roles of, and interactions between, government, corporation, safety management, and the worker, in the dynamic, economy driven environments of aviation and aerospace are central themes.

Aviation/Aerospace System Safety
Embry-Riddle Aeronautical University
EMRI#MAS611 Graduate   3 credits $840
This course emphasizes the specialized integration of safety skills and resources into all phases of a System's Lire Cycle. Accident prevention, beginning with systems engineering together with sound management, are combined in this course to enable the student to fully comprehend their vital roles in preventing accidents. The total program, from basic design concepts, through testing, maintenance/systems management and operational employment is fully examined and evaluated.

Behavioral Science in Engineering
New Jersey Institute of Technology
NJIT#IE603 Undergraduate   3 credits $1143*
The course focuses on human behavior in organizations. Students will study the processes and problems of communications in engineering activities. Through lecture, discussion and experiential exercises, students learn the nature of human behavior in organizations and techniques for developing interpersonal management skills. Prerequisite: Undergraduate probability & statistics course. Optional: 13 video lessons of 180 minutes each.
* NJ residents: $184/semester hour.

Bioceramic Materials
State University of New York
SUNY#CES486001 Graduate   3 credits $1038*
A survey of ceramic, metal and polymer materials and devices for repair and replacement parts in the human body. Emphasis on the nature of the materials, the design and fabrication of devices, properties, applications and the problems of introducing foreign materials into the biosystem.
* NY residents tuition: $137 per credit

Building Construction
Edmonds Community College
EDMO#FCA152 Undergraduate   3 credits $220
(Course description not available at press time.)

Building Materials and Construction
State University of New York
SUNY#FPT103 Undergraduate   3 credits $630*
Fundamentals of building construction methods and materials of construction. The approach is to study the stability of buildings and materials under fire conditions. The emphasis is upon safety under fire conditions and the technology of limiting fire spread in new and existing buildings.
* NY residents tuition: $105 per credit

Chemical Engineering Thermodynamics I
Texas Technical University
TETE#CHE3321 Undergraduate   3 credits $159
This course covers properties of pure substances, ideal gas behavior, first and second law analysis, and applications to energy conversion and power cycles Prerequisite: MATH2350, PHYS1308.

Compiler Design Theory
Nova Southeastern University
NOVA#CISC630 Graduate   3 credits $1,110
Language theory will be applied to the design of a compiler for a high-level language. Parsing, syntax analysis, semantic analysis, and code generation. Other areas of the compilation process will be covered, such as storage allocation, symbol table management, searching and sorting, and optimization.

Computer and Information Systems
New Jersey Institute of Technology
NJIT#CIS679 Undergraduate   3 credits $1143*
Management policies and practices associated with the acquisition, development, implementation, system testing, and acceptance of computer and information systems. Prerequisites: Course in evaluation of systems or equivalent knowledge. Optional: 14 video lessons of 180 minutes each.
* NJ residents: $184/semester hour.

Computer Architectures I
Strayer University
STRA#CIS312 Undergraduate   4.5 credits $665
Provides the fundamental concepts of the hardware and software in computer systems design. Includes number systems, machine structures, CPU, memory, cache memory and addressing modes. Prerequisite: CIS155.

Computer Concepts
New York Institute of Technology
NYIT#CS5641 Undergraduate   3 credits $???
A course designed to provide an understanding of what the computer can do and how it does it for the nontechnically oriented student. The course covers the basic concepts of computer operation and programming, applications of computers, and the effects of computers on society.

Computer Information Science I
Chemeketa Community College
CHEM#CIS120 Undergraduate   4 credits $159
This first course in a three-course sequence consists of an introduction to terminology and an overview of the historical development of computer and information science. The focus is the basic concepts of computer hardware and software systems, the science of information representation, and the fundamental elements of program design and computer language. Concepts are reinforced in a laboratory environment. Prerequisite: MTH070, Elementary Algebra; RD115, Accelerated Reading Tactics 1, or equivalent level of skill as demonstrated by satisfactory score on placement test.

Computer Information Science II
Chemeketa Community College
CHEM#CIS121 Undergraduate   4 credits $159
This second course of a three-course sequence consists of introduction to the fundamental logic in designing specific algorithms for processing information typified by management information systems. Concepts are reinforced in a laboratory environment. Prerequisite: CIS120, Computer Information Science I, or may take concurrently; or consent of instructor.

Computer Information Systems
Front Range Community College
FRCC#CIS115 Undergraduate   5 credits $1315
This is an overview of the need for and role of computer information systems. Emphasis is on computer requirements in organizations, history, hardware functions, programming, systems development, and computer operations. Introduces computer applications and programming. 7.5 Contact Hours.

Computer Information Systems
New Hampshire College
NEHA#CIS500 Undergraduate   3 credits $1656
The course focuses on the principles and practices underlying the analysis, design, implementation and management of computer-based information systems. Topics include: information system life-cycle, systems planning, requirements analysis, interface, data and process design, systems implementation, and software engineering. Background preparation: three credit hours in data processing, or equivalent.

Computer Information Systems
Nova Southeastern University
NOVA#MCIS620 Graduate   3 credits $1,110
Covers major concepts and architecture of computer information systems including information concepts; information flow; types of information systems; the role of information in planning operations, control, and decision-making; integrated information systems across a range of functional elements. Computer information systems in organizations.

Computer Information Systems
Rio Salado College
RISA#CIS105 Undergraduate   3 credits $186*
Overview of computer information systems, fundamental computer concepts, and programming techniques. Hands-on experience with selected business software and one programming language.
* AZ residents $37 per credit.

Computer Organization
New Jersey Institute of Technology
NJIT#CIS251 Undergraduate   3 credits $1143*
An introduction to computer system structure and organization. Topics include representation of information, circuit analysis and design, register transfer level, processor architecture and input/output. Prerequisites: NJIT#CIS113 or equivalent knowledge. Corequisite: NJIT#CIS231. Optional: 26 video lessons of 60 minutes each.
* NJ residents: $184/semester hour.

Computer Sci for Software Engineer
University of Alaska - Fairbanks
ALFA#CS670 Undergraduate   3 credits $474
An overview and survey of the theoretical underpinnings of computer science. Topics are taken from the areas of algorithms and data structures; computer architecture; computer networks, communications, and operating systems; computability and formal languages; languages and compilation. Prerequisite: Admission to the Computer Science MS program.

Computer Science with Problem Solving
New Jersey Institute of Technology
NJIT#CIS102 Undergraduate   3 credits $1143*
This is a three credit course in computer science with applications in engineering and technology problems, emphasis on programming methodology using the FORTRAN language as the vehicle to illustrate concepts. Requires FORTRAN 77 compiler. Optional: 32 video lessons of 60 minutes each.
* NJ residents: $184/semester hour.

Computing Fundamentals I
State University of New York
SUNY#CSC1591887 Undergraduate   4 credits $1038*
Students will learn algorithm development and structure program design using an object-oriented language such as C++ or Java. Topics include control structures, top-down design, program debugging, documentation, procedures and functions, parameter passing, recursion, arrays, records, and objects. Students spend a substantial amount of out-of-class time working on computer projects. Prerequisites: Essential reading and writing skills and a corequisite of MAT159 (College Algebra and Trigonometry).
* NY residents tuition: $137 per credit.

Construction Materials
Honolulu Community College
HONO#DRAF26 Undergraduate 3 credits $714*
A broad survey of materials used in construction and the buildings and other structures comprised of those materials. Materials and methods of light wood construction, lumber classifications and uses, plywood, concrete, metals, plaster and drywall, glass, equipment, and electrical and mechanical systems are some of the topics studied.
* Hawaiian residents tuition: $39 per credit.

Corporate Aviation Operations
Embry-Riddle Aeronautical University
EMRI#MAS622 Graduate 3 credits $840
The establishment and operations of a corporate flight department are examined along with the procedures and techniques generally accepted as standards by professional corporate flight operations. Included is a practical view of the corporate aviation mission of management mobility and use of the resources available to accomplish it.

DC Circuits
Northwest Technical College
NOTE#ELTR1802 Undergraduate 3 credits $240*
This course covers the fundamentals of direct current electricity progressing through a lecture/lab sequence of passive resistive components in series, parallel, and series-parallel configurations. Various circuit theorems relevant to circuit analysis and troubleshooting are also covered. This course not available to users with Macintosh platform.
* Residents rates may apply.

Deformable Body Mechanics
University of Minnesota
MINN#ENGR3016 Undergraduate 4 credits $400
Introductory treatment of stress and strain at a point. Stress-strain relationships in two dimensions. Linear theory of torsion. Bending stresses. Deflection of determinate and indeterminate beams. Instability. Prerequisite: ENGR3015, statics, and concurrent registration in MATH3380, Differential Equations I.

Digital Circuits
Greenville Technical College
GRTE#EET145A Undergraduate 3 credits $381*
A study of number systems, basic logic gates, Boolean algebra, logic optimization, flip-flops, counters and registers. Circuits are modeled, constructed and tested. Co-requisite: EET131 Active Devices.
* NC residents pay $48 per credit.

Dynamics
University of Colorado
CUON#ME2033 Undergraduate 0 credits $332*
(Course description not available at press time.)
* CO residents tuition: $136.

Engineering Graphics I
Brevard Community College
BREV#EGSC1110 Undergraduate 4 credits $575
Beginning course in drawing, involving lettering, sketching, orthographic projection, dimensioning, sections, pictorials, threads and fastener, charts and graphics, and a study of points, lines, and planes.

Engineering Mechanics (Statics)
State University of New York
SUNY#EGR271Y01 Undergraduate 3 credits $570*
Fundamental concepts of the statics of rigid bodies developed using a vector analysis approach. Force systems, centroids and centers of gravity, analysis of structures and machines, shear and bending moments, friction, moments of inertia, and the method of virtual work. Emphasis on problem solving. Projects will be included as part of this course. Prerequisites: Calculus I and Physics I or equivalent.
* NY residents tuition: $90 per credit

Engineering Mechanics-Dynamics
University of Missouri
MOCE#EN150 Undergraduate 2 credits $258
This course applies the principles of mechanics to engineering problems of motion and acceleration. Topics include plane motion; force; mass and acceleration; work and energy; and impulse and momentum. Perquisites: Basic Eng. 50 and Math/Statics 22.

Engineering Mechanics-Statics
University of Missouri
MOCE#EN50 Undergraduate 3 credits $387
This course applies the principles of mechanics to engineering problems of equilibrium. Topics include resultants; equilibrium; friction; trusses; center of gravity; and moment of inertia. Perquisites: Physics 23 or 21, preceded or accompanied by Math/Statics 22.

Federal Aviation Regulations
University of Alaska - Fairbanks
ALFA#AFPMF152 Undergraduate 1 credits $168
Federal Aviation Regulations for maintenance of aircraft. Maintenance forms and records, publications, privileges and limitations of aircraft mechanics. Prerequisite: Admission to A & P Program or permission of instructor.

Foundations of Computing I
Mercy College
MERC#CS131 Undergraduate 3 credits $900
The course offers an introduction to the fundamental aspects of the field of computing, focusing on algorithmic problem-solving, software design concepts and their realization as computer programs. Students are introduced to program modularization, stepwise refinement, and to the organization of the computer upon which the resulting programs run. Topics include control structures, data types and procedural abstraction using the programming language Pascal. Prerequisites: CS/MA120 Introduction to Computers and Application Software; MA116 College Algebra or high school intermediate algebra.

Fundamentals of Information Technology
New Hampshire College
NEHA#CIS100 Undergraduate 3 credits $1656
Use of a desktop computer with current important end-user software to solve problems within an organizational environment. Includes coverage of software and hardware components, operating system concepts, information structures and formal problem solving techniques.

Fundamentals of Petroleum
University of Alaska - Fairbanks
ALFA#SCIA101 Undergraduate   3 credits $213
This course is designed to give an overall view of the petroleum industry in terms that are understandable by the layperson as well as the professional. Included are lessons on petroleum geology, prospecting, leasing, drilling, production, pipelines, refining, processing, and marketing.

Human Factors in Aviation/Aero
Embry-Riddle Aeronautical University
EMRI#MAS604 Graduate   3 credits $840
This course presents an overview of the importance of the human role in all aspects of the aviation and aerospace industries. It will emphasize the issues, problems, and solutions of unsafe acts, attitudes, errors, and deliberate actions attributed to human behavior and the roles supervisors and management personnel play in these actions. The course will study the human limitations in the light of human engineering, human reliability, stress, medical standards, drug abuse, and human physiology.

Industrial Gas Cleaning
New Jersey Institute of Technology
NJIT#CHE687 Undergraduate   3 credits $1143*
Review of available tools for cleaning atmospheric effluents from manufacturing facilities and power plants; use of a systems approach to minimize gas cleaning cost; alternatives involving combination of process modification and effluent clean-up; methods for estimating key design parameters for cyclones, baghouses, electrostatic precipitators and scrubbers. Applications of design parameters through the solution of extensive problem-sets. Prerequisites: Undergraduate degree in chemical engineering, or permission of the instructor.. Optional: 13 video lessons of 180 minutes each.
* NJ residents: $184/semester hour.

Industrial Waste Control I
New Jersey Institute of Technology
NJIT#CHE685 Undergraduate   3 credits $1143*
Physical/chemical treatment of industrial wastewater's: ionic equilibria; surface characterization; thermodynamic applications; transport phenomena; and sludge treatment. Prerequisites: EVSC 610 or equivalent, or undergraduate degree in chemical engineering. Optional: 13 video lessons of 180 minutes each.
* NJ residents: $184/semester hour.

Industrial Waste Control II
New Jersey Institute of Technology
NJIT#CHE686 Undergraduate   3 credits $1143*
This telecourse will cover the biological treatment of industrial waste waters: biological mechanisms; kinetics, vapor-liquid equilibria, and settling phenomena. Prerequisites: EVSC 610 or equivalent, or undergraduate degree in chemical engineering. Optional: 13 video lessons of 180 minutes each.
* NJ residents: $184/semester hour.

Integrated Introduction to Computing
Michigan State University
MICH#01 Undergraduate   3 credits $???
Most computer science courses begin the way that computer science 'always has been taught,' with the syntax of a particular language. Our approach in this course is to see computer science as a tool for solving problems, the solutions of which are implemented as computer programs. Therefore, we emphasize design of computer programs and we introduce the computer language -- Visual Basic for DOS -- from the top down, beginning with the highest level words of the language.

Introduction to Computer Science
Indiana University
INDI#C211 Undergraduate   4 credits $358
A first course in computer science for those intending to take advanced computer science courses. Introduction to programming and to algorithm design and analysis. Using the SCHEME programming language, the course covers several programming paradigms. Prerequisite: two years of high school algebra or M014.

Introduction to Computer Science
Pima Community College
PIMA#CSC100 Undergraduate   3 credits $165*
This course is designed to acquaint students with general computer literacy and terminology, the workings of computers, problem solving techniques, computer operations and some BASIC programming. Prerequisite: MTH70 or similar competency level.
* AZ residents, $32/credit hour.

Introduction to Computer Science
State University of New York
SUNY#CSC1518223 Undergraduate   3 credits $1038*
Students will develop computer literacy by studying an overview of computing and a brief introduction to programming. Topics include a history of computers and computing, computer system components, data representation, the impact of computers on society, computer ethics, an introduction to data communications, networking, word processing, spreadsheets, programming in a structured language, and e-mail. Students will also use the Internet and a browser to access the World Wide Web.
* NY residents tuition: $137 per credit.

Introduction to Computer Science I
New Jersey Institute of Technology
NJIT#CIS113 Undergraduate   3 credits $1143*
Fundamentals of computer science are introduced, with emphasis on programming methodology and problem solving. Topics include concepts of computer systems, software engineering, algorithm design, programming languages and data abstraction with applications. The C++ language serves as the vehicle to illustrate many of the concepts. Corequisite: Math 111. Optional: 32 video lessons of 30 minutes each.
* NJ residents: $184/semester hour.

Introduction to Computer Science II
New Jersey Institute of Technology
NJIT#CIS114 Undergraduate   3 credits $1143*

A study of advanced programming topics with logical structures of data, their physical representation, design and analysis of computer algorithms operating on the structures, and techniques for program development and debugging. Prerequisites: Math 111, NJIT#CIS113 or completion of course of equivalent scope. Optional: 40 video lessons of 30 minutes each.

* NJ residents: $184/semester hour.

Introduction to Computers
Cerro Coso Community College
CECO#CSCI2 Undergraduate   3 credits $345*

Non-technical analysis of computer systems. Development and application of critical thinking through human and computer parallels. Computer literacy as a vehicle of communication through technology and methodology. Survey of computer history, terminology, application and social impact. Problem solving using an integrated computer software system; spreadsheet, word processing and database applications.

* California resident tuition: $13 per credit.

Introduction to Computers
College of DuPage
DUPA#CIS100 Undergraduate   5 qu. credits $150

A survey of the field of modern electronic computers. Emphasis on the role of the computer in today's society. Topics include computer concepts, hardware, software, database, data communications, system analysis and design, computer applications, and social implications of computers. Microcomputer applications include spreadsheets, word processing, data base and presentations along with a windows environment.

Introduction to Computers
Greenville Technical College
GRTE#CPT101 Undergraduate   3 credits $381*

Covers basic computer history, theory and applications, including word processing, spreadsheets, data bases and the operating system. Pre-requisite: Math placement into MAT100 or higher, access to a computer system with Windows 3.1, Microsoft Word 6.0, Microsoft Excel 5.0, Microsoft Access 2.0, and Microsoft PowerPoint 4.0.

* NC residents pay $48 per credit.

Introduction to Computers
Lansing Community College
LANS#CPSC120 Undergraduate   3 credits $315

In this survey course, the student learns of the application of computers in society, considers their social and economic implications, examines questions of privacy and security, and considers recent advances in computer technology. In addition, the student is exposed to beginning instruction and practice in word processing, spreadsheet and data base applications, programming, and user networks.

Introduction to Computers
Mercy College
MERC#CS120 Undergraduate   3 credits $900

An introduction to computers and computing including the history of computers, the role of computers in a technological society, descriptions of computers and associated hardware, binary and hexadecimal number systems, and use of a word processor, spreadsheet and database tools as in problem solving. Prerequisite: MA 105 or placement at MA114, MA115 or MA116 level and EN109 level or departmental approval.

Introduction to Computers
Northern State University
NOST#MIS105 Undergraduate   3 credits $248

Computer concepts, terminology, and data processing. Hands-on experience with microcomputers is gained through learning fundamental concepts of software packages such as word processing, electronic spreadsheets, database management, and desktop publishing. Basic keyboarding skills required.

Introduction to Computers
Pitt Community College
PITT#CIS110 Undergraduate   3 credits $???

This course provides an introduction to computers and computing. Topics include the computer as a system, impact on society, hardware, software applications, including spreadsheets, databases, word processors, graphics, the Internet, and operating systems. Upon completion, students should be able to demonstrate an understanding of the role and function of computers and the use of the computer to solve problems.

Introduction to Drafting
University of Minnesota
MINN#DHA0620 Undergraduate   0 credits $267

Beginning architectural instruction in the use of drafting instruments. Emphasis on drafting fundamentals: lines, lettering, introduction to orthographic and paraline drawings. Introduction to architectural symbols and vocabulary as related to interior design. Will serve as the prerequisite to DHA1621.

Introduction to Logic and Automata
New Jersey Institute of Technology
NJIT#CIS341 Undergraduate   3 credits $1143*

This course includes an introduction to logic and formal grammars. Theoretical models such as finite state machines, push-down stack machines, and Turing machines are developed and related to issues in programming language theory. Prerequisites: completion of a 100-level GUR course CIS; Math 226. Optional: 14 video lessons of variable length.

* NJ residents: $184/semester hour.

Introduction to Orbital Mechanics
University of North Dakota
NODA#SPST500 Graduate   3 credits $816*

A knowledge of how satellites orbit the Earth, of how planets orbit the Sun, and how the Solar System orbits the Milky Way is mandatory for a serious student in space studies. From the discoveries of Copernicus, Galileo, and Kepler to the demonstrated genius of Newton and Einstein, orbital mechanics is an important part of knowing how things work in space.

* ND residents, $102 per credit; may also be reduced for residents of adjoining states and provinces.

Law and Environmental Engineering
New Jersey Institute of Technology
NJIT#EM631 Undergraduate   3 credits $1143*
Control of air, water, and solid waste pollution by federal, state, and local government statutes and international law. Preparation of environmental impact statements and the right of private citizens to bring suit under federal clean air and water pollution legislation are discussed, as well as limitations on these rights. This course is part of the graduate certificates in Project Management and Environmental Infrastructure. Optional: 13 videos of 180 minutes each.
* NJ residents: $184/semester hour.

Mechanical Properties of Ceramics and Glass
State University of New York
SUNY#CES562001 Graduate   3 credits $1038*
Fundamental concepts concerning mechanical behavior are introduced and discussed with respect to their application to glasses and ceramics. Emphasis is placed on strength and fracture mechanics. Testing procedures, including non-destructive evaluation techniques, and problems associated with them are treated in detail. Part of the semester is devoted to a discussion of recent developments in the area of mechanical properties. Prerequisites: A basic understanding of mechanics and strength of materials and of the crystal structure and microstructure of glasses and ceramics is assumed.
* NY residents tuition: $137 per credit

Polymer Properties and Technology
State University of New York
SUNY#FCH552I Graduate   3 credits $1038*
Introduction to physical chemistry, physics, processing and technology of synthetic polymers. Polymer solutions, including molecular weight determinations and chain statistics. Polymer solid states, including rubber elasticity, viscoelasticity, the glassy state and the crystalline state. Properties, processing and technology of films, fibers, elastomers, and foams. Prerequisites: One year of organic chemistry and one year of physical chemistry.
* NY residents tuition: $137 per credit

Power Supplies
Northwest Technical College
NOTE#ELTR1812 Undergraduate   3 credits $240*
This course covers the operation of the devices and circuitry used in basic power supplies. Included are transformers, rectifiers, filters, and zener regulators. This course not available to users with Macintosh platform.
* Residents rates may apply.

Principles of Information Processing
City University
CITY#CS241 Undergraduate   5 qu. credits $785
Introduction to the world of information processing including programming logic, data types, structured programming, flow charting, the systems development life cycle, structured testing, user interface, algorithms, problem statements, ethics, and the professional role of the software developer. The foundation course for all computer systems courses.

Project in Computer Science
Nova Southeastern University
NOVA#CISC691 Graduate   3 credits $1,110
Students pursue a project, research study, or implementation under the supervision of a faculty member.

Solar Energy [Alternative Energy Sources]
University of Oregon
OREG#PHY162 Undergraduate   3 credits $294
This course will deal with the issues of alternative energy sources. The first half of the course will focus on Solar Energy as it is the most popular energy alternative. The intent is to perform an objective cost-benefit analysis on each form of alternative energy in order to determine what is practical on a large scale, as well as on the scale of the individual homeowner. We will pay particular attention to the efficiency of each alternative energy source as well as what limitations exist in terms of extracting usable energy.

Solar Energy and Systems
Mohave Community College
MOHA#BRT120 Undergraduate   3 credits $110
This course will cover fundamentals of alternative energy for the individual home owner. To educate students in the art and understanding of being independent using pollution free solar, wind and or Hydro generated energy. We will also educate students on what available equipment is necessary to change solar energy to usable electrical energy for their own home. We will cover fundamentals of solar, wind and hydro systems so that the student will also learn how to design, install and use their own alternative energy system.

Solid State Circuits
Northwest Technical College
NOTE#ELTR1814 Undergraduate   3 credits $240*
This course covers transistor operation, biasing, and specifications along with amplifier configurations and applications. Troubleshooting and design are emphasized. This course not available to users with Macintosh platform. Prerequisites: ELTR1804 or concurrent registration.
* Residents rates may apply.

Space Vehicle Design
University of North Dakota
NODA#SPST405 Graduate   3 credits $816*
A team design project to develop the requirements for a space mission. The specific mission will vary from time to time. Design teams will work on selected portions of the mission. Accompanying lectures will provide background materials.
* ND residents, $102 per credit; may also be reduced for residents of adjoining states and provinces.

Special Topics in Computer Science
Nova Southeastern University
NOVA#CISC690 Graduate   3 credits $1,110
This seminar will focus on the professor's current research interests. Prerequisite: prior consent of instructor and program director.

System Development Methodologies
City University
CITY#CS420 Undergraduate   **5 qu. credits**   **$785**

Analytical view of prevalent methods for developing software systems. Topics include CASE tools, structured programming, modular programming, Object-Oriented Design and the systems development life cycle. A comparison of these methodologies in terms of development time, system maintenance and life cycle costs is an integral part of this course. Prerequisite: CS322 or its equivalent; corequisite: CS090.

System Test and Evaluation
Nova Southeastern University
NOVA#MCIS640 Graduate   **3 credits**   **$1,110**

An analysis of the verification and validation process. Methods, procedures, and techniques for integration and acceptance testing. Reliability measurement. Goals for testing. Testing in the small and testing in the large. Allocation of testing resources. When to stop testing. Test case design methods. Black box software testing techniques including equivalence partitioning, boundary-value analysis, cause-effect graphing, and error guessing. White box software testing techniques including statement coverage criterion, edge coverage criterion, condition coverage criterion, and path coverage criterion. Test of concurrent and real-time systems.

System Test and Evaluation
Nova Southeastern University
NOVA#MMIS640 Graduate   **3 credits**   **$1,110**

An analysis of the verification and validation process. Methods, procedures, and techniques for integration and acceptance testing. Reliability measurement. Goals for testing. Testing in the small and testing in the large. Allocation of testing resources. When to stop testing. Test case design methods. Black box software testing techniques including equivalence partitioning, boundary-value analysis, cause-effect graphing, and error guessing. White box software testing techniques including statement coverage criterion, edge coverage criterion, condition coverage criterion, and path coverage criterion. Test of concurrent and real-time systems.

Systems & Procedures
Greenville Technical College
GRTE#CPT264 Undergraduate   **3 credits**   **$381***

Covers the techniques of system analysis, design, development and implementation.
* NC residents pay $48 per credit.

Systems Analysis & Design
Strayer University
STRA#CIS510 Undergraduate   **4.5 credits**   **$665**

Provides an integrated approach to the study of systems analysis and design Utilizes CASE tools of analysis as means of solving problems. Prerequisite: CIS 345, or equivalent.

Systems Analysis and Design
Nova Southeastern University
NOVA#MCIS660 Graduate   **3 credits**   **$1,110**

Analysis of requirements for information systems. Elicitation/fact-finding, problem analysis, decomposition, and the requirements document. Concepts, methods, techniques, and tools for systems analysis, modeling/simulation, and prototyping. Structured and object-oriented analysis. Role of the systems analyst in the organization. Gaining user commitment and fulfilling user needs. Concepts, tools, and techniques for systems design. Design principles, quality factors, decomposition of complex systems, and modularization techniques. Design methods such as object-oriented and function-oriented design. Comparison of analysis and design techniques.

Systems Analysis and Design
Nova Southeastern University
NOVA#MMIS660 Graduate   **3 credits**   **$1,110**

Analysis of requirements for information systems. Elicitation/fact-finding, problem analysis, decomposition, and the requirements document. Concepts, methods, techniques, and tools for systems analysis, modeling and simulation, and prototyping. Structured and object-oriented analysis. Role of the systems analyst in the organization. Gaining user commitment and fulfilling user needs. Concepts, tools, and techniques for systems design. Design principles, quality factors, decomposition of complex systems, and modularization techniques. Design methods such as object-oriented and function-oriented design. Comparison of analysis and design techniques.

Systems Analysis and Design
Rogers State University
ROGE#CS2133 Undergraduate   **3 credits**   **$495***

To be a successful computer science, professional, you need to know more than programming languages. You need to know how to analyze and organize the work. This is the course that teaches you those critical skills. In this course, engineering and computer science methods are applied to the production of software, according to problem specifications, and time and budget constraints. Methodologies for project definition, analysis, design, coding, testing and maintenance, are interrelated with management, costing, and communication considerations.
* OK residents $315.

Systems Analysis OOD
City University
CITY#CS450 Undergraduate   **5 qu. credits**   **$785**

System Analysis and design in an Object-Oriented environment. Topics include teamwork, security, problem solving, MIS management, project management, feasibility studies, financial management of MIS resources, object identity, Object-Oriented Design, system development life cycle, user involvement, software documentation, work metrics, work procedures and manuals, work flow analysis and Computer Aided Software Engineering (CASE). Prerequisite: CS322 or equivalent.

Systems Simulation
New Jersey Institute of Technology
NJIT#CIS461 Undergraduate   3 credits $1143*

This course introduces computer simulation as an algorithmic problem solving technique. It includes discrete simulation models, elementary theory, stochastic processes, use of simulation languages, random number generations, simulation of probabilistic processes, design of simulation experiments, validation of models, queuing systems, and applications to the design and analysis of operational systems. The GPSS language is covered in detail. Prerequisites: Completion of 100 level GUR course in CIS; Math 333. Optional: 25 video lessons of 60 minutes each.

* NJ residents: $184/semester hour.

Technical Writing for Engineers
University of Minnesota
MINN#COMP3031 Undergraduate   4 credits $391

Develops general strategies for engaging texts critically, both as a reader and as a writer. Three major assignments--abstract, critique, and synthesis--gradually teach the skills needed for precise understanding, critical analyses, and sophisticated use of texts. Students must have access to an Apple Macintosh with Hypercard.

The Air Transportation System
Embry-Riddle Aeronautical University
EMRI#MAS602 Graduate   3 credits $840

A study of air transportation as part of a global, multi-modal transportation system. The course reviews the evolution of the technological, social, environmental, and political aspects of this system since its inception at the beginning of this century. The long-term and short-term effects of deregulation, energy shortages, governmental restraints, and national and international issues are examined. Passenger and cargo transportation, as well as military and private aircraft modes, are studied in relation to the ever-changing transportation requirements.

The Mechanical Universe
University of Missouri
MOCE#SC275B Undergraduate   3 credits $387

This course provides an introduction to classical physics. The discipline's three components - mechanics, electromagnetics, and thermodynamics - are emphasized in this course. Topics studied include motion, vectors, gravity, work and energy, engines, waves, and angular momentum. Perquisites: college algebra or precalculus required; trigonometry or basic calculus recommended.

Theory of Computation and Its Applications
Harvard University
HARV#CSCIE207 Graduate   4 credits $1,200*

The fundamental concepts of the theory of automata, formal languages, computability, and computational complexity, and their relevance to the practice of computation. Practical applications include the parsing of natural and artificial languages, generative mechanisms in computer graphics, and identifying and coping with computationally hard problems. Homework assignments will include some programming assignments. Prerequisite(s): CSCI E-119 and MATH E-104 or equivalents.

* Noncredit option: $950.

Thermodynamics
New Jersey Institute of Technology
NJIT#CHE611 Undergraduate   3 credits $1143*

Principles of thermodynamics developed quantitatively to include thermodynamic functions and their application to chemical engineering processes. Prerequisites: Undergraduate courses in physical chemistry and thermodynamics, or equivalent. Optional: 13 video lessons of 150 minutes each.

* NJ residents: $184/semester hour.

Vehicles & Facilities Operations
University of North Dakota
NODA#SPST550 Graduate   3 credits $816*

A technically-oriented examination of the management issues involved in the planning, design, development and operation of new and existing vehicles and facilities. The course will include a review of present vehicles and those that will be required in the next two decades, from expendable launchers to the aerospace plane. Prerequisite: Survey   of   Space   Studies (NODA#SPST501).

* ND residents, $102 per credit; may also be reduced for residents of adjoining states and provinces.

X-Ray Powder Diffraction
State University of New York
SUNY#CHEM581B Graduate   2 credits $692*

An introduction to the basics of x-ray powder diffraction for characterizing solid materials. This will include lectures on the principle of x-ray diffraction of powders, and hands-on laboratories in the use of modern diffraction instruments for simple phase identification (finger printing) as well as the determination of simple structures. Prerequisite: An undergraduate course in Materials Science, Minerology or Solid State chemistry.

* NY residents tuition: $137 per credit

Health

Anatomy and Physiology

Child

Dental

Disease

General Health

Health Management

Nutrition and Fitness

Occupational

Other

Terminology

Advanced Disease State Management I
University of Colorado
CUON#PRDO5310 Undergraduate   4 credits $2604*
(Course description not available at press time.)
* CO residents tuition: $136 per credit.

Advanced Disease State Management V
University of Colorado
CUON#PRDO5350 Undergraduate   4 credits $2604*
(Course description not available at press time.)
* CO residents tuition: $136 per credit.

Advanced Health Data Systems
Dakota State University
DAKO#HIM444 Undergraduate   2 credits $298
In-depth study of collection and presentation of health data using manual and computerized methods. Development of case mix management reports as well as other reports requested by hospital administration and other outside agencies. Analysis and design of health information systems.

Applied Anatomy
Eastern Oregon University
EAOR#PEH321 Undergraduate   3 credits $240
Study of the musculoskeletal structure of the living human body; bones and their articulation; segments and their movements; muscles and their attachments and actions. Special emphasis is placed on musculoskeletal analysis of basic exercise and movement patterns. Prerequisite: BIOL231, BIOL232 or consent of instructor.

Applied Nutrition
University of Missouri
MOCE#HE212 Undergraduate   3 credits $387
This course covers feed composition and utilization; ration formulation; feed evaluation and identification; and practical problems. Perquisites: Animal Science 202 or concurrent enrollment.

Barrier Precautions and Infection Control Measures
State University of New York
SUNY#DEN113 Undergraduate   1 credits $210*
Focuses on the scientifically accepted principles and practices of infection control. This course will provide the students with the core elements on infection control and barrier precautions. Fall semester only.
* NY residents tuition: $105.

Basic Infection Control
Lake Superior College
LASU#CLTH1910 Undergraduate   4 CEUs $280
This course covers the basic concepts of infection control, Standard Precautions, and disease prevention. Using credible web sites, the student will have access to up-to-date information and statistics. This course meets the Minnesota Board of Nursing requirements for four hours of continuing education.

Basic Medical Terminology
Rio Salado College
RISA#HCC100AD Undergraduate   3 credits $186*
(Course description not available at press time.)
* AZ residents pay $37 per credit.

Basic Nutrition
State University of New York
SUNY#FSA102 Undergraduate   3 credits $630*
A study of nutrients-carbohydrate, protein, fat, vitamins, minerals, and water. The course provides students the opportunity to analyze their personal dietary intake. Food selection and energy needs are emphasized. Information about current research and literature is integrated into the course.
* NY residents tuition: $105 per credit.

Basic Principles of Occupational Health
Central Maine Technical College
CEMA#OHS101 Undergraduate   3 credits $512*
This survey course introduces students to basic principles of occupational health including the identification of common workplace health hazards, the effects of those hazards on the human body, methods of controlling exposures to health hazards and abatement procedures.
*Maine resident (and military) tuition: $269.

Basic Principles of Occupational Safety
Central Maine Technical College
CEMA#OHS106 Undergraduate   3 credits $502*
This survey course will introduce the student to basic principles of occupational safety including the identification of safety hazards, risk reduction measures, personal protection and safety attitudes and training. The course is based upon the standards adopted by the Occupational Safety and Health Administration.
*Maine resident (and military) tuition: $259.

Basics of Cancer Biology
University of Colorado
CUON#BIOL1352 Undergraduate   3 credits $1953*
This is an elective for non-science majors and could have practical applications in your life. This course will be exploring the biological nature of cancer, a disease that strikes one in three Americans. It also offers an overview of what recent research has revealed about the causes of cancer, about how it can be treated, and might be prevented. We'll also learn about early detection and diagnosis, as well as prospects for the future. This overview is based on a foundation of knowledge gained from basic research into the behavior and activities of cells.
* CO residents tuition: $136 per credit.

Biology of Aging
Western Illinois University
WEIL#BIO420G Undergraduate   3 credits $795*
This WIU teleclass examines the nature and theories of aging. Study the processes involved at the molecular, cellular, organ, and organismal levels of development and the changes that occur with time. In vitro aging is discussed in detail. Examine aging in respect to each human organ system: muscular, nervous, digestive, nutritional, excretory, endocrine, and reproductive. Relationships between aging and immunity, neoplasia, and pharmacology are considered. Geriatric medicine is examined. Prerequisite: Biology 101/102, 150/151, or 304, or Anatomy and Physiology I and II.
* IL residents tuition: $88 per credit.

Bones, Bodies and Disease
University of Colorado-Boulder
COBO#ANTH2070   Undergraduate   3 credits $240

Detailed study of the human skeleton and introduction to techniques used to evaluate demographic variables. Application of techniques through evaluation of photographic images of an excellently preserved mummified skeletal population from ancient Nubia to reconstruct prehistoric patterns of adaptation and biocultural evolution.

Breastfeeding and Human Lactation
Wichita State University
WIST#NUR001   Graduate   3 credits $603

The course is open to nursing and non-nursing graduate students and focuses on clinical topics that prepare the student for practice as a lactation consultant and for IBCLC certification.

Child Health and Safety
Bakersfield College
BAKE#CHDVB49   Undergraduate   2 credits $230*

For parents, aides, teachers, and directors of child care facilities. Health and safety assessments, needs issues, policies, and procedures addressed. Emphasis placed on application and demonstration of course content. Students will acquire American Red Cross Pediatric CPR and First Aid at the student's cost. Prerequisite: Reading Level 1 recommended.
* CA residents pay $40 per credit.

Child Nutrition and Health
Western Illinois University
WEIL#HEA303   Undergraduate   3 credits $795*

Discusses nutritional needs and problems of infants and preschool children. The course covers the development of food service and nutrition components in infant and preschool programs. Useful for anyone concerned with child nutrition and health, this course meets the teacher certification requirement for a course in child nutrition and health.
* IL residents tuition: $88 per credit.

Clinical Pharmocology in Nursing
State University of New York
SUNY#NUR211   Undergraduate   3 credits $1038*

The course introduces the basic principles of drug action, including absorption, distribution, metabolism, excretion and drug interactions. The role of the nurse and the application of the nursing process to the care of the patient receiving pharmacological therapy is reviewed and emphasized throughout. The course is organized according to major drug classifications, identified either by their clinical use or by body systems. For each classification, principles of drug action, use for specific disorders, and related nursing care will be considered. Prerequisites: Anatomy Physiology I and II.
* NY residents tuition: $137 per credit

Clinical Supervision
The Graduate School of America
TGSA#HS862W   Graduate   4 credits $795

This course provides a theoretical overview of the theory, basic functions, and methods of clinical supervision. Some of the topics to be covered are: the supervisory contract and relationship, the various styles of supervision, the legal and ethical issues related to clinical supervision, methods of supervision including case consultation, video supervision, live supervision and co-therapy as supervision.

Coed Personal Fitness
State University of New York
SUNY#PE101   Undergraduate   2 credits $420*

This course is designed to make the student aware of why they should be physically fit. It explores what physical fitness is and methods for developing the various component parts of physical fitness.
* NY residents tuition: $105 per credit.

Communication in Health Care Setting
Rio Salado College
RISA#HCC100AE   Undergraduate   3 credits $186*

(Course description not available at press time.)
* AZ residents pay $37 per credit.

Computers and Rehabilitation
University of Washington
WASH#REHABC496B   Undergraduate   3 qu. credits $222

Rehabilitation counselors, physical therapists, occupational therapists, teachers in K-12 and post-secondary education, librarians, and educational technologists will learn as part of a group. What you will learn: to understand the benefits of adaptive computer technology, to identify the costs of adaptation and funding sources, to understand the federal laws related to disability accommodation and to design a physical environment.

Consumer Nutrition
State University of New York
SUNY#HRMG110   Undergraduate   3 credits $1038*

This course studies specific nutrients and their functions, physiological, psychological, and sociological needs for food. It also involves the development of dietary standards for individuals of all ages. The use of nutritional standards in planning and analyzing menus will be included, as will current health nutrition problems.
* NY residents tuition: $137 per credit.

Contemporary Nutrition
University of Nebraska
NEBR#NUTR800   Masters   3 credits $467

Contemporary nutrition is designed for students interested in an overview of the field of nutrition, including the basis for current dietary recommendations and guidelines, nutrient functions, and current issues. By the end of the course, the student will be able to explain the principles underlying U.S. nutrition recommendations and dietary guidelines and list required nutrients, their food sources, functions, deficiency diseases, and toxicities when in high amounts.

CPR for Health Care Providers
Rio Salado College
RISA#HCC100AG Undergraduate   3 credits $186*
(Course description not available at press time.)
* AZ residents pay $37 per credit.

Current Issues in the Healthcare Professions
New Hampshire College
NEHA#ADB423 Undergraduate   3 credits $1656
Students will be challenged to contemplate and debate many of the complex issues facing the healthcare profession as it struggles to balance the needs of the individual, organization and local community. Issues such as hospital mergers, step-care retirement communities, ambulatory surgical centers and outpatient hospital centers represent a sampling of topics that will be discussed.

Current Trends In Health Care Delivery
Dakota State University
DAKO#HIM443 Undergraduate   3 credits $447
Current trends in health care delivery; recent research, theory, issues, and developments in health records, changing roles of health care providers.

Dental Epidemiology Update
Chemeketa Community College
CHEM#9435D Undergraduate   0 credits $50
An over-view of notifiable infectious diseases as they relate to dentistry. Includes etiology, signs and symptoms, and oral manifestations as well as the role of dental personnel in reporting and treatment.

Dental Ethics
Chemeketa Community College
CHEM#9435E Undergraduate   0 credits $40
An overview of professional standards of conduct in the dental environment. Presents and incorporates ethical principles with case studies.

Dental Materials
State University of New York
SUNY#DEN211 Undergraduate   2 credits $420*
A study of commonly used materials, physical and chemical properties, their manipulation, uses in dental practice. Fall semester only.
* NY residents tuition: $105 per credit.

Dental Radiology
State University of New York
SUNY#DEN111 Undergraduate   2 credits $630*
An introduction to physics and biology of radiation, radiation hygiene, equipment and materials, film exposure and processing, technique and chemistry. Intraoral projections only. Fall semester only.
* NY residents tuition: $105 per credit.

Directed Study
Central Maine Technical College
CEMA#OHS220 Undergraduate   3 credits $462*
This course provides students the opportunity to pursue a special new course project within the field of occupational health and safety OR pursue a third practicum. Specific goals and objectives are determined in conjunction with the faculty supervisor. An Advisor approved proposal is a necessary prerequisite to registration.
*Maine resident (and military) tuition: $219.

Economics for Health Care Executives
University of Missouri
MOCE#EC201 Undergraduate   3 credits $387
This course presents the basic theories, concepts, and tools of economics that can be used to evaluate systematically the characteristics, utilization patterns, delivery strategies, and financing mechanisms of an individual, organization, or industry.

Elements of Health Education
University of Missouri
MOCE#T85 Undergraduate   2 credits $258
Health needs of university students and school-aged children are investigated in this course through an examination of personal and community health problems.

Emerging Infectious Diseases
State University of New York
SUNY#1134501 Undergraduate   3 credits $1038*
This course will examine the infectious diseases whose incidence in humans has increased within the past two decades. We will explore our experiences with infectious diseases, identify significant factors that impact disease emergence and apply our growing knowledge of microbial life and epidemiology to critique proposed intervention strategies. Prerequisite: Successful completion of the first two years of an undergraduate general education program.
* NY residents tuition: $137 per credit

Ergonomics
Central Maine Technical College
CEMA#OHS160 Undergraduate   3 credits $472*
This course will deal with the issue that is most often associated with the lower back and upper body injuries that account for a large part of the lost-time work-related injuries in Maine. Ergonomics is the study of the relationship between the human body and the work that it does.
*Maine resident (and military) tuition: $229.

Exercise Physiology
State University of New York
SUNY#ES380 Undergraduate   4 credits $1038*
Analysis of physiologic responses and adaptations of the various body systems and structures to acute and chronic physical activity and to environmental stress. Cellular mechanisms that underlie these responses are emphasized.
* NY residents tuition: $137 per credit

Facts About Fluoride
Chemeketa Community College
CHEM#9435G Undergraduate   0 credits $40
An overview of fluoride products and their uses in dentistry. Includes topical fluoride applications, systemic fluoride, fluoride as a desensitizing agent, enamel fluoride uptake, and dispensing precautions.

Food Plant Sanitation
Auburn University
AUBU#NFS408 Undergraduate   2.4 credits $101
A thorough review of sanitary regulations and procedures for hazard control and quality assurance in the food industry.

Foundations of Health and Human Performance
Auburn University
AUBU#HHP201B Undergraduate   5 qtr. hrs. $210
A brief overview of significant ideas and events in the development of health education, physical education and recreation. Historical background of the fields of sports, physical education and health.

Greek and Latin Terminology in Medical Sciences
University of Minnesota
MINN#CLAS1048 Undergraduate   2 credits $178
Presentation in English contexts of Greek and Latin prefixes, suffixes, and root words in technical vocabularies, with special attention to medical terminology. No previous study of Greek or Latin required. Prerequisite: CLAS1045 recommended.

Health
Brevard Community College
BREV#HSC1100 Undergraduate   3 credits $485
The focus of this course is to help the student change health behaviors through presentation of material relating to family health, personal health, potential and limitations of drugs, values of sound nutritional practices, human sexuality and reproduction, functioning of the human body, and trends and techniques relating to current medical practices.

Health & Wellness for Children
Emporia State University
EMPO#HL700 Undergrad/Grad   1 credits $76
Involves exploring the Wide World Web for sites regarding health/wellness issues pertaining to children Preschool-8. Emphasis will be placed on issues, trends and curriculums involving school health education. Among the course requirements will be Internet "surfing" assignments, an instructor-approved independent project, and electronic forum discussion via the Internet.

Health Analysis and Improvement
Brevard Community College
BREV#HLP1081 Undergraduate   2 credits $345
To help students understand their current health status and to provide a functional program to obtain or maintain for optimal health. An analysis of current health status through a series of evaluation techniques. The student will be assisted in developing an individualized conditioning program and plan for life style modification.

Health and Fitness for Life
Chemeketa Community College
CHEM#HPE295 Undergraduate   3 credits $123
This course is designed for the person who would like to learn more about exercise and its effects on the human body. This information, presented through both lecture and hands on laboratory experiences, will provide students with an increased understanding of their own level of health, lifelong fitness, and wellness.

Health and Nutrition
Brevard Community College
BREV#HUN1100 Undergraduate   3 credits $485
This course introduces students to the scientific principles of nutrition. It covers the role of specific nutrients, their digestion, absorption, and metabolism, sources of the nutrients and requirements of different age groups.

Health Care Delivery in the United States
State University of New York
SUNY#HSM30135 Undergraduate   3 credits $1038*
A detailed study of the system and philosophy of health care in the United States. The areas of public health and community medicine are examined from a historical, current and future perspective. The rationale for the patterns and practices in the American system of health services is explored.
* NY residents tuition: $137 per credit

Health Care Organization and Management
Mercy College
MERC#BS308 Undergraduate   3 credits $900
(Course description not available at press time.)

Health Care Quality Assurance
Rochester Institute of Technology
ROCH#63543190 Undergraduate   4 credits $923
An Introduction to quality assurance in health care, including past and present definitions of quality and competing concepts of quality assurance.

Health Care Today
Rio Salado College
RISA#HCC100AA Undergraduate   3 credits $186*
(Course description not available at press time.)
* AZ residents pay $37 per credit.

Health Education
Barstow Community College
BARS#HEAL1 Undergraduate   3 credits $???
Introduction to health topics which include: health care systems; substances including alcohol, tobacco, caffeine, narcotics and other drugs; ecology; birth to death cycle; self-awareness; effective consumer practices; nutrition and physical conditioning.

Health Issues for Peace Officers
Rio Hondo College
RIHO#PAC43032 Undergraduate   0.5 credits $???
This course is designed to introduce the student to issues of health; an overview, health assessment, heart disease, and fitness tips. Note - no exercise or health program should be started without consulting a physician.

Health Problems in the Community
Indiana University
INDI#C366 Undergraduate   3 credits $268
Human ecology as it relates to the interaction of social and physical phenomena in the solution of community health problems. Considers the promotion of community health, programs of prevention, environmental health, and health services.

Health Psychology
Walden University
WALD#PSYC8400 Graduate   5 credits $1500
An examination of theoretical models and supporting research for a psychology of well-being and immunocompetence. Factors (personal and environmental) that impact on health and psychological interventions which modify them will be explored.

Health Science
Auburn University
AUBU#HHP195 Undergraduate   1.2 credits $50
Basic understanding concerning sound health practices and protection. Physical, mental and social aspects of personal and community health are considered.

Health, Culture, and Society
University of Southern Colorado
COSO#SOC401 Undergraduate   3 credits $210
Analysis of how social, cultural, and psychological factors influence health and health care. The goal of this class is to guide you through an examination of the sociology of health and its relationship to American society. The course will provide a guide to the issues that impact on your health care, the meaning of illness in our society, as well as how our social institutions influence your well-being. In the late 1990s the issues surrounding health care are topics of everyday conversations as well as political "hot potatoes" for our elected officials.

Health, Sport & Movement Science
Emporia State University
EMPO#PE707 Graduate   3 credits $315
This course is designed to examine the psychological aspects of exercise behavior and sport/athletic participation. Specifically, the areas of motivation, stress and stress-related problems, peak performance training, group dynamics, psychophysiological changes due to exercise, and retirement from sport will be addressed.

Healthcare Automation
University of Central Florida
FLCE#HSA4193 Graduate   3 credits $1305*
The course provides students with knowledge about computers and technology and how they can be useful in the healthcare industry. I use the term "healthcare automation" to mean the process of using computers and technology to get people away from paperwork and back to healthcare. This is not a computer literacy course. Its true, we do a lot of work with PC's and networks, and talk about them constantly. The objective of the course is teach you about "analysis and design of computerized systems for health data and health administration". Electronic commerce will be a constant theme.
* FL residents pay $129 per credit.

Healthcare Finance
Golden Gate University
GOLD#HM306 Graduate   3 credits $999
Examines financial decision making in the managed healthcare environment. Focuses on the impact of reimbursement and cost models on financial resource management and financial planning/control and techniques. Includes cost analysis, budgeting, variance analysis and pricing. Emphasizes the use of capital and cash management for strategic success in today's healthcare systems. Prerequisites: HM300 and HM301 or consent of the Department Chair.

Healthcare Financing Issues
State University of New York
SUNY#HCM194Y01 Undergraduate   3 credits $570*
This course will present the United States' health care system from a cost perspective. Students examine the history of health care costs in the U.S., the nature of competition, the characteristics of the market for medical services that influence competition, and the implications of these factors on the health care sector of our economy. Special emphasis will be placed on the most current legislative and administrative proposals/enactments. Prerequisite: HCM193, Introduction to US Healthcare Systems or permission of the Instructor.
* NY residents tuition: $90 per credit

Healthcare Information Systems
Golden Gate University
GOLD#HM312 Graduate   3 credits $999
Surveys computer systems and software available to managers for inpatient and ambulatory applications including: admissions, discharge, billing, medical records, budgeting, electronic claims submission, utilization analysis and capitation management. Emphasis is on evaluating data needs, defining and communicating information system needs, and managing information systems. Designed for non-technical managers; prior experience with computer applications is helpful, but not essential.

Healthcare Marketing
Golden Gate University
GOLD#HM308 Graduate   3 credits $999
Presents the principles of healthcare marketing in a managed care environment as well as the changing role and responsibilities of healthcare managers. You will learn current applications of core business marketing theories used by hospitals and other healthcare organizations to capture their target audience. Related topics include proper utilization of promotional tools, pricing strategies and healthcare advertising tactics for various delivery systems. Prerequisites: HM 300 and HM 301 or consent of the Department Chair.

HIV/Medial High Risk and Addiction
Kansas City Kansas Community College
KACI#AC1103 Undergraduate 1 credits $108*

HIV/AIDS has become a major epidemic in only twelve years and the link between drug abuse and infection is becoming more apparent everyday. This course is designed to give counselors the skills and understanding necessary to provide effective treatment to those clients who are both chemically dependent and HIV infected. In addition, the course will also cover other sexually transmitted diseases and their relation to chemical dependency. Fetal alcohol syndrome, cardiovascular, neurological and gynecological complications associated with chemical dependency. Medical detoxification techniques will also be reviewed.

* KS residents pay $40 per credit.

Human Anatomy
Eastern Oregon University
EAOR#BIOL210 Undergraduate 4 credits $320

Examination of the gross and microscopic anatomy of the human body. Includes the histology and development of the nervous, skeletal, circulatory, gastrointestinal, renal, reproductive, and the integumentary systems. The cat is used as a model in the laboratory portion of this course. Prerequisite: CHEM101, 102, 103.

Human Anatomy & Physiology
Brevard Community College
BREV#BSCC1092 Undergraduate 4 credits $625

Includes terminology; chemistry; cell biology and cellular respiration; tissues; survey of all organ systems. Meets the Biological Science requirement for A.A. degree. This course is recommended for non-science majors.

Human Anatomy and Physiology I
Rio Salado College
RISA#BIO201 Undergraduate 4 credits $248*

Study of structure and function of the human body. Topics include cells, tissues, integumentary system, skeletal system, muscular system, and nervous system. Prerequisites: BIO100, or BIO156, or BIO181, or equivalent, or permission of instructor.

* AZ residents $37 per credit.

Human Anatomy and Physiology II
Rio Salado College
RISA#BIO202 Undergraduate 4 credits $248*

Continuation of structure and function of the human body. Topics include endocrine, circulatory, respiratory, digestive, urinary, and reproductive systems. Prerequisites: BIO201 or permission of instructor.

* AZ residents pay $37 per credit.

Human Biology for Allied Health
Rio Salado College
RISA#BIO156 Undergraduate 4 credits $248*

An introductory biology course for allied health majors with an emphasis on humans. Topics include fundamental concepts of cell biology, histology, microbology, and genetics.

* AZ residents pay $37 per credit.

Human Nutrition & Health
University of Nebraska
NEBR#NSD151 Undergraduate 3 credits $467

A survey of the science of human nutrition and relationships between nutrition and health of individuals and groups throughout life and in special nutritional problems.

Human Physiology
Eastern Oregon University
EAOR#BIOL232 Undergraduate 4 credits $320

Introduction to the principles of human physiology, covering homeostatic control mechanisms, function and the fundamental interrelationships between interacting systems. Includes: gastrointestinal, renal, endocrine, neuromuscular, cardiovascular, respiratory systems; fluid-electrolyte and acid-base balance; and an introduction to cell biology. Prerequisite: BIOL231.

Immunology
University of Colorado
CUON#PRDO5010 Undergraduate 3 credits $1953*

This course includes basic concepts of immunology, immunopathology, immunopharmacology, and immunotherapy. It focuses on the pathogenesis of diseases associated with the immune system including hypersensitivity disorders, AIDS, autoimmune and rheumatic diseases, graft-versus-host disease and transplantation immunology, infectious diseases, and the role of the immune system in oncology. It addresses the effects and outcomes of drugs and drug therapy and their impact on the immune system. Clinical applications of immunology are included.

* CO residents tuition: $136 per credit.

Immunology
Western Illinois University
WEIL#BIO434 Undergraduate 3 credits $795*

Studies antigens and antibodies, the immune response and immunity, immunologic testing, allergy and hypersensitivity, transplantation, autoimmune diseases, and cancer immunology. Prerequisite: one year of chemistry and one introductory biology course.

* IL residents tuition: $88 per credit.

Industrial Hygiene and Occupational Health
New Jersey Institute of Technology
NJIT#IE615 Undergraduate 3 credits $1143*

Introduction to industrial hygiene. Recognition, evaluation and control of human exposure to noise, heat, bio-hazards, chemicals, radiation, and improper lighting, work practices, engineering designs, and the effects of excessive exposure on worker health and productivity. Prerequisites: one year of college physics and one semester of college chemistry or biology. Optional: video lessons.

* NJ residents: $184/semester hour.

Infection Control in the Dental Office
Chemeketa Community College
CHEM#9435H Undergraduate 0 credits $50
A study of infection control techniques used in the dental environment. Includes standard precautions, aseptic techniques, and sterilization and disinfection principles.

Information Systems and Computer Applications in Medicine
University of Central Florida
FLCE#HSA5198 Graduate 3 credits $1305*
Overview of Health Information Systems with an emphasis on computer applications. Discussion of hardware and software issues. We are going to study the contemporary issues related to information systems, and the healthcare business. We will examine the big picture of integrating clinical and traditional business systems. Electronic commerce is a theme throughout the course.
* FL residents pay $129 per credit.

Information Systems and Health Care I
Wichita State University
WIST#NUR775 Graduate 3 credits $603
Analyzes information systems in clinical management, administration, education and research. Emphasizes issues surrounding information systems and hands-on experience with selected health care information management exercises.

Information Systems and Health Care II
Wichita State University
WIST#NUR776 Graduate 3 credits $603
Provides an individualized opportunity for the student to apply the concepts/theories of information systems to a health care setting. Projects for this course include analyzing existing information programs, identifying applications for automation and undertaking small-scale development efforts. Prerequisite: Completion of Nursing 775 or concurrent enrollment.

Intro to Healthcare Management
Pitt Community College
PITT#HMT110 Undergraduate ?? credits $???
This course introduces the functions, practices, organizational structures, and professional issues in healthcare management. Emphasis is placed on planning, controlling, directing, and communicating within health and human services organizations.

Intro to Human Anatomy & Physiology
Northwest Technical College
NOTE#BIOL1404 Undergraduate 3 credits $240*
(Course description not available at press time.)
* Residents rates may apply.

Introduction to Anatomy and Physiology
New Hampshire College
NEHA#SCI217 Undergraduate 3 credits $1656
This course is intended to introduce the student to the fundamental principles of anatomy and physiology and the relationships of all the body systems and their functions. Prerequisite: ENG121 or permission of instructor.

Introduction to Dietary Management
Pennsylvania State University
PENN#DSM102 Undergraduate 1 credits $115
Introduction to the profession and exploration of the roles and responsibilities of the dietary manager. Note: All students must be approved by a Dietetic program adviser.

Introduction to HIV Mental Health
New York University
NEYO#X149300 Undergraduate 2.5 CEU $310
This on-line course is designed for social workers, pastoral counselors, psychiatric nurses, substance abuse counselors, and case managers who wish to get an edge in a competitive job market through specialized training. The course teaches you to understand HIV/AIDS using a biopsychosocial/spiritual model. Each component of the model is explained: the biomedical workings of the virus and new treatments; psychological and community responses to HIV/AIDS; and spiritual components of care. Other topics include: HIV dementia and other organic manifestations, psychological aspects of new medical treatments, and electronic sources of HIV information that can be quickly accessed.

Introduction to Nutrition
Western Illinois University
WEIL#HEA109 Undergraduate 3 credits $795*
Stresses basic nutrition concepts, the application of nutrition knowledge to everyday living, and world food problems.
* IL residents tuition: $88 per credit.

Introduction to Pharmacology
Delaware County Community College
DECO#PHA01 Undergraduate 3 credits $???
This course focuses on pharmacology the nurse needs to know in order to provide safe and effective care for clients taking medications. Basic principles of pharmacology are reviewed. Medications are grouped for study according to body system and drug action. Emphasis is on application of the nursing process, including patient education, to enhance effectiveness of medication therapy.

Introduction to Sports Medicine
State University of New York
SUNY#PPE170 Undergraduate 3 credits $630*
Covers the nature, philosophy, and practice of the field of sports medicine. Prevention, emergency care and rehabilitation as they pertain to certain athletic injuries will be the focus of the course.
* NY residents tuition: $105 per credit.

Law and Workplace Health & Safety
Central Maine Technical College
CEMA#OHS126 Undergraduate 3 credits $492*
This course will introduce the student to the laws and regulations which set out the rights and responsibilities of employers and employees for occupational health and safety. Legislative and legal processes will also be covered.
*Maine resident (and military) tuition: $249.

Legal & Ethical Aspects of Healthcare
Golden Gate University
GOLD#HM305 Graduate   3 credits $999
Examines principles and rules of law and ethics and their application to healthcare organizations. Specific legal and ethical responsibilities of the governing board and medical staff will be discussed in terms of admission and discharge of patients, consent for treatment, negligence and malpractice, employee relations, medical records and contracting. The question of who should receive medical treatment and under what circumstances also will be discussed. Prerequisites: HM300 and HM301 or consent of the Department Chair.

Managed Care Concepts
Golden Gate University
GOLD#HM302 Graduate   3 credits $999
Provides a survey and critical examination of insurance and managed care models. Emphasizes the unique financial and reimbursement practices in managed care: capitation analysis, sub-capitation, utilization analysis, payor mix, contract provisions and provider/payor relations. Includes current and future trends such as outcome measurement, government initiatives and legal structures.

Management Issues in Health Care
New School for Social Research
NEWS#8399 Undergraduate   3 credits $622
This course will focus on the organizational and interpersonal dynamics of managing systems, processes, people and change. The health care industry is in a state of organizational and structural flux. Issues to be discussed will include: Reorganization and Reengineering; Hierarchy and Flattened organizations; Team Building; Difference between Leadership and Management; How Leaders and Managers Facilitate Change; Diagnosing, Preventing and Overcoming Problems; Ethical Issues in Management; Negotiation Skills; How to Manage your Boss; How to Manage Others; Crisis Management; Unions and Management.

Management of Health Info. Centers I
Dakota State University
DAKO#HIM360 Undergraduate   3 credits $447
Application of the management principles of planning and organizing to health information settings. Concepts integrated into laboratory and computer experience.

Management of Health Info. Centers II
Dakota State University
DAKO#HIM361 Undergraduate   3 credits $447
Application of management principles of actuating, and controlling of health information settings. Concepts integrated into laboratory and computer experience.

Management of Health Services
State University of New York
SUNY#253734 Undergraduate   4 credits $586*
Review the basic concepts and theories related to the health services management functions of planning, organizing, staffing, leading, controlling, and decision making. After establishing the environmental, ethical, legal, and technical considerations that influence these activities in health service organizations, study how each of these management functions are applied in health service payor, provider, and consumer organizations. As a final course assignment, select a health service organization and relate the course materials to the actual management activities of the organization. Prerequisite: United States Health Systems (152104) or the equivalent.
* NY residents tuition: $515

Management of Healthcare Organizations
New Hampshire College
NEHA#ADB302 Undergraduate   3 credits $1656
This course focuses on teaching students the management and leadership theories, functions and skills that are required for success in the Healthcare profession in the decade of the 1990s. Recognizing that the healthcare industry faces tremendous pressures to control cost while continuing to deliver world class service, industry leaders struggle to find solutions that will meet with the approval of its many constituents. Students will be challenged to understand the complex problems of today's healthcare system and whenever possible to provide strategies that will result in added value to the market place.

Marketing of Dietetic Services
Pennsylvania State University
PENN#DSM304 Undergraduate   3 credits $345
Theories and applications of marketing principles to the design of consumer-oriented dietetic services. Note: All students must be approved by a Dietetic program adviser. The 1997 version of this course has been revised to emphasize marketing in the school food service environment.

Medical Emergency Preparedness
Chemeketa Community College
CHEM#9435A Undergraduate   0 credits $40
This course will emphasize prevention of medical emergencies in the dental office and will describe the preparation of the office and staff to deal with emergencies. It will include the gathering of patient information, including vital signs. Emergency kit supplies will be explained and demonstrated. Treatment of eight of the more common medical emergencies will be explained.

Medical Ethics
City University
CITY#PHI403 Undergraduate   5 qu. credits $785
A review of moral issues in the history of medicine, from the Campa Indians, to the Greeks, the Chinese, and modern medicine. Various schools of philosophy, from Aristotelian to utilitarianism, are related to medical issues. Topics examined include: AIDS, retardation, mental illness, human experimentation, abortion, suicide, organ transplants, and research on recombinant DNA. All issues are evaluated within the context of philosophical schools. Prerequisite: Strongly recommended: HUM200 or its equivalent.

Medical Ethics
Pennsylvania State University
PENN#PHIL432 Undergraduate 3 credits $345
Examination of such topics as euthanasia, the relationship between practitioner and patient, and the moral and political aspects of medicine. Note: 400-level courses are available only to students with junior or senior standing.

Medical Ethics
Pennsylvania State University
PENN#STS432 Undergraduate 3 credits $345
Examination of such topics as euthanasia, the relationship between practitioner and patient, and the moral and political aspects of medicine. Note: 400-level courses are available only to students with junior or senior standing.

Medical Office - Vocabulary
Rio Salado College
RISA#OAS181 Undergraduate 3 credits $186*
Basic medical vocabulary with emphasis on pronunciation, spelling, and definition.
* AZ residents $37 per credit.

Medical Terminology
Lake Superior College
LASU#ALTH1410 Undergraduate 1 credits $70
This course will provide you with a foundation of basic medical terms and abbreviations. It will focus on terminology used in anatomy and physiology for body systems, the appropriate abbreviations used for common medical and rehabilitative terms, and the principles for adding suffixes and prefixes to medical word roots.

Medical Terminology
Northwest Technical College
NOTE#HLTH1506 Undergraduate 3 credits $240*
(Course description not available at press time.)
* Residents rates may apply.

Medical Terminology
Rio Salado College
RISA#HIT170 Undergraduate 3 credits $186*
Basic tools for building a medical vocabulary and acquainting the student with medical terms as they pertain to anatomy, physiology, and diseases.
* AZ residents $37 per credit.

Medical Terminology
Rogers State University
ROGE#NURS1103 Undergraduate 3 credits $495*
The course presents a physiological systems approach to the principles of medical word building. Providing medical vocabulary for anatomy, physiology, systems, diagnostic testing and pharmacology, the course is appropriate for health science students such as nursing, dental hygiene, paramedic, and physical therapy assistant. Video: Medical Terminology.
* OK residents $315.

Medical Terminology and Pharmocology
State University of New York
SUNY#OT317 Undergraduate 1 credits $346*
Introduction to language used by health-care professionals whose medical decisions affect and determine the course of the rehabilitation and therapeutic process, includes four-week introductory unit on the fundamentals of pharmocology. Prerequisites: Human Anatomy and Physiology.
* NY residents tuition: $137 per credit

Medical Terms from Greek and Latin
Indiana University
INDI#C209 Undergraduate 2 credits $179
Basic vocabulary of some 1,000 words, together with materials for formation of compounds, enables students to build a working vocabulary of several thousand words. Designed for those intending to specialize in medicine, nursing, dentistry, or microbiology.

Medicare/Medicaid
Rochester Institute of Technology
ROCH#63579891 Undergraduate 4 credits $923
This overview course discusses the Medicare and Medicaid programs from a policy perspective.

Nursing Refresher Theory
Chemeketa Community College
CHEM#9410 Undergraduate 0 credits $320
This course has been developed to assist the inactive practical nurse or registered nurse to return to practice. Students review and acquire greater knowledge of concepts, skills, and values of contemporary licensed practical nursing. The nursing process is used in the management of nursing care in a variety of nursing situations. Prerequisite: Currently licensed as LPN or RN in Oregon (or) Eligibility for LPN or RN licensure and have applied for or obtained a limited license from the Oregon State Board of Nursing.

Nursing Research
University of Central Florida
FLCE#NUR3165 Undergraduate 3 credits $786*
Nursing Research is an undergraduate level course required of all nursing students enrolled in the School of Nursing, College of Health and Public Affairs at UCF. This course is now being offered as Web-based course. We recognize that regular and proficient use of the Internet is a competency and skill that will be required of professional nurses in practice. We understand the diverse needs of our students who desire flexibility in their school, work, and home schedules. This course emphasize the responsibility that students undertake for their own learning.
* FL residents tuition: $64 per credit.

Nutrition
Chemeketa Community College
CHEM#FN225 Undergraduate 3 credits $159
A study of the nutrients, their sources and body utilization to promote optimum health. Development of eating patterns, current dietary trends, evaluation of nutrition information in mass media, current national and international problems. Excellent for non-majors.

Nutrition
Eastern Oregon University
EAOR#PEH325   Undergraduate   4 credits $255
Essential dietary needs of individuals at different ages. Key emphasis is on the relationship of essential nutrients on digestion, absorption, and metabolism and its contribution to optimal health. Five-day computer dietary analysis and the development of different meal plans are included.

Nutrition
Kansas City Kansas Community College
KACI#BI145C   Undergraduate   3 credits $324*
For three hours of college credit, nutrition online is a computer-dependent, introductory general biology course for building knowledge about the science of nutrition. In order to participate fully in class, the student will need access to the World Wide Web and minimal computer literacy. The student will learn how nutrients are digested by the human body. Each vitamin and mineral will be analyzed in terms of functions source, deficiency and toxicity symptoms. A dynamic, interactive multimedia CD-ROM lets you explore and understand the world of nutrition as never before.
* KS residents pay $40 per credit.

Nutrition and Food
Texas Technical University
TETE#FN1410   Undergraduate   4 credits $???
Students examine the science of nutrition and food as applied to everyday living. The course is designed to convey basic nutrition concepts as they apply to individual students.

Nutrition Assessment Theory and Practice
Pennsylvania State University
PENN#NUTR359   Undergraduate   2 credits $230
Introduction to purpose, methods, and scientific basis for assessment of nutritional status and use of tools in a practice setting. Prerequisites: NUTR151 or NUTR251; all students must be approved by a Dietetic program adviser.

Nutrition Care of the Elderly
Pennsylvania State University
PENN#NUTR253   Undergraduate   3 credits $345
Introduction to the psychosocial, nutritional, and physiological needs of the elderly with emphasis on the delivery of nutrition care. Prerequisite: 3 credits of introductory nutrition.

Nutrition Throughout Life Cycle
University of Nebraska
NEBR#NUTR855   Masters   3 credits $467
The influence of normal physiological stresses on nutritional needs throughout the life span will be explored. Evaluating dietary intake and identifying appropriate community nutrition services will be included in discussions. Specific considerations such as the influence of age and cultural heritage will be incorporated. Each student will have the opportunity to plan, present and evaluate a mini education program which addresses a nutritional need(s) during a specific part of the life span.

Online Pharmacology
Delaware County Community College
DECO#AHA290   Undergraduate   3 credits $???
This course focuses on pharmacology the nurse needs to know in order to provide safe and effective care for clients taking medications. Basic principles of pharmacology are reviewed. Medications are grouped for study according to body system and drug action. Emphasis is on application of the nursing process, including patient education, to enhance effectiveness of medication therapy. Pre-requisite: Fundamentals of Nursing (NUS110), Anatomy (BIO117); corequisite: Nursing Concepts and Practice I (NUS111), Physiology (BIO118), or equivalent courses.

Oral Anatomy and Physiology I
State University of New York
SUNY#DEN112   Undergraduate   2 credits $420*
Gross anatomy of the teeth, tissues and organs of the oral cavity, related structures, innervation and blood supply, normal function, anatomical variation. Fall semester only.
* NY residents tuition: $105 per credit.

Organization & Administration for the Nurse Manager
Pennsylvania State University
PENN#NURS430   Undergraduate   3 credits $345
Introduction to organization and administration in nursing service and nursing management. Note: The student must be a registered nurse and provide a copy of his or her current nursing license for verification in order to be enrolled in this course.

Organizational Development
Golden Gate University
GOLD#PAD306   Graduate   3 credits $999
An examination of the development and current application of organization theory for healthcare and public sector agencies. This course will focus on the use of theory in public and healthcare administration as well as specific diagnostic and intervention toos/strategies for organizational development and change. Experiential and skill-building techniques are used extensively.

Personal Health
University of Alabama
ALAB#HHE270   Undergraduate   3 credits $250
This course is about enjoying life. It challenges you to increase your knowledge, strengths and skills in many areas - in self awareness, emotional health, stress management, nutrition fitness, intimate relationships, family planning, disease prevention, consumerism and many others. It aims to enhance your ability to take action in all these areas with confidence and competence. The course focuses on those choices that are yours to make. You make dozens of choices every day, and they determine your behaviors.

Personnel Issues in Health Care
New School for Social Research
NEWS#8564   Undergraduate   3 credits $622
This course examines the foundations, functions, and practices of human resource management. Special attention will be given to the effective techniques of supervision, moticationm delegation, monitoring and performance evaluation. Methods of staffing and physician recruitment, job descriptions and policy manuals will be developed. Various models of compensation will be examined.

Pharmacology and Addiction
Kansas City Kansas Community College
KACI#AC1101   Undergraduate   1 credits $108*
The purpose of this one credit hours course is to provide an overview of the primary processes involved in drug addiction. The focus will be on the terminology, methods of use, physiological effects of primary drugs of abuse including over the counter, prescription, and controlled substances.
* KS residents pay $40 per credit.

Practicum I in Occupational Health & Safety
Central Maine Technical College
CEMA#OHS200   Undergraduate   3 credits $512*
This course is designed to provide the student with field experience in an actual workplace under the supervision of a practicing occupational health and safety professional. Sites for this practical experience in the manufacturing, construction, insurance industries, consulting, or government agencies must be arranged prior to course registration. Special note: students choosing Practicums in Health Care Settings may have to meet the Immunization Requirements for Allied Health Students.
*Maine resident (and military) tuition: $269.

Practicum II in Occupational Health & Safety
Central Maine Technical College
CEMA#OHS210   Undergraduate   3 credits $512*
This course is designed to provide the student with additional field experience in the workplace under the continuing supervision of a practicing occupational health and safety professional. Special note: Students choosing Practicums in Health Care Settings may have to meet the Immunization Requirements for Allied Health Students.
*Maine resident (and military) tuition: $269.

Preclinical Dental Assisting
State University of New York
SUNY#DAS110   Undergraduate   4 credits $630*
This course will provide a broad background and application of basic dental terminology, four-handed dentistry, motion economy, medical emergencies, ethics, and jurisprudence. Preclinical practice will prepare the dental assisting student for clinical practice. Prerequisite: Must have CPR certification.
* NY residents tuition: $105 per credit.

Principles of Health
MiraCosta College
MIRA#HEAL101   Undergraduate   3 credits $357
A course about connections, the relationships between our individual lifestyles, the communities in which we live, and wellness. Further, since we do not live in a vacuum, we are citizens in a global community who are connected in a multitude of ways, many of which relate directly to our individual and collective wellness. The supports and barriers common to our society connect directly to our individual quality and quantity of life. While avoiding and preventing disease is critical to wellness, disease prevention is just one small part of the whole concept of wellness. Prerequisite: Mullen, K., McDermott, R., Gold, R., Belcastro, P. Connections for Health. Boston: WCB/McGraw-Hill. 1996.

Principles of Human Nutrition
Rio Salado College
RISA#FON241   Undergraduate   3 credits $186*
Scientific principles of human nutrition. Emphasis on nutrients, metabolism, and factors affecting utilization in the human body throughout the life cycle. Includes influence of food selection on health and evaluation of computerized dietary analysis. Prerequisites or Corequisites: One year high school chemistry with grade of "C" or better, or CHM130 and CHM130LL, or BIO100, or BIO181, or approval of instructor.
* AZ residents $37 per credit.

Reengineering Health Care Systems
Rochester Institute of Technology
ROCH#63579890   Undergraduate   4 credits $923
This course will introduce students to the concepts of reengineering as initiated in business and as currently being applied in the health care setting.

Research Methods in Healthcare
Dakota State University
DAKO#HIM350   Undergraduate   2 credits $298
An introduction to research methods in the healthcare industry that guides the student through the research process including developing problem statements, performing literature searches, evaluating and writing proposals and critiquing existing research articles. The course will also include an overview of existing statistical software applications used in research. Please check DSU's online catalog for prerequisite coursework information.

Research Problems in Health
Emporia State University
EMPO#PE868   Graduate   3 credits $315
A course designed to allow the graduate student to pursue an area of interest in health, physical education, recreation, or athletics. This course will result in an in-depth study or project that will be presented to the faculty. In addition, the project will result in some form of hard copy - bound paper, CD-ROM, Web Page, etc.

Science of Nutrition
University of Alaska - Fairbanks
ALFA#HLTH203   Undergraduate   3 credits $213
This is an introductory course in which the principles of nutrition and how they relate to the life cycle are studied. The effect this course has upon the student's thinking relative to nutrition and upon the student's dietary habits is an important outcome. An objective is improvement, if needed, in the student's nutritional status.

Seminar In Health Information Management
Dakota State University
DAKO#HIM498   Undergraduate   2 credits $298
Advanced research and presentation of an aspect of health information management.

Sports Physiology & Life Fitness
Rochester Institute of Technology
ROCH#69233190   Undergraduate   4 credits $923
Upon completion of this course, students will understand the biological composition of their bodies, how the musculoskeletal system functions, how energy is made and utilized during exercise.

Survey of Health Care Systems
Rochester Institute of Technology
ROCH#63531090 Undergraduate   4 credits $923
An overview of the current forces transforming health care, including physician practice and payment, etc...

The American Health Care System
University of Missouri
MOCE#HE210HM Undergraduate   3 credits $387
Students are provided with a basic understanding of the major components (financing, planning, and regulating) of the American health care system. Emphasis is on historical and current issues and their impact on the delivery system.

The Profession of Dietetics
Pennsylvania State University
PENN#DSM100 Undergraduate   1 credits $115
Introduction to the profession and exploration of the roles and responsibilities of dietetic professionals. Note: All students must be approved by a Dietetic program adviser.

Treating the Fearful Patient
Chemeketa Community College
CHEM#9435J Undergraduate   0 credits $40
This course is designed to teach dental personnel to assess and manage patients who experience dental fear. Includes techniques for alleviating and preventing patient anxiety.

Understanding Health Effects of Ionizing Radiation
Pennsylvania State University
PENN#NUCE497K Undergraduate   4 credits $460
(Course description not available at press time.) Note: 400-level courses are available only to students with junior or senior standing.

Vascular Access Devices
Kennesaw State University
KENN#FMV216A Undergraduate   3 credits $149
Because of the tremendous variety of vascular access devices available in clinical practice today, many healthcare practitioners are confused about how to choose the device most appropriate for each patient. Some would even question if a patient assessment falls within the scope of nursing practice. However, the nurse is the one routinely performing venipuncture and managing the infusion.

Weight Management
Chemeketa Community College
CHEM#PE185WABC Undergraduate   3 credits $153
A class to educate, support, and motivate individuals interested in managing their weight. Students will weigh-in once a week. Students will have theory, class discussion, and exercise management daily.

Women's Health
University of Massachusetts - Dartmouth
MADA#PSY490 Undergraduate   3 credits $408
Women's health is a timely and important topic. This course will focus on women's health issues, both physical and psychological. Topic areas will include those issues that affect women differentially, and course content will center on the unique contribution of gender to these biological and psychological concerns. The five topic areas that will be covered are breast cancer, HIV/AIDS, depression, trauma (domestic violence and sexual assault) and eating disorders.

Workplace Behavior in Health Care
Rio Salado College
RISA#HCC100AB Undergraduate   3 credits $186*
(Course description not available at press time.)
* AZ residents pay $37 per credit.

Worksite Evaluation
Central Maine Technical College
CEMA#OHS116 Undergraduate   3 credits $492*
This course covers methods of inspecting and evaluating health and safety hazards at a worksite including the analysis of specific job assignments. It also introduces the student to accident investigation techniques. The course will include hands-on worksite evaluation.
*Maine resident (and military) tuition: $249.

Languages

English

French

German

Italian

Latin

Other

Russian

Spanish

Academic Content via English
UCLA
UCLA#X325E Undergraduate 4.5 credits $460
Addresses the competencies needed by all content-area teachers of limited English proficient students. Provides strategies, techniques, and skills in teaching Specially Designed Academic Instruction in English (SDAIE). SDAIE is a method of teaching grade-level subject matter in and through English specifically designed for speakers of other languages. Participants develop materials related to their specific academic content areas.

Basic English
Barstow Community College
BARS#ENGL50 Undergraduate 3 credits $???
English composition with emphasis on paragraphing, the multi-paragraph essay, research skills. Designed to prepare students for English 1A or English 1A plus.

Basic English
Northwest College
NOCO#GE174 Undergraduate 5 credits $???
Students are provided with a thorough review of English grammar usage as well as an introduction to writing.

Beginning Ancient Greek I
University of Alaska - Fairbanks
ALFA#FL193A Undergraduate 3 credits $213
Study of ancient Greek language and culture through original Greek sources with emphasis on grammar and vocabulary building to competence and comprehension of texts.

Beginning Ancient Greek II
University of Alaska - Fairbanks
ALFA#FL193AA Undergraduate 3 credits $213
Continuation of the study of ancient Greek language and culture through original Greek sources with emphasis on grammar and vocabulary building to competence and comprehension of texts.

Beginning Finnish I
University of Minnesota
MINN#FIN1101 Undergraduate 5 credits $445
Teaches the beginnings of the Finnish language skills of listening, speaking, reading, and writing. Offers a two-tier approach to Finnish: communicative skills and the basics of vocabulary and grammar. Emphasizes social situations for which students learn useful, helpful phrases. Includes some composition. First in a series of three courses (FIN1101-1103) built around the new North American textbook, Mastering Finnish, which is accompanied by audiocassettes.

Beginning Finnish II
University of Minnesota
MINN#FIN1102 Undergraduate 3 credits $445
Continuation of FIN1101. Prerequisite: FIN1101 or equivalent.

Beginning Finnish III
University of Minnesota
MINN#FIN1103 Undergraduate 5 credits $445
Continuation of FIN1102. Prerequisite: FIN1102 or equivalent.

Beginning French I
University of Minnesota
MINN#FREN1101 Undergraduate 5 credits $445
Learn to understand and speak French while viewing 13 episodes of the video series French in Action, in which a young American man meets and interacts with a young French woman in Paris. Vignettes taken from French films, television, advertising, and cartoons. The audiotapes, texts, workbook, and study guide will help you learn authentic language for basic conversation, and familiarize you with French culture.

Beginning French II
University of Minnesota
MINN#FREN1102 Undergraduate 5 credits $445
Continuation of French 1101. Students view episodes 14 through 26 of French in Action. Prerequisite: FREN1101 or 1 year high school French.

Beginning French III
University of Minnesota
MINN#FREN1103 Undergraduate 5 credits $445
Continuation of French 1102. Students view episodes 27 through 38 of French in Action. Prerequisite: FREN1102 or 2 years high school French.

Beginning German I
University of Minnesota
MINN#GER1101 Undergraduate 5 credits $445
Introduction to reading through familiarity with "survival" situations; beginning listening with videos of everyday events; introduction to the frequently used constructions of German through a text and a computer tutorial on a 3.5-inch disk. Prerequisite: access to a Macintosh or an IBM/IBM-compatible computer with 256 K).

Beginning German II
University of Minnesota
MINN#GER1102 Undergraduate 5 credits $445
Continuation of GER1101. Building reading comprehension through expansion of topics related to travel and recent history; expanding listening comprehension with videos relating to broader topics; reviewing German constructions with a text and computer tutorial. Prerequisites: GER1101 or 1 year of high school German.

Beginning German III
University of Minnesota
MINN#GER1103 Undergraduate 5 credits $445
Continuation of GER1102. Pushing reading comprehension to the intermediate level with a work of popular fiction; intermediate listening comprehension practice with videos depicting contemporary German life; reviewing German constructions with a text and computer tutorial. Prerequisites: GER1102 or 2 years of high school German; access to a Macintosh or an IBM/IBM-compatible with 256 K.

Beginning Italian I
University of Minnesota
MINN#ITAL1101 Undergraduate   5 credits $445
This introductory course is designed to develop the language skills of listening, reading, writing, and speaking, and to introduce students to contemporary Italian culture and life. Students view seven episodes of the video series In Italiano, read its accompanying texts (a grammar textbook, a study guide, and an anthology of contemporary narrative), and listen to audiocassettes.

Beginning Italian II
University of Minnesota
MINN#ITAL1102 Undergraduate   5 credits $445
Continuation of Italian 1101. Prerequisite: ITAL1101 or equivalent.

Beginning Latin
University of Colorado
CUON#LATN1010 Undergraduate   5 credits $3255*
Introduces students to the basic grammar, syntax and vocabulary of Classical Latin. Designed for students with no previous knowledge of Latin, it is also useful for those whose Latin studies have been interrupted for more than one semester or who would like a good review of the basics.
* CO residents tuition: $136 per credit.

Beginning Latin I
University of Alaska - Fairbanks
ALFA#FL193B Undergraduate   3 credits $213
Introduction to ancient Latin language and Roman culture, development of competence through reading original authors with emphasis on vocabulary, recognition and correct use of grammar.

Beginning Latin I
University of Minnesota
MINN#LAT1101 Undergraduate   5 credits $445
Basic grammar and vocabulary, practice in reading and writing Latin, workbook exercises, easy Latin readings, and Roman legends in 38 Latin Stories.

Beginning Latin II
University of Alaska - Fairbanks
ALFA#FL193C Undergraduate   3 credits $213
Continuation of the introduction to ancient Latin language and Roman culture, development of competence through reading original authors with emphasis on vocabulary, recognition and correct use of grammar.

Beginning Latin II
University of Minnesota
MINN#LAT1102 Undergraduate   5 credits $445
Continuation of LAT1101. Similar in content and method, leading to connected reading in 38 Latin Stories. Prerequisite: LAT1101 or equivalent.

Beginning Norwegian I
University of Minnesota
MINN#NOR1101 Undergraduate   5 credits $445
An introduction to basic Norwegian grammar, pronunciation, sentence structure, reading, and writing. The emphasis in this course is placed on vocabulary and expressions used in everyday situations, while also providing a foundation for further study. The audiocassettes are at the Minnesota Book Center.

Beginning Norwegian II
University of Minnesota
MINN#NOR1102 Undergraduate   5 credits $445
A continuation of NOR1101. The audiocassettes are at the Minnesota Book Center. Prerequisite: NOR1101 or equivalent.

Beginning Norwegian III
University of Minnesota
MINN#NOR1103 Undergraduate   5 credits $445
A continuation of NOR1102 with emphasis on reading and writing skills. Prerequisite: NOR1102 or equivalent.

Beginning Russian I
University of Minnesota
MINN#RUSS1101 Undergraduate   5 credits $445
A multipurpose program of instruction in the fundamentals of the Russian language. Acquaints students with all four basic language skills: listening, reading, speaking, and writing.

Beginning Russian II
University of Minnesota
MINN#RUSS1102 Undergraduate   5 credits $445
Continuation of RUSS1101. Prerequisite: RUSS1101.

Beginning Russian III
University of Minnesota
MINN#RUSS1103 Undergraduate   5 credits $445
Continuation of RUSS1102. Prerequisite: RUSS1102.

Beginning Spanish I
University of Minnesota
MINN#SPAN1101 Undergraduate   5 credits $445
Fundamentals of Spanish. Students develop listening and speaking skills and learn about the cultures of Spain and Latin America by viewing 18 episodes of a Spanish soap opera, Destinos, reading its accompanying textbook and study guide, and listening to audiocassettes.

Beginning Spanish II
University of Minnesota
MINN#SPAN1102 Undergraduate   5 credits $445
Continuation of SPAN1101. Prerequisite: SPAN1101 or equivalent.

Beginning Spanish III
University of Minnesota
MINN#SPAN1103 Undergraduate   5 credits $445
Continuation of SPAN1102 Prerequisite: SPAN1102 or equivalent.

Beginning Swedish I
University of Minnesota
MINN#SWED1101 Undergraduate 5 credits $445
An introduction to written and spoken Swedish through basic grammar, workbook exercises, and easy composition. Vocabulary useful to everyday situations is covered.

Beginning Swedish II
University of Minnesota
MINN#SWED1102 Undergraduate 5 credits $445
Continued development of basic skills in reading, writing, and speaking. Exercises include grammar and oral assignments. Prerequisite: SWED1101.

Beginning Swedish III
University of Minnesota
MINN#SWED1103 Undergraduate 5 credits $445
A continuation of foundation skills in reading, writing, and listening. Prerequisite: SWED1102.

Communication for NonSpeakers
University of Washington
WASH#REHABC458 Undergraduate 3 qu. credits $222
Speech-language pathologists, therapists and educators who work with people with severe speech communication disorders learn practical solutions in augmentative and alternative communication (AAC) as part of a group. You will learn to identify candidates for AAC intervention and recognize obstacles to, participation, to identify the pros and cons of various technology approaches in AAC, and to connect via email and the World Wide Web to resources in AAC.

Elementary French I
University of Missouri
MOCE#LA1F Undergraduate 5 credits $645
This course gives an introduction to French grammar and composition; students practice hearing and speaking French through the use of audiocassette tapes.

Elementary French I
Western Illinois University
WEIL#LANF121 Undergraduate 4 credits $1060*
Learn French by seeing the language in action. This PBS telecourse combines video, audio, and print materials to provide a "planned immersion" course in French language and culture. Each of the half-hour video programs features an episode of an original romantic comedy entirely in French, followed by a cartoon, graphics, and film clips that use the same grammar and vocabulary.
* IL residents tuition: $88 per credit.

Elementary French II
University of Missouri
MOCE#LA2F Undergraduate 5 credits $645
This course is a continuation of French 1. Students practice hearing and speaking French through the use of audiocassette tapes. Perquisites: grade of C or better in French 1 or equivalent.

Elementary French II
Western Illinois University
WEIL#LANF122 Undergraduate 4 credits $1060*
Continuation of LANF121. Prerequisite: French 121 or 1 year of high school French.
* IL residents tuition: $88 per credit.

Elementary German I
University of Missouri
MOCE#LA1G Undergraduate 5 credits $645
This course covers the basics of speaking, reading, and writing German.

Elementary German II
University of Missouri
MOCE#LA2G Undergraduate 5 credits $645
This course is a continuation of German I. Perquisites: C or better in German 1 or equivalent.

Elementary German III
University of Missouri
MOCE#LA3G Undergraduate 3 credits $387
This course is a continuation of German II. Perquisites: German 2 or equivalent.

Elementary Latin I
University of Missouri
MOCE#LA1 Undergraduate 5 credits $645
This course covers the Latin language: forms, grammar, and syntax.

Elementary Russian I
University of Missouri
MOCE#LA1R Undergraduate 5 credits $645
This course covers the basics of speaking, reading, and writing Russian.

Elementary Spanish I
Cerro Coso Community College
CECO#SPAN1 Undergraduate 4 credits $460*
An introduction to the Spanish language. Basic grammar and vocabulary for speaking, reading, understanding and writing at the beginning level. The emphasis of the course is on communication and preparation for advanced reading and composition skills.
* California resident tuition: $13 per credit.

Elementary Spanish I
University of Missouri
MOCE#LA110S Undergraduate 4 credits $516
The goals of this course are to be able to speak and understand simple (spoken) Spanish, as well as to read and write simple prose.

Elementary Spanish I
University of Missouri
MOCE#LA1S Undergraduate 5 credits $645
This course gives an introduction to the Spanish language; students practice hearing and speaking Spanish through the use of audiocassette tapes.

Elementary Spanish I
Rio Salado College
RISA#SPA101 Undergraduate 4 credits $248*
Basic grammar, pronunciation and vocabulary of the Spanish language. Includes the study of the Spanish-speaking cultures. Practice of listening, speaking, reading, and writing skills.
* AZ residents $37 per credit.

Elementary Spanish I
Western Illinois University
WEIL#LANS121 Undergraduate 4 credits $1060*
Develop the four basic language skills--listening, speaking, reading, and writing. This PBS telecourse makes the Spanish language and culture come alive through video episodes of a mystery that help you develop basic language skills and an understanding of the gestures and cultural clues that enrich communication.
* IL residents tuition: $88 per credit.

Elementary Spanish II
Cerro Coso Community College
CECO#SPANC2 Undergraduate 4 credits $460*
A continuation of the basic grammar and vocabulary necessary for speaking, reading, understanding and writing Spanish. A continued emphasis on communicative skills. Some introduction to Latin American and Spanish culture is included. Prerequisite: SPANC1 with a grade of C or better, or appropriate placement on the college-level Spanish placement exam.
* CA residents pay $13 per credit.

Elementary Spanish II
Christopher Newport University
CHNE#SPAN102 Undergraduate 3 credits $993
An introduction to the Spanish language, with emphasis on reading, writing, speaking, and listening comprehension. Accompanying laboratory practice. One hour per week in the language laboratory is required. Prerequisite: SPAN101 or its equivalent or consent of instructor.

Elementary Spanish II
University of Missouri
MOCE#LA2S Undergraduate 5 credits $645
This course is a continuation of Spanish 1. Students practice hearing and speaking Spanish through the use of audiocassette tapes. Perquisites: grade of C or better in Spanish 1 or equivalent.

Elementary Spanish II
Rio Salado College
RISA#SPA102 Undergraduate 4 credits $248*
Continued study of grammar and vocabulary of the Spanish language and study of the Spanish-speaking cultures. Emphasis on speaking, reading, and writing skills. Prerequisites: SPA101 or departmental approval.
* AZ residents $37 per credit.

Elementary Spanish II
Western Illinois University
WEIL#LANS122 Undergraduate 4 credits $1060*
Continuation of LANS121. Prerequisite: Spanish 121 or 1 year of high school Spanish.
* IL residents tuition: $88 per credit.

Elementary Spanish III
University of Missouri
MOCE#LA3S Undergraduate 3 credits $387
This is a multi-skill course following Spanish II that highlights cultural/literary readings; it includes a grammar review and practice in the spoken language, as well as some practice in written expression. Perquisites: grade of C or better in Spanish 2 or equivalent.

English Grammar and Usage
UCLA
UCLA#X340G Undergraduate 2 credits $390
This course reviews the construction of standard English grammar and usage, exploring verb tenses; syntax; complete sentences; parallel construction; pronoun case, reference, and agreement; the use of modifiers; and some common idiomatic expressions. Instruction focuses on the grammar issues addressed in the GMAT examination.

English Grammar for ESL Teachers
New School for Social Research
NEWS#1092 Undergraduate 2 credits $1092
Permission required; call (212) 229-5372. This course is designed to improve understanding of English grammar in order to facilitate teaching the language.

English to Spanish Translation
New York University
NEYO#X278804 Undergraduate 5 credits $570
This course provides a survey of the reference materials, methods, and techniques of translation. Students are exposed to a wide range of texts and issues from a variety of fields so that they can become acquainted with the kinds of materials and problems that a translator actually encounters in professional life. The English to Spanish Translation Program is now offered to distance learning students. Students are admitted through the regular admissions exam (there is a $25 fee to take this exam by fax) and follow the standard curriculum, beginning with this course.

Foreign Language Learning on Net
The Heritage Institute
HEON#ED408O Undergraduate 3 qu. credits $215
Discover the global potential the Internet offers to increase motivation as well as help students enhance their foreign language skills. Learn successful Internet mining skills to find thousands of lesson plans to help you be successful in the classroom and motivate that "hard to reach" child. Navigate the World Wide Web and discover hundreds of pages filled with incredible information in the target language once only available within the boundaries of a foreign country.

France and the French-Speaking World
Pennsylvania State University
PENN#FR139 Undergraduate 3 credits $345
An introduction to the culture of France and its impact on the world.

Fundamentals of English
New School for Social Research
NEWS#1505 Undergraduate 0 credits $320
People who wish to improve their written English practice paragraph development and composition in a supportive atmosphere. The class studies effective sentence structure and explores different forms of the paragraph. Exercises are assigned weekly. This course is for native speakers only. Call (212) 229-5372 for suggested placement advising.

German Authors and/or Topics in Translation
University of Minnesota
MINN#GER3610 Undergraduate   4 credits $391
Through reading Böll's novels and short stories, students gain an understanding of the development of West German society since 1945. Students learn about postwar Germany through extensive study notes and some outside reading. Students also are asked to use media resources (films, magazines, videos, as available) to round out their knowledge of contemporary Germany. Students must have access to a large library to obtain the required texts.

Intensive Beginning Latin I
University of Missouri
MOCE#LA207L Undergraduate   3 credits $387
This course covers the Latin language: forms, grammar, and syntax.

Intensive Grammar Review
UCLA
UCLA#X401 Undergraduate   3.6 CEU $495
This online tutorial is intended for anyone who writes, edits, prepares final copy, or finds an interest in the structure and use of the English language. It presents the basic rules that apply in virtually every piece of writing as well as the fine points that occur infrequently but cause trouble when they do. Topics to be covered in the punctuation section include all the marks of punctuation, capitalization, numbers, abbreviations, plurals and possessives, and hyphens. In addition to the grammar and punctuation review, the course covers word usage, and spelling.

Intensive Grammar Review
UCLA
UCLA#X801 Undergraduate   1.1 CEU $315
This short online workshop succinctly explains basic sentence structure, the logic of rules of grammar, and the reasons for exceptions. It emphasizes the necessary skills to write and edit with accuracy. Topics include correct uses for punctuation and the elements of a sentence, as well as how to spot and correct such common-but serious-problems as run-on sentences, sentence fragments, dangling modifiers, and reference and agreement errors.

Intermediate Ancient Greek I
University of Alaska - Fairbanks
ALFA#FL293 Undergraduate   3 credits $213
Readings in great writers of the classical period of Ancient Greece. Authors such as Sophocles, Plato, Homer, Euripides, and Herodotus will be closely examined for understanding with excursions into grammar and vocabulary.

Intermediate Ancient Greek II
University of Alaska - Fairbanks
ALFA#FL293B Undergraduate   3 credits $213
Continuation of the readings in great writers of the classical period of Ancient Greece. Authors such as Sophocles, Plato, Homer, Euripides, and Herodotus will be closely examined for understanding with excursions into grammar and vocabulary.

Intermediate French I
Western Illinois University
WEIL#LANF223 Undergraduate   3 credits $795*
Continuation of LANF122. Prerequisite: French 122 or 2 years of high school French.
* IL residents tuition: $88 per credit.

Intermediate French II
Western Illinois University
WEIL#LANF224 Undergraduate   3 credits $795*
Continuation of LANF223. Prerequisite: French 223.
* IL residents tuition: $88 per credit.

Intermediate Latin I
University of Alaska - Fairbanks
ALFA#FL293C Undergraduate   3 credits $213
Study of great classical Roman prose writers and poets, including Cicero, Livy, Caesar, Vergil, Horace, Ovid, and Catullus. Emphasis will be on reading competence with minor note of vocabulary and grammar.

Intermediate Latin I
University of Colorado
CUON#LATN2010 Undergraduate   3 credits $1953*
Introduces students to the advanced grammar, vocabulary and stylistics of Republic prose authors via readings in Cicero or Caesar. Includes a review of basic grammar and an introduction to Latin prose composition. Emphasis on the historical, cultural, social and legal contexts of the authors and their works. Prerequisite: Latin 1020 or equivalent.
* CO residents tuition: $136 per credit.

Intermediate Latin II
University of Alaska - Fairbanks
ALFA#FL293D Undergraduate   3 credits $213
Continuation of the study of great classical Roman prose writers and poets, including Cicero, Livy, Caesar, Vergil, Horace, Ovid, and Catullus. Emphasis will be on reading competence with minor note of vocabulary and grammar.

Intermediate Norwegian I
University of Minnesota
MINN#NOR1104 Undergraduate   5 credits $445
Further development of reading, writing, listening, and speaking skills. Grammar review. Students will be exposed to a wide variety of sources, including newspaper and magazine articles, songs, folktales, short stories, poetry, travel brochures. Lessons center on specific aspects of Norwegian life and culture. Prerequisite: NOR1103 or equivalent The same audiocassettes are used for NOR1105 and 1106.

Intermediate Norwegian II (6307)
University of Minnesota
MINN#NOR1105 Undergraduate   5 credits $445
Continuation of NOR1104 with particular emphasis on reading, writing, and listening skills. Authentic Norwegian texts are made more accessible with prereading strategies and reading/comprehension tasks appropriate at this level. Prerequisite: NOR1104 or equivalent The same audiocassettes are used for NOR1104 and 1106.

Intermediate Norwegian III
University of Minnesota
MINN#NOR1106　Undergraduate　　　5 credits　　　$445

A continuation of NOR1105 that includes more advanced texts that center on social issues. Comprehension and expression of critical thought are promoted through reading and writing tasks. Pronunciation and grammar review. Advanced points of grammar. Prerequisite: NOR1105 or equivalent Uses the same audiocassettes as NOR1104 and 1105.

Intermediate Spanish I
University of Minnesota
MINN#SPAN1104　Undergraduate　　　5 credits　　　$445

Speaking and comprehension; development of reading and writing skills based on materials from Spain and Spanish America. Grammar review; composition; cultural aspects of the Spanish-speaking world. Prerequisite: SPAN1103 or equivalent.

Intermediate Spanish I
Rio Salado College
RISA#SPA201　Undergraduate　　　4 credits　　　$248*

Review of essential grammar of the Spanish language and study of the Spanish-speaking cultures and continued practice and development of reading, writing, and speaking skills. Emphasis on fluency and accuracy in spoken Spanish. Prerequisites: SPA102, two years of high school Spanish, or departmental approval.
* AZ residents pay $37 per credit.

Intermediate Spanish I
Western Illinois University
WEIL#LANS223　Undergraduate　　　3 credits　　　$795*

Continuation of LANS122. Prerequisite: Spanish 122 or 2 years of high school Spanish.
* IL residents tuition: $88 per credit.

Intermediate Spanish II
University of Minnesota
MINN#SPAN1105　Undergraduate　　　5 credits　　　$445

Continuation of SPAN1104. Prerequisite: SPAN1104 or equivalent.

Intermediate Spanish II
Rio Salado College
RISA#SPA202　Undergraduate　　　4 credits　　　$248*

Review of grammar, continued development of Spanish language skills with continued study of the Spanish-speaking cultures. Prerequisites: SPA201 or departmental approval.
* AZ residents pay $37 per credit.

Intermediate Spanish II
Western Illinois University
WEIL#LANS224　Undergraduate　　　3 credits　　　$795*

Continuation of LANS223. Prerequisite: Spanish 223.
* IL residents tuition: $88 per credit.

Intermediate Spanish III
University of Minnesota
MINN#SPAN1106　Undergraduate　　　5 credits　　　$445

Continuation of SPAN1105. Prerequisite: SPAN1105 or equivalent.

Intermediate Swedish I
University of Minnesota
MINN#SWED1104　Undergraduate　　　5 credits　　　$445

Further development of reading, writing, listening skills; grammar review; composition. Prerequisite: SWED1103.

Intermediate Swedish III
University of Minnesota
MINN#SWED1106　Undergraduate　　　5 credits　　　$445

Advanced texts focusing on four themes: Swedish history, Swedish culture, modern Sweden, and Swedish American immigration. Systematic review of grammar, as well as advanced points of grammar. Prerequisite: SWED1105.

Introduction to Language Study
State University of New York
SUNY#ENG201　Undergraduate　　　3 credits　　　$540*

An introductory course in the scientific study of human language. This course is designed to give you the basic tools for analyzing the components of language, covering basic phonetics and phonological analysis (the study of the sounds of language and how they are structured in particular languages), morphology (word formation), syntax (how words combine in larger units of discourse like sentences) and semantics (the study of linguistic meaning). We will also survey some of the major subdisciplines of modern linguistics.
* NY residents tuition: $90 per credit

Introduction to Linguistics
New School for Social Research
NEWS#1302　Undergraduate　　　3 credits　　　$1638*

This introductory course explores the nature and structure of human language, its biological and social aspects, and the ways it can change over time. Included are discussions about the structure of sounds, the forms of words and their meanings, and how sentences are formed. Attention is paid to how we acquire language, what happens to language when the brain is damaged, and how language can vary within a society.
* Non-credit option, tuition: $365.

Italian for Italian Speakers
New School for Social Research
NEWS#1133　Undergraduate　　　3 credits　　　$1638

Did you grow up speaking Italian without ever studying it? Have you lived in Italy and learned the language "the hard way," but not formally? This course is designed for students who speak Italian but would like to learn formal grammar and writing skills, broaden their vocabulary, and extend their knowledge of Italian culture.

Italian Syntax and Composition
State University of New York
SUNY#ITL412　Undergraduate　　　3 credits　　　$1038*

A course designed to acquaint students with the subtleties of Italian grammar and style. Extensive practice in composition and in translation from English to Italian. Prerequisite: For SB Students: ITL 311. For other students: proficiency at the fifth semester of college Italian.
* NY residents tuition: $137 per credit

Japanese Word Processing
Edmonds Community College
EDMO#OTA114 Undergraduate   5 credits $260
Basic word processing concepts and functions using the Japanese word processing program and a computer with a Japanese operating system. Includes converting copy from Romanji to Kana and Kanji. Designed for students with both Japanese and English elementary language skills. Keyboarding speed of 20 wpm is recommended.

Language and Composition
State University of New York
SUNY#ENGL101A Undergraduate   3 credits $1038*
An introduction to college writing, this course based on the assumption that critical thinking is the foundation of solid college level writing. One or more assignments incorporate research. Class methodology emphasizes writing as a process. Prerequisite: Grade of C or better in SKLS 088.
* NY residents tuition: $137 per credit

Language as a Listening Tool
New School for Social Research
NEWS#1627 Undergraduate   3 credits $1638*
This course teaches beginning writers of fiction or nonfiction how to use language to maximum advantage. The premise is that language is power. The course focuses on harnessing that power so that by the end of the term the students can write with clarity and impact and choose a form and style best suited to their message. All students are expected to submit manuscripts on a regular basis.
* Non-credit option, tuition: $365.

Language Development and Acquisition
UCLA
UCLA#X325C Undergraduate   3 credits $425
Provides the rationale for bilingual/English language acquisition and development programs. Covers historical and current theories of second language acquisition and models of language programs that have implications for second language development. Considers psychological factors affecting first- and second-language development.

Language Structure and Usage
UCLA
UCLA#X325D Undergraduate   3 credits $425
Covers the major theories and factors related to language structure and usage, as well as universals and differences, including those in the structure of English. Includes discussion of idioms and classroom applications of exercises. (Required course for TESOL, TEFL, and CLAD programs.)

Modern English Grammar
Western Illinois University
WEIL#ENG370 Undergraduate   3 credits $795*
Studies traditional English grammar as modified by the insights of descriptive linguistics and generative-transformational grammar. Required for English teacher certification.
* IL residents tuition: $88 per credit.

Pathophysiology
University of Iowa
IOWA#096118 Undergraduate   3 credits $240
This course examines the abnormal physiological health transitions which may be experienced by individuals over the lifespan and which have a well-documented physiological base. This knowledge builds upon information and concepts learned in each of the prerequisite courses and is necessary as one of the scientific bases for the practice of professional nursing. Emphasis will be placed on the transitions that occur in the human organism when ill, risk factors and contributing causes for these changes, and the methods used to correct or prevent these changes. Prerequisites: Physics 29:8, Chemistry 4:7 and 4:8, Biology 2:2.

Pratique de L'ecriture
State University of New York
SUNY#FRE312001 Undergraduate   3 credits $540*
Extensive writing in French on a wide range of topics explored through electronic resources, including online government documents, radio and television materials, and various other texts, both current and historical. Online discussions and written assignments submitted and evaluated in French. Emphasis on accuracy and clarity of expression; attention to various styles of writing (descriptive, expository, persuasive, narrative, etc.) Distance learning course open to on- and off- campus students. Prerequisites: FRE202, Intermediate French level. Basic skills in reading and writing French.
* NY residents tuition: $90 per credit

Reading & Writing-International Students
New York Institute of Technology
NYIT#EN1008 Undergraduate   3 credits $???
A course for international students whose English placement test reveals need for improved basic writing and reading skills. Students read and write various essays and practice prewriting, composing, revising and editing. The course will improve use of standard grammar and mechanics and develop comprehension strategies, vocabulary and study skills. Coursework includes a computer lab component. Prerequisite: English placement test.

Reading French
University of Minnesota
MINN#FREN0001 Undergraduate   0 credits $356
Fundamentals of grammar; reading of appropriate prose. Prepares for graduate reading examination in French. S/N grading only.

Reading Spanish
University of Minnesota
MINN#SPAN0221 Undergraduate   0 credits $356
Prepares students primarily for reading, especially general and technical nonliterary prose. The department will certify to the Graduate School a reading knowledge of Spanish on successful completion of the final examination.

Second Languages and Young Children
University of Minnesota
MINN#CI5620 Undergraduate   4 credits $400

Examines current approaches to teaching second languages to young children, with emphasis on innovative curricular models. Provides information about the way young children acquire language and the effects of bilingualism on child development, and presents rationales, advantages, and pedagogical theories of various program models, from full immersion to programs that emphasize cultural understanding. The video programs show visits to actual classrooms in action, bilingual and immigrant families, and interviews with a variety of outstanding specialists in the field.

Spanish Graduate Reading Course
New School for Social Research
NEWS#1253 Undergraduate   0 credits $385

This course is for graduate students preparing for the reading examination and for those who would like to read books and articles in Spanish. Included in the course are the essentials of Spanish grammar. Students are offered intensive practice in reading and translation and the selection of reading materials is geared to students' interests whenever possible. No previous knowledge of Spanish is required.

Teaching English Abroad
UCLA
UCLA#X325 Undergraduate   3 credits $425

The key difference between English as a Second Language (ESL) and English as a Foreign Language (EFL) is the societal setting in which the course is taught to non-English speakers. This course explores the role of the teacher in the EFL classroom: to provide extensive and effective opportunities in the minimum amount of time, develop reading and writing skills in English, and practice listening and speaking.

Teaching English Language Learners
UCLA
UCLA#X325B Undergraduate   3 credits $425

Provides the rationale and methodologies for teaching the basic skills of listening, speaking, reading, and writing to English language learners. Focuses on the major themes of current research that relate to the connections among the language arts. Emphasizes the development of a repertoire of strategies that promote academic and functional language opportunities for English language learners.

The English Language
University of Minnesota
MINN#ENGL3851 Undergraduate   4 credits $391

An introduction to the English language that examines grammatical structure (phonetics, phonology, morphology, syntax, semantics), language acquisition, historical change, regional variation, and other aspects of the social life of English. The course uses linguistic theory and emphasizes a descriptive approach to the subject matter.

The Origin of English Words
University of Minnesota
MINN#ENGL3860 Undergraduate   4 credits $391

An introduction to the origins of English words. Explains how the words of English emerged, clashed, combined, lost their initial freshness, and died, to give way to upstarts whose day will come.

The Structure of English Words
University of Oregon
OREG#LING150 Undergraduate   4 credits $374

In this course we will use linguistic principles to study English vocabulary. This involves studying the morphemes, or meaningful elements, in English words and examining how these elements combine to form words. We will also investigate the sounds of English and their pronunciation, and the historical development of English (both sound changes and meaning changes) and its relationship to other Indo-European languages.

Writing for Non-Natives
College of DuPage
DUPA#EN070 Undergraduate   3 qu. credits $90

Prepares students whose first language is not English for college-level writing. Intended for students who hold a high school certificate or its equivalent and have previously studied English in the United States or their native country. Recommended for students who have at least an advanced level of English.

Writing Spanish for Professionals
UCLA
UCLA#X400 Undergraduate   3 credits $450

Learn to compose letters, reports, descriptions, and summaries related to your professional needs in this ten week online course geared to those in business and education, as well as other fields. Provides theory and examples of how to write expository prose, narration, and argumentation, supplemented by writing samples, concepts, grammar review, technical vocabulary, and some of the Spanish resources available on the Internet.

Law

Business

Civil

Constitutional

Criminal Justice

General

International

Justice Administration

Legal Studies

Other

Tax

Administration of Correctional Institutions
Christopher Newport University
CHNE#GOVT345 Undergraduate   3 credits $993
An examination of the political, ideological, and organizational issues associated with crime control in a free society. Some emphasis is placed on issues of organizational effectiveness, community relations, and crime prevention strategies. Examination of policies designed to promote community support for crime prevention.

Administration of Justice
Rio Hondo College
RIHO#AJ101 Undergraduate   ?? credits $???
This is a comprehensive discourse on crime and its causes, including the history and philosophy of the Administration of Justice in America, the development of criminal justice, identification of the various subsystems, role expectations, and their interrelationships, theories of crime, punishment, adjudication, and rehabilitation and training for professionalism in the entire system. The basic course provides the student with an orientation to the criminal justice system.

Administration of Justice
Rio Hondo College
RIHO#AJ102 Undergraduate   ?? credits $???
This is an in-depth study of the legal responsibilities of the law enforcement and judicial segment of the administration of justice system which includes a past, present, and future analysis of the procedures of each subsystem within the administration of justice system from initial entry to final disposition, and the relationship each segment maintains with its system members.

Administration of Justice
Rio Hondo College
RIHO#AJ41 Undergraduate   ?? credits $???
This is a basic course designed to assist students in perfecting their writing and communication skills.

Administrative Law
Christopher Newport University
CHNE#GOVT367 Undergraduate   3 credits $993
An examination of judicial and non-judicial control of the administrative process, procedural due process and the right to an administrative hearing, rules and rule making, and procedures for obtaining judicial review.

Advanced Federal Income Taxation
Golden Gate University
GOLD#TA318 Graduate   3 credits $1404
Examines the basics of federal income taxation with emphasis on statutory materials; special attention to problems of individual taxpayers and specific rules regarding gross income, adjusted gross income, taxable income, deductions, exemptions and credits. You are required to take this course as one of the first two advanced graduate seminars in Taxation.

Advanced Federal Taxation
Strayer University
STRA#ACC220 Undergraduate   4.5 credits $665
Covers federal taxation as it relates to partnerships, corporations, estates, and gift taxes. Comprehensively covers the preparation of the partnership returns and related schedules, allocation of partnership taxable income and other deductions, credits, and applicable self-employment taxes. Comprehensively covers the preparation of the corporation return, loss carrybacks and carryforwards. Introduces the treatment of Sub-S corporations. Involves the Federal estates and gift tax filing process. Prerequisite: ACC215.

Advanced Income Tax Accounting
State University of New York
SUNY#ACC61135 Graduate   3 credits $1038*
This course will focus on the study of federal tax legislation and IRS regulation of corporations, partnerships, estates and trusts. Special attention is given to capital gains and losses, normal tax and surtax, income and deductions for domestic, international, and multinational corporations. Prerequisite: Income Tax I (ACC310) or equivalent.
* NY residents tuition: $137 per credit

Advanced Investigative Techniques
Rio Hondo College
RIHO#PAC4328 Undergraduate   0.5 credits $???
This course allows the individual student, investigator, to develop a course of study that they wish to take but is not offered.

Advanced Law
Bellevue University
BELL#MBA665 Graduate   3 credits $825
Emphasis on common law and its use in the day-to-day operations of business.

Advanced Officer Development
Rio Hondo College
RIHO#PAC43001 Undergraduate   0.5 credits $???
This course allows the individual student, law enforcement officer, to develop a course of study that they wish to take but is not offered.

Advanced Police Video/Photography
Rio Hondo College
RIHO#PAC4355 Undergraduate   0.5 credits $???
This course is designed to introduce the use of video/photography in recording the crime scene and evidence. Topics and activities include; the role of the photographer as a member of the team; techniques for recording evidence, photography under special conditions, and the application in a simulated crime scene.

Advanced Security Investigation
Rio Hondo College
RIHO#PAC4354 Undergraduate   0.5 credits $???
This course allows the individual student, security officer, to develop a course of study that they wish to take but is not offered.

American Constitutional Law
City University
CITY#PLS401 Undergraduate   5 qu. credits $785
A detailed examination of the most significant decisions of the United States Supreme Court and other federal courts dealing with a wide spectrum of constitutional issues. The topics of judicial power, federalism, separation of powers, the commerce power and the taxing power are emphasized. Coverage also includes the constitutional rights of criminal defendants and the freedoms of speech and religion. Prerequisite: Strongly recommended: SSC218 or equivalent.

American Constitutional Law I
Indiana University
INDI#Y304 Undergraduate   3 credits $268
Nature and function of law; selected Supreme Court decisions interpreting American constitutional system.

American Criminal Justice Systems
Brevard Community College
BREV#CCJ1020 Undergraduate   3 credits $435
Philosophical and historical background of criminal justice agencies; evaluating their purpose, functions, administration, and related programs.

American Juvenile Justice System
Indiana University
INDI#P375 Undergraduate   3 credits $268
Structure and operation of the juvenile justice system in the United States, past and present. Analysis of the duties and responsibilities of the police juvenile officer, the juvenile court judge, and the juvenile probation officer. Prerequisites: P290 and P291.

American Law
Western Illinois University
WEIL#HIS303 Undergraduate   3 credits $795*
American law does not exist in a vacuum. It is a mirror of American life, a reflection of the ever-changing needs and aspirations of our society. The course examines the evolution of American law through four epochs: the colonial period, the early republic, the post- Civil War years of urbanization and industrialization, and the twentieth-century's reform eras.
* IL residents tuition: $88 per credit.

Bankruptcy Law
City University
CITY#PL207 Undergraduate   5 qu. credits $785
The Federal Bankruptcy Act, proscribed procedures for debtors, creditors, trustees and attorneys, voluntary bankruptcy and wage earner plans, and legal services in bankruptcy proceedings.

Business Law
Eastern Oregon University
EAOR#BA254 Undergraduate   4 credits $320
This course studies the nature, origin, and philosophy of law and procedures. Study of law of contracts and sales.

Business Law
Edmonds Community College
EDMO#BUS240 Undergraduate   5 credits $260
This course is intended to enable the student to understand the fundamental concepts, structures and function of the American legal system as it relates to commercial and personal business activities. We will examine the role of law and legal process as it relates to our society and its effect on our individual daily existence. We will study the various sources of law, court systems, dispute resolution techniques, fundamental constitutional rights and guarantees, business torts, contracts, business organizations, consumer laws and the foundation and processes of legal reasoning.

Business Law
Marylhurst College
MARY#MGT515B Undergraduate   3 credits $651
A practical survey of the legal aspects of business relationships. Students will learn that successful management of business relationships rarely involves hiding behind clever legal strategies and that the benefits to be derived from pursuing even a strong legal case must be weighed against not only the risks and costs of litigation but also the resulting damage to such relationships.

Business Law and Ethics
City University
CITY#MLA412 Undergraduate   5 qu. credits $785
A survey of the concepts and principles affecting business organizations and commercial transactions, contracts and agency and employment relationships. Emphasis is given to the Uniform Commercial Code's provisions regarding sales, commercial paper and transactions involving security interests. The course also covers real property, personal property, bankruptcy, estates and trusts and environmental regulation.

Business Law I
Cerro Coso Community College
CECO#BSADC18A Undergraduate   3 credits $345*
Rules of law as related to business transactions. Origins of American legal system; definition and classifications of law; court systems and procedure; law of contracts; essentials of enforceable agreements, operation and discharge; law of agency and employer-employee; creation of relationship, rights and liabilities of parties and termination of relationship. The Law of Torts and the concept of negligence.
* CA residents pay $13 per credit.

Business Law I
Fayetteville Technical Community College
FAYE#BUS115 Undergraduate   3 credits $489*
This course introduces the ethics and legal framework of business. Emphasis is placed on contracts, negotiable instruments, Uniform Commercial Code, and the working of the court systems. Upon completion, students should be able to apply ethical issues and laws covered to selected business decision-making situations.
* North Carolina residents and non-resident US military personnel stationed within the state tuition: $60; NC senior citizens: free.

Business Law I
New Hampshire College
NEHA#ADB206 Undergraduate 3 credits $1656
The background, foundation and structure of the United States legal system is examined. In addition, the following topics are explored: torts, product liability, criminal law, contracts, sales.

Business Law I
New York Institute of Technology
NYIT#BUS3529 Undergraduate 3 credits $???
An introductory course with emphasis on the law of contracts and agency. Designed to give a basic understanding of the legal aspects of contractual obligations and agency relationships.

Business Law I
Waukesha County Technical College
WAUK#102160007 Undergraduate 3 credits $193
Surveys the legal and ethical environments of business. These environments include positive law, criminal and tort law, contracts, comparative law, agency, business formation, government regulation, property (including bailment), ethics and social responsibility and the international legal environment. This specific class section of Business Law I can be characterized as "non-traditional" in the sense that lecture and discussion and all class activities are carried out entirely "online".

Business Law I, Basic Principles
Lansing Community College
LANS#LEGL215 Undergraduate 3 credits $315
Covers fundamental principle of our law for business and non-business students. To Develop understanding of our legal system (Federal, state, and local), its purposes and importance to society. Course contents include study of the nature and sources of law, study of courts and court procedure, torts, crimes, contracts, no-fault auto insurance, landlord-tenant relations, personal property and bailments.

Business Law II
Christopher Newport University
CHNE#ACCT342 Undergraduate 3 credits $993
A study of the primary legal principles and their applicability to ordinary commercial transactions, with emphasis on contracts, legal forms of business enterprise, agencies, negotiable instruments, and labor and anti-trust legislation.

Business Law II
Fayetteville Technical Community College
FAYE#BUS116 Undergraduate 3 credits $489*
This course continues the study of ethics and business law. Emphasis is placed on bailments, sales, risk-bearing, forms of business ownership, and copyrights. Upon completion, students should be able to apply ethical issues and laws covered to selected business decision-making situations.
* North Carolina residents and non-resident US military personnel stationed within the state tuition: $60; NC senior citizens: free.

Business Law II
New Hampshire College
NEHA#ADB307 Undergraduate 3 credits $1656
The study begun in Business Law I continues as the following topics are explored: commercial paper, real and personal property, creditors' rights and bankruptcy, agency, business organizations, estate planning and government regulation of business. Prerequisite: ADB206.

Business Law II
New York Institute of Technology
NYIT#BUS3532 Undergraduate 3 credits $???
Law of property, bailments, secured transactions, bankruptcy, and related subjects. An analysis of the Uniform Commercial Code as it applies to the law of sales. Designed to give a basic understanding of legal problems in the marketing and transportation of goods. Prerequisite: BUS3529.

Business Law III
New York Institute of Technology
NYIT#BUS3533 Undergraduate 3 credits $???
A study of the forms of business organization with emphasis on the law of partnership and corporations. An analysis of the Uniform Commercial Code with respect to commercial paper. When appropriate, problems from professional examinations will be introduced. Prerequisite: BUS3532.

Civil Law and Procedure
Brevard Community College
BREV#PLA2203 Undergraduate 4 credits $575
A survey of the litigation process relating to the court system, with focus on the function of the law, the role of the attorney, and substantive law as well as procedural law in civil and criminal litigation. Students learn practical skills and concepts to effectively assist the lawyer in litigation procedures.

Civil Litigation
Front Range Community College
FRCC#PAR221 Undergraduate 3 credits $790
(Course description not available at press time.)

Civil procedure
City University
CITY#PL202 Undergraduate 5 qu. credits $785
The study of civil investigative techniques. The course will focus on proper pleading discovery and pre-trial motion practice, interrogatories, requests for admission and production, and deposition summaries.

Computer Applications For Paralegals
Front Range Community College
FRCC#PAR125 Undergraduate 3 credits $790
(Course description not available at press time.)

Contract Law
Northwest College
NOCO#BU111A Undergraduate 3 credits $???
Students will be introduced to the basic concepts of law and how it operates. Emphasis will be on contract law and the Uniform Commercial Code and its impact on business.

Contracts
Brevard Community College
BREV#PLA1423 Undergraduate   3 credits $485
This course introduces the student to laws involving contract information and terminology. This course, while part of the A.S. degree, Legal Assistant Program, is open to all and could be of special interest to those in business or planning to be there.

Controlled Substances-Drugs
Rio Hondo College
RIHO#PAC43012 Undergraduate   0.5 credits $???
This course is designed to introduce the student to the study of controlled substances, drug. Topics covered in the course will include; drugs and crimes, abuse trends, enforcement, and treatment and resistance programs.

Corrections and Criminal Justice
Indiana University
INDI#P303 Undergraduate   3 credits $268
Historical and comparative survey of prison confinement and the various alternatives within the scope of the criminal justice system's policies and methods of implementation.

Crime Scene Investigation
Rio Hondo College
RIHO#PAC4317 Undergraduate   0.5 credits $???
This course is designed to present a detailed study of various investigative and scientific aspects of crime scene investigation: including collection, preservation, identification, and packaging of evidence.

Criminal Behavior
City University
CITY#SOC302 Undergraduate   5 qu. credits $785
This course will cover five broad but related areas of study: 1) the origins of laws and definitions of criminal behavior, 2) techniques used to measure crime, 3) demographic characteristics of criminals and crime trends, 4) sociological theories of crime and 5) the effectiveness of the criminal justice system as an institution of social control.

Criminal Investigation
Fox Valley Technical College
FOVA#504-112 Undergraduate   3 credits $200
This class presents the study of fundamentals of criminal investigation, protection, search and recording of the crime scene, and principles involved in collection and preservation of physical evidence. Knowledge, use and function of scientific aids in crime detection, the importance of the criminal's "modus operandi," development of sources of information, and the place of the criminal informant in law enforcement are described. Criminal investigation procedures for various crimes are discussed.

Criminal Investigation
New York Institute of Technology
NYIT#BES2318 Undergraduate   3 credits $???
Introduction to criminal investigation in the field. Analysis and explanation of conduct at the crime scene, strategies for interviewing and interrogating witnesses and suspects, techniques of surveillance and preservation of evidence for presentation in court.

Criminal Justice
Auburn University
AUBU#PCJ36 Undergraduate   1.8 credits $76
This course focuses on the three major components of the American criminal justice system: the police, courts, and jails or prisons. Information concerning the legal process is also presented. In particular, the rights of individuals who come in contact with the criminal justice system are examined. Individuals who hope to become law enforcement officers, lawyers, or social workers will find this course to be useful as part of their pre-professional training.

Criminal Justice Policy
Rio Hondo College
RIHO#WWW3 Undergraduate   ?? credits $???
This course is designed to explore the use of the Internet in researching criminal law and justice issues. The focus of the class is on the Criminal Justice services on the Internet. The course addresses networks (e-mail, mailing, list, USNET groups) and information retrieval (Gopher, FTP, Telnet, and the World Wide Web).

Criminal Law
City University
CITY#PL208 Undergraduate   5 qu. credits $785
The course is divided into two parts. The first part will examine criminal procedure and attendant rights, the second part will examine substantive criminal law, including elements of crimes, defenses, and constitutional requirements for criminal statutes.

Criminal Law
Fox Valley Technical College
FOVA#504-115 Undergraduate   3 credits $200
This course covers the general principles of criminal law and elements of specific crimes in the resident state of the student. Students will learn to recognize when a crime has occurred under their state law and determine what charge is appropriate.

Criminal Law and Proceeding
New York Institute of Technology
NYIT#BES2301 Undergraduate   3 credits $???
A study of the elements of the Penal Law particularly relevant to police officers, including a review and analysis of major criminal offenses with consideration given to the available defenses and judicial interpretations.

Criminal Law, Litigation, Discovery
Brevard Community College
BREV#PLA1303 Undergraduate   3 credits $485
A study of the substantive crimes and their respective elements, criminal procedure and related constitutional considerations. Prerequisite: PLA1003.

Criminology
Brevard Community College
BREV#CCJ1010 Undergraduate   3 credits $435
In-depth examination of crime and criminality in our society. Criminology examines causes and types of crime and means by which our society copes with it. Domestic violence, murder, and several other areas of criminology are highlighted.

Criminology
University of Colorado-Boulder
COBO#SOCY4014   Undergraduate   3 credits $240
Scientifically studies criminal behavior with special attention given to development of criminal law and its use to define crime, the causes of law violation, and methods used to control criminal behavior.

Criminology
New York Institute of Technology
NYIT#BES2477   Undergraduate   3 credits $???
An examination of crime and theories of crime causation. Topics include: the white collar criminal, the professional criminal, and the structure of organized crime. The criminal justice process is analyzed, including the role of the police, the criminal courts, the probation officer, correctional services, and the re-entry of the offender into society. Prerequisites: BES2401 and BES2411.

Custodial Services in Corrections
Rio Hondo College
RIHO#PAC43031   Undergraduate   0.5 credits $???
This course is designed as a study of correctional issues. Topics include; special, alternatives, juvenile detention, and trends.

Customs Law Issues for Importers
Pace University
PACE#OL704   Undergraduate   3 credits $500
This study of U.S. Customs and trade laws and their application to imports focuses on structuring the import transaction to minimize customs duties. Emphasis will be on a detailed analysis of the Customs Valuation Statute including: various bases of appraisement, commissions, foreign offices, subsidiaries, interest charges, assists, CMT operations, royalties, defective goods, manufacturer's pricing, etc.

Domestic Violence
Rio Hondo College
RIHO#PAC43025A   Undergraduate   0.5 credits $???
This course is designed to present a study of Domestic Violence. Topics include; facts and myths about domestic violence, the relationship between violence and other aspects of our lives, the 'cycle of violence" and responses of various agencies, and the response of the criminal justice system.

Ethics in Law Enforcement
Rio Hondo College
RIHO#PAC43007   Undergraduate   0.5 credits $???
This course is designed to introduce the student to the study and application of ethics in decision making. Topics include the various theories of ethics, survey of personal applications, ethical decision making, and resources for exploring issues in ethics.

Evidence
National American University
NAAM#PL340D   Undergraduate   4.5 credits $900
This course introduces the student to the intriguing and complex rules that govern the admission of evidence at trial. Through study of the federal rules of evidence, supplemented by numerous examples, students acquire a fundamental knowledge and understanding of the purpose and procedures related to the law of evidence.

Family Law
City University
CITY#PL206   Undergraduate   5 qu. credits $785
A study of the legal issues and procedures involved in the dissolution of marriage, including legal separation and show-cause hearings, child custody, client interviews and pro-dissolution legal problems.

Federal Income Taxation I
City University
CITY#AC421   Undergraduate   5 qu. credits $785
The income tax returns of individuals; exemptions; basic concepts of gross income, exclusions, deductions and credits; analysis of property transactions; federal tax research; history of federal taxation. Recommended: college course in financial accounting.

Federal Income Taxation II
City University
CITY#AC422   Undergraduate   5 qu. credits $785
The income tax returns of corporations, partnerships, estates and trusts; federal estate and gift taxes; installment sales; cash basis and accrual basis taxation. Prerequisite: AC421 or its equivalent.

Federal Tax Procedure
Golden Gate University
GOLD#TA319   Graduate   3 credits $1404
Examines federal tax procedure at the administrative level and in litigation; organization of the I.R.S.; legal and practical aspects of Treasury regulations; administrative rulings; closing and compromise agreements; deficiency and jeopardy assessments; waivers; refund claims; mitigation of statute of limitations; pretrial, trial and appellate processes; tax collections; civil penalties; and the rights and privileges of the taxpayer. Prerequisite: TA318 and TA329.

Federal Taxation
Strayer University
STRA#ACC215   Undergraduate   4.5 credits $665
Includes a comprehensive study of the federal income tax structure and the practical application of income tax accounting to specific problems as related to individuals and proprietorships. Emphasizes the general filing status, includable and excludable income, analysis of the categories of itemized and other deductions, tax treatment of sales and exchange of property, available depreciation methods and recapture provisions. Introduces the alternative minimum tax on individuals, the earned income credit, child care credit, and credit for the elderly. Prerequisite: ACC105.

Federal Taxation I
New Hampshire College
NEHA#ACC415   Undergraduate   3 credits $1656
A detailed presentation is made of the theory and practice applicable in the preparation of federal income tax returns for corporations, partnerships, estates and trusts. Prerequisite: ACC 102.

Federal Taxation II
New Hampshire College
NEHA#ACC416 Undergraduate   3 credits $1656
A detailed presentation is made of the theory and practice applicable in the preparation of federal income tax returns for corporations, partnerships, estates and trusts. Prerequisite: ACC415.

Forensic Technology
New York Institute of Technology
NYIT#BES2317 Undergraduate   3 credits $???
An introduction to problems and techniques of scientific criminal investigation. Emphasis on values and assistance of various scientific aids to the investigator. Included are such topics as fingerprint identification, lie detector usage, hypnosis, blood typing, hair analysis, DNA typing and crime scene analysis.

Fundamentals of Law
State University of New York
SUNY#LAW101 Undergraduate   3 credits $630*
A study of how civil and criminal law governs society. Purchases, leases, contracts, divorces, environmental issues, and criminal offenses will be explored. Emphasis will be on development of those skills necessary to recognize and better deal with common legal problems to be confronted throughout adult life.
* NY residents tuition: $105 per credit.

Hazardous Materials Regs I - OSHA
Brevard Community College
BREV#EVS1640 Undergraduate   3 credits $435
This course will provide a historical overview of occupational, consume, and environmental health and safety issues. The student will be introduced to past and present governmental regulations which helped shape the work, consume, and environmental protection programs in the United States. Emphasis will be placed on identifying applicable occupational safety and health regulation, interpreting them and recommending compliance strategies.

Homicide Investigation
Rio Hondo College
RIHO#PAC4323 Undergraduate   0.5 credits $???
This course is designed to introduce you to homicide crime scene investigation. Topics and activities include; the role of the investigator, techniques for recording evidence, and the application of investigative techniques in a simulated crime scene. In addition, the course reviews much of the research that have been conducted into the crime of homicide and who commits them.

Individual Income Taxation
Eastern Oregon University
EAOR#BA333 Undergraduate   5 credits $400
A study of the Federal income tax system as it relates to the taxation of the individual, including a survey of the historical development of the tax law, tax research techniques, technical tax provision and tax planning. Prerequisite: BA213.

Intellectual Property Law
University of Colorado
CUON#ARTS3150 Undergraduate   3 credits $1953*
This is an interdisciplinary course which covers the fields of visual art, music, theater, dance and literature. The course is designed as an intensive, in-depth analysis of the laws protecting artistic creations. Copyright and trademark law are emphasized and privacy rights and free speech issues are also covered.
* CO residents tuition: $136 per credit.

International Law
City University
CITY#INT304 Undergraduate   5 qu. credits $785
An examination and analysis of the fundamental concepts of international law.

International Law
Salve Regina University
SALV#INR504 Grad   3 credits $???
Students examine the role international law plays in today's dynamic world. Topics include the ever-evolving concepts of legal order, jurisdiction, territoriality, nationality, extradition, and sovereignty over land, sea, and air space, as well as the broadening impact of human rights, statehood, diplomacy, treaties, and international economic regulations. Students examine, too, the ongoing quest to regulate the use of force, including United Nations peacekeeping operations.

Interview and Interrogation
Rio Hondo College
RIHO#PAC4320 Undergraduate   0.5 credits $???
This course is designed to focus on interviewing and confrontation-interrogation techniques. Students will become more skilled at retrieving information from witnesses and victims, including children.

Intro to Legal Studies
Front Range Community College
FRCC#PAR121 Undergraduate   3 credits $790
(Course description not available at press time.)

Introduction to Administration of Justice
Cerro Coso Community College
CECO#ADMJC50 Undergraduate   3 credits $345*
History and philosophy of administration of justice in America; recapitulation of the system; identification of sub-systems, role expectations, and interrelationships; theories of crime, punishment and rehabilitation; ethics, education and training for professionalism in the system.
* CA residents pay $13 per credit.

Introduction to Business Law
University of Missouri
MOCE#LE254 Undergraduate   3 credits $387
This course introduces the legal aspects of business as they relate to society - the legal system; constitutional, criminal, and torte law; contracts and sales law cases and problems; and administrative regulation of business and consumer issues. Perquisites: junior standing.

Introduction to Corrections
Rio Hondo College
RIHO#CORR101 Undergraduate   ?? credits $???
This course is designed to provide the student with an overview of the history and trends of adult and juvenile corrections including probation and parole. It will focus on the legal issues, specific laws and general operation of correctional institutions. The relationship between corrections and other components of the justice system will also be examined. The basic course provides the student with an orientation to the corrections system.

Introduction to Criminal Justice
University of Alabama
ALAB#CJ100 Undergraduate   3 credits $250
Criminal justice is not a separate body of theories such as one would find in the study of sociology or psychology. Rather, it is a problem area. In the study of criminal justice, one normally finds theories from psychology, sociology, political science, law, and other disciplines applied to the types of social problems that we define as within the realm of regulation by means of criminal sanctions.

Introduction to Criminal Justice
Fox Valley Technical College
FOVA#504-121 Undergraduate   3 credits $200
This course introduces the student to the study of crime and the administration of justice in the United States. The course focuses on the roles of police, prosecution, courts and corrections in dealing with people charged with the commission of crimes. Upon completion of this course, students will have a better understanding from an historical perspective of how the criminal justice process evolved and is carried out in the U.S. today.

Introduction to Criminal Justice
Indiana University
INDI#P100 Undergraduate   3 credits $268
Historical and philosophical background, structure, functions, and operation of the criminal justice system in the United States. Introduction to and principles of formal behavior control devices. Prerequisite: Freshman or sophomore standing.

Introduction to Criminal Justice
New York Institute of Technology
NYIT#BES2316 Undergraduate   3 credits $???
An introduction to the contemporary American criminal justice system. Discussion of the role of police, courts and prisons. Also examined is the juvenile justice system. General issues considered include: police discretion, due process and change as an integral element of the American criminal justice system.

Introduction to Criminal Justice I
University of Nevada-Reno
NERE#C101 Undergraduate   3 credits $210
This course is the first semester of a two semester introductory survey course on criminal justice, where we will be examining crime, the Criminal Justice system, the police, and the law. Generally, this course has two primary purposes. The first is to familiarize the student with standard concepts, definitions, systematic relationships, and key court cases which define the structure and process of American criminal justice (within the scope of the aforementioned areas). The second purpose of this course is to introduce the complex relationships between the social, economic, political and criminal justice arenas.

Introduction to Criminalistics
State University of New York
SUNY#CHEM131 Undergraduate   3 credits $735*
Criminalistics, also referred to as forensic science, is the application of science to the examination of physical evidence obtained in the investigation of a crime. This course emphasizes the scientific principles utilized by the evidence examiner, as well as the role of forensic science within the criminal justice system. Some of the topics to be covered include the crime scene, collection of physical evidence, fingerprints, firearms, and serology.
* NY residents tuition: $98 per credit.

Introduction to Criminology
University of Minnesota
MINN#SOC1300 Undergraduate   4 credits $356
Analysis of social justice with emphasis on the criminal justice system in the United States. Special attention to nature, extent of crime, and social factors related to criminal behavior.

Introduction to Criminology and Criminal Justice
University of Missouri
MOCE#CR010 Undergraduate   3 credits $387
This is a survey of the historical development and the current status of American criminal justice. Processes, institutions, and significant problems of the various components are analyzed.

Introduction to Paralegalism
State University of New York
SUNY#PARA101 Undergraduate   3 credits $1038*
This course will examine the role of paralegals in the legal system, with a particular emphasis on the New York State court system. The following topics will be studied: an overview of the courts system and administrative agencies; legal terminology; law office management; and ethical and professional practice standards.
* NY residents tuition: $137 per credit.

Introduction to Private Investigations
Fox Valley Technical College
FOVA#504-142 Undergraduate   3 credits $200
In this course, students learn about investigations in the private and corporate sectors. Topics include investigative techniques relating to open record laws and searches, techniques of surveillance, employee screening, evidence collection, interviewing techniques, sources of information, and computer and other technology used in research. Applicable state statutes of attendees will be researched, and licensing requirements discussed.

Introduction to the Criminal Justice System
Mercy College
MERC#CJ102 Undergraduate   3 credits $900
Students will be given an overview of the criminal justice system, commencing with a discussion of law, its sociology, its functions, etc; then moving on into the historical origins of the system, current practices, and prognosis for the future of the criminal justice system.

Investigative Report Writing
Rio Hondo College
RIHO#PAC43018 Undergraduate   0.5 credits $???
This course is designed as a study of Investigative Report Writing. Topics include; mechanics of writing, getting started, planning and self-editing. The course will expose the student to researching and writing a research paper.

Judicial Process
University of Minnesota
MINN#POL3309 Undergraduate   4 credits $391
The structure of the American judiciary; selection of judges; process of litigation; influences on judicial decisions; impact of and compliance with decisions; role of the Supreme Court in the American political system. Prerequisite: POL1001 or equivalent.

Justice Information & Statistics
Rio Hondo College
RIHO#WWW7 Undergraduate   ?? credits $???
This course is designed to introduce the you to SEARCH; The National Consortium for Justice Information and Statistics. This organization provides assistance to justice agencies in the areas of public domain software for justice related activities, online databases, publications, U.S. Supreme Court decisions, email and public forums on such topics as new technology, law and policy, training issues, and research and statistics. 1. Program Areas - Law and Policy, Systems and Technology. Research and Statistics. 2. Publications - Newsletters, Briefing Papers, and Training Bulletins.

Justice Information Sources Online
Rio Hondo College
RIHO#WWW1 Undergraduate   ?? credits $???
This course is designed to introduce the you to the Internet and World Wide Web (WWW) as a source of information and a research tool. The focus of the class is two fold: 1) Search tools - various search tools or engines that search for sites based on the criterion selected by the user. 2) Specific sites - various sites that are useful in researching specific areas of the criminal justice system.

Juvenile Justice
Rio Hondo College
RIHO#PAC4336 Undergraduate   0.5 credits $???
This course is examines the Juvenile Justice system. Topics include how juveniles enter into the system, what type of criminal activities they are involved in, and what prevention programs hold promise for the reduction of delinquency and crime.

Juvenile Justice and Delinquency
State University of New York
SUNY#264604 Undergraduate   4 credits $586*
Examine in depth the nature, causes and control of juvenile delinquency, one of the most significant social problems of our time. First examine the history of delinquency and juvenile justice in this country. Then investigate how delinquency is defined and measured, and compare and contrast these sources of information. Evaluate the major theories of the causes of delinquency, focusing on sociological theories. Concentrate on the relationship between social context and delinquency, specifically, gender, school, families, peers and drugs. Prerequisite: Introduction to Criminal Justice or equivalent.
* NY residents tuition: $515

Labor Law
Indiana University
INDI#L201 Undergraduate   3 credits $268
A survey of the law governing labor-management relations. Topics include the legal framework of collective bargaining, problems in the administration and enforcement of agreements, protection of individual employee rights.

Law for Business I
National American University
NAAM#LA216D Undergraduate   4.5 credits $900
This course examines numerous legal issues encountered in business today. Course content includes an overview of the American legal system, including civil and criminal law, torts, contracts, product liability, agency, employer liability, and selected areas of the Uniform Commercial Code.

Law of Evidence
New York Institute of Technology
NYIT#BES2300 Undergraduate   3 credits $???
An explanation and analysis of the rules of evidence. The course presents recent U.S. Supreme Court decisions concerning the rights of the citizen against unreasonable search and seizure, the rules of giving testimony, and the protecting and safeguarding of evidence. In addition to instruction in the law of evidence, time is devoted to visiting court to view demonstrations of proper and improper presentation of evidence. Prerequisite: BES2301 or Dean's approval.

Legal & Ethical Communication
City University
CITY#COM305 Undergraduate   5 qu. credits $785
This course examines the historical background and development of freedom of speech and freedom of the press. Discussion will focus on the limitations that have been imposed on those freedoms by statute, by common law, and by the courts' interpretation of constitutional law. The case study approach is used, with emphasis on the principles and philosophy that underlie the various topics comprising communications law and ethics. Prerequisite: Strongly recommended: BSK210 or its equivalent.

Legal Aspects in Construction
New Jersey Institute of Technology
NJIT#EM632 Undergraduate   3 credits $1143*
Introduction to the legal factors affecting construction activities. This course is part of the graduate certificate in Construction Management. Optional: 13 video lessons 180 minutes each.
* NJ residents: $184/semester hour.

Legal Aspects of Evidence
Rio Hondo College
RIHO#AJ104 Undergraduate   ?? credits $???
This course is a through study of the evidence rules with specific emphasis on the application of these rules in preparing and presenting evidence. This includes a discussion of the history and approach to the study of evidence; proof by evidence by way of witness testimony, documents, and real evidence; and exclusion of evidence on constitutional grounds. For a better understanding of the evidence rules judicial decisions are cited, and students are required to brief cases.

Legal Environment of Business
Pennsylvania State University
PENN#BLAW243 Undergraduate   3 credits $345
Social control through law: courts, basic policies underlying individual and contractual rights in everyday society. Prerequisite: third-semester standing.

Legal Issues in the Workplace
City University
CITY#BSC403 Undergraduate   5 qu. credits $785
A survey of the crucial legal concepts and principles which impact business organizations. Topics studied include: the rules which influence planning decisions and commercial transactions; rights of employers and employees; and the impact of unions on an organization.

Legal Research
Brevard Community College
BREV#PLA1104 Undergraduate   3 credits $435
This course provides the students with knowledge of basic legal research tools and methods necessary to research any legal issues.

Legal Research
State University of New York
SUNY#PAL11271 Undergraduate   3 credits $1038*
This course is designed to equip students with the skills necessary to accurately and efficiently research virtually any topic in the law. In addition to providing a background for understanding the tools used, students are taught the fundamental techniques of how to find applicable legal principles and authority among primary and secondary sources of law. Methods for updating the law, through the use of Shepard's Citations and other tools, are presented so that the legal research product will be accurate and timely. Prerequisite: Survey of American Law.
* NY residents tuition: $137 per credit.

Legal System & Legal Assistantship
Brevard Community College
BREV#PLA1003 Undergraduate   3 credits $485
A study of the American Court system, and the roles of judges, lawyers, and legal assistants within that legal system. The course will also survey the emergence of the paralegal/legal assistant as a new career. Included will be a look at employment and career opportunities for the future.

Legal Terminology
Brevard Community College
BREV#OST1435 Undergraduate   3 credits $435
This course covers common legal terminology and vocabulary drawn from general principles of law.

Legal Update - Court Decisions
Rio Hondo College
RIHO#PAC43008 Undergraduate   0.5 credits $???
This course is designed to explore the Bill of Rights and the decisions of the US Supreme Court. The course will focus on an overview of the Bill of Rights, 4th Amendment and Search and Seizure, 14th Amendment and Due Process, and the Miranda Decision.

Legal Writing and Research
City University
CITY#PL204 Undergraduate   5 qu. credits $785
The foundations of legal research. The course emphasizes the function and uses of the law library, the fundamentals of legal writing, computer research, and the abstracting and briefing of cases.

Litigation/Civil Procedure
State University of New York
SUNY#PARA205 Undergraduate   3 credits $1038*
This course is designed to have the upper level paralegal student develop an understanding of the basic concepts, rules and principles as well as some of the basic practical applications that form the foundation of civil procedure and practice. This background is deemed a fundamental part of the paralegal course of study. Topics covered include terminology, courts, statutes of limitations, jurisdiction, venue, parties, pleadings, motions, judgements, remedies, discovery, pre-trial procedures, trial, judgement, enforcement, appeals, special proceedings, etc. Prerequisite: Grade C or better in Business Communications, Introduction to Paralegalism and Legal Research and Drafting.
* NY residents tuition: $137 per credit.

Management of Criminal Justice
Bellevue University
BELL#CJAC303 Undergraduate   4 credits $1000
Presents approaches to management to include leadership styles and key principles of management.

Management of Criminal Justice
Bellevue University
BELL#CJAC420 Undergraduate   3 credits $750
Examines facility and resource requirements for law enforcement, court systems and correctional functions of criminal justice. Discusses principles of resource management and forecasting.

Mass Media Law & Regulation
University of Alaska - Fairbanks
ALFA#JB413 Undergraduate   3 credits $237
Common law, statutory law, and administrative law that affects the mass media, including libel, copyright, access to the media, constitutional problems, privacy, shield laws, and broadcast regulations. Prerequisite: JB301 or permission of instructor.

Morality and the Law
City University
CITY#PHI405 Undergraduate   5 qu. credits $785
An overview of the historical and cultural background of legal ideas and regulations for understanding the formal, complex rules of human interaction and their impacts. Specific cases are related to legal philosophies and to contemporary decisions. Prerequisite: Strongly recommended: HUM200 or its equivalent.

Objects as Property
George Mason University
GEMA#LRNG731 Graduate   3 credits $851
This course explores the practical, theoretical, economic, and paradigmatic implications of object technology on the building blocks of the software developer's craft and trade, with a special emphasis on ownership paradoxes posed by objects made of bits. This is a chance to anticipate the challenges that we face as the global economy leaps headlong into an information age, an age where property is increasingly composed of bits instead of the atoms that commerce has been concerned with since antiquity.

Occupational Health and Safety
Indiana University
INDI#L240 Undergraduate   3 credits $268
Elements and issues of occupational health and safety. Emphasis is on the union's role in the implementation of workplace health and safety programs, worker and union rights, hazard recognition techniques, and negotiated and statutory remedies--in particular the Occupational Safety and Health Act (OSHA) of 1970.

Office of Justice Programs
Rio Hondo College
RIHO#WWW2 Undergraduate   ?? credits $???
This course is designed to introduce the you to the Office of Justice programs resources on the Internet and World Wide Web; Bureau of Justice Assistance (BJA), Bureau of Justice Statistics (BJS), National Institute of Justice (NIJ), Office of Juvenile Justice and Delinquency Prevention (OJJDP), and the Office for Victims of Crimes (OVC).

Overview of Criminal Justice System
Bellevue University
BELL#CJAC302 Undergraduate   3 credits $750
Provides a common foundation for the entire criminal justice administration course. Presents unique system terminology, subsystem processes and relationships, and application of theory. Looks at successes and failures of the criminal justice system.

Patrol Function
New York Institute of Technology
NYIT#BES2310 Undergraduate   3 credits $???
A course devoted to an analysis of the objectives and functions of the uniformed police. Emphasis is placed on detailed examination of many typical patrol problems and consideration of both the sociological and psychological factors which facilitate or impede effective performance.

Personal Injury Litigation and Torts
City University
CITY#PL201 Undergraduate   5 qu. credits $785
The study of torts, including intentional torts, negligence and professional negligence. Personal injury litigation practices will be emphasized.

Philosophy of Law
Western Illinois University
WEIL#PHI420 Undergraduate   3 credits $795*
Examines the philosophical problems raised by law including the nature and aims of law, the relation of law and morality, the rationale of legal responsibility and punishment, and legal obligation and the rule of law. Prerequisite: one philosophy course or permission of instructor.
* IL residents tuition: $88 per credit.

Police & Society
University of Central Florida
FLCE#CCJ4105 Graduate   3 credits $1305*
This course will examine a collection of readings on policing: what it means, what can it mean, where it has been, where it is, and where it is going. The second is a vision of students: what do you need to learn, what can you learn, and how should it be taught. This course will approach such topics as: the images and expectations of police, origins and comparisons of police, the police and serious crime, policing in everyday life, police discretion, the moral hazards of policing, and future prospects for policing.
* FL residents pay $129 per credit.

Police Administration
New York Institute of Technology
NYIT#BES2305 Undergraduate   3 credits $???
An introduction to the organization and structure of a police department. Topics include an overview of the police departments, an analysis of the police function, tables of organization, chains of command and lines of authority, division of labor, and the informal police organization. Attention centers on typical problems of police administration and the coordination of police services. Prerequisites: Dean's approval.

Police and Community Relations
New York Institute of Technology
NYIT#BES2320 Undergraduate   3 credits $???
This course analyzes the complex relationship between police and community, community attitudes toward police, the efforts of the police organization to create a more favorable public image, the emergence of a civil rights and civil rights and civil liberties movement, and the contribution of the individual police officer to police-community relations.

Practical Law
University of Minnesota
MINN#GC1534 Undergraduate   4 credits $356
Designed to acquaint students with common legal problems. The topics examined include: definition and sources of law, formation and discharge of contracts, torts (personal injury/property damage), criminal law, bailments, nature and classification of real and personal property, joint ownership and tenancy.

Probate Law
City University
CITY#PL205 Undergraduate   5 qu. credits $785
An examination of the jurisdiction of probate courts, probate administration, the forms of wills and trusts, and applicable legal and equitable principles.

Probation and Parole
New York Institute of Technology
NYIT#BES2350 Undergraduate   3 credits $???
An examination of organization and management in probation and parole systems. Topics include: distinctions between probation and parole in terms of organizational function and types of clients served.; client relationships and interactions with other social control agencies; case loads, case work methods, and case supervision; problems in pre-sentence investigation; and job requirements and performance standards for probation and parole officers with particular emphasis on recruitment, training, and assignment. Prerequisites: BES2401, BES2411.

Property Law
Brevard Community College
BREV#PLA1503 Undergraduate   3 credits $485
A survey course introduces students to real estate transactions and terminology. Prerequisite: PLA1003.

Real Estate Law
University of Alaska - Fairbanks
ALFA#ABUS223 Undergraduate   3 credits $213
A practical course surveying the various kinds of deeds and conveyances, mortgages, liens, rentals, appraisals, and other transactions in the field of real estate and the law.

Real Estate Law
City University
CITY#PL209 Undergraduate   5 qu. credits $785
An examination of the legal principles controlling real estate transactions; the acquisition and sale of property, lease and rental agreements, escrow, landlord-tenant relationships, title searches, deed and closings.

Real Estate Law
Waukesha County Technical College
WAUK#194182003 Undergraduate   3 credits $193
(Course description not available at press time.)

Remote Sensing Policy & Law
University of North Dakota
NODA#SPST575 Graduate   3 credits $816*
This course focuses on the evolving laws, policies, and institutions that have long-term ramifications for Earth observations. Some topics addressed are the United Nations Principles on Remote Sensing; the United Kingdom's 1984 National Remote Sensing Policy; the Montreal Protocol; and, the U.S. Land Remote Sensing Policy Act of 1992. Ground segment institutions considered are the Landsat Ground Stations Operations Working Group and the Global Land 1-KM AVHRR Project.
* ND residents, $102 per credit; may also be reduced for residents of adjoining states and provinces.

Research For Paralegals
Front Range Community College
FRCC#PAR124 Undergraduate   3 credits $790
(Course description not available at press time.)

Sex Discrimination and the Law
Indiana University
INDI#Y200A Undergraduate   3 credits $268
An examination of the many ways the law affects women and the advantages and disadvantages of trying to use the law to effect social change. Not a specialized law course but does analyze some law-related articles and legal cases.

Sociology and Law
California State University - San Marcos
CASA#SOC313B Undergraduate   3 credits $315
The focus of the course is to explore the origin and development of legal norms in various social settings. We will employ different perspectives to assess the interactions between law and society, such as through morality, jurisprudence and sociology. We will pay attention to how law evolves as a result of social change and how different legal systems are used as means to accomplish certain political and economical goals. The course, however, emphasizes the social construction of law and many of its intended and unintended consequences.

Special Problems in Criminal Justice
Bellevue University
BELL#CJAC450 Undergraduate   3 credits $750
Analyzes professional project research in progress and allows for fulfillment of project objective. Students will gain instruction in professional presentations, present their professional project and discuss current criminal justice topics.

Special Topics in Criminal Justice
Bellevue University
BELL#CJAC440 Undergraduate   3 credits $750
Presents students with the opportunity to discuss criminal justice research topics in an open forum. Prevention, control and investigation; Detention and corrections; Adjudication and the Courts.

Stress and the Peace Officer
Rio Hondo College
RIHO#PAC4343 Undergraduate   0.5 credits $???
This course is designed to introduce the student to issues related to stress: an overview, personal assessment, burnout, and coping techniques. Note - no exercise or health program should be started without consulting a physician. Seek professional health for mental problems.

Survey of Law Enforcement
Auburn University
AUBU#CJ260 Undergraduate   3 credits $126
Introduction to the philosophical and historical backgrounds; agencies and processes; purposes and functions; administration and technical problems; career orientation. More specifically, this course provides the opportunity for a student to become informed about the wide areas of activity which today's law enforcement official encounters as a public servant.

Tax Characterization
Golden Gate University
GOLD#TA330 Graduate   3 credits $1404

Analyzes federal income taxation of capital assets, including definition and mechanics of capital transactions; nonrecognition property transactions, including I.R.C. Sections 1031, 1033 and 1034; examination of the at risk and passive loss rules.

Tax Research and Decision Making
Golden Gate University
GOLD#TA329 Graduate   3 credits $1404

Examines the primary sources of income tax law; the I.R.C. and administrative and judicial interpretations. The research process will be analyzed, using both paper products as well as electronic resources. Practical written and computerized assignments will be completed using research tools to locate, understand and interpret primary source materials. You are required to take this course as one of the first two Advanced Program seminars in Taxation.

Tax Research and Planning
Strayer University
STRA#ACC565 Undergraduate   4.5 credits $665

Provides a basis for examining additional, more complex topics in corporate and partnership taxation. Additional topics such as estate and gift taxes, fiduciary accounting, tax-exempt entities and qualified and nonqualified plans are discussed. Ethics, research and tax planning are an integral part of the course. Prerequisite: ACC215 or equivalent.

Tax Timing
Golden Gate University
GOLD#TA338 Graduate   3 credits $1404

Examines issues related to the allocation of items of income and deduction to the proper taxable year, including adoption of tax year end; definition of method of accounting; the annual accounting concept; cash, accrual and installment methods of accounting; time value of money; and the Uniform Capitalization Rules. Prerequisite: TA318 and TA329.

Torts
Brevard Community College
BREV#PLA2273 Undergraduate   3 credits $435

An introduction to the rules governing situations in which a person has injured or caused harm to another person. Students will learn the specific laws that state when an injured person is entitled to get money as compensation from the person who has caused harm or injury.

US Constitutional Civil Liberties
City University
CITY#PLS402 Undergraduate   5 qu. credits $785

A detailed examination of the major civil rights and liberties guaranteed by the United States Constitution. Leading judicial decisions are studied in their overall political/social context. A broad spectrum of civil liberties are examined, including the right to vote, religious liberty, freedoms of speech, expression and assembly, civil rights, and the rights to political participation, privacy and reproduction.

Victimology
Rio Hondo College
RIHO#PAC43004 Undergraduate   0.5 credits $???

This course is designed as a study of "victims." Topics include; understanding the consequences, the reaction to being a victim, assistance programs, and the impact. This course uses online resources for instruction.

Wills, Trusts, Estates & Probate
Brevard Community College
BREV#PLA2604 Undergraduate   3 credits $485

Presents a survey of estate planning and administration including preparation of wills, trusts, probate forms and guardianship procedures.

Other

Home and gardening

Journalism

Municipal

Other

Sports and Recreation

Telecommunications

Advanced Study in Research Methods
The Graduate School of America
TGSA#RM502W Graduate   4 credits $795
In this course, you will gain an understanding of the principles according to which you choose a specific method of research to use in your master's thesis or doctoral dissertation. The method you will select should be both appropriate to the research problem you intend to explore and possible to accomplish within your resources and time schedule.

An Introduction to Culinary History
New School for Social Research
NEWS#3872 Undergraduate   3 credits $1638*
An overview of Western culinary history, from antiquity and the civilizations of the Mediterranean Basin through the Renaissance in Europe and the confluence of New World and Old World foods to the culinary multiculturalism and global cuisine of today. Presentations are varied and include lectures, tastings, guest speakers, and discussions of readings drawn from the works of writers who have pioneered the field.
* Non-credit option, tuition: $365.

Applying Telecommunications
University of Alaska - Fairbanks
ALFA#ED593C Undergraduate   1 credits $100
Design and implementation of an approved project using telecommunications in the classroom or work place, or an in-depth research paper. Prerequisite: ED593 or permission of instructor.

Basic Home Horticulture
University of Missouri
MOCE#HO25 Undergraduate   3 credits $387
This course includes discussions of and scientific rationale for current cultural practices for growing home horticultural plants.

Broadcast Journalism
State University of New York
SUNY#BRC225 Undergraduate   3 credits $1038*
Analysis of network and local news operations. Emphasis on social issues and their implications for the broadcast equipment.
* NY residents tuition: $137 per credit

Broadcasting and Society
Western Illinois University
WEIL#COM323 Undergraduate   3 credits $795*
This two-part course introduces you to the broadcast industry in America, including business practices, history, and regulation. The course also surveys the social impact of the broadcast media. Topics covered include broadcast journalism, violence on television, and the stereotyped portrayal of characters on television.
* IL residents tuition: $88 per credit.

Broadcasting Management and Programming
Lake Superior College
LASU#BDCT1670 Undergraduate   2 credits $140
Who makes the programming decisions at radio and TV stations and what factors do they consider? Why do so many TV stations look alike - and so many radio stations sound alike - all over the country? This course provides the answers. It is designed for both serious mass communication students or just for those who wish to better understand the electronic media. Previous students say they never watch or listen to radio/TV the same way again.

Coaching Theory and Techniques
State University of New York
SUNY#PPE209 Undergraduate   3 credits $630*
The course is designed to examine theories and techniques in coaching through developing information, organization and management skills. Development of technical information, safety aspects and human relationships will be studied. The practicum experience brings the student to an on site awareness and participation. This course satisfies the state guidelines for elementary and secondary coaching certification.
* NY residents tuition: $105 per credit.

Communications I
Brevard Community College
BREV#ENC1101 Undergraduate   3 credits $435
The first of two writing courses which teach principles of pre-writing, organizing, revising, and editing essays. Includes basic research and documentation methods.

Communications II
Brevard Community College
BREV#ENC1102 Undergraduate   3 credits $485
A continuation of ENC 1101 with emphasis on writing about literature using different rhetorical strategies. Selections from the areas of the short story, essay, novel, poetry, or drama provide the basis for advanced essay writing, research, and practice in literary analysis.

Communications III
Strayer University
STRA#ENG310B Undergraduate   4.5 credits $665
Covers the principles of composition through essays and presents methods for compiling, writing, and documenting a research paper. The course enhances oral as well as written communication skills. Prerequisite: ENG105.

Communications III
Strayer University
STRA#ENG320 Undergraduate   4.5 credits $665
Covers the principles of composition through essays and presents methods for compiling, writing, and documenting a research paper. The course enhances oral as well as written communication skills. Prerequisite: ENG105 or ENG106.

Computer Applications in Telecommunications
State University of New York
SUNY#01920588R Undergraduate   3 credits $675*
An introductory course in the basic computer orientation and implementation of hardware and software applications in telecommunications. Students will use various software packages to create documents, spreadsheets, graphs, databases, and presentations. The students will utilize this knowledge to solve problems and transfer information via electronic medium. Lectures, interactive learning, demonstrations will be employed.
* NY residents tuition: $98 per credit.

Digital Electronics For Telecommunications
State University of New York
SUNY#01915588R   Undergraduate   4 credits $900*
This course will prepare students in digital electronics with topics related to number systems and codes, logic functions, and Boolean algebra. IC building blocks are used in applications ranging from logic gates to flip-flops, counters, registers, and arithmetic circuits. Computer simulation of digital circuits will be used to verify actual hardware setups. Prerequisites: Telecommunications Electronics I and Mathematical Applications II.
* NY residents tuition: $98 per credit.

Digital Telecommunications Networks
University of Denver, University College
DEUC#TELE4846   Undergraduate   3 qtr. hrs. $885
This course will focus on the T-1 bit stream and associated network components, including channel banks, DSU/CSUs and intelligent multiplexors. DS-1 framing, formatting, signaling, and line coding will be fully explored. Digital voice and data applications will be discussed. The use of T-1 for access to packet and switched services such as Frame Relay and ISDN will be introduced. The student will gain an in-depth knowledge of T-1 communications principles and what features to look for from vendors and carriers. (Prerequisite: Computer Networks I or Telephony I.)

Directed Study
Humboldt State University
HUMB#NRPI318   Undergraduate   4 credits $500
This course will be a correspondence practicum that provides a bridge between course work of NRPI x218 and the field trip of NRPI x418. The practicum will involve each student in a special ecological tourism study project. The instructor will provide ongoing direction, feedback and support for the students while they are developing their projects. Instructor contact may involve telephone, FAX, personal meetings, mail, E-mail and telecommunication technology thereby enabling students considerable scheduling flexibility.

Directed Study Project
Strayer University
STRA#ACC590   Undergraduate   4.5 credits $665
Enables student to complete a research project in the field of major concentration. The research project will be monitored by a supervising faculty member and must be defended by the student in an oral examination. The oral defense may be conducted in a conference-style meeting of student, instructor, and second reader or technical advisor. A second type of defense allows students to present a synopsis of their projects during one of the last two scheduled class meetings. Students are encouraged to discuss the project with an instructor or academic officer early in their program.

Directed Study Project
Strayer University
STRA#BUS590   Undergraduate   4.5 credits $665
Enables the student to complete a research project in his or her field of major concentration. The research project will be monitored by a supervising faculty member and must be defended by the student in an oral examination. The oral defense may be conducted in a conference-style meeting of student, instructor and second reader or technical advisor. A second type of defense allows students to present a synopsis of their project during one of the last two scheduled class meetings.

Dynamics of Outdoor Recreation
Indiana University
INDI#R271   Undergraduate   3 credits $268
Philosophical orientation to the field of outdoor recreation; camping, outdoor/environmental education, and natural resource management, with emphasis on programs, trends, resources, and values. Prerequisite: R160.

Electronics for Telecommunications
University of Denver, University College
DEUC#TELE4800   Undergraduate   3 qtr. hrs. $885
This course and its sequel (TELE 4801-Principles of Electronic Communications), provide a survey of the technical basis of modern telecommunications systems. An understanding of these basic technical fundamentals is vital to the success of the modern telecommunications manager. The course emphasis is on applications of basic electronic knowledge for the telecommunications professional, and is intended for those new to electronics and circuits. (Prerequisite: Mathematics Essentials for Information Technology.)

Environmental and Societal Issues in Telecommunications
The Graduate School of America
TGSA#OM892W   Graduate   4 credits $795
The relationship of telecommunications to the environment and society is examined. Topics that are considered include a consideration of free speech and privacy, the impact of chemicals, noise, and recycling. International and global issues are included.

Fire Protection Systems
Fox Valley Technical College
FOVA#503-160   Undergraduate   3 credits $200
The student will survey and examine the various suppression and detection systems used in the United States. A thorough study of sprinkler systems, standpipe systems, fire extinguishers, foam systems, carbon dioxide systems, dry and wet chemical systems, halogenated agent systems, explosion suppression systems and the most common types of detection systems are included in this course.

Fundamentals of Copy Editing
New School for Social Research
NEWS#1515   Undergraduate   1 credits $546
Skillful copy editing can turn a flawed piece of writing into a polished editorial product. By applying the rules of grammar, word usage, and sentence clarity, the copy editor ensures the integrity of the written word. Whether you edit text for a newspaper, website, or newsletter, this course aims to improve your editing skills and give you techniques for writing sharp, vivid headlines.

Graduate Writing II
Golden Gate University
GOLD#ENGL301 Graduate   3 credits $960
Prepares MBA students to write in both academic and professional settings. Reviews unity, coherence, clarity, conciseness, audience analysis and document formatting. Based on library and online research, you will prepare documents appropriate for presentation in your professional field. Required of all MBA students who score either 2.5 or on the GMAT or who have completed ENGL300. Prerequisite: ENGL300 for those students who scored below 2.5 on the GMAT.

Hazardous Materials and the EMT
State University of New York
SUNY#EMS113 Undergraduate   2.5 credits $525*
This course provides students with the knowledge that will enable them to respond to and take a defensive role at an incident involving hazardous materials. The response role they will fulfill will help reduce the effects of the incident to the environment, community, and themselves.
* NY residents tuition: $105 per credit.

Hotel Catering and Sales
University of Nevada-Reno
NERE#C379 Undergraduate   3 credits $210
This course will acquaint the student with the role of the catering department within a hotel. Students will be exposed to the selling, servicing and logistical planning that goes into producing a catered event in the on-premise environment. Basic principles will apply in any on-premise setting, including private clubs, banquet halls, restaurants and convention centers. Each lesson in this syllabus correlates to a chapter in the textbook. Lesson One in this syllabus should be read with chapter one in the book. The lessons are intended to update and supplement the information in the textbook.

Hypertext Poetry and Fiction
New School for Social Research
NEWS#1827 Undergraduate   3 credits $1638*
The course surveys published interactive poetry and fiction, which uses the computer monitor as its medium instead of the printed page. Students then have an opportunity to create and discuss their own writing in this genre. They explore how the resources of the computer can take literature in new directions not possible in print. Focus is on hypertext, but students also explore the literary possibilities of kinetic text, decision-making algorithms, randomization functions, graphics, and audio.
* Non-credit option, tuition: $365.

Independent Study
Christopher Newport University
CHNE#GOVT499 Undergraduate   3 credits $993
The purpose of this course is to enable a qualified student to enrich his/her program through independent work. The topic and evaluation are agreed upon in writing by the student and faculty member supervising the effort. Prerequisite: Junior standing and consent of instructor.

Intro to Mass Communications
University of Alaska - Fairbanks
ALFA#JB101 Undergraduate   3 credits $210
History and principles of mass communications and the role of information media in American society. Introduction to professional aspects of mass communications, including print and broadcast.

Intro to Mass Media
State University of New York
SUNY#TELC101601 Undergraduate   3 credits $1038*
Introduces the student to the practices and business aspects of American mass media industries. Explore the history, structure, organization, function and effects of mass media. Prerequisite: Readiness for Freshman English.
* NY residents tuition: $137 per credit

Introduction to Broadcasting
University of Alaska - Fairbanks
ALFA#JB102 Undergraduate   3 credits $210
Principles of broadcasting as they relate to the US, including history, government involvement, and social effects.

Introduction to Digital Transmission
The Graduate School of America
TGSA#OM883W Graduate   4 credits $795
This course presents an introduction to concepts of digital transmission techniques involved in voice, data, and video systems. Topics include a review of pulse code modulation, frequency division multiplexing, T-1 lines, and digital hierarchy; an introduction to ISDN, frame relay, asynchronous transfer mode (ATM), and SONET.

Introduction to Financial Reporting
University of Minnesota
MINN#ACCT1050 Undergraduate   5 credits $445
In this course, students learn the basic concepts of measurement and valuation that underlie the development of financial reports for external users. Financial statement preparation, analysis of alternative valuation approaches, and interpretation of financial statement information are examined.

Introduction to Journalism
New York Institute of Technology
NYIT#CA5540 Undergraduate   3 credits $???
Survey of evolution of the American press and its influence in our democratic society. Freedom of the press and social responsibilities. Professional goals, professional qualities, and professional ethics of a journalist. Technical developments and organizational structure in print and broadcast journalism. Survey of various types and styles of journalism and profiles of the prominent journalists. Survey of literature and vocational opportunities in journalism.

Introduction to Mass Communications
University of Minnesota
MINN#JOUR1001 Undergraduate   4 credits $356
A survey of the means of delivering information, opinion, and entertainment. The course explores the historical roots, current structures, and principal issues in modern mass media.

Introduction to Recreation
Kansas City Kansas Community College
KACI#RT171 Undergraduate   3 credits $324*
An introductory course to the philosophical foundation of play and leisure; various career opportunities in the recreation field are explored such as Therapeutic Recreation, Community or Public Recreation, Park Management, Outdoor Recreation, Voluntary Youth Organizations and Commercial Recreation.
* KS residents pay $40 per credit.

Introduction to Technical Writing
Roane State Community College
ROAN#ENG231 Undergraduate   3 credits $459*
An introduction to the field of technical writing that covers purpose, audience, outlining and organization, clarity and conciseness, editing, a grammar and punctuation review and research methods. A proposal and several types of reports are required related to the student's field of specialization. As much of today's technical writing takes place online, the course is held in an online environment to additionally enhance computer and electronic communications skills.
* Tennessee residents tuition: $48 per semester hour.

Introduction to Telecommunications
Cerro Coso Community College
CECO#CSCIC30 Undergraduate   3 credits $345*
An overview of telecommunications as it relates to modern uses, hardware devices, software, protocols, local area networks, security and management. Prerequisite: CSCI C2 or equivalent. Level 1 reading, level 2 writing classification recommended.
* CA residents pay $13 per credit.

Introduction to Telecommunications
New York Institute of Technology
NYIT#TN4701 Undergraduate   3 credits $???
An overview of the telecommunications field. Brief historical overview of major events in the technology, regulation, and business applications. The roles of telecommunications management in the organization describes and introduces the terminology of voice and data transmission, media, switching and signaling, networks, terminals, and codes, traffic engineering, etc. An overview of telecommunications function.

Journalistic Writing
City University
CITY#COM301 Undergraduate   5 qu. credits $785
Fundamental and practical techniques of information gathering, interviewing, writing and editing for various audiences via the print and broadcast media. Perfect journalistic writing, grammatical and editing skills. Form news stories based on accurate observation and interviews. Prerequisite: Strongly recommended: BSK210 or its equivalent.

Landscape Gardening and Design
University of Minnesota
MINN#HORT1010 Undergraduate   4 credits $356
Working knowledge of propagation and culture of common landscape materials: turf, flowers, trees, and shrubs. Principles and practices of gardening. Prepared for beginners but also valuable for advanced or experienced gardeners. Text assignments and home projects with plants for the garden are required. Topics: planting, transplanting, seeds, soils, fertilizers, preparing beds and planting areas, selecting a good garden site, controlling garden pests, weeding, watering, cultivating, vegetable gardening, and landscape maintenance. Discusses annuals, perennials, bulbs, and roses for northern gardens. The final project provides the fundamentals for home landscape design.

Magazine and Feature Writing
Western Illinois University
WEIL#ENG330 Undergraduate   3 credits $795*
Provides experience with reporting, writing, and marketing of factual articles for general or specialized print publications. Interviewing and research, manuscript preparation, and ethics appreciation are covered with an emphasis on narrative-style journalism. Prerequisite: competency in sophomore-level writing.
* IL residents tuition: $88 per credit.

Magazine Article Writing
University of Alaska - Fairbanks
ALFA#JB311 Undergraduate   3 credits $237
Writing articles for publication. Students repeating the course limited to six credits. Prerequisite: JB301 or permission of instructor.

Magazine Article Writing
Rio Salado College
RISA#ENG235 Undergraduate   3 credits $186*
Basic skills and techniques used by professional writers for publication in magazines. Includes analyzing markets, identifying article slant, writing query letters, research techniques, editing, and submission procedures. Emphasis on nonfiction.
* AZ residents $37 per credit.

Magazine Writing
University of Colorado
CUON#ENGL3416 Undergraduate   3 credits $1953*
An intensive, Practical course in writing nonfiction with an emphasis on journalistic approaches for daily, weekly, and monthly publications. Prerequisite: ENGL1020.
* CO residents tuition: $136 per credit.

Magazine Writing
University of Minnesota
MINN#JOUR3173 Undergraduate   4 credits $391
Writing nonfiction feature articles for adult consumer and trade publications is covered, as is a study of marketing one's freelance writing, including the construction and submission of query letters. Students write, revise, and submit three articles to magazines or newspaper feature sections of their choice.

Mass Communication
Rochester Institute of Technology
ROCH#53548290 Undergraduate   4 credits $923
An Introduction to the study of the mass media.

Media in Developing Countries
New School for Social Research
NEWS#2653 Undergraduate   3 credits $1638*
Technology has brought the world closer than ever. We learn about countries and peoples from regions previously distant and closed to external observers. But what exactly do we know? From whose perspective is the story told? This course contrasts what foreign coverage tells us about life in African, Asian, Latin American, and Eurasian countries with local reporting of their own lives. We explore the print and broadcast media in countries self-consciously building new, more democratic states.
* Non-credit option, tuition: $365.

Modern Police Management
New York Institute of Technology
NYIT#BES2319 Undergraduate   3 credits $???
The essentials of personnel management and fundamentals of supervision and leadership as applied to the administration of police organizations. The course will examine such issues as the decision making processes, leadership styles, budgetary and union problems, motivation, discipline, public policy, performance management, and organizational development.

Outdoor Recreation Perspectives
Western Illinois University
WEIL#REC376 Undergraduate   3 credits $795*
Introduces outdoor recreational use of lands for the outdoor enthusiast and conservationist as well as the person planning a career in recreation leadership or park management. Topics include psychological, social, and economic factors of outdoor recreation in America; future leisure environments and equipment; the role of private enterprise; state and national parks, forest, refuges, and reservoirs; recreation carrying capacity, multiple use, and other administrative tools; wilderness, scenic rivers, etc.
* IL residents tuition: $88 per credit.

Philosophy & Principles of PE & Athletics
State University of New York
SUNY#PPE175 Undergraduate   3 credits $630*
Designed to expose the professional preparation student to the history and development trends of the field. Specifically, exposure to the subfields of Physical Studies will be explored. These will include, but not be limited to, Physical Education, Sport Medicine, Sport Psychology, Exercise Physiology, Motor Learning, History of Sport, Sociology of Sport, Recreation, Health Education, Adapted P.E., Coaching. Special emphasis is on the role of coaching as part of the education system, legal and health consideration, and local, state, and national roles.
* NY residents tuition: $105 per credit.

Praxis and Policy
University of Nebraska
NEBR#HRFS900 Undergraduate   3 credits $467
This course will focus on the role of research as the basis for improving policies and services which for individuals, families and consumers in society.

Principles of Safety
Fox Valley Technical College
FOVA#196-121 Undergraduate   2 credits $150
This course explains the supervisor's role in developing and implementing safety procedures and accident prevention programs in all types of work environments. Other topics include ergonomics, office safety, health care costs and Occupational Safety and Health Administration (OSHA) standards.

Principles of Telecommunications
University of Denver, University College
DEUC#TELE4810 Undergraduate   3 qtr. hrs. $885
This course is primarily a survey of fundamental topics of concern to telecommunications managers. An overview of key issues and technologies, it is a foundation for more detailed courses. It should be taken as early as possible in the student's educational program. Topics to be explored include the history, structure and regulation of the telecommunications industry. Basic principles of telephony, networks and telecommunications services will be examined.

Principles, Ethics, and Issues of Athletic Coaching
Pennsylvania State University
PENN#KINES493 Undergraduate   3 credits $345
Integration of the practical and theoretical knowledges necessary for effective coaching, through classroom and field experiences. Prerequisite: KINES 390. Note: 400-level courses are available only to students with junior or senior standing.

Public Service Report Writing
Fox Valley Technical College
FOVA#801-125 Undergraduate   2 credits $150
The purposes, principles and components of public safety/security reports are examined. Relevant applications of course content are designed to give students the proficiency to write narrative reports which meet the minimum standards of investigative reports. Prerequisite: Written Communication, with a grade of C or better.

Recreational Sports Programming
Indiana University
INDI#R324 Undergraduate   3 credits $268
Overview of programmatic elements and techniques in recreational sports. Topics include informal, intramural, club, extramural, and instructional sports programming; values of recreational sports; terminology and career opportunities in various recreational sport settings.

Rendering the Ordinary Extraordinary
New School for Social Research
NEWS#1649 Undergraduate 3 credits $1638*
Often great poems render what is generally considered ordinary, extraordinary. Neruda wrote an ode to his socks; in Whitman's Song of Myself a child asks: "What is the grass? Fetching it to me with full hands,/How could I answer the child? I do not know what it is more/than he." In discussing student work, we address the relationships between our vision of the everyday world and the images that inhabit our poems. How do we learn to elaborate on the most ordinary of objects or situations? How do we recognize the extraordinary in what is commonplace? How do we write inventively about a pair of scissors or a train ride?.
* Non-credit option, tuition: $365.

Research Writing
Golden Gate University
GOLD#ENGL1B Undergraduate 3 credits $960
Provides extensive practice in research and writing techniques that can be applied in both academic and professional settings. You will learn to critically analyze various types of reading material and will practice information gathering techniques, library and online research strategies, and the use of surveys, interviews and field observations. Prerequisite: ENGL1A with a grade of "C" or better.

Senior Seminar
University of Colorado
CUON#SOC4831 Undergraduate 3 credits $1953*
Seminar for senior sociology majors considering important concepts, issues, and problems in sociology. Prerequisite: SOC3111, 3121, 3151, and 3161.
* CO residents tuition: $136 per credit.

Sport Psychology
Walden University
WALD#PSYC8560 Graduate 5 credits $1500
(Course description not available at press time.)

Strategies for Telecommunications I
University of Denver, University College
DEUC#TELE4835 Undergraduate 3 qtr. hrs. $885
This course focuses on management planning strategies for the future, focusing on business opportunities which may emerge as a result of new telecommunications technologies or other technologies, and management changes which will result from utilization of these technologies. Developing competitive strategies, gaining competitive advantage and the critical issue of time will be explored. (Prerequisite: Principles of Telecommunications or equivalent experience.)

Technical Communications
Great Basin College
GRBA#ENG107 Undergraduate 3 credits $186*
(Course description not available at press time.)
* NV residents tuition: $43 per credit.

Technical Editing
UCLA
UCLA#X439 Undergraduate 3.3 credits $495
An introduction to technical editing as a skill and profession. Examines the job of the technical editor, the politics of editing, and editorial techniques and standards. Features instruction and practice in content editing, copy editing, proofreading, designing the printed page, and making an editing guide. Addresses specific problems of editing in various technical fields.

Technical Report Writing
University of Colorado
CUON#TC4120 Undergraduate 3 credits $1953*
This on-line course will study various aspects of technical communication through technical document analysis, readings, and writing assignments. The course will be conducted in an electronic classroom using software that will allow you to send assignments to the instructor, read lectures, exchange papers with fellow students, and be part of group instructions. We will examine the writing process and in particular report writing. Required readings will cover theoretical research of technical communication and will be applied to writing assignments.
* CO residents tuition: $136 per credit.

Technical Report Writing
Dakota State University
DAKO#ENGL405 Undergraduate 3 credits $447
Technical Report Writing is a professionally-oriented writing course which teaches students to prepare technical reports in their major fields of study. Students will learn the basics of technical writing by preparing a variety of technical communications. Prerequisite: ENGL101 (Composition) and ENGL301 (Advanced Composition).

Technical Writing
Chemeketa Community College
CHEM#WR227 Undergraduate 3 credits $123
This course is the report writing class for transfer students. Students write a variety of reports that include format, organizational, supplemental, bibliographical, and illustrative considerations. These reports emphasize factual content, objective presentation, and a defined purpose for specific readers/audiences. Prerequisite: WR121 or consent of instructor.

Technical Writing
University of Colorado
CUON#CMMU3154 Undergraduate 3 credits $1953*
This course introduces the study and writing of technical documents. The emphasis will be on the processes, style, structure, and forms of technical writing. Attention will be paid to audience analysis, organization, clarity, and precision. Section OL1. Prerequisite: ENGL1020.
* CO residents tuition: $136 per credit.

Technical Writing
University of Colorado
CUON#ENGL3154 Undergraduate 3 credits $1953*
This course introduces the study and writing of technical documents. The emphasis will be on the processes, style, structure, and forms of technical writing. Attention will be paid to audience analysis, organization, clarity, and precision. Section OL1. Prerequisite: ENGL1020.
* CO residents tuition: $136 per credit.

Technical Writing
University of Colorado
CUON#TC3154 Undergraduate   3 credits $1953*
This course introduces the study and writing of technical documents. The emphasis will be on the processes, style, structure, and forms of technical writing. Attention will be paid to audience analysis, organization, clarity, and precision. Section OL1. Prerequisite: ENGL1020.
* CO residents tuition: $136 per credit.

Technical Writing
University of Denver, University College
DEUC#COMM4120 Undergraduate   3 qtr. hrs. $885
In this course, students will improve and refine the skills necessary for producing technical documents, which synthesize, distill and translate complex information from technical to non-technical terminology. Topics include: situation and audience analysis; preparation and organization; and document formatting, drafting and revising. Appropriate language style, and English usage for technical documents will also be covered. Assignments, created to meet the needs of students in specific technical professions or industries, may include short reports, standard abstracts, annotated bibliographies, white papers, and business or academic proposals.

Technical Writing
Eastern Oregon University
EAOR#WR320 Undergraduate   3 credits $220
Emphasis on the structure and style of scientific and technical writing, including reports, proposals, instructions, correspondence and documentation. WR320 is for those interested in the rapidly growing field of "technical writing" and for anyone who wants to be a better language user at work. Prerequisites: WR121 or equivalent, and upper-division standing; or instructor consent.

Technical Writing
University of Massachusetts - Dartmouth
MADA#ENL650 Undergraduate   3 credits $483
This graduate level course explores the many purposes, audiences, forms, and formats of technical documents written for lay audiences. An in-depth writing workshop, focusing on advanced principles of technical writing, this graduate-level course introduces students to the many purposes, audiences, forms, and formats of technical documents written for lay audiences. The type of writing taught during a particular semester will vary, and principles covered will include: audience analysis, writing ethics, organization and style. Prerequisite: B.S. or B.A. degree, or permission of the instructors.

Technical Writing
University of Missouri
MOCE#EN161 Undergraduate   3 credits $387
This course teaches advanced composition dealing with the fundamentals and applications of technical writing; it includes work with outlines and abstracts, graphic aids, formal proposals, and progress reports. Perquisites: English 20 or equivalent, and junior standing.

Technical Writing
New Hampshire College
NEHA#COM341 Undergraduate   3 credits $1656
This course trains students to produce technical documents that are commonly found within a business context. Students are required to prepare a variety of technical reports including audits, manuals, and feasibility studies. Prerequisite: ENG121.

Technical Writing
New York Institute of Technology
NYIT#EN1043 Undergraduate   3 credits $???
An intermediate-level writing course for students of the physical and life sciences and technology. Emphasis on style in technical writing, modes of technical discourse (definition, description, analysis, interpretation), and strategies for effective business communication, including resume writing and technical reports. Methods and procedures of research are explored in- depth. Recommended for all science and technology majors. Coursework includes a computer lab component. Prerequisite: EN1020.

Technical Writing
Rio Salado College
RISA#ENG111 Undergraduate   3 credits $186*
Analysis, planning, organization, research, and writing of technical reports and oral presentations for specific job-related audiences. Preparation of recommendation and feasibility reports, proposals, and applications of graphics in documents and oral presentations. Prerequisites: ENG101 with a grade of "C", or better, or permission of instructor.
* AZ residents pay $37 per credit.

Technical Writing
UCLA
UCLA#X439B Undergraduate   3 credits $495
This online tutorial is designed for beginning technical writers, those interested in a technical writing career, and technical specialists who write documents as part of their job. The course covers the stages in document preparation, from concept to print (audience analysis, document planning, gathering information, formatting documents, drafting and revising, and managing the review cycles). Students learn how to evaluate documents for usability and how to tailor a document's style, format, and content to a technical and nontechnical audience. Students analyze documents, complete a series of writing assignments, plus plan and draft one short technical document.

Technical Writing I
Front Range Community College
FRCC#ENG132A Undergraduate   3 credits $790
This course develops proficiency in technical writing, emphasizing principles for organizing, drafting, and revising a variety of documents for industry, business, and government. 45 Contact Hours.

Technical Writing II
Front Range Community College
FRCC#ENG132B Undergraduate   3 credits $790
This course expands and refines the objectives of ENG131 for students whose jobs or majors require advanced skills in technical writing. 45 Contact Hours. Prerequisite: ENG 131 or permission of instructor.

Telecommunications
International Society for Technology in Education
ISTE#EDUC510E Grad   4 qu. credits $540*
This course explores electronic mail, conferencing, distance education, and information access using the Internet through a school, Internet provider, or commercial network such as America Online. It discusses ways these tools can be used for classroom and personal use. Topics covered include: exploring the network and the information age, uses of electronic mail, conferencing for educators and students, curriculum-based telecommunication projects, distance education and remote database searching.
* Non-credit option, tuition: $460.

Telecommunications
State University of New York
SUNY#BRC330 Undergraduate   3 credits $1038*
This course deals with telecommunications and its relationship to information science. Topical areas include government regulation, wide area network systems and related technologies.
* NY residents tuition: $137 per credit

Telecommunications and Networking
Nova Southeastern University
NOVA#MMIS653 Graduate   3 credits $1,110
The role of telecommunications and computer networks in management information systems. Technical fundamentals and design of telecommunications and computer networks. Strategies, tools, and techniques for network planning, implementation, management, maintenance, and security. Topics include ISDN and B-ISDN, the OSI Model, transmission media, network operating systems, topologies, configurations, protocols, and performance characteristics. Trends in standardization, internetworking, downsizing, and the development of local area networks (LANs), wide area networks (WANs), metropolitan area networks (MANs), and enterprise-wide networks are examined.

Telecommunications Applications
The Graduate School of America
TGSA#OM893W Graduate   4 credits $795
This course examines a variety of telecommunications applications including teleshopping, video conferencing, desktop video, call centers, help desks, message management, telecommuting, telemedicine and multimedia applications.

Telecommunications Management
Golden Gate University
GOLD#TM301 Graduate   3 credits $1404
Investigates the history and recent developments in industry regulation and technology. Major aspects of domestic and international telecommunications, including voice services and facilities, data and computer communications are discussed. Examines the role of the telecommunications manager in a dynamic environment.

Telecommunications Policy
University of Denver, University College
DEUC#TELE4830 Undergraduate   3 qtr. hrs. $885
This course is the first in a sequence of two courses examining telecommunications policy and regulation. The course concentrates on policy-making institutions, the policy-making process, and values and goals for telecommunications policy-making in an information society. It will evaluate alternative theories of regulation in terms of their economic incentives and market impacts. (Prerequisites: None, but Information Industry Finance recommended.)

Telephony I
University of Denver, University College
DEUC#TELE4811 Undergraduate   3 qtr. hrs. $885
Students in this class will discuss voice telephone systems including characteristics of speech, network hierarchy, customer premises equipment, transmission systems and impairments, multiplexing, signaling, alerting and supervision, traffic engineering, network optimization and switching fundamentals.

Telephony I
The Graduate School of America
TGSA#OM882W Graduate   4 credits $795
This course introduces the concepts of telephony including theory of sound and noise, types of circuits, impedance, traffic engineering, telephone equipment, modulation, modems, and signaling systems. An overview of the history of telecommunications is included.

Television as a System
New School for Social Research
NEWS#3935 Undergraduate   3 credits $455
This course focuses on television as a system: formal, narrative, ideological and experiential. Using the concept of desire as a broad theoretical framework, our aim is to explore the various ways in which the forms and processes of television bind us as viewers to the screen. From its beginnings, television has evoked contradictory scenarios, captured perhaps most succinctly by the metaphors of "vast wasteland" on the one hand and "global village" on the other. Television criticism has also reflected a similar uncertainty as it struggles to account for television's everydayness and omnipresence in today's societies.

Theory of Coaching Baseball
University of Alabama
ALAB#HCA383 Undergraduate   3 credits $250
This course has been designed to acquaint the interested learner with the rudimentary knowledge they would need to be able to impart baseball skills and techniques to youthful players. Fundamentals are extremely important and must be learned from the little leagues to the major leagues. These same fundamentals can also be of help to aspiring softball players, since hitting, running, fielding and throwing make up the basics of this increasingly popular sport.

Theory of Coaching Basketball
University of Alabama
ALAB#HCA382 Undergraduate   3 credits $250
Those with basketball coaching intentions will have to understand where basketball has been, where it stands now and where it is heading into the Twenty-First Century. Current strategies and training methods will enable the aspiring basketball coach to compete at the highest levels. This course has been designed to help young coaches research and refine the latest in basketball coaching techniques to accomplish these goals.

To be A Technical Writer
Kennesaw State University
KENN#FMV204 Undergraduate   3 credits $149
The field of technical writing offers many opportunities to those people with an interest in technology and a talent for explaining technical concepts in writing. In this workshop, you'll explore the opportunities available to technical writers, find out the types of work that technical writers do and the industries they work in, and learn about the skills you must develop to succeed in this exciting field. You'll also have the opportunity to try your hand at technical writing by preparing a simple technical documentation project, which will be evaluated by an experienced technical writer.

Transmission Systems
Golden Gate University
GOLD#TM315 Graduate   3 credits $1404
Analyzes information transport systems encompassing microwave radio, coaxial cable, satellite circuits, submarine cable, high-frequency radio, tropospheric scatter circuits, short-distance radio, waveguide systems, optical-lightwave communications, cellular radio, networking and infrared technology. Prerequisite: TM301 or consent of the instructor or the Department Chair.

Travel Journal Writing
University of Colorado-Boulder
COBO#ENGL3081 Undergraduate   3 credits $240
Take advantage of the privileged point of view of the world you enjoy while traveling. Capture the observations of your trip in a journal to preserve and get the most out of the full impression of each scene and situation of your trip beyond its static image. Each entry allows you to focus on a different aspect of travel writing as a process of transforming observation into language.

Travel Journalism
UCLA
UCLA#X447 Undergraduate   3 credits $450
Structural guides in approaches and techniques for turning a weekend trip, vacation, or other travel experience into features for newspapers and magazines, as well as techniques for capturing atmosphere, color, and mood with words and camera. Includes extensive guided practice in writing queries, feature stories, and columns, with individual editorial and marketing suggestions. The goal is to generate publishable material. Lectures and discussion cover research methods; information sources; techniques and markets; recordkeeping; finding and keeping the focus; and deciding on length, content, and style.

Trends in Technology
Fayetteville Technical Community College
FAYE#CIS226 Undergraduate   2 credits $326*
This course introduces emerging information systems technologies. Emphasis is placed on evolving technologies and trends in business and industry. Upon completion, students should be able to articulate an understanding of the current trends and issues in emerging technologies for information systems.
* North Carolina residents and non-resident US military personnel stationed within the state tuition: $40; NC senior citizens: free.

Writing for Magazine & Newspapers
Kennesaw State University
KENN#FMV207 Undergraduate   3 credits $149
This online Freelance Writing workshop is ideal for people looking to write newspaper or magazine articles, and launch a full-time or part-time freelance writing business. After an introduction to what freelance writers do and how they market their services, several exercises will be used to help you develop article ideas, pitch article ideas to editors, develop your interview skills and write articles.

Writing Short Newspaper Articles
Kennesaw State University
KENN#FMV206 Undergraduate   3 credits $149
This course will familiarize students with the basic process for writing a newspaper article, concentrating on the need to communicate information quickly, vividly and coherently. The course will approach the short article not simply as a story that takes fewer words to tell than a longer feature piece, but as a distinct sub-genre of newspaper writing that is particularly challenging for writers.

Personal

Career

Other

Personal

Test Preparation

Writing and Communications

Academic & Field Research Writing
Marylhurst College
MARY#WR306 Undergraduate   3 credits $651
For those wanting an update on their academic and field research skills, this course is designed to acquaint students with solid academic and field research strategies for the 1990s. Writing and footnoting styles are emphasized, as well as research ethics and other skills needed for undertaking simple or complex research papers.

Academic Writing I
State University of New York
SUNY#ENGL101B Undergraduate   4 credits $1484*
This course is required of all students in degree programs (AT TCCC) and is meant to be taken during the first semester of study. Students practice basic strategies of academic discourse: planning, drafting, revising, and editing expository essays in response to reading on significant issues. Students will learn to summarize, paraphrase, quote, and document sources as they analyze, evaluate, and synthesize ideas. The course will enable students to choose the appropriate rhetorical and stylistic approaches to respond effectively to writing assignments with clarity, coherence, and sound reasoning.
* NY residents tuition: $137 per credit.

Advanced Composition
University of Colorado
CUON#ENGL3084 Undergraduate   3 credits $1953*
Reading, discussion, and writing about the ways writers use language to affect others. Focus on the power of language in such areas as politics, sexism, advertising, prejudice, and propaganda. Equal focus on developing individual student writing styles at advanced levels. Prerequisite: ENGL1020 or 2030.
* CO residents tuition: $136 per credit.

Advanced Composition
Dakota State University
DAKO#ENGL301 Undergraduate   3 credits $447
In a technologically sophisticated environment, students refine and practice skills needed for effective communication in academic, personal, and professional writing. Substantial research compositions are included. Prerequisite: ENGL101 and 48 hours of course work completed.

Advanced Composition
Ohio University
OHIO#ENG308JW Undergraduate   4 credits $256
Focuses on skills in writing expository prose, with regular practice and evaluation supplemented by attention to professional prose and concepts of rhetoric and style. OU students cannot take this course pass/fail if used to satisfy the junior-level composition requirement.

Advanced Composition
State University of New York
SUNY#ENG200 Undergraduate   3 credits $630*
Course focuses on written analysis, evaluation, and argument. Assignments develop depth and proficiency in using language. Basic composition skills are assumed. Can be taken in place of ENG101 to satisfy the composition requirement for graduation (applicable to matriculated MCC students).
* NY residents tuition: $105 per credit.

Advanced Writing and Editing
New York Institute of Technology
NYIT#EN1049 Undergraduate   3 credits $???
An advanced workshop in business and technical writing techniques including technical aspects of editing and interpersonal skills employed by successful editors. Participants practice revising writing for specific audiences; strengthen their techniques in revising for style, clarity, and conciseness; increase their command of grammar and mechanics; practice production editing and using style manuals; utilize word processors and computerized text editors; and develop important interpersonal editing skills through the use of role playing and peer evaluation. Participants also continue to be exposed to a variety of common forms of career-oriented business and technical writing.

Advanced Writing for Grad School
UCLA
UCLA#X340E Undergraduate   2 credits $390
This online course explores the variety of formats required for graduate papers and reports, focusing on development of ideas, primary and secondary support materials, and discussion of implications. Students read exemplary graduate-level projects and model two short papers on standard formats used in business school.

Adventures in Writing a Novel
Kennesaw State University
KENN#FMV222 Undergraduate   3 credits $149
Each week we will read a piece by an established writer about the creative process. Brewster Ghiselin's The Creative Process: A Symposium is a great source for this kind of essay, but I will draw from other sources as well. Writers such as Henry James, Alice Walker, Katherine Anne Porter, Thomas Wolfe, Virginia Woolfe, and Henry Miller have written helpful essays on tapping potential and inspiration in the writing process. In addition to reading, of course, we will exchange drafts of manuscripts in progress, including brainstorming and bare-bones ideas to completed chapters.

American Nature Writing
Western Illinois University
WEIL#ENG400G Undergraduate   3 credits $795*
Introduces you to some of the finest American nature writers, including such figures as John James Audubon, Henry David Thoreau, John Muir, Aldo Leopold, Rachel Carson, Loren Eiseley, Mannie Dillard, and Barry Lopez. The course emphasizes changing perspectives on the natural world from the late eighteenth century to the present, focusing on such matters as the early American landscape, the impact of evolution, the preservation of wilderness, the coming of a biocentric perspective, and the quest for religious experience in nature.
* IL residents tuition: $88 per credit.

Applied Discourse Theory
Eastern Oregon University
EAOR#WR206 Undergraduate   3 credits $240
Study of the theoretical approaches and materials for composition studies. Emphasis on analyzing texts and applying discourse theory to the student's own writing and writing pedagogy. Prerequisite: ENGL104 or equivalent, and WR121 or equivalent.

Basic Reading and Writing
New York Institute of Technology
NYIT#EN1007 Undergraduate   3 credits $???

A course designed for students whose English placement test reveals the need for improved basic writing and reading skills. Students will read and write various kinds of essays, and practice prewriting, composing, revising and editing. The course will improve the use of standard grammar and mechanics and develop comprehension strategies, vocabulary and study skills. Prerequisite: English placement test.

Basic Speech Communication
New York Institute of Technology
NYIT#SP1023 Undergraduate   3 credits $???

Study of the fundamentals of verbal communication including public communication, interpersonal communication, and small group interaction. Training in methods of obtaining and organizing materials and ideas for effective verbal communication.

Basics of Investing
University of Alaska - Fairbanks
ALFA#ABUS120 Undergraduate   3 credits $213

This covers personal financial planning, goal setting, and investing. Also, a study will be made of stocks, bonds, trusts, securities, options, real estate and other investment vehicles. Inflation, taxes, interest rates, retirement, and selecting financial planners are covered.

Becoming a Master Student
Pima Community College
PIMA#HDE101 Undergraduate   3 credits $165*

Development of personal and academic skills to maximize learning and success in a college setting. Includes personal skills, library skills, learning styles, study skills, can critical thinking skills.
* AZ residents pay $32 per credit.

Career and Life Planning
Mercy College
MERC#BS120 Undergraduate   3 credits $900

(Course description not available at press time.)

Career and Life Planning for Returning Adult Students
State University of New York
SUNY#CDL101 Undergraduate   2 credits $420*

An in-depth examination of the elements in career decision-making with emphasis on the process of career and life planning for the returning adult student. Topics include life renewal, functional learning, skills assessment, values, interests, decision-making, goal-setting, and the world of work.
* NY residents tuition: $105 per credit.

Career Discovery & Testing
Brevard Community College
BREV#MFAX0792 Undergraduate   0 credits $100

This course is for people who are searching for a new career or coming to the job market for the first time. To provide information that will lead you to intelligent and guided career choices, you'll take three career surveys, including: the Myers-Briggs Preference Indicator, the Strong Interest Inventory, the Career Ability Placement Survey, provided with the materials of the course to learning more about your career opportunities and preferences, including: Skill Identification, Work Values, Current Labor Market Trends, Transferable Skills.

Career Exploration
Rio Salado College
RISA#CPD102AB Undergraduate   2 credits $124*

Designed to assist students making career choices. Focus on an awareness of self in terms of educational opportunities and reasonable possibilities in the world of work. Includes testing for personal/vocational interests, attitudes, skills, and potential, and exploration of career information to establish career objectives.
* AZ residents pay $37 per credit.

Career Planning
Dakota State University
DAKO#SOC110 Undergraduate   1 credits $149

Individual interest, values and skills as they relate to possible career choices. Individual exploration of potentially compatible occupations and development of job seeking skills.

Career Planning and Development
New York University
NEYO#X489571 Undergraduate   2.0 CEU $325

Designed to provide students with a framework for advising adults of all ages on career-related issues, this course begins with theories of adult and career development, which are then woven into a step-by-step view of career planning and advising processes. Topics include: the impact of age, gender, culture, and labor market trends; and, techniques for helping clients identify career problems, explore alternatives, make decisions, and choose or change careers. This course is for career development specialists and other professionals who wish to develop and broaden their skills in working with adults on career development issues.

Career Planning for Adults
University of Missouri
MOCE#A170 Undergraduate   3 credits $387

This course, written by educators and career planning professionals, is designed for adults interested in their own career planning. Through readings and exercises, students learn about adult developmental issues and about dealing with life's transitions. They assess barriers to their career planning; determine their interests, skills, and work values; and explore career options and lifestyle patterns. Students learn survival and enhancement skills for college; resume writing; interviewing skills; and job-hunting strategies. Adults taking this course receive personalized comments and feedback on each lesson from career planning professionals.

Clinical Skills Foundations
University of Colorado
CUON#PRDO5700 Undergraduate   1.5 credits $976*

This course combines two important areas that together form an appropriate foundation for the Advanced Disease State Management blocks. The first component(formerly Special Topics in Pharmacokinetics) is a lecture format course. It includes a review of basic applied pharmacokinetics principles and individualization of drug dosing as preparation for the advanced pharmacokinetics portions of individual therapeutics modules. The main focus of the course will be to address issues of pharmacodynamics, physiologic determinants of drug disposition, protein binding, drug disposition in liver disease, and the use of assays in applied pharmacokinetics.

* CO residents tuition: $136 per credit.

College Composition
State University of New York
SUNY#ENG1011 Undergraduate   2 credits $420*

This course emphasizes essay writing with special attention on the writing process. Students generate, revise and edit several short essays. They also study research techniques and practice writing in ways that challenge their reading and thinking skills.

* NY residents tuition: $105 per credit.

College Composition I
New York Institute of Technology
NYIT#EN1010 Undergraduate   3 credits $???

Instruction in and application of the principles and skills involved in effective expository writing, with most readings from nonfiction prose. Required of all freshmen. Coursework includes a computer lab component. Prerequisite: English placement test.

College Composition II
New Hampshire College
NEHA#ENG120 Undergraduate   3 credits $1656

English 120 is a college-level writing course which introduces students to various forms of academic discourse. Students are required to prepare essays in a variety of rhetorician modes including exposition, description and argumentation. In addition to out-of-class writing assignments, students will also be required to compose in-class essays in response to readings and other prompts. English 120 introduces students to process writing techniques, library research and documentation procedures. The primary focus of English 120 is to help students acquire the writing skills necessary to succeed in an academic environment. Prerequisite: ENG101.

College Composition II
New York Institute of Technology
NYIT#EN1020 Undergraduate   3 credits $???

Further development of the expository writing and reading skills taught in English 1010. Introduction to literature and library research. Prerequisite: EN1010.

College Composition III
New Hampshire College
NEHA#ENG121 Undergraduate   3 credits $1656

This course concentrates on argumentative writing and requires students to prepare a major research report, one which reveals fluency with argumentative strategies and rhetorical conventions. In addition, students are introduced to analytical reading techniques, critical research methods, and current documentation procedures. Although other kinds of writing are commonly assigned in ENG121, argumentation remains the major focus of study. The final exam will require students to compose a documented essay complying with prescribed MLA guidelines. Prerequisites: ENG120.

College Preparatory Writing II
Brevard Community College
BREV#ENCV0001 Undergraduate   3 credits $258

A course in developing logical, effective sentence structure skills in a variety of sentence types with emphasis on grammar, punctuation, spelling and appropriate word choice. For students not ready for college level English.

College Writing
State University of New York
SUNY#221624 Undergraduate   4 credits $586*

Learn essential writing skills such as how to create ideas, choose a focus for writing, develop and organize ideas, and choose appropriate language for the writing purpose and situation. Prepare to write competently in any academic discipline by focusing on writing skills within the context of the larger writing process. Learn how to approach and work through a writing task from prewriting through revising. Work on research and personal interest essays. Develop a more objective view of writing by learning how to apply basic revision criteria for college writing.

* NY residents tuition: $515

College Writing I
Western Illinois University
WEIL#ENG180 Undergraduate   3 credits $795*

Prepares you to write at the level expected of those in the academic community. Emphasis is on both the mechanics of writing and on the content of the essays. The course provides practice in developing an awareness of yourself as a writer, creating a comfortable writing process, using invention techniques, revising, editing, combining sentences, and using conventions of edited American English. You will write six assignments designed to provide practice using specific writing skills and steps in the writing process.

* IL residents tuition: $88 per credit.

College Writing II
Christopher Newport University
CHNE#ENGL102 Undergraduate   3 credits $993

Prepares student for advanced reading and writing in the University's four colleges. Continues College Writing I emphasis on writing summaries and critiques. Develops skills in reading and writing arguments connected to academic disciplines. Provides frequent guided practice, inside and outside of class, in writing analyses of arguments and creating extended written arguments with various aims. Prerequisite: Grade of C- or higher in ENGL101 or ENGL103 or the equivalent transfer credit.

Colloquium in Scholastic Journalism
Indiana University
INDI#J525   Undergraduate   3 credits $???
Examination of techniques and problems in supervising school publications. Topics covered include impact on scholastic journalism of changes in educational philosophy, law, financial support, management and technology. At the conclusion of J525, students should have both an understanding of and the competencies to advise secondary school newspapers, yearbooks and other media. Learning packet includes learning guide, videos and audio lecture tape.

Communication and Public Opinion I
University of Minnesota
MINN#JOUR5501 Undergraduate   4 credits $391
This course covers understanding and interpreting public opinion polls; persuasion; theories and models of mass communication; and how researchers study the media.

Communication I
Strayer University
STRA#ENG102 Undergraduate   4.5 credits $665
Uses an integrated approach to the acquisition of effective oral and written communications skills. Requires presentation of ideas in both oral and written formats. Within shorter structured units, emphasizes effective organization, unity and coherence as well as standard grammatical forms.

Communication II
Strayer University
STRA#ENG106 Undergraduate   4.5 credits $665
Combines critical reading and written analysis to help students develop into better writers of the types of papers most often required both in college and in the world of work. Develops realization that seemingly disparate skills (i.e., reading, analytic and argumentative skills) are interrelated. Stresses essay writing. Prerequisite: ENG102.

Communication Skills for Employees
Kennesaw State University
KENN#FMV200 Undergraduate   3 credits $149
The objective of this course is to help workplace employees be more effective in their oral and written communication skills. At the outset of this workshop a series of questions are posed regarding the student's workplace environment. From this information, students are sensitized to gauge where current communication problems exist. Once targeted, the correct remedy is applied though written exercises and participation in the virtual conference room.

Computer Literacy
Great Basin College
GRBA#COT105 Undergraduate   3 credits $186*
Defines the relationship between computer hardware and software, the process of saving, retrieving, revising, deleting, and copying files, the resources on a typical local area network, techniques for avoiding, detecting, and eradicating a computer virus, etc.
* NV residents tuition: $43 per credit.

Computers in Food Service
University of Nebraska
NEBR#NSD272 Undergraduate   3 credits $467
Demonstrations and work assignments using word processing, spreadsheet, database and nutrient analysis software in applications relevant to food service management and dietetics.

Critical and Evaluative Reading I
Rio Salado College
RISA#CRE101 Undergraduate   3 credits $186*
Emphasis on applying critical inquiry skills to varied and challenging reading materials. Includes analysis, synthesis, and evaluation through written discourse. Prerequisites: Reading placement test score of 41 or higher (ASSET), or grade of "C" or better in RDG091, or permission of instructor.
* AZ residents $37 per credit.

Critical Thinking
Eastern Oregon University
EAOR#PHIL203 Undergraduate   5 credits $400
An introduction to critical thinking and argument analysis. The primary goal of this course is to develop a technique for the evaluation of practical arguments in the real world.

Developing Career Options
UCLA
UCLA#X765C Undergraduate   0 credits $425
This online course provides an introduction to various career interests inventories. Students are given a hands-on opportunity to administer and score these inventories. The interpretation of these results and their application to each student's situation are discussed. Designed for those deciding on a career, those making a career transition, or those who work with people who are making such career developments.

Development   of   Mutual   Resources   Parenting
Western Illinois University
WEIL#FAM426G Undergraduate   3 credits $795*
Examines the principles and philosophies relevant to the process of parenting with emphasis on changing roles and responsibilities, child-rearing decisions, and diverse parenting perspectives.
* IL residents tuition: $88 per credit.

Directed Studies in Stress Management
University of Minnesota
MINN#PSY3970 Undergraduate   4 credits $391
The concept of stress, various ways of measuring stress levels, the concept of coping, and various methods of coping. Information is incorporated from diverse medical and psychological research to show how the brain, beliefs, moods, and thoughts affect one's physical and psychological well-being. Techniques for dealing with stress directly and for health maintenance. Appropriate for health-care providers who work with patients with stress-related problems or individuals suffering from stress who want to understand the problem.

Dynamics of Communication
Lansing Community College
LANS#SPCH120 Undergraduate   3 credits $315
Introduction to the theory and practice of communicating effectively in interpersonal, group, and public settings. The course utilizes readings, discussions (forum), chats, learning activities, and oral and written assignments to help students both understand the communication process and become more skillful interpersonal, group (team), and public communicators.

Effective Human Communications
Kennesaw State University
KENN#FMV201 Undergraduate   3 credits $149
General Principles of Human Communication in which we explore "Talk" (conversation), Interpersonal Relational Behavior (dyadic), Conflict, Nonverbal Communication, and elements of effective oral presentation. The class will consist of a number of applied assignments that are theory guided. Students will conduct their own investigations/observations of Human Communication principles as experienced in their own lives and social settings. They will complete the course having gained increased awareness of the influences of Human Communication and enhanced skills when interacting with others.

Effective Listening
Marylhurst College
MARY#CM323 Undergraduate   3 credits $651
Careful and discriminating listening is essential to effective communication. In this course, students explore listening skills and strategies for effectiveness in various interpersonal and professional contexts. Through a series of practical activities, students assess their own listening strengths and weaknesses and work to improve their listening.

Effective Speech
Pennsylvania State University
PENN#SPCOM100C Undergraduate   3 credits $345
Principles of communication, demonstrated through analysis and evaluation of messages made by others, with some attention to preparing your own speech.

Efficient and Effective Self-expression
City University
CITY#BC302 Undergraduate   5 qu. credits $785
Creative, problem-solving approaches to writing. Concepts examined include the preparation of effective presentations; fostering innovation; writing under pressure; and implementing rational and creative solutions.

Embalming Theory I
Fayetteville Technical Community College
FAYE#FSE210 Undergraduate   3 credits $489*
This course introduces various embalming procedures and the purpose, history, and need for embalming. Emphasis is placed on laboratory equipment, post mortem changes, and the proper use of embalming chemicals. Upon completion, students should be able to identify various instruments and relate theoretical case analysis to embalming procedures used in the funeral home.
* North Carolina residents and non-resident US military personnel stationed within the state tuition: $60; NC senior citizens: free.

Embalming Theory II
Fayetteville Technical Community College
FAYE#FSE212 Undergraduate   3 credits $489*
This course is a continuation of FSE210 and covers more detailed embalming procedures. Topics include anatomical consideration for embalming, case analysis, positioning features, arterial injection, cavity treatment, autopsies, and other post mortem conditions. Upon completion, students should be able to demonstrate knowledge of embalming theory and sanitation to protect the public health. Prerequisites: FSE210 or FSE211.
* NC residents pay $20 per credit.

Emergency Operations Planning
Rio Hondo College
RIHO#PAC43055B Undergraduate   0.5 credits $???
This course is designed to address Emergency Operations Planning (EOP); considerations, process, format, annexes, and preparing a draft plan. Topics will also include various types of emergencies; earthquakes, floods, fire, hazardous materials incidents, etc.

Entertainment Industry Careers
UCLA
UCLA#X474 Undergraduate   3 credits $450
If you are set on working in the entertainment industry--whether you have a clearly defined goal or only a vague notion of where to position yourself--this course provides the knowledge, information, resources, and skills to embark on a career path best suited to your talents and ambitions. Whether you are a college senior ready to cross the threshold into the world of work or an active professional in another field and want to make a career change into entertainment, the presentations, assignments, and interactive discussion conducted by top industry professionals in this course give you.

Exposition and Argumentation
University of Missouri
MOCE#SO20 Undergraduate   3 credits $387
This course stresses writing as a process, with due attention given to the critical reading and thinking skills needed to succeed in college. Course covers inventing, drafting, revising, and rewriting skills as well. Perquisites: English 20 is a prerequisite for any writing-intensive course.

Extended Preparation for the GMAT
UCLA
UCLA#X740 Undergraduate   0 credits $515
This online course provides thorough instruction in each of the six parts of the GMAT-essays, reading comprehension, sentence correction, critical reasoning, problem solving, and data sufficiency. Covers recommendations for the new essay performance section in addition to error recognition in sentences (poor diction, verbosity, and faulty grammar), logical reasoning, arithmetic, algebra, geometry, data interpretation, reading comprehension, and writing the personal statement for business school admissions. Includes a complimentary editing service.

Extended Preparation for the LSAT
UCLA
UCLA#X740B Undergraduate   0 credits $475

This online course includes in-depth modules on reading comprehension, analytical reasoning, logical reasoning, and the writing sample. Diagnostic testing is incorporated into the program to help students best determine his/her level of preparedness. The course also includes a segment on writing the personal statement for law school admissions and a complimentary editing service.

Family Financial Management
University of Nebraska
NEBR#FACS907 Masters   3 credits $467

More than ever before, consumers are realizing that investing is critical to the achievement of long-term goals like providing for a child's education, or enjoying a secure retirement. How does a household go about developing an investment strategy? This class will explore the evolution of the financial marketplace, develop criteria for judging investments, and critically examine alternate ratings systems for a popular investment product, the mutual fund.

Family Strengths
University of Nebraska
NEBR#FACS987 Masters   3 credits $467

Living in a family is a microcosm of life itself. Our family can bring us both great joy and excruciating pain. A healthy family can be a valuable resource during difficult times. Conversely, an unhealthy or dysfunctional family can create problems for family members that will last for generations. This course focuses on how families develop their inherent potential for health and how professionals in fields serving families can best help in the quest for emotional well-being.

Find a Creative Job in the Real World
University of Massachusetts - Dartmouth
MADA#CMP325 Undergraduate   0 credits $135

This course is aimed at helping graphic designers, illustrators, photographers, copywriters, and others involved in related creative fields find a job. It covers the skills necessary to help you stand out in your search for that job of your dreams. The course goes beyond the usual how to organize your portfolio and how to write a resume.

Food Service Preparation I
State University of New York
SUNY#HRMG101 Undergraduate   3 credits $1038*

Basic procedures and techniques for large quantity food preparation and service are covered. The study of sanitation, safety, equipment operation, food purchasing and preparation techniques and table service are assigned an integral part of this course. Special projects in menu planning, purchasing, preparation, and services are required.
* NY residents tuition: $137 per credit.

Fund Raising
Dakota State University
DAKO#NFP315 Undergraduate   3 credits $447

Designed to cover fund raising fundamentals including: funding sources, methodology and goal setting. Prerequisite: CSC105 or concurrent registration.

Fundamental Principles of Financial Freedom
New School for Social Research
NEWS#9999 Undergraduate   0 credits $1638*

This course offers a holistic approach to financial planning. Quantitative and qualitative analysis helps establish participants' financial and personal profiles. All areas of financial planning-- including cash-flow management, risk management, tax planning, benefits coordination, and retirement and estate planning--are addressed. The participants' relationship to money and financial matters is explored to facilitate reaching true financial freedom.

Fundamentals of Communication
University of Colorado
CUON#CMMU1011 Undergraduate   3 credits $1953*

A lecture-discussion-recitation approach to communication theory and its application. Specific topics such as communication models, interpersonal communication and the concept of self, nonverbal communication, message preparation and analysis, problem solving, and decision making.
* CO residents tuition: $136 per credit.

Gender Communication
University of Minnesota
MINN#COMM3220 Undergraduate   4 credits $391

Using a symbolic-cultural approach, this course explores the difficulties women and men have in relating with themselves and each other. Obstacles are explored and alternatives proposed.

General Internship
State University of New York
SUNY#CEL200 Undergraduate   3 credits $630*

The Internship Program gives you an opportunity to learn from a work environment and gain practical experience in your prospective career field. Generally, students are placed in non-paid positions. Internships require a minimum of nine hours of internship placement hours per week as well as participating in the on-line seminar throughout the semester, dealing with problems and issues related to work (approximately two hours per week). Prerequisite: Students must have a 2.0 GPA and permission from the office of Experiential and Adult Learning at MCC to register for this course.
* NY residents tuition: $105 per credit.

Getting Results with Time Management
Chemeketa Community College
CHEM#BA062G Undergraduate   1 credits $140

Getting Results with Time Management focuses on methods to help boost productivity and efficiency by better utilizing time and organizational skills. Emphasis will be on creating extra time for planning, evaluation, and decision making. Designed for managers and supervisors in business, industry and government.

Identity Design
Marylhurst College
MARY#MGT502 Undergraduate   3 credits $651
This course examines how an organization articulates and embodies a sense of vision and purpose, how it represents itself in terms of its messages, its goods and services, and the ways in which it does business. As new business conditions and contexts, such as the Internet, arise, identity design must be adapted extended, and re-envisioned.

Individual Differences
Marylhurst College
MARY#PSY360WS Undergraduate   3 credits $651
(Course description not available at press time.)

Internship in Professional Writing
New York Institute of Technology
NYIT#EN1080 Undergraduate   3 credits $???
An advanced elective course which permits the student to gain supervised on-the-job experience as a technical communicator in a professional environment. Prerequisites: EN1048, EN1049, and/or permission of advisor.

Interpersonal Communication
Front Range Community College
FRCC#SPE125 Undergraduate   3 credits $790
This course examines communication in interpersonal relationships in family, social, and career situations. Topics include self-concept, perception, listening, nonverbal communication, and conflict negotiation. 45 Contact Hours.

Interpersonal Communication
Marylhurst College
MARY#CM322B Undergraduate   3 credits $651
Increase your effectiveness in both personal and professional interaction by focusing on awareness, adaptation, social roles, conflict management, and systems of relating.

Interpersonal Communication
Rio Salado College
RISA#COM110 Undergraduate   3 credits $186*
Theory and practice of communication skills which affect day-to- day interactions with other persons. Topics may include using verbal and nonverbal symbols, interactive listening, resolving interpersonal conflict, developing and maintaining personal and professional relationships.
* AZ residents $37 per credit.

Interpersonal Relations
University of Wisconsin
WISC#EDUC388 Undergraduate   3 credits $312
Interpersonal relations applied to teaching. Myers-Briggs personality theory and True Colors (tm), interaction skills, gender differences and relations, negotiation, colleague and long-term relations. Outside reading, projects, writing and exchange of views electronically. This course is available for enrollment whenever it is of interest. Once a student enrolls, there are 120 continuous calendar days in which to complete the course.

Interviewing and Employment Skills
Northwest College
NOCO#OP153 Undergraduate   1 credits $???
Students are assisted in developing personal skills and technical tools needed to obtain entry-level positions after graduation. The writing of resumes and letters of application will be covered.

Interviewing Techniques
Edmonds Community College
EDMO#JOBDV120 Undergraduate   1 credits $45
This course prepares you to interview effectively. You'll develop your own answers to frequently asked questions, including "behavior based" questions which require specific examples. You'll find out how to write a thank you letter and learn the principles of salary negotiation.

Interviewing Techniques
New York Institute of Technology
NYIT#BES2460 Undergraduate   3 credits $???
The examination of communication from various standpoints, as illustrated by different types of interviews. Interviewing techniques employed for personnel selection are compared with those used in interrogation and those used for the therapeutic purposes. Practice in interviewing. Prerequisites: BES2401, BES2411.

Introduction to Professional Editing
University of Minnesota
MINN#ENGW5401 Undergraduate   4 credits $391
Beginning editing, from substantive editing to the nature of the editor-writer relationship: manuscript reading, author queries, rewrite and style, extensive discussion of different kinds of editing, including substantive editing and mechanical editing. Students develop editing awareness and skills by working on varied writing samples.

Introduction to Stock Market Investing
State University of New York
SUNY#BUS107 Undergraduate   1 credits $1038*
This one credit course will cover the basic topics involved with investing and incorporates a stock market simulation that will enable the student to create a stock portfolio from the stocks listed on the new York State Stock Exchange, the American Stock Exchange, or the Over-The-Counter Market. The course covers general introductory principles of investing and topics such as: investment goals and objectives, information sources, common and preferred stock, participation in the market, investment strategies, fundamental and technical analysis, bonds and fixed income fundamentals, mutual funds and other investments.
* NY residents tuition: $137 per credit

Introduction to Technical Writing
Edmonds Community College
EDMO#ENG231 Undergraduate   5 credits $260
This practical course covers the principles of organizing, developing, and expressing technical information and ideas in writing. Attention is given to (1) report forms and rhetorical patterns common to scientific and technical disciplines and (2) technical writing conventions including headings, illustrations, style, and tone. This class teaches writing skills that will be required of science and engineering students during their academic and professional careers. Prerequisite: ENGL105 or equivalent (Compositional English) with a grade of 2.0 or higher.

Investing and Trading on the Internet
Syracuse University
SYRA#HSC0011 Undergraduate   0 credits $299
This course is designed for individuals who wish to learn the art of investing and trading and the practical skills for using the Internet for data gathering and trade execution. The goal is to develop the ability to manage personal investment portfolios including brokerage accounts, IRAs, 401ks, and TIAA-CREFs. The focus of the course is twofold. 1) the theory of investing and 2) the effective use of technology.

Investing in Securities
UCLA
UCLA#X433 Undergraduate   4 credits $500
For beginners and new investors, this online course examines investment policies, mechanics, and techniques of the market. Participants examine types of securities, factors influencing price changes, timing purchases/sales, preparing investment programs to meet objectives, portfolio balancing, and the markets and their behaviors with an emphasis on the New York Stock Exchange.

Investment Basics
New School for Social Research
NEWS#2982 Undergraduate   0 credits $390
This course provides a basic introduction to investments, beginning with discussion of what investing is and why you should invest. Concepts such as creating an appropriate investment strategy and constructing your portfolio are covered. The importance of determining goals, deciding on risk, and setting yardsticks against which to measure your portfolio are discussed thoroughly.

Job Search
Waukesha County Technical College
WAUK#102113013 Undergraduate   1 credits $64*
Beginning a new career, finding employment, or advancing within your current organization can be challenging in a job market affected by downsizing and reorganizing. Students enrolled in Job Search will learn how to assess the needs of a targeted employer and then design an application package that addresses these "needs" in a professional manner. Participants will write cover letters; chronological or functional resumes; participate in a videotaped employment interview; and write follow-up correspondence that is persuasive and polite. Prerequisites: 4th semester student or instructor permission.
* WI residents pay $54 per credit.

Job Search Preparation
Chemeketa Community College
CHEM#FE205A Undergraduate   1 credits $51
Intro, objectives, syllabus, grading, What do I want to achieve from this class - goal statement, The job market and future trends, Portfolios as a job search tool, Benefits and usage, Self-assessment exercises, What do I have to offer?.

Job Search-Job Survival
Edmonds Community College
EDMO#JOBDV115 Undergraduate   3 credits $220
During this course you'll explore a variety of techniques to use when looking for a job, including using the Internet. Investigate the hidden job market. Discover resources that will help you identify potential employers. You'll also examine the skills required to keep the job once you're working.

Keyboarding
Chemeketa Community College
CHEM#CA121 Undergraduate   3 credits $123
Basic touch keyboarding skills on standard microcomputer or typewriter keyboards. Emphasizes speed and accuracy, understanding the basic vocabulary of entering or retrieving information, and formatting business letters and reports.

Keyboarding II
Northwest Technical College
NOTE#ADMS1304 Undergraduate   1 credits $80*
(Course description not available at press time.)
* Residents rates may apply.

Life Planning & Career Development
The Graduate School of America
TGSA#HS879W Graduate   4 credits $795
This course is designed to provide theory, research and opportunities for application appropriate for counselors working with individuals responding to life transitions. Included will be theory and research related to career and life development, improvement and transition.

Life/Work Planning
Marylhurst College
MARY#LPS270 Undergraduate   3 credits $651
Life/Work Planning is designed for individuals changing careers, wanting more fulfillment in their lives and work, entering or re-entering the job market, or returning to school. Learn about your skills, interests, and values. In exploring your personality style, learn how it affects your life and career choices. Recommended for anyone thinking of making personal or professional changes.

Lifestyle for Better Health
Pennsylvania State University
PENN#KINES015 Undergraduate   1 credits $115
Concepts of health, lifestyle, and risk factors; development and implementation of personal action plans.

Logic and Language
University of Colorado
CUON#PHIL2441 Undergraduate   3 credits $1953*
An introduction to logic which will assist students in learning to think more clearly by examining topics such as deduction, fallacies, syllogisms, and rules of inference.".
* CO residents tuition: $136 per credit.

Logic, Business & Everyday Life
Marylhurst College
MARY#PHL325 Undergraduate   3 credits $651
This course aims at teaching the skills to help you come to intelligent, reasoned opinions, to make correct decisions, and to choose the best courses of action in you life and business. This course is not designed to tell you what to think, but to give you sound strategies on how to think; in short, how to think critically. While attending to the skills basic to reasoning in general, this class will focus its efforts on the practical skills necessary for critical thinking in Business and Everyday life.

Logical Thinking
Mercy College
MERC#PL112 Undergraduate   3 credits $900
An introduction to logic, both deductive and inductive, with emphasis on the ways it is most commonly useful: the identification of arguments in context; common fallacies in argument; deductive validity; categorical propositions and their interpretation; the categorical syllogism in standard form and its interpretation; disjunctive an hypothetical syllogisms, and other common argument forms; the nature of inductive arguments; reasoning from analogy; Mill's canons, scientific method.

Managing Creativity
The Graduate School of America
TGSA#OM829W Graduate   4 credits $795
This course focuses on theories and methods for encouraging and rewarding creativity in the organization, its managers and personnel.

Networking for Career Advancement
UCLA
UCLA#X765B Undergraduate   0 credits $400
This course explores the philosophy, processes, and techniques of effective career networking. This is not your typical how to meet people' or sales-lead development course. Networking is redefined to be more accessible and practical for professionals who are seeking to expand and re-energize their career and social networks. This course introduces new online networking strategies, but it is primarily focused on the real-time/real-life issues of connecting with other people face-to-face in order to advance and clarify one's career goals.

Nonverbal Communication
Marylhurst College
MARY#CM324 Undergraduate   3 credits $651
This class explores the nonverbal messages that are intrinsic to interpersonal and public communication settings. Students increase awareness of their own body language as well as their understanding of concepts and principles of non-verbal communication.

Occupational Information
Auburn University
AUBU#VED510 Undergraduate   1.8 credits $76
Occupational Structure, job qualifications and requirements, sources of occupational information, current trends, industrial and occupational surveys. Preparation, evaluation and dissemination of occupational information.

Occupational Information
University of South Florida
FLSO#VED510 Undergraduate   3 qtr. hrs. $???
Occupational Structure, job qualifications and requirements, sources of occupational information, current trends, industrial and occupational surveys. Preparation, evaluation and dissemination of occupational information. (AU students required to have junior standing).

Options on Futures
Western Illinois University
WEIL#AGR456G Undergraduate   1 credits $265*
Explores the trading of options on futures contracts for hedging or speculative purposes. Familiarization with the jargon is followed by consideration of risk/return and effective-price profiles of option positions, hedging strategies for long and short cash positions, trading strategies, and an introduction to the Black pricing model. Registrants should have an understanding of basis hedging.
* IL residents tuition: $88 per credit.

Oral Communications
Strayer University
STRA#ENG221 Undergraduate   4.5 credits $665
Concentrates on the elements and functions of oral communications, studying and practicing various types of oral presentations. Leads the student to first present short speeches (unwritten), and then longer, more formal speeches. Involves student participation in group presentations through planning, organization, and final delivery.

Oral Presentations
Northwest College
NOCO#GE272 Undergraduate   3 credits $???
A comprehensive study of planning presentations using verbal and nonverbal communications, emphasis will be on presenting various types of speeches. Prerequisite: GE179 and GE180 (as applicable).

Personal & Workplace Safety
Rio Salado College
RISA#HCC100AC Undergraduate   3 credits $186*
(Course description not available at press time.)
* AZ residents pay $37 per credit.

Personal and Exploratory Writing
Rio Salado College
RISA#ENG217 Undergraduate   3 credits $186*
Using writing to explore one's self and the world one lives in; emphasis on expository writing as a means of learning. Prerequisites: ENG101 and ENG102.
* AZ residents $37 per credit.

Personal and Family Finance
University of Missouri
MOCE#FI183 Undergraduate   3 credits $387
This course introduces the basic concepts of consumer and family economics. The topics discussed include budgeting, estate planning, cash management, credit, housing, and investing. Perquisites: Math 10 with grade of C or better and sophomore standing.

Personal and Interpersonal Skills
Pennsylvania State University
PENN#HDFS216 Undergraduate   3 credits $345
Conceptions of life-span personal and interpersonal skill enhancement.

Personal Finance
Bakersfield College
BAKE#BUSB40 Undergraduate   3 credits $345*
Teaches the principles and skills of budgeting, making intelligent consumer choices related to consumer credit, banking services, insurance, taxes, transportation, investing for personal retirement, and real estate planning.
* CA residents pay $40 per credit.

Personal Finance
Indiana University
INDI#F260 Undergraduate   3 credits $268
Financial problems encountered in managing individual affairs; family budgeting, installment buying, insurance, home ownership, investing in securities.

Personal Finance
University of Massachusetts - Dartmouth
MADA#FIN320 Undergraduate   3 credits $408
This course is an introduction to the personal financial planning process of setting goals, developing action plans, creating budgets and measuring results. The student will become familiar with the techniques of financial analysis necessary to make choices when considering housing, insurance, retirement plans, borrowing and other personal finance issues. There will be an emphasis on investing in stocks, bonds, and mutual funds. The Internet/Web will be used to study financial planning issues and to communicate with the instructor. No prerequisites.

Personal Finance
Pennsylvania State University
PENN#FIN108 Undergraduate   3 credits $345
Personal management of budgets, bank accounts, loans, credit buying, insurance, real estate, and security buying. May not be scheduled by students in The Smeal College of Business Administration. Prerequisite: third-semester standing.

Personal Financial Planning
Strayer University
STRA#FIN215 Undergraduate   4.5 credits $665
Discusses spending, saving, investing and borrowing decisions within the household life cycle framework. Examines choices among investment alternatives including risk exposure and suitability. Covers real estate transactions, taxes, insurance (life, health, automobile, property, and fire), personal property, securities (stocks and bonds), and estate planning. Applies budgeting techniques to the management of personal finances.

Personal Financial Planning
Western Illinois University
WEIL#FIN301 Undergraduate   3 credits $795*
This introductory personal money management course is intended for the non-finance major. Topics include managing cash income, home ownership, investments, insurance, income and estate planning. Prerequisite: Junior standing.
* IL residents tuition: $88 per credit.

Personal Selling
Pennsylvania State University
PENN#MKTG220 Undergraduate   3 credits $345
Principles underlying the sales process and practical application of these principles to selling situations. Studies role of selling in total marketing process. Prerequisite: third-semester standing.

Personal Taxes
Northwest College
NOCO#AC110 Undergraduate   3 credits $???
The major emphasis of this course is on the individual income tax laws and regulations so that the students will be qualified to prepare their own federal income tax returns.

Personal Writing
Lansing Community College
LANS#WRIT118 Undergraduate   3 credits $315
Develops composition skills, self-expression and sharpened awareness through writing in standard English about personal observations and life experiences. Emphasizes broad choice in subject matter and sensitivity to the language and styles appropriate to description, story telling, and memoirs.

Preparation for Writing Practice
University of Minnesota
MINN#ENGC0011 Undergraduate   0 credits $267
This course is for students who need to build confidence in their writing ability. Exercises emphasize writing as a process--from generating and developing ideas, to writing clearly, to revising.

Preparing for the TOEFL
UCLA
UCLA#X931 Undergraduate   1 credits $150
Assists in preparing non-native speakers of English for the listening, grammar, and reading sections of the TOEFL. Also covers developing good test-taking strategies.

Principles of Communication
Marylhurst College
MARY#CM300 Undergraduate   3 credits $651
Explore central concepts and applications of communication and discover the individual's roles and responsibilities in relating communication to self and society. Prerequisites: advanced standing in a communication major, CM 200, and WR 306 or equivalent.

Principles of Finance
University of Missouri
MOCE#FI123 Undergraduate   3 credits $387
Topics in this course include budgeting, taxes, housing and auto loans, credit, insurance, mutual funds, stocks and bonds, and retirement planning.

Principles of Funeral Service
Fayetteville Technical Community College
FAYE#FSE112 Undergraduate   3 credits $489*
This course covers the principles of funeral service and various religious and cultural customs of funeral service in the US. Emphasis is placed on Protestant, Catholic, Jewish, and other religious groups and the professional and ethical obligations of the profession. Upon completion, students should be able to demonstrate an understanding of religious and cultural traditions and how various funeral services are conducted.
* NC residents pay $20 per credit.

Principles of Real Estate
Western Illinois University
WEIL#FIN321 Undergraduate   3 credits $795*
In the United States, the total value of real estate exceeds that of all stocks, bonds, savings, and currency. The course stresses personal aspects, including information for decision making about home ownership, apartment rental, or selection of a condominium or mobile home. Real estate careers and those in brokerage, property management, appraising, investment counseling, and mortgage lending are introduced and reviewed. Other important course topics deal with the current status of land use controls and zoning, mortgages and financing, private property rights, and real estate contracts.
* IL residents tuition: $88 per credit.

Principles of Risk and Insurance
Indiana University
INDI#N300 Undergraduate   3 credits $268
Nature of risk; insurance as method of dealing with risk; property-liability and life-health insurance; insurance as an economic and social institution.

Principles of Speech Communication
Front Range Community College
FRCC#SPE115 Undergraduate   3 credits $790
This course combines basic theory of speech communication with public speech delivery, preparation, organization, support, and audience analysis. 45 Contact Hours.

Prior Learning Resume
Chemeketa Community College
CHEM#CPL120 Undergraduate   3 credits $123
This course helps students in the process of obtaining credit for prior learning. The course focuses on: identifying career and educational goals, defining college level learning, identifying prior learning, describing prior learning, writing competency statements, documenting prior learning, and preparing one's CPL resume for credit evaluation.

Private Pilot Ground School
University of Alaska - Fairbanks
ALFA#AVTY100 Undergraduate   4 credits $284
Study of aircraft and engine operation, flight instruments, navigation computers, national weather information service. Federal Aviation Regulations, flight information publications, radio communications, radio navigation to prepare for FAA Private Pilot exam.

Problem Solving and Critical Thinking
UCLA
UCLA#X340 Undergraduate   2 credits $415
This 24-hour equivalent online course includes in-depth modules on problem solving and the more general field of critical thinking. The problem-solving modules emphasize multiple-choice problem-solving skills necessary for standardized tests (e.g., GMAT, TOEFL). The critical-thinking modules emphasize logical reasoning, argument analysis, and creative problem solving. Incorporating examples along a continuum of problems from standardized tests to creative open-ended conundrums, the course provides extensive practice and valuable techniques to enhance problem solving, decision making, test taking, and academic performance.

Professional Communication
State University of New York
SUNY#ENG250 Undergraduate   3 credits $630*
Concentration of practical business and professional communication skills, including writing, speaking, and listening. Emphasis is on clarity, organization, format, appropriate language, and consideration of audience, for both written and oral assignments. Prerequisites: English 101 or Advanced Composition.
* NY residents tuition: $105 per credit.

Professional Development
Eastern Oregon University
EAOR#OADM264 Undergraduate   3 credits $240
This course is designed to help the student recognize the importance of intellectual, social, and emotional dimensions of business situations. Emphasis is placed on oral and nonverbal communications, values, ethics, organizational conflict and change, and personal development. Prerequisite: OADM262.

Professional Project Presentation
Bellevue University
BELL#MGTC460 Undergraduate   1 credits $250
(1) Results of student research on a management topic, presented as an oral and written professional project or (2) results of in-depth analysis of a specific company presented as an oral and written Case Study.

Qualitative Analysis
Walden University
WALD#PSYC8130 Graduate   5 credits $1500
This course has been designed to provide academic background information to the doctoral student who plans to use qualitative methodolgy for her/his dissertation research.

Quantitative & Qualitative Analysis
Walden University
WALD#PSYC8120 Graduate   5 credits $1500
An analysis of quantitative statistical designs. Careful attention will be given to the appropriate application of experimental and correlational statistical models. Specific techniques such as data screening, testing assumptions, and analysis will be studied.

Quantitative Reasoning Skills
UCLA
UCLA#X340F Undergraduate   2 credits $390
This 18-hour equivalent online course is designed for students seeking a review of the basic mathematical skills required to successfully take the GMAT and begin a graduate business school course of study. Basic math concepts from arithmetic, algebra, and geometry are presented to reacquaint students who have not had a math class recently or who experience math anxiety.

Research Methods and Statistics
Embry-Riddle Aeronautical University
EMRI#MAS605 Graduate   3 credits $840
A study of current aviation research methods that includes techniques of problem identification, hypothesis formulation, design and use of data gathering instruments, and data analysis. Research reports that appear in professional publications are examined through the use of statistical terminology and computations. A formal research proposal will be developed and presented by each student as a basic course requirement.

Resumes That Get Results
Edmonds Community College
EDMO#JOBDV110 Undergraduate   3 credits $220
During this course, you will learn how to develop a resume that demonstrates your strengths and gives examples of how you've used them at school and paid or volunteer work. You'll find out how to prepare your resume for the Internet and post it at various sites. The class also teaches you the basics of writing a clear, concise cover letter.

Retirement Planning
Rio Salado College
RISA#CPD122 Undergraduate   2 credits $124*
Focuses on cultural and social aspects of retirement planning with emphasis on financial planning, legal concerns, attitude and role adjustments.
* AZ residents pay $37 per credit.

Retirement Planning/Employee Benefits
Waukesha County Technical College
WAUK#114120003 Undergraduate   3 credits $192*
The purpose of this course is to describe the Social Security System and the benefits available through the system. Other topics included are the features of employer retirement plans such as pension, profit sharing, stock bonus, stock option, and stock purchase plans, and retirement plans of self-employed persons. Prerequisite:114105.
* WI residents pay $54 per credit.

Self Managed Career
UCLA
UCLA#X765 Undergraduate   0 credits $450
This online course provides an overview of the steps needed to actively manage one's career. The goal is to build competency in achieving career goals through development of specific career management skills. This course involves the development of realistic career options through the use of self-assessment tools and labor market data. The research techniques and resources available that are necessary to narrow the options also are covered. Resume writing (with instructor feedback) and creating a network are other skills developed in this course.

Skillbuilding I
Northwest Technical College
NOTE#ADMS1308 Undergraduate   1 credits $80*
(Course description not available at press time.)
* Residents rates may apply.

Skills for Healthy Living II
Eastern Oregon University
EAOR#PEH351 Undergraduate   3 credits $240
The course studies contemporary wellness issues that include consumer health, community health, prevention and control of disease, health careers, HIV-AIDS, and environmental health.

Speed Reading
Rio Salado College
RISA#RDG105 Undergraduate   2 credits $124*
Development of skills that result in increased reading speed while maintaining satisfactory comprehension of a variety of materials. Prerequisites: A grade of "C" or better in RDG091 or permission of instructor.
* AZ residents $37 per credit.

Strategies for Effective Communication
Syracuse University
SYRA#ETS400 Undergraduate   3 credits $960
An opportunity to understand the complex ways in which language works as well as to improve written/oral communication skills via the office or home computer. Participants learn the fascinating history, variety, and politics of "standard" English grammar and usage; understand and use skillfully the language/communication "codes" of various discourse communities; understand how language embeds attitudes toward gender and race, and encodes power relationships; practice rhetorical analysis in several venues such as business, the professions, and various forms of popular culture learn strategies for effective communication of complex information.

Stress Management
Chemeketa Community College
CHEM#HS152 Undergraduate   1 credits $59
An introduction to stress management, relaxation techniques, and their impact on health and well-being. It covers a variety of the major relaxation techniques and emphasizes the analysis of life stressors and the development of a personalized stress management plan.

Stress Management
State University of New York
SUNY#PEC253 Undergraduate   2 credits $420*
A course designed to make the student aware of stress and how it impacts his/her quality of life. It will provide methods for identifying stressors and strategies to effectively manage them. Students will be able to construct a personalized life style management program.
* NY residents tuition: $105 per credit.

Study Skills
Chemeketa Community College
CHEM#HD112 Undergraduate   3 credits $123
Develop practical and efficient strategies for learning in order to succeed in college. Learn note taking, listening, textbook study-reading, and time management. Improve test-taking skills, reduce test anxiety, improve concentration and learn memory strategies. Campus resources and learning styles are also included. Prerequisite: Reading Placement Test Score of 34 or Instructor approval.

Teach Yourself Anything
Kennesaw State University
KENN#FMV214A   Undergraduate   3 credits $149
In this dynamic interactive course, self learning expert Art Nieman will share his insights into the enlightening world of learning-by-doing. Nieman, author of The Ultimate Lesson - 10 Point Guide on How to Teach Yourself Anything, taught himself piano at age 5, started a business at 9, and began programming computers at 14. He will inspire you with the courage to take on virtually any subject whether or not formal instruction is available.

Technical Analysis of Securities
Golden Gate University
GOLD#FI352   Undergraduate   3 credits $???
Examines empirical evidence concerning non-efficient markets in which technical analysis is thought to apply. Topics include trend analysis, turning-point analysis, charting techniques, volume and open interest indicators, contrary opinion theories, and technical theories such as Dow theory and Elliot waves. Prerequisite: FI203 or FI300.

Techniques For Improving Imagining Ability
University of Colorado
CUON#ARCH6290   Undergraduate   1 credits $651*
(Course description not available at press time.)
* CO residents tuition: $136 per credit.

Techniques of Study
Lansing Community College
LANS#SDEV124   Undergraduate   2 credits $210
Students will examine their study habits and work toward practicing skills to enhance classroom performance.

The Autonomous Individual
California State University - Dominguez Hills
CADO#HUX543   Undergraduate   3 credits $405
Interdisciplinary study of the nature of the creative act, including the following: the artist's vision of self; the defenses of personalism; notions of aesthetics; and abstract of symbolic thought.

The Craft of Reading
New York University
NEYO#Y20624103   Undergraduate   4 credits $450
In this course, students learn to read various forms of literature with critical attention. They gain a working knowledge of the evolution and structural features of the major literary genres beginning with oral and epic forms, moving to classical and Shakespearean tragedy, as well as various poetic forms, the short story, and the novel. At the same time, students learn to do close, attentive textual analysis of style. As students become sensitive to the subtleties of literary language, they gain skills applicable to any situation. Prerequisite: Writing Workshop I and II or placement testing.

The Individual and Society
California State University - Dominguez Hills
CADO#HUX544   Undergraduate   3 credits $405
Exploration of the position of the individual in the classic and modern models of social and political organization; conservatism, liberalism, socialism, anarchism; study of the Utopian tradition; and study of aesthetic theories that connect the artist with society.

Training and Development
Strayer University
STRA#BUS222   Undergraduate   4.5 credits $665
A practical treatment of the theory and application of training techniques used to develop employees. Topics include the Training Director's job, methods used to identify training and development needs and the design, implementation, and evaluation of training programs. On and off-site training methods, assessment centers, and management development are discussed.

Writing in the Workplace
Waukesha County Technical College
WAUK#801463002   Undergraduate   3 credits $193
(Course description not available at press time.)

Writing in Your Profession
University of Minnesota
MINN#RHET3562   Undergraduate   4 credits $400
Projects in writing professional documents. Analyses of audience and situation; writing effectively to meet the needs of particular readers. Course assignments include writing instructions, feasibility report or proposal, memorandum, letter of application, and resume. Prerequisite: RHET1101, COMP1011, or equivalent.

Science and Mathematics

Advanced Math

Algebra

Basic Math

Basic Science

Biology

Calculus

Chemistry

Earth Science

Geometry

Other

Physics

Trigonometry

Advanced Environmental Science
City University
CITY#SCI301 Undergraduate   5 qu. credits $785
An advanced study of how environmental conditions impact the physical, biological and sociological aspects of life. The impact of current environmental problems such as greenhouse effect, nuclear weapons, and indoor pollution will be explored. Prerequisite: Strongly recommended: NAS215 or its equivalent.

Advanced Topics in Space Studies
University of North Dakota
NODA#SPST570 Graduate   1 credits $272*
These are some topics which show the variety of topics taught for this course: The Planet Mars, The Planet Venus, Outer Planets, Volcanoes of the Planets, Manned Exploration of Moon & Mars, Life in the Universe, Professional Skills Practium. Some are one time only classes.
* ND residents, $102 per credit; may also be reduced for residents of adjoining states and provinces.

Analytic Geometry and Calculus I
Bakersfield College
BAKE#MATHB6A Undergraduate   4 credits $460*
Elements of analytic geometry, differential calculus, and introduction to integration of algebraic functions. Prerequisite: MATH I or equivalent with a grade of C required.
* CA residents pay $40 per credit.

Analytic Geometry and Calculus I
University of Missouri
MOCE#MA80 Undergraduate   5 credits $645
This course gives an introduction to the differentiation and integration of algebraic functions; elementary analytic geometry; functions; limits; continuity; derivatives; antiderivatives; and definite integrals. Perquisites-grade of C or better in Math 14 or equivalent.

Analytic Geometry and Calculus II
Bakersfield College
BAKE#MATHB6B Undergraduate   4 credits $460*
Transcendental functions, polar coordinates, sequences, infinite series and methods of integration. Further exposure to techniques and applications of differential and integral calculus. Prerequisite: MATH6A or equivalent with a grade of "C"; Reading level 1 recommended.
* CA residents pay $40 per credit.

Analytic Geometry and Calculus II
University of Missouri
MOCE#MA175 Undergraduate   5 credits $645
This course discusses select topics from plane analytic geometry and calculus. Perquisites-grade of C or better in Math 80 or equivalent.

Analytic Geometry and Calculus III
University of Missouri
MOCE#MA180 Undergraduate   5 credits $645
Topics in this course include vectors, solid analytic geometry, and calculus of several variables. Perquisites-Math 220; UMR-Math 21; UMSL-Math 175.

Analytical Geometry & Calculus I
University of Colorado
CUON#MATH1401 Undergraduate   4 credits $2604*
The first course of a three-semester sequence (MATH 1401, 2411, 2422/2423) in calculus. Students cannot receive credit for both MATH 1080 and 1401. Topics covered include an introduction to differential and integral calculus, including applications of the derivative and the definite integral. Prerequisite: MATH1120 or 1130; or placement exam.
* CO residents tuition: $136 per credit.

Animal Behavior
University of Missouri
MOCE#HO330 Undergraduate   3 credits $387
This course presents a comparative study of animal behavior. It teaches how behavior relates to bodily structure and environment. Perquisites: Psych. 1 plus eight hours of psychology or biological sciences.

Applied Regression Analysis
Golden Gate University
GOLD#MATH104 Undergraduate   3 credits $960
Applies multiple regression and correlation analysis to forecasting (in particular, managerial interpretation of the regression equation) using a case-study approach. Other topics include: time-series analysis and regression of time-series data. Prerequisite: MATH40.

Asteroids, Meteorites, & Comets
University of North Dakota
NODA#SPST520 Graduate   3 credits $816*
The small bodies of the solar system are clues to its origin. All planets and larger moons have been chemically transferred, but many asteroids, meteorites and comets are apparently little modified from the time of their origin 4.5 billion years ago. Each of these classes of objects is investigated separately, and relationships between them are examined.
* ND residents, $102 per credit; may also be reduced for residents of adjoining states and provinces.

Astronomy
City University
CITY#SCI302 Undergraduate   5 qu. credits $785
An evaluation of the field of Astronomy with emphasis on the creation of the universe and study of the solar system. Topics addressed are: Planetary Motion, Stellar Structure, Star Formation, Milky Way, Terrestrial Planets and UFOs. Prerequisite: Strongly recommended: NAS215 or its equivalent.

Astronomy
Rogers State University
ROGE#PHYS2003 Undergraduate   3 credits $495*
Course includes history of astronomy, techniques and tools of the astronomer, and structure of the universe. A knowledge of basic algebra is helpful but not required. Video: Universe, the Infinite Frontier from Saunders Publishing.
* OK residents $315.

Astronomy
State University of New York
SUNY#1230101 Undergraduate   4 credits $1038*
Introduction for science majors. Spherical trigonometry, planetary motions, solar system, formation of stars, H-R diagram, binaries, brightness scale, distance ladder, Dippler effect, stellar masses, parallax, proper motion, radial motion, mass-luminosity, black-body radiation, spectroscopy, telescopes, dense stars, black holes, galaxies, relativity and cosmology. Prerequisites: General Physics and Calculus II.
* NY residents tuition: $137 per credit

Astronomy
Western Illinois University
WEIL#GEO325 Undergraduate   3 credits $795*
Astronomy has been called the oldest and most comprehensive of sciences. Study major developments from the time of the Babylonians to the present. Requiring no prior knowledge of physics, the course emphasizes the Earth and our solar system. The last part of the course, however, is devoted to other stars and extragalactic astronomy, including clusters, super clusters of galaxies, quasars, and black holes.
* IL residents tuition: $88 per credit.

Astronomy and the WWW
The Heritage Institute
HEON#SC404I Undergraduate   3 qu. credits $215
Astronomy is a science that easily captures the imagination but it is poorly understood by young people and adults. In this course, teachers will take advantage of the great variety of fascinating resources on the WWW to help teach astronomy to all students K-12. You'll learn the major concepts in astronomy, including black holes, comets and meteors, and will learn how to do moon observations. Classroom projects using the WWW which are part of the course will help make astronomy come alive as never before for you and your students.

Basic Algebra
Marylhurst College
MARY#MTH111 Undergraduate   3 credits $651
This class brings you a thorough, but gentle study of the ideas and techniques of algebra, if you've forgotten it or perhaps never had it. It will help you develop skills in the manipulation of polynomial and rational expressions and the solution of linear and quadratic equations. You'll gain an appreciation of the broad range of applications of algebra in professional as well as everyday experiences. The course is also ideal for students planning to study statistics and economics or for those who are preparing for pre-calculus mathematics.

Basic Mathematics
Rogers State University
ROGE#MATH0013 Undergraduate   3 credits $495*
Pre-college math; preparation for college level courses. Includes operations with real numbers, percentages, volumes, areas, perimeters of simple geometric figures, metric system, English system, scientific notation, basic rules of exponents, and solving algebraic equations. This course is for students who need a refresher course in basic mathematics. Video: Topics in Basic Mathematics (DC Heath).
* OK residents $315.

Basic Mathematics Online
Great Basin College
GRBA#MATH091 Undergraduate   3 credits $186*
This course is a review of basic mathematics. Topics include operations with whole numbers, fractions, mixed numbers, decimals, percents, and measurement. This course does not fulfill the math requirement of any degree, nor will it count as an elective for any program.
* NV residents tuition: $43 per credit.

Behavioral Genetics
University of Colorado
CUON#BIOL4104 Undergraduate   3 credits $1953*
Lecture. Interdisciplinary course on relationships between behavior and heredity with an emphasis on human behavioral genetics. Prerequisite: General biology or general psychology.
* CO residents tuition: $136 per credit.

Behavioral Genetics
University of Colorado
CUON#PSY4104 Undergraduate   3 credits $1953*
(Course description not available at press time.)
* CO residents tuition: $136 per credit.

Biology of Nature
State University of New York
SUNY#BIO103 Undergraduate   3 credits $528*
This television course introduces basic ecological principles and applies them to the natural environment of New York State and the Northeast. Topics include basic botany and zoology, food chains, ecosystems, population and community interactions, and terrestrial and aquatic biology. Students receive extensive study guides and thirty half-hour video-taped programs.
* NY residents tuition: $89 per credit.

Calculus
City University
CITY#MTH220 Undergraduate   5 qu. credits $785
An introduction to the basic concepts and theory of differential and integral calculus of one variable, with emphasis on applications to business and economics. Additional application examples are drawn from the natural and social sciences. Prerequisite: Strongly recommended: BSK200 or its equivalent.

Calculus I
University of Alaska - Fairbanks
ALFA#MATH200 Undergraduate   4 credits $284
Techniques and application of differential and integral calculus, vector analysis, partial derivatives, multiple integrals, and infinite series. Prerequisite: MATH107-108.

Calculus I
Golden Gate University
GOLD#MATH100 Undergraduate   3 credits $960
MATH 100 CALCULUS I -3 UNITS Introduces the concepts of differential and integral calculus including the derivative and the definite integral, and differentiation of algebraic, exponential and logarithmic functions. You will apply concepts to business and social sciences. Prerequisite: MATH30 (or equivalent).

Calculus I
University of Minnesota
MINN#MATH1211 Undergraduate   5 credits $445
Analytical geometry and calculus of functions of one variable. Prerequisite: MATH1201 with a grade of C or better, or MATH1008 and 1111 with grades of C or better, or four years of high school MATH and MATH placement score.

Calculus I
New Jersey Institute of Technology
NJIT#MATH111 Undergraduate   4 credits $1524*
A four credit telecourse in calculus, the first in a series of calculus for students in mathematics, quantitative science, or engineering curricula. Considers the theory and techniques of differentiation and integration with application of both processes to engineering and science. Prerequisites: Two years high school algebra, one year geometry, and at least one half year of trigonometry (or college equivalent). Optional: 44 video lessons of 30 and 60 minutes each.
* NJ residents: $184/semester hour.

Calculus I w/ Analytic Geometry
State University of New York
SUNY#MAT171Y03 Undergraduate   4 credits $570*
A University parallel calculus course covering functions, limits, and continuity. Differentiation of algebraic and trigonometric functions with applications including curve sketching, rectilinear motion, related rates, maxima and minima. Summation, integration, and the Fundamental Theorem of Calculus. Differentiation, integration, and graphing logarithmic, exponential, and hyperbolic functions. Analysis of problems using a graphing calculator is part of this course. Prerequisites: Algebra and Trigonometry for Calculus or equivalent.
* NY residents tuition: $90 per credit

Calculus I with Analytic Geometry
Brevard Community College
BREV#MAC1311 Undergraduate   5 credits $765
Limits, continuity, differentiation and integration of algebraic and trigonometric functions, and application of derivatives and integrals. Prerequisite: MCA1104 and 1114 or 1142.

Calculus II
University of Alaska - Fairbanks
ALFA#MATH201 Undergraduate   4 credits $284
Techniques and application of differential and integral calculus, vector analysis, partial derivatives, multiple integrals, and infinite series. Prerequisite: MATH107-108.

Calculus II
New Jersey Institute of Technology
NJIT#MATH112 Undergraduate   4 credits $1524*
This is a four credit telecourse in calculus, the second in a series of calculus for students in mathematics, quantitative science, or engineering curricula. Topics considered include the differentiation and integration of inverse trigonometric, exponential, and logarithmic functions, further methods of integration, infinite series, Taylor series and applications of the definite integral to physical problems. Prerequisites: Calculus I (NJIT#MATH111 or equivalent). Optional: 66 video lessons of 30 minutes each.
* NJ residents: $184/semester hour.

Calculus III
University of Alaska - Fairbanks
ALFA#MATH202 Undergraduate   4 credits $284
Techniques and application of differential and integral calculus, vector analysis, partial derivatives, multiple integrals, and infinite series. Prerequisite: MATH107-108.

Calculus III
Bakersfield College
BAKE#MATHB6C Undergraduate   4 credits $460*
Continuation of Calculus II. Vectors and parametric equations, vector-valued functions, partial differentiation, multiple integrals, vector analysis, including theorems of Green, Gauss, and Stokes. Prerequisite: MATH 6B or equivalent with a grade of "C".
* CA residents pay $40 per credit.

Calculus III
University of Minnesota
MINN#MATH1261 Undergraduate   4 credits $356
In this course, students explore vectors, matrices, linear algebraic equations, Gaussian elimination, determinants and their applications, linear transformations, subspaces, quadratic forms, rigid motions, and orthogonal matrices. Prerequisite: MATH1252, 1353, or equivalent.

Calculus Offered On Line
University of Wisconsin
WISC#MATH221 Undergraduate   5 credits $???
Students take COOL (Calculus Offered On Line) at their high school or at home by joining the class electronically via the WWW. Class materials, which consist of the text "Calculus & Mathematica" and the computer program "Mathematica", are sent by regular mail to each student.

Carbohydrate Chemistry I
State University of New York
SUNY#FCH540 Graduate   2 credits $692*
Two hours of lecture/discussion on the structure, reactions, and analysis of carbohydrates and polysaccharides. Introduction to carbohydrate structure and nomenclature. Overview of important oligosaccharides and major classes of polysaccharides. Reactions of carbohydrates, derivatization, polymerization, degradation. Analysis of carbohydrate molecules - sequence and linkages size, shape, distribution of functional groups. Course Prerequisites: One year of introductory organic chemistry, or permission of Instructor.
* NY residents tuition: $137 per credit

Cell Biology
University of Minnesota
MINN#BIOL5004 Undergraduate   4 credits $400
Structures and functions of membranes, organelles, and other macromolecular aggregates found in plant, animal, and bacterial cells. Cell form and movement, intercellular communication, transport, and secretion. Prerequisite: BIOL5001 or BIOC3021 or BIOC5331, and BIOL5003 or BIOC5333.

Chemistry
Rogers State University
ROGE#CHEM1115 Undergraduate 4 credits $495*
Study of the basic concepts involved in chemical combination, valences, gas laws, liquids, solids, and solutions. For students who have not had high school chemistry. Prerequisites: College Algebra. Video: The World of Chemistry.
* OK residents $315.

Classification of Birds
Northern State University
NOST#BIOL363 Undergraduate 4 credits $329
The course will consist of a series of Internet lectures with links to the Internet. Each student will be required to write a term paper on the natural history of any bird species. Students are asked to submit weekly lists of birds they have identified, as a fulfillment of the laboratory aspect of the class. In addition each student will be required to take three essay exams during the course.

Climatology
Western Illinois University
WEIL#GEO327 Undergraduate 3 credits $795*
The elements of weather and climate are basic to our comfort. This course focuses on the causes and distribution of climatic regions, with special emphasis on the application of climatology to our everyday lives.
* IL residents tuition: $88 per credit.

Coastal Geography
University of South Florida
FLSO#GEO4201 Undergraduate ?? credits $???
This course is designed to introduce upper-division undergraduate students to the field of coastal geography. Coastal geography encompasses a wide diversity of fields, including biology, ecology, geology, geomorphology, marine science, and physical oceanography. It is a topic that has warranted a great deal of attention in geography over the past two decades. A broad overview of the concepts of coastal geography and scientific research in this field will be the focus of the course.

College Algebra
Auburn University
AUBU#MH140 Undergraduate 3 credits $126
The primary goal is to teach basic mathematical skills. Topics include algebraic techniques, coordinate geometry, functions and their graphs, logarithms and exponential functions. A hand-held calculator is required. Enrollees are assumed to have had high school geometry and second-year high school algebra.

College Algebra
Brevard Community College
BREV#MAC1104 Undergraduate 3 credits $485
An in-depth course in linear and quadratic equations and inequalities and their systems, exponential, logarithmic and other functions, matrices and determinants, complex numbers, the binomial theorem. Intended for student who are transferring to any program requiring a calculus or statistics sequence and who do intend to complete the calculus or statistics at BCC.

College Algebra
Fayetteville Technical Community College
FAYE#MAT161 Undergraduate 3 credits $489*
This course provides an integrated technological approach to algebraic topics used in problem solving. Emphasis is placed on equations and inequalities; polynomial, rational, exponential and logarithmic functions; and graphing and data analysis/modeling. Upon completion, students should be able to choose an appropriate model to fit a data set and use the model for analysis and prediction. This course has been approved to satisfy the Comprehensive Articulation Agreement general education core requirement in natural sciences/mathematics. Prerequisites: MAT080 or MAT090.
* NC residents pay $20 per credit.

College Algebra
University of Missouri
MOCE#MA30 Undergraduate 3 credits $387
Course topics include algebra and probability, polynomial functions, the binomial theorem, logarithms, exponentials, and solutions to systems of equations.

College Algebra
Rogers State University
ROGE#MATH1513 Undergraduate 3 credits $495*
Includes special products, factoring, fractions, exponents, radicals, functions, inequalities, polynomials, systems of equations, matrices, determinants, and progressions. Prerequisite: MATH0013 Video: College Algebra from Rogers State College.
* OK residents $315.

College Algebra and Trigonometry
New York Institute of Technology
NYIT#MA3014 Undergraduate 3 credits $???
A study of relations and functions; inequalities; complex numbers; quadratic equations; linear and quadratic systems; trigonometric functions; identities; functions of composite angles; graphs of the trigonometric functions; logarithm; and binomial formula. Prerequisite: Math placement test.

College Algebra and Trigonometry
State University of New York
SUNY#MAT1593408 Undergraduate 4 credits $1038*
Students will learn algebra and trigonometry topics necessary to prepare them for the study of precalculus. Topics include one-to-one functions and their inverses and graphs, polynomial and rational functions and their applications, radicals and exponents, and trigonometric functions, including graphs and basic identities. Problem-solving and applications are emphasized. Prerequisite: Intermediate Algebra. Special Requirement: An approved graphing calculator is required.
* NY residents tuition: $137 per credit.

College Chemistry I
New Jersey Institute of Technology
NJIT#CHEM108 Undergraduate 3 credits $1143*
This course provides the first of a two-semester sequence of college chemistry for high school students and other distance learners seeking college credit and/or preparation for the AP Examination. Prerequisites: One year College-Prep H.S. Chemistry and Math including Algebra and Trigonometry. Optional: 28 video lessons of 30 minutes each.
* NJ residents: $184/semester hour.

College Chemistry II
New Jersey Institute of Technology
NJIT#109 Undergraduate   3 credits $1143*
A continuation of Chem 108. Prerequisites: One year College-Prep H.S. Chemistry and Math including Algebra and Trigonometry. Optional: 28 video lessons of 30 minutes each.
* NJ residents: $184/semester hour.

College Geometry
City University
CITY#MTH120 Undergraduate   5 qu. credits $785
An examination of the definitions, postulates, theorems and corollaries that make up the study of geometry as written by Euclid. Topics covered include: planes, angles, parallel lines, quadrilaterals, circles, cylinders, spheres and coordinates.

College Mathematics
Rio Salado College
RISA#MAT142 Undergraduate   3 credits $186*
Working knowledge of college-level mathematics and its applications to real-life problems. Emphasis on understanding mathematical concepts and their applications rather than on manipulative skills. Appropriate for the student whose major does not require college algebra or pre-calculus. Prerequisites: Grade of "C" or better in MAT120 or MAT122 or equivalent, or satisfactory score on District placement exam.
* AZ residents $37 per credit.

College Physics I
University of Colorado
CUON#PHYS2010 Undergraduate   4 credits $2604*
Mechanics, heat, and sound. Prerequisite: College algebra and trigonometry; Coreq: PHYS2030.
* CO residents tuition: $136 per credit.

College Physics Lab I
University of Colorado
CUON#PHYS2030 Undergraduate   1 credits $651*
(Course description not available at press time.) Prerequisite: Coreq: PHYS2030.
* CO residents tuition: $136 per credit.

Commercialization of Space
University of North Dakota
NODA#SPST440 Graduate   3 credits $???
A study of the current state of commercial space activities, with analysis of the possibilities and the barriers. Key areas include launch services, satellite communications, remote sensing, microgravity materials processing, and interaction with the government. Global competition against subsidized or government-sponsored entities is examined. This course investigates the economic aspects of the space industry, including who purchases equipment and services and why, the structure of the space industry, national and international competition, different market segments and products, factors of production (labor, capital), and technology generation and diffusion.

Comprehensive Introductory Physics with Calculus I
University of Minnesota
MINN#PHYS1311 Undergraduate   4 credits $356
Calculus-level general physics stressing the use of fundamental principles. Topics: vectors, kinematics in two and three dimensions, particle dynamics, work, energy, collisions, and gravitation. This course does not include a lab, and the physics department does not offer a separate lab. Prerequisite: completion or concurrent registration in introductory calculus.

Comprehensive Introductory Physics with Calculus II
University of Minnesota
MINN#PHYS1321 Undergraduate   4 credits $356
Calculus-level general physics stressing the use of fundamental principles. Topics: rigid-body kinematics and dynamics, statics, elasticity, oscillations, mechanical waves, sound, fluid statics and dynamics, heat and thermodynamics. This course does not include a lab, and the physics department does not offer a separate lab. Prerequisite: PHYS1311 or equivalent.

Comprehensive Introductory Physics with Calculus III
University of Minnesota
MINN#PHYS1331 Undergraduate   4 credits $356
Calculus-level general physics stressing the use of fundamental principles. Topics: the electric field, electric potential, capacitors, dielectrics, DC circuits, magnetic fields, induction, magnetic materials, and AC circuits. This course does not include a lab, and the physics department does not offer a separate lab. Prerequisite: PHYS1321 or equivalent.

Comprehensive Introductory Physics with Calculus IV
University of Minnesota
MINN#PHYS1341 Undergraduate   4 credits $356
Calculus-level general physics stressing the use of fundamental principles. Topics: Maxwell's equations, electromagnetic waves, nature and propagation of light, reflection, refraction, lenses, mirrors, optical instruments, interference, diffraction, special relativity, quanta, atomic spectra, nuclei, fission, and fusion. Does not include a lab, and the physics department does not offer a separate lab. Prerequisite: PHYS1331 or equivalent.

Computer Algebra with Mathematica
University of Massachusetts - Lowell
MALO#92419 Undergraduate   3 credits $395
Mathematica is an extremely powerful computer-based tool for solving problems. Computer algebra systems like Mathematica are used by engineers, scientists and mathematicians to assist them in attacking problems that require complicated and involved symbolic or numeric computations. Requirements for the course: Mathematica (Version 2.0 or later) Your version should have a Notebook interface. A computer that will run your version of Mathematica (most likely a Macintosh or PC) An Internet connection with email and web browser software.

Concepts & Applications of Math
University of Alaska - Fairbanks
ALFA#MATH131 Undergraduate   3 credits $213
Applications of math in modern life, including uses of graph theory in management science; probability and statistics in industry, government, and science; geometry in engineering and astronomy. Problem solving emphasized. Requires access to a VCR. Prerequisite: High school geometry and algebra II.

Concepts of Math
University of Alaska - Fairbanks
ALFA#MATH132 Undergraduate   3 credits $213
Mathematical thought and history for students with a limited math background. Mathematical reasoning rather than formal manipulation. May include number theory, topology, set theory, geometry, algebra, and analysis. Prerequisite: MATH131.

Concepts of Physical Science
Cerro Coso Community College
CECO#PHSCC11 Undergraduate   3 credits $345*
A survey of concepts in physics and chemistry, with applications to the earth sciences and astronomy, for the nonscience major. Topics are developed with a minimum of mathematical presentation. Prerequisite: Level 1 reading, level 3 mathematics classification recommended.
* CA residents pay $13 per credit.

Conservation and Management of Natural Resources
Western Illinois University
WEIL#GEO426G Undergraduate   3 credits $795*
Examines U.S. environmental problems in their physical and regulatory contexts. Specific topics addressed are air and water quality, wildlife and soil conservation, waste and toxic substance management, and public lands management. Particular emphasis is given to forest management and the preservation of biological diversity. A short history of the conservation movement in the Unites States is also presented.
* IL residents tuition: $88 per credit.

Conservation of Natural Resources
University of Minnesota
MINN#NRES1201 Undergraduate   3 credits $267
Current status, utilization, and sound management of natural resources with emphasis on the ecological approach. Conservation principles and their application to soil, water, forests, grasslands, wildlife, minerals, energy sources.

Contemporary Environmental Issues
City University
CITY#INT303 Undergraduate   5 qu. credits $785
A critical survey of leading environmental issues facing the contemporary world and particular regions at risk. Topics include the use and misuse of world energy resources, natural resource exploitation and air and water quality use. Emphasis is on the effects that environmental policy and resource use have on the structure and stability of the world's political, economic and social order. The course concludes with an examination of current topics such as acid rain, species extinction and the destruction of the world's oceans, rain forests and atmosphere.

Contemporary Science - Oceanus
Rochester Institute of Technology
ROCH#69223490 Undergraduate   4 credits $923
An introduction to the fundamental principles of oceanography for non-science majors and the application of those concepts to areas of interest and concern in our contemporary technological society.

Cosmology and the Origin of Life
University of Oregon
OREG#AST123 Undergraduate   4 credits $374
This course is designed to be an exploration of the process by which the universe grows; more specifically, it is a study in the evolution of ideas, based on observations, and the development of a non-unique evolutional model that describes the origin of the universe and the development of life. The final exam will be quite different and will hopefully force you to reflect on how you think everything in the universe fits together.

Data Analysis & Statistics
The Graduate School of America
TGSA#RM500W Graduate   4 credits $795
This course addresses data skills and analytical capabilities as applied to management decisions. It covers an overview of data sources and data analysis, inferential procedures, regression analysis and the use of statistical packages. (This course fulfills the requirements for RM501).

Descriptive College Physics
Barstow Community College
BARS#PHYS2 Undergraduate   3 credits $???
Basic physics principles and concepts. Energy, momentum, electromagnetic radiation, gravity and Newton's Laws of Motion.

Developmental Mathematics I/II
New York Institute of Technology
NYIT#MA3013 Undergraduate   3 credits $???
Designed for the accelerated student who has had some skills in algebra and is more motivated to finish at a faster pace. Topics covered include basic operations of signed integers and fractions, factoring, basic operation of algebraic fractions, exponents and radicals, functions and graphs, and equations. Prerequisite: Math placement test.

Differential Equations
New Jersey Institute of Technology
NJIT#MATH222 Undergraduate   4 credits $1524*
Methods of solving ordinary differential equations are studied together with physical and geometrical applications, Laplace transforms, numerical and series solutions are included. Prerequisites: Calculus III and knowledge of a programming language. Optional: 60 video lessons of 30 minutes each.
* NJ residents: $184/semester hour.

Discrete Analysis
New Jersey Institute of Technology
NJIT#MATH226 Undergraduate   4 credits $1524*
An introduction to discrete mathematics. Topics include elementary set theory, logic, combinatorics, relations, graphs and trees, algebraic systems. Prerequisite: Calculus II. Optional: 37 video lessons each 60 minutes in length.
* NJ residents: $184/semester hour.

Earth Science
University of Missouri
MOCE#EA56 Undergraduate   3 credits $387
This is a general study of the earth: its origin; the development of its crustal features and the processes that shape them; its oceans; its climates; and its neighbors in the solar system.

Earth System Science
University of North Dakota
NODA#SPST430 Graduate   3 credits $816*
Space Exploration has fundamentally altered how humans perceive their home. Individual scientific disciplines are no longer studied as isolated fields; rather, we have gained a greater understanding of the important interrelationships between all of the physical sciences.
* ND residents, $102 per credit; may also be reduced for residents of adjoining states and provinces.

Ecological Philosophy
City University
CITY#PHI408 Undergraduate   5 qu. credits $785
An historical and cultural convergence of philosophy and ecology which examines common concerns. The course shows how philosophies have shaped human attitudes and uses of nature and how an understanding of ecological philosophies can be applied to resolve environmental problems. Prerequisite: Strongly recommended: HUM200 or its equivalent.

Elementary Algebra
University of Alaska - Fairbanks
ALFA#DEVM060 Undergraduate   3 credits $213
First year high school algebra. Evaluating and simplifying algebraic expressions, solving first degree equations and inequalities, integral exponents, polynomials, factoring, rational expressions. Prerequisite: DEVM050 or placement.

Elementary Algebra
Rogers State University
ROGE#MATH0113 Undergraduate   3 credits $495*
Includes signed numbers, exponents, and algebraic expressions through quadratic equations. Prerequisite: MATH0013 or a firm understanding of basic mathematics. Video: Elementary Algebra from Rogers State College.
* OK residents $315.

Elementary Physics II
Christopher Newport University
CHNE#PHYS104 Undergraduate   3 credits $993
Fall and spring. A survey of classical and modern physics with discussion of their historical development and implication to society. Analysis of problems in mechanics, heat, sound, electromagnetism, and modern physics. Influence of physics on art, literature, and values. Satisfies distribution requirements in the field of science.

Elementary Probability and Statistics
University of Alaska - Fairbanks
ALFA#STAT200 Undergraduate   3 credits $213
Descriptive statistics, frequency distributions, sampling distributions, elementary probability, estimation of population parameters, hypothesis testing (one and two sample problems), correlation, simple linear regression, and one-way analysis of variance. Parametric and nonparametric methods. Prerequisite: MATH107, MATH161, MATH181 or consent of the instructor.

Elementary Probability and Statistics
Bakersfield College
BAKE#MATHB22 Undergraduate   5 credits $575*
Graphical methods of description of data, finite probability; discrete and continuous random variables; sampling distributions; hypothesis testing for large and small samples, analysis of variance, nonparametric statistics; linear regression and correlation. Prerequisite: MATH D or equivalent with grade of "C"; Reading Level 1 recommended.
* CA residents pay $40 per credit.

Elementary School Teacher Math I
University of Alaska - Fairbanks
ALFA#MATH205 Undergraduate   3 credits $213
Elementary set theory, numeration systems, and algorithms of arithmetic, divisors, multiples, integers, introduction to rational numbers. Prerequisite: Two years high school math, including at least one year of algebra.

Elementary School Teacher Math II
University of Alaska - Fairbanks
ALFA#MATH206 Undergraduate   3 credits $213
A continuation of MATH205. Real number systems and subsystems, logic, informal geometry, metric system, probability, and statistics. Prerequisite: MATH205.

Elementary Statistics
University of Missouri
MOCE#MA31 Undergraduate   3 credits $387
Topics in this course include the collection and presentation of data; averages; and dispersion. This course also provides an introduction to statistical inference, estimation, hypothesis testing, and correlation. Perquisites: grade of C or better in Math 10, 14, or 15, or an MMPT score of 26 or better.

Elements of Calculus
University of Missouri
MOCE#MA61 Undergraduate   3 credits $387
This course introduces analytic geometry, derivatives, and definite integrals.

Elements of Physical Geography
University of Alaska - Fairbanks
ALFA#GEOG205 Undergraduate   3 credits $213
Analysis of the processes that form the physical environment and the resulting physical patterns. Study of landforms, climate, soils, water resources, vegetation, and their world and regional patterns. Prerequisite: GEOG101, GEOG103 or permission.

Entomology
Auburn University
AUBU#ENT204 Undergraduate   3 qtr. hrs. $126
Life processes, occurrence and importance of insects.

Environmental Biology
Rio Salado College
RISA#IO105 Undergraduate   4 credits $248*
Fundamentals of ecology and their relevance to human impact on natural ecosystems. Field trips may be required at students' expense.
* AZ residents $37 per credit.

Environmental Ethics
Christopher Newport University
CHNE#PHIL395A Undergraduate   3 credits $993
The course will analyze the major philosophical issues in the field of environmental ethics. Topics will include the role of science and the scientific method, the aesthetic value of nature, animal rights, strong and weak anthropocentrism, Ecotheology, Deep Ecology, Ecofeminism, environmental economics, Buddhist and Taoist attitudes toward nature, the political concept of the Commons. In addition to Western metaphysical and ethical systems, non-Western cultures and primal societies will be considered. Prerequisite: Three hours of philosophy or consent of instructor.

Environmental Ethics
City University
CITY#PHI406 Undergraduate   5 qu. credits $785
An historical and cultural assessment of attitudes towards nature from the archaic to the postmodern. The course examines how philosophies have shaped attitudes toward and uses of nature and how an understanding of philosophies can be applied to resolve current environmental problems. Prerequisite: Strongly recommended: HUM200 or its equivalent.

Environmental Geology
New School for Social Research
NEWS#0809 Undergraduate   3 credits $1638*
Environmental geology emphasizes the interrelationship of humans and their planet. This course provides the non-scientist with an understanding of how natural geological processes and hazards influence human activities. Environmental questions such as acid rain, PCBs in the Hudson River, waste disposal, pollution, earthquakes on the East Coast, energy resources, and nuclear energy for New York are addressed. Classic problems like volcanic eruptions, flooding, glaciation, threats to shoreline environments, and the development of mineral resources are also studied.
* Non-credit option, tuition: $365.

Environmental Geology
Western Illinois University
WEIL#GEO375 Undergraduate   3 credits $795*
Is an in-depth treatment of our relations with the physical environment. Subjects range from the philosophical basis for the study of environmental geology to the geological and human aspects of natural hazards such as flooding, landslides, earthquakes, and volcanoes. Other materials include water and human use; solid, liquid, and nuclear waste disposal; the geologic aspects of environmental health; mineral and energy resources; and environmental law. Prerequisite: Geology 110.
* IL residents tuition: $88 per credit.

Environmental Problems
University of Minnesota
MINN#GEOG3355 Undergraduate   4 credits $391
Defining and "solving" environmental problems; implementing "solutions.".

Environmental Report Writing
Eastern Oregon University
EAOR#GEOG319 Undergraduate   3 credits $250
Data collection and analysis, design and writing of land use and environmental reports for public and private agencies. Individual and/or class projects. Prerequisite: GEOG317, GEOG318.

Environmental Research
Eastern Oregon University
EAOR#GEOG01 Undergraduate   1-5 credits $80-400
(Course description not available at press time.)

Environmental Science
Eastern Oregon University
EAOR#SCI241 Undergraduate   4 credits $320
This course is designed to introduce students to the interdisciplinary field of environmental science. Concepts fundamental to the study of the physical sciences as they apply to the environment will be emphasized. Additionally, there will be some investigation of the social, political, and economic impact of environmental policies. Prerequisite: High school biology and chemistry.

Environmental Science
Mercy College
MERC#BI112 Undergraduate   3 credits $900
Students will study the basic biological concepts and scientific methodology as exemplified in the study of the present-day environmental problems such as air and water pollution, food control and populations, and their effects on humans.

Environmental Science
New Jersey Institute of Technology
NJIT#EVSC602 Undergraduate   3 credits $1143*
An introduction to pollution prevention, life cycle analysis and industrial metabolism topics with an emphasis on case study work. The focus of the course will be on industrial profiles and other issues including: technology and industry, budget and cycles, process and product audit, "green" economics, regulatory topics, unit operations and future outlooks. Prerequisites: Approval of graduate advisor in environmental science. Optional: 13 video lessons 180 minutes each.
* NJ residents: $184/semester hour.

Environmental Sciences
New York Institute of Technology
NYIT#LS9500 Undergraduate   3 credits $???
A multidisciplinary approach to the environmental and ecological sciences emphasizing principles, problems, and alternative approaches to situations. The issues are treated in sufficient depth to permit quantitative reasoning and assessment, especially in such vital topics as the demographic trends of humanity in a resource-limited biosphere. Human physiological and behavioral requisites are interwoven with the fabric of culture and technology in modern society. In addition to lectures and seminars, students are required to become involved in a term activity, project, or paper which may integrate several disciplines.

Environmental Studies
University of Minnesota
MINN#BIOL3051 Undergraduate 4 credits $400
Principles of ecology and current environmental issues, including air and water pollution, human population growth, toxic and hazardous wastes, urbanization, land use, biological diversity, energy, environmental health, conservation history, attitudes toward nature, environmental politics, and ethics. Meets environmental theme for liberal education curriculum. Students may receive credit for only one of these courses: BIOL3051 or BIOL1051. Biological Sciences students may not apply these credits to the major. Read a detailed description of BIOL3051.

Equine Genetic Principles
Waukesha County Technical College
WAUK#091112 Undergraduate 1 credits $105
With the recent rapid advances in Equine genetic testing, the horse enthusiast and student can no longer pass over equine genetics as only important to the breeder. The trainer and barn manager must now understand the consequences of certain genetically inherited traits in order to advise owners and manage horses effectively. Genetics is currently ranked as one of the most important and rapidly advancing fields in human medicine. While equine advances are slower, researchers will take advantage of techniques learned in other fields and utilize them to advance equine genetic understanding.

Finite Mathematics
University of Missouri
MOCE#MA60 Undergraduate 3 credits $387
This course introduces matrices and linear programming and probability. It is recommended that students taking this course have access to a scientific calculator. Perquisites: one year of high school algebra or equivalent.

Finite Mathematics
New Hampshire College
NEHA#MAT120 Undergraduate 3 credits $1656
This course serves to both prepare students for other courses in the core curriculum and in their major as well as provide a basis for making decisions which they will encounter after graduation. Topics include solving equations, modeling with linear, quadratic, exponential and logarithmic functions, solving simple linear systems of equations, mathematics of finance, and probability. While these topics obviously are prerequisite to more advanced mathematics, they increasingly play a part in quantitatively sophisticated discussions of difficult and controversial public policy issues. Prerequisite: competency in high school algebra.

Finite Mathematics
New York Institute of Technology
NYIT#MA3010 Undergraduate 3 credits $???
Review of elementary algebra and selected topics in statistics and probability. Sets, real numbers, graphing, linear and quadratic equations and inequalities, relations and functions, solving systems of linear equations, descriptive statistics, frequency distribution, graphical displays of data, measures of central tendency and dispersion, introduction to probability. Prerequisite: MA3008 or MA3013 or Math placement test.

Forecasting
The Graduate School of America
TGSA#OM861W Graduate 4 credits $795
This introduces managers to quantitative and qualitative forecasting methods.

Foundations of Elementary Math I
Eastern Oregon University
EAOR#MATH211 Undergraduate 4 credits $320
Introduction to the basic concepts of elementary mathematics designed to initiate the building of an understand ing and appreciation of the nature, structure, philosophy, and history of mathematics. Prerequisite: MATH095.

Foundations of Elementary Math II
Eastern Oregon University
EAOR#MATH212 Undergraduate 4 credits $320
Introduction to the basic concepts of elementary mathematics designed to initiate the building of an understand ing and appreciation of the nature, structure, philosophy, and history of mathematics. Prerequisite: MATH095.

Foundations of Elementary Math III
Eastern Oregon University
EAOR#MATH213 Undergraduate 4 credits $320
Introduction to the basic concepts of elementary mathematics designed to initiate the building of an understand ing and appreciation of the nature, structure, philosophy, and history of mathematics. Prerequisite: MATH095.

Functions for Calculus
University of Alaska - Fairbanks
ALFA#MATH107 Undergraduate 3 credits $213
A study of algebraic, logarithmic, and exponential functions, together with selected topics from algebra. Prerequisite: 2 years of high school algebra and MATH107 placement or higher.

General Biology
Brevard Community College
BREV#BSCC1010 Undergraduate 4 credits $625
An introduction to principles of biology to include a study of cell structure, function and reproduction; inheritance; development; energy transformation; evolution and ecology of populations and communities.

General Biology
University of Minnesota
MINN#BIOL1009 Undergraduate 5 credits $445
An introduction to the general principles of biology. Topics: the cell, metabolism, heredity, reproduction, ecology, and evolution. Eight lab exercises, most of which students can perform in their own kitchens.

General Biology
University of Missouri
MOCE#BI1 Undergraduate 3 credits $387
This course covers general principles of biology; it studies the cell through organisms, ecosystems, and man.

General Chemistry I
Fayetteville Technical Community College
FAYE#CHM151C Undergraduate 3 credits $489*

This course covers fundamental principles and laws of chemistry. Topics include measurement, atomic and molecular structure, periodicity, chemical reactions, chemical bonding, stoichiometry, thermochemistry, gas laws, and solutions. Upon completion, students should be able to demonstrate an understanding of fundamental chemical laws and concepts as needed in CHM152. This course has been approved to satisfy the Comprehensive Articulation Agreement general education core requirement in natural sciences/mathematics.

* North Carolina residents and non-resident US military personnel stationed within the state tuition: $60; NC senior citizens: free.

General Chemistry I
University of Massachusetts - Dartmouth
MADA#CHM101 Undergraduate 3 credits $408

An introduction to the fundamental chemical laws and theories covering inorganic and organic chemistry with some descriptive chemistry. (For non-science majors, nurses and technologists) course? Prerequisites: Although there are no formal prerequisites, two years of high school algebra are strongly recommended. A background in high school chemistry is desirable, but not required.

General Environmental Biology
Rogers State University
ROGE#BIOL1134 Undergraduate 4 credits $545*

A general survey of environmental science. Includes an introduction to basic ecological principles with an emphasis on major modes of environmental pollution.

* OK residents $420.

General Geology
MiraCosta College
MIRA#GEOL101 Undergraduate 3 credits $357

This course is designed for students who wish to study geology using computer resources and information technology. Students use on-line field trips, CD associated with the textbook and other computer-based resources to learn geology. Prerequisite: Tarbuck & Lutgens; The Earth: An Introduction to Physical Geology, 5th ed.

General Physics
University of Minnesota
MINN#PHYS1104 Undergraduate 4 credits $356

Primarily for premedical and biological science students. Topics: motion, Newton's laws, work and energy, momentum and the pressure of gases, mechanical properties of matter, temperature, thermal properties of matter, thermodynamics, sound, entropy. No credit for IT students. Prerequisite: MATH1142 and high school trigonometry or MATH1008.

General Physics
University of Minnesota
MINN#PHYS1105 Undergraduate 4 credits $356

Second course in the series. Topics: fluid statics, fluid dynamics, elastic properties of solids, vibration, traveling, standing, and sound waves, reflection and refraction of light, optical instruments, interference, electric fields, and electrical energy. No credit for IT students. Prerequisite: PHYS1104.

General Physics
University of Minnesota
MINN#PHYS1106 Undergraduate 4 credits $356

Third course in the series. Topics: direct-current circuits, capacitors, magnetic fields and forces, alternating-current circuits, special relativity, wave-particle duality, Bohr model of the atom, quantum mechanics, nuclear physics, and elementary particle physics. Prerequisite: PHYS1105.

General Physics
Pennsylvania State University
PENN#PHYS201 Undergraduate 4 credits $460

Mechanics. Concurrent: MATH140.

General Physics
Pennsylvania State University
PENN#PHYS202 Undergraduate 4 credits $460

Electricity and magnetism. Student must supply: electronic calculator with trigonometric functions in both degrees and radians, base 10 and base e logarithms, and reciprocals. Ruler, protractor, and three-ring loose-leaf binder also are needed. Concurrent: MATH 141 Prerequisite: PHYS 201.

General Physics
Pennsylvania State University
PENN#PHYS203 Undergraduate 3 credits $345

Wave motion and thermodynamics. Student must supply: electronic calculator with trigonometric functions in both degrees and radians, base 10 and base e logarithms, and reciprocals. Ruler, protractor, and three-ring loose-leaf binder also are needed. Prerequisite: PHYS202.

Genetics
University of Minnesota
MINN#BIOL5003 Undergraduate 4 credits $400

Introduction to the nature of genetic information, its transmission from parents to offspring, its expression in cells and organisms, and its course in populations. Students may receive credit for only one of these courses: BIOL5003, GCB3022, or GCB5022. Prerequisite: BIOL5001 or BIOC3021 or BIOC5331.

Genetics
University of Minnesota
MINN#GCB3022 Undergraduate 4 credits $400

Mechanisms of heredity, their implications for biological populations, and applications to practical problems are examined. Not intended for biology majors. Students may receive credit for only one of these courses: GCB3022 or BIOL5003. Prerequisite: BIOL1009 or BIOL1202.

Genetics
University of Missouri
MOCE#SC224 Undergraduate 4 credits $516

This course studies the principles of heredity and reasons for variation in plants and animals. A study of Mendelian principles and population genetics with emphasis on the human is included. Perquisites-Biological Science 10, Chemistry 31, and sophomore standing.

Geographic Technical Methodology
University of South Florida
FLSO#GEO4114   Undergraduate   ?? credits $???
This course is designed to introduce upper-division undergraduate geography students to the basic concepts and principles of geographic information systems. Since geographic information systems are presently being used in many different fields of study, including criminology, ecology, geography, marine science, remote sensing, and urban planning, it is important that geography majors understand what geographic information systems are and how they are utilized. This course is intended to give future professional geographers a 'taste' for what a geographic information system can do for them now and for their forthcoming endeavors.

Geography of Alaska
University of Alaska - Fairbanks
ALFA#GEOG302   Undergraduate   3 credits $237
Regional, physical and economic geography of Alaska. Special consideration of the state's renewable and nonrenewable resources, and of plans for their wise use. Frequent study of representative maps and visual materials. Prerequisite: GEOG101 & GEOG205.

Geography of the United States and Canada
University of Minnesota
MINN#GEOG3101   Undergraduate   4 credits $391
Learn the tools of geographic analysis through readings and exercises focused on ten major regions of the United States and Canada. The emphasis in this course is on a comparison and analysis of road maps, landform maps, and thematic maps to decipher the cultural, physical, and economic nuances that make all locations geographically unique.

Geology of Oregon and the Pacific Northwest
University of Oregon
OREG#GEO308   Undergraduate   4 credits $374
Written around a brand new text on the Geology of the Pacific Northwest by Orr and Orr. Despite the fascinating nature of geological features and history of this area, this is the first comprehensive book on NW geology that has been written in over two decades.

Geology of the National Parks
University of Oregon
OREG#GEO303   Undergraduate   4 credits $374
Modeled after a popular large enrollment course taught annually at the University of Oregon. It is designed for students with limited science backgrounds and can be taken without prerequisites. Material presented in the text is to give the reader an overview of the general geology of over 50 national parks. For each introductory section and chapter, students are directed to focus on what geologic events and history at each site make the area attractive as a national park.

Global Change
University of North Dakota
NODA#SPST435   Graduate   3 credits $816*
Investigation of environmental changes, often occurring locally, which contribute to large scale transformations. Some of these changes are natural, others are a consequence of human activity. Topics include comet impacts, population growth, volcanic eruptions, deforestation, biodiversity, water management, global warming, and ozone and sustainable societies.
* ND residents, $102 per credit; may also be reduced for residents of adjoining states and provinces.

Global Environment & Change I
Thomas Edison State College
THED#OLENS311   Undergraduate   3 credits $397*
This course examines a number of the environmental changes that may result from human activities and possible effects of and responses to those changes. Two central themes are considered. First, the need for a variety of resources: food & the soil to produce it; fresh water; atmospheric processes; and energy to support the subsistence, social & economic activities of humankind. The second theme is the exponentially increasing global human population & relationship of factors influencing global environment to the number of humans the environment must support.
* NJ residents tuition: $33 per credit.

Global Environment and Change II
Thomas Edison State College
THED#OLENS312   Undergraduate   3 credits $397*
This course examines a number of the environmental changes that may result from human activities and possible effects of and responses to those changes. Two central themes are considered. First, the need for a variety of resources: food & the soil to produce it; fresh water; atmospheric processes; and energy to support the subsistence, social & economic activities of humankind. The second theme is the exponentially increasing global human population & relationship of factors influencing global environment to the number of humans the environment must support.
* NJ residents tuition: $33 per credit.

Historical Geology
University of Minnesota
MINN#GEO1002   Undergraduate   4 credits $356
Evolution of the earth and its inhabitants from their origins to the present, emphasizing the past 600 million years. The course outlines the fundamentals of geology, evolution, and paleontology.

Human Biology
Front Range Community College
FRCC#BIO116   Undergraduate   3 credits $790
This course is an introduction to human anatomy and physiology for students who have little or no background in science. It does not substitute for a year long Anatomy and Physiology course with a lab. Topics covered are atoms, molecules, cells, energetics, genetics, and a brief survey of systems. 45 Contact Hours (lecture).

Human Biology
Marylhurst College
MARY#BIO162 Undergraduate   3 credits $651

The workings of the human body are an intricate choreography. Responses to external changes and challenges occur at many levels from molecular to that of the organ system. The body is always working to maintain a constant internal environment. This course explores human biology with an emphasis on physiology. Taking advantage of resources and communications unique to the Internet, we will examine the latest findings on the structure and function of the human body as well as how it responds to factors such as disease and aging.

Human Biology
Western Illinois University
WEIL#BIO304 Undergraduate   4 credits $1030*

Includes topics on human evolution, behavior, ecology, and physiology in detail. Human genetics, including inheritance of chromosomes, sex determination, molecular genetics, mutations, and genetic engineering are also developed. There are 7 required laboratory experiments that include dissecting a preserved fetal pig and following chicken egg development.
* IL residents tuition: $88 per credit.

Human Factors in Space
University of North Dakota
NODA#SPST515 Graduate   3 credits $816*

A review of the major stresses experienced by humans on entering the new and alien environment of space. Examples will be taken from the psychological and physiological impacts experienced by U.S. and Soviet crews with emphasis on longer flights. How to avoid and/or overcome these stresses will be examined as an essential and growing need in the future development and settlement of the space frontier.
* ND residents, $102 per credit; may also be reduced for residents of adjoining states and provinces.

Human Genetics and Values
State University of New York
SUNY#BIO144 Undergraduate   3 credits $545*

An interdisciplinary course that is designed to present the basic concepts of human genetics that relate to understanding the mechanism of genetic disorders, cytogenetics, genetic biotechnology issues of public policy and the law. In addition, certain personal, social and legal issues/consequences will be considered.
* NY residents tuition: $278

Human Geography
Rogers State University
ROGE#GEOG2243 Undergraduate   3 credits $495*

An introduction and general education course which emphasizes the interrelationship of the physical environment and human responses.
* OK residents $315.

Humanity and the Biological Universe
New York Institute of Technology
NYIT#LS4422 Undergraduate   3 credits $???

This course acquaints students with basic biological, health and environmental issues of the modern world. To achieve intended awareness, students will study basic anatomy, physiology, genetics and microbiology. Special attention will be given to contemporary problems such as AIDS, genetic engineering, cancer, heart disease, and pollution. The student will use basic mathematical, computer and quantitative reasoning skills to present cohesive written summations of learning.

Humanity and the Physical Universe
New York Institute of Technology
NYIT#PH4024 Undergraduate   3 credits $???

A survey course in the physical sciences for the non-technical student. The course will examine conceptually a broad range of topics including: motion; electromagnetism; optics; atomic physics; heat; energy and power generation; earth science and modern concepts (relatively and quantum physics). The interactions between physical science and technology and their impact upon society and the quality of life will be considered.

Individual Research in Space Studies
University of North Dakota
NODA#SPST593 Graduate   1 credits $272*

Individual student projects designed to develop advanced knowledge in a specific area of expertise. A written report is required. May be repeated for up to 6 credits.
* ND residents, $102 per credit; may also be reduced for residents of adjoining states and provinces.

Insects in the Environment
University of Missouri
MOCE#SC110 Undergraduate   3 credits $387

This course introduces the study of insects, with emphasis on those species important to humans and on the general principles of integrated insect control. This course is designed for students interested in a study of insects and how they are affecting the environment.

Introduction to Biology I
State University of New York
SUNY#SCI1103S Undergraduate   4 credits $532*

This course provides an understanding of basic biological processes and principles. Topics covered include the chemical and cellular basis of life, evolution, cellular control systems, genetics, ecology, and behavior. Basic laboratory work will be incorporated into the course material.
* NY residents tuition: $90 per credit.

Integrated Science
Lansing Community College
LANS#ISCI131 Undergraduate   4 credits $420

A general education course designed to provide students with a basic understanding of the methods and applications of science. Topics include basic chemistry, thermodynamics, the hydrologic cycle, climate, and weather. Critical thinking and problem-solving skills are applied to environmental issues. Laboratory activities illustrate and amplify lecture topics.

Intermediate Algebra
University of Alaska - Fairbanks
ALFA#DEVM070 Undergraduate   3 credits $213
Second year high school algebra. Operations with rational functions, radicals, rational exponents, complex numbers, quadratic equations, and inequalities. Cartesian coordinate system and graphing, systems of equations, determinants and logarithms. Prerequisite: DEVM060 or placement.

Intermediate Algebra
Bakersfield College
BAKE#MATHBD Undergraduate   4 credits $460*
Sets and operations, signed numbers, factoring, linear equations, simple and complex fractions, functional notation, simple graphs, exponents and radicals, quadratic equations, the conics, variation, determinants, logarithms, exponential equations, sequences and series and the binomial expansion. Prerequisite: MATH A or one year of high school Algebra or equivalent with a grade of C required.
* CA residents pay $40 per credit.

Intermediate Algebra
Kansas City Kansas Community College
KACI#MA104 Undergraduate   3 credits $324*
This course continues the study of the real number system. Topics studied will include a review of basic algebra, factoring, functions and graphs, rational expressions and equations, radicals and complex numbers, quadratic functions and equations, circles, and an introduction to logarithmic functions. Prerequisite: Elementary Algebra MA099 or one year of high school algebra, each with a grade of C or higher.
* KS residents pay $40 per credit.

Intermediate Algebra
Marylhurst College
MARY#MTH125 Undergraduate   3 credits $651
This course continues the gentle study of algebra in an entertaining manner. Activity centers on polynomials, rational expressions, integers exponents, and radicals. Further exploration of quadratic equations and systems in two variables will also help the student to understand how to solve real-life problems.

Intermediate Algebra
University of Missouri
MOCE#MA5 Undergraduate   3 credits $387
This course prepares students for college algebra. It covers graphs, functions, linear equations, inequalities, polynomials, systems, exponents, and quadratic equations. Problem solving is emphasized.

Intermediate Algebra
Northeastern Oklahoma A&M College
NOOK#MATH0123 Undergraduate   3 credits $315*
(Course description not available at press time.)
* OK residents tuition: $42 per credit.

Intermediate Algebra
Rogers State University
ROGE#MATH0213 Undergraduate   3 credits $495*
This course covers the real numbers system, exponents and polynomials, factoring polynomials, rational expressions, linear equations, absolute value, linear inequalities, linear functions and their graphs, rational exponents and radicals. Prerequisite: MATH0013 or a firm understanding of elementary algebra. Preparatory for College Algebra Video: Intermediate Algebra for College Students from Rogers State College.
* OK residents $315.

Intermediate Algebra Accelerated
Rio Salado College
RISA#MAT122 Undergraduate   3 credits $186*
Algebraic operations on polynomial, rational, and radical expressions and complex numbers; graph polynomial, exponential and logarithmic functions; solve linear, quadratic, rational and absolute value equations and inequalities algebraically and graphically, solve systems of linear equations algebraically and graphically; and real world applications and use of current technology. May receive credit for only one of the following: MAT120 or MAT122. Prerequisites: Grade of "B" or better in MAT090, or MAT091, or MAT092, or equivalent, or satisfactory score on District placement exam.
* AZ residents pay $37 per credit.

Intermediate Algebra I
University of Minnesota
MINN#GC0625 Undergraduate   0 credits $445
For students needing additional preparation in algebra before Intermediate Algebra, Part II. Sets, real numbers, linear equalities, linear inequalities, absolute values, polynomials, rational expressions, exponents, radicals and radical expressions, complex numbers, systems of equations, word problems. Prerequisite: GC0621 or MATH0006.

Intermediate Algebra II
University of Minnesota
MINN#GC0631 Undergraduate   0 credits $445
Assumes basic knowledge of linear and quadratic equations and inequalities, exponents, factoring, rational expressions, roots, radicals, complex numbers, and graphing. Topics: quadratic equations, matrix solutions to linear systems, general inequalities, conic sections, functions and inverse functions, logarithmic and exponential functions, introduction to sequences, series, and binomial theorem. Prerequisite: GC0625 with a grade of C or better.

Interpreting Statistics
State University of New York
SUNY#MAT150 Undergraduate   3 credits $528*
This course will develop the statistical skills necessary to evaluate studies done in various disciplines in which statistics and statistical thinking get used and abused in a variety of ways. Statistical concepts rather than computations will be emphasized. Current newspaper and magazine articles from areas such as public health, politics, economics and science will be analyzed. Many of the articles are available on-line. Prerequisite: Students should have taken college level Algebra and English, or their equivalents.
* NY residents tuition: $89 per credit.

Interpreting Statistics and Data
City University
CITY#BC303 Undergraduate   5 qu. credits $785
Interpreting, organizing, and illustrating data. Present-day applications for interpreting reports, surveys, charts, graphs, and opinion polls.

Intro to Environmental Science
Brevard Community College
BREV#EVR1001 Undergraduate   3 credits $435
A survey of basic chemical, biological, and physical principles of environmental science and ecology and the application of these principles to current political, scientific and economic issues.

Introduction to Astronomy
Brevard Community College
BREV#AST1002 Undergraduate   3 credits $485
A study of the solar system, stars, galaxies, and cosmology. An elementary survey of astronomy as both a human activity and a physical science. Primarily for non-science majors. Meets one of the A.A. degree Physical Science requirements. Prerequisite: High School Algebra within past 3 years.

Introduction to Astronomy
University of Massachusetts - Dartmouth
MADA#PHY151 Undergraduate   3 credits $408
A descriptive introduction to the planets, stars, galaxies, and general concepts of astronomy for the non-science major. Topics will include brief historical glimpses of the earliest concepts of the universe, contributions of Galileo, Newton and others. Following topics will include the nature of the earth and moon, the physical environments of selected planets, moons, comets, and asteroids. The general nature of the stars and stellar evolution will also be investigated.

Introduction to Astronomy
New School for Social Research
NEWS#0814 Undergraduate   3 credits $1638*
The beauty, serenity, and majesty of the night sky have inspired astronomers from the earliest times. Study has yielded answers to questions as old as humanity itself. Sophisticated optical instruments are not needed to do it justice; the unaided eye can discover much of the grandeur. With the help of star maps, you learn how to locate and identify the constellations, stars, and planets visible from your latitude. Attention is given to the real and apparent motions of all the heavenly bodies, including signs of the zodiac, especially to understanding their predictability.
* Non-credit option, tuition: $365.

Introduction to Astronomy
State University of New York
SUNY#SCI1030S Undergraduate   4 credits $532*
Introduces the tools, history, methods and objects of astronomy, including study of the origins of modern astronomy, telescopes, spectroscopes, space probes, and other astronomical tools, structures, characteristics and cycles of the sun, moon and other solar system members, properties, structure, formation, and death of stars, galaxies, constellations, and cosmology. Laboratory activities include work with astronomical models, telescopes, and spectroscopes, computers simulations and to obtain current astronomical data, use of photographs, maps, models and first-hand observations to study the moon, the sun and sunspots, seasons, planets, constellations, and galaxies, and several outdoor observing sessions.
* NY residents tuition: $90 per credit.

Introduction to Basic Mathematics
University of Minnesota
MINN#GC0611 Undergraduate   0 credits $445
In-depth review of mathematics from whole numbers to geometry. Emphasizes computation and understanding basic concepts. Ideal for students who plan to study elementary algebra.

Introduction to Calculus
State University of New York
SUNY#272754 Undergraduate   4 credits $586*
Study the concepts of limits, derivatives and integrals through intuitive and graphical arguments rather than through mathematically rigorous derivations. Focus on applications in the business area, including minimum-maximum problems, present value calculations, and inventory models. Using a standard text and graphing software or calculator and assigned problems, learn techniques to compute derivatives and elementary integrals of algebraic, logarithmic and exponential functions. Prerequisite: A working knowledge of algebra, including factoring and solving algebraic equations (e.g. CDL Algebra course or its equivalent). Note: Requires a computer which can run MATHCAD software.
* NY residents tuition: $515

Introduction to Cell Biology
Lake Superior College
LASU#BIOL1100 Undergraduate   2 credits $140
This is a laboratory course which will develop your understanding of the function, chemistry, metabolism, and structure of the basic unit of life, the cell. This course will also prepare you for taking further courses in anatomy, physiology, and microbiology.

Introduction to Contemporary Mathematics
Chemeketa Community College
CHEM#MTH105 Undergraduate   4 credits $159
Surveys the application of mathematics as a problem solving tool in the real world. Problems that are explored come from fields including business, consumerism, ecology and city planning. The tools included are probability, statistics. geometry, graph theory, linear programming and game theory. Prerequisite: Grade of "c" or better in MTH095 or equivalent.

Introduction to Ecology
University of Minnesota
MINN#EEB3001 Undergraduate   4 credits $400
Ecology is the science that investigates the interactions of living things with each other and their environments. Students learn the ways that ecologists explore these interactions as they take place between individuals and within ecosystems, communities, and populations of organisms. Attention is given to the overwhelming importance of evolution in shaping ecological relationships, as well as the impact of human beings on natural systems.

Introduction to Environmental Science
City University
CITY#NAS215 Undergraduate   5 qu. credits $785
An exploration of environmental change on a global scale, emphasizing the fundamental concepts of matter, energy and ecology as applied to contemporary environmental concerns. Environmental issues impacting 29 countries around the world are illustrated to develop an international perspective on the environmental challenges facing our planet.

Introduction to Environmental Technology
Bakersfield College
BAKE#ENVTB1B Undergraduate   3 credits $345*
An introduction to the overall scope of Environmental Technology. Emphasizes legal definitions, terminology, and regulatory framework. Included are: historical background, career opportunities, governmental processes, health effects, basic ecology, air, water and wastewater, hazardous materials and waste, occupational health and safety, and pollution prevention. Prerequisite: The successful completion of ET01A.
* CA residents pay $40 per credit.

Introduction to Geology
Bakersfield College
BAKE#GEOLB10 Undergraduate   3 credits $345*
An introduction to the principles of geology with emphasis on the structure and origin of the earth, its present and past landscapes and the processes at work changing its surface. Includes identification of rocks and minerals, topographic and geologic map exercises demonstrating the work of water, wind, ice and gravity and effects of colcanism and earthquakes. Prerequisite: Reading Level 1 recommended.
* CA residents pay $40 per credit.

Introduction to Geology
University of Minnesota
MINN#GEO1001 Undergraduate   4 credits $356
An introduction to general geology. Survey of the main features of the physical world and the processes that have evoked them. Topics: plate tectonics, rock formation, weathering, soils, deserts, oceans, and the phenomena of earthquakes, glaciers, and volcanoes. Rock and mineral collection recommended.

Introduction to Geoscience
City University
CITY#NAS201 Undergraduate   5 qu. credits $785
A survey of earth science, emphasizing recent developments in atmospheric chemistry, geology and astrophysics. The course will also explore the impact humans will continue to have on the fate of the earth.

Introduction to Ideas of Statistics
University of Minnesota
MINN#STAT1001 Undergraduate   4 credits $356
Incorporates World Wide Web resources in the online study guide. Contains built-in interactive software that gives students the chance to practice statistics problems on their own computers. A computer capable of running Windows 3.1 or a Macintosh is necessary, with 8 megabytes of RAM and 10 megabytes of hard drive space and a direct or modem Internet connection. Students must be able to access the Netscape World Wide Web browser, version 1.1 or higher (available at no cost from the course Web site). Prerequisite: high school algebra.

Introduction to Logic
University of Minnesota
MINN#PHIL1001 Undergraduate   5 credits $445
Rules and procedures of sound argument and valid inference. Relationship of formal patterns of reasoning to such uses of ordinary language as argument, propaganda, and persuasion. How formal logic can be employed as a tool for critical thinking.

Introduction to Marine Biology
University of Alaska - Fairbanks
ALFA#BIOL150 Undergraduate   3 credits $213
A general survey of marine organisms, evolution of marine life, habitats and communities of ocean zones, productivity, and marine resources. Course designed for non-science majors.

Introduction to Organic Evolution
Western Illinois University
WEIL#BIO319 Undergraduate   4 credits $1030*
Although this course is intended for the general student, it covers enough basic genetics to allow appreciation of how the evolutionary process works. Topics include a brief introduction to the role of development in the evolutionary process and microevolution, including basic genetics, mutation, natural selection, speciation, kin selection, and sociobiology. The basic tenets of scientific creationism are outlined, and the nature of the creation/evolution debate examined.
* IL residents tuition: $88 per credit.

Introduction to Physical Geography
University of South Florida
FLSO#GEO3013 Undergraduate   ?? credits $???
This course is designed to introduce upper-division undergraduate students to the field of physical geography. Physical geography encompasses a wide diversity of fields, including climatology, geology, geomorphology, and oceanography. It is a topic that has warranted a great deal of attention in geography over the past four decades. A broad overview of the concepts of physical geography and their applications will be the focus of the course. We will look at both regional and global perspectives. The course is intended as a 'lead-in' course for the advanced geography courses taught on all USF campuses.

Introduction to Physical Geography
Laramie County Community College
LARA#GR1010 Undergraduate   ?? credits $???
The Internet feature of Introduction to Physical Geography is straightforward. First, access the home page of Tom McKnight's textbook, Physical Geography: A Landscape Appreciation at http://www.prenhall.com/~mcknight. Once there, find the menu for the Chapter Reviews. Try going into the Chapter Review for Chapter One. You will find a list of questions, many of them linked to sites for the review questions.

Introduction to Physical Geography
Rio Salado College
RISA#GPH111 Undergraduate   4 credits $248*
Spatial and functional relationships among climates, landforms, soils, water, and plants.
* AZ residents $37 per credit.

Introduction to Probability
New York Institute of Technology
NYIT#MA3017 Undergraduate   3 credits $???
Functions, curve equation relationship, set theory, random events, probability functions, mathematical expectation, conditional probability, special distributions (e.g. binomial, normal, and notion of a statistic). Prerequisite: MA3014 or equivalent.

Introduction to Research
Bellevue University
BELL#MGTC303 Undergraduate   3 credits $750
Library research skills, introduction to APA style, and writing a professional project or case study proposal.

Introduction to Sports Science
State University of New York
SUNY#PPE100 Undergraduate   4 credits $820*
A course designed to expose the students to the components of the sports sciences, including anatomy, physiology, biomechanics, sports medicine and sports technology as the relate to human exercise. This class includes both the theory and practice through a lecture and laboratory experience.
* NY residents tuition: $105 per credit.

Introduction to Statistics
Bellevue University
BELL#MGTC360 Undergraduate   3 credits $750
The research process and analysis of data. In-depth study of statistical methods and processes as a basis for logical business decision-making.

Introduction to Statistics
University of Colorado
CUON#PSY2090 Undergraduate   4 credits $2604*
Research methods and analysis of date. Intended for those who plan to major in psychology. Prereq: completion of college algebra course such as MATH 1070 or MATH 1110 or intermediate algebra from a community college.
* CO residents tuition: $136 per credit.

Introduction to Statistics
Rio Salado College
RISA#PSY230 Undergraduate   3 credits $186*
An introduction to basic concepts in descriptive and inferential statistics, with emphasis upon application to psychology. Consideration given to the methods of data collection, sampling techniques, graphing of data, and the statistical evaluation of data collected through experimentation. Required of psychology majors. Prerequisites: PSY101 with a grade of "C" or better and MAT092 or equivalent, or permission of instructor.
* AZ residents pay $37 per credit.

Introductory Algebra
Lansing Community College
LANS#MATH107 Undergraduate   4 credits $420
Emphasizes technology and applications. Learning tools include the Internet and computer software, textbook, graphing calculator, and videotapes.

Introductory Algebra
Rio Salado College
RISA#MAT092 Undergraduate   3 credits $186*
Basic axioms of algebra, linear equations in one and two variables, operations on polynomials, rational expressions, graphing of linear equations and the solving of linear equations. May receive credit for only one of the following: MAT090, MAT091, or MAT092. Prerequisites: Grade of "C" or better in MAT082, or MAT102, or equivalent, or satisfactory score on District Placement exam.
* AZ residents $37 per credit.

Introductory Astronomy
Bakersfield College
BAKE#ASTRB1 Undergraduate   3 credits $345*
Introductory course dealing with the fundamental observations and scientific models of astronomy. Among topics included: The motions and properties of the sun, moon, earth, planets, stars, galaxies, the properties of electromagnetic radiation, astronomical instruments, and stellar and cosmic evolution. Prerequisite: *CA residents pay $40 per credit.
* CA residents pay $40 per credit.

Introductory Astronomy
University of Missouri
MOCE#AS999 Undergraduate   4 credits $516
This course highlights several topics. Planets: A brief survey of their motions and properties. Stars: Observations, including stellar spectra and colors; stellar evolution; and star clusters. Galaxies: Structure and content of the Milky Way Galaxy, and its relationship to other galaxies. Cosmology: The origin and evolution of the universe. Some activities in this course require students to view the sky and record their observations. Perquisites: Two years of high school algebra and one year of high school physics are strongly recommended.

Introductory Concepts of Math
New York Institute of Technology
NYIT#MA3015 Undergraduate   3 credits $???
A course on selected topics in mathematics for students of the humanities, especially in communication arts. Topics include: graphs, matrices, elements, of liner programming, finite probabilities, introduction to statistics. Applications to real-life situations are emphasized. The place of these topics in the history of mathematics are outlined.

Introductory Meteorology
University of Missouri
MOCE#ME50 Undergraduate   3 credits $387
This course studies physical processes of the atmosphere in relation to the day-to-day changes in weather. Perquisites: Although there are no prerequisites for this course, students should have a good background in mathematics and physics and some background in chemistry.

Introductory Physics I
University of Minnesota
MINN#PHYS1041 Undergraduate   5 credits $445
Primarily for students interested in a general, non-calculus physics course, but also for CLA distribution requirements. Topics: uniformly accelerated motion, Newton's laws of motion, work, energy, motion of rigid bodies, mechanical properties of matter, temperature, gas law, thermal properties of matter, thermodynamics, vibratory motion, wave motion, and sound. A laboratory component is included and involves experiments in graphical analysis of data, geometry of motion, gravitational field, energy, power, and sound waves. Replaces old PHYS1032. Students who have completed PHYS1031 should take PHYS1041 to complete the series. Prerequisite: high school algebra, geometry, and trigonometry.

Introductory Physics II
University of Minnesota
MINN#PHYS1042 Undergraduate   5 credits $445
Topics: electric fields, direct current circuits, magnetism, electromagnetic induction, alternating currents, electromagnetic waves, properties of light, optical devices, interference, diffraction, atomic structure, the atomic nucleus, and physics of the universe. A laboratory component is included and involves experiments in probability and statistics, direct current circuits, magnetic fields, optics, and diffraction. Prerequisite: PHYS1041 or equivalent.

Issues in Sustainable Agriculture
University of Minnesota
MINN#AGRO5500 Undergraduate   3 credits $300
An overview of issues related to sustainable agriculture: agroecology, impacts on the environment and public health, alternate farming practices, economic issues and government policies, and sociological factors. The sustainable agriculture movement is driven by the belief that our food production system will be sustaining only when on-farm practices and agricultural policies balance profitability with concern for the environment and the well-being of farm families and rural communities.

Life In The Universe
University of North Dakota
NODA#SPST570B Graduate   3 credits $816*
The course examines life as a natural consequence of events that were set in motion at the Big Bang origin of the Universe. The biological evolution occurring on Earth's biosphere will be treated as one facet of the overall evolution of the entire cosmos. A cosmic perspective will show Earth's status is not special but ordinary. The conditions under which life can exist will also be considered.
* ND residents, $102 per credit; may also be reduced for residents of adjoining states and provinces.

Life Support Systems
University of North Dakota
NODA#SPST410 Graduate   3 credits $816*
A review of the physiological effects of living in space including a discussion of current and near-term life support systems for the provision of oxygen, water, food, and radiation protection. In addition, a review will be made of the issues associated with the development of fully closed ecological life support systems, which will be essential to the long-term development of space.
* ND residents, $102 per credit; may also be reduced for residents of adjoining states and provinces.

Marine Biology
Rio Salado College
RISA#BIO183 Undergraduate   4 credits $248*
A survey of marine environments and their biotic communities with emphasis on the natural history of marine organisms.
* AZ residents $37 per credit.

Mars
University of North Dakota
NODA#SPST570A Graduate   3 credits $816*
The Red Planet has captivated human imagination throughout history. Mars displays huge volcanoes, canyons, and terrains that have no terrestrial counterparts. There are still significant fundamental questions about Mars (that will also teach us about Earth) that await the upcoming Mars Gloabal Surveyor and Mars Pathfinder missions.
* ND residents, $102 per credit; may also be reduced for residents of adjoining states and provinces.

Math Applications I
State University of New York
SUNY#06332588R Undergraduate   4 credits $900*
The course is part one in a two-semester sequence of intermediate algebra and trigonometry with technical applications. Topics included are: The trigonometry functions, vectors, units of measurement and approximate numbers, fundamental concepts of algebra, functions and graphs, systems of linear equations, determinants, factoring and fractions, quadratics, variation and geometry. Special Requirement: Students must have a T185 or T186 graphing calculator. Prerequisite: Two units of high school math or equivalent.
* NY residents tuition: $98 per credit.

Math Concepts
State University of New York
SUNY#MAT13071 Undergraduate   3 credits $1038*
This course includes solving equations, U.S. Customary and Metric systems of measurement, geometry, consumer mathematics, statistics and probability, and applications in various fields. Prerequisite: Basic Arithmetic.
* NY residents tuition: $137 per credit.

Math for Information Technology
University of Denver, University College
DEUC#TELE3800 Undergraduate   3 qtr. hrs. $885
This class presents a review of algebra, trigonometry, and statistical functions which apply to Telecommunications course work. Students will be exposed to mathematical concepts and formulas which are used extensively in the electronics series and the Telecommunications Technology courses. The CIS Quantitative Analysis course does not contain all of the information necessary to succeed in the Telecommunications program and should not be substituted for this course. (Prerequisite: high school algebra or the equivalent.)

Math Principles
Waukesha County Technical College
WAUK#804160008 Undergraduate   3 credits $193
Math skills are developed in the area of algebra and introductory statistics. Additional topics include percentages, simple and compound interest, annuities and sinking funds. Prerequisite: Knowledge of basic Algebra.

Mathematical Concepts/Applications
Rio Salado College
RISA#MAT102 Undergraduate   3 credits $186*
A problem solving approach to mathematics as it applies to life and the world of work. Development, demonstration, and communication of mathematical concepts and formulas that relate to measurement, percentage, statistics, and geometry. Prerequisites: Grade of "C" or better in MAT082, or equivalent, or satisfactory score on District placement exam.
* AZ residents pay $37 per credit.

Mathematical Models
Fayetteville Technical Community College
FAYE#MAT115 Undergraduate   3 credits $489*
This course develops the ability to utilize mathematical skills and technology to solve problems at a level found in non-mathematics-intensive programs. Topics include applications to percent, ratio and proportion, formulas, statistics, functional notation, linear functions and their groups, probability, sampling techniques, scatter plots, and modeling. Upon completion, students should be able to solve practical problems, reason and communicate with mathematics, and work confidently, collaboratively, and independently. Prerequisites: MAT070.
* NC residents pay $20 per credit.

Mathematics for Decision Making
State University of New York
SUNY#271754 Undergraduate   4 credits $586*
Focus on problem-solving as a process. An effective problem solving methodology includes identifying, defining, and understanding the problem, and then modeling, validating, and documenting its solution. Modeling this process will improve and refine problem-solving skills, including analytical and critical thinking and quantitative reasoning. Use a learning journal throughout the course as a strategy for reflection and self-assessment. This course provides an opportunity for improving quantitative reasoning skills in a problem-solving context. Includes use of tables, data management and analysis, graphical analysis, and modeling using computer software.
* NY residents tuition: $515

Mathematics for Management
UCLA
UCLA#X110 Undergraduate   4 credits $500
This online course provides a fundamental background for administrators in the public and private economic sectors, as well as a solid review of pre-MBA mathematics. Topics include linear and matrix algebra (with special emphasis on demand/supply and cost/revenue analysis) and differential calculus.

Mathematics for the Liberal Arts
University of Colorado
CUON#MATH2000 Undergraduate   3 credits $1953*
Designed to give liberal arts students the skills required to understand and interpret quantitative information that they encounter in the news and in their studies, and to make quantitatively based decisions in their lives. Topics include a survey of logic and analysis of arguments, identifying fallacies in reasoning, large and small numbers in the world around us, linear and exponential relation, essentials of probability and statistics, networks, and applications and modeling with case studies in economics, finance, environmental sciences, health, music, and science.
* CO residents tuition: $136 per credit.

Mathematics for the Liberal Arts
Mercy College
MERC#MA115 Undergraduate   3 credits $900
Introduction to mathematical applications in the real world and as they relate to the liberal arts; stressing logical thinking and problem solving. Topics include numeration, number theory, logic, geometry, counting methods, probability, statistics, matrices and others. Prerequisite MA 105 or by mathematics placement exams.

Mathematics in Computing
Nova Southeastern University
NOVA#MCIS502 Graduate   3 credits $1,110
Graph theory, lattices and boolean algebras, state models and abstract algebraic structures, logical systems, production systems, computability theory, recursive function theory.

Mathematics on the WWW
University of Nevada-Reno
NERE#C120 Undergraduate   3 credits $210
Sets, logic; probability, statistics; consumer mathematics; variation; geometry and trigonometry for measurement; linear, quadratic, exponential and logarithmic functions; emphasis on problem solving and applications.

Measurement Concepts
New York Institute of Technology
NYIT#BES2421 Undergraduate   3 credits $???
The construction, validation, and interpretation of test results. Group and individual tests of aptitude, intelligence, and personality are analyzed. Each student will develop and administer a measure for a specific diagnostic or research purpose. Perquisite: BES2401.

Meteorology
City University
CITY#SCI304 Undergraduate   5 qu. credits $785

This course will examine the earth's atmosphere, with emphasis on weather observations and forecasting. Topics include physical processes involved in weather phenomena, such as highs, lows, fronts, clouds, storms, jet streams and air pollution. Prerequisite: Strongly recommended: NAS201 or its equivalent.

Methodology for the Social and Behavioral Sciences
Mercy College
MERC#BS248 Undergraduate   3 credits $900

(Course description not available at press time.)

Modern Physics
University of Minnesota
MINN#PHYS3501 Undergraduate   4 credits $400

Descriptive modern physics. Topics: quantum mechanics, hydrogen atom, multi-electron atoms, molecular structure, quantum statistics, thermal radiation, solid state physics, nuclear physics. No credit for physics majors. Prerequisites: Physics 1253, 1453, Chem 1052, MATH3261.

Multivariable Differential Calculus
University of Minnesota
MINN#MATH3251 Undergraduate   4 credits $400

Differentiation of parametric curves. Partial differentiation and the derivative as a local linear approximation. The chain rule. Applications to max/min problems with attention to boundaries and constraints include Lagrange multipliers. Taylor's theorem (multivariable) and the second derivative test. Prerequisite: MATH1261.

Multivariable Integral Calculus
University of Minnesota
MINN#MATH3252 Undergraduate   4 credits $400

Double and triple integrals; change of variable procedures emphasizing polar and spherical coordinates; mass and centoid; integration on curves and surfaces; vectors fields and the theorems of Green, Gauss, and Stokes. Prerequisite: MATH3251 or equivalent.

National Parks Biology
State University of New York
SUNY#SC119 Undergraduate   3 credits $435*

A natural history study of America's parklands featuring the biology, geology and ecology and accompanying principles illustrated by these unique areas. Included is a discussion of the park movement in the U.S. Examples are taken from selected national parks and the Adirondack Park.

* NY residents tuition: $80 per credit.

Number Systems and Applications
University of Missouri
MOCE#MA130 Undergraduate   3 credits $387

Designed for elementary school teachers, this course presents a constructive development of the real number system that includes the system of whole numbers, concepts from elementary number theory, and applications of quantitative systems to problems in discrete mathematics. Perquisites: high school algebra and geometry.

Observational Astronomy
University of North Dakota
NODA#SPST425 Graduate   3 credits $816*

This course will provide an overview of observational astronomy with particular emphasis on planetary astronomy. Students will learn to use the departmental observatory (near Grand Forks AFB), the 18" telescope there, and digital imaging with a CCD camera. Each student will set up the telescope and camera, acquire a target, record the image data, and process it in the laboratory.

* ND residents, $102 per credit; may also be reduced for residents of adjoining states and provinces.

Oceanography
City University
CITY#SCI303 Undergraduate   5 qu. credits $785

This is an upper division science course which evaluates oceanography and its influences upon life on earth. Topics examined include: storms, sea level, food and mineral sources, and their role in controlling earth's environment. Prerequisite: Strongly recommended: NAS201 or its equivalent.

Oceanography
University of Oregon
OREG#GEO307 Undergraduate   4 credits $374

An introduction to the physical, chemical and biological processes in the world's oceans. There will be emphasis on the history and geology of the ocean basins, as well as the human impact and exploitation of the resources. This offering has been designed for the non-science student desiring a one-course overview of the ocean sciences. Material will be presented with the assumption that students enrolled have a limited science background.

One-Variable Differential and Integral Calculus I
University of Minnesota
MINN#MATH1251 Undergraduate   4 credits $356

Calculus of functions of one variable and related geometry and applications. Prerequisite: four years of high school math, including trigonometry, or a grade of C or better in MATH1201 or 1008 and 1111, or equivalent.

One-Variable Differential and Integral Calculus II
University of Minnesota
MINN#MATH1252 Undergraduate   4 credits $356

Calculus of functions of one variable and related geometry and applications. Prerequisite: MATH1251 with a grade of C or better.

Ordinary Differential Equations
Bakersfield College
BAKE#MATHB6D Undergraduate   3 credits $345*

Vector spaces and linear transformation; elementary differential equations; Laplace transforms; series solutions and systems of differential equations; matrices and eigen values. Prerequisite: MATH 6c or equivalent with grade of "C".

* CA residents pay $40 per credit.

Our Planet and Its Future
Indiana University
INDI#G116 Undergraduate   3 credits $268
The interaction between geologic and environmental processes in the Earth. Special emphasis on how these processes affect public policies and laws. Multimedia exercises and videotape presentations (made specifically for this course) are included. Learning packet includes learning guide, CD-ROM, video, lab kit and dilute hydrochloric acid. No refunds given on learning packets after 30 days. For refunds on learning packets within 30 days, the CD-ROM must not be opened. Students must have access to a camera, VCR, and CD-ROM drive. National award winner.

Perspectives in Biology
Auburn University
AUBU#BI105 Undergraduate   3 credits $126
Principles of biology with emphasis upon the relationship between man and modern biological science. Specific subject areas include cellular structure, biologically important organic molecules, photo-synthesis, cellular respiration, inheritance, evolution and ecology. These topics are all developed with a view toward understanding how the human organism exists as both an individual biological entity and as an important interacting member of the natural world. Laboratory work is primarily in the areas of cell biology and inheritance.

Physical Geography
University of Missouri
MOCE#GE111 Undergraduate   3 credits $387
This is an introductory study of the physical environment: maps, landforms, water, elements of climate, climatic types, soils, and vegetation. The course examines the effects of human behavior on natural environmental systems. Perquisites: Geog. 1 or 2 or sophomore standing.

Physical Geology
University of Missouri
MOCE#GE51 Undergraduate   4 credits $516
This course studies the materials of the earth's crust; structures; geologic features of the earth's surface; common minerals and rocks; and topographic and geologic maps.

Physics I
New Jersey Institute of Technology
NJIT#PHYS111 Undergraduate   3 credits $1143*
This course deals with the study of elementary mechanics. Emphasis is placed on the fundamental concepts and laws of mechanics especially the conservation laws. Topics discussed are: scalar and vector quantities of mechanics; rectilinear and circular motion; equilibrium and Newton's laws of motion; work, energy, momentum; the conservation laws. Prerequisite: NJIT#MATH111. Optional: 15 video lessons of 90 minutes each.
* NJ residents: $184/semester hour.

Physics I for Engineers & Scientists
State University of New York
SUNY#PHY17101 Undergraduate   4 credits $570*
A calculus-based physics course. Vectors, equilibrium, kinematics in one and two dimensions, Newton's Laws (linear and rotational systems), work and energy, impulse and momentum, rotation, elasticity, harmonic motion, hydrostatics, and heat. Simulated laboratory experiences are included as part of this course. Prerequisite: Calculus I or equivalent.
* NY residents tuition: $90 per credit

Physics II for Engineers & Scientists
State University of New York
SUNY#PHY17201 Undergraduate   4 credits $570*
A calculus-based physics course. Coulomb's and Gauss' Laws, electric potential and energy, capacitance, magnetic forces and torques, induced fields, self and mutual inductance, DC and AC circuits, thermodynamics, wave motion, optics, sound, relativity, and other selected topics in modern physics. Simulated laboratory experiences are included as part of this course. Prerequisite: Calculus-based Physics I or equivalent.
* NY residents tuition: $90 per credit

Physics of Energy and Environment
University of Oregon
OREG#PHY161 Undergraduate   3 credits $289
This course will deal with the use of energy in a Technology Society and will examine, in detail, the various physical feedback loops that are present in nature but witch Technology disrupts. We will examine our present understanding of the nature of energy and energy efficiency in order to establish what the limitations are:.

Physics of Materials
New Jersey Institute of Technology
NJIT#PHYS687 Undergraduate   3 credits $1143*
This course discusses quantum mechanics fundamentals: energy bonds on solids; electrical conduction in metals and alloys; semiconduction: optical, magnetic and thermal properties of materials; novel approach to chemical bonding in solids. Prerequisite: Introductory course in materials. Optional: 12 video lessons of 180 minutes each.
* NJ residents: $184/semester hour.

Plane Geometry
University of Minnesota
MINN#GC0623 Undergraduate   0 credits $356
Elements of plane geometry with some geometry of solids. Equivalent to one year of high school plane geometry. Prerequisite: GC MATH placement score or elementary algebra.

Planet Earth
University of Massachusetts - Dartmouth
MADA#PHY171 Undergraduate   3 credits $408
An introduction to the basics of Earth Sciences. Through the use of text and exploration of numerous web sites, Planet Earth explores such diverse topics as continental drift, plate tectonics, glaciation, volcanic activity, earthquakes, paleontology, deserts, the fundamentals of weather and an introduction to the principles of planetary geology. Related topics such as the Mars Pathfinder mission or recent volcanic activity will also be included within the course.

Planet Earth
Western Illinois University
WEIL#GEO422 Undergraduate   3 credits $795*
Explore our planet--its interior, oceans, continents, mountains and volcanoes, energy and mineral resources, climate, sun, and atmosphere. As you move through the PBS telecourse sequence, you climb from the depths of the oceans to the heights of our solar system in all its magnificence. Internationally recognized experts share their theories, models, and opinions; on-location film footage takes you to places and events you might not otherwise experience; and animation and graphic displays let you "see" more difficult concepts.
* IL residents tuition: $88 per credit.

Plant Propagation
Pennsylvania State University
PENN#HORT202 Undergraduate   3 credits $345
Principles and practices of asexual and sexual plant propagation. Laboratory.

Pre Algebra
University of Alaska - Fairbanks
ALFA#DEVM050 Undergraduate   3 credits $213
Operations with whole numbers, fractions, decimals and signed numbers. Percents and ratios. Evaluating algebraic expressions. Introduction to geometric figures. Metric system.

Prealgebra
Pima Community College
PIMA#MAT086 Undergraduate   3 credits $165*
This course helps to ease the transition from arithmetic to algebra. The topics covered include basic operations of fractions and decimals, signed numbers, percents, rations, and applications. Class topics also include order of operations, solution of linear equations, as well as inequalities in one variable. Prerequisites: MAT082 or placement via the math assessment test.
* AZ residents, $32/credit hour.

Precalculus
University of Minnesota
MINN#MATH1201 Undergraduate   5 credits $445
Inequalities; analytical geometry; complex numbers; binomial theorem; mathematical induction; functions and graphs; trigonometric, exponential, logarithmic functions. Intended for students who need to review higher algebra and trigonometry before taking a calculus sequence. May be substituted for MATH1051-1151. Prerequisite: GC0631 or high school higher algebra, trigonometry, and mathematics placement score.

Preparation for General Chemistry
Pima Community College
PIMA#CHM080 Undergraduate   3 credits $165*
Fundamentals of chemistry. Includes nomenclature, atomic structure, bonding, chemical equations, moles, stoichiometry, the periodic table, conversions, problem-solving techniques, and study skills. Designed to prepare students for CHM151 Prerequisites: MTH092.
* AZ residents pay $32 per credit.

Principles of Biology I
State University of New York
SUNY#BIOL101 Undergraduate   3 credits $1038*
The first semester of a two-semester sequence which presents an overview of biological principles. Major topics include chemistry as it relates to organisms, cell morphology and physiology, and human anatomy and physiology. This course is intended for non-majors and presumes no prior experience in biology. Substantial outside preparation for laboratories may be required.
* NY residents tuition: $137 per credit.

Principles of Chemistry
University of Minnesota
MINN#GC1166 Undergraduate   5 credits $445
Fundamental principles and laws of chemistry; problem-solving techniques applied to chemistry. Topics: classification of matter, elements, atomic and molecular structure, compounds and chemical bonding, mole calculations, percent composition and empirical formulas, chemical equations and reactions, stoichiometry, solutions and solution concentrations, acids and bases, gases and gas laws, organic chemistry. Students become acquainted with everyday applications of chemistry, the contributions chemistry makes to modern society, and gain a general understanding of both the content and process of the science of chemistry. Prerequisite: elementary algebra.

Probability & Statistics
Bellevue University
BELL#IBMC320 Undergraduate   3 credits $750
A course that discusses probability concepts and their application in statistics.

Probability and Statistics
New Jersey Institute of Technology
NJIT#MATH333 Undergraduate   3 credits $1143*
A course in descriptive statistics and statistical inference. Specific topics include discrete and continuous distributions of random variables, probability models in science, and statistical inference. Prerequisite: Calculus III. Optional: 40 video lessons of 30 minutes each.
* NJ residents: $184/semester hour.

Professional Research & Reporting
Fayetteville Technical Community College
FAYE#ENG114 Undergraduate   3 credits $489*

This course, the second in a series of two, is designed to teach professional communication skills. Emphasis is placed on research, listening, critical reading and thinking, analysis, interpretation, and design used in oral and written presentations. Upon completion, students should be able to work individually and collaboratively to produce well-designed business and professional written and oral presentations. This course has been approved to satisfy the Comprehensive Articulation Agreement general education core requirement in English composition.
* North Carolina residents and non-resident US military personnel stationed within the state tuition: $60; NC senior citizens: free.

Race to Save the Planet
Western Illinois University
WEIL#BIO422 Undergraduate   3 credits $795*

Explores the relationships between human society and the earth's natural resources. From fossil fuels to rain forests, from intensive agriculture to industrial pollutants, this PBS telecourse demonstrates how dramatically human activities are influencing the global web of ecosystems. Examine the major environmental questions facing the world today--among them deforestation, the loss of species' diversity, soil erosion and climate change--probe the human dimensions of international environmental issues, and explore new approaches that can create a more sustainable future.
* IL residents tuition: $88 per credit.

Regional Geography
State University of New York
SUNY#SS172 Undergraduate   3 credits $435*

An analysis of both the formal and functional world regions, concentrating on the social, political, and economic problems as they relate to the geographic characteristics of those areas.
* NY residents tuition: $80 per credit.

Remote Sensing
Emporia State University
EMPO#ES771 Graduate   4 credits $420

Remote sensing of the Earth's surface utilizing the electromagnetic spectrum. Techniques of photography, multispectral scanning, and microwave imagery from airplane, satellite, and manned-spacecraft platforms. Image interpretations, practical applications in earth science, and use of remotely sensed data in geographic information systems. Prerequisite, MA112 and GE371 or ES545 or by consent of instructor.

Resampling Statistics
University of Wisconsin
WISC#EDUC796 Undergraduate   3 credits $518

An alternative or second statistics course. The course involves simulating the main techniques of a first course with the computer program called "Resampling Stats." The program is available on DOS, Mac, Windows 3.1 and Windows 95 operating systems. This course is available for enrollment whenever it is of interest. Once a student enrolls, there are 120 continuous calendar days in which to complete the course.

Research Methodology
Nova Southeastern University
NOVA#MCTE690 Graduate   3 credits $1,110

This course is an introduction to research, statistical analysis and decision-making. Close attention is paid to data types, data contributions, the identification of variables and descriptive data presentation techniques. Students are introduced to both parametric and non-parametric data analysis procedures including independent and dependent sample t-tests, chi-square analysis and simple analysis of variance. Hypothesis testing and the use of statistical software packages are emphasized.

Research Methods
University of Nebraska
NEBR#HRFS875 Masters   3 credits $467

Research Methods addresses practical and theoretical issues involved in designing, conducting and evaluating research in the areas of human resources and family sciences. By the end of this course the student will be able to understand the dominant modes of inquiry, understand the usefulness of theoretical frameworks to research design and methodology, understand the basics of the scientific method and its application to the inquiry paradigms, develop abilities to become critical consumers of research.

Research Problems in Earth Science
Emporia State University
EMPO#ES739 Graduate   1-3 credits $105

For graduate students wishing to work on research problems of special interest in the field of earth science.

Review of Basic Geometry
University of Alaska - Fairbanks
ALFA#DEVM081 Undergraduate   1 credits $71

High School geometry without formal proofs. Definitions, measurements, parallel lines, triangles, polygons, circles, area, solid figures and volume. Prerequisite: DEVM060.

Review of Elementary Algebra
University of Alaska - Fairbanks
ALFA#DEVM061 Undergraduate   1 credits $71

This course is designed to assist students in reviewing material covered by DEVM060. Individuals who have not previously taken an elementary algebra course are recommended to enroll in DEVM060.

Review of Intermediate Algebra
University of Alaska - Fairbanks
ALFA#DEVM071 Undergraduate   1 credits $64

Reviews material in DEVM070. Individuals who have not taken an intermediate algebra course on the high-school level should enroll in DEVM070.

Satellite Information Processing
University of North Dakota
NODA#SPST535 Graduate   3 credits $816*

Earth orbit provides a "high-ground" perspective that has led to enormous advances in space-based communication, navigation, meteorological forecasting and climate studies, and remote sensing. In this class, we will concentrate on all of those, particularly remote sensing, with a hands-on emphasis towards applications of satellite data.
* ND residents, $102 per credit; may also be reduced for residents of adjoining states and provinces.

Science and Society
Strayer University
STRA#HUM300 Undergraduate 4.5 credits $665
Examines the impact of science and technology on our everyday experience. Focuses on the recent technological discoveries in the fields of communication, transportation, aerospace, artificial intelligence, and medicine.

Science of Human Movement
State University of New York
SUNY#ES200 Undergraduate 3 credits $1038*
Provides students with an introduction to the biological and physical bases of exercise responses and adaptations to chronic physical activity in humans. Examination of appropriate exercise principles and concepts is accompanied by critical examination of misconceptions, fads and myths that pervade exercise and fitness activities.
* NY residents tuition: $137 per credit

Scientific and Technical Writing
New York Institute of Technology
NYIT#EN1048 Undergraduate 3 credits $???
Continued training and practice in the techniques and forms of scientific and technical writing. Topics covered include: longer report forms, manuals, patent disclosures, preparation of forms, promotional materials, business and product plans, specification writing graphic techniques, information gathering, strategic planning, group problem solving, legal aspects of technical publishing, introduction to new technologies, including industrial use of film/videotape, audience analysis, rhetorical techniques, logical organization and clarity.

Scientific and Technical Writing
Western Illinois University
WEIL#ENG381 Undergraduate 3 credits $795*
Primarily serves those who will be writing various types of scientific and technical papers, reports, and memoranda. However, since good technical writing is basically clear and correct expository prose, the course would be valuable to anyone who wants to improve his or her writing to communicate more effectively. Prerequisite: Freshman composition or consent of instructor.
* IL residents tuition: $88 per credit.

Scientific Approaches to Organic Gardening
Auburn University
AUBU#H204 Undergraduate 3 qtr. hrs. $126
An introduction to the basic principles and practices of organic gardening including planting, maintenance, harvesting and storage of organically grown fruits, vegetables and herbs.

Selected Topics in Physical Studies
State University of New York
SUNY#PPE240 Undergraduate 3 credits $630*
An overview and introduction to various methods of presentation in the sport sciences. The ability to effectively communicate ideas, information and teach skills are fundamental to the field of Physical Studies. The goal of this course is to provide theoretical and practical experience in group presentation and written communication of a selected topic. Topics this semester will include: Gender in Sport, Amateurism vs Professionalism, Aggression and Violence in Sport, Nature vs. Nurture - are athletes born or made' Other timely topics will be included.
* NY residents tuition: $105 per credit.

Short Calculus
University of Minnesota
MINN#MATH1142 Undergraduate 5 credits $445
For students in pre-business administration, pre-pharmacy, and others requiring a minimal amount of calculus; students who plan to take several quarters of mathematics should register for MATH1251-1252. Prerequisite: MATH1111 or 1031 or mathematics placement score.

Society, Culture and the Environment
University of South Florida
FLSO#U101 Undergraduate 3 qtr. hrs. $???
An interdisciplinary course introducing concepts and processes relating to society, culture and the environment as studied by anthropology, geography and sociology.

Solar System Astronomy
University of Minnesota
MINN#GC1161 Undergraduate 4 credits $356
An introductory survey of the solar system, including a study of the earth, planets, satellites, asteroids, comets, and meteorites. Topics: the celestial sphere, coordinate systems, time intervals, motions and physical attributes of the planets and their satellites in the solar system, and instruments used by the astronomer. Observations of the night sky included. Knowledge of elementary algebra suggested.

Solar System Geology
University of Oregon
OREG#AST121 Undergraduate 4 credits $374
The study of the Solar System is primarily an exercise in planetary geology. The input data, in most cases, consists only of images of planetary surfaces from which we attempt to reconstruct its particular geological history. Each planetary surface in our Solar System has a unique geological history and a wealth of network accessible information now exists. Well over 10,000 individual images of planetary surfaces are now available via the World Wide Web and Internet system.

Solar System Laboratory
Pima Community College
PIMA#AST111 Undergraduate 1 credits $55*
Laboratory for AST101, involving exercises, star gazing sessions and field trips to plantaruims and observatories. Students will link electronically to Dr. Iadevaia's observatory in Patagonia, AZ.
* AZ residents pay $32 per credit.

Solid State Physics I
State University of New York
SUNY#CES541001 Graduate   3 credits $1038*

This course is the first half of a two-semester course, which discusses the microscopic origins of the physical properties of solids. This section focuses on the atomic lattice and associated mechanical, thermal and dielectric properties. Prerequisites: The complete undergraduate sequence of courses in Physics and Mathematics plus Thermal and Mechanical Properties and Electrical, Magnetic and Optical Properties or equivalent.

* NY residents tuition: $137 per credit

Space Science and Exploration
University of North Dakota
NODA#SPST420 Graduate   3 credits $816*

Human and robotic exploration of space has profoundly expanded our view of the Universe and has revealed the gross characteristics of most of the planetary surfaces (moons, too) in the Solar System. In this course we will review the present state of knowledge in planetary science, how that knowledge was obtained, and the potential future of space exploration and its attendant social and economic benefits.

* ND residents, $102 per credit; may also be reduced for residents of adjoining states and provinces.

Space Studies Seminar
University of North Dakota
NODA#SPST590 Graduate   1 credits $272*

A series of invited lectures presented by UND faculty. May be repeated for up to 4 credits. Seminars offered in the past have included: Telerobotics: A unique distance-education course on Telerobitcs. Produced jointly with NASA Ames Research Center, the Telerobotics course will be presented over the Internet using CU-SeeMe and Real Audio software. Distance students will have the opportunity to communicate questions and comments online through Internet Chat.

* ND residents, $102 per credit; may also be reduced for residents of adjoining states and provinces.

Statics
University of Colorado
CUON#ME2023 Undergraduate   3 credits $1953*

A vector treatment of force systems and their resultants; equilibrium of trusses, beams, frames, and machines, including internal forces and three-dimensional configurations; static friction; properties of areas; distributed loads; hydrostatics.

* CO residents tuition: $136 per credit.

Statistical Analysis
New York Institute of Technology
NYIT#BES2422 Undergraduate   3 credits $???

This course covers descriptive and inferential statistics, frequency distributions, percentile rank, measure of central tendency and variability, correlation and regression and tests of significance. Using computer software students will directly apply these statistics to specific problems common to the behavioral sciences.

Statistical Methods for Experimental Sciences
Western Illinois University
WEIL#FIN470 Undergraduate   3 credits $795*

Statistics is a necessary tool for students in all fields. This PBS telecourse focuses on the application of statistics. Learn how statisticians collect, organize, and draw inferences from data. The concepts and techniques you learn enable you to analyze and solve real everyday problems in a wide variety of applied fields. Prerequisite: Mathematics 100 or high school advanced algebra.

* IL residents tuition: $88 per credit.

Statistics
Brevard Community College
BREV#STA2023 Undergraduate   3 credits $485

An elementary statistics course with emphasis on mathematical concepts and suitable for students of business, mathematics, education and the sciences. Topics include measures of central tendency and spread, probability binomial, normal and t-distributions, statistical inference, and linear regression and correlation.

Statistics
University of Colorado
CUON#SOC3121 Undergraduate   4 credits $2604*

Quantitative techniques used in analyzing social phenomena. Prerequisite: MATH1070 or its equivalent.

* CO residents tuition: $136 per credit.

Statistics
Golden Gate University
GOLD#MATH40 Undergraduate   3 credits $960

(Course description not available at press time.)

Statistics
University of Minnesota
MINN#GC1454 Undergraduate   5 credits $445

Introduction to modern statistics, emphasizing exploratory data analysis. The topics examined in this course include methods of organizing, graphing, and interpreting data; measures of center and variability; sampling; probability and probability distributions; estimation, correlation, and hypothesis testing. Prerequisite: elementary algebra.

Statistics
New Hampshire College
NEHA#MAT220 Undergraduate   3 credits $1656

A fundamental course in the application of statistics including descriptive statistics, probability distributions, hypothesis testing and basic linear regression. Prerequisite: MAT120.

Statistics - An Activity Based Approach
State University of New York
SUNY#272384 Undergraduate   4 credits $586*

Cover the fundamental concepts and methods of data analysis, including both descriptive and inferential statistics. Gain an understanding of the data analysis processes used by statisticians and other researchers. Includes the use of technology based tools commonly used by researchers (a graphing calculator or statistical software, spreadsheets are not an acceptable tool) to assist in summarizing and interpreting data and information. Understand how to evaluate which statistical analyses are appropriate for a given set of data.

* NY residents tuition: $515

Statistics and Quantitative Methods
Bellevue University
BELL#MBA522 Graduate   3 credits $825
An introductory course to essentials of statistics and basic quantitative tools.

Statistics for Everyone
New School for Social Research
NEWS#0849 Undergraduate   3 credits $1638*
This is a gentle, compassionate introduction to statistics and a perfect starter course for those who want to use them in daily life, office, and academic research. We explain the concepts of statistics and probability and define them in accessible language. The textbook, by focusing on key ideas rather than mathematical formulations, shows the students how a sound understanding of statistics can help them make better decisions--as consumers, students, parents, or professionals. We emphasize reasoning rather than memorizing. We utilize studies drawn from newspapers to stimulate students to grasp the statistical concepts.
* Non-credit option, tuition: $365.

Statistics I
Mercy College
MERC#MA122 Undergraduate   3 credits $900
(Course description not available at press time.)

Stellar Astronomy
University of Minnesota
MINN#GC1162 Undergraduate   4 credits $356
An introductory survey of the large-scale structures of the universe, including the definition of certain properties of stars (magnitude, luminosity, brightness). Topics: the sun, the spectral classification of stars, white dwarfs, neutron stars, black holes, clusters, nebulae, galaxies, quasars, cosmology, and cosmogony. Observation of the night sky included. Knowledge of elementary algebra helpful.

Survey of Astronomy
Honolulu Community College
HONO#AST110 Undergraduate   3 credits $714*
Survey of the nature of the astronomical universe for non-science majors, with emphasis on the scientific method and the development of scientific thought.
* Hawaiian residents tuition: $39 per credit.

Survey of Probability and Statistics
New Jersey Institute of Technology
NJIT#MATH225 Undergraduate   3 credits $1143*
Topics include: descriptive statistics, elements of probability, random variables and distribution; mean and variance; introduction to estimation and inference. Note: This course satisfies the General University Requirement (GUR) in probability and statistics. Any higher level mathematics course in probability and statistics also will satisfy the GUR in probability and statistics. Credits will not be grated for both Math 225 and any such upper level course. Prerequisite: Calculus II. Optional: 15 video lessons of 30 minutes each.
* NJ residents: $184/semester hour.

Survey of Research Methodology
The Graduate School of America
TGSA#RM501W Graduate   4 credits $795
This course presents an overview of the general approaches to research methodology at the graduate level. It deals with the quantitative and qualitative approaches to rigorous scholarly inquiry and the major research methodologies.

Survey of Space Studies
University of North Dakota
NODA#SPST501 Graduate   3 credits $816*
A broad, multidisciplinary survey of our space program and its meaning for the future economic and national security of the nation. Emphasis will be placed on the multinational aspects of humanity's move into this new milieu and what this means in terms of cooperation and competition for the United States. The course will include a survey of the major scientific and technical issues involved. SPST501 is a prerequisite/co-requisite to all other 500 level courses.
* ND residents, $102 per credit; may also be reduced for residents of adjoining states and provinces.

Technical Issues in Space
University of North Dakota
NODA#SPST525 Graduate   3 credits $816*
An examination of the highly developed technological base required for the exploration and development of space. An understanding of this technology and of its impact upon humans is essential to an appreciation of many of the issues and problem areas that are and will be associated with our continuing efforts to explore and settle this new frontier. Prerequisite: Survey of Space Studies (NODA#SPST501).
* ND residents, $102 per credit; may also be reduced for residents of adjoining states and provinces.

Technical Mathematics I
New York Institute of Technology
NYIT#MA3310 Undergraduate   3 credits $???
Review of algebra: exponents, factoring, fractions. Linear equations, ratio, proportions. Applications to concrete problems. Coordinate systems and graphs of functions: straight line, slope. Systems of linear equations and their applications. Complex numbers. Quadratic equations. Introduction to Trigonometry. Application to problems in engineering technology are emphasized throughout. Prerequisite: MA3008 or MA3013 or Math placement test.

Technical Mathematics II
New York Institute of Technology
NYIT#MA3320 Undergraduate   3 credits $???
Topics include trigonometric functions, identities and equations, the sine and cosine laws; graphs of the trigonometric functions; functions of a composite angle; DeMoivre's Theorem; logarithms; binomial theorem; and Cramer's rule. Prerequisite: MA3310.

Technology 2002
Northwest Technical College
NOTE#CPTR1404 Undergraduate 3 credits $240*
(Course description not available at press time.)
* Residents rates may apply.

The Changing Physical World
University of Minnesota
MINN#PHYS1003 Undergraduate 4 credits $356
Introduces nonscience students to the changing world of 20th-century physics. Against a background of history and philosophy, it highlights the new ideas and discoveries of relativity, cosmology, and quantum theory as seen on the vast scale of stars and galaxies, in everyday realm of matter and energy, and down to the submicroscopic level of atoms and nuclei.

The Fossil Record
University of Oregon
OREG#GEO304 Undergraduate 4 credits $374
This course looks at the systematic treatment of the history of life as it is read from the fossil record. This offering is intended for non-science students desiring a one-course summary of earth history specifically as it is seen in the record of plants and animals.

The Physical World
University of Minnesota
MINN#PHYS1001 Undergraduate 4 credits $356
Fundamental laws and principles of the physical world discussed in the context of modern science and technology. Topics: motion of particles, laws of motion, momentum and energy conservation, gravity, fluids, temperature, heat, wave motion, the nature of light, optics, electricity, magnetism. Prerequisite: one year high school algebra.

The Science of Physics
Pennsylvania State University
PENN#PHYS001 Undergraduate 3 credits $345
Historical development and significance of major concepts and theories, with emphasis on the nature of physical science and its role in modern life. For students in nontechnical fields.

The Solar System
Pima Community College
PIMA#AST101 Undergraduate 3 credits $165*
Descriptive and historical introduction to the science of astronomy focusing on the sun and its family of planets. Includes comets, origin of the solar system, the space program and critiques of related pseudosciences, e.g. astrology. Prerequisites: None.
* AZ residents pay $32 per credit.

Theory and Concepts of Plant Pathology
University of Missouri
MOCE#HO305 Undergraduate 3 credits $387
This course investigates the diseases of plants. Topics include viruses, prokaryotes, fungi, gene regulation, plant metabolism, and the genetics of plant disease. Perquisites: 5 hours of biology; junior, senior, or graduate standing.

Topics in Technical Math
Northwest Technical College
NOTE#MATH1404 Undergraduate 3 credits $240*
(Course description not available at press time.)
* Residents rates may apply.

Trigonometry
University of Alaska - Fairbanks
ALFA#MATH108 Undergraduate 3 credits $213
A study of the trigonometric functions. Prerequisite: MATH107.

Trigonometry
City University
CITY#MTH130 Undergraduate 5 qu. credits $785
An introductory course designed to prepare the student for further studies in technical fields such as electronics, surveying and physical design, and for studies in higher mathematics, engineering and natural sciences. The topics include: basic theory and properties of relations and functions; graphing; angular measure; right triangle applications; laws of sines and cosines; rectors and polar coordinates.

Trigonometry
University of Minnesota
MINN#MATH1008 Undergraduate 4 credits $356
Analytic trigonometry, identities, equations, properties of functions; right and oblique triangles without logarithmic computations. Calculator with trig and inverse trig functions necessary. Prerequisite: plane geometry, higher algebra, mathematics placement score.

Trigonometry
University of Missouri
MOCE#MA9 Undergraduate 2 credits $258
This course covers the basics of trigonometry.

Trigonometry and Analytic Geometry
Honolulu Community College
HONO#MATH140 Undergraduate 3 credits $714*
A study of angles; trigonometric and circular functions; solutions of triangles; graphical representation; identities; inverse trigonometric functions; polar coordinates; conic sections; graphs of exponential and logarithmic functions.
* Hawaiian residents tuition: $39 per credit.

Volcanoes and Earthquakes
University of Oregon
OREG#GEO306 Undergraduate 4 credits $374
A one-course summary of the fundamental geologic phenomena and is written for students with a limited science background. The course focus will be on the processes surrounding and causing these events as well as their impact on human culture. In addition to historical perspectives on earthquakes and volcanoes, their prediction and mitigation will be considered.

Volcanology
City University
CITY#SCI401 Undergraduate 5 qu. credits $785
This introductory course in volcanology will examine the characteristics and impacts of volcanoes on Earth as well as other planets. Topics include: the creation and location of volcanoes and the impacts of volcanoes on the environment and climate. Prerequisite: Strongly recommended: NAS201 and NAS215 or their equivalents.

Weather in the Pacific Northwest
Marylhurst College
MARY#ATM124 Undergraduate   3 credits $651
Examine the general principles of atmospheric activity and focus on the peculiarities of the Pacific Northwest Weather and climate in the northwest corner of the United States is so variable that it can serve as a model within the global perspective.

Writing about Science
University of Minnesota
MINN#COMP3015 Undergraduate   4 credits $391
Designed to improve the writing ability of students interested in science, this course focuses on writing about science (general) and writing for science (special). The tasks and forms of science writing are discussed and practiced. Also considers the writing process and what makes for rhetorical effectiveness: organization, support, clarity, cleanliness, and appropriateness for the audience. The course attempts to respond to individual student needs, interests, and abilities. Prerequisite: Writing Practice requirement or equivalent.

Social Sciences

Abnormal Psychology

Anthropology

Child Psychology

Economics

General Psychology

Geography

Government

International Relations

Labor

Other

Public Policy

Sociology

Abnormal Psychology
University of Alaska - Fairbanks
ALFA#PSY345 Undergraduate   3 credits $237
A study of abnormal behavior, its causes, treatment, and social impact. The major classifications of disorder. Prerequisite: PSY101.

Abnormal Psychology
City University
CITY#PSY402 Undergraduate   5 qu. credits $785
This course assesses both past and present models of psychological abnormality including the current diagnostic system, DSM-III-R. Other topics addressed include: problems of anxiety, mood, mind and body, social impact, psychosis, and personality. Prerequisite: Strongly recommended: SSC205 or its equivalent.

Abnormal Psychology
Fayetteville Technical Community College
FAYE#PSY281 Undergraduate   3 credits $489*
This course provides an examination of the various psychological disorders, as well as theoretical, clinical, and experimental perspectives of the study of psychopathology. Emphasis is placed on terminology, classification, etiology, assessment, and treatment of the major disorders. Upon completion, students should be able to distinguish between normal and abnormal behavior patterns as well as demonstrate knowledge of etiology, symptoms, and therapeutic techniques. This course has been approved to satisfy the Comprehensive Articulation Agreement general education core requirement in social/behavioral sciences. Prerequisites: PSY150.
* NC residents pay $20 per credit.

Abnormal Psychology
Indiana University
INDI#P324 Undergraduate   3 credits $268
A first course in abnormal psychology, with emphasis on forms of abnormal behavior, etiology, development, interpretation, and final manifestations. Prerequisites: P101 and P102, or P106.

Abnormal Psychology
Mercy College
MERC#PY212 Undergraduate   3 credits $900
The course surveys the causes, symptoms, treatments and prevention of abnormal behavior. A variety of theoretical perspectives of abnormal psychology will be examined, along with the problems of diagnosis and research. Other topics include the history of mental illness, ethical and legal problems and new approaches to therapy.

Abnormal Psychology
University of Missouri
MOCE#PS245 Undergraduate   3 credits $387
This course introduces major symptom complexes, theories of etiology, and treatment of behavior disorders. Perquisites: Psych. 3.

Abnormal Psychology
New York Institute of Technology
NYIT#BES2465 Undergraduate   3 credits $???
A study of mental health and abnormal behavior. The topics covered include: definitions of mental health and mental illness; problems of adjustment; the causes, diagnosis, treatment, and prevention of mental disorders. Case studies supplement and illustrate the theoretical parts of the course material. Prerequisites: BES2401.

Abnormal Psychology
State University of New York
SUNY#SS155 Undergraduate   3 credits $435*
An examination of behavior patterns which interfere with personal efficiency. Emphasis is placed on the characteristics, probable etiologies and common modes of treatment of the behavior patterns studied.
* NY residents tuition: $80 per credit.

Abnormal Psychology
Texas Technical University
TETE#PSY4305 Undergraduate   3 credits $159
This course is a study of personality deviations and maladjustments with an emphasis on clinical descriptions of abnormal behavior, etiological factors, manifestations, interpretations, and treatments. Prerequisite: PSY 3306 or consent of instructor.

Abnormal Psychology
Walden University
WALD#PSYC8220 Graduate   5 credits $1500
The course will discuss the bases for identifying behavior as normal or abnormal, focusing on the etiology, major signs and symptoms of maladaptive behaviors and potential treatment approaches, both traditional and alternative.

Abnormal Psychology
Western Illinois University
WEIL#PSY424G Undergraduate   3 credits $795*
Examines the complex factors that cause behavioral disorders and the problems of recognizing, understanding, treating, and preventing these disorders. This PBS telecourse combines video case studies of mental disorders with the insights of psychologists involved in current research.
* IL residents tuition: $88 per credit.

Activity Ideas for Elementary Phy Ed
Emporia State University
EMPO#PE700A Undergrad/Grad   1 credits $76
The course will be a sharing vehicle for PE/Classroom teachers looking for new ideas for their elementary PE classes or recesses. We will explore the internet for various sites containing activity ideas for children. Also, we will have forum discussions with our classmates via the internet to share ideas and activities.

Administration of Ministries
Marylhurst College
MARY#PMT410 Undergraduate   3 credits $651
(Course description not available at press time.)

Administration of Programs for Children and Families
University of Missouri
MOCE#SO358 Undergraduate   3 credits $387
This course examines the design, operation, and evaluation of family programs. Perquisites: Human Develop. 264 or instructor's consent.

Adolescent Development
University of Missouri
MOCE#A208 Undergraduate   2 credits $258
The psychological, intellectual, social, and physical development of adolescents is studied in this course. Perquisites: Psych. 1 or 2.

Adolescent Development
Pennsylvania State University
PENN#HDFS239 Undergraduate   3 credits $345
Social, behavioral, and biological development and intervention throughout adolescence.

Adolescent in the Family
University of Nebraska
NEBR#FACS872 Masters   3 credits $467
Adolescent in the Family is a five session multi-media series designed to provide the student with a knowledge of normal adolescent development and problem conditions often associated with adolescence. A series of 19 lecturettes have been prepared by the course instructor. In addition, the course instructor has collaborated with Boys Town to develop a series of videotapes concerned with teaching parents of adolescents useful parenting skills.

Adolescent Psychology
University of Minnesota
MINN#CPSY5303 Undergraduate   4 credits $400
Survey of the behavior and psychological development of the adolescent, including biological factors, cognition and creativity, moral development, parent-child relations, peers, ego identity, sexual development, school adjustment, social-cultural considerations, and the adolescent subculture. Prerequisite: 5 credits introductory psychology.

Adolescent Psychology
University of Missouri
MOCE#PS271 Undergraduate   3 credits $387
This course studies the principles of biological, behavioral, and personality development from puberty to maturity. Perquisites: Psych. 3.

Adolescent Psychology
New York Institute of Technology
NYIT#BES2441 Undergraduate   3 credits $???
An introduction to the study of that portion of human development called adolescence. Some of the topics treated: significance of puberty, biological and social sex roles, adolescent image, the emergence of new figures such as peers and idols, society at large as agents of socializations in place of parents and family, the extinction of old habits and practices and their replacement with new behavioral patterns. Theoretical consideration will be supplemented with observational experience. Prerequisites: BES2401.

Adult Development and Aging
Pennsylvania State University
PENN#HDFS249 Undergraduate   3 credits $345
Physiological, psychological, and social development and intervention from young adulthood through old age.

Advanced Fire Administration
State University of New York
SUNY#264014 Undergraduate   4 credits $586*
Review the history and development of the American fire service. Consider the evolution of management theory and its fire service applications. Addresses personnel administration, goal setting, control, coordination, direction, and organization of a fire department, and matching human and physical resources. Includes value engineering for capital resources; cost effectiveness in service delivery; management by objectives, quality circles, fire prevention, suppression, and investigation; emergency medical services; the utilization of computers in data collection, retrieval, and analysis; budgeting; and productivity. Prerequisites: Introduction to Public Administration (162164) or equivalent or have significant practical background in administration and management.
* NY residents tuition: $515

Advanced Fire Administration
Western Illinois University
WEIL#IND481A Undergraduate   3 credits $795*
offers an overview of organization and management in the modern fire service. Topics include management of equipment and personnel, fire department functions, planning, resource development, labor relations, communications, financial management, and community relations.
* IL residents tuition: $88 per credit.

Advanced Psychological Testing
Walden University
WALD#PSYC8270 Graduate   5 credits $1500
An in-depth examination of advanced psychological test procedures and research for the assessment of intelligence, personality, achievement, and sensory abilities.

Advanced Psychology
Northwest College
NOCO#GE275 Undergraduate   3 credits $???
Continuing the study of the theories of psychology and human development, particular attention is given to the major figures in the advancement of modern psychology. Students will also examine the role of healthy emotions and personality in the development of human behavior, as well as look at abnormal psychology and its effect on the individual. Prerequisite: GE177.

Advanced Psychopathology
Walden University
WALD#PSYC8230 Graduate   5 credits $1500
An in-depth examination of current theory and research associated with major psychological disorders. The transition from the concepts and terminology of DSM-IV to actual clinical situations will be emphasized.

Africa and the Global Perspective
Salve Regina University
SALV#INR524 Grad   3 credits $???
Students analyze the fundamental factors in influencing the relations of contemporary African states within the continent and with the outside world. Such factors as African social, economic, political, and cultural developments are considered, as well as reaction to African developments by other states.

Aging in Contemporary Society
University of Missouri
MOCE#SO410R Graduate   3 credits $489
Topics in this course include attitudes and stereotypes associated with the aged; the status of the aged in American society; the social psychology of the aging process; and the response of social institutions such as the family and political system to the aging of the population as a whole.

Alaska Native Claims Settlement
University of Alaska - Fairbanks
ALFA#AKNP151 Undergraduate   3 credits $237
A general survey of the Alaska Native Claims Settlement Act. It will include a brief historical overview of land claims of various tribes in the Lower 48 and in Alaska leading to the Settlement Act of 1971. We will examine the current status of the various Native corporations, including regional, village and non-profit corporations. We will also give special attention to the discussion of future issues related to implementation of ANCSA.

Alaska, Land and Its People
University of Alaska - Fairbanks
ALFA#HIST115 Undergraduate   3 credits $213
A survey of Alaska from earliest days to present, its peoples, problems, and prospects.

Alienation Estrangement Subcultures
California State University - Dominguez Hills
CADO#HUX546 Undergraduate   3 credits $405
Survey of the elements and historical implications of alienation and examination of subcultures as they exist in America. Readings from social Philosophy as well as from Chicano and African-American studies.

American & Wyoming Government
Laramie County Community College
LARA#POLS1000 Undergraduate   ?? credits $???
The Internet version of the American and Wyoming (State) Government class offers political science students an exciting interactive approach to the traditional American Government course. Throughout the semester the class will visit a variety of political web sites focusing on the presidential elections, visit the home pages of the presidential candidates, tap into alternative electronic media, and follow major legislation from Congress and Supreme Court decisions. In addition to traditional class assignments and readings, class members will have weekly online chat sessions with the instructor and each other.

American Federal Government
Rogers State University
ROGE#POLSC1113 Undergraduate   3 credits $495*
Course topics cover the development of the national government with emphasis on state origins, constitutionalism and basic structures and theories of the federal government. Video: Government by Consent.
* OK residents $315.

American Foreign Relations
University of Missouri
MOCE#IN361 Undergraduate   3 credits $387
Following a rapid survey of major principles and actions in American diplomatic affairs before 1900, this course analyzes developing principles, problems, methods, and factors in American foreign relations since that date. Attention is given to the interrelationships of domestic factors and foreign relations, with an attempt to discover principal influences that have shaped this area of American development.

American Government
Edmonds Community College
EDMO#POLSC104 Undergraduate   5 credits $260
This course is designed to help you understand, think critically about, and participate in the American political process. It will introduce you to the institutions of national government, the contemporary politics of our nation, and to what is unique about American political thought, culture, and traditions. The goal of this course is to help you become critical consumers and active participants in American politics.

American Government
University of Missouri
MOCE#GO1 Undergraduate   3 credits $387
Topics in this course include the Constitution, federalism, civil liberties, political attitudes, interest groups, political parties, nominations, elections and campaigns, voting behavior, Congress, the Presidency, and the judiciary.

American Government & Politics
University of Alaska - Fairbanks
ALFA#PS101 Undergraduate   3 credits $213
Principles, institutions, and practices of American national government; the Constitution, federalism, interest groups, parties, public opinion, and elections.

American Government and Politics
University of Minnesota
MINN#POL1001 Undergraduate   5 credits $445
This course provides student with an introduction to the ways in which the goals of political actors and the structures of government combine to influence American national policy making. Attention is given to the major actors (both institutions and individuals), the mechanics of elections and governing, and the values and standards of democratic rule in the United States. The course concludes with two case studies of recent events in American politics.

American Government and Politics
New York Institute of Technology
NYIT#SS2700 Undergraduate   3 credits $???
An introduction to the processes of the American form of government. The nature and structure of government, its characteristics and functions. The intimate relation of government to other interests.

American Government and Politics
State University of New York
SUNY#7721607 Undergraduate 3 credits $1038*
Structure and processes of the American system of government and politics. Basic constitutional principles, the theory and practice of representative government, and the organization and function of the political system.
* NY residents tuition: $137 per credit

American Government and Politics
Western Illinois University
WEIL#POL122 Undergraduate 3 credits $795*
Examines the structure and operation of the national government of the United States. The powers and limitations of the central government are analyzed through a detailed discussion of Congress and its committees, the Presidency with its bureaucracy, and the federal court system. In addition, the part played by the extra-constitutional agencies of political parties and interest groups in the proper functioning of the government is discussed. Finally, the current status of individual rights and liberties is catalogued and defined.
* IL residents tuition: $88 per credit.

American National Government
Eastern Oregon University
EAOR#POLS101 Undergraduate 5 credits $400
An introductory analysis of American politics, including the historical and philosophical origins of the system, institutions of government, political processes and contemporary issues.

American National Government
University of South Carolina-Aiken
SCAI#APLS201 Undergraduate 3 credits $???
To give you an opportunity to learn how the American political system actually works, as opposed to how you are often told it should work. To do this, there are many facts you should know, but they are not worth knowing unless you understand the forces that tie them together in a meaningful way. For example, understanding how a bill becomes law is a series of facts that helps us understand why the status quo is so hard to change, and that in turn helps us understand why we are so cynical about politics and politicians.

American Political Institutions
Barstow Community College
BARS#POLI1 Undergraduate 3 credits $???
The fundamental principles of American federal, state and local government. Governmental structure, political parties and public policies.

American Political Parties
University of Minnesota
MINN#POL5737 Undergraduate 4 credits $391
Party activities in the United States--recruiting, nominating, and campaigning. Parties in power. Party organization and membership, party identification, third parties, and independents. Party reform and the functions of parties. Attention throughout to the impact of parties on democratic government. Prerequisite: POL1001 or consent of instructor.

American Political Process
Christopher Newport University
CHNE#GOVT201 Undergraduate 3 credits $993
An examination of political dynamics within the American system. Consideration is given to American political institutions, such as the President, Congress, judiciary, bureaucracy, elections, political parties, and interest groups.

American Political System
Lansing Community College
LANS#POLS120 Undergraduate 3 credits $315
This class will give each student a complete analysis of the American political system. Emphasis is given to the federal system, with special attention to American government at the national level. The textbook for the class American Government and Politics Today uses the excitement of current events such as the 1996 national elections, citizen militias, and the debate over the flat tax to capture and maintain your interest in the material.

American Politics
New Hampshire College
NEHA#GOV110 Undergraduate 3 credits $1656
GOV110 is the study of policy-making in the American national political system. Emphasis is placed on interest groups, PACs, and on the activities of sub-governments in the formulation of policy.

American Politics
Rochester Institute of Technology
ROCH#51321190 Undergraduate 4 credits $923
This course is a study of the American national political system, its theoretical foundations and institutions and the contemporary issues that confront it.

American Public Policy
Texas Technical University
TETE#POLS2302 Undergraduate 3 credits $159
This Internet-delivered course covers the policy-making process in the governments of the United States, the states in general, and Texas in particular.

American Urban Minorities
New York Institute of Technology
NYIT#BES2435 Undergraduate 3 credits $???
An in-depth analysis of the diverse ethnic structure of the urban community. Major attention is given to black, Puerto Rican, and Mexican groups. Topics include: a survey of each group's social and economic structure, an examination of ghetto conditions and their effects, the impact of urban conditions on the new arrival, a comparison with the adaptation and treatment accorded earlier migrants, the validity of the melting pot concept, and a comparison of the life styles of various minority groups. Prerequisites: BES2411.

An Introduction to Jung
New School for Social Research
NEWS#0388 Undergraduate   3 credits $1638*

Jung, a philosopher as well as the father of modern psychology, wrote on dreams, soul, mythology, religion, and the unconscious, and was often at odds with theologians and much of the medical establishment. He saw his work as pedagogic and he was concerned about the future of the world. This course introduces students to Jung through his most accessible writings--Memories, Dreams, Reflections and Man and His Symbols--and two books by the British psychiatrist and analyst, Dr. Anthony Stevens--On Jung and the small paperback Jung. The emphasis is on experiencing Jung and discussing his ideas.

* Non-credit option, tuition: $365.

Analytic Approaches to Public Fire Protection
Western Illinois University
WEIL#IND482 Undergraduate   3 credits $795*

Gives you a broad understanding of the characteristics of systems analysis and of its uses and limitations in fire protection and other problem areas. The course is illustrated with case studies and models using the systems approach to fire suppression and prevention.

* IL residents tuition: $88 per credit.

Analyzing Society
University of Colorado-Boulder
COBO#SOCY1001 Undergraduate   3 credits $240

An exploration of U.S. society in global context, using basic sociological ideas, focusing on the nature of group life, social and moral order, social institutions, social disorganization, social problems, and social change.

Anthropology
New York Institute of Technology
NYIT#BES2405 Undergraduate   3 credits $???

An introduction to the study of ancient man and primitive cultures. Major topics include: the origins and evolution of man; the evolution of different cultural forms in terms of craft and technology, magic, religion, and government.

Anthropology of Women
Western Illinois University
WEIL#ANT315 Undergraduate   3 credits $795*

Examines women's roles in different types of societies. This course emphasizes economic roles and considers activity in the public realm as well as the domestic. Questions about whether animal behavior can give us any clues to human sex roles and what the life of the earliest human females was like are considered. Whether social theory adequately explains women's roles will also be reviewed. An introductory cultural anthropology course is recommended.

* IL residents tuition: $88 per credit.

Applications of Fire Research
Western Illinois University
WEIL#SOC487 Undergraduate   3 credits $795*

Involves the understanding of fire research and its application. The transfer and implications of available research results for fire prevention and protection programs are studied. A major emphasis is to encourage fire personnel to become aware of research studies at the national level and international levels.

* IL residents tuition: $88 per credit.

Approaches to Critical Thinking
City University
CITY#BC301 Undergraduate   5 qu. credits $785

The critical thinking process is used to analyze today's issues and aid the student in identifying rational solutions. Topics examined include: argument analyzing and building; forms and standards of critical thinking; and evaluating sources of information.

Arizona Constitution
Rio Salado College
RISA#POS221 Undergraduate   1 credits $62*

Examination of the Constitution of the State of Arizona. Equivalent to the second part of POS220. May not enroll in POS220 and POS221 concurrently.

* AZ residents $37 per credit.

Assessment of Sociotechnological Problems and Issues
State University of New York
SUNY#CEN580 Graduate   3 credits $1038*

This examination of studies that relate to current socio-technical issues includes a look at world population, medical technology, environmental resources, and information technology.

* NY residents tuition: $137 per credit

Basic Economics
New York Institute of Technology
NYIT#EC2011 Undergraduate   3 credits $???

A basic introduction to economic analysis, with emphasis on the problems and issues of a modern economy. This course is not available to business, economics, and political science majors.

Basic Fire Investigation
Edmonds Community College
EDMO#FCA120 Undergraduate   3 credits $220

A basic study of fire scene investigation procedures and techniques used to determine the origin and cause of fire. The course will cover the reasons for accurately determining the origin and cause of fire, the systematic approach to fire scene examination, the chemistry of fire, determining the origin, major accidental and incendiary fire causes, scene sketching, scene photography, note taking, and Washington State Criminal statutes. Other topics that will be covered are basic scene security, major fire scene control, report writing, interviewing, and courtroom demeanor for the firefighter and investigator.

Basic Police Armorer Certification
Yavapai Community College
YAVA#GST160 Undergraduate   2 credits $???

(Course description not available at press time.)

Behavior Modification
State University of New York
SUNY#PSY227Y02 Undergraduate   3 credits $570*

A study and survey of the development and especially the application of practical approaches to behavior management and change based on modern learning theories. Special attention will be given to the application of principles of operant and classical learning to all social milieus including behavior change at home, school, rehabilitative, corrective and recreational institutions, and other social settings. Self-control techniques are also analyzed.

Prerequisite: PSY110 General Psychology

* NY residents tuition: $90 per credit

Behavioral Psychology
City University
CITY#PSY303 Undergraduate   5 qu. credits $785
An introduction to behaviorism, designed so that students will gain a thorough grounding in the basic principles of conditioning and behavior. Topics include: the importance of context in conditioning, choice, cognition and self-control. Prerequisite: Strongly recommended: SSC205 or its equivalent.

Biological Bases of Behavior
The Graduate School of America
TGSA#HS811W Graduate   4 credits $795
Biological Bases of Behavior explores the latest information in our understanding of the brain and its relationship to human thought, feeling, and behavior. No particular background in science is required or expected of learners. The course will make general knowledge about the brain accessible; and, will show how behavior and psychological phenomena are related to the brain's cellular structure, chemical signals, and operations. Knowledge gained from this course has relevance for the general understanding of behavior, as well as for those learners in the human services field where the clinical assessment and effective treatment of individuals.

Biological Psychology
University of Alaska - Fairbanks
ALFA#PSY393 Undergraduate   3 credits $237
All behavior, thought, and feelings are the result of complex patterns of brain activity. Brain structure, major functions of the brain and the mechanisms responsible for them. The work of neuroscientists in studying the brain. Brain diseases and disorders and how they are treated. Prerequisite: Beginning biology or psychology course.

Biological Psychology
Walden University
WALD#PSYC8050 Graduate   5 credits $1500
A review of the structure and function of the nervous system and the brain. Special attention is given to neuro-transmitter systems, the endocrine system, the relationship of cognitive and sensory process to brain functioning, and the effects of brain damage on behavior.

Biological Psychology 1
University of Colorado-Boulder
COBO#PSYC2012 Undergraduate   3 credits $240
Broad survey of biological bases of learning, motivation, emotion, sensory processes and perception, movement, comparative animal behavior, sexual and reproductive activity, instinctual behavior, neurobiology of language and thought, and neurophysiology and neuroanatomy in relation to behavior.

Biological Psychology 2
University of Colorado-Boulder
COBO#PSYC2022 Undergraduate   3 credits $240
Continuation of PSYC 2012. Integrates knowledge and facts presented in PSYC 2012 into current topics in biopsychology. Prerequisite: PSYC2012.

Borders of Identity
New School for Social Research
NEWS#0514 Undergraduate   3 credits $1638*
Who exactly is "the Other"? Terms like "multiculturalism" and "cultural globalization" are becoming part of everyday language that describes the changes recently occurring on a worldwide scale. The right to be "diverse" is meanwhile voiced by more and more people who do not fit the image of the "average" citizen. Our main objective is to examine how issues of ethnicity, culture, and diversity are not only crucial in our own construction of personal identity, but also inform literary works from all over the world. Novels and short stories from different cultures and backgrounds are discussed and analyzed.
* Non-credit option, tuition: $365.

Bureaucracy and Regulation
City University
CITY#PLS404 Undergraduate   5 qu. credits $785
The purpose of this course is to introduce the student to the role and complexities of bureaucracy in the United States political system. The focus will be on the political/administrative responses to policy problems in the American government system. Public bureaucracy is one of the most important governmental institutions involved in the formation, implementation and output of policy decisions.

Business, Government and Society
City University
CITY#BSM302 Undergraduate   5 qu. credits $785
A study of how contemporary business enterprises are influenced and shaped by the cultural, political and ethical norms of societies and how business success or failure is directly affected by the struggle among these forces.

Business, Society & Ethics
Bellevue University
BELL#IBMC360 Undergraduate   3 credits $750
A study of the interface between business and the social environment, including social responsibility, ethics, public policy and government regulation.

Celebrating Differences - Disability Culture
New School for Social Research
NEWS#0517 Undergraduate   3 credits $1638*
What's there to celebrate about disability? Why are more people with disabilities saying they don't want to be cured? What do they mean when they speak of "disability pride"? Is there really a "disability culture"? Are the values of this culture different from those of the non-disabled majority? This course examines the radical cultural changes that have emerged during the thirty-year struggle for disability rights. We consider the rejection of the medical model of disability and the redefinition of disability as a social construct.
* Non-credit option, tuition: $365.

Central and South America
Salve Regina University
SALV#INR561 Grad   3 credits $???
Students focus on the major political, social, and economic problems facing Central and South America today. They examine the political culture and processes, political interest groups, and the solutions proposed by constitutional, military, and leftist regimes to the problem of political instability. Other issues discussed are economic underdevelopment and dependency, including demographic problems, unbanization, and agrarian reform.

Central Asia and India
Salve Regina University
SALV#INR535 Grad   3 credits $???
Central Asia, long divided between Russia and China, has partially returned to the international system. Five ex-Soviet republics - Turkmenistan, Tadzhikistan, Kyrgystan, Uzbekistan, Kazakhstan - as well as Out Mongolia must rapidly develop their weak economies, revive fragile cultures, and devise astute foreign policies if they are to survive. This course considers their history, politics, and relationships with neighboring states, stressing their impact upon the Indian Sub-continent.

Change Theory and Human Behavior
Walden University
WALD#EDUC6310 Undergraduate   4 credits $920
Focus on change theory and learning behavior and processes which facilitate their integration. Analysis of effective educational practices and the conditions of educational change which improve systems.

Chemical Dependency - Youth at Risk
Pennsylvania State University
PENN#CNED420 Undergraduate   3 credits $345
Study of youth who are at risk of developing chemical dependency, including the characteristics and factors related to chemical dependency. Prerequisite: CNED401; 400-level courses are available only to students with junior or senior standing.

Child Abuse
Rio Hondo College
RIHO#PAC4362 Undergraduate   0.5 credits $???
This course is designed as a study about Child Abuse. Topics include; understanding the problem, investigation, death investigation teams, services and intervention, and prevention.

Child Abuse and Neglect
Chemeketa Community College
CHEM#HDFS260 Undergraduate   3 credits $123
An overview of the problems of child abuse for students interested in child care, teaching and other areas. Students will look at causes of abuse, the abused child, the abusive parents, the role of teachers, areas of treatment, education and locally available organizations that can assist the abused child and the abusive parent.

Child Abuse Workshop
Chemeketa Community College
CHEM#9924 Undergraduate   0 credits $30
This course is designed to meet the State of Oregon two-hour training requirement and to provide an introduction to how to prevent, identify and report abuse and neglect for all those who are interested.

Child Development
University of Alaska - Fairbanks
ALFA#EC245 Undergraduate   3 credits $213
Study of development from prenatal through middle childhood including the cognitive, emotional, social, and physical aspects of the young child. Course includes child observations. Emphasis is on the roles of heredity and environment in the growth process. Prerequisite: PSY101 or permission of the instructor.

Child Development
Cerro Coso Community College
CECO#CHDVC50A Undergraduate   3 credits $345*
The child from prenatal life through adolescence with emphasis on the years between two and five. Prerequisite: Level 1 reading classification recommended.
* CA residents pay $13 per credit.

Child Development
University of Missouri
MOCE#A207 Undergraduate   2 credits $258
The psychological, intellectual, social, and physical development of children is studied in this course. Perquisites: Psych. 1 or 2.

Child Psychology
Mercy College
MERC#ED130 Undergraduate   3 credits $900
The course considers theories and research findings on physical growth, sensorimotor, emotional and intellectual development and cultural influences in children prior to adolescence. The course emphasizes developmental, psychoanalytic, and cognitive theories in child psychology.

Child Psychology
University of Missouri
MOCE#PS170 Undergraduate   3 credits $387
This course introduces the scientific study of the physical, cognitive, and psychosocial development of the child from the point of conception until adolescence. Perquisites: Psych. 1.

Child Psychology
New York Institute of Technology
NYIT#BES2439 Undergraduate   3 credits $???
The study of human growth and development. This course is designed to give the student an understanding of children and how they change while passing through the major phases of growth. Emphasis is placed on physical, emotional, and personality development with an aim toward understanding the period of human growth on which adulthood is founded. Special topics include: identification of conditions in childhood leading to normal psychological development. Prerequisite: BES2401.

Child Psychology
Texas Technical University
TETE#PSY2301 Undergraduate   3 credits $159
This course examines the developmental processes and environmental factors that shape the personality and affect the achievement of the child. Prerequisite: PSY 1300 or EPSY 3330 or F S 2320.

Child Psychology and Development
State University of New York
SUNY#3837107 Undergraduate   3 credits $1038*
Considers theoretical positions regarding growth, learning and personality development as they relate to the education of children. Examines general characteristics and individual differences of the infant and preschool child and the school-age child up to adolescence. Includes child observation and discussion of such factors as sex, role, ethnic and linguistic difference, handicapping conditions and abuse and neglect. Prerequisite: Matriculated status or permission of college.
* NY residents tuition: $137 per credit

Child Socialization
University of Colorado
CUON#SOC3550 Undergraduate   3 credits $1953*
Topics in Sociology. Special topics in sociology to be selected by the instructor. Can be taken more than once when topics vary.
* CO residents tuition: $136 per credit.

China, Japan, and the Pacific Rim
Salve Regina University
SALV#INR528 Grad   3 credits $???
Students examine the major political, economic, military, and cultural factors influencing the current relations of China and the Asian states. Special emphasis is on the broader Asian and global trends, including Japan and the developing impact of the Pacific Rim states.

Codependency
College of DuPage
DUPA#HUMS291 Undergraduate   1 qu. credits $30
(Course description not available at press time.)

Codes & Inspection Procedures
Edmonds Community College
EDMO#FCA195 Undergraduate   3 credits $220
This class is designed to give the Firefighter/Company Officer the skills and knowledge necessary to perform basic fire inspections. The Uniform Fire Code is used as the basis for acquiring the knowledge necessary to conduct these inspections. In addition, the student will learn basic inspection procedures, recording the findings of an inspection, and making a report of actions taken based on the findings.

Cognitive-Affective Bases of Behavior
The Graduate School of America
TGSA#HS812W Graduate   4 credits $795
Introduction to the normal and psychopathological factors of cognitive and emotional functions on behavior. These include learning, perception, imagining, language, memory, reasoning, and judging. The course examines the organization of the perceptual world into a unified and hierarchical pattern of belief, attitudes and expectancies. These dynamics will be applied to contemporary issues and problems within human services.

Community
Western Illinois University
WEIL#SOC312 Undergraduate   3 credits $795*
Is a group larger than family yet smaller than society or nation that helps to meet the needs of both. What holds a community together and enables it to function? Examine small towns, villages, neighborhoods, suburbs, and groups held together by religious, ethnic, tribal, and communal bonds. By comparing the characteristics of communities and what scholars say accounts for variations in community life, you will learn what circumstances create the communities and enable them to meet human needs. Prerequisite: Sociology 100 or consent of instructor.
* IL residents tuition: $88 per credit.

Community Oriented Policing
Rio Hondo College
RIHO#PAC43021 Undergraduate   0.5 credits $???
This course is designed to introduce the student to Community Oriented/Based Policing as an alternative to more traditional policing techniques. Topics will include; pre implementation, integration of the community, problem solving-strategies, managing change, strategic planning, the transition plan. The course uses online resources for instruction.

Community Psychology
Walden University
WALD#PSYC8470 Graduate   5 credits $1500
This course will examine Community psychology and how psychologists can function as agents of change within the community. Students will analyze and evaluate communities from the anthropological, sociological, physical and psychological points of reference.

Community Relations
Rio Hondo College
RIHO#AJ105 Undergraduate   ?? credits $???
The course covers the role of modern police in a metropolitan community. It is intended for police science students and the general public, especially teachers, city employees, ministers, and others who are interested in the relationship between community welfare and law enforcement. Students majoring in Psychology, Sociology, Government, and Education can benefit from the subject matter presented.

Community Relations
Rio Hondo College
RIHO#PAC43003 Undergraduate   0.5 credits $???
This course is designed to introduce the student to Community Relations, Police Community Relations (PCR) or the concept of both the community and the police experiencing each other in their relationship to crime prevention, community oriented programs, and as an integral part of the criminal justice system. Various programs will be examined and how they effect the relationship. The course uses online resources for instruction.

Comparative Government
New York Institute of Technology
NYIT#SS2710 Undergraduate   3 credits $???
An introduction to comparative political structures and institutions covering the major European governments as well as non-Western political systems. Prerequisite: SS2700.

Comparative Labor Movements
Indiana University
INDI#L375 Undergraduate   3 credits $268
Labor movements and labor relations in industrial societies from historical, analytical, and comparative perspectives. Emphasis on interaction between unions and political organizations, national labor policies, the resolution of workplace problems, the organization of white-collar employees, and the issues of worker control and codetermination.

Comparative Politics
Eastern Oregon University
EAOR#POLS200 Undergraduate   5 credits $400
A comparative study of political culture, institutions and processes in a selected group of countries.

Compulsive & Addictive Behavior
The Graduate School of America
TGSA#HS875W Graduate   4 credits $795
This course will focus on the specific issues involved in systemically-oriented treatment of the compulsive or addictive client. Issues to be covered are: family assessment, engaging the family in treatment, treatment planning, working with family resistance, boundary issues in family therapy and development of a cohesive clinical orientation based on current research and theory.

Compulsive Behavior & the Disturbance of Self
The Graduate School of America
TGSA#HS866W Graduate   4 credits $795
This course defines the nature of addictive and compulsive behavior problems, discusses the development of the addiction model and its tenets, and reviews the literature on the validity and efficacy of treatment approaches based on the addiction model. Alternatives to the addiction model will be discussed including cognitive behavior therapy. An understanding of the Compulsive Behavior model, a psychodynamically oriented model, will be developed in detail.

Computers and Society
New Jersey Institute of Technology
NJIT#CIS350 Undergraduate   3 credits $1143*
Examines the historical evolution of computer and information systems and explores their implications in the home, business, government and science. Impacts on the individual, the organization and society are considered. Topics include: automation and job impact; applications in electronic fund transfer, government education, medicine and others; professional ethics, and legal issues. This course satisfies an NJIT GUR. Prerequisites: Completion of a 100-level GUR course in computer science or equivalent and one basic SS course. Optional: 14 video lessons of 60 minutes each.
* NJ residents: $184/semester hour.

Computers and Society
Northwest College
NOCO#DP127 Undergraduate   3 credits $???
This survey course introduces computer hardware, software, procedures, systems and human resources and explores their integration and application in business and other segments of society. This course is an overview of computer information systems. Note: This is a course for non-data-processing majors.

Computers and Society II
Thomas Edison State College
THED#OLSOC160 Undergraduate   3 credits $397*
A continuation of GSCOS100 "Computers and Society I".
* NJ residents tuition: $33 per credit.

Computers for the Social and Behavioral Sciences
Mercy College
MERC#BS226 Undergraduate   3 credits $900
An introduction to computers as a professional tool in the social and behavioral sciences. Topics include data collection, data description and data analysis (with statistical software SPSS for Windows), use of the Internet, on-line bibliographic searching, computers in teaching and learning and computerized techniques in psychological testing. Prerequisite: CS120 Introduction to Computers and Application Software.

Conflict Management in Social Systems
University of Colorado-Boulder
COBO#SOCY4025 Undergraduate   3 credits $240
Explores conflict resolution theory and method as applied to interpersonal, intergroup, and interorganization conflict. Course available via World Wide Web only.

Conflict Resolution
Emporia State University
EMPO#SP500 Undergraduate   3 credits $228
The course examines the ineffective responses individuals make in a conflict situation, responses such as flight behavior, defensiveness, and manipulation. Particular emphasis upon theoretical models and communication techniques that will assist the student in handling conflict constructively. All course activities are online.

Congress
Eastern Oregon University
EAOR#POLS311 Undergraduate   3 credits $240
A study of decision-making processes in legislative bodies with an emphasis on the U.S. Congress.

Congressional Politics
University of Missouri
MOCE#PO231 Undergraduate   3 credits $387
A study of legislative institutions, procedures, and behavior, this course emphasizes the role of the U.S. Congress in the context of political representation theories.

Consumer and Family Economics
University of Nebraska
NEBR#FACS906 Masters   3 credits $467
Diverse family types face the challenge of acquiring and using economic resources to achieve their goals. To attain the level of living needed and desired, an increasing number of women have entered the paid work force, bring with them the need for family-related employee benefits and the challenge of balancing work, family and leisure. This course focuses on the economics of women, men and work; employee benefits needed for a changing work force; and the problem of the overworked American.

Consumer Behavior
City University
CITY#MK387 Undergraduate   5 qu. credits $785
An investigation of the influences on and processes of buying in both consumer and industrial markets. Emphasis is placed on awareness of and utilization of concepts in practical strategic applications.

Consumer Economics
Western Illinois University
WEIL#FAM331 Undergraduate   3 credits $795*
Explores such topics as consumers in the global economy; protection for consumers--rights and responsibilities; rational decision making; budgeting; consumption patterns; financial management; risk management; and retirement planning.
* IL residents tuition: $88 per credit.

Contemporary American Economic History
Strayer University
STRA#ECO200 Undergraduate   4.5 credits $665
Investigates the historical development of the U.S. economy. Emphasizes the nature and sources of the U.S. economic growth, and the social and economic consequences of economic change in U.S. since 1865. Topics include a survey of leading economic issues in U.S. history, population trends, and the nature of agriculture.

Contemporary International Issues
Salve Regina University
SALV#INR568 Grad   3 credits $???
Major problems in international relations are analyzed in a seminar on a selected case-study basis. Topics include global concerns ranging from nuclear proliferation through international terrorism to world overpopulation, hunger, degradation of the global environment, and a new international economic order.

Contemporary Political Ideologies
University of Minnesota
MINN#POL1041 Undergraduate   4 credits $356
A systematic survey of the major competing ideologies of the 20th century --communism, conservatism, liberalism, fascism, "liberation" and "green" ideologies, and others. Special emphasis is placed on the historical sources, philosophical foundations, and argumentative structure of these influential ideologies.

Contemporary Social Issues
University of Colorado
CUON#SOC2010 Undergraduate   3 credits $1953*
Consideration of controversial issues from various sociological perspectives: alienation, degradation of work, racism, sexism, ageism, class exploitation, social control, oppression and repression, imperialism, and underdevelopment. Student nomination and exploration of issues salient to him/her are encouraged.
* CO residents tuition: $136 per credit.

Contemporary Social Theory
University of Colorado
CUON#SOC3161 Undergraduate   3 credits $1953*
(Course description not available at press time.)
* CO residents tuition: $136 per credit.

Contemporary Sociological Theory
City University
CITY#SOC403 Undergraduate   5 qu. credits $785
The course will focus on the writings of three major figures in the area of macro-sociological theory. First, the work of Emile Durkheim and his theory of social integration, second, Karl Marx's critique of capitalism and his crisis theory, and finally, the writings of Max Weber on charisma and institutionalization.

Contemporary Sociological Theory
University of Colorado
CUON#SOC5160 Undergraduate   3 credits $1953*
Study of contemporary sociological theory, with emphasis on how it applies to related fields.
* CO residents tuition: $136 per credit.

Contingency Planning
Brevard Community College
BREV#EVS2611 Undergraduate   3 credits $435
Development of an emergency response plan for a facility or community including analyzing potential hazards, writing and implementing contingency plans, training employees for an emergency and evaluating the effectiveness of the contingency plan.

Corrections
University of Missouri
MOCE#LE260 Undergraduate   3 credits $387
This course studies the correctional setting as an aspect of the criminal justice system; it analyzes the administrative involvement and studies the modes of organization and management that seem applicable to this type of setting. Perquisites: Crim. 010.

Counseling Psychology-Integrative Career Planning
University of Minnesota
MINN#EPSY5400 Undergraduate   4 credits $400
Based on profound changes occurring in work, technology, education, family, and society, this course provides students with an in-depth approach to career planning called "Integrative Life Planning" (ILP). Up-to-date information about labor market trends and workforce and work pattern changes is combined with the latest knowledge of how to plan for work and other life roles in the 21st century. Other topics include life span career development, assessing individual and cultural identities, career socialization and stereotyping, and career change/transitions.

Credit Analysis
New York University
NEYO#Z813170 Undergraduate   2 credits $225
This course, held exclusively on-line, focuses on the classical bank-credit concepts and its application to the lending situation, bridging the gap between credit analysis and lending. The on-line format, which replaces the blackboard with a PC, is designed to allow students 24-hour access to lectures and assignments. Through e-mail, Web pages, and chat room discussions, students learn a variety of topics which include evaluation and analysis of loan purpose; repayment source and schedule; short- and intermediate-term credit; financial statement projection; cash flow; and liquidity and solvency.

Crime and Police
Western Illinois University
WEIL#HIS310 Undergraduate   3 credits $795*
Surveys the history of crime and police in the United States, France, Germany, Britain, and Ireland since the eighteenth century. The course compares the different policing traditions of these countries and examines the development of crime in its social and cultural contexts.
* IL residents tuition: $88 per credit.

Criminal Justice Agency Accounting
Bellevue University
BELL#CJAC421 Undergraduate   3 credits $750
Provides understanding of financial planning and budgeting from a criminal justice viewpoint. Covers zero-based, line item and planning, programming and budgeting systems.

Criminal Justice Human Resources
Bellevue University
BELL#CJAC310 Undergraduate   3 credits $750
Explores the allocation of people in organizational structures, interpersonal relations, evaluation of performance, and collective bargaining in the criminal justice field. Extensive use of case studies and real-world applications.

Criminology
University of Missouri
MOCE#CR211 Undergraduate   3 credits $387
Topics in this course include the sociology of law; the constitutional, psychological, and sociological theories of criminal behavior; the process of criminal justice; the treatment of corrections; and the control of crime.

Cultural Anthropology
Front Range Community College
FRCC#ANT101 Undergraduate   3 credits $790
Studies human cultural patterns and learned behavior. Includes linguistics, social and political organization, religion, culture and personality, culture change, and applied anthropology. Cultural Anthropology deals with issues of cultural diversity, pluralism, and relativism as a component of multi-cultural studies. 45 Contact Hours.

Cultural Anthropology
Ohio University
OHIO#ANTH101 Undergraduate   5 credits $320
Basic concepts; introduction to various world cultures; nature of cultural diversity; evolution of sociocultural systems. The course has an optional VHS videotape.

Cultural Anthropology
Pennsylvania State University
PENN#ANTH045 Undergraduate   3 credits $345
Beginnings of human culture; economic life, society, government, religion, and art among traditional peoples.

Cultural Diversity in the Modern World
University of Colorado
CUON#ANTH3142 Undergraduate   3 credits $1953*
An in-depth analysis of the phenomena of culture and application of the culture concept to understanding cultural diversity in the modern world. The course will apply the concept of culture to several basic aspects of human social life, for example: social class and gender relations, ethnicity, racism and sexism, education, health, and economic behavior. Students will explore these issues in the context of case studies of particular groups and /or communities, focusing primarily on the diversity of cultural expression in contemporary U.S.
* CO residents tuition: $136 per credit.

Cultural Geography
Bellevue University
BELL#IBMC310 Undergraduate   3 credits $750
A survey of traditional and popular culture, including a study of cultural regions, cultural diffusion, cultural ecology, cultural integration and cultural landscape.

Culture and Society
Indiana University
INDI#E105 Undergraduate   3 credits $268
Introduction to the ethnographic and comparative study of contemporary and historical human society and culture.

Current Economic Issues
Great Basin College
GRBA#ECON104 Undergraduate   3 credits $186*
Participants in the Current Economic Issues course engage in a spirited analysis of current economic issues and discuss their relevance to individuals in their roles as consumers, workers, businessmen, and voters. Economic theories and concepts are utilized in explaining important social interaction relating to such topics as medical care, anti-trust policy, price controls, drug prohibition, protectionism, environmentalism, tax policy, public debt, and income distribution. This course is required of all those pursuing the Associate of Applied Science degree in business, and is also suggested for students in other areas.
* NV residents tuition: $43 per credit.

Customs Entry Preparation Workshop
Pace University
PACE#OL703 Undergraduate   3 credits $500
This workshop approach on proper preparation of customs entries includes: detailed analysis of customs processing procedures pertaining to the ABI system; step-by-step hands-on flow chart of Delivery Authorize Documents (DAD) release; calculations of Harbor Maintenance Fee and merchandise processing fee; and full in-class discussion on proper techniques and rules used in the preparation of entries.

Death and Dying in American Society
University of Southern Colorado
COSO#SOC491C Undergraduate   3 credits $210
Issues of life and death in our society are difficult and perplexing for most. Is dying the same for a child as it is for an elder? Who decides when enough is enough? What role does (or should) your physician play? Why is Jack Kevorkian wrong (or is he right?) to help others? These and other topics will be researched and discussed.

Depression and Melancholia

New School for Social Research

NEWS#0353 Undergraduate   3 credits $1638*

With increased social emphasis on quelling the difficult symptoms of depression, we neglect its prominence as a historical phenomenon. First thought to be a disorder of the "humors," melancholia has for centuries interested philosophers, theologians, and physicians as a significant reflection of human development. Only during the current era has society attempted to suppress this baffling symptom, rather than addressing the phenomenon itself. We trace the historical relationship between depression and society, discussing its clinical manifestations, as well as its ever-shifting implications for both society and the individual.

* Non-credit option, tuition: $365.

Deregulation - Do Market Solutions Really Work'

State University of New York

SUNY#213224 Undergraduate   4 credits $586*

Investigate several markets and groups of firms and how they respond to a deregulated environment. Emphasis is placed on a broad range of perspectives and issues surrounding deregulation in industries such as airline, electric utilities and telecommunications. Students apply concepts from micro economics analysis and also examine the politics of regulation. Prerequisite: Microeconomics or permission of Instructor.

* NY residents tuition: $515

Development - Adulthood to Aging I

Salve Regina University

SALV#HDV539 Grad   3 credits $???

An examination of adult behavior in the context of the person's attempts to lead an independent and autonomous existence in society. An analysis of the roles of cultural norms and values as well as an individual's developmental history in the shaping of adult behavior, with some attention given to the common emotional and social problems confronted by adults in their relations to family, employers, and the larger society.

Development - Adulthood to Aging II

Salve Regina University

SALV#HDV540 Grad   3 credits $???

A study of the normal process of aging in terms of social, psychological, biological, and cultural factors, including problems of accommodation and adjustment of the aged.

Development of Social Thought

City University

CITY#SOC402 Undergraduate   5 qu. credits $785

This course focuses on broad sociological concepts, theories, and research, emphasizing development achieved through socialization, deviance and social control, stratification and inequality, and the impact of population growth and decline upon society.

Developmental Psychology

Auburn University

AUBU#PG212 Undergraduate   5 qtr. hrs. $210

Introduction to cognitive, social and emotional development across life span.

Developmental Psychology

Fayetteville Technical Community College

FAYE#PSY241 Undergraduate   3 credits $489*

This course is a study of human growth and development. Emphasis is placed on major theories and perspectives as they relate to the physical, cognitive, and psychosocial aspects of development from conception to death. Upon completion, students should be able to demonstrate knowledge of development across the life span. This course has been approved to satisfy the Comprehensive Articulation Agreement general education core requirement in social/behavioral sciences.

* NC residents pay $20 per credit.

Developmental Psychology

Mercy College

MERC#PY233 Undergraduate   3 credits $900

A consideration of human development and behavior throughout the life span: childhood, adolescence, and the adult years; emphasis on normal growth and development focusing on the critical issues involved in each stage of development including cultural influence. (Primarily for students not taking PY130; PY131; PY239).

Developmental Psychology

Rio Salado College

RISA#PSY240 Undergraduate   3 credits $186*

Human development from conception through adulthood. Includes: physical, cognitive, emotional and social capacities that develop at various ages. Recommended for students majoring in nursing, education, pre-med, and psychology. Prerequisites: PSY101 with a grade of "C" or better or permission of the instructor.

* AZ residents pay $37 per credit.

Developmental Psychology

State University of New York

SUNY#PSY210Y05 Undergraduate   3 credits $570*

This course covers human development from the moment of conception through childhood, adolescence, early adulthood, middle adulthood, late adulthood, dying and death. Intellectual growth, personal and social adjustment, the relationship between physical and mental development, and typical challenges in various states of the life-cycle are considered. Prerequisite: Students should have taken General Psychology.

* NY residents tuition: $90 per credit

Developmental Psychology

Walden University

WALD#PSYC8030 Graduate   5 credits $1500

A study of social and cultural theories influencing the practice of psychology. Examination of factors which tend to enhance and retard social change. Techniques and approaches applicable for psychologist as advocates of social change.

Deviance

Charter Oak State College

CHOA#SOC371 Undergraduate   3 credits $390*

This course analyzes the social processes and structural factors that form deviance in society. The course includes the study of how behaviors and attributes come to be defined as deviant as well as how patterns of deviance come to be organized. These topics are linked to the reaction to deviance to outline the relationship between deviance and social order.

* CT residents pay $95 per credit.

Deviant Behavior and Social Control
Indiana University
INDI#S320 Undergraduate   3 credits $268
Analysis of deviance in relation to formal and informal social processes. Emphasis on deviance and respectability as functions of social reactions, characteristics of rules, and power and conflict. Prerequisite: 3 credit hours of sociology or consent of instructor.

Diagnostic Procedures for Communication Disorders
University of Oregon
OREG#CDS658 Undergraduate   4 credits $374
(Course description not available at press time.)

Disaster and Fire Defense Planning
Western Illinois University
WEIL#SAF477 Undergraduate   3 credits $795*
Covers the relationship of structural, climatic, and topographic variables to group fires, conflagrations, and natural disasters. The course includes concepts and principles of community risk assessment.
* IL residents tuition: $88 per credit.

Drama of Diversity
University of Colorado
CUON#THTR3611 Undergraduate   3 credits $1953*
An investigation of the creation and reinforcement of gender, ethnic, and racial stereotypes in theatre, film, and television in the United States. The course will explore how popular images are created by writers, directors, and performers, and become "reality" for the audiences for which they are intended.
* CO residents tuition: $136 per credit.

Drugs and Drug Dependence
University of Alaska - Fairbanks
ALFA#PSY370 Undergraduate   3 credits $237
Multidisciplinary approach to study of drugs and drug abuse emphasizing acute and chronic alcoholism, commonly abused drugs, law enforcement and legal aspects, medical use of drugs, physiological aspects of drug abuse, psychological and sociological causes and manifestations of drug abuse, recommended drug education alternatives and plans, and treatment and rehabilitation of acute and chronic drug users. Prerequisite: PSY101, SOC101 or permission of instructor.

Drugs, Alcohol, and Behavior
Texas Technical University
TETE#PSY4325 Undergraduate   3 credits $???
This course is a survey of psychological factors involved in drug use and an introduction to chemotherapy used in the treatment of mental illness. Prerequisite: PSY1300 or consent of instructor.

East Asia for Educators
UCLA
UCLA#X400B Undergraduate   3 credits $425
This online course introduces teachers to the history and cultures of East Asia, focusing on China, Japan, South Korea, and Taiwan, including a brief look at Asian-American communities in the U.S. that originate from these areas. The two goals of the course are to attain a basic knowledge and understanding of East Asia and to become familiar with resource materials (text, multimedia, and Web resources) on East Asia that can be integrated into the K-12 or community college curriculum.

Eastern Europe after 1989
Marylhurst College
MARY#HUM425 Undergraduate   3 credits $651
This course will survey the changing cultural discourse of post-1989 Eastern Europe. Taking into account the rapid disintegration of the East Bloc into East-Central European and Balkan realms, the focus will be on the substantial changes in the field of culture.

Econometrics
Strayer University
STRA#ECO470 Undergraduate   4.5 credits $665
Examines applications of statistical techniques to economic data, regression analysis and estimation of economic models. Includes violations of the regression model and analysis of variance. Prerequisite: ECO101 and ECO102 and MAT300.

Economic Development
Strayer University
STRA#ECO415 Undergraduate   4.5 credits $665
Looks at some of the major issues in the economics of development, including: developing human resources; the role of population growth, health, nutrition, the world food problem, sources of capital; financial intermediation; inflation; public and private enterprises. Special attention is given to African, Latin American, and Asian experience.

Economic Problems and Issues
Strayer University
STRA#ECO405 Undergraduate   4.5 credits $665
Applies conventional economic theory to national and international economic issues and events. Utilizes the policy ideas and stances of contemporary economists to provoke discussion of prevailing economic issues. Applies economic tools to the business decision making process.

Economic Theory and Transformation
New School for Social Research
NEWS#0263 Undergraduate   3 credits $1638*
There is debate around our current economic circumstances, but nearly unanimous agreement that we are in a period of transformation. This introductory course examines the nature of the economic forces leading to transformations by introducing microeconomic and macroeconomic theory in a historical context. We use microeconomic theory to understand the economy of the 19th century and the transformation that followed. We use macroeconomic theory to determine the dominant economic forces of the 20th century and contemporary transformations.
* Non-credit option, tuition: $365.

Economics
Heriot-Watt University
HERI#02 Graduate   4 credits $???
Economics is an important and exciting subject which pervades many facets of human behavior. Economics can be split into micro and macro components. The objective of the microeconomics section is two-fold: to spell out the strengths and weaknesses of the free enterprise system in a politically unbiased fashion and to highlight the economics principles and tools essential for rational decision making in a company.

Economics
New Jersey Institute of Technology
NJIT#SS201 Undergraduate   3 credits $1143*

The nature of a market economy. Microeconomics-demand theory, production possibilities, cost and price, equilibrium analysis, and applications to decision making in the firm. Macroeconomics-national income accounts, consumption, investment, government monetary and fiscal policy, and problems of employment and price levels. Economic analysis leading to an understanding of current developments in the United States economy and international trade and currency problems. Prerequisite: Three credits of basic social science. Optional: 28 video lessons of 30 minutes each.

* NJ residents: $184/semester hour.

Economics
Waukesha County Technical College
WAUK#809195016 Undergraduate   3 credits $193

This course provides a general introduction to major institutions and principles which underlie our contemporary American economic system. Topics covered are the free enterprise system, supply and demand, circular flow, government involvement, the Federal Reserve system, economic growth and development, and effects of international trade.

Economics and Management
Strayer University
STRA#ECO550 Undergraduate   4.5 credits $665

Provides a consistent framework of economic analysis to help decision makers adapt to government regulations and other external factors influencing economic variables. Systematically analyzes the complex nature of firms and organizations. Applies relevant economic theory to business problems, and develops general principles that can be applied to the business decision making process. Prerequisite: ECO100, or equivalent.

Economics I
Auburn University
AUBU#EC200 Undergraduate   3 credits $126

Economic principles with emphasis upon the macro-economic aspects of the national economy.

Economics I - Macroeconomics
Rogers State University
ROGE#ECON2113 Undergraduate   3 credits $495*

Does economics affect your life? Of course it does, and if you'd like to know how, this course will let you find out. Understanding economics will enable you to address issues ranging from national and international politics to your professional and personal life. Economics I is a theory-oriented course that introduces basic economic principles and develops them through the study of important social issues: inflation, unemployment, consumer expectations, surpluses, shortages, and international trade.

* OK residents $315.

Economics II
Auburn University
AUBU#EC202 Undergraduate   3 credits $126

A continuation of economic principles with emphasis upon the microeconomic aspects of the economy. Prerequisite: EC200.

Economics II - Microeconomics
Rogers State University
ROGE#ECON2114 Undergraduate   3 credits $495*

A theory-oriented approach to the study of economics. Elementary principles of price theory and national income theory are developed systematically with emphasis on their use in analyzing economic issues and for recommending appropriate economic policy. Prerequisite: Math proficiency at the level of College Algebra Video: Economics U$A from Dallas Community College Telecourses.

* OK residents $315.

Economics of a Sustainable Society
Humboldt State University
HUMB#ECON309 Undergraduate   3 credits $345

Interprets meaning of sustainable economy. Introduces techniques for measuring economic performance using sustainability standard. Analyzes domestic and international policies consistent with a sustainable economy.

Economics of Energy
Strayer University
STRA#ECO440 Undergraduate   4.5 credits $665

Studies economic theory of the use of energy resources in the less developed as well as the developed countries. Examines the use of theory in determining optimal pricing and use of different types of energy resources, both in the current period and overtime. Focuses on actual energy markets and institutions for selected resources, such as petroleum. Prerequisite: ECO100 or equivalent.

Economics of Labor
Strayer University
STRA#ECO310 Undergraduate   4.5 credits $665

Focuses on theoretical and policy issues that relate to the operation of labor markets. Topics include labor demand, labor mobility, unemployment, and the effect of various government policies on labor markets. Prerequisite: ECO101 and ECO102.

Economics of Transportation
Strayer University
STRA#ECO455 Undergraduate   4.5 credits $665

Studies the development of the various modes of transport; the problems that they have created; the attempts to deal with these problems through the regulatory process; the era of railroad building; the theory of railroad rates; the various transportation acts; the fair value and rate of return; the weak and strong road problem; the development of competition; the problems of water transportation and motor carrier regulations along with the trends and choices of transport policy.

Economics of Urban Development
Strayer University
STRA#ECO425 Undergraduate   4.5 credits $665

Provides and analytical presentation of the nature of major urban problems in the context of U.S. economic growth. Examines theories and solutions offered by well-known urban experts and economists for eliminating and/or diminishing the major economic problems besetting the urban centers in the U.S. Emphasizes critical treatment of a broad range of public programs designed to reduce certain urban problems, such as poverty, public health, and housing.

Economics, Micro
State University of New York
SUNY#212224 Undergraduate 4 credits $586*
Develop an understanding of the micro aspects of economics--the study of components of larger aggregates--by investigating a wide range of problems from prices to monopolies and from urban decay to industrial pollution. Includes the anatomy of the market system, prices and allocation of resources, competition and the firm, big business, market imperfections, income distribution, trade, the underdeveloped world, and economic planning. Prerequisite: Knowledge of Algebra is useful but not required.
* NY residents tuition: $515

Educational Psychology
Marylhurst College
MARY#PSY360WT Undergraduate 3 credits $651
(Course description not available at press time.)

Electoral Politics and the Mass Media
City University
CITY#COM401 Undergraduate 5 qu. credits $785
Examines the historical role print and broadcast media have played in the American political process. Assesses ways the media have informed and mobilized the electorates, their candidates, issues and political parties. Ascertains the increasing dominance and influence the media have had in defining electoral issues. Prerequisite: Strongly recommended: BSK210 or its equivalent.

Elementary French I
University of Iowa
IOWA#009001 Undergraduate 3 credits $240
This course, 009:001 Elementary French, and its sequel, 009:002, correspond to a typical university-level first-year program in French. In particular, both 009:001 and 009:002 in the Guided Correspondence Study program correspond to the content of 009:001 and 009:002 in the Department of French and Italian at the University of Iowa. The course is an introduction, intended for those who have never studied French or who seek a thorough review of the language.

Emergency Planning & Methodology
Rochester Institute of Technology
ROCH#69447190 Undergraduate 4 credits $923
Comprehensive emergency planning and methods of risk and hazard analysis.

Emergency Response
Brevard Community College
BREV#EVS2613 Undergraduate 3 credits $435
Coordination and implementation of emergency response procedures to assess the incident, respond to the emergency, supervise clean-up, and meet reporting requirements. Simulated emergency activities are utilized. Prerequisite: EVS1640, 1641.

Emotional Intelligence
Pima Community College
PIMA#EDU198 Undergraduate 3 credits $165*
New research on the different kinds of intelligences, male and female differences in emotions, brain functions that cause our emotions, people without feelings, our subconscious, moods and behavior, anger and rage, anxiety disorders, balm for anger, mood lifters, optimism, empathy, outward expressions of our emotions, social intelligence, emotional brilliance, our intimate enemies, non-defensive listening, violence, dealing with diversity, stress and emotional control, stress and anxiety, the healing powers of emotions, depression, and ways to re-educate our brain to deal with emotions.
* AZ residents, $32/credit hour.

Energy and Society
New Hampshire College
NEHA#SCI220 Undergraduate 3 credits $1656
This course surveys various forms of energy which are available in an industrial society. The environmental impact as well as the continued availability of each form of energy will be discussed. Special emphasis will be given to conservation of energy sources and the development of alternative sources of energy in the home and industry. Prerequisite: ENG121.

Environmental & Natural Resources Economics
Humboldt State University
HUMB#ECON423 Undergraduate 3 credits $345
Environmental economics and implications for public policy. Economic principles applied to public policies and management of natural resources: water, air, fisheries and forestry. Benefit/cost and economic impact analysis.

Environmental Economics
Pennsylvania State University
PENN#ECON428 Undergraduate 3 credits $345
Environmental pollution, the market economy, and optimal resource allocation; alternative control procedures; levels of environmental protection and public policy. Prerequisite: ECON302 or ECON323; 400-level courses are available only to students with junior or senior standing.

Environmental Ethics
Marylhurst College
MARY#ENV328 Undergraduate 3 credits $651
In the wake of the vast discoveries in science, we desperately need an ethic that can help us define our relationship with the earth. This course will trace the development of environmental ethics in this country, survey the range of ethical values before us, and apply our understanding of the land ethic to specific land-use dilemmas we face today.

Environmental Psychology
University of Missouri
MOCE#PS315 Undergraduate 3 credits $387
This course studies the psychological effects of various environmental and socially relevant problems. Course topics include: environmental perception, attitudes toward the environment, effects of the environment on work performance, environmental stressors, crowding, and the effects of urban environments on interpersonal relations. Perquisites: Psych. 50.

Environmental Psychology
New York Institute of Technology
NYIT#BES2467   Undergraduate   3 credits $???
A study of man's relationship to the physical environment. Topics include the effects of architecture on behavior, design in selective environments, social uses of space, urban and environmental stressors encouraging ecological behaviors. Prerequisites: BES2401.

Ethical Perspectives on Global Issues
Salve Regina University
SALV#HUM501   Grad   3 credits $???
Students examine and compare the ethical standards and approaches of Western and non-Western moralists in the resolution of major moral issues. Readings include such topics as nuclear proliferation, the search for peace, ecological issues, world hunger, and genetic engineering.

Ethics and Addiction
Kansas City Kansas Community College
KACI#AC1102   Undergraduate   1 credits $324*
The purpose of this course is to familiarize the student with state and national professional codes of ethics, state and federal regulations regarding client rights, and the state and national processes for professional credentialing.
* KS residents pay $40 per credit.

Ethics and Society - The Person and the Community
University of Colorado
CUON#PHIL1020   Undergraduate   3 credits $1953*
In this course, the student will study some of the traditional problems in ethics which tend to be focused on individual morality within the larger context of social and political philosophy. Some of the more specific contemporary moral problems will be addressed, such as: AIDS, abortion, famine, and individual rights versus the collective rights of society.
* CO residents tuition: $136 per credit.

Ethics, Policy, Law & Criminal Justice
Bellevue University
BELL#CJAC304   Undergraduate   4 credits $1000
Sensitizes students to the complexities of creating, implementing and administering public policy. Includes study of theory and case applications.

Ethnic & Cultural Awareness
The Graduate School of America
TGSA#HS834W   Graduate   4 credits $795
This course involves examination of ethnic and cultural issues that influence the etiology, perception of, and treatment of mental illness. Topics to be reviewed are needs for specialized training, needs of various special populations, the impact of racial identity on self-perception, and specialized methods of treatment.

European Heritage - Greece
University of Minnesota
MINN#HUM1111   Undergraduate   4 credits $356
Greek culture and Greece as the birthplace of reason. The course traces the development of Greek thought and literature from the Homeric epic, through Greek tragedy and comedy, to the dialogues of Plato.

Evolution of Human Culture
California State University - Dominguez Hills
CADO#HUX540   Undergraduate   3 credits $405
An examination of the nature of change and cultural unfolding, using the development of the city as a key concept, and looking into three representative types of cities: ancient, medieval, and modern.

Experimental Psychology
Mercy College
MERC#PY372   Undergraduate   3 credits $900
An introduction to experimental methods in psychology, including: the logic and nature of experimental investigation; the basic concepts in the experimental process, such as hypotheses, sampling, bias, and control, a review of simpler experimental designs that statistical methods applied to each design; psychophysical methods and research use of the computer. Students are sensitized to the rights of subjects in research and in particular to concerns of minorities. Prerequisite: PY370.

Exploration of Controversial Issues
Northwest College
NOCO#GE284   Undergraduate   3 credits $???
The purpose of this course is to encourage students to think critically by learning how to support logically both the pro and con perspectives of such issues as Capital Punishment, the Environmental Crisis, Criminal Justice, Economics in America, SDI, Nuclear Power, the Arms Race, War and Human Nature, Censorship, America's Prisons, Euthanasia, the Farm Crisis, Welfare, Deregulation, the Budget Deficit, Public Schools, Sports, etc. Prerequisite: GE180.

Family - Cross-Cultural Perspective
University of Alaska - Fairbanks
ALFA#SOC242   Undergraduate   3 credits $213
The study of comparative patterns of marriage and family relationships. Various approaches such as the developmental, systems, and social psychological are used to analyze these relationships. The family is followed through the stages of the family life cycle, such as mate selection, marriage, early marital interaction, parenthood, the middle and later years, and possible dissolution. Attention is given to cross-cultural differences in Alaska as well as in other parts of the world. Prerequisite: SOC101 or permission of instructor.

Family - Cross-Cultural Perspective
University of Nebraska
NEBR#FACS980   Masters   3 credits $467
This course is about patterned differences based on the national, cultural, religious, and racial identification of groups of people who do not set the dominant style of life or control the majority in any given society. Ethnicity usually is displayed in the values, attitudes, lifestyles, customs, rituals, and personality types of individuals who identify with particular ethnic groups. Identification with and membership in an ethnic group has far reaching effects on both groups and individuals.

Family and Society
University of Colorado-Boulder
COBO#SOCY4086 Undergraduate   3 credits $240
Studies the changing relationship between the family and the economic structure, historically and sociologically. Examines households that differ from the nuclear family, taking into account the political, social, ideological, demographic, and economic determinants of family formation.

Family Literacy
New School for Social Research
NEWS#1322 Undergraduate   0 credits $190
Permission required; call (212) 229-5372. When adults improve their own literacy skills, they can positively affect the educational attainments of their children. This course explores the issues that gave rise to this concept and examines several models of family literacy that are now in place in various settings such as community-based organizations and public schools. Students learn how to develop a family literacy class and how to integrate family literacy into ongoing adult education classes.

Family Systems
University of Minnesota
MINN#FSOS5200 Undergraduate   5 credits $489
Examination of the family as an institution and system of relationships. Current developments in the study of family, changes in American society, and their influence on family life. The course includes lectures, simulated family interaction, and participation of a studio audience on videocassettes. Prerequisites: SOC1001 and PSY1001 or equivalents.

Federal Acquisition Systems and Process
Strayer University
STRA#BUS209 Undergraduate   4.5 credits $665
Examines the federal procurement process and introduces concepts, policies, and procedures associated with government and commercial contracting. Discusses the programming, planning and justification of program funding, formulation and earmarking procurement requirements, preparation of work statements and specifications, procurement requests and acquisition planning.

Federal Personnel
Strayer University
STRA#BUS225 Undergraduate   4.5 credits $665
Covers the principles and procedures of Federal Personnel Administration including personnel structure and organization, rules and regulations of the Office of Personnel Management, and other procedural sources. Explains Civil Service examinations and recruitment, appointments, transfers, promotion, reduction in force, leave and hours of duty, and disciplinary actions through practical application in classroom exercises.

Fire Dynamics
Western Illinois University
WEIL#IND444 Undergraduate   3 credits $795*
Is a study of fire propagation phenomenon in both fuel and air regulated phases. Variables in pre- and post-flashover fire development are discussed. The study of geometric, material, gaseous, fluid flow, and thermodynamic parameters enhances the course.
* IL residents tuition: $88 per credit.

Fire Prevention Organization and Management
Western Illinois University
WEIL#IND484 Undergraduate   3 credits $795*
Is an examination and evaluation of the techniques, procedures, programs, and agencies involved with fire prevention. Consideration is given to related governmental inspection and education procedures.
* IL residents tuition: $88 per credit.

Fire Protection Structures and Systems Design
Western Illinois University
WEIL#IND443 Undergraduate   3 credits $795*
Examines the design principles involved in the protection of the structure from fire, the empirical tests and prediction procedures, control detection and suppression system design practices, and fundamentals of the hydraulic design of sprinkler and water spray systems with recent innovations.
* IL residents tuition: $88 per credit.

Fire Protection Systems
Edmonds Community College
EDMO#FCA137 Undergraduate   3 credits $220
(Course description not available at press time.)

Fire Service Management
Edmonds Community College
EDMO#FCA232 Undergraduate   3 credits $220
This is an introductory course in management theory and practice. Management is presented as a discipline and as a process. The purpose of this class is to build comprehension of the roles and responsibilities of shift commanders and staff officers through concepts, examples, and practice. Major topic areas will include the scope and evolution of management, decision making, planing, organizing, leading, and controlling. The objectives of this course are to acquaint the student with the management process, as applied to the fire service.

Fire Service Supervision
Edmonds Community College
EDMO#FCA231 Undergraduate   4 credits $240
Fire Service Supervision The purpose of this class is to build comprehension of the roles and responsibilities of company officers through concepts, examples, and practice. Topics covered in the class are related to those skills necessary for effective supervision in any organization, including goal setting, delegating, counseling, coaching, problem solving, decision making, total quality management, leadership, communications, and the supervisors role in labor relations.

Fire-Related Human Behavior
Western Illinois University
WEIL#IND481B Undergraduate   3 credits $795*
Examines human behavior in fire incidents. The course discusses occupant behaviors, fire setting, public education and fire prevention, eyewitness reports, and post-fire interviewing; it also looks at aspects of building design as related to evacuation, communication, and safety in fire situations.
* IL residents tuition: $88 per credit.

Foundations of Chemical Dependency Counseling
Pennsylvania State University
PENN#CNED401 Undergraduate   3 credits $345
Overview of diagnosis and assessment models for chemical dependency prevention, counseling, and recovery; and contexts of chemical dependency treatment. Note: 400-level courses are available only to students with junior or senior standing.

Foundations of Feminism
New School for Social Research
NEWS#0207 Undergraduate   3 credits $1638*
As we approach the millennium and assess our century, we find a major revolution in progress: the worldwide re-evaluation of woman's condition. What is the nature of and reason for this fundamental upheaval? Why have women's studies gained status in academia? What have women accomplished, and what remains to be achieved? What obstacles impede progress in this and other societies? In order to analyze and understand questions of gender, we turn to women who have inspired women's studies.
* Non-credit option, tuition: $365.

Foundations of Guidance and Counseling Processes
Pennsylvania State University
PENN#CNED403 Undergraduate   3 credits $345
Factors in personal choice making; rationale for an elements of guidance and counseling processes in school, college, and rehabilitation settings. Prerequisites: 6 credits in psychology and/or sociology.

Foundations of International Relations
Salve Regina University
SALV#INR502 Grad   3 credits $???
Students explore the salient issues involving conflict or cooperation in contemporary international politics. The major topics include nation-state systems; struggle for power among nations; continuities and changes in current international relations; the role of diplomacy, ideology, economics, military force, war, nuclear weapons, international law and organizations; the quest for community; and the relationship of moral and religious values to some of the problems of international relations.

Foundations of Psychology
New School for Social Research
NEWS#0344 Undergraduate   3 credits $1638*
Modern psychology is distinguished from earlier psychology by its concerted effort to define itself as a science. That effort has created definitions that form the foundations of present-day psychology. The diversity of modern psychology is presented along with the foundational principles that hold the various parts together. Topics include the nervous system, sensation, perception, emotion, motivation, learning, development, personality, social processes, and mental/behavioral disorders. Special attention is given to foundational principles and methods that explain these phenomena and show many applications to everyday life.
* Non-credit option, tuition: $365.

Gang Awareness
Rio Hondo College
RIHO#PAC43038 Undergraduate   0.5 credits $???
This course is designed as a study of gangs. Topics include; awareness, specific ethnic gangs, contending with gangs, and the future issues and impact.

Gender Roles
Western Illinois University
WEIL#SOC360 Undergraduate   3 credits $795*
Is a critical, sociological exploration of the social and historical origins of gender roles from a feminist perspective. Specific attention is paid to the process and the results of socialization that separate women from men and that undercut gender stratification in the United States. Cross-cultural and historical comparisons are included as a means of illustrating recurrent themes of gender differences throughout the world and through time. Prerequisite: Sociology 100 or permission of instructor.
* IL residents tuition: $88 per credit.

General Anthropology
University of Missouri
MOCE#AN1 Undergraduate   3 credits $387
This is a general course that surveys fields of anthropological concern: archaeology, cultural anthropology, physical anthropology, and linguistics; it emphasizes underlying concepts and principles in these fields. Examples from peoples of the world are included.

General Psychology
Cerro Coso Community College
CECO#PSYC1A Undergraduate   3 credits $345*
An introduction to the scientific study of behavior; perceptions, thinking, motivation, emotion, intelligence and learning; general psychological principles.
* California resident tuition: $13 per credit.

General Psychology
Chemeketa Community College
CHEM#PSY201 Undergraduate   3 credits $123
This course focuses on psychology as a science stressing history, methodology, the biological foundations of behavior, human development, sensation and perception.

General Psychology
Fayetteville Technical Community College
FAYE#PSY150 Undergraduate   3 credits $489*
This course provides an overview of the scientific study of human behavior. Topics include history, methodology, biopsychology, sensation, perception, learning, motivation, cognition, abnormal behavior, personality theory, social psychology, and other relevant topics. Upon completion, students should be able to demonstrate a basic knowledge of the science of psychology. This course has been approved to satisfy the Comprehensive Articulation Agreement general education core requirement in social/behavioral sciences.
* North Carolina residents and non-resident US military personnel stationed within the state tuition: $60; NC senior citizens: free.

General Psychology
Laramie County Community College
LARA#PSYC1000 Undergraduate ?? credits $???
This basic introductory survey course is offered two ways: through the Internet or in the traditional classroom. The information on this page describes General Psychology as an Internet class. Students will complete chapter review sessions through Internet delivery by accessing the Prentice-Hall online chapter review site listed in the assignments section of this site.

General Psychology
University of Missouri
MOCE#PS3 Undergraduate 3 credits $387
This course gives a historical background of the psychology and principles of human behavior. It includes an introduction to human growth and development; intelligence; motivation; psychological measurement; emotions; personality development and adjustment; and related research methods.

General Psychology
Northeastern Oklahoma A&M College
NOOK#PSY1113 Undergraduate 3 credits $315*
(Course description not available at press time.)
* OK residents tuition: $42 per credit.

General Psychology I
Brevard Community College
BREV#PSY2013 Undergraduate 3 credits $485
A survey of the scientific field of psychology including learning, motivation, emotion, human development, personality, psychopathology and therapy techniques. Requires placement scores.

General Psychology I
Front Range Community College
FRCC#PSY101 Undergraduate 3 credits $790
Scientific study of behavior including motivation, emotion, physiological psychology, stress and coping, research methods, consciousness, sensation, perception, learning and memory. 45 Contact Hours.

General Psychology I
Roane State Community College
ROAN#PSY101 Undergraduate 3 credits $459*
Definition of psychology and its relationship to the scientific method. Study of brain processes, sensation, perception, motivation, emotion, learning, memory, language, and thought as aspects of behavior.
* Tennessee residents tuition: $48 per semester hour.

General Psychology II
Front Range Community College
FRCC#PSY102 Undergraduate 3 credits $790
Scientific study of behavior including cognition, language, intelligence, psychological assessment, personality, abnormal psychology, therapy, life span development and social psychology. 45 Contact Hours.

Geography of Latin America
University of Minnesota
MINN#GEOG3121 Undergraduate 4 credits $391
This course provides students with an opportunity to study and evaluate the character and diversity of Mexico, Central America, the Caribbean, and South America. The individual countries and major regions within them are analyzed. Emphasizes the influence of cultural and physical elements on people and their use of the land. Problems are considered on a national and regional basis. Students view one of two videos, Missing or Official Story.

Geography of Latin America
Syracuse University
SYRA#GEO3211 Undergraduate 3 credits $960
This course introduces students to the fascinating diversity of contemporary Latin America. It includes a review of the historical processes of socio-economic and political change upon which twentieth century development has been founded, as well as examining the changing use and misuse of the environmental heritage of the region. The complex geography of this major world region will be examined by means of case studies including such issues as: deforestation of Amazonia; urban growth and crises of employment; the roles of the nation state in development; new economic structures - NAFTA, Mercosur; etc.

Geography of Missouri
University of Missouri
MOCE#GE225 Undergraduate 3 credits $387
Topics in this course include the physical, human, economic, and political geography of Missouri. This course also studies how geography applies to current state issues. Perquisites: Geog. 1 or junior standing.

Geriatric Psychology
Walden University
WALD#PSYC8430 Graduate 5 credits $1500
(Course description not available at press time.)

Global Economics
City University
CITY#BSM406 Undergraduate 5 qu. credits $785
An investigation of how goods and services are produced and regulated in a globalized economy. Topics addressed include the dynamics of international trade exchange rates; growth and development; monetary systems; competition; and resource allocation.

Gov't & Politics of Russia & the CIS
Rochester Institute of Technology
ROCH#51344290 Undergraduate 4 credits $923
Course provides an analysis of the politics and governmental systems in Russia.

Government & Metropolitan Problems
New York Institute of Technology
NYIT#SS2705 Undergraduate   3 credits $???
The first part compromises the political framework; state governmental structure, its functions, services, and financing; local, rural, and urban government, their structures, services, and functions. The second half focuses on metropolitan problem and their interaction with metropolitan government; housing, schooling, transportation, sanitation, pollution, and taxation. Social parameters stemming from ethnic, religious, class, and employment factors, among others, will be interwoven in the analysis. Prerequisite: SS2700.

Government and Business
New York Institute of Technology
NYIT#SS2708 Undergraduate   3 credits $???
A consideration of relationships between business enterprise and the societal and political milieu in which these enterprises operate. New concepts in business ethics and corporate responsibility. Government regulation of business activity. Prerequisite: SS2700.

Government and Politics of Canada
Syracuse University
SYRA#PSC3311 Undergraduate   3 credits $960
Canada has a complex and rich history, where average citizens are engaged in arguments about citizenship and who is a Canadian. We will study the political culture and processes in Canada, such as political socialization, the party system, interest groups, leadership, elections, the nature of Canadian federalism, and current issues such as the existence of an independence movement in Quebec, but not elsewhere in Canada. We will pay special attention to the nature of citizenship in multicultural and multilingual Canada.

Grief and Bereavement Counseling
The Graduate School of America
TGSA#HS845W Graduate   4 credits $795
This Course investigates research on death and dying. Students will examine psychological stages of dying common to all losses, symptomatology of grief, death trajectory, hospice model of treatment, and dealing with death in the family. Case consultations with dying children and parents will be featured utilizing techniques of drawing therapy and storytelling which elicit, respectively, psychological material in the form of unfinished business and techniques for coping with losses of all types.

Grief Therapy
Walden University
WALD#PSYC8570 Graduate   5 credits $1500
This course will explore various approaches to Grief Counseling. Grief tasks and Grief processes and mediating factors such as type of death, character styles, age of the bereaved and deceased, quality of the relationship with the deceased, etc. will be analyzed.

Group Counseling and Psychotherapy
The Graduate School of America
TGSA#HS841W Graduate   4 credits $795
This course reviews the historical development, major theories, current research and clinical procedures of group counseling and psychotherapy. Course content also includes the role of the leader and leadership styles, mechanics of co-therapy, designing special function groups, and handling of critical incidents within groups.

Group Psychology
Walden University
WALD#PSYC8490 Graduate   5 credits $1500
The course consists of a review of basic group leadership competencies, techniques supporting clinical and counseling uses of group procedures with various client populations researched effectiveness of different models of groups.

Health Psychology
Mercy College
MERC#PY159 Undergraduate   3 credits $900
(Course description not available at press time.)

Heredity and Human Society
University of Minnesota
MINN#BIOL1101 Undergraduate   4 credits $356
Principles of heredity and their social and cultural implications.

History and Systems of Psychology
Walden University
WALD#PSYC6020 Undergraduate   4 credits $1200
An examination of the historical and contemporary schools of psychology, with an emphasis on the key contributors to the profession of psychology.

History and Systems of Psychology
Walden University
WALD#PSYC8010 Graduate   5 credits $1500
This course examines historical and contemporary schools of psychology with an emphasis on key contributor to the discipline. Paradigmatic approaches (e.g., behavioral, cognitive, psychoanalytic, humanistic, etc.) are analyzed in relation to the cultural context existing in the United States at the close of the twentieth century.

History of American Foreign Relations 1760-1865
University of Minnesota
MINN#HIST3881 Undergraduate   4 credits $391
An investigation of foreign policy and diplomacy during the period of independence and territorial expansion. The topics covered include diplomacy of the American Revolution, the War of 1812, the Monroe Doctrine and territorial expansion, American commercial expansion, foreign relations with American Indians, the Mexican War, and the diplomacy of sectionalism and the Civil War.

History of American Foreign Relations, 1945-95

University of Minnesota

MINN#HIST3883 Undergraduate   4 credits $391

American foreign relations from the end of World War II to the most recent international affairs. Examines the cold war and the changes that have taken place with the end of that ideological conflict. Primary issues: the decision to drop the atomic bomb; American-Soviet relations; the Vietnam War; the Reagan years and the fall of communism, and present concerns regarding trade and international economic issues.

History of Economic Thought

Strayer University

STRA#ECO400 Undergraduate   4.5 credits $665

Provides and analytical presentation of the origin and development of economic theories and concepts in history, with special emphasis on contemporary economic principles and thoughts.

Human Development and Behavior

The Graduate School of America

TGSA#HD501W Graduate   4 credits $795

This course reviews the major theories of human development and behavior across the entire lifecycle. The developing person is the focus of inquiry and connects such areas of study as psychology, anthropology, and biology. Some of the research will approach human development from the point of view of personality theory, developmental "tasks," or "moral" development.

Human Development and Family Studies Interventions

Pennsylvania State University

PENN#HDFS311 Undergraduate   3 credits $345

Survey of individual and family formal and informal intervention efforts; historical and current perspectives and approaches. Prerequisites: HDFS129.

Human Geography

Ohio University

OHIO#GEOG121W Undergraduate   4 credits $256

This course is an introduction to cultural geography. Various elements such as population, agricultural, social and political organization, urbanization, and industrialization are examined from the perspective of five themes: culture region, cultural diffusion, cultural ecology, cultural integration, and cultural landscape.

Human Growth and Development

New Hampshire College

NEHA#PSY211 Undergraduate   3 credits $1656

Studies physical and psychological development from the prenatal period to death. In addition, the course considers the human patters of development. Prerequisite: PSY108 or permission of instructor.

Human Origins

University of Minnesota

MINN#ANTH1111 Undergraduate   5 credits $445

World prehistory as investigated by archaeologists is the course's major topic. The methods and concepts employed by archaeologists in the study of human origins and prehistoric biological and cultural development are also considered. Students need to obtain some reading materials from a large library. This course does not fulfill the Liberal Education Requirements at the University; it has no lab. Students will receive credit for only one of these courses: ANTH1101 or ANTH1111.

Human Origins and Prehistory

Indiana University

INDI#A105 Undergraduate   3 credits $268

Human biological evolution and prehistory from the earliest archaeological record through the rise of civilization.

Human Sexual Behavior

University of Minnesota

MINN#FSOS5001 Undergraduate   5 credits $489

Exploration of biological, psychological, and social aspects of human sexuality. Topics: sexual development over the life span; anatomy and physiology; reproduction; birth control and abortion; sexual response, arousal, and communication; love; sex research; gender roles and sex differences; heterosexuality, homosexuality, and bisexuality; sexual variations and economics; sexual coercion and abuse; dysfunction and therapy; sexually transmitted diseases; ethics, religion, and law; and sex education.

Human Sexuality

State University of New York

SUNY#SOCE201 Undergraduate   3 credits $1038*

This course covers the biological, psychological and sociological aspects of human sexuality. Evolving norms and customs, cross cultural comparisons, sexual development and sexual choices are some of the topics covered. Controversial issues such as abortion and pornography will also be discussed, with an emphasis on understanding the complexity of issues rather than teaching a particular perspective.

* NY residents tuition: $137 per credit.

Human Sexuality

Walden University

WALD#PSYC8565 Graduate   5 credits $1500

(Course description not available at press time.)

Human Sexuality and Social Behavior

University of Southern Colorado

COSO#SOC403 Undergraduate   3 credits $210

Sexuality and sexual conduct from a sociological and developmental perspective. The goal of this class is to guide you through an examination of the how sex and sex roles influence all aspects of modern society, including salaries, mortgages, suburbs, and social classes.

Human Societies - A Global View
Christopher Newport University
CHNE#SOCL201G Undergraduate 3 credits $993
An ecological-evolutionary approach to the study of human societies, from hunting and gathering through horticultural, agrarian, industrial, and industrializing. Includes: a) study of societal change, its nature, causes, and consequences, and b) cross-cultural study of institutions, ideologies, norms, values, socialization processes, social interaction, and everyday life. SOCL201G uses ethnographic analyses of historic and contemporary hunting and gathering, horticultural, and agrarian societies. Prerequisite: ENGL101.

Humanistic Psychology
Walden University
WALD#PSYC8500 Graduate 5 credits $1500
(Course description not available at press time.)

Hysteria - Her Story
New School for Social Research
NEWS#0382 Undergraduate 3 credits $1638*
Throughout history, hysteria has served as a way of expressing in the language of the body what is inexpressible through words. It has long been viewed as primarily a woman's affliction. The term comes from the Greek word for womb, and in early times, hysteria was thought to be caused by a sexually dissatisfied uterus that had become dislodged and wandered through the body in search of satisfaction. Hysteria was frequently the diagnosis for Victorian woman subject to the vapors and fainting fits.
* Non-credit option, tuition: $365.

Ideologies and Politics
Christopher Newport University
CHNE#GOVT359 Undergraduate 3 credits $993
An analysis of such contemporary ideologies as capitalism, liberalism, democratic socialism, Marxism, fascism, conservatism, and nationalism in relation to their significance for contemporary political movements and international affairs.

Ideology and Culture - Racism and Sexism
University of Colorado
CUON#PHIL3500 Undergraduate 3 credits $1953*
Surveys the different ways we look at race and sex or gender. Possible areas of focus include: the concept of ideology, feminist theory, race theory, and the standpoint debate." The basic theme of this course will revolve around unmasking the ways in which the overt power relations obtained in society and a particular moment in history are made to seem part of the natural, external order of things, thus serving to promote and legitimate racism and sexism.
* CO residents tuition: $136 per credit.

Incendiary Fire Analysis and Investigation
Western Illinois University
WEIL#IND486 Undergraduate 3 credits $795*
Examines the procedures and techniques for the collection, comparison, and analysis of the physical evidence relative to the area of fire origin. Also studied are principles of evidence of ignition phenomenon and propagation variables; legislative, economic, psychological, and sociological variables of the incendiary fire; the role of insurance and government programs; and data analysis and prediction techniques, including pattern analysis.
* IL residents tuition: $88 per credit.

Incident Management I
Edmonds Community College
EDMO#FCA161 Undergraduate 3 credits $220
A study of the Emergency Incident Management process as it applies to the fire service at the fire company level. Emphasis to include basic command structure and components, incident safety considerations, personnel accountability and application of the management process to a variety of emergency situations.

Incident Management II
Edmonds Community College
EDMO#FCA261 Undergraduate 3 credits $220
A study of the Emergency Incident Management process as it applies to Emergency Response services at the Disaster Management level. Emphasis to include advanced command structure and components, pre-incident planning and application of the management process to a variety of large scale emergency situations.

Individual, Society, and Culture
University of Alaska - Fairbanks
ALFA#ANTH100X Undergraduate 3 credits $213
An examination of the complex social arrangements guiding individual behavior and common human concerns in contrasting cultural contexts.

Individual, Society, and Culture
University of Alaska - Fairbanks
ALFA#SOC100 Undergraduate 3 credits $213
An examination of the complex social arrangements guiding individual behavior and common human concerns in contrasting cultural contexts.

Infancy
University of Minnesota
MINN#CPSY3302 Undergraduate 4 credits $400
This course provides an examination of the perceptual, motor, emotional, social, and cognitive development during the first two years of life, and the developing infant in his or her social and physical environment. Prerequisite: CPSY1301.

Infancy to Adolescence
Salve Regina University
SALV#HDV519 Grad 3 credits $???
The course will trace the ontogenesis of major developmental processes such as intelligence, motivation, language, personality, and social abilities, with selected reference to relevant theory and research through stags from infancy to adolescence.

Infants, Toddlers, & Twos
Fayetteville Technical Community College
FAYE#EDU234 Undergraduate   3 credits $489*
This course covers the skills needed to effectively implement group care for infants, toddlers, and two-year olds. Emphasis is placed on child development and developmentally appropriate practices. Upon completion, students should be able to identify, plan, select materials and equipment, and implement and evaluate a developmentally appropriate curriculum.
* NC residents pay $20 per credit.

Info Management in Criminal Justice
Bellevue University
BELL#CJAC425 Undergraduate   3 credits $750
Develops an understanding of information management within police/law enforcement agencies, corrections systems and court systems. Addresses future information management needs.

Information Needs of Seniors
Emporia State University
EMPO#LI861 Graduate   2 credits $210
Senior citizens are the fastest growing segment of our population. But what do we know about their information needs? This course will focus on typical changes taking place during the years of 55-75, the knowledge requirements of the elderly and how information specialists might best serve those. Major topics include: aging and dying, health care, housing arrangements, legal rights and assistance, volunteerism and the leisure activities, retirement financial planning, etc. The class will "meet" electronically. Students who do not have WWW access will be sent course materials via email.

Insanity, Psychiatry, and Society
New School for Social Research
NEWS#0404 Undergraduate   3 credits $1638*
"Insanity"--and psychiatry's efforts to cure or control it--has a fascinating history. Like all history, it varies depending on who tells it. We examine several scholarly approaches to this subject. Our readings reach back to ancient Israel, Greece, and India. Some texts address the political, economic, or legal determinants of "insanity," while other emphasize the nodal points between "insanity," art, religion, and ideas. We ask if art merely reflects or shapes attitudes toward insanity, or if it offers an alternative reality.
* Non-credit option, tuition: $365.

Instructional Theory in Family Sciences
University of Nebraska
NEBR#FACS815 Undergraduate   3 credits $467
Family and Consumer Sciences' unique contribution to education is instruction in the work of the family, family systems of action, and the use of practical reasoning to resolve recurring concerns of the family. These concepts can be applied in many educational settings such as secondary education, post secondary education, extension, or social service agencies. This course is designed to provide educators with a framework based on critical science on which to build an educational program. Practical applications of these theoretical concepts will be explored and demonstrated.

Integrated Studies
Rio Salado College
RISA#IGS290 Undergraduate   3 credits $186*
Integrated nature of human experience. Critical inquiry of a particular theme from a wide variety of academic viewpoints. Synthesis of knowledge and skills. Evaluation of experience and decisions from ethical, aesthetic, and intellectual perspectives. Preparation of three formal papers.
* AZ residents $37 per credit.

Intellectual Development Across the Lifespan
The Graduate School of America
TGSA#ED828W Graduate   4 credits $795
This course covers the major theories of development and learning styles and is meant as a complement to the Human Development and Behavior Foundation course. Various learning and motivation theories and how they apply to the different developmental stages are explored.

Intelligence and Mental Retardation
State University of New York
SUNY#PSY223Y04 Undergraduate   3 credits $570*
This course introduces atypical social, emotional and cognitive development. It focuses on the problems, etiologies and expectancies of the social and /or emotional maladjustments and the cognitive atypicalities (Learning Disabilities, Mental Retardation, Savants, etc.) Special consideration is given to intelligence testing and the educational, social, legal and placement needs of the atypical individual. Prerequisite: General Psychology
* NY residents tuition: $90 per credit.

Intercultural Communication
Marylhurst College
MARY#CM333 Undergraduate   3 credits $651
Just what does it mean to be thrown into contact with others whose lifestyles and values differ dramatically from one's own? Such interactions are often complex and confusing. This seminar examines face-to-face intercultural communication - focusing on cultural awareness, values, perception, and recognizing differences as a resource.

Intercultural Communication
University of Missouri
MOCE#CO332 Undergraduate   3 credits $387
This course studies culture as a variable in both interpersonal and collective communicative situations. Emphasis is placed upon opportunities and problems arising from similarities or differences in communication patterns, processes, and codes among various cultural groups.

Intercultural Communication
New School for Social Research
NEWS#3936 Undergraduate   3 credits $455

Cultural diversity impacts communication processes between different cultural groups. Cultural groups can also be defined by various characteristics, such as nationality, ethnicity, gender, age, sexuality, disability, etc. These cultural groups have unique set of cultural norms, beliefs, values, attitudes, as well as languages, perceptions, and expectations. It is commonly believed that cultural differences in these factors become "barrier" to competent communication. But does it? If cultural diversity hinders effective communication between people of different cultural groups, why and how does it negatively impact our communication processes?.

Intermediate Macroeconomics
Strayer University
STRA#ECO302 Undergraduate   4.5 credits $665

Covers systematic study of the theory of aggregate economics including the level and growth of national income and employment, the degree of utilization of productive capacity, and the general level of prices. Prerequisite: ECO101 and ECO102.

Intermediate Microeconomics
Strayer University
STRA#ECO301 Undergraduate   4.5 credits $665

Examines economic theory of consumer behavior, production and costs, the firm, price, distribution, general equilibrium, and welfare. Deals with more advanced microeconomic theories and concepts. Prerequisite: ECO101 and ECO102.

International Economic Problems
City University
CITY#INT302 Undergraduate   5 qu. credits $785

The course focuses on the applied aspects of international trade and economics, after a short review of economic theory. The course is divided into two sections: international trade and international finance. International trade discusses the impact of protectionist policies, cartels, and other multinational policies on world trade. International finance covers the foreign exchange markets and the complexities of different types of exchange rates. The course also examines the impact that world debt and the multinational corporation have on the world economy. Prerequisite: ECN301 and ECN302 or their equivalents.

International Economics
Bellevue University
BELL#IBMC430 Undergraduate   3 credits $750

A survey of international trade and finance, including study of contemporary international economic problems.

International Economics
Strayer University
STRA#ECO305 Undergraduate   4.5 credits $665

Provides a comprehensive account to the theory and practice of modern international economic relations among nations. Emphasizes the basic issues and concepts concerning the traditional and new international economic orders. Prerequisite: ECO100.

International Economics
Thomas Edison State College
THED#OLECO490 Undergraduate   3 credits $397*

Inside the Global Economy presents an in-depth examination of the basic principles of international economics. The course broadens viewers' perspectives on the growing economic interdependence of nations - how it happens and how it affects lives around the globe. Such topics as industrial policy and strategic trade policy, comparative advantage theory, exchange rate determination and forecasting, international trade in services, environmental regulatory policies and international competitiveness are covered.

* NJ residents tuition: $33 per credit.

International Economics and Finance
New York Institute of Technology
NYIT#EC2088 Undergraduate   3 credits $???

A study of international trade, investment, finance and economic cooperation. Topics will include theory and techniques of international trade, the U.S. in international trade, tariffs and quotas, foreign aid programs, foreign exchange markets and hedging exposure to foreign exchange risk. Operations of multinational corporations, economic integration and cooperation, balance of payments and international adjustment mechanisms and international indebtedness. Prerequisite: EC2072.

International Relations
Christopher Newport University
CHNE#GOVT321 Undergraduate   3 credits $993

Fundamental elements of international politics and an examination of the structure of the international system. Includes the role of states as political actors, their inter-relationships with one another, and the major problems of the contemporary period.

International Relations
City University
CITY#INT301 Undergraduate   5 qu. credits $785

This is an upper division social science course which evaluates the political and economic behavior of nations in the international arena. Topics examined include: U.S. world leadership, nuclear politics, terrorism, and contemporary trends in the international political economy.

International Relations
Eastern Oregon University
EAOR#POLS221 Undergraduate   5 credits $400

Covers the contemporary nation-state system with an emphasis on the sources of national power, the causes of war and the prospects for peace, economic relations, inequality, and the problems of development.

International Relations
Mercy College
MERC#IB370 Undergraduate   3 credits $900

The course focuses on international relations using case studies to illuminate problems faced by companies, industries and countries. Topics covered include: historical background; East-West and North-South conflicts; international organizations, law and diplomacy; economic power; environmental issues; nongovernmental organization; and, ideology.

International Relations
University of Missouri
MOCE#IN55 Undergraduate   3 credits $387

This course provides theories and analyses on various international topics. Included are three schools of thought in the area of international relations: idealism, realism, and transnationalism. The concept of power and how political leaders use it to achieve goals is studied, as well as the role of the public in shaping foreign policy. In addition, the arms race and nuclear deterrence are discussed, with commentary on the Cuban missile crisis, the cold war, and the Persian Gulf War. The course concludes with a look at current problems in the world.

International Relations
New Hampshire College
NEHA#GOV211 Undergraduate   3 credits $1656

The study of international politics is considered from a national interest perspective. The means of formulating and executing policy in the context of a system of sovereign states are emphasized. Included as well is a consideration of the influence of recent entrants in international relations such as multinational corporations, the European Economic Community and free trade systems. Prerequisite: GOV109 or GOV110.

Internet Literacy
George Mason University
GEMA#LRNG592A Graduate   3 credits $410

Internet Literacy (LRNG592) is a one credit-hour minicourse that the GMU Program on Social and Organizational Learning offers at the beginning of each semester to provide the skills and software to access instructional materials via dialup phone lines or MasonNet. It is a service course; a resource for faculty and staff who want to produce instructional material for distribution via the web and email. Its goal is to facilitate distance learning courses across the curriculum.

Interpersonal Relationships, Alcohol, and Drugs
Pennsylvania State University
PENN#CNED416 Undergraduate   3 credits $345

This course examines families with chemically dependent members: dynamics, appropriate interventions, and treatment. Prerequisite: CNED401 or CNED403.

Interpretive Social Science
George Mason University
GEMA#LRNG792 Graduate   3 credits $???

This is a course in the philosophy of the social sciences which takes place entirely over the internet. A more detailed description of the procedures will be supplied later, but the main idea is that the student registers for the course via the world wide web, pays the university for the course by check, pays the teacher for the "books" by check, and gets mailed to them a set of disks which contain all the readings in hypertext form.

Introductory Sociology
State University of New York
SUNY#SS161 Undergraduate   3 credits $435*

A study of the concepts of sociology with an emphasis on theory and research including culture, socialization, social processes, population and ecology, aging and the family.
* NY residents tuition: $80 per credit.

Intro to Community Planning
Christopher Newport University
CHNE#GOVT331 Undergraduate   3 credits $993

Examines the general nature of community planning and its development in the United States, including a survey of the problems with which planning seeks to cope.

Intro to International Relations
University of Colorado-Boulder
COBO#PSCI2223 Undergraduate   3 credits $240

Introductory conceptual approaches, national and international dynamics of the international environment, problems, and issues.

Intro to Sociology
Fayetteville Technical Community College
FAYE#SOC210 Undergraduate   3 credits $489*

This course introduces the scientific study of human society, culture, and social interactions. Topics include socialization, research methods, diversity and inequality, cooperation and conflict, social change, social institutions, and organizations. Upon completion, students should be able to demonstrate knowledge of sociological concepts as they apply to the interplay among individuals, groups, and societies. This course has been approved to satisfy the Comprehensive Articulation Agreement general education core requirement in social/behavioral sciences.
* North Carolina residents and non-resident US military personnel stationed within the state tuition: $60; NC senior citizens: free.

Introduction to Abnormal Psychology
University of Minnesota
MINN#PSY3604 Undergraduate   4 credits $391

This course focuses on the theoretical causes of human behavior, the description of behavioral disorders, the etiologies of behavioral disorders, and treatment alternatives. Prerequisite: PSY1001.

Introduction to American Government
Auburn University
AUBU#PO209 Undergraduate   5 qtr. hrs. $210

Constitutional principles, federalism; elections and public opinion; legislative, executive and judicial departments; principal functions.

Introduction to American National Government
Pennsylvania State University
PENN#PLSC001 Undergraduate   3 credits $345

Introduction to development and nature of American political culture, constitutional/structural arrangements, electoral/policy processes; sources of conflict and consensus.

Introduction to American Politics
Indiana University
INDI#Y103 Undergraduate   3 credits $268

Introduction to the nature of government and the dynamics of American politics. Origin and nature of the American federal system and its political party base.

Introduction to Anthropology
University of Alaska - Fairbanks
ALFA#ANTH101 Undergraduate 3 credits $213
Introduction to the study of human societies and cultures based on the findings of the four subfields of the discipline: archeological, biological, cultural, and linguistic.

Introduction to Biological Anthropology
University of Colorado
CUON#ANTH1303 Undergraduate 4 credits $2604*
Introduction to the study of human biological evolution, both processes and outcomes, from primate ancestors to fossil hominids to contemporary human populations. Methods of obtaining and interpreting data concerning the genetic, biological, and evolutionary basis of physical variation in living and skeletal populations. There will be both a lecture and lab component.
* CO residents tuition: $136 per credit.

Introduction to Biological Psychology
University of Minnesota
MINN#PSY3061 Undergraduate 4 credits $391
This course is an introduction to the biology of behavior. Topics include basic neuroanatomy and neurophysiology; the neural basis of learning, memory, and motivation; biology of abnormal behavior, dementia, and drug addiction. It also explores how behavior can be analyzed by studying the nervous system. Prerequisites: PSY1001, BIOL1009, or permission.

Introduction to Comparative Politics
University of Oregon
OREG#POL204 Undergraduate 4 credits $374
This is an introductory course in comparative politics that is designed to give students an understanding of cross-national differences in the structure of political systems and how these structures affect social, economic, and political outcomes. During the course we will examine the basic elements of political systems as well as the contemporary changes these systems are undergoing. A focus on specific policy areas, like economic development and performance, and on the institutions of politics will provide us with further mechanisms for analyzing these political systems.

Introduction to Criminal Justice Systems
State University of New York
SUNY#PSCJ101 Undergraduate 3 credits $735*
The focus of this course will be to introduce the student to a survey of the criminal justice institutions and their operational roles within the system. The three main components are analyzed with respect to the accomplishments of their goals as mandated by the New York State Criminal Procedure Law, Penal Law and Corrections Law.
* NY residents tuition: $98 per credit.

Introduction to Cultural and Social Anthropology
Rio Salado College
RISA#ASB102 Undergraduate 3 credits $186*
Principles of cultural and social anthropology, with illustrative materials from a variety of cultures. The nature of culture; social, political, and economic systems; religion, aesthetics and language.
* AZ residents pay $37 per credit.

Introduction to Economics
Lake Superior College
LASU#ECON1100 Undergraduate 3 credits $210
The best things in life are free. Everything else is economics. This course is a survey of economics with an emphasis on applying economics to the stuff of everyday life.

Introduction to Economics II
University of Missouri
MOCE#EC202 Undergraduate 3 credits $387
This course focuses on microeconomics, firm analysis, the principles of supply and demand, elasticity, price determination, costs, income distribution, market structures, trade, and other related social and economic issues.

Introduction to Fire Safety
Brevard Community College
BREV#FFP1000 Undergraduate 3 credits $435
Course is designed to benefit the fire technician as well as city officials and private citizens; included are chemistry and physics of fire, effects on economy, examination of basic classification, fire causes and leading fire problems.

Introduction to Human Geography
Auburn University
AUBU#GY215 Undergraduate 3 credits $126
An introduction to the various subfields of human/cultural geography, including population, agricultural geography, linguistic geography, the geography of religion, ethnic geography, and economic and urban geography.

Introduction to Human Geography
University of Colorado-Boulder
COBO#GEOG1992 Undergraduate 3 credits $240
Systematic introduction to the broad field of human-environment relationships. Includes growth and distribution of populations; locational analysis of economic activities' origin, development, and problems of urban communities; and spatial analysis of cultural, historical, and political phenomena.

Introduction to Human Geography
Indiana University
INDI#G110 Undergraduate 3 credits $268
An introduction to the principles, concepts, and methods of analysis used in the study of human geographic systems. Examines geographic perspectives on contemporary world problems, such as population growth, globalization of the economy, and human-environmental relations.

Introduction to Human Origins
University of Colorado
CUON#ANTH103 Undergraduate 3 credits $1953*
Evolution of humanity and its cultures from their beginnings through the early metal ages. Covers human evolution, race, prehistory, and the rise of early civilization.
* CO residents tuition: $136 per credit.

Introduction to International Relations
Indiana University
INDI#Y109 Undergraduate 3 credits $268
Causes of war, nature and attributes of the state, imperialism, international law, national sovereignty, arbitration, adjudication, international organization, major international issues.

Introduction to Macroeconomics
University of Oregon
OREG#ECON202 Undergraduate   4 credits $374
This is a self-paced study course, designed to introduce students to macroeconomics. Macroeconomics is the analysis of the aggregate economic variables including GDP, inflation, growth, unemployment. The aim of this course is to develop an understanding of how these important variables are determined.

Introduction to Mental Retardation
University of Missouri
MOCE#L385 Undergraduate   3 credits $387
This introductory course describes the characteristics, classification, and causes of mental retardation and severe handicaps. Perquisites-Spec. Ed. L311, L332. Concurrent L333, L342; UMSL-Spec. Ed. 313.

Introduction to Microeconomics
University of Oregon
OREG#ECON201 Undergraduate   4 credits $374
Microeconomics involves the analysis of how consumers make decisions about what to consume, how firms decide what and how much to produce, and how the interactions of consumers and firms determine how much of a good will be sold, and at what price. Many interesting questions can be approached by applying the methodology developed by microeconomists. For example, what are the economic implications of the recent rise in Oregon's minimum wage? How can we explain the see-sawing of gasoline prices we have witnessed in the past year?.

Introduction to Personality
University of Minnesota
MINN#PSY3101 Undergraduate   4 credits $391
Introduction to the study of personality--how people are and how they got that way. A look at how the major theorists explain personality development; a review of important research; a discussion of how different schools of personality study and assess individual personality and do psychotherapy. Exploration of some special topics in the field. Prerequisite: PSY1001.

Introduction to Political Futures
Honolulu Community College
HONO#POLS110 Undergraduate   3 credits $714*
This course focuses on "images of the future" - ideas and beliefs about the future which come largely determined by how people act in the present.
* Hawaiian residents tuition: $39 per credit.

Introduction to Political Futures
Honolulu Community College
HONO#POLS171 Undergraduate   3 credits $714*
This course is an introduction to political problems, systems, ideologies, and processes. Consequently, the course will seek to familiarize you, the student, with four things: 1) the basic underpinnings of politics and government; 2) understanding of how politics has evolved in modern times; 3) consideration of the current milieu given the interaction of the forces identified; and 4) impact of current trends if extended in duration. Prerequisites or Required Preparation: ENG10 or 15 or placement in ENG22/60.
* Hawaiian residents tuition: $39 per credit.

Introduction to Political Science
City University
CITY#SSC218 Undergraduate   5 qu. credits $785
An introduction to the historical, legal and psychological methods of understanding politics. Questions as fundamental as why do people behave as they do in the political process are examined. The course also compares different political ideologies, forms of government, and the role of the individual in the state.

Introduction to Political Science
University of Missouri
MOCE#PO11 Undergraduate   3 credits $387
This course discusses the scope and content of politics, and it studies the theory and operation of democratic and nondemocratic governments. This course meets state law that requires students to successfully complete a constitutional course.

Introduction to Political Theory
Indiana University
INDI#Y105 Undergraduate   3 credits $268
Perennial problems of political philosophy, including relationships between rulers and ruled, nature of authority, social conflict, character of political knowledge, and objectives of political action.

Introduction to Politics
New Hampshire College
NEHA#GOV109 Undergraduate   3 credits $1656
Introduction to Politics examines theories of government, the nature of the state and the citizen. The course surveys American government, comparative politics and international relations.

Introduction to Psychology
University of Alaska - Fairbanks
ALFA#PSY101 Undergraduate   3 credits $213
Fundamentals and basic principles of general psychology emphasizing both the natural science orientation and the social science orientation including the cultural, environmental, heredity, and psychological basis for integrated behavior; visual perception and its sensory basis; audition and the other senses; motivation and emotion; basic processes in learning, problem solving, and thinking; personality; psychological disorders; and the prevention, treatment, and therapeutic strategies.

Introduction to Psychology
Charter Oak State College
CHOA#PSY101 Undergraduate   3 credits $390*
This course emphasizes psychology as a constantly changing behavioral science with the goals of describing, explaining, predicting and influencing behavior and mental processes. The emphasis in on research methods, and the goal is to assist learners in becoming active learners and researchers. Topics include history of psychology, experimental methods, statistics, central nervous system, learning, intelligence, personality, behavioral disorders and therapies.
* CT residents pay $95 per credit.

Introduction to Psychology
Lansing Community College
LANS#PSYC200 Undergraduate   4 credits $420
The basic orientation to the field of psychology, designed as a general survey and as preparation for advanced courses in the field. Topics include methods, nervous systems, sensation, perception, development, learning, motivation, emotion, cognition, personality, abnormality, therapy, and social behavior.

Introduction to Psychology
University of Minnesota
MINN#PSY1001 Undergraduate   5 credits $445
A computer version of PSY1001. The interactive software provides a variety of self-check exercises that enable students to master key concepts and receive immediate feedback. Optional use of course Web site for class discussion. Topics: psychology's methods, biological roots of behavior, the developing child, adolescence and adulthood, sensation, perception, states of consciousness, social psychology, social diversity, and more. The disks are for Macintosh (System 7 or higher) or Windows users.

Introduction to Psychology
New Hampshire College
NEHA#PSY108 Undergraduate   3 credits $1656
This class is an introduction to various areas of psychology including scientific investigation, motivation, personality, intelligence, behavioral deviation, perception, learning, and human development. It provides a basis for further study in psychology and related areas.

Introduction to Psychology
New York University
NEYO#Y20680103 Undergraduate   4 credits $450
An introduction to the fundamental principles of psychology, with emphasis on psychology1s major areas of study: personality, development, learning, social psychology, physiology, learning, and motivation. Current schools of thought are examined in an historical context. Psychoanalytic, behavioral, humanistic, and cognitive approaches to psychology are reviewed.

Introduction to Psychology
Pima Community College
PIMA#PSY101 Undergraduate   4 credits $220*
This class is a survey of general psychology. It includes psychology history and systems of thought. Some topics covered are physiology, sensation and perception, learning, motivation, cognition, development, and personality. Twelfth grade reading level (or above) is strongly recommended. This class will be enriched through the use of the internet to visit sites of particular interest in the study of psychology.
* AZ residents, $32/credit hour.

Introduction to Psychology
Rio Salado College
RISA#PSY101 Undergraduate   3 credits $186*
To acquaint the student with basic principles, methods and fields of psychology such as learning, memory, emotion, perception, physiological, developmental, intelligence, social and abnormal.
* AZ residents $37 per credit.

Introduction to Psychology
Rogers State University
ROGE#PSY1113 Undergraduate   3 credits $495*
A survey of the scientific study of human behavior.
* OK residents $315.

Introduction to Psychology
Strayer University
STRA#PSY105 Undergraduate   4.5 credits $665
Introduces psychology as a human and scientific endeavor. Included, among other topics, examination of concepts and methods in learning, motivation, development, personality, and social behavior.

Introduction to Psychology
State University of New York
SUNY#PSYC103 Undergraduate   3 credits $1038*
This course is a survey of the fundamentals of psychology including scientific method, measurement, motivation, learning, sensation and perception, behavioral disorders treatment, biological basis of disorder, social determinants of behavior, and child development.
* NY residents tuition: $137 per credit.

Introduction to Psychology I
University of Colorado
CUON#PSY1000 Undergraduate   3 credits $1953*
Introduction to the scientific study of behavior, including and overview of the biological basis of behavior, densatio/perception, states of consciousness, learning and memory, thinking and language, intelligence, motivation, and emotion.
* CO residents tuition: $136 per credit.

Introduction to Psychology II
University of Colorado
CUON#PSY1005 Undergraduate   3 credits $1953*
Introduction to the scientific study of behavior, including an overview of the history of psychology, development, personality, psychological disorders, therapy, health psychology, and social behavior.
* CO residents tuition: $136 per credit.

Introduction to Public Finance
Strayer University
STRA#FIN250 Undergraduate   4.5 credits $665
Applies fundamental economic analysis to government spending, taxes and social regulation programs. Provides working knowledge to techniques needed to examine and evaluate public sector activity in the context of the government budget. Topics include public goods, externalities, income transfers and social insurance programs, and benefit-cost analysis.

Introduction to School Food Service
Pennsylvania State University
PENN#DSM105 Undergraduate   2 credits $230
History of school food service programs and exploration of management opportunities, methods, and concepts of various food service systems. Note: All students must be approved by a Dietetic program adviser.

Introduction to Social Development
University of Minnesota
MINN#CPSY3331 Undergraduate   4 credits $400

Processes of individual change from infancy through adolescence are investigated. Also explores the development of capacities for and influences of social relations. Research, methodology, and theoretical perspectives are examined. Students enrolling in the 5xxx-level course will be expected to do extra work. Prerequisite: CPSY1301 or equivalent.

Introduction to Social Psychology
University of Colorado
CUON#SOC2462 Undergraduate   3 credits $1953*

Study of the development and functioning of persons, especially within a group context, and the dynamics of small groups. Emphasis is on import of symbols for human behavior, development of self-concepts, and the processes of competition and cooperation in group dynamics.

* CO residents tuition: $136 per credit.

Introduction to Social Psychology
University of Minnesota
MINN#SOC5201 Undergraduate   4 credits $391

An intensive examination of the major issues in social psychology. Covers substantive areas of self, personality, person perception, interpersonal attraction, attitudes, social influence, prosocial behavior and aggression, small groups, and collective behavior. Emphasis on application of theories and concepts to everyday life. Sociology majors may not receive credit for this course. Prerequisites: 8 credits in Soc, Anth, Psy, Pol, or Econ.

Introduction to Social Psychology
New School for Social Research
NEWS#0363 Undergraduate   3 credits $1638*

Social psychology focuses on the social dimension of human action and society's role in the formation of individual and group behavior. This course explores the influence of current cognitive and information-processing theories in the development of consciousness, and the role of such processes as attention, memory, and social perception in explaining human behavior. The focus is on contemporary research and the theoretical perspectives underlying its scientific and experimental approach. As background, research in psychoanalysis, behaviorism, phenomenology, and social cognition is presented, as are the foundations of contemporary social research and practice.

* Non-credit option, tuition: $365.

Introduction to Social Welfare and Community Services
University of Minnesota
MINN#SW1001 Undergraduate   5 credits $445

History of American social services; rise of professional social work in response to human need. Social, political, and economic factors influencing public policy and services. Role of social workers with individuals, families, groups, and communities; values and ethics of professional helping role.

Introduction to Sociology
University of Alaska - Fairbanks
ALFA#SOC101 Undergraduate   3 credits $213

An introduction to the science of the individual as a social being, emphasizing the interactional, structural, and normative aspects of social behavior. An attempt is made to construct a cross-cultural framework in understanding and predicting human behavior.

Introduction to Sociology
Cerro Coso Community College
CECO#SOCI1 Undergraduate   3 credits $345*

Concepts and research findings of contemporary sociology; understanding human groups, such as the family, the play group, the work group, social class, institutions, mass behavior and culture. Discussion is centered around the effects of social change in an industrial society.

* California resident tuition: $13 per credit.

Introduction to Sociology
University of Colorado
CUON#SOC1001 Undergraduate   3 credits $1953*

A survey course in which the main concepts that define the sociological perspective are presented, and a picture of society is provided by examining major social institutions and forms of social organization within society.

* CO residents tuition: $136 per credit.

Introduction to Sociology
University of Iowa
IOWA#034001 Undergraduate   3 credits $240

The objectives for this course are a) to allow you to discover what relationship there is between you and society and how this relationship may be affected by your own volition; b) familiarize you with the field, i.e. familiarize you with the sociological perspective; c) demonstrate how the sociological perspective is applied via the scientific method; and d) promote critical thought.

Introduction to Sociology
Lansing Community College
LANS#SOCL120 Undergraduate   4 credits $420

Sociology is the scientific study of human social behavior. Sociology studies the processes and patterns of individual and group interaction, the forms of organizations and social groups, the relationship among groups and group influences on individual behavior. In short, sociology is the science of society. Sociologists seek to understand social behavior.

Introduction to Sociology
University of Missouri
MOCE#SO1B Undergraduate   3 credits $387

This course examines the organization and activities of human groupings such as the family, community, crowd and social class; the structure and function of institutions; and the social influences that shape personality, behavior, and social change.

Introduction to Sociology
New Hampshire College
NEHA#SOC112 Undergraduate   3 credits $1656

This course studies the organization of social behavior and relationship of society and social conditions. Emphasis is placed on culture, norm stratification, systems, structure, social institutions, and social change.

Introduction to Sociology
New York University
NEYO#Y20720107 Undergraduate   4 credits $450
A study of society, groups, and culture, and an introduction to sociological theory as a means for interpreting and understanding human behavior and the human condition. Topics of discussion include: the process of social and cultural change, social structure and stratification, roles and gender, the family, and social control.

Introduction to Sociology
Northwest College
NOCO#GE286 Undergraduate   3 credits $???
An introductory approach to the field of sociology, topics include a study of the individual's behavior in diverse social groups, ranging from family to bureaucracies, social stratification, group personality and social change. Prerequisite: GE180.

Introduction to Sociology
New York Institute of Technology
NYIT#BES2411 Undergraduate   3 credits $???
An analysis of the social and cultural forces which govern human behavior. The principal topics include: social interaction and organization, socialization processes, primary groups and the family (associations, bureaucracy, and other social institutions), collective behavior, population, and ecology.

Introduction to Sociology
Rio Salado College
RISA#SOC101 Undergraduate   3 credits $186*
Fundamental concepts of social organization, culture, socialization, social institutions and social change.
* AZ residents $37 per credit.

Introduction to Sociology
Strayer University
STRA#SOC100 Undergraduate   4.5 credits $665
Provides a critical survey of contemporary social, political and economic problems facing American society. Emphasizes the urban crises, military-industrial complex, racism, and distribution of income.

Introduction to Sociology
State University of New York
SUNY#SOC110Y01 Undergraduate   3 credits $570*
Sociological facts and principles dealing with the scientific study of human relationships. Emphasis on analysis and study of culture and human society, socialization, groups and group structures, collective behavioral patterns, and the concept of social institutions. Initial experiences for students who desire an introduction to the sociological perspective.
* NY residents tuition: $90 per credit

Introduction to Sociology
State University of New York
SUNY#SOCI101 Undergraduate   3 credits $1038*
This is an introductory study of the basic concepts, theoretical principles, and methods used within the discipline of sociology. Emphasis will be placed on group interaction, social and cultural processes, and the structure and organization of American social institutions.
* NY residents tuition: $137 per credit.

Introduction to Sociology
Waukesha County Technical College
WAUK#809196016 Undergraduate   3 credits $193
Introduction to the basic concepts of sociology as one of the intercultural disciplines. Emphasis is given to the following specific areas: culture, socialization, social stratification and the five institutions including family, politics, economics, religion and education. Examples of other topics include: the sociology of the workplace, domestic and international issues associated with social change, demography, technology and deviance.

Introduction to the American Economy
University of Missouri
MOCE#EC40 Undergraduate   3 credits $387
An introduction to economic analysis that examines the development and operation of the American economy, this course studies its evolutions, institutions, and principal problems.

Introduction to Women's Studies
University of Central Florida
FLCE#WST3010 Undergraduate   3 credits $786*
This is an interdisciplinary course introducing students to key achievements, issues and problems regarding women and gender relations in past and present societies. The course also traces the development of laws and policies that have helped women to become more equal participants in their societies. We will both look at the actual lives of women past and present and at theories concerning women and gender.
* FL residents tuition: $64 per credit.

Introductory Child Psychology
University of Minnesota
MINN#CPSY1301 Undergraduate   4 credits $400
This course is designed to provide an understanding of children and their development, the methods used by child psychologists, and the critical evaluation of research. The topics explored include personality and social behavior, biological bases and cognitive development, and the work of Jean Piaget. Prerequisite: CPSY1301, 5 credits introductory psychology; CPSY3309, PSY1001.

Introductory Geography
University of Alaska - Fairbanks
ALFA#GEOG101 Undergraduate   3 credits $213
World regions, an analysis of environment, with emphasis on major culture realms.

Introductory Psychology
Auburn University
AUBU#PG201 Undergraduate   5 qtr. hrs. $210
An introduction to the scientific study and interpretation of human behavior. Consideration of topics such as learning, motivation, emotion, intelligence, perception, personality and interpersonal relationships is included in the reading and related exercises.

Introductory Psychology
New York Institute of Technology
NYIT#BES2401 Undergraduate   3 credits $???
An introduction to selected concepts, methods, and vocabulary of psychology. Focus of study will be on the individual and the conditions that influence behavior. Topics that will be covered include: growth and development, learning and thinking, emotions and motivations, personality and assessment, maladjustment and mental health, groups and social interactions, and social influence and society.

Introductory Psychology I
Indiana University
INDI#P101 Undergraduate   3 credits $268
Introduction to psychology; its methods, data, and theoretical interpretations in areas of learning, sensory psychology, and psychophysiology.

Introductory Psychology II
Indiana University
INDI#P102 Undergraduate   3 credits $268
Continuation of P101. Developmental, social, personality, and abnormal psychology. Equivalent to B104. Prerequisite: P101.

Introductory Research Methods
New York Institute of Technology
NYIT#BES2470 Undergraduate   3 credits $???
This course stresses the classical approach to experimental research on human behavior. Students conduct and report on experiments in the fields of psychophysics, psychomotor learning, memory, and perceptions. These laboratory experiments permit the student to apply knowledge gained in former courses about measurements, statistical inference, and the design of experiments. Prerequisites: BES2401, BES2421 and BES2428.

Introductory Social Psychology
Pennsylvania State University
PENN#SOC003 Undergraduate   3 credits $345
The impact of the social environment on perception, attitudes, and behavior.

Introductory Sociology
Pennsylvania State University
PENN#SOC001 Undergraduate   3 credits $345
The nature and characteristics of human societies and social life. Prerequisite: .

Issues in Applied Psychology I
Barstow Community College
BARS#PSYC99 Undergraduate   1 credits $???
This course will use personality theory to explain the complexities of human behavior, especially those actions or impulses which seem to be inconsistent or out of character.

Juvenile Delinquency
City University
CITY#SOC304 Undergraduate   5 qu. credits $785
This course will trace the origins of laws and definitions of juvenile delinquency. The techniques used to measure delinquency, sociological theories of crime, and institutions of social control for juveniles, including the juvenile justice system and delinquency prevention programs, will be covered.

Juvenile Delinquency
New York Institute of Technology
NYIT#BES2473 Undergraduate   3 credits $???
An inquiry into the causes of juvenile delinquency and the social and psychological factors involved in the predictive studies and theories concerning the development of delinquency. Topics also include formation of youth gangs, methods of coping with gang activity, the types of crime committed by children and youths, narcotics problems, neglected and retarded children, the youthful offender and wayward minor, the operation of the Children's Court, crime prevention programs. Prerequisites: BES2401, BES2411 and BES2477.

Labor and the Media
Indiana University
INDI#L290A Undergraduate   3 credits $268
An investigation of images of labor in the media. Topics include the media and the economy, corporate bias and the manufacturing of news, and labor's response to the corporate image.

Labor and the Political System
Indiana University
INDI#L203 Undergraduate   3 credits $268
Federal, state, and local governmental effects on workers, unions, and labor-management relations; political goals; influences on union choices of strategies and modes of political participation, past and present; relationships with community and other groups.

Labor Economics
Pennsylvania State University
PENN#ECON315 Undergraduate   3 credits $345
Economic analysis of employment, earnings, and the labor market; labor relations; related government policies. Prerequisite: ECON002.

Labor Institutions and Public Policy
Western Illinois University
WEIL#ECO340 Undergraduate   3 credits $795*
Provides a broad perspective on the role of "labor institutions" in modern industrialized society, particularly the United States. The topics in the course are organized in three general areas: (1) the institution--the structure and growth of labor organizations, the evolution of public policy toward unions in the United States, and an international comparison of labor movements; (2) an economic analysis of trade unions--sources of economic power, impact on relative wages and overall inflation; and (3) a focus on some contemporary issues--public sector unions and antidiscrimination policies. Prerequisite: Economics 232 or consent of instructor.
* IL residents tuition: $88 per credit.

Latin America on the Brink of the 21st Century
State University of New York
SUNY#HUM215 Undergraduate   3 credits $528*
In this course, the student will discover Latin American culture through literature and film, as well as through an analysis of recent social and political developments. Students will examine Mexico, Puerto Rico, Costa Rica, Chile, and Argentina as these societies face the new millennium. Prerequisite: Freshman English Composition. Special Requirement: Students are required to have access to a VCR and to rent films from the local video store.
* NY residents tuition: $89 per credit.

Leisure Services for the Elderly
Western Illinois University
WEIL#REC452G Undergraduate   3 credits $795*
Explores the theories and concepts of leisure and aging. This course is an introduction to the exciting and emerging field of gerontology as it relates to leisure. Study the meaning of leisure during the different stages of life, especially as a means of social integration and as a source of personal meaning for the elderly. Learn about the various leisure service settings available to senior citizens, the large number of leisure activities, and the future leisure environment and its effect on older persons.
* IL residents tuition: $88 per credit.

Life Span Growth and Development II
University of Minnesota
MINN#NURS3691 Undergraduate   2 credits $200
Introductory course that incorporates biological, sociological, and psychological perspectives of human lifespan development from young adulthood through aging and the death experience. NURS3690/5690 and NURS3691/5691 may be taken concurrently. Prerequisite: general psychology and general biology, NURS3690/5690 or equivalent, or consent of instructor).

Life Span Human Development
Texas Technical University
TETE#HD2303 Undergraduate   3 credits $???
This course is an introduction to the theories, processes, and enhancement of development for infants, young children, adolescents, and adults.

Lifespan Development - Adulthood
City University
CITY#PSY305 Undergraduate   5 qu. credits $785
This course will introduce the student to adult development and aging. Both psychological and physiological factors concerning the nature of adult development and aging will be presented. The material will be presented from a life-span developmental approach and inherent in this approach is the view that positive developmental changes occur in all major periods of life. A complete picture of development is presented and most variables that affect this development are identified and discussed. Prerequisite: Strongly recommended: SSC205 or its equivalent.

Lifespan Development Psychology
University of Alaska - Fairbanks
ALFA#PSY240 Undergraduate   3 credits $213
The development of persons is examined from both a psychological and cross-cultural perspective. Key topics will be the development of cognition, personality, and social behavior with attention to relevant research on those cultures found in Alaska. No more than one lesson may be submitted at a time and a second lesson may not be submitted until the first is graded and returned. Not available on a semester basis. Prerequisite: PSY101.

Lifespan Development Psychology
City University
CITY#PSY401 Undergraduate   5 qu. credits $785
This course evaluates the issues relevant to child psychology and physiology, with an approach designed for studying this topic in the 1990s. The nature and scope of child psychology is extensively examined along with integrated material on the family, school, and other environmental influences. In this way, a complete picture of development is presented and most variables that affect this development are identified and discussed. Prerequisite: Strongly recommended: SSC205 or its equivalent.

Lifespan Growth and Development I
University of Minnesota
MINN#NURS3690 Undergraduate   2 credits $200
Introductory course that incorporates biological, sociological, and psychological perspectives of human lifespan development from conception through adolescence. NURS3690/5690 and NURS3691/5691 may be taken concurrently. Prerequisite: general psychology and general biology.

Lifestyle Abuse
Eastern Oregon University
EAOR#PEH350 Undergraduate   3 credits $240
Study of contemporary issues that result from unhealthy lifestyle practices. Topics include alcohol and drug abuse, sexually transmitted diseases, nutritional issues, safety and injury prevention, tobacco abuse, steroid abuse, and family relationship issues.

Macro-Economics
Mercy College
MERC#EC220 Undergraduate   3 credits $900
A study of the modern mixed American economy, national income, employment, output, price levels, economic growth and fluctuations, monetary and fiscal policies, current events relating to the American economy. Prerequisite: MA116.

Macroeconomics
College of DuPage
DUPA#ECO201 Undergraduate   5 qu. credits $150
A study of the major factors that determine levels of economic activity, resource allocation, national production, introduction to price functioning, income levels, government, money and banking, policy implications, and economic growth.

Macroeconomics
Eastern Oregon University
EAOR#ECON375 Undergraduate   5 credits $490

An intensive analysis of the functioning of the economy at the aggregate level. Issues such as inflation, unemployment, economic growth, and the role of the government will be investigated as they affect the stability of the economy. Prerequisites: ECON201, MATH241, STAT315/STAT316, or STAT327.

Macroeconomics
New Hampshire College
NEHA#ECO202 Undergraduate   3 credits $1656

This course explores the manner in which the overall levels of output, income, employment and prices are determined in a capitalist economy. After a brief exposure to alternative economic systems, the focus becomes the nature and performance of American capitalism. Primary emphasis is placed upon the development of models which explain the behavior of consumers, producers, and resource suppliers in various market structures.

Macroeconomics
Northwest College
NOCO#GE115 Undergraduate   3 credits $???

Macroeconomics is the level of economic analysis that deals with the activity of the whole economy and with the interaction between the major sectors of the economy, such as all households, all businesses or all governments.

Macroeconomics
Strayer University
STRA#ECO102 Undergraduate   4.5 credits $665

Examines aggregate relationships of economic activity, institutional background, examination of public sector, income determination, inflation, unemployment, fiscal and monetary policy. Discusses economic growth and income distribution. Prerequisite: ECO100.

Managerial Economics
Eastern Oregon University
EAOR#ECON340 Undergraduate   5 credits $400

Case study approach to decisions involving productions optimization, cost minimization, resource allocation, pricing, demand analysis, long-range forecasting, and capital budgeting by public and private organizations. Prerequisites: ECON201, MATH241, STAT315, STAT316.

Market Logic
Western Illinois University
WEIL#AGR459G Undergraduate   2 credits $530*

In 1987, WIU became the first academic institution in the nation to teach the CBOT Market Profile (R). This approach to market analysis was formulated by J. Peter Steidlmayer, developed by the Chicago Board of Trade, and can be used for day-trading and overnight positions. Registrants should possess an understanding of technical analysis.

* IL residents tuition: $88 per credit.

Marriage & Family Systems
The Graduate School of America
TGSA#HS871W Graduate   4 credits $795

Families will be studied as systems which evolve over time and develop patterns of intergenerational connectedness. This course emphasizes an examination of the developmental stages of the American family life cycle, from a theoretical, clinical and research perspective. The impact of divorce, remarriage and the development of new family forms will be explored. Included is an in-depth perspective on the impact of gender on family life at each stage in the life cycle and on cultural variations in life patterns. The application of interventions to the life cycle issues will be addressed.

Marriage and Family Interaction
Indiana University
INDI#F258 Undergraduate   3 credits $268

Basic personal and social factors influencing the achievement of satisfying marriage and family experiences.

Marriage and Family Relationships
University of Southern Colorado
COSO#SOC231 Undergraduate   3 credits $210

Marriage and family form an institutional and relationship perspective, involving cross-cultural diversity, mate selection, marital dynamics, parenting, divorce, remarriage, and emerging patterns. Students will examine the history of how the American family has evolved to what it is today. Many scholars are concerned that the family is in demise; others feel that the family is changing to suit other aspects of society.

Marriage and Family Therapies
Walden University
WALD#PSYC8450 Graduate   5 credits $1500

This course is designed to examine perspectives related to the treatment of couples and families. These perspectives include

Marriage and the Family
New York Institute of Technology
NYIT#BES2425 Undergraduate   3 credits $???

This course covers historical changes in family patterns, contemporary family life in different cultures and subcultures, evolution of the American family pattern, functions of the family, the family as a primary group, kinship patterns, and nuclear and extended families. Other topics include: dating, mate selection, family disorganization, and marital success. Prerequisites: BES2411.

Marriage and the Family
Thomas Edison State College
THED#OLSOC210 Undergraduate   3 credits $397*

Few topics are more popular in conversation and in the mass media than the American family. This course looks sociologically at definitions and varieties of families, explores the family life cycle, and considers some of the problems facing the contemporary family including stress, divorce, and the role of the elderly.

* NJ residents tuition: $33 per credit.

Media and Politics
Honolulu Community College
HONO#POLS190 Undergraduate   3 credits $714*

This course seeks to discern how the organization and operation of our political system is related to, and affected by, the media. Throughout our readings and videos we will ask how today's and tomorrow's media and politics interact, and what this means for our society. Thus the course seeks to familiarize and clarify the student's understanding of five things: 1) A historical overview of the role of media in politics; 2) The difference between data, information, knowledge, understanding, and wisdom; etc.

* Hawaiian residents tuition: $39 per credit.

Media Economics
State University of New York
SUNY#BRC320 Undergraduate   3 credits $1038*

A comprehensive overview of economic issues that affect the funding and operation of media systems, an introduction to standard methods for quantifying media usage and effects. Students will learn and apply a variety of techniques for measuring media usage and effects.

* NY residents tuition: $137 per credit

Memory and Cognition
City University
CITY#PSY301 Undergraduate   5 qu. credits $785

An analysis of the relation between the mind and the brain. A systematic introduction to the theoretical and experimental foundations of perception, memory, reasoning, language structure, and their relation to cognitive development. Prerequisite: Strongly recommended: SSC205 or its equivalent.

Mental Health Counseling
The Graduate School of America
TGSA#HS821W Graduate   4 credits $795

This course reviews the basic skills, methods and practices related to mental health counseling. Topics included are basic counseling skills, treatment planning, special issues in working with diverse populations, and various methods of therapeutic interventions. The course will apply current theory and research to clinical practice.

Microcounseling
University of Iowa
IOWA#07C178 Undergraduate   1 credits $80

This course demystifies the counseling process by breaking counseling into single skills. The basic concept of microcounseling was developed by Allen Ivey of the University of Massachusetts and has been taught at the University of Iowa for the past twenty-five years. This one-hour course provides you with the group of core communication skills essential to any interview. The single-skills focus has been proven to be an effective process in developing communication skills in professional and lay workers.

Microeconomics
New Hampshire College
NEHA#ECO201 Undergraduate   3 credits $1656

The course examines the role of economic systems in allocating scarce resources to satisfy the needs and wants of individual members of society. After a brief exposure to alternative economic systems, the focus becomes the nature and performance of American capitalism. Primary emphasis is placed upon the development of models which explain the behavior of consumers, producers, and resource suppliers in various market structures.

Microeconomics
New Jersey Institute of Technology
NJIT#ECON265 Undergraduate   3 credits $1143*

The theory of price determination and resource allocation under various market structures. The theory of demand, production, costs, factor and product pricing, income distribution, market failure, implications of government intervention in the market, and comparison of the free enterprise and alternative systems. Students who have received credit for NJIT#SS201 may not subsequently receive credit for NJIT#ECON265. Optional: video lessons.

* NJ residents: $184/semester hour.

Microeconomics
Northwest College
NOCO#GE116 Undergraduate   3 credits $???

Microeconomics is the study of the activity of individual agents of the economic system, such as households and business firms. This course presents students with the basic material necessary in understanding economics.

Microeconomics
Strayer University
STRA#ECO101 Undergraduate   4.5 credits $665

Examines economic decision-making process, theory of consumer behavior, economics of the firm, and market structure. Discusses major issues of welfare economics, comparative systems, and other microeconomics topics. Prerequisite: ECO100.

Minority Peoples
Western Illinois University
WEIL#SOC300 Undergraduate   3 credits $795*

Meets the practical, as well as the theoretical, need for a more fundamental understanding of the dynamics of majority/minority relations. The focus is on those racial and ethnic groups of greatest national concern and interest in the United States plus certain groups (for example, women) who are subordinated in the social structure. Attention is given to the role of the white ethnic groups and immigration in the United States and race relations in other nations as well. Prerequisite: Sociology 100 and one additional sociology course or consent of the instructor.

* IL residents tuition: $88 per credit.

Modern East Asian Civilization
Indiana University
INDI#H207 Undergraduate   3 credits $268

Contrasting patterns of indigenous change and response to Western imperialism in East Asia during the nineteenth and twentieth centuries. China and Japan receive primary consideration; Korea and Vietnam, secondary. Emphasis on the rise of nationalism and other movements directed toward revolutionary change.

Modern Political Systems
Christopher Newport University
CHNE#GOVT103G Undergraduate   3 credits $993
This course furnishes an overview of the concepts and issues necessary to understand politics in the world today. It begins by surveying the principle ideologies of political debate and analysis. It then discusses a variety of topics in comparative politics, including the nature and origins of dictatorships and democracies. Class discussions, along with required readings, concentrate upon countries in sub-Sahara Africa, Asia, Europe, Latin America and the Middle East.

Modern Political Theory
Western Illinois University
WEIL#POL382 Undergraduate   3 credits $795*
Studies modern political thought--from Machiavelli in the 16th century to American political ideologies in the late 20th century. The main text is a collection of original writings by Machiavelli, Hobbes, Locke, Rousseau, Mill, Marx, etc. The readings center around questions of authority, power, justice, liberty, equality, human nature, social contract, state of nature, and community.
* IL residents tuition: $88 per credit.

Modern Psychology in Historical Perspective
Mercy College
MERC#PY210 Undergraduate   3 credits $900
The course offers an analysis of the major systematic viewpoints in the history of psychology.

Money and Banking
Eastern Oregon University
EAOR#ECON318 Undergraduate   5 credits $400
An investigation of the operation of financial institutions and the governmental agencies responsible for their regulation as they affect the stability of the economic system. Issues such as the control of the money supply, the financing of governmental operations, the impact of taxation, and the public debt will be examined using Keynesian and monetarist economic theory. Prerequisite: ECON202.

Money and Banking
University of Minnesota
MINN#ECON3701 Undergraduate   4 credits $391
Money, banks, and financial intermediaries as economic institutions; the mechanics of monetary transactions; the value of money; international monetary relationships; issues relating to monetary policy.

Money and Banking
New York Institute of Technology
NYIT#EC2072 Undergraduate   3 credits $???
The structure and function of the banking system and financial markets in the United States. The use of monetary policy in the regulation of the national economy. The role of the Federal Reserve System. Prerequisites: EC2020.

Money and Banking
Ohio University
OHIO#ECON360 Undergraduate   4 credits $256
Role of money and banking system in determination of national income and output. Monetary theory and policy emphasized. Prereq: ECON104.

Money and Banking
Pennsylvania State University
PENN#ECON351 Undergraduate   3 credits $345
Money, credit, commercial and central banking; financial intermediaries, treasury operations, monetary theory and policy, and foreign exchange. Prerequisites: ECON002, ECON004.

Money and Banking
Strayer University
STRA#ECO320 Undergraduate   4.5 credits $665
Discusses the role of financial institutions, the banking system, the Federal Reserve System, and the nature and effectiveness of monetary policy tools. Prerequisite: ECO100.

Money, Banking, and Credit
Western Illinois University
WEIL#ECO325 Undergraduate   3 credits $795*
Focuses on the monetary aspects of the U.S. economy, with emphasis on the role of depository financial institutions and the Federal Reserve System. The course's major intent is to provide you with an overview of the purpose and structure of depository institutions; the development of the American banking system; the organizational aspects of commercial banks; the role of depository institutions and the Federal Reserve System in the creation of money; and the determinants of prices and output in the economy. Prerequisite: Economics 231. Social Science credit.
* IL residents tuition: $88 per credit.

Money, Banking, and Monetary Theory
University of Missouri
MOCE#FI220 Undergraduate   3 credits $387
This course discusses American monetary and banking systems and their influence on economic activities.

Motivation
Eastern Oregon University
EAOR#PSY345 Undergraduate   5 credits $400
Motivational concepts as explanations of behavior: homeostasis, drive, instinct, and dynamic psychology. Prerequisite: PSY201 and 202 or consent of instructor.

Multicultural Counseling
Walden University
WALD#PSYC8420 Graduate   5 credits $1500
This course will examine the cross-cultural factors that influence the delivery of counseling and psychological services. Diversity issues will be explored and their impact on the therapeutic relationship will be discussed.

Multicultural Study of Children and Families
University of Missouri
MOCE#SO241 Undergraduate   3 credits $387
This course studies multicultural groups within the context of their unique cultural heritage. Special attention is focused on the external conditions that affect the internal workings of these families. Prerequisites: HDFS 175 or instructor's consent.

Multicultural Voices
Northwest College
NOCO#GE291 Undergraduate   3 credits $???
In this course students experience customs, food, history and literature of several cultures. The subject matter will vary. The course is team taught. Prerequisite: GE180.

Multiculturalism in American Politics
New School for Social Research
NEWS#0239 Undergraduate   3 credits $1638*
"Diversity" and "multiculturalism" are the catch-phrases of the 1990s. Identities have proliferated, and various groups have organized to make new kinds of demands on political systems, educational institutions, and the media. A new form of politics has emerged. Where did this trend come from? Where is it leading? This course examines how the offspring of the movements for civil rights, gay liberation, and gender equality-- as well as the challenges posed by mass immigration--have precipitated a sea change in the way Americans think about identity.
* Non-credit option, tuition: $365.

Native American Studies
Dakota State University
DAKO#HIST379 Undergraduate   3 credits $447
A basic knowledge of Indian history with emphasis on the Lakota, Dakota, and Nakota speaking peoples. Current cultural issues are presented with emphasis on learning styles and teaching Native American people.

Native Cultures of Alaska
University of Alaska - Fairbanks
ALFA#ANTH242 Undergraduate   3 credits $213
Introduction to traditional Aleut, Eskimo, and Indian (Athabaskan, Tlingit) cultures of Alaska. Comparative information on Eskimo and Indian cultures in Canada. Discussion of linguistic groupings as well as cultural groups; presentation of population changes through time; subsistence patterns, social organization and religion in terms of local ecology. Precontact interaction between native groups of Alaska. General introduction presenting an overall view of the cultures of Native Alaskans.

Nature of Language
University of Alaska - Fairbanks
ALFA#LING101 Undergraduate   3 credits $213
The study of language: systematic analysis of human language and description of its grammatical structure, distribution, and diversity.

Neurological and Behavioral Pathology
University of Iowa
IOWA#096119 Undergraduate   3 credits $240
This course examines the abnormal physiological and psychological health transitions which may be experienced by individuals over the lifespan and which have a well-documented physiological and/or behavioral base. It focuses on neurobiological and behavioral disorders. This knowledge builds upon information and concepts learned in each of the prerequisite courses and is necessary as one of the scientific bases for the practice of professional nursing.

Neuropsychology
Walden University
WALD#PSYC8540 Graduate   5 credits $1500
(Course description not available at press time.)

Northern Minnesota Women Myths and Realities
University of Minnesota
MINN#WS1990 Undergraduate   3 credits $267
This course examines the stereotypes and realities of life for Northern Minnesota Indian, Yankee, and immigrant women from early settlement times to the present. The assignments include historical research projects, which can be written using topics from a student's own geographical location.

Operation of Therapeutic Recreation
University of Missouri
MOCE#HE327B Undergraduate   3 credits $387
This course covers the theories and principles of leadership and programming as they apply to recreation services for the ill, handicapped, and aged.

Organized Crime
University of Central Florida
FLCE#CCJ4641 Graduate   3 credits $1305*
This course will examine the topic of organized crime, its emergence in American Society, its activities, and its relationship to other principal social institutions and components of the criminal justice system. It will include a consideration of the historical, economic, social, legal, and political events which lead to the precedents of organized crime and its history; the relationship of organized crime to federal, state and local politics; the activities of organized crime figures; policies designed to combat organized crime; and some explanations for the persistence of organized crime.
* FL residents pay $129 per credit.

Out of the Fiery Furnace
Pennsylvania State University
PENN#EMSC150 Undergraduate   3 credits $345
A history of materials, energy, and humans, with emphasis on their interrelationships. For nontechnical students.

Parent-Child Relationships
University of Minnesota
MINN#GC1722 Undergraduate   4 credits $356
An interdisciplinary course to help students develop their own philosophy of child rearing--attitudes, principles, and perspectives--that will guide them in their relations to their children and performance of their parental responsibilities. Focuses on helpful information related to crises of parenthood. Research emphasizes principles of parent-child relations and prepares students for the tasks of parenthood.

People with Disabilities
Indiana University
INDI#A201A Undergraduate   3 credits $268
Americans with disabilities from both a historical and a contemporary perspective. An examination of the architectural, institutional, and attitudinal environment encountered by disabled persons.

Personal Emergency Planning
Rio Hondo College
RIHO#PAC43055A Undergraduate   0.5 credits $???
This course is designed to assist the student in developing a personal Emergency Plan. Topics will include: preparedness, response, recovery, and mitigation. The student will assess risk by applying the 4 Phases of Emergency Management. The student will also address what local governments and business are doing to prepare for emergencies.

Personality
University of Alaska - Fairbanks
ALFA#PSY304 Undergraduate   3 credits $237
Psychological and social/cultural determinants of personality formation including appropriate theories. Prerequisite: PSY101.

Personnel Management for the Fire Service
Western Illinois University
WEIL#IND483 Undergraduate   3 credits $795*
Covers personnel practices and management procedures. It investigates collective bargaining, binding arbitration, applicable legislative procedures, and administrative and supervisory procedures.
* IL residents tuition: $88 per credit.

Personnel Management in Public Sector
Indiana University
INDI#V373 Undergraduate   3 credits $268
The organization and operation of public personnel management systems with emphasis on concepts and techniques of job analysis, position classification, training, affirmative action, and motivation.

Physiological Basis of Behavior
New York Institute of Technology
NYIT#BES2412 Undergraduate   3 credits $???
A basic course to familiarize students with the bodily processes involved in various aspects of human behavior. Physiological psychology studies the biological basis of psychological functions such as sleeping, emotions, motivations, perceptions, learning, memory, and problem solving. The two major biological systems most relevant to psychology are the nervous system and the glandular system. Prerequisites: BES2401; LS9501 and LS9502 are recommended.

Physiological Psychology
University of Central Florida
FLCE#PSB3002 Undergraduate   3 credits $786*
In this course, you will learn more about the mechanisms behind everyday influences of physiology on behavior and cognition. Therefore, what you will learn here will have implications for you and your life beyond learning isolated facts in a textbook for a college class.
* FL residents tuition: $64 per credit.

Play Therapy
Walden University
WALD#PSYC8545 Graduate   5 credits $1500
(Course description not available at press time.)

Pluralism and Diversity In America
State University of New York
SUNY#PDA101 Undergraduate   3 credits $1038*
Intended to help the student appreciate and better understand the historical and social realities of diversity and pluralism in these United States, analyze the concepts and language of this complex legacy, and develop a greater awareness of the significance of both community and interdependence necessary for successful living and working in the 21st century. The basic argument is that we have a shared national culture which is the basis of our shared national identity. Our capacity to enjoy and carry on our individual/collective ethnic or national heritages is guaranteed by our constitutional democracy.
* NY residents tuition: $137 per credit.

Political and Economic Geography of the World
Strayer University
STRA#ECO105 Undergraduate   4.5 credits $665
Surveys diverse historical developments, socioeconomic systems, natural/mineral sources, the structure of population, and the geopolitical map throughout the world.

Political and Legal Foundations of Fire Protection
Western Illinois University
WEIL#IND485 Undergraduate   3 credits $795*
Studies the legal basis for the police power of government related to public safety, legal limitations and responsibility, and liability of fire prevention organizations and personnel. It also reviews judicial decisions.
* IL residents tuition: $88 per credit.

Political Economy
City University
CITY#PLS403 Undergraduate   5 qu. credits $785
Political economy is the study of the political management of a nation's economic affairs and how political and governmental decisions affect the allocation and distribution of goods and services within a nation. The course covers the major theories of political economy, including the classical, Marxian, neoclassical and Keynesian approaches. The course also covers the topic of the international political economy regarding the inequality of assets between nations and how various political systems allocate resources among their people.

Political Economy
University of South Florida
FLSO#U102 Undergraduate   3 qtr. hrs. $???
The institutional setting of U.S. economy and U.S. political system and interaction between the two. Course offered intermittently.

Political Economy of the Third World
City University
CITY#INT405 Undergraduate   5 qu. credits $785

The course examines the basic workings of the international political economy. A historical perspective on the development of the present international political economy is provided. Various development options for the world economy are considered. Current topics regarding the development of the Third World economy are addressed, including the role of financial assistance to Third World nations, the role of debt owed by such nations and the role of trade and investment by multinational corporations in the development process.

Political Geography
Western Illinois University
WEIL#GEO444G Undergraduate   3 credits $795*

Investigates the geographic foundations of political phenomena. This course focuses on significant geographic factors in the growth and development of states, boundary problems, and other international problems. It provides insights into politico-geographic realities of the new world order. Lessons include assignments in place-name and location knowledge. Two previous geography courses recommended but not required.

* IL residents tuition: $88 per credit.

Political Parties and Interest Groups
City University
CITY#PLS405 Undergraduate   5 qu. credits $785

A theoretical treatment of interest groups, factions and political parties and their relationship to the dominant paradigm in American political science. The course provides a historical and analytical interpretation of the role of interest groups in American politics and focuses on how special interests have affected the American political system, its goals and predominant themes. Consideration is given to how democratic societies provide for change and the linkage between elites and masses.

Political Parties and Interest Groups
Indiana University
INDI#Y301 Undergraduate   3 credits $268

Theories of American party activity; behavior of political parties, interest groups, and social movements; membership in groups; organization and structure; evaluation and relationship to the process of representation. Prerequisite: Y103 recommended.

Political Power in America
Mercy College
MERC#GV101 Undergraduate   3 credits $900

The use of political science theory and method to investigate American political institutions: executives, legislatures, judiciaries, bureaucracies, mass media, parties, interest groups, elites, and publics; comparisons with foreign political institutions, including their relationship to American institutions as manifested in foreign politics and international relations; the importance of political institutions, American and foreign, to the lives of students.

Political Science Internship
Pennsylvania State University
PENN#PLSC495 Undergraduate   1–6 credits $115

Combining experience in government offices, related agencies, or law firms, with appropriate readings, and a research paper/report. Prerequisites: prior consent of supervisor, adviser, or department head; applicable departmental internship requirements, such as satisfactory completion of required 300- and 400-level course appropriate for the internship program selected. Note: 400-level courses are available only to students with junior or senior standing.

Political Sociology
University of Southern Colorado
COSO#SOC355 Undergraduate   3 credits $210

Analysis of the major sociological variables associated with political decision making and other political processes. The goal of this class is to guide you to analyze the major sociological variables associated with political decision making and other political processes. Politics is a fascinating subject for most of us; many (maybe even most) of us tend to argue our political beliefs from a personal, not scholarly, perspective.

Political Terrorism
Indiana University
INDI#Y200B Undergraduate   3 credits $268

Probes the evolution of terrorism from a residual event in the margins of society to almost an epidemic in the forefront of the political stage. Looks at terrorism from both a historical and theoretical aspect.

Political Theory for the 21st Century
New School for Social Research
NEWS#0225 Undergraduate   3 credits $1638*

Contemporary politics often appears as a Babel of competing ideals and goals. We examine a variety of political frameworks-- conservatism, liberalism, libertarianism, Marxism, anarchism, feminism, and eco-politics--and evaluate their philosophical presuppositions about human nature, freedom, political authority, and social change. To what extent do any of these frameworks help us make sense of the upheavals and crises of the 20th century? Which offer hope for freedom and justice as we approach the 21st century? Will we need a new political paradigm for the 21st century?.

* Non-credit option, tuition: $365.

Political Violence and Terrorism
University of Nevada-Reno
NERE#C410 Undergraduate   3 credits $210

This course will attempt to understand and focus on the nature of terrorism in contemporary society. It will examine the definition of international terrorism, its underlying social, political and economic causes, its use as a political tool, its manifestations in the world and the measures to be taken for its prevention. It will examine the aims and activities of several terrorist organizations and consider the various measures adopted by individual nation-states and the international community in response. Emphasis will be placed upon the social and political factors which produce terrorism, and on the domestic repercussions of counter-terrorist measures.

Politics of War and Peace
City University
CITY#INT403 Undergraduate   5 qu. credits $785
This course provides a theoretical examination of the impact of political and economic interests in the international arena and specifically focuses on how the threat and actual existence of modern warfare have impacted national and international politics. The course examines contemporary theories regarding the causes of war and concludes with a review of possible means to avoid future wars.

Popular Culture
University of Southern Colorado
COSO#SOC308 Undergraduate   3 credits $210
Advertising, television, radio, books, and news media all influence the lives of Americans. This course will use current popular materials to explore the effects of these influences on the individual in society.

Population
Indiana University
INDI#S305 Undergraduate   3 credits $268
Population composition, fertility, mortality, natural increase, migration; historical growth and change of populations; population theories and policies; techniques in manipulation and use of population data; and the spatial organization of populations. Prerequisite: 3 credit hours of sociology or consent of instructor.

Postmodern Sociology Thought
California State University - San Marcos
CASA#SOC485 Undergraduate   3 credits $315
The purpose of this course is to provide an introductory exploration of postmodernist influences in contemporary social thought. A key feature of the course is that it is delivered exclusively via the internet (there is one required textbook that can be obtained via the CSUSM bookstore or directly through the publisher). We will the engage the material primarily by reading secondary descriptions of postmodern imagery in social theory, mini cyber-lectures, and by discussing these perspectives in an on-line chatroom format.

Power & Politics in Organizations
The Graduate School of America
TGSA#OM834W Graduate   4 credits $795
This course examines the role of power and politics in organizations. It emphasizes especially the impact of political action and coalition formation in management decision making and organizational behavior.

Practicum in Governmental Admin.
Christopher Newport University
CHNE#GOVT491 Undergraduate   3 credits $993
Part-time internship with a government, military, private, or non-profit organization. Periodic conferences, written evaluations, and final paper relating theory and practice. A maximum of six credits may be counted toward a degree. Prerequisite: GOVT201-202, or GOVT103G-104G and senior standing, or consent of instructor.

Preparation for Marriage and Family
Western Illinois University
WEIL#FAM321 Undergraduate   3 credits $795*
Is an in-depth study of intimate relationships, marriage, and family. The focus is on building relationships, effective communications, conflict management, decision making, and changing roles through the life cycle.
* IL residents tuition: $88 per credit.

Principles of Banking
Mercy College
MERC#BK112 Undergraduate   3 credits $900
The course examines the role of a commercial bank in today's economy and the regulatory environment in which it exists. Topics include the deposit and payment function; bank loans and investments; non-credit financial services (cash management, international banking services, fiduciary services, and technology-based services); new customer products; the Federal Reserve System and Governmental supervision. The definition and correct use of banking terminology are stressed.

Principles of Development-Lifespan
Eastern Oregon University
EAOR#PSY311 Undergraduate   5 credits $400
Principles of human development from birth to late adulthood. Physical, intellectual, and social development will be examined, with a consideration of maturation, learning, the environment, and individuality at each stage. Prerequisite: PSY201, 202, Sophomore standing.

Principles of Economics
University of Alaska - Fairbanks
ALFA#ECON200 Undergraduate   4 credits $284
Goals, incentives, and outcomes of economic behavior with applications and illustrations from current issues: operation of markets for goods, services, and factors of production; the behavior of firms and industries in different types of competition; and income distribution. The functioning and current problems of aggregate economy, determination and analysis of aspects of international exchange. (Prereq: Sophomore standing or permission of instructor.) Prerequisite: Sophomore standing or permission of instructor.

Principles of Economics
Strayer University
STRA#ECO100 Undergraduate   4.5 credits $665
Covers general synopsis of micro as well as macroeconomics theories and policies. Examines major economic topics, including market forces, capitalism contrasted with other systems, government influences on economy, national income analysis, and contemporary international trade problems and policies.

Principles of Economics
Strayer University
STRA#ECO250 Undergraduate   4.5 credits $665
Analyzes the main economic systems operative today and their effect on international trade policies. compares economic internal growth in centrally planned, mixed, and capitalist countries. Prerequisite: ECO102.

Principles of Economics - Macroeconomics
University of Colorado
CUON#ECON2012 Undergraduate   3 credits $1953*
Purpose is to teach fundamental principles, to open the field of economics in the way most helpful to further a more detailed study of special problems, and to give those not intending to specialize in the subject an outline of the general principles of economics. Subject matter includes topics of inflation, unemployment, national income, growth and problems of the national income, growth and problems of the national economy, stabilization policy, plus others at the discretion of the instructor.
* CO residents tuition: $136 per credit.

Principles of Economics - Micro
Lansing Community College
LANS#ECON201 Undergraduate   4 credits $420
This course is designed to develop objective consideration of economic issues and provides information and understanding of how resources are allocated by prices. Topics for study include price theory, consumer demand, cost and market structure, the role of government in the market, resource pricing, and international trade.

Principles of Economics I
Brevard Community College
BREV#ECO2013 Undergraduate   3 credits $485
Macroeconomics: introduction to the general theories of economics with practical applications. Topics include determination of prices, national income computation, economic stabilization growth, money and banking, and monetary policy.

Principles of Economics I
Cerro Coso Community College
CECO#ECONC1A Undergraduate   3 credits $345*
Principles of economic analysis, institutions, and issues of economic policy. Micro economics, including the price system allocation of resources and the distribution of income throughout the economic system. Prerequisite: MATHC70 recommended, or equivalent, with a grade of C or better.
* CA residents pay $13 per credit.

Principles of Economics I
New York Institute of Technology
NYIT#EC2010 Undergraduate   3 credits $???
A study of basic economic concepts emphasizing analysis of the aggregate economy. The fundamental concepts of national income and its determination, economic fluctuations, monetary and fiscal policies, and economic growth are covered.

Principles of Economics I - Micro
Texas Technical University
TETE#ECO2301 Undergraduate   3 credits $???
This course emphasizes theories of the firm, value and price determination, and functional distribution, and applies these theories to the problems of particular firms, industries, and markets.

Principles of Economics II
Brevard Community College
BREV#ECO2023 Undergraduate   3 credits $435
Microeconomics: introduction covering theory and practical applications. Topics include economic growth, resource allocation, economics of the firm and international economics.

Principles of Economics II
Christopher Newport University
CHNE#ECON201G Undergraduate   3 credits $993
An introduction to the analytical tools commonly employed by economists in determining the aggregate level of economic activity and the composition of output, prices, and the distribution of income. Problems related to these subjects are considered, and alternative courses of public policy are evaluated. Macroeconomics.

Principles of Economics II
New York Institute of Technology
NYIT#EC2020 Undergraduate   3 credits $???
An examination of the processes of price determine, output, and resource allocation in perfect and in imperfect competition. Also covers labor economics, international trade and finance, and alternative economic systems. Prerequisites: EC2010.

Principles of Economics Macro
University of Minnesota
MINN#ECON1005 Undergraduate   4 credits $356
National income accounting and theory, public finance, money, monetary policy, international trade, economic growth. Students must have access to an Apple Macintosh computer. Of value to general education students and required for economics majors and minors.

Principles of Learning
Eastern Oregon University
EAOR#PSY343 Undergraduate   5 credits $400
This course includes a thorough survey of modern learning and conditioning principles. The course emphasizes the experimental analysis of learning and adaptive behavior and demonstrates how experimental research can be, and is, applied to the understanding and modification of human behavior. Prerequisite: PSY 201 & 202 or consent of instructor.

Principles of Macroeconomics
University of Colorado-Boulder
COBO#ECON2020 Undergraduate   4 credits $320
An overview of the economy, examining the flows of resources and outputs and the factors determining the levels of income and prices. Policy problems of inflation, unemployment, and economic growth are explored.

Principles of Macroeconomics
Fayetteville Technical Community College
FAYE#ECO252 Undergraduate   3 credits $489*
This course introduces economic analysis of aggregate employment, income, and prices. Topics include major schools of economic thought; aggregate supply and demand; economic measures, fluctuations, and growth; money and banking; stabilization techniques; and international trade. Upon completion, students should be able to evaluate national economic components, conditions, and alternatives for achieving socioeconomic goals. This course has been approved to satisfy the Comprehensive Articulation Agreement general education core requirement in social/behavioral sciences.
* NC residents pay $20 per credit.

Principles of Macroeconomics
University of Minnesota
MINN#ECON1102 Undergraduate 4 credits $356

Determinants of national income, national income accounting, unemployment, inflation. Classical and Keynesian theories. Money and banking, monetary and fiscal policy, international economic relations, and less-developed nations. Students may receive credit for only one of these courses: ECON1102 or ECON1001. Prerequisite: ECON1101.

Principles of Microeconomics
University of Colorado-Boulder
COBO#ECON2010 Undergraduate 4 credits $320

Examines basic concepts of microeconomics, or the behavior and interactions of individuals, firms, and government. Topics include determining economic problems, how consumers and businesses make decisions, how markets work and how they fail, and how government actions affect markets.

Principles of Microeconomics
University of Colorado
CUON#ECON2010 Undergraduate 4 credits $2604*

Economics is a social science that examines decision making and human interaction. Recognizing and understanding basic economics should help you not only professionally but in your personal life. Macroeconomics views the economy from a national perspective, focusing on current issues such as economic growth, unemployment, inflation, and many others. Microeconomi-0cs, on the other hand, looks at individual economic decision makers, such as households, businesses, and politicians.

* CO residents tuition: $136 per credit.

Principles of Microeconomics
Fayetteville Technical Community College
FAYE#ECO251 Undergraduate 3 credits $489*

This course introduces economic analysis of individual, business, and industry choices in the market economy. Topics include the price mechanism, supply and demand, optimizing economic behavior, costs and revenue, market structures, factor markets, income distribution, market failure, and government intervention. Upon completion, students should be able to identify and evaluate consumer and business alternatives in order to efficiently achieve economic objectives. This course has been approved to satisfy the Comprehensive Articulation Agreement general education core requirement in social/behavioral sciences.

* NC residents pay $20 per credit.

Principles of Microeconomics
University of Minnesota
MINN#ECON1101 Undergraduate 4 credits $356

A study of the basic economic principles of pricing and resource allocation. Includes demand and supply, consumer choice, costs of production; competition, monopoly, oligopoly; determination of wages, rent, interest, profits; income distribution; farm and urban problems.

Principles of Sociology
Rogers State University
ROGE#SOC1113 Undergraduate 3 credits $495*

This course covers the fundamental concepts of sociology; foundations of group life; social change, processes and problems.

* OK residents $315.

Principles of Urban Economics
Indiana University
INDI#G330 Undergraduate 3 credits $268

An introduction to basic concepts and techniques of urban economic analysis to facilitate understanding of current urban problems: urban growth and structure, public provisions of urban services, housing, employment, transportation, relationships between public and private sectors. Prerequisite: E201 or consent of instructor.

Psychoanalysis and Literature
New School for Social Research
NEWS#0663 Undergraduate 3 credits $1638*

Freud knew it all along--"Creative writers ... know a whole host of things between heaven and earth of which our philosophy has not yet let us dream. In their knowledge of the mind they are in advance of us everyday people, for they draw upon sources which we have not yet opened for science." Psychoanalysis systematized that knowing as a distinct body of knowledge grounded in the belief that a behavior is psychically determined and that a dynamic unconscious influences that behavior.

* Non-credit option, tuition: $365.

Psychological Anthropology
University of Minnesota
MINN#ANTH5141 Undergraduate 4 credits $391

Examines the relation between culture and personality, with emphasis on recent work in psychoanalytic anthropology. Topics include human nature, child development, personality, mental illness, group psychodynamics, religious ritual and symbolism, and war.

Psychological Appraisals
Walden University
WALD#PSYC8250 Graduate 5 credits $1500

An examination of testing methods, interviewing procedures, and observational techniques associated with formulating diagnostic impressions and treatment plans. Emphasis will be given to multimodal appraisals of cognitive, affective, social, vocational, interest/aptitude, achievement, intellectual and personality functioning.

Psychological Consultations
Walden University
WALD#PSYC8460 Graduate 5 credits $1500

(Course description not available at press time.)

Psychological Research Designs
Walden University
WALD#PSYC8140 Graduate 5 credits $1500

An examination of the philosophical, logical, and scientific assumptions of behavioral science as they apply to empirical research conducted by psychologists.

Psychology
Northwest College
NOCO#GE177 Undergraduate   3 credits $???
Focusing on scientific aspects of human behavior, students will examine the history, methods and theories of psychology as a behavioral science. The brain and the senses will be explored as they relate to human development.

Psychology and Education of Exceptional Individuals
University of Missouri
MOCE#PS313 Undergraduate   3 credits $387
This course studies the psychology and education of individuals with special problems and/or abilities. It surveys theories and strategies for the learning-teaching process and sources of assistance to educators and parents. A seminar is required for a grade of A or B. Seminars are usually held in St. Louis or at group enrollment sites; students will be notified of seminars nearest them. Prerequisites: Psych. 270 or 271 or equivalent.

Psychology and Social Change
Walden University
WALD#PSYC8020 Graduate   5 credits $1500
A study of social and cultural theories influencing the practice of psychology. Examination of factors which tend to enhance and retard social change. Techniques and approaches applicable for psychologist as advocates of social change.

Psychology in the 21st Century
Walden University
WALD#PSYC8550 Graduate   5 credits $1500
This course will examine the social, political, and economic forces influencing the delivery of psychological services in the 21st century. The role of practice guidelines to the future of the practice of psychology will be explored.

Psychology of Abnormal Behavior
New Hampshire College
NEHA#PSY215 Undergraduate   3 credits $1656
The course offers students an opportunity to better understand human behavior. It also studies the similarities and differences between normal and abnormal reactions to environmental stimuli. Prerequisite: PSY108.

Psychology of Addictions
State University of New York
SUNY#PSY234Y02 Undergraduate   3 credits $570*
This course is an introductory course which will focus on the nature of addiction, the many types of addiction and the effects on individuals, family and ultimately society. Some of the topics being addressed are anatomy, physiology and human development issues, pharmacology of various classifications of drugs, e.g. alcohol, prescription medications, and illegal drugs. Also addressed are eating disorders, gambling and sexual addiction and the current theories about the process and treatment of addiction as well as family and social issues related to addiction.
* NY residents tuition: $90 per credit

Psychology of Adulthood and Aging
Western Illinois University
WEIL#PSY423G Undergraduate   3 credits $795*
This PBS telecourse explores the biopsychosocial aspects of the aging person by focusing on six themes of development: (1) identification of the stability and change shown in the growth processes throughout adulthood, (2) how the aging person interacts with and influences the environment, (3) how aging is studied empirically, (4) what similarities and differences in aging exist among societies, (5) how older persons can experience an optimal quality of life, and (6) how the changes in society have affected the aging person.
* IL residents tuition: $88 per credit.

Psychology of Death and Dying
Fayetteville Technical Community College
FAYE#PSY141 Undergraduate   3 credits $489*
This course presents psychological perspectives on death and dying. Topics include the culturally diverse aspects of death and the grieving process, adjustment mechanisms, interventions, and the psychological and ethical dimensions of death and dying. Upon completion, students should be able to demonstrate an understanding of the psychosocial aspects of death and dying.
* NC residents pay $20 per credit.

Psychology of Discipline
Pennsylvania State University
PENN#PSYCH497E Undergraduate   3 credits $345
Provides theory and practice for effective discipline of children in a variety of situations. Note: 400-level courses are available only to students with junior or senior standing.

Psychology of Human Development
University of Minnesota
MINN#GC1283 Undergraduate   5 credits $445
Explores the growth and development of an individual from conception through old age. Emphasizes physical, motor, social, emotional, and psychological growth. Integration of facets of development helps students to understand a human being as a complex organism functioning in a complex environment.

Psychology of Human Relations
Waukesha County Technical College
WAUK#809199016 Undergraduate   3 credits $193
This course covers principles of interaction as applied to human relations at home and on the job. Topics include self concept/personality development, learning, motivation, emotions, stress, human relations processes, and special relationships. Classroom interaction and discussions are emphasized along with cognitive achievement in this introductory psychology course.

Psychology of Individual Differences and Special Needs
New Hampshire College
NEHA#PSY320 Undergraduate   3 credits $1656
This course provides knowledge and understanding of exceptional children and adolescents. The approach is both theoretical and practical. Prerequisite: PSY108.

Psychology of Personality
Indiana University
INDI#P319 Undergraduate 3 credits $268
Methods and results of scientific study of personality. Basic concepts of personality traits and their measurements, developmental influences, and problems of integration. Prerequisites: P101 and P102, or P106.

Psychology of Personality
New Hampshire College
NEHA#PSY216 Undergraduate 3 credits $1656
Personality is studied from the standpoint of theories, applications, and individual and group patterns of behavior formation. Prerequisite: PSY108 or permission of the instructor.

Psychology of Personality
Salve Regina University
SALV#HDV541 Grad 3 credits $???
Students investigate personality theories within the philosophical context of psychoanalysis, behaviorism, and existentialism. The development of healthy personalities is studied in detail.

Psychology of Personality
Wichita State University
WIST#PSY324 Graduate 3 credits $603
This course is intended to provide the student a knowledge of major personality theories and to stimulate critical thinking: present a clear and concise picture of the important personality theories; focus on significant ideas and themes that structure the context of the different personality theories; and provide criteria to guide the evaluation of each theory.

Psychology of Sensation and Perception
University of Missouri
MOCE#PS220 Undergraduate 3 credits $387
This course studies the general characteristics of the senses and the basic conditions and principles of human perception, with an emphasis on auditory and visual perception. The role of sensation and perception on affectivity and motivation is stressed. Prerequisites: Psych. 216; UMR-Psych. 50.

Psychology of Women
Walden University
WALD#PSYC8580 Graduate 5 credits $1500
n/a

Psychology Principles I
State University of New York
SUNY#PSY111 Undergraduate 3 credits $545*
Emphasis is on the major aspects of human behavior and its adaptation to the environment. Topics include learning, motivation, emotional behavior, maturation, personality, behavior disorders and therapies.
* NY residents tuition: $278

Psychopathology, Assessment and Treatment
The Graduate School of America
TGSA#HS831W Graduate 4 credits $795
This course examines the assessment and treatment of various forms of psychopathology. The etiology of psychopathology, current methods of psychological assessment, research on psychodynamics, and existing treatment methods will be reviewed. The politics of mental disorders, emerging diagnoses, and other contemporary issues will be addressed.

Psychopharmacology
Walden University
WALD#PSYC8410 Graduate 5 credits $1500
An introduction to psychotropic medications, their neurochemical effects, mode of action, clinical application. Principles of use and modern applications of psychopharmacology will be discussed.

Public Administration
Eastern Oregon University
EAOR#POLS351 Undergraduate 5 credits $400
This course is an investigation of the role of public management in the political process; including the social and political environment of public administration and issues of organizational behavior, efficiency, responsiveness, and ethics. Prerequisite: POLS101, POLS110, POLS200 or POLS221.

Public Administration
University of Missouri
MOCE#A140 Undergraduate 3 credits $387
This course includes a survey of public administration, with reference to financial administration, personnel management, and judicial control of the administrative requirement. This course meets state law that requires students to successfully complete a constitutional course. Prerequisites: Pol. Sci. 11 or consent of instructor.

Public Budgeting
Christopher Newport University
CHNE#GOVT391 Undergraduate 3 credits $993
A critical study of the theories and practices of budgeting. Particular emphasis will be directed toward the role of politics in the budgetary process, value issues in tax policy, and related contemporary issues. Prerequisite: GOVT371 recommended.

Public Contracting
Strayer University
STRA#BUS350 Undergraduate 4.5 credits $665
Focuses on public purchasing and contracting at the buyer level with emphasis on methods of procurement, types of contracts and grants used by government, and implementation including sealed bidding. Topics include specifications and standards, competitive bidding, administration of purchase orders, procurement codes, ordinances and regulation, planning and scheduling purchasing requirements, quality assurance, and inventory management.

Public Finance
Strayer University
STRA#ECO450 Undergraduate 4.5 credits $665
Covers economics of the public sector and analytical framework for government involvement, official budgeting process, benefit-cost analysis, taxes and their economic impact, national debt, fiscal policy, negative income tax, and other current topics. Prerequisite: ECO101 or equivalent.

Public Policy
Eastern Oregon University
EAOR#POLS350 Undergraduate 5 credits $400
An evaluation of the American political system following individual programs through their origins, design and formation, and implementation. Prerequisite: POLS101, POLS110, POLS200 or POLS221.

Quantitative Political Analysis
Christopher Newport University
CHNE#GOVT352 Undergraduate   3 credits $993
Data analysis techniques, including statistical analysis, measurement, hypothesis testing, multivariate analysis, and measures of association. Prerequisite: MATH25 or consent of instructor.

Quantitative Political Analysis
Christopher Newport University
CHNE#SOCL392 Undergraduate   3 credits $993
Data-analysis techniques, including statistical analysis, measurement, hypothesis testing, multivariate analysis, and measures of association. Prerequisite: MATH125, SOCL201G or consent of department.

Race and Ethnic Relations
California State University - San Marcos
CASA#SOC313A Undergraduate   3 credits $315
This course focuses on race and ethnic relations paying close attention to how these relations are structured in the United States. Students will use the Internet to unearth racial discourse in the United States and to explore alternative underlying assumptions of how race structures U.S. public policy. In addition, the Internet will be used to examine how racist counter discourses are also produced. These counterdiscourses are then explored to understand how they affect structures of equality, democracy and social citizenship in multi-racial nation-states.

Race and Ethnic Relations in the US
City University
CITY#SOC303 Undergraduate   5 qu. credits $785
This course evaluates the sociological theories and concepts used to explain and describe race and ethnic relations. It will also consider the sources of racial and ethnic conflict, and the historical experiences and current conditions for various minority groups in the United States. Special emphasis is placed upon the African-American experience.

Race and Ethnicity in the U.S.
University of Colorado
CUON#SOC3020 Undergraduate   3 credits $1953*
A sociological examination of race and ethnicity in contemporary U.S. society. Includes a focus on the nature and causes of prejudice and discrimination. Dominant-minority relations are examined, with emphasis on current status of minority groups and issues. Prerequisite: Six hours of social science.
* CO residents tuition: $136 per credit.

Race, Gender, Ethnicity in US Politics
Mercy College
MERC#GV366 Undergraduate   3 credits $900
History and political status of race, sex, and ethnicity in the United States; the relationship of such groups as blacks, Hispanics, Jews, Italian-American, Irish-Americans, and women to the larger political environment; application of theories in political science, such as pluralism and class analysis; the rise of political action and consequent social change.

Racial and Ethnic Diversity in Families
University of Minnesota
MINN#FSOS5500 Undergraduate   4 credits $391
Sociological overview of family structures and family values of various American racial and ethnic groups, including African Americans, Native Americans, Mexican Americans, Jews, and Asian Americans. Combines a study of research and case studies with individual projects to develop and enrich understanding of cultural diversity. Students may receive credit for only one of these courses: FSOS5500 or FSOS3240. Prerequisite: FSOS3600.

Regulatory Issues
The Graduate School of America
TGSA#OM891W Graduate   4 credits $795
This course presents an overview of telecommunications law including regulations, public policy, regulatory agencies and current regulatory issues.

Relationship of the Individual to the World
University of Colorado
CUON#PHIL1012 Undergraduate   3 credits $1953*
An introductory course in philosophy, in which the main focus is on some of the central questions in any body of philosophic work regarding: theories of reality, the nature of knowledge, an its limits. The knowledge of these areas of philosophy is essential to the student for informed participation in the resolution of contemporary problems in today's society.
* CO residents tuition: $136 per credit.

Remarriage and Stepfamilies
University of Colorado
CUON#SOC4600 Undergraduate   3 credits $1953*
A sociological examination of remarriages and stepfamilies. History, demographics, family structure and process, adjustment of partners, stepparents-stepchildren, and role of extended family are among the topic to be studied. Special attention will be directed at current research issues. Prerequisite: Three hours of sociology.
* CO residents tuition: $136 per credit.

Remed Invest & Corrective Action
Rochester Institute of Technology
ROCH#63044490 Undergraduate   4 credits $923
Delineates and describes the sequence of events required in remedial investigations (RI), feasibility studies and corrective actions at hazardous waste sites.

Research and Statistics
Bellevue University
BELL#CJAC307 Undergraduate   4 credits $1000
Provides instruction on conducting research in the criminal justice field. Students will develop their thesis proposal.

Rights of the Offender
University of Missouri
MOCE#LE345 Undergraduate   3 credits $387
This course addresses the constitutional protection of the accused, including an analysis of the rights guaranteed under the Fourth, Fifth, Sixth, and Fourteenth Amendments. Perquisites: Crim. 110, 120, 130, 210, 220, or consent of instructor.

Rural Sociology
University of Missouri
MOCE#SO1 Undergraduate   3 credits $387
This course introduces students to the sociology of rural and small towns. The structure, functioning, and trends of rural society are discussed. Basic sociological principles are also emphasized.

Russia and Eastern European Politics
Salve Regina University
SALV#INR518 Grad   3 credits $???
Students establish a conceptual framework for understanding the international relations of the Eastern European states since 1945. Special attention is devoted to recent changes in the Russian government's approach toward foreign policy. The global impact of these developments is considered.

Russia and Environs
University of Minnesota
MINN#GEOG3181 Undergraduate   4 credits $391
An introduction to the diverse characteristics and regions of the former Soviet Union. Emphasizes analysis of the physical, cultural, and economic phenomena in the former U.S.S.R., including the impact of present political and economic trends.

Sanitation Techniques
State University of New York
SUNY#HOT13271 Undergraduate   2 credits $692*
This course emphasizes the importance of proper sanitation techniques in the food service industry. Special emphasis will be placed upon proper food handling techniques. Topics covered will be HACCP, food-borne illnesses, proper cooking, handling and storage of food, the knowledge of correct temperatures to prevent food contamination, and safe personal hygiene for food handlers. Successful completion of a test will result in a food service sanitation procedures certification awarded by the Educational Foundation of the National Restaurant Association.
* NY residents tuition: $137 per credit.

Science Fiction (From Frankenstein to the Future)
University of Iowa
IOWA#008182 Undergraduate   3 credits $240
(Course description not available at press time.)

Science, Technology, Community
City University
CITY#BC304 Undergraduate   5 qu. credits $785
Scientific method, the origins of applied science and their impact on everyday life and work.

Seasons of Life
Western Illinois University
WEIL#PSY423A Undergraduate   3 credits $795*
Studies the stages of human development from the "terrible twos" through "mid-life crisis" into the "twilight years." Modern psychology emphasizes that not just childhood and youth, but every stage of human life offers opportunities for personal growth and enrichment. This PBS telecourse examines the drama of human development that unfolds under the influence of three "clocks": physical (the timeline our bodies follow), social (the age norms dictated by family and society), and psychological (each individual's unique sense of timing).
* IL residents tuition: $88 per credit.

Setting Limits for Toddlers to 5-Year-Olds
New York University
NEYO#X489467 Undergraduate   2.0 CEU $210
Working with young children is a joy and a challenge. As children grow and develop, they move through stages that create stress and frustration. Positive limit setting helps children to meet their needs, learn, and develop social skills while building their self-esteem. This course explores the concept of positive discipline and its relationship to healthy, well-functioning children, and strategies for positive limit setting. Participants observe child behavior outside of class and relate it to limit-setting strategies discussed in the course.

Social Change
Indiana University
INDI#S215 Undergraduate   3 credits $268
Introduction to theoretical and empirical studies of social change. Explores such issues as modernization; rationalization; demographic, economic, and religious causes of change; and reform and revolution.

Social Environment of Business
New Hampshire College
NEHA#ADB326 Undergraduate   3 credits $1656
This course discusses in detail the interrelationships among business, government, and society. Considerable time is spent discussing how these relationships change. The potency of change comes from both forces in the business environment and from the actions of business. The impact of these changes affects the daily lives of all Americans. Through the use of readings, supplemental cases and class discussions students will gain an understanding of he many significant issues facing the business community today.

Social Influences of Behavior
The Graduate School of America
TGSA#HS813W Graduate   4 credits $795
Overview of behavior that is influenced by the presence of others, or behavior that is under the control of society. Culture and society, large and small group behavior, cross cultural factors, and interpersonal relationships will be considered. The social psychology of decision making, attitude formation, and social attribution will be reviewed and applied to contemporary issues.

Social Influences on Human Sexual Behavior
Syracuse University
SYRA#PSY5771 Graduate   3 credits $1587
The primary objective of the course is to introduce the student to the scientific study of human sexual behavior. The perspective taken is a social psychological one. Theory and research linking social and cultural variables to sexuality-related beliefs, attitudes, and behavior will constitute the major content of the course. How social influences build on and interact with biological capacities will be analyzed in an effort to understand individual variability in sexual expression. Within-cultural and cross-cultural variations in sexual beliefs, attitudes, and behavior will be considered.

Social Institutions
University of Alaska - Fairbanks
ALFA#SOC102 Undergraduate   3 credits $213
Continuation of SOC101: application of concepts learned by developing and implementing short surveys of sociological phenomena. Institutions of society, such as family, political and economic order, examined, including their operation in the Alaska rural and cross-cultural milieu. Prerequisite: SOC101.

Social Institutions
Dakota State University
DAKO#SOC380 Undergraduate   3 credits $447
The major institutions in society (Political, Economic, Family, Science, Religion, and Education). The impact of computer information and technology on each. Prerequisite: SOC285.

Social Justice and Social Policy
University of Missouri
MOCE#SO310 Undergraduate   3 credits $387
Based on the concepts of human need and social justice, this course provides a historical and analytical approach to social welfare policies and programs. Perquisites: Social Work 125.

Social Policy and Service Delivery in Social Work
University of Missouri
MOCE#SO410 Graduate   3 credits $489
This course covers historic and contemporary issues in social welfare policy. It focuses on relationships among social problems, public policies, private actions, poverty, racism, sexism, and social work practice/values. Perquisites: graduate standing; consent required.

Social Problems
Fayetteville Technical Community College
FAYE#SOC220 Undergraduate   3 credits $489*
This course provides an in-depth study of current social problems. Emphasis is placed on causes, consequences, and possible solutions to problems associated with families, schools, workplaces, communities, and the environment. Upon completion, students should be able to recognize, define, analyze, and propose solutions to these problems. This course has been approved to satisfy the Comprehensive Articulation Agreement general education core requirement in social/behavioral sciences.
* NC residents pay $20 per credit.

Social Problems
University of Central Florida
FLCE#SYG2010 Undergraduate   3 credits $786*
This course is intended to provide students with a better understanding of a number of important social issues. The course begins by developing a sociological foundation from which social issues may be considered. We will explore such fundamental sociological concepts as social systems and their components, social stratification, the world system of societies, and the relationship between human societies and the global ecosystem. The remaining two-thirds of the semester will be devoted to the application of these fundamental concepts to a variety of social issues including poverty, race and ethnic relations, and drugs.
* FL residents tuition: $64 per credit.

Social Problems
Indiana University
INDI#R121 Undergraduate   3 credits $268
Selected current "problems" of American society are analyzed through the use of basic sociological data and the application of major sociological frameworks. Policy implications are discussed in the light of value choices involved in various solutions. Prerequisite: R100 or consent of instructor.

Social Problems
University of Iowa
IOWA#034002 Undergraduate   3 credits $240
The objectives for this course are to examine the nature and cause of a number of social issues from a sociological perspective and to examine and consider the various policy implications tied to these social issues. This is an introductory level course which requires no previous exposure to the discipline. What is required is a willingness to step outside your own beliefs about the various social issues we will examine and step into the role of sociologist and begin to take a sociological perspective on these issues.

Social Problems
New York Institute of Technology
NYIT#BES2475 Undergraduate   3 credits $???
A sociological analysis of social problems in American society. All social problems will be viewed from a structural perspective, i.e., the root cause of a social problem lies in the institutional arrangements of American society that give rise to social problems will be evaluated in terms of value conflicts, power structures, and economic institutions. Major topics include: inequality, poverty, environmental destruction, ageism, educational institutions, social deviance, unemployment, problems of the city. Prerequisites: Complete12 BES credits including BES2401 and BES2411.

Social Psychology
City University
CITY#PSY302 Undergraduate   5 qu. credits $785
This course presents Social Psychology in a concise, yet intellectually stimulating way. It is designed so that students will gain a thorough grounding in the basic principles of social psychology; an understanding of the importance of context when interpreting research findings, and other complex topics such as conformity, self-justification, and prejudice. Prerequisite: Strongly recommended: SSC205 or its equivalent.

Social Psychology
Indiana University
INDI#P320 Undergraduate   3 credits $268
Principles of scientific psychology applied to individual in social situation. Prerequisites: P101 and P102, or P106.

Social Psychology
University of Missouri
MOCE#PS190 Undergraduate   3 credits $387
This course provides an introduction to how people's thoughts, feelings, and behaviors are influenced by the actual or imagined thoughts, feelings, and behaviors of others. Perquisites: Psych. 1.

Social Psychology
Walden University
WALD#PSYC8090 Graduate   5 credits $1500
Social Psychology is the scientific study of the experience and behavior of individuals in relation to social stimulus situations. Social stimulus situations are comprised of individuals and groups of people and objects of the sociocultural setting.

Social Psychology I
Thomas Edison State College
THED#OLPSY370 Undergraduate   3 credits $397*
This course enables students to gain an understanding of and perspective on the study of individuals as they influence and are influenced by the groups to which they belong. Topics include attribution and heuristics; bargaining, negotiation, and persuasion; friendships; prejudice; conformity; group decision making and leadership; aggression; and altruism.
* NJ residents tuition: $33 per credit.

Social Psychology II
Thomas Edison State College
THED#OLPSY371 Undergraduate   3 credits $397*
A continuation of Social Psychology I. [GSPSY370].
* NJ residents tuition: $33 per credit.

Social Research for Professionals
State University of New York
SUNY#283504 Undergraduate   4 credits $586*
Professionals in the fields of human services, public affairs, education, law, and business who have occasion to read scientific reports on social research will find this course helps them to understand the findings. This course covers the structuring of social inquiry and addresses the modes of observation: experiments, survey research, field research, unobtrusive research, and evaluation research. Examine the logic of analysis and understand the ethical questions about social research. Prerequisite: Course work in such fields as sociology, political science, anthropology, or psychology. Prior knowledge of statistics is not required.
* NY residents tuition: $515

Social Systems and Technology
Dakota State University
DAKO#SOC360 Undergraduate   3 credits $447
The changes in human values that take place because of technological innovations in Biology, biochemistry, medical science, and engineering. Prerequisite: Three hours of Social Systems and eight hours of science.

Social Theory
Indiana University
INDI#S340 Undergraduate   3 credits $268
Sociological theory, with focus on content, form, and historical development. Relationships between theories, data, and sociological explanation. Prerequisite: 3 credit hours of sociology or consent of instructor.

Social Welfare and Social Work
University of Missouri
MOCE#SO25 Undergraduate   3 credits $387
This course examines the nature of social welfare institutions and social work, and the relationship between them. It focuses on policy issues, with special references to poverty, racism, and sexism.

Social Work with Involuntary Clients
University of Minnesota
MINN#SW5424 Undergraduate   3 credits $293
Designed for students and professionals practicing with involuntary clients in many fields, such as chemical dependency, mental health, public schools, criminal justice and those in nursing, social work, psychology, and psychiatry. This course will help students and practitioners understand the dynamics of involuntary status and improve their contact with clients in involuntary situations.

Social, Political, Cultural Controversies
City University
CITY#BC305 Undergraduate   5 qu. credits $785
How debates surrounding controversial issues stimulate change. Topics examined include the origins of present day controversies; freedom of expression; and the interaction of people and political policies.

Society and the Rights of Animals
New School for Social Research
NEWS#0501 Undergraduate   3 credits $1638*
The ethic of "animal rights" was formalized in the 1970s in the writings of philosophers Peter Singer and Tom Regan. These writings provided a conceptual model that became a rallying point for people who had long empathized in silence with the suffering other species. Also spurred by these writings were individuals who had never before realized the extent of animal exploitation in our society. This course presents the philosophical foundations of the modern animal rights movement in the writings of many great philosophers and humanitarians, such as Schopenhauer, Henry Salt, and Albert Descartes.
* Non-credit option, tuition: $365.

Society, Culture and the Environment
Auburn University
AUBU#U101 Undergraduate   3 qtr. hrs. $126
An interdisciplinary course introducing concepts and processes relating to society, culture and the environment as studied by anthropology, geography and sociology.

Society, Technology and Environment
New Jersey Institute of Technology
NJIT#HSS202 Undergraduate   3 credits $1143*
This course uses case studies to examine the relationships between the creation and use of technologies, the human and natural environment, and the development of social and cultural institutions. Its central theme is the manner in which human society structures the environment in which it lives: nature and culture, city and country, civilization and development. Optional: 12 lessons of 30 minutes in length plus 6 summary lectures.
* NJ residents: $184/semester hour.

Sociolinguistics
University of Minnesota
MINN#LING5831 Undergraduate   4 credits $391
Focuses on the relationship between language and social identity: how we define ourselves and others through the use of language. Close examination of various regional, social, ethnic, and gender varieties of American English. Introduction to linguistic field methods and practical applications to teaching and testing.

Sociology - Tools for Understanding the World
New School for Social Research
NEWS#0325 Undergraduate   3 credits $1638*
Sociology? Why sociology? Sociology is not social psychology. Sociology is a set of theoretical tools we can use to make sense of the society in which we live. By using the theoretical tools of sociology, we can interpret the social world in which we spend our lives, and make sense out of the complexities of social life. In this introduction to sociology, we open the tool box, identify some theoretical tools, and begin to learn to use them.
* Non-credit option, tuition: $365.

Sociology and Social Problems
University of Minnesota
MINN#SOC1100 Undergraduate   5 credits $445
Provides students with the tools of the sociological imagination. Introduction to the process by which sociological theories are developed and tested and shows how those theories may be applied usefully to major social problems.

Sociology of Deviant Behavior
New Hampshire College
NEHA#SOC326 Undergraduate   3 credits $1656
The sociological analysis of the nature, cause, and societal reactions to deviance such as mental illness, suicide, drug and alcohol addiction, and sexual deviations. Prerequisite: SOC112 or permission of the instructor.

Sociology of Evil
Syracuse University
SYRA#SOC4004 Undergraduate   3 credits $960*
This course examines the following questions: What are the social conditions and social processes that systematically allow human beings to be treated without human dignity? What does it mean to be systematically dehumanized in this way? How is this dehumanization accounted for from the perspectives of victims, perpetrators, and audiences? By studying extreme examples of evil such as enslavement, genocide, and sexual violence, what can we learn about the more subtle ways we dehumanize one another on a routine basis?.
* Graduate level course tuition: $1587.

Sociology of Mental Health
Western Illinois University
WEIL#SOC424 Undergraduate   3 credits $795*
Imparts a fundamental understanding of the problems of mental health in the United States. Major topics include the history of the mental health movement; the evolution of the concept of mental illness and treatment strategies; the association of mental illness with age, sex, marital status, class, religion, and other sociological variables; and recent trends in mental health treatment practices and rehabilitative policies and programs. Prerequisite: Sociology 100 and one additional sociology course or consent of instructor.
* IL residents tuition: $88 per credit.

Sociology of the Third World
City University
CITY#INT404 Undergraduate   5 qu. credits $785
A study of the varied forms in inequality among the nations and regions of the world and how those inequalities in wealth, power and prestige affect the world economy and political structure. Emphasis is given to the social and economic inequalities of life in the developing nations in the areas of race, gender, ethnic origin and class. The course considers how inequalities among nations give rise to resistance, protest, group mobility and world conflict.

Sociology of Work
City University
CITY#SOC405 Undergraduate   5 qu. credits $785
This course will serve as a broad overview of sociological theories and research regarding work and occupations. Several areas will be examined and evaluated: 1) the historical context of work, and the rise of the industrial age, 2) sociological theories of work and organization, 3) the decline of leisure in relation to the growth of capitalism, 4) issues of stratification and work, 5) the impact of work on the individual, and 6) the determinants of the structure of occupations and organizations.

Soviet/Russian Space Program
University of North Dakota
NODA#SPST450 Graduate   3 credits $816*
From the launch of the world's first satellite to the present space station, the Soviet Union and Russia have dominated the world's space stage. A study of the Soviet/Russian Space Program determines why this country has been so successful in its space exploration despite economic and cultural chaos. This course presents the development of the Russian Space Program from its earliest roots to its plans for collaboration with the U.S. on an international space station.
* ND residents, $102 per credit; may also be reduced for residents of adjoining states and provinces.

Space Policy & Internat. Implications
University of North Dakota
NODA#SPST545 Graduate   3 credits $816*
A review of U.S. space policy since the beginning of the Cold War. Specific technology applications, for example remote sensing, communications, transportation, etc., are addressed within a policy context. Emphasis on the evolution of space policy in the Post-Cold War era.
* ND residents, $102 per credit; may also be reduced for residents of adjoining states and provinces.

Space Treaties & Legislation
University of North Dakota
NODA#SPST565 Graduate   3 credits $816*
A survey of international and U.S. domestic law that governs space activities. Among the topics addressed are the five major international space treaties, the ABM Treaty, the National Aeronautics and Space Act of 1958, The Commercial Space Launch Act, etc.
* ND residents, $102 per credit; may also be reduced for residents of adjoining states and provinces.

Sport Psychology
State University of New York
SUNY#PPE208   Undergraduate   3 credits $630*
As the demand for enhanced sport performance continues, the cognitive or mental aspects within sport are being exposed. Sport Psychology has evolved through this need. Specifically, this course will relate the application of conventional psychological areas (personality, motivation, aggression, etc.) to the arena of sport. This course satisfies the requirement for a social science elective. Prerequisite: PSY101 or equivalent.
* NY residents tuition: $105 per credit.

State & Local Government
Eastern Oregon University
EAOR#POLS314   Undergraduate   5 credits $400
Analysis of the politics and the organization of American state and local government. Prerequisite: POLS101, 110, 200 or 221.

State & Local Government
State University of New York
SUNY#POLSC107   Undergraduate   3 credits $735*
This course is a survey of the institutions of state and local governments, federalism and regionalism, the structure and operation of governments at various levels below the national, current problems of the cities. It is designed for students with a special interest or need in understanding local politics and particularly recommended for police science students.
* NY residents tuition: $98 per credit.

State & Local Government and Politics
City University
CITY#PLS304   Undergraduate   5 qu. credits $785
A detailed review of the politics and operations of state and local governments. The course focuses on current topics such as the influences affecting the development of state policy, the politics of governors and state legislatures, the function and role of legislative committees, reform strategies for metropolitan areas, the selection of judges and the role of special interest groups in politics. The course will be composed of a general perspective on state and local governments and a specific case history regarding political developments in Washington state.

State and Local Government
Christopher Newport University
CHNE#GOVT202   Undergraduate   3 credits $993
A survey of the structure, functions, and issues of state and local governments in the U. S. Includes such topics as federalism, the new role of the states, local government structures and elections, reform movements, and problems of modern local governments.

State Politics in the United States
Indiana University
INDI#Y306   Undergraduate   3 credits $268
Comparative study of politics in the American states. Special emphasis on the impact of political culture, party systems, legislatures, and bureaucracies on public policies. Prerequisite: Y103 recommended.

Statistics & Research in Psychology
University of Colorado-Boulder
COBO#PSYC2101   Undergraduate   4 credits $320
Introduces descriptive and inferential statistics and their roles in psychological research. Topics include correlation, regression, t-test, analysis of variance, and selected non-parametric statistics. Prerequisite: MATH1000 or equivalent is highly recommended.

Statistics in Psychology
Walden University
WALD#PSYC6110   Undergraduate   4 credits $1200
(Course description not available at press time.)

Strategic and Tactical Planning Systems
Bellevue University
BELL#CJAC430   Undergraduate   3 credits $750
Provides theory and application opportunities in strategic planning. Utilizes PERT. Discusses advantages of sound planning and disadvantages of poor planning.

Strategic Implications of Space
University of North Dakota
NODA#SPST555   Graduate   3 credits $816*
An analysis of the increasing strategic importance of space to the U.S. and other nations. Some topics addressed are the structure and missions of U.S. Space Command; the Russian military space program; SDI; and other historic programs. The course also addresses the surveillance/reconnaissance missions and issues surrounding the introduction of offensive and defensive weapons into space.
* ND residents, $102 per credit; may also be reduced for residents of adjoining states and provinces.

Strategic Planning
Heriot-Watt University
HERI#07   Graduate   4 credits $???
Strategic Planning is the process of setting company objectives, choosing among alternative courses of action, allocating resources and evaluating outcomes. The objective of this course is to incorporate the transferable management skills developed in the compulsory discipline courses into a decision making structure. In business schools planning is usually taught using the case approach in an interactive class environment.

Study of Africa, Asia, and Latin America
Strayer University
STRA#SOC300   Undergraduate   4.5 credits $665
Analyzes the main cultural strata in selected societies of the Third World. Emphasis their unique historical background and development, their traditional ethos, national characteristics, family structures, and religious beliefs, as well as, their political, economic, and foreign policy views.

Study of Crimes Against Women
New School for Social Research
NEWS#0334   Undergraduate   3 credits $1638*
This course considers the effects on the individual of crimes associated with women as victims, such as rape and domestic violence. We study gender, crime, and identity. We explore how victimization affects the lives of women, specifically what the victimized woman thinks of crime, victimization, and herself as and result of her experience. Theories on social structure and processes are studied relevant to crime, gender, and locating the feminine victim's social status and roles.
* Non-credit option, tuition: $365.

Substance Abuse Therapies
Walden University
WALD#PSYC8440 Graduate   5 credits $1500
The etiology of drug dependence and different methods of assessment, treatment, and relapse prevention will be investigated. Differential treatments for addiction will be one focus.

Surface Water Management
University of Missouri
MOCE#WA201 Undergraduate   3 credits $387
Topics in this course include water management and its role in maintaining soil productivity; farm surveying; and the design and layout of terrace systems. Perquisites: Math 10 and junior standing.

Survey of Economics
Fayetteville Technical Community College
FAYE#ECO151 Undergraduate   3 credits $489*
This course introduces basic concepts of micro- and macroeconomics. Topics include supply and demand, optimizing economic behavior, prices and wages, money, interest rates, banking system, unemployment, inflation, taxes, government spending, and international trade. Upon completion, students should be able to explain alternative solutions for economic problems faced by private and government sectors. This course has been approved to satisfy the Comprehensive Articulation Agreement general education core requirement in social/behavioral sciences.
* NC residents pay $20 per credit.

Survey of Research in Societal and Cultural Change
The Graduate School of America
TGSA#SC501W Graduate   4 credits $795
This course concerns research and theories relating to societal and cultural evolution. The dynamics of cultural development are studied within the broader context of societal issues. The study of societal issues emphasizes an understanding of cultural dynamics and change.

Survey of Social Psychology
Eastern Oregon University
EAOR#PSY310 Undergraduate   5 credits $400
An overview of Social Psychology focusing on three major areas: 1) social psychological explanations of human activity, based on theory, scientific research or both; 2) major empirical studies; and 3) how social psychological studies pertains to real-life situations. Prerequisite: General Psychology would be helpful.

Technology and Society
Western Illinois University
WEIL#HIS312 Undergraduate   3 credits $795*
Explores how technology has influenced and advanced our society. The course views technology as a process of continuity, integration, and accommodation rather than as a series of disconnected inventions and inventors. It investigates major technological innovations against the background of concurrent social and ideological influences and population movements. You can study the impact of various technologies upon past, present, and future societies.
* IL residents tuition: $88 per credit.

Technology, Society and Values
New York Institute of Technology
NYIT#SS1535 Undergraduate   3 credits $???
Concerned with the impact of machines on man, of technological systems on social structures, and modes of production on values. Special attention is paid to the link between new technologies and the study of ethics.

Tests and Measurements
Walden University
WALD#PSYC8100 Graduate   5 credits $1500
This course was designed to give the student an overview of psychometric methods. Emphasis is on understanding what tests measure and how well they do it.

Textile Economics
University of Nebraska
NEBR#TXCD870 Masters   3 credits $467
Areas to be discussed are: Current status of the domestic textile and apparel complex; current theories of textile consumption and demand within the global market, factors influencing textile and apparel production, distribution, and expenditures; the role of international trade and its influence on the domestic textile and apparel industry and foreign policy. Course objectives: To provide a multidimensional perspective of the U.S. textile and apparel complex. To acquire an understanding of trade theory and the role of international trade concerning the textile and apparel complex.

The Adult Years
Western Illinois University
WEIL#PSY423B Undergraduate   6 credits $1590*
The experience of being an adult differs depending on sex, age, race, social class, and personal interpretation of events. This IUC video course explores adulthood as a period of variability and change rather than as stages of sequential development. It examines the inner lives of adults and their relationship to family, work, education, and the community.
* IL residents tuition: $88 per credit.

The American Constitution
University of Missouri
MOCE#LE320 Undergraduate   3 credits $387
This course examines leading constitutional principles as they have evolved through important decisions of the U.S. Supreme Court. This course meets state law that requires students to successfully complete a constitutional course. Perquisites: Pol. Sci. 1 or 11, and junior standing.

The American Political Scene
Northwest College
NOCO#GE274 Undergraduate   3 credits $???
This course is designed to inform students about government and politics in America: how the system works, its history and its strengths and weaknesses. It attempts to integrate the traditional with the modern approach so that students can understand the interconnection between political thought/the formal structure of politics on one hand and the policy making process/political behavior on the other.

The American Political System
University of Colorado-Boulder
COBO#PSCI1101 Undergraduate   3 credits $240
Emphasizes interrelations among levels and branches of government, formal and informal institutions, processes, and behavior.

The Bill of Rights and the Supreme Court
New School for Social Research
NEWS#0243 Undergraduate   3 credits $1638*
This course examines some basic and controversial issues of U.S. constitutional law. The focus is the Bill of Rights. Topics include freedom of speech, the press, and religion, and related issues such as libel and obscenity and freedom of communication over the Internet; civil rights and various types of discrimination; affirmative action; and the right to privacy (including the abortion controversy). Another important topic is the rights of people accused of crime. We explore the most important Supreme Court decisions concerning the meaning of procedural safeguards.
* Non-credit option, tuition: $365.

The Community
Indiana University
INDI#S309 Undergraduate   3 credits $268
Introduction to the sociology of community life, stressing the processes of order and change in community organization. Major topics include the community and society, the nonterritorial community, analysis of major community institutions, racial-ethnic differences in community behavior, community conflict and community problems. Prerequisite: 3 credit hours of sociology or consent of instructor.

The Community and Fire Threat
Western Illinois University
WEIL#SOC488 Undergraduate   3 credits $795*
Covers the sociological, economic, and political characteristics of communities and their influence on the fire problem. It includes a review of the urban studies related to housing, structure abandonment, rent control, crime, false alarm and incendiary rates, and the fire problem. The roles of the fire department and fire prevention programs are examined, as are community and fire service role conflicts.
* IL residents tuition: $88 per credit.

The Congress
City University
CITY#PLS302 Undergraduate   5 qu. credits $785
An examination of the organization and procedures of Congress as well as the changing and constant roles of Congress in both national and state political systems.

The Counselor as Scientist-Practitioner
The Graduate School of America
TGSA#HS838W Graduate   4 credits $795
This course presents a theoretical and practical review of ways in which counselors can demonstrate accountability in a broad range of settings. The application of scientific methods to problems of human behavior will be demonstrated. Topics considered are methods of field research, program evaluation, the role of empirical validation of treatment methods, the efficacy of psychotherapeutic methods and the strengths and limitations of various methods of inquiry.

The Economy, Jobs, and You
Mercy College
MERC#EC115 Undergraduate   3 credits $900
This course will introduce the student to the ways different economists view the free market economy of the American society and help solve its problems; and an understanding of the variety of economic policies and their impact on public policy issues. A knowledge of diverse economic approaches to public questions ranging across the political spectrum will help the student critically evaluate the diversity of opinion on today's economic issues.

The Family
City University
CITY#SOC301 Undergraduate   5 qu. credits $785
This course will cover five broad but related areas of study: (1) the origins of the family, as well as basic concepts and theories underlying the family; (2) the relationship between the family and society through history; (3) work roles for men and women both within and outside the home; (4) trends in marriage, divorce and childbearing; and the outlook for the future of the family.

The Four Levels of Evaluation
The Graduate School of America
TGSA#ED850W Graduate   4 credits $795
This course deals with Kirkpatrick's four levels of evaluation. It will enable learners to understand what each level accomplishes and will provide techniques for accomplishing the goals of each level. Included in the course is a section devoted to preparing effective tests for measuring knowledge and skills (level 2 evaluation). This includes preparing test blueprints and writing effective items.

The Human Environment
Cerro Coso Community College
CECO#BIOLC34 Undergraduate   3 credits $345*
Human interaction with the lives and activities of other organisms and with the environment. The human role, place, and responsibility in the environmental issues and problems facing our contemporary world. Prerequisite: Level 1 reading, level 2 writing classification recommended.
* CA residents pay $13 per credit.

The Individual and Society
Strayer University
STRA#PSY100 Undergraduate   4.5 credits $665
Presents the various ways in which the individual constructs his self-awareness. Studies how social institutions, such as the family and religion, influence the psychological make-up of the individual.

The Information Society
Dakota State University
DAKO#SOC285 Undergraduate   3 credits $447
Analysis for the present and future impact of computerized information on social relationships and fabric of society. Prerequisites: General education computer literacy requirement.

The Middle East
Salve Regina University
SALV#INR586 Grad   3 credits $???
Students examine the following interrelated subject areas in an effort to better understand how they influence and shape events in the Middle East: the Peoples of the Middle East, Islam, the Arab-Israeli Problem, Oil, Iran's Revolution, the Iran-Iraq War, the Iraq-Kuwait War, and Gulf Security.

The Nature of Human Language
University of Minnesota
MINN#LING1001 Undergraduate   4 credits $356
A survey of the nature of human language, its properties, its possible origins, and how it differs from animal communication. Methods of describing the sounds, structures, and meanings of language are examined, along with a consideration of the relationship between language and the brain, how children acquire language, and the different roles of language in society. Whenever possible, points are illustrated with examples from the everyday use of English.

The Non-Western World
California State University - Dominguez Hills
CADO#HUX545 Undergraduate   3 credits $405
Interdisciplinary examination of the non-western world by focusing on cultural characteristics of China and Japan.

The Politics of the Third World
University of Missouri
MOCE#PO350 Undergraduate   3 credits $387
This course explores the processes and problems of the developing nations of the world. It examines the internal political processes of third world nations, as well as the position of the third world in international affairs. Perquisites: Pol. Sci. 90, or History 112 or 175 or 176.

The Presidency
City University
CITY#PLS301 Undergraduate   5 qu. credits $785
This is an upper division political science course which evaluates the nature of the contemporary American President. An examination of the presidency since 1932 will illustrate how economics, public policy, and the personal and political character of the men who have held the office have influenced and changed the office of the Presidency.

The Supreme Court
City University
CITY#PLS303 Undergraduate   5 qu. credits $785
The course examines the history, structure, processes, and personalities of the United States Supreme Court. Particular emphasis is on the nomination and confirmation process with focus on recent controversial nominations. The course will also emphasize the changing composition and direction of the Court under the leadership of different Chief Justices. Prerequisite: Strongly suggested: SSC218 or its equivalent.

The United States Congress
University of Minnesota
MINN#POL3308 Undergraduate   4 credits $391
This course examines the internal organization, committee system, party leadership, norms, and recruitment; legislative policy making; the relationship of Congress with the president and bureaucracy; and interest group, political party, and constituency influences on the congressional process. Prerequisite: POL1001 or equivalent.

The United States in World Affairs
City University
CITY#INT401 Undergraduate   5 qu. credits $785
An examination of the current role and position of the United States in the modern post-Cold War era. The course emphasizes the recent changes in the world political and military structure and how they will affect American foreign policy into the 21st Century. The strengths and weaknesses of the United States in a complex and interdependent global economy are reviewed, as is the role of the U.S. as the last superpower.

The World Around Us
University of Minnesota
MINN#GEOG1302 Undergraduate   5 credits $445
This course in world regional geography examines the world by dividing it into regions that share certain basic characteristics. Provides a geographic perspective on contemporary world issues such as population growth and environmental degradation.

Theories of Crime and Deviance
Indiana University
INDI#P200 Undergraduate   3 credits $268
Critical examination of biological, psychological, and sociological theories of crime and deviance. Examination of individual, group, and societal reactions to norm-violating behaviors.

Theories of Personality
New York Institute of Technology
NYIT#BES2445 Undergraduate   3 credits $???
A survey of the major theoretical approaches to understanding the development, structure, and dynamics of personality. Prerequisites: BES2401.

Theories of Personality
The Graduate School of America
TGSA#HS814W Graduate   4 credits $795
An examination of the assumptions, constructs, and processes of personality as these are expressed in the major theoretical writings. Reviewed are the psychodynamic, behavioral, structuralist, humanistic/existential, social, feminist, and cognitive theories of personality. Research on normal and abnormal constructs of personality will be reviewed. Contemporary issues and problems in personality theory and types will be addressed.

Theories of Personality
Walden University
WALD#PSYC8200 Graduate   5 credits $1500
Major theories of personality and supporting research to understand behavior in a therapeutic setting. Emphasis is placed on current thinking and research as applicable to the practice of psychology.

Theories of Psychotherapy
The Graduate School of America
TGSA#HS839W Graduate   4 credits $795
This course provides an examination of major psychotherapy theories, procedures, and techniques. The course reviews various schools of therapeutic intervention, their philosophical tenets and the therapeutic skills. Emphasis will be placed on applying current theory, research and techniques to a variety of clinical problems.

Theories of the Labor Movement
Indiana University
INDI#L380 Undergraduate   3 credits $268
Perspectives on the origin, development, and goals of organized labor. Theories include those that view the labor movement as a business union institution, an agent for social reform, a revolutionary force, a psychological reaction to industrialization, a moral force, and an unnecessary intrusion.

Theorizing Intellect
New School for Social Research
NEWS#0357 Undergraduate   3 credits $1638*
The what and how of the concept of intelligence is heatedly debated in the social sciences. We examine the major trends in intelligence theory and research, including the cutting-edge approaches. We explore the history of the concept of intelligence, theories of its development, research on thinking in pre-literate and non-Western cultures, and current findings on the biological underpinnings of intellective skills. Students administer IQ tests and score them as a practical introduction to standardized and alternative assessment methods, including consideration of so-called culture-fair and anxious-fair measures.
* Non-credit option, tuition: $365.

Therapeutic Psychology
Walden University
WALD#PSYC8240 Graduate   5 credits $1500
This course is designed to facilitate critical thinking about psychotherapy and methods of behavior change, in this age of managed care.

Thinking and Cognition
University of Missouri
MOCE#PS356 Undergraduate   3 credits $387
This course focuses on basic research in human perception, memory, attention, and thought.

U.S. Foreign Policy
Western Illinois University
WEIL#POL331 Undergraduate   3 credits $795*
Since the end of World War II, the United States has been involved in cold wars, military conflicts, nuclear arms summits, and peace missions. What decisions were made to get us involved in these situations? This course focuses on the theoretical concepts involved in developing and implementing American foreign policies and explores the U.S. role in the major events in international relations from the latter stages of World War II to the present.
* IL residents tuition: $88 per credit.

UN Crime and Justice Info. Network
Rio Hondo College
RIHO#WWW4 Undergraduate   ?? credits $???
The focus of the class is international; United Nations Crime and Justice Information Network (UNCJIN), United Nations Online Crime and Justice Clearinghouse (UNOJUST), International Association of Correctional Officers (IACO), United Nations International Drug Control Programme (UNDCP), Office of International Criminal Justice (OICJ), and the International Association for the Study of Organized Crime (IASOC). Many of these sites maintain journals and publications that are available for searches.

Understanding Consumer Behavior
City University
CITY#BSC300 Undergraduate   5 qu. credits $785
An investigation of consumer demand and consumer behavior. Marketing planning, research, and policy implementation will be emphasized.

Understanding Cultures
University of Minnesota
MINN#ANTH1102 Undergraduate   5 credits $445
Introduction to the ways the cross-cultural, comparative, and holistic study of contemporary societies and cultures across the world can provide an understanding of human diversity, adaptation, and condition. This course considers social, political, economic, technological, and religious institutions.

Understanding Gender
New School for Social Research
NEWS#0377 Undergraduate   3 credits $1638*
How different are men and women? Are men from Mars and women from Venus, as some suggest? In the early days of the contemporary women's movement, women argued that perceived gender differences in cognition and personality were superficial, constructions of a repressive culture. As women's influence grows, these assertions are reconsidered and new questions are posed. Do men and women have different styles for learning about the world and communicating that knowledge?.
* Non-credit option, tuition: $365.

Understanding War Causes and Consequences
University of Minnesota
MINN#POL3810 Undergraduate   4 credits $391
An exploration of the normative and ethical issues surrounding international violence; the types and the causes of war between the 18th and the 20th centuries; and the mechanisms for creating peace and limiting future violence.

United States and Canada
Western Illinois University
WEIL#GEO461G Undergraduate   3 credits $795*
Analyzes the regional variations in the physical environments of the U.S. and Canada and studies human beings and their activities in the two countries.
* IL residents tuition: $88 per credit.

United States Politics
University of Oregon
OREG#POL201   Undergraduate   4 credits $374
This introductory course is designed to provide a comprehensive overview of U.S. politics. We will discuss the constitutional foundations of the U.S. government. Once we understand these foundations, we will explore key political institutions in U.S. politics--Congress, the Presidency, bureaucracies, and the media. Other topics to be covered include: an examination of political participation in the U.S., via voting behavior, elections, interest groups and social movements, and an assessment of the overall status of democracy in America.

Urban Politics
Indiana University
INDI#Y308   Undergraduate   3 credits $268
Political behavior in modern American communities; emphasizes the impact of municipal organization, city officials and bureaucracies, social and economic notables, political parties, interest groups, the general public, and protest organizations on urban policy outcomes. Uses SimCity software.

Urban Sociology
University of Southern Colorado
COSO#SOC354   Undergraduate   3 credits $210
How did the city evolve? In what ways are cities different in various parts of the world? Who lives in cities? Are city folk different? How could you plan a city? An in-depth look at urban development throughout history up to modern society, with thoughts on the future of the urban sprawl.

Urban Sociology
University of Missouri
MOCE#SE202   Undergraduate   3 credits $387
This course studies urbanism as a world phenomenon; the ecological and demographic characteristics of cities; and the organization of urban society. Urban topics include status systems; occupational structure; formal and informal associations; racial and cultural relations; forms of communication; housing; and city planning.

Urban Sociology
University of Missouri
MOCE#SO216   Undergraduate   3 credits $387
This course studies urbanism as a world phenomenon; the ecological and demographic characteristics of cities; and the organization of urban society. Urban topics include status systems, occupational structure, formal and informal associations, racial and cultural relations, forms of communication, housing, and city planning. Perquisites: Rural Soc. 1 or equivalent or Soc. 1 or 4.

US Government Organization
Texas Technical University
TETE#POLS1301   Undergraduate   3 credits $???
This course covers constitutions and organization of the governments of the United States, the states in general, and Texas in particular.

Violence in Movies
Christopher Newport University
CHNE#PHIL395B   Undergraduate   3 credits $993
The course will analyze violence in the movies from a philosophical, religious, ethical and aesthetic standpoint. Films will include Pulp Fiction, Unforgiven, Clockwork Orange, Reservoir Dogs, Natural Born Killers, True Romance, among others. Conceptions of violence will be examined, such as violence conceived as spiritual liberations, catharsis, sacrimental participation, expiatory sacrifice, as transgression of societal norms, as social decadence, as a phenomenon that is impervious to scientific and rational analysis, etc.

Vocational Psychology
Walden University
WALD#PSYC8510   Graduate   5 credits $1500
(Course description not available at press time.)

War and Human Experience
California State University - Dominguez Hills
CADO#HUX530   Undergraduate   3 credits $405
An examination, through readings in history and literature, of the nature of war and its effects on individuals, families, groups and communities. The course will draw on a wide range of examples, including conflicts in the ancient world, modern Europe and the United States. Prerequisite: HUX501 is recommended.

Women and Men in a Changing Society
Rio Salado College
RISA#SOC212   Undergraduate   3 credits $186*
A study of the way culture shapes and defines the positions and roles of both men and women in society. Major emphasis on social conditions which may lead to a broadening of sex roles and a reduction of sex-role stereotypes and the implications of these changes. Open to both men and women.
* AZ residents pay $37 per credit.

Women and the American Experience
Pennsylvania State University
PENN#WMNST104   Undergraduate   3 credits $345
Selected aspects of the role of women in U.S. history and culture from colonial to modern times.

Women in Contemporary Society
University of Southern Colorado
COSO#SOC491D   Undergraduate   3 credits $210
From traditional to contemporary, today's woman struggles to define herself in her own way. It's a journey that has been taken by others who have written about their way. This course will help women or men who wish to understand the road contemporary women take. Topics covered will include the history of the women's movement, women in the workforce, women in the home, and more.

Women in Muslim Society
University of Minnesota
MINN#SOC3340 Undergraduate   5 credits $489

Introduction to the role of women in Muslim society from a sociological perspective. Explores what it is to be a woman in a society dominated by Islamic religious values and third world cultures. Topics: literature of women's studies in general, Islamic values in regard to the status of women in particular, and sociological theories of sex roles. Provides comparison of the effects of different political and economic structures on the roles of women in different Muslim societies, including some African, Asian, and Middle Eastern countries. Readings in anthropological and sociological literature, and the autobiographies of Muslim women.

Women in Popular Culture
University of Missouri
MOCE#SO201 Undergraduate   3 credits $387

Drawing on the theoretical framework created by feminist scholars, this course investigates the ways women are portrayed in today's media. Topics include women in television and film, women's magazines, fashion and beauty, self-help books, advertising aimed at women, psychology and women, and ways to reverse traditional views of women. Perquisites: junior standing or Women Studies 105.

Women, Medicine, and Society
University of Iowa
IOWA#131135 Undergraduate   3 credits $240

Like the group enrolled in that first topics course at the University of Iowa, the students who have taken this course through the GCS Program have given it strength through the diversity of their backgrounds. They have included Women's Studies students, women of color, lesbians, "non-traditional" students and those completing a traditional degree, health care workers in a variety of traditional fields from nurses to physicians, healers from methodologies and traditions whose perspectives challenge Western, "scientific" practices, and students who are new to many of these issues. All have contributed important insights.

Working in Modern America
University of Southern Colorado
COSO#SOC431 Undergraduate   3 credits $210

Exploring the changing patterns, structure, and attitudes toward work in the United States today. Contemporary readings will focus on social group identification, the nature of work, unemployment, leisure, and one- and two-family wage earners.

Workplace Violence
Rio Hondo College
RIHO#PAC43025B Undergraduate   0.5 credits $???

This course is designed to present a study of Workplace Violence. Topics include; analysis of characteristics, recognition of potential violent employees and indicators, how to plan and combat violence in the workplace, and examples of workplace plans.

World Geography
Auburn University
AUBU#GY102 Undergraduate   3 credits $126

An examination of the socio-economic patterns of development in Europe, the Pacific World, Latin America, North Africa and the Middle East, and Asia.

World Geography
University of South Florida
FLSO#GY102 Undergraduate   5 qtr. hrs. $???

An examination of the socio-economic patterns of development in Europe, the Pacific World, Latin America, North Africa, the Middle East, and Asia. Important characteristics of the land and people of the major regions of the world. This course is available via correspondence or presented by the computer via the internet/WWW. Students signing up for the Internet version must have access to the Internet e-mail, and Gopher for this version of this course.

World Regional Geography
Indiana University
INDI#G120 Undergraduate   3 credits $268

Analysis of population, culture, environment, and economics of major world regions. Examination of issues of global importance, including development, demographic change, urbanization and migration, and international conflict.

Writing in the Social Sciences
University of Minnesota
MINN#COMP3014 Undergraduate   4 credits $391

Strategies for expressing quantitative or statistical information in clear prose. How statistical tables and summaries interact with written text. How to develop narrative and descriptive techniques for producing case studies and histories. Emphasizes the proper use of qualitative information and case histories in the analysis of complex situations, and how writing should change for different audiences. Intended for social science majors. Prerequisite: Writing Practice requirement or equivalent.

Writing in the Social Sciences
Pennsylvania State University
PENN#ENGL202A Undergraduate   3 credits $345

Instruction in writing persuasive arguments about significant issues in the social sciences. Prerequisites: ENGL015 or ENGL030; fourth-semester standing.

Accredited Course Providers

Auburn University   (AUBU)

Distance Learning and Outreach Technology
204 Mell Hall, Auburn University AL 36849
Accred.: Southern Association of Colleges and Schools
Email: audl@uce.auburn.edu

(334) 844-5103 –   fax:(334) 844-4731
URL: http://www.auburn.edu:80/outreach/dl/

Description: The faculty of Auburn University is pleased to provide you with educational programs that enable you to achieve your educational goals without having to sacrifice other central aspects of your life. Through distance education you can participate in quality educational experiences in your own locale and at times that are convenient to you. Through the use of a variety of delivery options Auburn University academic departments make available to you programs for college credit, personal enrichment and professional development.
Courses: (22) College Algebra (MH140) Criminal Justice (PCJ36) Developmental Psychology (PG212) Economics I (EC200) Economics II (EC202) Entomology (ENT204) Food Plant Sanitation (NFS408) Foundations of Health and Human Performance (HHP201B) Health Science (HHP195) History and Principles of Phys. Ed. (HHP201) International Travel and Tourism (GY320) Introduction to American Government (PO209) Introduction to Film Studies (RTF235) Introduction to Human Geography (GY215) Introductory Psychology (PG201) Occupational Information (VED510) Perspectives in Biology (BI105) Psychology (PG201) Scientific Approaches to Organic Gardening (H204) Society, Culture and the Environment (U101) Survey of Law Enforcement (CJ260) World Geography (GY102)

Bakersfield College   (BAKE)

1801 Panorama Drive, Bakersfield CA 93305
Accred.: Western Association of Schools and Colleges
Email: kloomis@bc.cc.ca.us

(805) 395-4011 (805) 325-6900 fax:
URL: http://www.bc.cc.ca.us/distance/index.html

Description: Online courses provide an opportunity for students to complete all course requirements from their home or office. Depending on the course, students may be required to take proctored or non-proctored examinations. Participants will have the chance to interact with the instructor and other students, regardless of location using a variety of technologies. Online courses allow students with non-traditional work schedules and/or home responsibilities to take college courses and pursue their education. Are online courses right for you?
Courses: (15) Analytic Geometry and Calculus I (MATHB6A) Analytic Geometry and Calculus II (MATHB6B) Basic Functions and Calculus for Business (MATHB2) Calculus III (MATHB6C) Child Health and Safety (CHDVB49) Elementary Probability and Statistics (MATHB22) Expository Composition (ENGLB1A) Financial Accounting (BSADB1A) Intermediate Algebra (MATHBD) Introduction to Computer Information Systems (COMSB2) Introduction to Environmental Technology (ENVTB1B) Introduction to Geology (GEOLB10) Introductory Astronomy (ASTRB1) Ordinary Differential Equations (MATHB6D) Personal Finance (BUSB40)

Barstow College   (BARS)

2700 Barstow Road, Barstow CA 92311
Accred.: Western Association of Schools and Colleges
Email: nolson@bcconline.com

(760) 252-2411 ext. 7319   fax:
URL: http://www.barstow.cc.ca.us/

Description: None of our courses are open entry/open exit. The courses are taught over the Internet through the use of email, discussion groups, interactive forms and online calendars. The cost to take these courses is $13 per unit if the student is a resident of California or is in the military and is based in California. Students may take these courses using either a PC or a Macintosh computer.
Courses: (17) Advanced Internet (COMP101) American Political Institutions (POLI1) Art History & Appreciation (ARTS2) Basic English (ENGL50) Beginning Internet (COMP100) Business Communications (BUSI75) Creative Writing (ENGL7) Descriptive College Physics (PHYS2) Elements of Supervision (MGMT50) English Composition (ENGL1A) Health Education (HEAL1) Introduction to Business (BADM5) Introduction to Literature (ENGL1B) Introduction to Online Courses (COMP111) Issues in Applied Psychology I (PSYC99) Leadership/Human Relations (BADM53) Survey of U.S. History (HIST2A)

Bellevue University   (BELL)

Admissions Office, 1000 Galvin Road South, Bellevue NE 68005
Accred.: North Central Association of Colleges and Schools
Email: bellevue_u@scholars.bellevue.edu

(800) 756-7920 (402) 293-2000 fax:(402) 293-2020
URL: http://www.bellevue.edu/

Description: Bellevue University is an information-age, learning institution that is committed to creating optimum learning environments and assisting students in an accelerated process of life-long learning. With Internet access, students download online software to open the online classroom, interact with professors and students, use online library services and advising.
Courses: (67) Accounting and Information Systems (MBA541) Accounting and Information Systems (MBA642) Advanced Human Resource Management (LDR661) Advanced Law (MBA665) Business Information Systems (MGTC310) Business Processes and Functions (MBA501) Business, Society & Ethics (IBMC360) Capstone Project in IS Technology (MISC460) Communication Skills for MIS (MISC320) Concepts of Leadership and Power (LDR601) Consumer Behavior (BA656) Criminal Justice Agency Accounting (CJAC421) Criminal Justice Human Resources (CJAC310) Cultural Geography (IBMC310) Developing Management Skills (MGTC340) Essentials of Management (MGTC350) Essentials of Marketing (MGTC420) Ethical Issues in Information Systems (MISC440) Ethics, Policy, Law & Criminal Justice (CJAC304) Financial Strategy (MBA612) Fiscal Management (MGTC410) Global Issues of Quality Management (IBMC340) Global Management (BA637) Global Purchasing (IBMC410) Info Management in Criminal Justice (CJAC425) Information Systems Planning (MISC340) International Business (IBMC350) International Economics (IBMC430) International Finance (IBMC420) International Marketing (IBMC450) International Trade Policy (IBMC440) Introduction to Research (MGTC303) Introduction to Statistics (MGTC360) Leadership and Organizational Change (LDR651) Leadership in Formal Organizationals (LDR611) Leadership Models for Organizations (LDR641) Leadership Strategy and Policy (LDR671) Legal & Ethical Issues in Management (MGTC450) Management Essentials (MISC300) Management of Criminal Justice (CJAC303) Management of Criminal Justice (CJAC420) Managerial Finance and Accounting (MISC360) Marketing Research & Communication (IBMC330) Marketing Strategy (MBA652) Operations Management (MGTC440) Operations Management Methods (MISC400) Operations of Markets (MISC420) Organizational Behavior (MBA633) Organizational Theory (MBA634) Overview of Criminal Justice System (CJAC302) Probability & Statistics (IBMC320) Production and Operations Management (MBA626) Professional Leadership Project (LDR681) Professional Project Presentation (MGTC460) Quantitative Methods (BA623) Research and Statistics (CJAC307) Security for Investment Environment (BA616) Seminar in International Business (IBMC460) Special Problems in Criminal Justice (CJAC450) Special Topics in Criminal Justice (CJAC440) Statistics and Quantitative Methods (MBA522) Strategic and Tactical Planning Systems (CJAC430) Strategic Communication Leadership (LDR621) Strategic Management (MBA639) Strategic Management (MGTC411) Survey of the Environment of Business (MBA565) Team and Group Dynamics (LDR631)

Brevard Community College   (BREV)

c/o The Electronic University Network, 1977 Colestin Road, Hornbrook CA 96044

Accred.: Southern Association of Colleges and Schools
Email: euncouncil@aol.com

(800) 225-3276 (541) 482-5871 fax:(541) 482-7544
URL: http://www.wcc-eun.com/brevard/

Description: Brevard Community College, located in the nation's space capital, is a publicly-supported community college that provides degrees, certificates, courses (credit and noncredit), professional training, lifelong learning, and community and cultural services. BCC has campuses in Melbourne, Titusville, and Palm Bay, centers at Patrick Airforce Base and Kennedy Space Center, and the Online Campus through the Electronic University Network. Altogether, the college serves more than 53,000 people, including more than 22,000 credit students, annually. BCC's mission is to provide educational resources for all: the transfer student who plans to go on to a senior college after graduation, the adult who wishes to learn the techniques and skills necessary to enhance current job skills and technical knowledge, the high school student in a remote area who seeks courses not available in his community or wants to earn Advanced Placement college credits, the student outside the U.S. who wants a college education of American style and quality but is unable or unwilling to come to the U.S. for one or two years, the homebound and those with mobility limitations, the adult working on variable or swing-shifts and working parents.

Courses: (55) American Criminal Justice Systems (CCJ1020) American Literature I (AML2012) Art of Being Human (HUM2390) Business Communications (OST2335) Business Mathematics (MTB1103) Business Organizations (PLA2433) C Programming - Advanced C++ (COP1002) Calculus I with Analytic Geometry (MAC1311) Career Discovery & Testing (MFAX0792) Civil Law and Procedure (PLA2203) College Algebra (MAC1104) College Preparatory Writing II (ENCV0001) Communications I (ENC1101) Communications II (ENC1102) Contingency Planning (EVS2611) Contracts (PLA1423) Criminal Law, Litigation, Discovery (PLA1303) Criminology (CCJ1010) Emergency Response (EVS2613) Engineering Graphics I (EGSC1110) Experiential Learning Portfolio I (SLS1371) Financial Accounting (ACG2021) General Biology (BSCC1010) General Psychology I (PSY2013) Hazardous Materials Regs I - OSHA (EVS1640) Health (HSC1100) Health Analysis and Improvement (HLP1081) Health and Nutrition (HUN1100) Hospitality Management (HFT1000) Human Anatomy & Physiology (BSCC1092) Humanities I (HUM2210) Humanities II (HUM2230) Intro to Environmental Science (EVR1001) Introduction to Astronomy (AST1002) Introduction to Data Processing (CGS1000) Introduction to Fire Safety (FFP1000) Legal Research (PLA1104) Legal System & Legal Assistantship (PLA1003) Legal Terminology (OST1435) Logistic Support Analysis (ETI2203) Managerial Accounting (ACG2071) Mastering Microsoft Office (CFPX0448) Material Management II (ETI2228) Materials Management I (ETI2227) Microcomputer Applications (CGS1530) Principles of Economics I (ECO2013) Principles of Economics II (ECO2023) Property Law (PLA1503) Records Management and Filing (OST2335) Statistics (STA2023) Torts (PLA2273) United States History I (AMH2010) United States History II (AMH2020) Western Civilization I (EUH1000) Wills, Trusts, Estates & Probate (PLA2604)

California State University - Dominguez Hills   (CADO)

Humanities External Degree Program, 1000 E. Victoria SAC2-2126, Carson CA 90747

Accred.: Western Association of Schools and Colleges
Email: huxonline@dhvx20.csudh.edu

(310) 243-3300 –   fax:–
URL: http://hux.csudh.edu/

Description: What we offer is a Master of Arts in the Humanities; we are a fully-accredited correspondence program which does NOT require on-campus attendance of any kind. Students can specialize in one of five areas: Art, Music, Literature, Philosophy or History, or they can do a generalized or interdisciplinary study in all five areas. Students must complete 30 units (up to 9 graduate-level units in Humanities can be transferred in) and finish within five years to earn the degree. At present we offer our introductory level courses, as well as selected core courses, with a computer online instruction option, so that students can do assignments and correspond with their instructors and other students via the Internet.

Courses: (36) 19th Century American Literature (HUX575) Alienation Estrangement Subcultures (HUX546) Ancient Mayan Art (HUX576) Archetypal Criticism in Literature (HUX573) Art & Lit of Harlem Renaissance (HUX531) Art Aesthetics and Theory (HUX504) Baroque Music (HUX571) Beethoven (HUX551) Carnegie, Rockefeller and Ford (HUX554) Concert Music (HUX522) Contemporary Art (HUX570) Evolution of Human Culture (HUX540) Female Coming of Age in World Lit. (HUX578) Film Encounter (HUX524) Frank Lloyd Wright (HUX550) Hemingway and Faulkner (HUX553) History (HUX501) History (HUX523) History of the Arab World (HUX579) Literature (HUX502) Morality in 20th Century Thought (HUX548) Music (HUX503) Philosophy (HUX505) Rousseau (HUX552) Stalin (HUX555) Studies in Modern World Literature (HUX556) The Age of Revolution (HUX574) The Autonomous Individual (HUX543) The Biblical Movement (HUX572) The Individual and Society (HUX544) The Living Theatre (HUX521) The Non-Western World (HUX545) The Para-Rational Perspective (HUX542) The Rational Perspective (HUX541) War and Human Experience (HUX530) World Religious Perspectives (HUX547)

California State University - San Marcos   (CASA)

Extended Studies, San Marcos 92096

Accred.: Western Association of Schools and Colleges
Email: es@mailhost1.csusm.edu

(760) 750-4020 (760) 750-4002 fax:(760) 750-3138
URL: http://www.csusm.edu/Extended_Studies/coming.htm

Description: California State University San Marcos Office of Extended Studies offers academic credit and non-credit programs, on-line classes, test preparation workshops and professional certificate programs.

Courses: (7) California History (HIST347) Data-based Instruction (EDUC596) Instructing Special Needs Students (EDUC501) Postmodern Sociology Thought (SOC485) Race and Ethnic Relations (SOC313A) Riding Information Super Highway (HTM423) Sociology and Law (SOC313B)

Carlow College   (CARL)

Office of Continuing Education, 3333 Fifth Avenue, Pittsburgh PA 15213

Accred.: Middle States Association of Colleges and Schools
Email: ehof@carlow.edu

(412) 578.6092 (412) 578.6000 fax:(412) 578.6321
URL: http://www.carlow.edu

Description: Carlow College as a private, Catholic Liberal Arts College located in Pittsburgh, PA. Committed to innovation with regard to access, Carlow has begun to develop online courses with the goal of delivering entire degree programs online.

Courses: (1) Introduction to Application Software (IM101)

Cerro Coso Community College (CECO)
3000 College Heights Blvd. Ridgecrest CA 93555
Accred.: Western Association of Schools and Colleges
Email: jboard@cc.cc.ca.us

(888) 537-6932 (760) 384-6203 fax:(760) 375-6219
URL: http://www.cc.cc.ca.us/cconline/dised.htm

Description: Cerro Coso is committed to serving students with a quality online program. Courses are offered over the internet using a carefully designed class format, that is intuitive for the student and maintains the focus on class content and learning. Online faculty are experienced educators, well versed with online delivery.

Courses: (31) Beginning Database (CSCI52A) Beginning Spreadsheets (CSCI51A) Beginning Word Processing (CSCI50A) Business Correspondence (BSADC55) Business Correspondence (ENGLC55) Business Law I (BSADC18A) C++ Programming (CSCIC28A) Child Development (CHDVC50A) Concepts of Physical Science (PHSCC11) Developing a Web Page Using HTML (CSCIC56C) Developing a Web Page With HTML2 (ART56C) Elementary Spanish I (SPAN1) Elementary Spanish II (SPANC2) Expository Composition (ENGL1A) General Psychology (PSYC1A) History of the US (HIST17A) History of the US II (HISTC17B) Human Relations in Business (BSADC40) Introduction to Administration of Justice (ADMJC50) Introduction to Art (ART10) Introduction to Computers (CSCI2) Introduction to Philosophical Problems (PHILC1) Introduction to Sociology (SOCI1) Introduction to Telecommunications (CSCIC30) Introduction to the Internet (CSCIC56A) Introduction to Windows NT (CSCIC69NT) Music Appreciation (MUSC22) Presentation Software (CSCIC53) Principles of Economics I (ECONC1A) Search Bank Remote Access (INST89SB) The Human Environment (BIOLC34)

Charter Oak State College (CHOA)
66 Cedar Street Newington CT 06111
Accred.: New England Association of Schools and Colleges
Email: mwoodman@commnet.edu

(860) 666-4595 x26   (860) 666-4595 x28   fax:(860) 666-4852
URL: http://www.ctdlc.org

Description: Charter Oak State College is an external degree granting institution specializing in adult learners. We offer personal advising and a variety of ways of earning credits including Portfolio Review, Independent Guided Study and web-based online courses. We are offering the latter through the Connecticut Distance Learning Consortium which we have founded to create an online degree program using over 20 of Connecticut's institutions of higher education.

Courses: (5) Composition (ENG101) Critical Thinking (IDS110) Deviance (SOC371) Introduction to Psychology (PSY101) Western World Literature (ENG252)

Chemeketa Community College (CHEM)
400 Lancaster Dr. P. O. Box 14007 Salem OR 97309
Accred.: Northwest Association of Schools and Colleges
Email: admissions@chemek.cc.or.us

(503) 399-5000 (503) 399-7873 fax:(503) 399-6992
URL: http://bbs.chemek.cc.or.us

Description: Online courses allow you to schedule class time at your convenience from your home or work place. You'll need access to a computer and internet, students participate in class discussions, receive instruction, submit assignments and interact with their instructor. The electronic classroom is available 24 hours per day, seven days per week. Students choose when and from where they will participate.

Courses: (51) Bed & Breakfast Management (HTM112) Child Abuse and Neglect (HDFS260) Child Abuse Workshop (9924) Computer Information Science I (CIS120) Computer Information Science II (CIS121) Cultural Heritage Tourism (HTM111) Current Office Software - Database (CS118C) Current Office Software - Worksheets (CA118B) Dental Epidemiology Update (9435D) Dental Ethics (9435E) Desktop Publishing I - Pagemaker (CA205) English Composition - Logic and Style (WR122) English Composition - Research Writing (WR123) English Composition Exposition (WR121) Facts About Fluoride (9435G) Financial Accounting I (BA211) General Psychology (PSY201) Getting Results with Time Management (BA062G) Health and Fitness for Life (HPE295) History of World Civilization (HST110) How to Delegate Effectively (BA062H) Infection Control in the Dental Office (9435H) Internet For Office Professionals (CA118D) Introduction to American Literature (ENG253) Introduction to Composition (WR115) Introduction to Contemporary Mathematics (MTH105) Introduction to Fiction (ENG104) Introduction to Microcomputer Applications (CS101) Introduction to the Hospitality Industry (HTM100) Introduction to the Leisure and Recreation Industry (HTM108) Job Search Preparation (FE205A) Keyboarding (CA121) Medical Emergency Preparedness (9435A) Meeting and Convention Management (HTM126) Micro Database Software - Access (CS125) Nursing Refresher Theory (9410) Nutrition (FN225) Office Microcomputer Applications (CA210) Office Microcomputer Applications - Windows (CA210W) Philosophical Problems -Metaphysics (PHL201) Prior Learning Resume (CPL120) Stress Management (HS152) Study Skills (HD112) Technical Writing (WR227) Treating the Fearful Patient (9435J) Web Graphics (VC137) Web Photography (VC199P) Web Publishing (0615W) Weight Management (PE185WABC) Word Processing Procedures I - Word for Windows (CA201D) Writing for Management Success (BA062M)

Christopher Newport University (CHNE)
CNU Online 50 Shoe Lane Newport News VA 23606
Accred.: Southern Association of Colleges and Schools
Email: info@cnuonline.cnu.edu

(757) 594-7607 (757) 594-7015 fax:--
URL: http://cnuonline.cnu.edu/

Description: Christopher Newport University offers a variety of courses online through a computer - managed communication system. Using a computer, modem, and regular telephone lines, students are networked with other students, instructors, and teaching resources. Christopher Newport University offers general education, elective and major courses leading to the Bachelor of Science Degree in Governmental Administration (BSGA) and Bachelor of Arts in Philosophy and Religious Studies entirely online. Degree concentrations for the BSGA program include Public Management, Criminal Justice, and International Studies. The B.A. in Philosophy also includes a concentration in Religious Studies. Students may enroll for a combination of online and classroom courses. Online courses may be used to fulfill requirements for any university degree program, transfer to other institutions, or satisfy full degree requirements for the Government and Philosophy departments. Individualized interaction with the instructor and discussions with other class members are available 24 hours a day, 7 days a week through this message based system. Learners are not blocked from pursuing a college degree because of distance from the classroom, care of children, shift work, or employment travel.

Courses: (29) Admin. of Correctional Institutions (GOVT345) Administrative Law (GOVT367) American Political Process (GOVT201) Business Law II (ACCT342) College Writing II (ENGL102) Critical Thinking (PHIL101) Elementary Physics II (PHYS104) Elementary Spanish II (SPAN102) Environmental Ethics (PHIL395) Ethics in Government and Politics (GOVT355) History of Ancient Philosophy (PHIL201G) History of Modern Philosophy (PHIL202G) Human Societies - A Global View (SOCL201G) Ideologies and Politics (GOVT359) Independent Study (GOVT499) International Relations (GOVT321) Intro to Community Planning (GOVT331) Introduction to World Religions (RSTD211) Leadership in Public Organizations (GOVT401) Literature and Ideas II (ENGL208G) Modern Political Systems (GOVT103G) Practicum in Governmental Admin. (GOVT491) Principles of Economics II (ECON201G) Public Budgeting (GOVT391) Quantitative Political Analysis (GOVT352) Quantitative Political Analysis (SOCL392) Research (GOVT492) State and Local Government (GOVT202) Violence in Movies (PHIL395)

City University

(CITY)

c/o The Electronic University Network 1977 Colestin Road Hornbrook CA 96044

Accred.: Northwest Association of Schools and Colleges
Email: euncouncil@aol.com

(800) 225-3276 (541) 482-5871 fax:(541) 482-7544
URL: http://www.wcc-eun.com/city/

Description: City University is a private, non-profit institution of higher education. Its primary purpose is to provide educational opportunities for those segments of the population not being fully served through traditional processes. City University is based on these philosophical principles: education is a lifelong process and must be relevant to the student's aspirations; education should be affordable and offered, as much as possible, at the student's convenience; opportunity to learn should be open to anyone with the desire to achieve.

Courses: (127) Abnormal Psychology (PSY402) Advanced Accounting (AC405) Advanced Environmental Science (SCI301) Advanced Internet Publishing and Web Design (CS350) Advanced Windows Appl. Development (CS464) Advertising (MK390) American Constitutional Law (PLS401) Approaches to Critical Thinking (BC301) Astronomy (SCI302) Auditing (AC411) Bankruptcy Law (PL207) Behavioral Psychology (PSY303) Broadcast Script and News Writing (COM403) Bureaucracy and Regulation (PLS404) Business Ethics (PHI404) Business Law and Ethics (MLA412) Business Organizations (PL203) Business, Government and Society (BSM302) Calculus (MTH220) Civil procedure (PL202) College Geometry (MTH120) Communication and Public Relations (COM303) Consumer Behavior (MK387) Consumer Psychology (PSY307) Contemporary Environmental Issues (INT303) Contemporary Sociological Theory (SOC403) Cost Accounting (AC312) Criminal Behavior (SOC302) Criminal Law (PL208) Data Communications (TM304) Data Structures (CS366) Database Management (CS416) Decision Modeling and Analysis (BSC400) Development of Social Thought (SOC402) Ecological Philosophy (PHI408) Effective Org Communications (BSM304) Efficient and Effective Self-expression (BC302) Electoral Politics and the Mass Media (COM401) Enterprise Networking (CS494) Environmental Ethics (PHI406) Family Law (PL206) Federal Income Taxation I (AC421) Federal Income Taxation II (AC422) Financial Accounting I (AC210) Financial Accounting II (AC220) Financing Organizations (BSC402) Global Economics (BSM406) History of US Mass Communications (COM402) Information Systems (MG416) Intermediate Accounting I (AC301) Intermediate Accounting II (AC302) Intermediate Accounting III (AC303) International Business (BSM404) International Economic Problems (INT302) International Law (INT304) International Marketing (MK388) International Relations (INT301) Internet Client/Servers (CS443) Interpretation of Financial Accounting (BSC401) Interpreting Statistics and Data (BC303) Intro to Internet and Web Publishing (CS340) Introduction to Environmental Science (NAS215) Introduction to Geoscience (NAS201) Introduction to Philosophy (HUM200) Introduction to Political Science (SSC218) Introduction to Visual Basic (CS220) ISDN and Broadband ISDN (TM490) JAVA Programming (CS440) Journalistic Writing (COM301) Juvenile Delinquency (SOC304) LAN Implementation (CS394) Legal & Ethical Communication (COM305) Legal Issues in the Workplace (BSC403) Legal Writing and Research (PL204) Lifespan Development - Adulthood (PSY305) Lifespan Development Psychology (PSY401) Local Area Networks (CS390) Marketing Research (MK386) Marketing Strategy (MK400) Medical Ethics (PHI403) Memory and Cognition (PSY301) Meteorology (SCI304) Morality and the Law (PHI405) Network Design (CS490) Network Operating Systems Survey (CS392) Object-Oriented Programming C++ (CS364) Oceanography (SCI303) Operating Systems (CS470) Operations Management (BSM405) Personal Injury Litigation and Torts (PL201) Philosophy of Corporations (PHI409) Political Economy (PLS403) Political Economy of the Third World (INT405) Political Parties and Interest Groups (PLS405) Politics of War and Peace (INT403) Principles of Information Processing (CS241) Probate Law (PL205) Program Design in C (CS362) Programming Language Survey (CS423) Race and Ethnic Relations in the US (SOC303) Real Estate Law (PL209) Research and Business Applications (CS445) Science, Technology, Community (BC304) Services Marketing (MK389) Social Psychology (PSY302) Social, Political, Cultural Controversies (BC305) Sociology of Education (SOC401) Sociology of the Third World (INT404) Sociology of Work (SOC405) Software Project Management (CS480) State & Local Government and Politics (PLS304) System Development in Visual Basic (CS322) System Development Methodologies (CS420) Systems Analysis OOD (CS450) The Congress (PLS302) The Effective Organization (BSC407) The Family (SOC301) The Philosophy of Cultures & Nations (PHI407) The Presidency (PLS301) The Supreme Court (PLS303) The United States in World Affairs (INT401) Trigonometry (MTH130) Understanding Consumer Behavior (BSC300) US Constitutional Civil Liberties (PLS402) Uses and Abuses of Ethics (BC306) Visual/Photo Communication (COM304) Volcanology (SCI401)

College of DuPage

(DUPA)

425 22nd St. Glen Ellyn IL 60137-6599

Accred.: North Central Association of Colleges and Schools
Email: schiesz@cdnet.cod.edu

(630) 942-2800 (630) 942-3326 fax:(630) 942-3764
URL: http://www.cod.edu/online

Description: The College of DuPage is a fully accredited local community college offering 2-year degrees and certificates. The college is located in the far western suburbs of Chicago Illinois. Overall the college serves an enrollment of 34,000 each 10-week academic term. Twelve online courses are offered to distance learning students through our Center for Independent Learning as of Fall term 1998. The center has an overall enrollment of 5,000 distance learning students who are enrolled in 140 different courses which are delivered in a variety of alternative learning formats such as telecourses, local cable and radio broadcast courses. The 12 courses offered online are in the subject areas of Computer training, English composition, Business courses, Economics, Office Technology and Human Services. The college is planning and working toward offering an entire AA degree option through online course delivery in the near future.

Courses: (10) Business Correspondence (OFC150) Codependency (HUMS291) Composition (EN101, 102, 103) Introduction to Business (BUS100) Introduction to Computers (CIS100) Introduction to Local Area Networks (CIS151) Macroeconomics (ECO201) Principles of Management (MGT210) Supervision (MGT100) Writing for Non-Natives (EN070)

Dakota State University

(DAKO)

Mundt Library Madison SD 57042

Accred.: North Central Association of Colleges and Schools
Email: dsuinfo@columbia.dsu.edu

(800) 641-4309 (605) 256-5049 fax:(605) 256-5208
URL: http://www.courses.dsu.edu/disted/internet.htm

Description: Dakota State University, established in 1881, has offered Web courses since 1990 and recently expanded a distance education program to provide technology-based education to students nationally and internationally. Located in southeast South Dakota, DSU offers a variety of courses with an emphasis in Information Systems and English for Information Systems. A fully accredited bachelor degree will be available in 1998 and there are plans for additional baccalaureate degrees and two masters degrees in the future.

Courses: (25) Advanced Composition (ENGL301) Advanced Health Data Systems (HIM444) Basic Programming (CSC130) Career Planning (SOC110) COBOL I (CSC221) Computer Text Analysis (ENGL350) Computers in the Humanities (CHUM650) Current Trends In Health Care Delivery (HIM443) English Composition (ENGL101) Fund Raising (NFP315) Grant and Report Writing (ENGL305) Introduction to Literature (ENGL210) Introduction To Music (MUS100) Management of Health Info. Centers I (HIM360) Management of Health Info. Centers II (HIM361) Native American Studies (HIST379) Principles of Programming (CSC150) Programming for GUI (CSC403) Research Methods in Healthcare (HIM350) Seminar In Health Information Management (HIM498) Social Institutions (SOC380) Social Systems and Technology (SOC360) Technical Report Writing (ENGL405) The Information Society (SOC285) Writing SBIR Proposals (ENGL670)

Darton College (DART)

2400 Gillionville Road Albany GA 31707

Accred.: Southern Association of Colleges and Schools
Email.: robbinsc@mail.dartnet.peachnet.edu

(912) 430-6730 (912) 430-6732 fax:(912) 430-6698
URL: http://www.dartnet.peachnet.edu/

Description: The geographic location of Darton's Primary Service Area and the demographic composition of its population make distance learning a critical component of the College's outreach program and enhances the College's mission to provide prebaccalareate instructional programs. Darton College currently offers college credit instruction at a distance via compressed video conferencing, cable television, video tape, and the World Wide Web.

Courses: (1)English Composition I (ENG101)

Delaware County Community College (DECO)

Registrar's Office 901 S. Media Line Road Media PA 19063

Accred.: Middle States Association of Colleges and Schools
Email: rsmolens@dcccnet.dccc.edu

(610) 359-5365   fax:
URL: http://www.dccc.edu/cyber/cyber.html

Description: Delaware County CyberCollege is designed to provide accessible and cutting-edge technology training and services to a broad-based constituency. Recognizing the increasingly competitive higher education market, the dissolution of geographic boundaries, and the proliferation of "virtual" courses and programs, CyberCollege was created in the fall of 1997 to respond to these challenges. Its goal is to design and deliver cutting-edge technology-based instruction and training on campus, in educational and corporate settings, and via distributed learning technologies. Our current projects include a multimedia/web development certificate program, staff "exchange programs" with corporate partners, and the creation of 5-10 web-based courses by January 1999. In addition, we are actively pursuing partnership and grant opportunities with several local, national, and international corporations.

Courses: (7) C++ Programming (DPR226) Introduction to Pharmacology (PHA01) Multimedia Design and Development I (MCR20151) Multimedia Design and Development II (MCR20253) Online Pharmacology (AHA290) Publishing on WWW with HTML (DPR999) Visual Basic (DPR222)

Eastern Oregon University (EAOR)

Extended Programs, Zabel Hall, Rm. 232 1410 L Ave. La Grande OR 97850

Accred.: Northwest Association of Schools and Colleges
Email: jhart@eou.edu

(541) 962-3614   fax:(541) 962-3627
URL: http://www.eou.edu/dep

Description: Eastern embeds its distance learning program within its regional mission to serve a sparsely populated (140,000) ten-county area of Eastern Oregon that is approximately the size of the state of Pennsylvania; this unification of on-campus and off-campus efforts has lead to a remarkably high participation rate (67%) by the on-campus faculty in the off-campus delivery programs. The university has recently been mandated to create, in collaboration with Treasure Valley CC and Blue Mountain CC, a model virtual institution for the state system—the Eastern Oregon Collaborative Colleges Center. Eastern is now extending its rural delivery expertise into the delivery of degrees to other parts of Oregon and to wider partnerships with virtual institutions such as the Western Governors University.

Courses: (70) American Labor and Unions (ECON481) American National Government (POLS101) American Women's History (HIST410A) Applied Anatomy (PEH321) Applied Discourse Theory (WR206) Approaches to Grammar (ENGL316) Business Communication (OADM225) Business Law (BA254) Cartography I (GEOG201) Cartography II (GEOG306) Comparative Politics (POLS200) Computerized Accounting (OADM210A) Congress (POLS311) Critical Thinking (PHIL203) Desktop Publishing Applications (OADM210E) Environmental Report Writing (GEOG319) Environmental Research (GEOG01) Environmental Science (SCI241) Expository Prose Writing (WR121) For All Practical Purposes I (MATH110) For All Practical Purposes II (MATH110) Foundations of Elementary Math I (MATH211) Foundations of Elementary Math II (MATH212) Foundations of Elementary Math III (MATH213) Foundations of Visual Literacy (ART101) History of the American West (HIST410B) History of the Pacific Northwest (HIST410C) Human Anatomy (BIOL210) Human Physiology (BIOL232) Individual Income Taxation (BA333) International Relations (POLS221) Introduction to Expository Writing (WR115) Introduction to Literature (ENGL104) Introduction to Literature (ENGL104) Lifestyle Abuse (PEH350) Machine Transcription (OADM222) Macroeconomics (ECON375) Major American Writers I (ENGL253) Major American Writers II (ENGL254) Management Science (BA366) Managerial Economics (ECON340) Money and Banking (ECON318) Motivation (PSY345) Non-Profit Accounting (BA420) Nutrition (PEH325) Office Procedures I (OADM261) Office Procedures II (OADM262) Principles of Development-Lifespan (PSY311) Principles of Finance (BA313) Principles of Learning (PSY343) Professional Development (OADM264) Public Administration (POLS351) Public Policy (POLS350) Report Writing (BA225) Retailing Management (BA350) Screenwriting Fundamentals (WR310) Selected Topics in Writing (WR210) Skills for Healthy Living II (PEH351) State & Local Government (POLS314) Survey of Social Psychology (PSY310) Tao, Zen & Baseball - Asian Influences on Management Thought (BA407) Technical Writing (WR320) The Middle and Far East, The Mediterranean, Medieval Europe (HIST101) Word Processing - Executive (OADM210B) Word Processing - Legal (OADM210C) Word Processing - Medical (OADM210D) Word Processing I (OADM123) Word Processing II (OADM124) World Civilization Since 1500 (HIST102) Writing Fundamentals of Screenwriting (WR310)

Edmonds Community College (EDMO)

Center for Continuing Education 20000 68th Avenue West Lynnwood WA 98036

Accred.: Northwest Association of Schools and Colleges
Email: sloreen@edcc.edu

(425) 640-1010 (425) 640-1361 fax:(425) 640-1496
URL: http://www.cce.edcc.edu/cce/edol.htm

Description: Join a growing number of students on the EdCC campus and throughout the nation who are earning college credits and completing a degree or certificate through Distance Learning. Distance Learning classes at Edmonds are taught as either Telecourses (video-based) or Online (computer/Internet based) courses. Register for these self-support courses through the regular registration process or through Continuing Education.

Courses: (42) Access/Windows (PCAPP118) Accounting Fundamentals (OTA121) American Government (POLSC104) Basic Fire Investigation (FCA120) Building Construction (FCA152) Business English (OTA107) Business Law (BUS240) Codes & Inspection Procedures (FCA195) Employee Skills Assessment (JOBDV105) Excel On Line (PCAPP167) Financial Accounting I (ACCT201) Financial Accounting II (ACCT202) Fire Protection Systems (FCA137) Fire Service Management (FCA232) Fire Service Supervision (FCA231) Greek and Roman History (HIST111) Greek Mythology (HUM109) History of Washington/Pacific NW (HIST204) Incident Management I (FCA161) Incident Management II (FCA261) Intermediate Business Computing (CIS102) Interviewing Techniques (JOBDV120) Introduction to Business (BUS100) Introduction to Business Computing (CIS100) Introduction to Technical Writing (ENG231) Introduction to the Internet (PCAPP256) Japanese Word Processing (OTA114) Job Search-Job Survival (JOBDV115) Managerial Accounting (ACCT203) On Line Internet Basics (PCAPP155G) Powerpoint On Line (PCAPP194) Practical Accounting (ACCT101) Resumes That Get Results (JOBDV110) Small Business Management (MGMT260) Teaching On Line (PCAPP257) The Ancient World (ENGL140) Transition to College (BR111) Web Page Design-HTML (PCAPP155) Western Civilization I (HIST104) Western Civilization III (HST106) Windows 95 (PCAPP157) Word 7.0 On Line (PCAPP185)

352

Embry-Riddle Aeronautical University   (EMRI)

Department of Independent Studies 600 South Clyde Morris Blvd. Daytona Beach FL 32114

Accred.: Southern Association of Colleges and Schools
Email: galloglj@cts.db.erau.edu

(800) 866-6271 (904) 226-6263 fax:(904) 226-7627
URL: http://ec.db.erau.edu/

Description: The Department of Independent Studies is an integral part of the Extended Campus with close links to the College of Career Education (CCE). It was established in July 1980 in response to the realization that even the rapidly growing number of CCE resident centers in the United States and abroad would never be able to reach everyone who had an ambition for higher education degree programs in aviation and aerospace related fields. Some prospective students lived in small communities where establishment of a resident center was not feasible; others lived and worked in isolated areas around the world. Still others worked in professions where the word "schedule" had no real meaning. The Department of Independent Studies was developed to extend to these people the opportunity to complete an Embry-Riddle degree at their own locations and their own schedules, but still continue to adhere to all University requirements.

Courses: (16) Advanced Aviation/Aero Planning (MAS636) Air Carrier Operations (MAS620) Aircraft and Spacecraft Development (MAS603) Airport Operations and Management (BA645) Airport Operations Safety (MAS613) Aviation/Aero Accident & Safety (MAS608) Aviation/Aerospace Communications (MAS606) Aviation/Aerospace Distribution (MAS640) Aviation/Aerospace Industrial Safety (MAS612) Aviation/Aerospace System Safety (MAS611) Corporate Aviation Operations (MAS622) Graduate Research Project (MAS690) Human Factors in Aviation/Aero (MAS604) Research Methods and Statistics (MAS605) Seminar in Aviation Labor Relations (BA632) The Air Transportation System (MAS602)

Emporia State University   (EMPO)

Campus Box 4052 1200 Commercial St. Emporia KS 66801

Accred.: North Central Association of Colleges and Schools
Email: conted@emporia.edu

(316) 341-5385 (316) 341-5314 fax:(316) 341-5744
URL: http://www.emporia.edu/conted/home.htm

Description: The Office of Lifelong Learning is the organizational and managerial support system for extending ESU's resources beyond its campus to those who want to further their education. Students may pursue undergraduate and graduate degrees, seek professional development, or meet recertification requirements through our offerings.

Courses: (19) Activity Ideas for Elementary Phy Ed (PE700) Advanced Techniques in HPER (PE700) Business & Computer Curriculum (BE882) Computer Networks & Internets (CS410) Conflict Resolution (SP500) Health & Wellness for Children (HL700) Health, Sport & Movement Science (PE707) Information Needs of Seniors (LI861) Instructional Design (IT841) Internet for Math Educators (IT743) Internet Resources & Tools for Educators (IT744) Introduction to PASCAL (CS250) Principles of Career/Technical Education (E581) Remote Sensing (ES771) Research Problems in Earth Science (ES739) Research Problems in Health (PE868) Scenarios & Information Planning (LI863) Shakespeare Online (EN540) Using the World Wide Web (SP370)

Fayetteville Technical Community College   (FAYE)

P. O. Box 35236 Fayetteville NC 28303

Accred.: Southern Association of Colleges and Schools
Email: bervin@atlas.faytech.cc.nc.us

(910) 678-8425   fax:–
URL: http://www.faytech.cc.nc.us/infodesk/vcampus/vcampus.html

Description: FTCC's Virtual Campus is a selection of standard, full-credit college and continuing education classes being offered to the global audience of the Web. Classes are kept to a size where instructors can provide the same level of personal interaction they do in the traditional classroom. The Virtual Campus uses the World Wide Web, email, and other Internet resources to provide opportunities for meaningful student-to-faculty and student-to-student interaction.

Courses: (41) Abnormal Psychology (PSY281) American Literature II (ENG232) Art Appreciation (ART111) Basic PC Literacy (CIS111) British Literature I (ENG241) Business Finance (BUS225) Business Law I (BUS115) Business Law II (BUS116) College Algebra (MAT161) Cost Accounting (ACC225) Creative Writing I (ENG125) Developmental Psychology (PSY241) Embalming Theory I (FSE210) Embalming Theory II (FSE212) Expository Writing (ENG111) General Chemistry I (CHM151C) General Psychology (PSY150) Human Resource Management (BUS153) Infants, Toddlers, & Twos (EDU234) Intermediate Accounting I (ACC220) Intro to Sociology (SOC210) Introduction to Audio Concepts (MIT120) Introduction to Business (BUS110) Introduction to Distance Learning (MIT110) Introduction to the Internet (CIS172) Literature-Based Research (ENG113) Mathematical Models (MAT115) Principles Of Accounting I (ACC120) Principles of Funeral Service (FSE112) Principles of Macroeconomics (ECO252) Principles of Management (BUS137) Principles of Marketing (MKR120) Principles of Microeconomics (ECO251) Principles of Supervision (BUS135) Professional Research & Reporting (ENG114) Psychology of Death and Dying (PSY141) Social Problems (SOC220) Spreadsheets I (CIS120) Survey of Economics (ECO151) Trends in Technology (CIS226) World Literature I (ENG261)

Front Range Community College   (FRCC)

Distance Education 3645 West 112th Ave. Westminster CO 80030

Accred.: North Central Association of Colleges and Schools
Email: gertrude@cccs.cccoes.edu

(303) 404-5554 (303) 404-5513 fax:(303) 404-5156
URL: http://www.frcc.cc.co.us/

Description: In its Distance Learning program, FRCC seeks to enhance its basic mission of providing high quality educational services for students. The use of telecommunications technologies for instruction allows FRCC to reach out to a large population that has been for the most part unserved by traditional delivery methods. Within the program, we are engaged in an ongoing process of balancing the extension of access and attempting to keep up with technological advances on the one hand with the maintenance of high standards for quality and rigor on the other.

Courses: (30) C Language Programming (CSC230) Civil Litigation (PAR221) Computer Applications For Paralegals (PAR125) Computer Information Systems (CIS115) Cooperative Education (LST297) Creative Writing I (ENG221) Cultural Anthropology (ANT101) English Composition I (ENG121) English Composition II (ENG122) General Psychology I (PSY101) General Psychology II (PSY102) Human Biology (BIO116) Interpersonal Communication (SPE125) Intro to Java Programming (CSC226) Intro to Legal Studies (PAR121) Intro to UNIX Administration (CIS178) Introduction to Business (BUS115) Introduction to Literature I (LIT115) Organizational Communication (SPE225) Principles of Speech Communication (SPE115) Principles of Supervision (MAN116) Research For Paralegals (PAR124) Special Topics - Education (LST290) Technical Writing I (ENG132) Technical Writing II (ENG132) U.S History I (HIS201) U.S. History II (HIS202) UNIX (CIS175) Western Civilization I (HIS101) Western Civilization II (HIS102)

The Internet University - Accredited Course Providers

George Mason University   (GEMA)
Program on Social and Organizational Learning Fairfax VA 22030
Accred.: Southern Association of Colleges and Schools
Email: bcox@gmu.edu
(703) 993-1142   fax:–
URL: http://www.virtualschool.edu/courses
Description: Virtual School and Taming the Electronic Frontier is a project of George Mason University and Alternative Technology Corporation to offer web and video based courses on a not-for-credit basis. Three courses are currently offered to commercial and Graduate School, USDA customers worldwide.
Courses: (5) Economy as Ecosystem (LRNG592) Internet Literacy (LRNG592) Interpretive Social Science (LRNG792) Objects as Property (LRNG731) Taming the Electronic Frontier (LRNG572)

Golden Gate University   (GOLD)
536 Mission Street San Francisco CA 94105
Accred.: Western Association of Schools and Colleges
Email: cybercampus@ggu.edu
(888) 874-2923 (415) 442-7060 fax:(888) 896-2394
URL: http://cybercampus.ggu.edu/
Description: CyberCampus is the latest, cutting edge endeavor of Golden Gate University. CyberCampus is designed to provide a comprehensive team-based, high quality environment, which allows students to improve the quality of their lives by making education a more flexible and convenient experience. Courses are taught entirely over the World Wide Web in combination with textbooks and articles of the instructor's selection. Lectures for web-based courses may take the form of step-by-step modules through web pages designed by faculty. Access to these web pages is strictly limited to class participants. As a CyberCampus student you will receive exceptional instructional, technical and administrative support.
Courses: (41) Accounting Information Systems (ACCTG319A) Advanced Federal Income Taxation (TA318) Applied Regression Analysis (MATH104) Business Internet Access and Usage (TM396F) Business Policy and Strategy (MGT362) Business Writing (ENGL120) Calculus I (MATH100) Database Management Systems (CIS315) Electronic Commerce via the Internet (TM396H) Elements of Arts Administration (AA300) Expository Writing (ENGL1A) Federal Tax Procedure (TA319) Finance & Budgeting in Arts Admin (AA303) Financial Analysis for Management (FI203) Financial Management (FI100) Fund Raising in Arts Administration (AA304) Graduate Writing II (ENGL301) Healthcare Finance (HM306) Healthcare Information Systems (HM312) Healthcare Marketing (HM308) International Business Management (MGT304) Legal & Ethical Aspects of Healthcare (HM305) Legal Aspects of Arts Administration (AA302) Managed Care Concepts (HM302) Management Information Systems (CIS125) Management Information Systems (CIS301) Management Theory & Applications (MGT310) Managerial Communications (MGT300) Marketing & PR in Arts Administration (AA301) Marketing Management (MKT300) Organizational Development (PAD306) Quantitative Analysis for Mgmt (MATH106) Research Writing (ENGL1B) Statistics (MATH40) Tax Characterization (TA330) Tax Research and Decision Making (TA329) Tax Timing (TA338) Technical Analysis of Securities (FI352) Telecommunications Management (TM301) Transmission Systems (TM315) Worldwide Special Event Tourism (HRTM138)

Great Basin College   (GRBA)
Admissions Office 1500 College Parkway Elko NV 89801
Accred.: Northwest Association of Schools and Colleges
Email: hyslop@scs.unr.edu
(702) 753-2305 (702) 738-8493 fax:(702) 738-8771
URL: http://www.scs.unr.edu/gbc/
Description: Great Basin College is a community college located in Elko, Nevada. It has been offering online courses for the last four years via a BBS. In Fall semester, 1997, 170 students participated in fourteen courses taught by seven instructors in English, Nursing, Philosophy, Accounting and Computer Applications. We are moving all online classes onto the Internet. The course offerings are constantly expanding, making it difficult to maintain an up-to-date list on CASO. Visit our web page to see a current list of classes.
Courses: (16) Basic Mathematics Online (MATH091) Building Web Pages (COT207B) Computer Literacy (COT105) Current Economic Issues (ECON104) English Composition (ENG101) Exploring the Internet (COT133B) Intro to Spreadsheets – MS Excel 97 (COT134) Introduction to QuickBooks (COT198B) Introduction to Windows 95 (COT204) Introduction to WordPerfect 6.1 for Windows (COT198B) Microcomputer Accounting Systems (ACC220) PowerPoint for Microsoft Office 95 (COT136B) Religion in American Life (PHIL145) Science Fiction (ENG190) Spreadsheets in the Workplace (COT132B) Technical Communications (ENG107)

Greenville Technical College   (GRTE)
506 South Pleasantburg Drive P. O. Box 5616 Greenville SC 29606
Accred.: Southern Association of Colleges and Schools
Email: moreinfo@college-online.com
(800) 723-0670 (864) 250-8130 fax:–
URL: http://college-online.com/
Description: The new opportunities brought about by the Internet gave Greenville Tech another way to offer courses. College Online offers the ultimate in convenience and flexibility for the student. This program is perfect for the student that, for whatever reason, cannot make it to campus to take a course. Currently the college is focusing our online effort in the Computer Technology and Office Systems Technology areas. More courses will be added in these areas each semester. Courses in other areas will be added regularly also. An acceptable ASSET/ACT/SAT score will be necessary for you to be formally admitted into a certificate or degree program. However you may take up to two courses as a Personal/Career Development or transfer.
Courses: (12) Computers and Programming (CPT114) Digital Circuits (EET145) Information Processing (EET145) Introduction to Computers (CPT101) Introduction to Internet Searching (CPT105) Microcomputer Applications (CPT270) Office Communications (OST234) Office Procedures I (OST141) Office Spreadsheet Applications (OST261) Operating Systems Fundamentals (CPT255) Systems & Procedures (CPT264) Western Civilization to 1689 (HIS101)

Harvard University Extension   (HARV)
The Distance Education Program 1 Oxford Street, Science Center 906 Cambridge MA 02138
Accred.: New England Association of Schools and Colleges
Email: dep@fas.harvard.edu
(617) 496-4836   fax:(617) 495-0975
URL: http://lab.dce.harvard.edu/~dep
Description: The Distance Education Program (DEP) at the Harvard University Extension School offers a series of calculus courses via the Internet. Through DEP, high school, college-level and adult students learn calculus, gain valuable skills and interact with instructors and other students throughout the country – without leaving their own home or school. The courses are taught remotely using Calculus & Mathematics (C&M), an interactive computer-based calculus course developed at the University of Illinois by NetMath, a coalition of universities based at the University of Illinois dedicated to the teaching of the mathematical sciences via the Internet.
Courses: (7) Approximations (MATHE14B) Differential Equations (MATHE13) Internet Architecture and Protocols (CSCIE131) Multivariable Functions (MATHE13B) Multivariable Functions (MATHE20B) The Derivative (MATHE13A) The Integral (MATHE4A)

Heriot-Watt University   (HERI)

c/o The Electronic University Network   1977 Colestin Road   Hornbrook CA 96044

Accred.: NONE

Email: euncouncil@aol.com

(800) 225-3276 (541) 482-5871 fax:(541) 482-7544
URL: http://www.wcc-eun.com/heriotwatt/

Description: The Heriot-Watt University MBA by Distance Learning is one of the largest and best-known MBAs in the world, with over 10,000 students in more than 100 countries. The University operates under a Royal Charter, granted in 1966, the highest accreditation possible in the United Kingdom. The MBA program is highly ranked by the US Graduate Management Admissions Council. The University's technological base and Business School are located at Riccarton, about eight miles west of the center of Edinburgh, Scotland. Course materials are built on learning materials already proven very successful for training within business and industry (for such organizations as American Express, Atlantic Container Lines, BP, Digital, Hewlett-Packard, IBM, and Rolls-Royce. The courses are designed to equip managers with practical skills, and can be completed while students remain fully employed. Courses are written at the highest academic standards and are demanding both of time and intellectual energy. To succeed, students need to be highly motivated and committed. The MBA Program requires no campus attendance. The rigorous, internationally recognized program can be done on your schedule, at home or while traveling with online Instructor Guidance. Yet the costs of the program are substantially less than on-campus counterparts. The curriculum consists of nine courses. The seven required courses are: Accounting, Economics, Finance, Marketing, Organizational Behavior, Quantitative Methods, and Strategic Planning. Two electives can be chosen from a growing list, which currently includes: Decision-Making Techniques, Government and Industry, International Trade and Finance, Negotiation, Strategies for Change, and Strategic Information Systems. Courses may be taken in any order. Exams are given in late June and late November each year at locations selected for easy access by students. Taking three courses each six months the program can be completed in 18 months, though two years is more typical of distance learning students.

Courses: (14) Accounting (01) Decision-Making Techniques (08) Economics (02) Finance (03) Financial Risk Management (09) Government, Industry & Privatization (10) International Trade & Finance (11) Marketing (04) Negotiation (12) Organizational Behavior (05) Quantitative Methods (06) Strategic Information Systems (13) Strategic Planning (07) Strategies for Change (14)

Honolulu Community College   (HONO)

874 Dillingham Boulevard Honolulu HI 96817

Accred.: Western Association of Schools and Colleges

Email: beryl@hcc.hawaii.edu

(808) 845-9211   fax:(808) 845-9173
URL: http://www.hcc.hawaii.edu/

Description: HCC Online is Honolulu Community College's web site for the delivery of online courses and course materials. Some courses are offered totally online, and at most you may need to come to campus to take examinations. Other courses provide online materials as supplements to classroom instruction. In most cases, the online materials provided include links to other web sites directly related to the courses.

Courses: (8) Construction Materials (DRAF26) Introduction to Internet Resources (CENT102) Introduction to Political Futures (POLS110) Introduction to Political Futures (POLS171) Media and Politics (POLS190) Survey of Astronomy (AST110) Trigonometry and Analytic Geometry (MATH140) World Civilization (HIST151)

Humboldt State University   (HUMB)

Academic Information and Referral Center   Siemens Hall 210,1 Harpst St.   Arcata CA 95521

Accred.: Western Association of Schools and Colleges

Email: extended@laurel.humboldt.edu

(707) 826-3731 (707) 826-4241 fax:(707) 826-5885
URL: http://www.humboldt.edu

Description: Registration in classes requires no formal application to the university. Transcripts or high school diplomas are not required to enroll. However, students may be required to provide proof of completion of course prerequisites. There are no residency requirements. Upon recommendation of their principal or counselor, high school students who have completed their sophomore year with a B (3.0) grade point average or better may register for courses at HSU. Registration forms and information are available at the Office of Extended Education. Credit earned may be applied toward a degree at HSU or other collegiate institutions.

Courses: (10) Directed Study (NRPI318) Economics of a Sustainable Society (ECON309) Environmental & Natural Resources Economics (ECON423) First Year Reading and Composition (ENGL100) Geographic Information Systems (CIS499) Goddesses in World Mythology (RS390) Introduction to Ecotourism Planning & Management (NRPI218) Living Myths (RS300) Streaming Internet Technologies (CIS180) Symbols, Themes and Traditions in Mythology (RS399)

Indiana University   (INDI)

Director of Continuing Studies 202 Owen Hall Bloomington IN 47405

Accred.: North Central Association of Colleges and Schools

Email: bulletin@indiana.edu

(800) 334-1011 (812) 855-2292 fax:(812) 855-8680
URL: http://www.extend.indiana.edu/univ/internet.htm

Description: Indiana University's Division of Extended Studies offers a national award-winning selection of university independent study courses. Whether you are in school, employed, or busy being a parent, you'll find that taking an independent study course from IU is a great way to enrich and simplify your life. Whatever your situation, you can gain something from this nationally recognized program. Who knows–you may even discover a new you. Indiana University and the School of Continuing Studies are committed to providing educational opportunities to all interested citizens in the state and elsewhere through quality programs. The School brings the resources of the University to serve people who cannot take advantage of the traditional formal programs at fixed campus locations. We continually update and revise our programming to provide personal, intellectual, and professional enrichment through independent study courses and associate's and bachelor's degrees in general studies. The student is given one year to complete a course once enrolled (18 months for international students and there are extensions).

Courses: (100) Abnormal Psychology (P324) American Constitutional Law I (Y304) American Juvenile Justice System (P375) American Labor History (L101) American Literature since 1914 (L354) American Politics through Film and Fiction (Y373) American Social History, 1865 to Present (A317) An Introduction to Film (C190) Ancient Greek Philosophy (P201) Basic Accounting Skills (A100) Business & Professional Communication (S223) Business Communications (X204) Children's Literature (L390) Classical Mythology (C205) Collective Bargaining (L250) Colloquium in Scholastic Journalism (J525) Comparative Labor Movements (L375) Contemporary Labor Problems (L105) Corrections and Criminal Justice (P303) Culture and Society (E105) Deviant Behavior and Social Control (S320) Dynamics of Outdoor Recreation (R271) English Literature from 1600 to 1800 (L298) Europe - Napoleon to the Present (H104) Europe - Renaissance to Napoleon (H103) Europe in the Twentieth Century II (B362) Grievance Arbitration (L320) Grievance Representation (L220B) Health Problems in the Community (C366) History of Africa II (E432) History of Women in the United States (H260) Human Origins and Prehistory (A105) Introduction to American Politics (Y103) Introduction to Computer Science (C211) Introduction to Criminal Justice (P100) Introduction to Fiction (L204) Introduction to Folklore (F101) Introduction to Folklore in the US (F131) Introduction to Human Geography (G110) Introduction to International Relations (Y109) Introduction to Marketing (M300) Introduction to Poetry

(L205) Introduction to Political Theory (Y105) Introduction to Shakespeare (L220) Introductory Psychology I (P101) Introductory Psychology II (P102) Labor and the Economy (L230) Labor and the Media (L290A) Labor and the Political System (L203) Labor Law (L201) Late Plays of Shakespeare (L314) Latin American Culture and Civilization I (H211) Marriage and Family Interaction (F258) Medical Terms from Greek and Latin (C209) Modern East Asian Civilization (H207) Nineteenth-Century British Fiction (L348) Occupational Health and Safety (L240) Operations of International Enterprises (D302A) Our Planet and Its Future (G116) People with Disabilities (A201A) Personal Finance (F260) Personnel Management in Public Sector (V373) Political Parties and Interest Groups (Y301) Political Terrorism (Y200B) Population (S305) Principles of Risk and Insurance (N300) Principles of Urban Economics (G330) Psychology of Personality (P319) Recreation Activities and Leadership (R272) Recreational Sports Programming (R324) Religion and Society (S313) Retail Management (M419) Science Fiction (L230B) Sex Discrimination and the Law (Y200A) Social Change (S215) Social Problems (R121) Social Psychology (P320) Social Theory (S340) Sports in History (H233) State Politics in the United States (Y306) Supervision of School Publications (J425) Survey of Unions and Collective Bargaining (L100) Teaching Secondary School Reading (L517) The Community (S309) The Community (S309) The International Business Environment (D301) The International Business Environment (D301A) The Occult in Western Civilization (X207) The Occult in Western Civilization (X207) The United States, 1917-1945 (A314) The United States, 1917-1945 (A314) Theories of Crime and Deviance (P200) Theories of the Labor Movement (L380) Union Government and Organization (L270) Unions & Collective Bargaining (L100) United States, 1829-1865 II (A304) Urban Politics (Y308) US Politics through Film and Fiction (Y373) Using Instructional Media & Technology (R503) World Regional Geography (G120)

International Society for Technology in Education   (ISTE)
1787 Agate Street Eugene OR 97403
Accred.: Northwest Association of Schools and Colleges
Email: iste@oregon/uoregon.edu

(800) 336-5191   fax:–
URL: http://www.iste.org/

Description: The International Society for Technology in Education (ISTE) is the largest teacher-based, nonprofit organization in the field of educational technology. Its mission is to help K-12 classroom teachers and administrators share effective methods for enhancing student learning through the use of new classroom technologies. ISTE members truly are redefining the boundaries of the K-12 classroom. They form an ever-expanding network of dedicated professionals sharing classroom-proven solutions to the challenge of incorporating computers, the Internet, and other new technologies into their schools. Classes conducted by the University of Oregon.
Courses: (7) ClarisWorks (EDUC508K) Computers in Math Education (EDUC510A) Hypermedia in the Classroom (EDUC508T) Instructional Software (EDUC508B) Internet for Educators (EDUC508M) Planning Technology in Schools (EDUC507B) Telecommunications (EDUC510E)

Kansas City Kansas Community College   (KACI)
7250 State Ave. Kansas City KS 66112
Accred.: North Central Association of Colleges and Schools
Email: kckccinfo@toto.net

(913) 334-1100   fax:
URL: www.kckcc.cc.ks.us/online/

Description: Acceptance to KCKCC is the first step towards enrolling for classes. To apply for admission to the College follow these steps. New Students: 1. Complete and submit a student information form; 2. Have official high school and college transcripts sent to the Admissions and Records Office; and 3. Complete the ASSET placement process, which is given on campus. Former students: if you have previously attended KCKCC but did not attend classes during the last semester, you must complete and submit a readmission form to the Admissions and Records Office before enrolling. High school students: students with junior and senior status in high school are eligible to enroll in college courses provided they have a 3.0 GPA and approval from the principal and counselor at their high school.
Courses: (8) Ethics and Addiction (AC1102) HIV/Medial High Risk and Addiction (AC1103) Intermediate Algebra (MA104) Introduction to Recreation (RT171) Marketing (BU113) Microcomputer Business Software (BU111) Nutrition (BI145C) Pharmacology and Addiction (AC1101)

Kennesaw State University   (KENN)
1000 Chastain Road Kennesaw GA 30144
Accred.: Southern Association of Colleges and Schools
Email: mvickery@KSCmail.kennesaw.edu

(800) 869-1151 (770) 423-6598 fax:(770) 423-6524
URL: http://www.student.org/ksu/

Description: Kennesaw State University in a joint Venture with JER Group, Inc. a private sector educational service provider offer a variety of courses that are available to adult and lifelong learners. Courses span approximately 5-7 weeks and are facilitated by both industry leaders/practitioners and academics worldwide.
Courses: (31) A Virtual Tour of The Internet (FMV218) Advanced Web Design (FMV227) Adventures in Writing a Novel (FMV222) Careers in Cyberspace (FMV223) Communication Skills for Employees (FMV200) Creating Messages that Get Results (FMV202) Creative Writing - Getting Started (FMV203) Dramatica Screenplay Writing (FMV208) Effective Business Management (FMV221) Effective Human Communications (FMV201) Evolving Technical Communication (FMV235) How to Write Television Soap Opera (FMV209) Internet Search Strategies (FMV215) Into Technical Writing for Industry (FMV233) Intro to World Women's Poetry (FMV211) Introduction to HTML (FMV001) Introduction to Photoshop (FMV224) Introduction to the Internet (FMV219) Leadership for Entrepreneurs (FMV213A) Powerpoint 7 Beginning Workshop (FMV225) Small Business Marketing on Internet (FMV220) Teach Yourself Anything (FMV214A) Teaching Online (FMV217) To be A Technical Writer (FMV204) Vascular Access Devices (FMV216A) Web Page with Java Applets and CGI (FMV226) Writing for Magazine & Newspapers (FMV207) Writing Short Newspaper Articles (FMV206) Writing through Childhood (FMV210) Writing Tools for Consultants (FMV205) Writing Tools for Independent Consultants (FMV234)

Lansing Community College   (LANS)
Admissions Office P. O. Box 40010 Lansing MI 48901
Accred.: North Central Association of Colleges and Schools
Email: lccvcollege@voyager.net

(800) 644-4522 (517) 483-1620 fax:(517) 483-9668
URL: http://vcollege.lansing.cc.mi.us/

Description: Welcome to Lansing Community College's Virtual College. Whether you live in our community, across the state or country, or around the world, your Internet connection is your gateway to a quality college education at Lansing Community College. If your are an independent learner, highly self-motivated and interested in accelerating your course of study, the Lansing Community College Virtual College Degree program may be appropriate for you. Since the coursework can be completed any time of the day or night, it is ideal for those who are unable to attend classes in the evenings or on weekends. Virtual College courses limit enrollment to 20 students and will close when full.
Courses: (39) Advanced Internet for Business and Ed (CISB202) Advanced RPG on the AS/400 (CISB275) American Political System (POLS120) Beginning RPG on the AS/400 (CISB175) Business Communications (WRIT127) Business Law I, Basic Principles (LEGL215) Composition I (WRIT121) Computer Information Systems (CISB100) Data Communications (CISB130) Developing Multimedia for WWW (CISB258) Dynamics of Communication (SPCH120) Information Systems Problem Solving (CISB200) Integrated Science (ISCI131) Intro to Algebra (MATH107) Intro to AltaVista Forum (CABS100) Intro to Computer Info - Software Apps (CISB099) Intro to Computer Information Systems (CISB100) Intro to Local Area Networks (CISB230) Intro to the Internet in Business (CISB 102) Introduction to Computers (CPSC120) Introduction to Internet in Business (CISB102) Introduction to Psychology (PSYC200) Introduction to Sociology (SOCL120) Introductory Algebra (MATH107) Math for Business (MATH117) Multimedia Home Pages for WWW (CISB258) Personal Writing (WRIT118) Personal Writing (WRIT118) Principles of Accounting I (ACCG210) Principles of Economics - Micro (ECON201) Principles of Economics-Micro (ECON201) Techniques of Study (SDEV124) Techniques of Study (SDEV124) Web Site Management (CISB204) World Philosophies I (PHIL211) World Philosophy I (PHIL211) Writing (WRIT121) Writing Skills Review (WRIT119) WWW Interactive Programming (CISB253)

Laramie County Community College   (LARA)
1400 East College Drive Cheyenne WY 82007
Accred.: North Central Association of Colleges and Schools
Email:

(307) 778-1212 (307) 637-2400 fax:–
URL: http://www.lcc.whecn.edu/Internet/internet.html

Description: The mission of Distance Education at Laramie County Community College is to utilize effective technologies to meet the needs of distant learners who, because of time, geographic, or other constraints, choose not to attend the traditional classroom.
Courses: (3) American & Wyoming Government (POLS1000) General Psychology (PSYC1000) Introduction to Physical Geography (GR1010)

Marylhurst College   (MARY)
P. O. Box 261 Marylhurst OR 97036
Accred.: Northwest Association of Schools and Colleges
Email: learning@marylhurst.edu

(800) 634-9982 (503) 636-8141 fax:–
URL: http://www.marylhurst.edu/

Description: Marylhurst is dedicated to making innovative post-secondary education accessible to students of any age. Animated by its Catholic and liberal arts heritage, Marylhurst emphasizes the uniqueness and dignity of each person, and is committed to the examination of values, as well as to quality academic and professional training. Transfer credit, employment and other prior learning experience are integrated into degree plans and teaching methodologies.
Courses: (50) Academic & Field Research Writing (WR306) Administration of Ministries (PMT410) Basic Algebra (MTH111) Beginning & Advanced Screenwriting (WR327) Building Visual Collections (HUM449) Business Law (MGT515B) Business Writing (WR214) Creating Culture (HUM355) Eastern Europe after 1989 (HUM425) Educational Psychology (PSY360WT) Effective Listening (CM323) Effective Writing for Public Presentations (CM431) Environmental Ethics (ENV328) Film & International Culture (HUM322) Film Criticism (HUM323) From Con Man to Death of a Salesman (LIT385) Grant & Proposal Writing (WR305) Human Biology (BIO162) Identity Design (MGT502) Individual Differences (PSY360WS) Information in an Era of Overload (CLL373C) Information Systems Applications (CIS345) Information Systems Strategies (CIS445B) Intercultural Communication (CM333) Intermediate Algebra (MTH125) Interpersonal Communication (CM322B) Introduction to Communication Studies (CM200) Issues in Ethics & Leadership (MGT418) Learning Organizations in Practice (MGT564) Life/Work Planning (LPS270) Logic, Business & Everyday Life (PHL325) Management Foundations (MGT500B) Managerial Accounting & Control Systems (FIN510) Managerial Finance (FIN420B) Managing in the Wired Organization (MGT454) Marketing (MKT438B) Nonverbal Communication (CM324) Organizationals & Gender (MGT508) Organizations of Continual Learning (MGT463) Perspectives on American Culture (HUM357) Philosophy of Religion (PHL327) Principles of Communication (CM300) Project Management (MGT303B) Quality Management Methods (MGT532) Research and Discovery in Communication (CM400) Scenarios & Information Planning (MGT516) Selling (MKT425) Small Group Communication (CM321) Weather in the Pacific Northwest (ATM124) Writing Fiction (WR341)

Mercy College   (MERC)
Director of Distance Learning 555 Broadway Dobbs Ferry NY 10522
Accred.: Middle States Association of Colleges and Schools
Email: admission@merlin.mercynet.edu

(914) 674-7527   fax:(914) 674-7518
URL: http://merlin.mercynet.edu

Description: Mercy College offer courses you can take whenever you have the time. Mercy College's Distance Learning Network allows you to take courses without physically attending classes. If you have some familiarity with computers and can work on your own, you should could consider taking a course on Distance Learning. If you think you're too busy or find commuting to a college too difficult, consider distance learning. It could change your life and provide you with opportunities for success.
Courses: (45) Abnormal Psychology (PY212) American History since 1877 (HI106) American History through 1877 (HI105) Art History Survey (AR107) Artificial Intelligence (CS339) Career and Life Planning (BS120) Child Psychology (ED130) Computers for the Social and Behavioral Sciences (BS226) Creative Basics for Direct Marketing (MK322) Desktop Publishing (CS240) Developmental Psychology (PY233) Environmental Science (BI112) European History to 1500 (HI101) Experimental Psychology (PY372) Foundations of Computing I (CS131) Harlem Renaissance (HU224) Health Care Organization and Management (BS308) Health Psychology (PY159) International Business (IB250) International Relations (IB370) Introduction to Computers (CS120) Introduction to Direct Marketing (MK321) Introduction to Management Accounting (AC121) Introduction to Religion (RE109) Introduction to the Criminal Justice System (CJ102) Issues in Teaching & Learning with Technology (ED675) Logical Thinking (PL112) Macro-Economics (EC220) Mathematics for the Liberal Arts (MA115) Methodology for the Social and Behavioral Sciences (BS248) Modern Psychology in Historical Perspective (PY210) Music Appreciation (MU107) Political Power in America (GV101) Principles of Banking (BK112) Principles of Business Finance (FI320) Principles of Management (MG120) Principles of Marketing (MK220) Race, Gender, Ethnicity in US Politics (GV366) Software for the Office - Evaluation and Use (CS353) Statistics I (MA122) Strategic Media Planning for Direct Marketing (MK323) Survey of Telecommunications for Teaching and Learning (ED575) The Economy, Jobs and You (EC115) The Economy, Jobs, and You (EC115) Written English and Literary Studies I (EN111)

Michigan State University (MICH)
c/o The Electronic University Network 1977 Colestin Road Hornbrook CA 96044
Accred.: North Central Association of Colleges and Schools
Email: euncouncil@aol.com
(800) 225-3276 (541) 482-5871 fax:(541) 482-7544
URL: http://www.wcc-eun.com/msu/
Description: Michigan State University is offering one of the most popular and useful courses in computer programming online through the Electronic University Network. The course earns you 3 semester credits from MSU, which can be applied to your degree from MSU or another institution. For example, the credit can be applied to the Computer Science Associate Degree program at Rogers University - Claremore or toward a Bachelor Degree program at City University. Michigan State University is located in East Lansing, Michigan. MSU is accredited by the North Central Association of Colleges and Schools.
Courses: (1) Integrated Introduction to Computing (01)

MiraCosta College (MIRA)
One Barnard Drive Oceanside CA 92056
Accred.: Western Association of Schools and Colleges
Email: commservices@miracosta.cc.ca.us
(888) 201-8480 (760) 757-2121 fax:(760) 795-6823
URL: http://www.miracosta.cc.ca.us
Description: MiraCosta College is a California State Community College. We are proud to be part of the public, not-for-profit network of colleges and universities that includes the University of California and the California State University system. Our physical location is sunny San Diego County, but our online classes are attended by students from all around the globe! MiraCosta College Community Services offers a wide variety of results-oriented non-credit online workshops designed specifically to harness the education potential of the Internet. Thanks to the Internet's powerful capabilities for interactive communication, it is now possible for you to upgrade your work skills, learn a new talent, or chart a career path at your own pace and from the convenience of your own home!
Courses: (7) Contemporary Moral Problems (PHIL02) CyberCinema - Introduction to Film (FILM101) General Geology (GEOL101) Knowledge and Reality (PHIL101) Principles of Health (HEAL101) The College Library (LIBR101) US History 1865 to present (HIST111)

Mohave Community College (MOHA)
P. O. Box 980 Colorado City AZ 86021
Accred.: Western Association of Schools and Colleges
Email: elizcraw@et.mohave.cc.az.us
(800) 678-3992 (520) 875-2799 fax:
URL: http://www.mohave.cc.az.us/
Description: Mohave Community College is fully accredited and has been providing educational programs and services in Mohave County since 1971. MCC offers you the opportunity to learn with a student-teacher ratio of about 18-to-1. We also offer one of the lowest rates for tuition and fees of any community college in Arizona, which is designed to assist our students, especially the working adult, with financing their education. Programs and services are offered through campuses in Bullhead City, Kingman, Lake Havasu City, Colorado City, and its various sites throughout the fastest growing county in Arizona.
Courses: (1) Solar Energy and Systems (BRT120)

National American University (NAAM)
Coordinator for Distance Learning 321 Kansas City St. Rapid City SD 57701
Accred.: North Central Association of Colleges and Schools
Email: sluckhurst@national.edu
(800) 843-8892 (605) 394-4943 fax:(605) 394-4871
URL: http://online.national.edu/classroom.htm
Description: Welcome to National American University where keeping pace with the changing needs of working adults continues to be a top priority. On-line courses provide you with the flexibility and convenience of continuing your education through an accredited university. We invite you to join our world-wide community of on-line learners. Attend college at a time and place that suits you. Join others from around the world in your quest for perpetual learning. NAU is now offering several courses on-line for students just like you who wish to continue their college education, on-line, from an accredited University. In small groups, no more than sixteen, students will discuss issues and share ideas just as in a on-campus course but with a difference – no commuting. With your PC, and any phone or Internet connection, you'll be able to "hook up" with your classmates and faculty 24 hours a day, seven days a week, anywhere you might be.
Courses: (10) Accounting Principles I (AC105D) Business Statistics I (MA210D) Business Statistics II (MA220D) Evidence (PL340D) Finance I (FN201D) Fundamentals of Marketing (MG105D) Introduction to Visual Basic (CI202D) Law for Business I (LA216D) Management Across Cultures (MT430D) Principles of Supervision (MT330D)

New Hampshire College (NEHA)
Distance Education Program 2500 No. River Rd. Manchester NH 03106
Accred.: New England Association of Schools and Colleges
Email: leewil@nhc.edu
(603) 437-1711 (603) 645-9766 fax:(603) 645-9706
URL: http://www.dist-ed.nhc.edu/home.html
Description: Although we do not currently offer an entire bachelor's program online, we do offer certificates in Computer Programming, Accounting, and Human Resources Management. In the very near future, because we are adding new courses every term, we will have the ability to present bachelor and associate degrees to our distance education students. The courses we have selected for our DE Program are taken from New Hampshire College's core curriculum, business curriculum, or liberal arts curriculum, and apply readily to the various degrees offered by New Hampshire College.
Courses: (96) Advanced Web Technology (CIS271) American Politics (GOV 110) Application Design and Implementation (CIS310) Application Development (CIS210) Baroque through Modern Arts (HUM202) Business Communication (ENG220) Business Ethics (PHL216) Business Law I (ADB206) Business Law II (ADB307) C Advanced Programming Language (CIS231) C Programming (CIS230) College Composition II (ENG120) College Composition III (ENG121) Compensation and Benefit Administration (ADB325) Computer Information Systems (CIS500) Consumer Behavior (MKT345) Cost Accounting I (ACC207) Cost Accounting II (ACC208) Culture and Politics of International Business (INT316) Current Issues in the Healthcare Professions (ADB423) Desktop Publishing (COM331) Elementary Accounting I (ACC101) Elementary Accounting II (ACC102) Energy and Society (SCI220) Entrepreneurship (ADB320) Ethical Issues in Marketing (MKT350) Federal Taxation I (ACC415) Federal Taxation II (ACC416) Finite Mathematics (MAT120) Fundamentals of Information Technology (CIS100) Graphics and Layout in Print Media (COM330) Greece through Renaissance (HUM201) Human Growth and Development (PSY211) Human Relations in Administration (ADB125) Human Resource Management (ADB211) Human Resource Management and Development (ADB442) Information Systems Concepts (CIS200) Intermediate Accounting I (ACC203) Intermediate Accounting II (ACC204) International Management (INT315) International Relations (GOV211) Introduction to

Anatomy and Physiology (SCI217) Introduction to Business (ADB110) Introduction to Business Finance (FIN320) Introduction to International Business (INT113) Introduction to Marketing (MKT113) Introduction to Operations Management (ADB331) Introduction to Philosophy (PHL110) Introduction to Politics (GOV109) Introduction to Psychology (PSY108) Introduction to Sociology (SOC112) Introduction to UNIX Operating System (CIS350) Labor Relations and Arbitration (ADB318) Macroeconomics (ECO202) Management of Healthcare Organizations (ADB302) Management of Information Technology (CIS430) Managing Organizational Change (ADB322) Market Research (MKT630) Marketing Strategies (MKT500) Mass Communication (COM226) Mathematical Concepts and Techniques for Business (MAT121) Microeconomics (ECO201) Modern Authors (ENG334) Multinational Corporate Finance (INT336) Object Oriented Programming in C++ (CIS232) Organizational Behavior (ADB342) Organizational Leadership (ADB328) Principles of Advertising (MKT329) Principles of Management (ADB215) Principles of Public Relations (COM335) Principles of Retailing (MKT222) Psychology of Abnormal Behavior (PSY215) Psychology of Individual Differences and Special Needs (PSY320) Psychology of Personality (PSY216) Sales and Persuasion (MKT335) Sales Management (MKT320) Seminar in Advanced Writing (ENG330) Small Business Management (ADB317) Social Environment of Business (ADB326) Sociology of Deviant Behavior (SOC326) Statistics (MAT220) Strategic Management (MBA700) Survey of American Literature I (ENG213) Survey of American Literature II (ENG214) Survey of English Literature I (ENG223) Survey of English Literature II (ENG224) Survey of World Literature in Translation (ENG202) Technical Writing (COM341) The Nature Writers (ENG332) Total Quality Management (ADB324) United States History I, 1607-1865 (HIS113) Visual Basic (CIS125) Visual Basic (CIS260) Western Civilization I - Prehistory to 1648 (HIS109) Western Civilization II -1648 to Present (HIS110) World-Wide Web Technology (CIS270)

New Jersey City University   (NJCU)
Continuing Education Department   2039 Kennedy Boulevard   Jersey City NJ 07305
Accred.: Middle States Association of Colleges and Schools   (201) 200-3306 (201) 200-3449 fax:(201) 200-2188
Email: conted@njcu.edu   URL: http://conted4.njcu.edu/
Description: New Jersey City University currently provides several graduate level online courses through its Continuing Education department. These courses are designed for educators and the EDTC courses listed apply toward the University's new Master of Arts degree program in Educational Technology. The format consists of weekly lessons which are posted to each course's home page on the World Wide Web. A listserv offers a forum for discussion and clarification of assignments through email. Each course will also have its own Web Board which provides an opportunity for discussion and class interaction.
Courses: (4) Integrated Software Across Curriculum (EDTC625) Introduction to Hypermedia (EDTC642) Using Child & Adolescent Literature (LTED642) Using the Internet in Education (EDTC621)

New Jersey Institute of Technology   (NJIT)
Office of Distance Learning Guttenburg Information Center   Newark NJ 07102
Accred.: Middle States Association of Colleges and Schools   (800) 624-9850 (973) 642-7015 fax:(973) 596-3203
Email: dl@njit.edu   URL: http://www.njit.edu/dl/
Description: NJIT has been a leader in distance learning for over a decade, first with groundbreaking work in the development of the EIES computerized conferencing system; next with ACCESS NJIT production of academically rigorous telecourses in the sciences, mathematics, computer science, engineering and management; and recently with its membership in the National Technological University (NTU). NTU is a visionary educational organization which provides advanced technology education through satellite delivery. Each course consists of two components : a tele-lecture and an electronic discussion. The tele-lecture can be delivered by leased VHS tape.
Courses: (76) Advanced Data Structures (CIS435) Advanced Professional Communication (ENG601) Advanced Programming Environments (CIS786) Applications to Commercial Problems (CIS365) Behavioral Science in Engineering (IE603) Business Process Innovation (CIS684) C Programming (CIS105C) C++ Programming (CIS105E) Calculus I (MATH111) Calculus II (MATH112) Client/Server Architecture (CIS785P) College Chemistry I (CHEM108) College Chemistry II (109) Computer and Information Systems (CIS679) Computer Organization (CIS251) Computer Programming Languages (CIS635) Computer Science with Problem Solving (CIS102) Computer Systems Management (CIS455) Computer Techniques for MIS (CIS465) Computers and Society (CIS350) Computing Concepts for Managers (MIS620) Cost Estimating for Capital Projects (EM691) Culture from Reformation to Present (HUM231) Data Management System Design (CIS631) Decision Support Systems (MIS648) Design Of Interactive Systems (CIS732) Differential Equations (MATH222) Discrete Analysis (MATH226) Document Design & Desktop Publishing (ENG605) Economics (SS201) Environmental Science (EVSC602) Evaluation of Information Systems (CIS675) Guided Design in Software Engineering (CIS490) Industrial Gas Cleaning (CHE687) Industrial Hygiene and Occupational Health (IE615) Industrial Management (EM501) Industrial Quality Control (IE672) Industrial Waste Control I (CHE685) Industrial Waste Control II (CHE686) Information System Principles (CIS677) Introduction to Computer Science I (CIS113) Introduction to Computer Science II (CIS114) Introduction to Database Systems (CIS431) Introduction to Logic and Automata (CIS341) Law and Environmental Engineering (EM631) Legal Aspects in Construction (EM632) Machine and Assembly Language (CIS231) Management Information Systems (MIS545) Management Science (EM602) Managerial Economics (ECON565) Microeconomics (ECON265) MIS Operations & Planning (MIS645) Multimedia Systems (CIS658) Object-Oriented Programming in C++ (CIS601) Object-Oriented Software Development (CIS683) Open Systems Networking (CIS456) Organizational Behavior (HRM301) Physics I (PHYS111) Physics of Materials (PHYS687) Principles of Management (MGMT390) Principles of Marketing (MRKT330) Principles of Operating Systems (CIS332) Probability and Statistics (MATH333) Programming and Problem Solving (CIS101) Programming Language Concepts (CIS280) Project Control (EM637) Project Management (EM636) Proposal Writing (ENG620) Requirements Analysis (CIS390) Society, Technology and Environment (HSS202) Software Design and Production (CIS673) Survey of Probability and Statistics (MATH225) Systems Simulation (CIS461) Thermodynamics (CHE611) Total Quality Management (IE673) Western Culture and History I (HUM112)

New Mexico Highlands University   (NMHI)
Registrar's Office Las Vegas NM 87701
Accred.: North Central Association of Colleges and Schools   (505) 454-3437   fax:(505) 454-3552
Email: registrar@merlin.nmhu.edu   URL: http://www.nmhu.edu
Description: Our philosophy is to reach out and address student needs where the student is located. New Mexico Highlands University began Distance Education offerings fall of 1996 through the interactive television medium. Effective Summer 1998, two courses from our School of Business will be taught on-line through the Internet. It is anticipated that the number of course offerings will increase as more professors become accustomed to this method of instruction.
Courses: (2) Electronic Commerce (8552A) Internet Marketing (8523A)

New School for Social Research (NEWS)
DIAL Program 66 West 12th Street New York NY 10011

Accred.: Middle States Association of Colleges and Schools
Email: dialexec@dialnsa.edu

(800) 319-4321 (212) 229-5880 fax:(212) 239-5852
URL: http://www.dialnsa.edu/

Description: DIAL, the New School's Distance Learning program, is an opportunity for people all over the world to take New School courses at their own convenience. Connecting through the Internet's World Wide Web to our cyberspace campus, students receive instruction, ask questions of their instructors and each other, discuss issues, and actively participate in their classes. Students and faculty connect to the WWW and participate in class discussion from their homes, offices or wherever they may be. The process is asynchronous (that is, people log in to their courses and add their contributions to the dialogue at different times.) Without the constraints of time and place, students and faculty come to The New School from places around the world. The New School's electronic campus reaches wherever the web reaches.

Courses: (118) Adobe Illustrator Level 1 (Macintosh) (3226) Adobe Illustrator Level 2 (Macintosh) (3234) Advanced Microcomputer Applications (8592) Advertising 101 (4010) An Introduction to Culinary History (3872) An Introduction to Jung (0388) Art Nouveau (4013) Basic Photography (2514) Borders of Identity (0514) Buddhist Influences in American Literature (0686) Business Writing (ESL) (1492) C Language Programming (3127) Celebrating Differences - Disability Culture (0517) Crime and Punishment (9998) D.H. Lawrence and the Language of Love (0666) Depression and Melancholia (0353) Economic Theory and Transformation (0263) Elements of Business Writing (1518) English Grammar for ESL Teachers (1092) Environmental Geology (0809) Ethics and the Family (0333) Family Literacy (1322) Feminine and Masculine in Native America (0498) Fiction Writing - Memory, Imagination, Desires (1695) Financial Management of Practice Groups (8563) Forbidden Literature (0675) Foundations of Feminism (0207) Foundations of Psychology (0344) Four American Classics (0641) Four European Classics (0643) From Silence to Poem (1645) Fundamental Principles of Financial Freedom (9999) Fundamentals of Copy Editing (1515) Fundamentals of English (1505) Harlem Writers Guild On-Line Fiction Workshop (1706) History of 20th Century Fashion (4008) History of Communication Technologies (3937) How and Why My Family Came to This Country (1743) How To Do Research Online (2687) Hypertext Poetry and Fiction (1827) Hysteria - Her Story (0382) Insanity, Psychiatry, and Society (0404) Intercultural Communication (3936) Intermediate Photography (2516) International Business Management (8635) Introduction to Astronomy (0814) Introduction to AutoCAD (4002) Introduction to Business Management (2862) Introduction to CGI (4005) Introduction to Fashion Computing with Photoshop (4004) Introduction to Interior Design (4014) Introduction to Linguistics (1302) Introduction to MiniCAD (4001) Introduction to Page Design with QuarkXPress (4000) Introduction to Social Psychology (0363) Investment Basics (2982) Italian for Italian Speakers (1133) Language as a Listening Tool (1627) Learner Assessment (1318) Live Picture (3275) MacroMedia DreamWeaver (3347) Management Issues in Health Care (8399) Media Ethics (3939) Media in Developing Countries (2653) Media Management and Leadership (3938) Memorializing Vietnam (0699) Methods and Techniques of Teaching ESL/EFL 1 (1333) Microsoft PowerPoint (3165) MS Word Level 2 (Windows 95) (3179) Multiculturalism in American Politics (0239) Multigenre Writing From Multicultural Roots (1804) Online Drawing Workshop for Beginners (2305) Organizational Behavior (8643) Personnel Issues in Health Care (8564) Photoshop 4.0 Level 1 (Macintosh) (3248) Photoshop for Artists (2287) Photoshop for the Photographer (2526) Playwriting (1786) Political Theory for the 21st Century (0225) Preparatory Writing (1612) Principles of Language Learning and Teaching (1345) Psychoanalysis and Literature (0663) Published ESL/EFL Materials (9997) QuarkXPress Level 1 (Macintosh) (3208) Rendering the Ordinary Extraordinary (1649) Screenwriting 1 - Fundamentals (2816) Screenwriting 2 - Facing the Blank Page (2823) Secrets of the South (0679) Seven Visionary Poets (0655) Six African-American Women Writers (0658) Society and the Rights of Animals (0501) Sociology - Tools for Understanding the World (0325) Spanish Graduate Reading Course (1253) Statistics for Everyone (0849) Study of Crimes Against Women (0334) Teaching ESL Writing On Line (1363) Teaching the Sound System of English (1348) Teaching Writing (1352) Television as a System (3935) The 1920s - The Emergence of Modern America (0307) The Bill of Rights and the Supreme Court (0243) The Grammar of Business Writing (1512) The Historic Country Houses of England (4012) The Lesbian Literary Tradition (0711) The Mother/Daughter Theme in Literature (0715) The Pacific Century (0302) Theorizing Intellect (0357) Troubleshooting Web Graphics (3341) Understanding Gender (0377) UNIX Operating System (3123) Web Design / Production (3940) Web Design for Architects & Designers (4003) Webmaster (3332) William Blake (0629) Women's Autobiographical Writing (0645) World Wide Web Page Design and Construction (3312) Writing Creative Nonfiction (1732) Writing Experimental Fiction (1702)

New York Institute of Technology (NYIT)
On-Line Campus P. O. Box 9029 Central Islip NY 11722

Accred.: Middle States Association of Colleges and Schools
Email: ssilverman@acl.nyit.edu

(800) 222-6948 (516) 348-3059 fax:–
URL: http://www.nyit.edu/olc/

Description: Welcome to the On-Line Campus (OLC) of the New York Institute of Technology. If you want to complete a college degree but cannot attend conventional college classes on a traditional campus because of obstacles such as time, geography, dependent children or work conflicts, we have a distance learning program tailored just for you. The OLC/NYIT offers the following degrees: Bachelor of Arts in Interdisciplinary Studies, Bachelor of Science in Interdisciplinary Studies, Bachelor of Science in Business Administration (Management Option)Bachelor of Science in Behavioral Sciences (Options: Psychology, Sociology, Community Mental Health and Criminal Justice), Studying both independently and in organized groups, you will interact with your instructors and classmates via an electronic or virtual seminar. Since the system remains accessible 24-hours-a-day, your only schedule will be the deadline set for assignments and exams.

Courses: (104) Abnormal Psychology (BES2465) Accounting I (BUS3511) Accounting II (BUS3521) Adolescent Psychology (BES2441) Advanced Writing and Editing (EN1049) American Government and Politics (SS2700) American History I (SS2500) American History II (SS2510) American Urban Minorities (BES2435) Anthropology (BES2405) Basic Economics (EC2011) Basic Reading and Writing (EN1007) Basic Speech Communication (SP1023) Behavioral Science in Marketing (BES2451) Business Law I (BUS3529) Business Law II (BUS3532) Business Law III (BUS3533) Business Organization and Admin. (BUS3900) Business Policy Seminar (BUS3909) Business Writing (EN1042) Child Psychology (BES2439) Collective Bargaining (BUS3902) College Algebra and Trigonometry (MA3014) College Composition I (EN1010) College Composition II (EN1020) Comparative Government (SS2710) Computer Concepts (CS5641) Contemporary World (SS2540) Corporate Finance (BUS3630) Criminal Investigation (BES2318) Criminal Law and Proceeding (BES2301) Criminology (BES2477) Data Communications (TN4704) Developmental Mathematics I/II (MA3013) Environmental Psychology (BES2467) Environmental Sciences (LS9500) Ethics and Social Philosophy (SS1530) Finite Mathematics (MA3010) Forensic Technology (BES2317) Government & Metropolitan Problems (SS2705) Government and Business (SS2708) Human Resources Management (BUS3917) Humanity and the Biological Universe (LS4422) Humanity and the Physical Universe (PH4024) International Economics and Finance (EC2088) Internship in Professional Writing (EN1080) Interviewing Techniques (BES2460) Intro to International Business (BUS3907) Intro. to Computer Conferencing (EN1006) Introduction of Marketing (BUS3400) Introduction to Business (BUS3906) Introduction to Criminal Justice (BES2316) Introduction to EDP in Business (BUS3801) Introduction to Journalism (CA5540) Introduction to MISs (BUS3811) Introduction to Probability (MA3017) Introduction to Sociology (BES2411) Introduction to Telecommunications (TN4701) Introductory Concepts of Math (MA3015) Introductory Psychology (BES2401) Introductory Research Methods (BES2470) Juvenile Delinquency (BES2473) Law of Evidence (BES2300) Learning Theory (BES2413) Literature Seminar (EN1100) Logic and Scientific Method (SS515) Making Managerial Decisions (BUS3803) Management of Promotion (BUS3405) Managerial Accounting (BUS3501) Marketing Research (BUS3406) Marriage and the Family (BES2425) Measurement Concepts (BES2421) Modern Police Management (BES2319) Money and Banking (EC2072) New Product Management (BUS3904) Organizational Behavior (BUS3903) Patrol Function (BES2310) Philosophy and History of Religion (SS1525) Physiological

Basis of Behavior (BES2412) Police Administration (BES2305) Police and Community Relations (BES2320) Principles of Economics I (EC2010) Principles of Economics II (EC2020) Probation and Parole (BES2350) Problems of Philosophy (SS1510) Production & Operation Mgmt (BUS3916) Quantitative Methods in Business (MA3019) Reading & Writing-Internatl Students (EN1008) Report Writing (EN1044) Sales Management (BUS3401) Scientific and Technical Literature (EN1056) Scientific and Technical Writing (EN1048) Shakespeare (EN1083) Small Business Management (BUS3905) Social Problems (BES2475) Statistical Analysis (BES2422) Technical Mathematics I (MA3310) Technical Mathematics II (MA3320) Technical Writing (EN1043) Technology, Society and Values (SS1535) The Art of Drama (EN1053) The Art of Fiction (EN1054) Theories of Personality (BES2445) Voice Communications (TN4703)

New York University (NEYO)
SCPS Registration Office P.O. Box 1206 Stuyvesant Station, NY NY 10009
Accred.: Middle States Association of Colleges and Schools
Email: sce.advise@nyu.edu
(212) 998-7088 (212) 998-7277 fax:(212) 995-3060
URL: http://www.sce.nyu.edu/on-line/
Description: Whether you're a busy professional who needs "just in time" learning or you simply prefer the convenience of taking a course from your office or home, New York University's School of Continuing Education (SCE) has exciting online opportunities this spring. Our distance learning courses provide students with a flexible alternative to traditional classroom learning and allow our resources and innovative programming to reach beyond geographical boundaries. Courses are taught by the same faculty of experts you'll meet on campus, and the learning experience is equally rewarding. You'll participate in discussions with your classmates, receive lectures, and interact with an instructor who asks and answers questions, assigns work, and provides feedback.
Courses: (19) Career Planning and Development (X489571) Credit Analysis (Z813170) Data Communications (X529028) English to Spanish Translation (X278804) Fundamentals in Electronic Commerce (X529027) Internet and Intranet Business Applications (X529418) Introduction to HIV Mental Health (X149300) Introduction to Psychology (Y20680103) Introduction to Sociology (Y20720107) Java for C++ Programmers (X529269) Meeting and Conference Management (X659560) New Information Technologies (Y26607401) Object-Oriented Analysis and Design (X529267) Organizational Behavior (Y10130101) Principles of Accounting (Y10014203) Setting Limits for Toddlers to 5-Year-Olds (X489467) Site Search, Inspection, and Selection (X659513) The Craft of Reading (Y20624103) The Elements of Fiction Writing (X329354)

Northeastern Oklahoma A&M College (NOOK)
200 "I" Street, NW Miami OK 74354
Accred.: North Central Association of Colleges and Schools
Email: jgenandt@neoam.cc.ok.us
(918) 540-6208 (918) 540-6296 fax:(918) 542-7065
URL: http://www.neoam.cc.ok.us
Description: It is the belief of NEO A&M College that every person should have an opportunity for furthering their education beyond secondary education. Every person should be able to access excellent educational experiences regardless of whether they reside in a major American city or rural areas of the world. It is our aim to provide this opportunity through distance learning which includes interactive instructional television courses; video courses; or interactive Internet courses delivered on the World Wide Web. Every person, whether physically challenged or fully mobile, will be able to pursue intellectual growth through NEO A&M's distance learning efforts.
Courses: (2) General Psychology (PSY1113) Intermediate Algebra (MATH0123)

Northern State University (NOST)
Office of Continuing Education 1200 S. Jay Street, Box 870 Aberdeen SD 57401
Accred.: North Central Association of Colleges and Schools
Email: winthert@wolf.northern.edu
(605) 626-2568   fax:(605) 626-2542
URL: http://www.northern.edu/
Description: At Northern State University, each student makes a difference. With an enrollment of about 3,000, Northern students represent 36 states and 20 foreign countries. Northern State University also offers a variety of programs and activities which allow you to learn, explore and contribute to the adventure called college.
Courses: (3) Classification of Birds (BIOL363) Introduction to Computers (MIS105) Introduction to Theatre (THE100)

Northwest Technical College (NOTE)
Distance Education Section 2022 Central Ave SE East Grand Forks MN 56721
Accred.: Northwest Association of Schools and Colleges
Email: webmaster@mail.ntc.mnscu.edu
(800) 451-3441 x 575(218) 773-3441 x 575fax:(218) 773-4502
URL: http://www.ntc-online.com/
Description: Welcome to the Northwest Technical College Online. You are among a growing number of students who are choosing to access their education using a distance education format. NTC is committed to bringing you the best education available by utilizing the latest technologies. Our Internet Distance Education program is part of this commitment. The faculty and staff of the college want you to have a superior experience as a distance education student at NTC Distance Education Program. We all wish you the greatest success in achieving your educational/career goals.
Courses: (12) AC Circuits (ELTR1804) Advanced AC Circuits (ELTR1806) DC Circuits (ELTR1802) Intro to Human Anatomy & Physiology (BIOL1404) Keyboarding II (ADMS1304) Medical Terminology (HLTH1506) Power Supplies (ELTR1812) Skillbuilding I (ADMS1308) Solid State Circuits (ELTR1814) Technology 2002 (CPTR1404) Topics in Technical Math (MATH1404) Written Business Communications (ADMS1342)

Northwestern College (NOCO)
1441 N. Cable Road Lima OH 45805
Accred.: North Central Association of Colleges and Schools
Email: info@nc.edu
(419) 227-3141   fax:-
URL: http://www.nc.edu/virtual/
Description: With simple Internet connectivity, students can access the Virtual College homepage where they can enroll in classes, view current course material, look at instructor profiles, and communicate with their classmates. With the use of proctors and limited on-line testing, Northwestern College ensures that you will receive the highest quality education possible. The Virtual College also has an extensive on-line Student Services Department and Library. This is our way of making sure that you receive all of the same opportunities and services that our traditional students do.
Courses: (50) Accounting I (AC100) Accounting II (AC101) Advanced Psychology (GE275) Advertising (MT120) Automotive Aftermarket Management (MA215) Basic English (GE174) Beginning Keyboarding (TY139) Business Math (MH169) Business Statistics (MH267) Civil War Literature (GE261) Computer-Assisted Management (MA127) Computers and Society (DP127) Contract Law (BU111) Creative Writing (GE279) English Composition (GE180) Ethics (GE281) Exploration of Controversial Issues (GE284) Film and Literature (GE280) Human Resources

Management (MA226) International Business I (BU240) Interpersonal Communications (GE179) Interviewing and Employment Skills (OP153) Introduction to Automotive Industry (MA130) Introduction to Business (BU120) Introduction to Microcomputing (DP105) Introduction to Sociology (GE286) Macroeconomics (GE115) Marketing I (MH169) Marketing II (MT230) Marketing Management (MT232) Marketing Research (MT231) Microeconomics (GE116) Multicultural Voices (GE291) Oral Presentations (GE272) Parts & Service Management (MA210) Personal Taxes (AC110) Principles of Management (MA121) Professional Selling (BU111) Psychology (GE177) Religions of the World (GE270) Retail Management (MA225) Short Stories (GE278) Skills for College (GE070) Small Business Management (BU120) Special Topics in History (GE260) Spreadsheet Applications (DP150) The American Political Scene (GE274) U.S. History - 1870-Present (GE285) Women and Literature (GE290) Written Communications (BU271)

Nova Southeastern University   (NOVA)

School of Computer and Information Sciences 3100 SW 9th Avenue Fort Lauderdale FL 33315

Accred.: Southern Association of Colleges and Schools

Email: scisinfo@scis.nova.edu

(800) 986-2247, Ext. 2000 (954)262-2001 fax:(954)262-3872

URL: http://www.scis.nova.edu/

Description: The School of Computer and Information Sciences offers programs that enable professionals to pursue advanced degrees without career interruption. Ranked by Forbes Magazine as one of the nation's top 20 cyber-universities, the School pioneered online graduate education with its creation of the Electronic Classroom and has been offering online programs and programs with an online component since 1983. MS programs are offered on-campus or online (computer science, computer information systems, management information systems, and computing technology in education). Ph.D. programs use a hybrid on-campus/online format (computer science, information systems, information science, and computing technology in education).

Courses: (90) Advanced Instructional Delivery (MCTE661) Applications of the Internet (MCIS654) Artificial Intelligence (CISC670) Artificial Intelligence (MMIS670) Artificial Intelligence, Expert Systems (MCIS670) Assembly Language and Architecture (MCIS500) Authoring Systems Design (MCTE626) C++ Programming Language (MCIS501) Client-Server Computing (CISC665) Client-Server Distributed Computing (MMIS626) Compiler Design Theory (CISC630) Compiler Implementation C (ISC632) Computer Graphics for Information Managers (MCIS625) Computer Graphics for Managers (MMIS625) Computer Information Systems (MCIS620) Computer Integrated Manufacturing (MMIS624) Computer Networks (MCTE650) Computer Operating Systems (MCIS615) Computer Security (MCIS652) Computer Security (MMIS652) Computer Structures and COBOL (MMIS611) Computer-Aided Software Engineering (MMIS672) Computing Technology in Education (MCTE691) Computing Technology in Education (MCTE695) Data and Computer Communications I (CISC650) Data and Computer Communications I (MCIS650) Data and Computer Communications II (CISC651) Data and Computer Communications II (MCIS651) Data and File Structures (MCIS610) Data Center Management (MMIS683) Data Structures and Algorithms for CIS (MCIS503) Data Warehousing (MMIS642) Database Management Systems (CISC660) Database Management Systems Practicum (CISC661) Database Systems (MCIS630) Database Systems (MCTE630) Database Systems Practicum (MCIS631) Databases in MIS (MMIS630) Databases in MIS Practicum (MMIS631) Decision Support Systems (MCIS671) Decision Support Systems (MMIS671) Design and Analysis of Algorithms (CISC615) Distributed Computing Systems (CISC646) Distributed Database Management (MCIS632) Distributed Database Management (MMIS632) Distributed Databases (CISC662) Electronic Commerce on the Internet (MMIS654) Human-Computer Interaction (CISC685) Human-Computer Interaction (MCIS680) Human-Computer Interaction (MCTE680) Human-Computer Interaction (MMIS680) Information Systems Projects (MCIS621) Information Systems Projects (MMIS621) Interactive Computer Graphics (CISC681) Language Theory and Automata (CISC631) Learning Theory and Computers (MCTE670) Legal and Ethical Aspects of Computing (MCIS623) Legal and Ethical Aspects of Computing (MMIS623) Management Information Systems (MMIS620) Management Information Systems (MMIS691) Mathematics in Computing (MCIS502) Multimedia and Emerging Technologies (MCTE660) Multimedia and Emerging Technologies (MMIS681) Object-Oriented Applications for CIS (MCIS661) Object-Oriented Applications for MIS (MMIS661) Object-Oriented Database Systems (CISC663) Object-Oriented Design (CISC683) Office Automation Systems (MMIS622) Operating Systems Implementation (CISC644) Operating Systems Theory and Design (CISC640) Programming Languages (CISC610) Project in Computer Science (CISC691) Project in Information Systems (MCIS682) Project in MIS (MMIS682) Quantitative Methods (MMIS615) Research Methodology (MCTE690) Software Engineering (CISC680) Software Engineering Implementation (CISC682) Special Topics in Computer Science (CISC690) Special Topics in Information Systems (MCIS691) Spreadsheet, Database, and Graphing Applications (MCTE645) Survey of Computer Languages (MMIS610) Survey of Courseware (MCTE625) Survey of Programming Languages (MCIS611) System Test and Evaluation (MCIS640) System Test and Evaluation (MMIS640) Systems Analysis and Design (MCIS660) Systems Analysis and Design (MMIS660) Telecommunications and Networking (MMIS653) The Internet (MCTE615)

Ohio University   (OHIO)

Independent Study Office 302 Tupper Hall Athens OH 45701

Accred.: North Central Association of Colleges and Schools

Email: indstudy@ouvaxa.cats.ohiou.edu

(800) 444-2910 (740) 593-2910 fax:(740) 593-2901

URL: http://www.cats.ohiou.edu/~indstu/index.htm

Description: Ohio University was founded in 1804, the first institution of higher learning in the Northwest Territory. The university has been providing learning opportunities for nontraditional students since 1919, including more than seventy years of distance learning programs: correspondence courses, credit for experiential learning, the external student degree program, and now Internet courses.

Courses: (11) Advanced Composition (ENG308JW) Advertising Concepts (BMT270) Business and Its Environment (BA101) Concepts of Marketing (BMT140) Cultural Anthropology (ANTH101) Elements of Supervision (BMT150) Hinduism (PHIL370) Human Geography (GEOG121W) Human Geography (GEOG121W) Islam (PHIL372) Money and Banking (ECON360)

Pace University   (PACE)

WTI School of International Trade and Commerce One World Trade Center, 55th Fl. New York NY 10048

Accred.: Middle States Association of Colleges and Schools

Email: advising@paceonline.edu

(800) 874-7223 (212) 346-1200 fax:

URL: http://paceonline.edu/pub/

Description: Through Pace Online, The School of International Trade and Commerce is now available for your convenience over the Internet. WTI, recognized as a leader in the field of international business education, now offers you the flexibility to earn Program or Course Certificates whenever it is convenient for you. The School of International Trade and Commerce Online: Your source for professional, job-oriented training in this complex and ever-changing field.

Courses: (8) Customhouse Brokers License Preparation (OL705) Customs Entry Preparation Workshop (OL703) Customs Law Issues for Importers (OL704) Export/Import Letters of Credit (OL706) Import Regulations and Documentation (OL702) Import Transportation Management (OL708) Importing Techniques (OL707) Introduction to World Trade (OL701)

Pennsylvania State University   (PENN)
Office of Distance Education 207 Mitchell Building University Park PA 16802

Accred.: Middle States Association of Colleges and Schools   (800) 252-3592 (814) 865-5403 fax:
Email: psude@cde.psu.edu   URL: http://www.outreach.psu.edu/de/catalog/

Description: In just two decades, the availability of technology to facilitate teaching and learning has seen unprecedented growth. Today, educators can use technologies such as audioconferencing, videoconferencing, computer-mediated communication, and the Internet, all of which can link—more effectively than ever—teacher and student. The information revolution is in full force and profoundly influencing the way we teach and learn. At Penn State, we are dedicated to continuing the evolution of distance education, using our historic strength in correspondence study and our leadership in the use of technology in the classroom.

Courses: (66) Accounting and Business (ACCTG211) Adolescent Development (HDFS239) Adult Development and Aging (HDFS249) Basic Problems of Philosophy (PHIL001) Business Logistics Management (BLOG301) Chemical Dependency - Youth at Risk (CNED420) Commentary on Art (ART122W) Critical Thinking and Argument (PHIL010) Cultural Anthropology (ANTH045) Effective Speech (SPCOM100C) Environmental Economics (ECON428) Ethics and Social Issues (PHIL103W) Evolution of Jazz (MUSIC007) Foundations of Chemical Dependency Counseling (CNED401) Foundations of Guidance and Counseling Processes (CNED403) France and the French-Speaking World (FR139) General Physics (PHYS 202) General Physics (PHYS201) General Physics (PHYS203) Global Sourcing (BLOG297B) History of Education in the United States (EDTHP430) Human Development and Family Studies Interventions (HDFS311) Interpersonal Relationships, Alcohol, and Drugs (CNED416) Introduction to American National Government (PLSC001) Introduction to Creative Writing (ENGL050) Introduction to Dietary Management (DSM102) Introduction to Finance (FIN100) Introduction to School Food Service (DSM105) Introductory Social Psychology (SOC003) Introductory Sociology (SOC001) Labor Economics (ECON315) Legal Environment of Business (BLAW243) Lifestyle for Better Health (KINES015) Management and Analysis of Quantity Food (DSM260) Marketing of Dietetic Services (DSM304) Masterpieces of Western Literature Since the Renaissance (CMLIT002) Medical Ethics (PHIL432) Medical Ethics (STS432) Money and Banking (ECON351) Nutrition Assessment Theory and Practice (NUTR359) Nutrition Care of the Elderly (NUTR253) Organization and Administration for the Nurse Manager (NURS430) Out of the Fiery Furnace (EMSC150) Personal and Interpersonal Skills (HDFS216) Personal Finance (FIN108) Personal Selling (MKTG220) Plant Propagation (HORT202) Polish Culture and Civilization (POL100) Political Science Internship (PLSC495) Principles, Ethics, and Issues of Athletic Coaching (KINES493) Problems of Small Business (BA250) Psychology of Discipline (PSYCH497E) Purchasing Management (BLOG297A) Reading Poetry (ENGL263) Rhetoric and Composition (ENGL015) Sanitation Practices in Food Service Operations (DSM101) Security Markets (FIN204) Social and Political Philosophy (PHIL108) Social, Legal, and Ethical Environment of Business (BA243) Survey of Western Art I (ART111) The Profession of Dietetics (DSM100) The Science of Physics (PHYS001) Understanding Health Effects of Ionizing Radiation (NUCE497K) Vietnam at War (HIST173) Women and the American Experience (WMNST104) Writing in the Social Sciences (ENGL202A)

Pima Community College   (PIMA)
Community Campus 401 North Bonita Ave. Tucson AZ 85709

Accred.: North Central Association of Colleges and Schools   (800) 860-7462 x6453   (520) 206-6453 fax:(520) 206-6542
Email: ddavidson@pimacc.pima.edu   URL: http://www.pima.edu/~coadmissions/internet.htm

Description: Pima Community College is a five campus district located in Tucson, Arizona. The Community Campus, responsible for the District's distance education programs, coordinates the online offerings through its NetLearning Division. Presently, thirteen classes are offered with more being added each semester. An A.A. degree in General Studies will be available online in the near future. Please visit our website for more information.

Courses: (17) Art & Culture II (ART131) Becoming a Master Student (HDE101) Emotional Intelligence (EDU198) Independent Studies in Humanities (HUM130) Instructional Applications of Internet (CSC103) Internet for New Computer Users (CSC110) Introduction to Computer Science (CSC100) Introduction to Music Theory (MUS102) Introduction to Psychology (PSY101) Prealgebra (MAT086) Preparation for General Chemistry (CHM080) Solar System Laboratory (AST111) Survey of Microcomputer Uses (CSC105) The Solar System (AST101) Writing Fundamentals (WRT100) Writing I (WRT101) Writing II (WRT102)

Pitt Community College   (PITT)
P. O. Drawer 7007 Greenville NC 27835

Accred.: Southern Association of Colleges and Schools   (919) 321-4245   fax:–
Email: pittadm@pcc.pitt.cc.nc.us   URL: http://sphynx.pitt.cc.nc.us:8080/home.htm

Description: Pitt Community College has emerged as a leader in the North Carolina Information Highway (NCIH) to provide interactive distance education and telecommunications services and instruction to locations around the state of North Carolina. Pitt Community College also provides Internet instruction to recipients around the United States. It is our goal to provide instruction to those who might not otherwise have the opportunity to gain knowledge, certification, or degrees in various areas of instruction. We were one of the first in the state of North Carolina, and were the first in our region to be certified as a distance education site. Pitt Community College is a resource for future NCIH sites and personnel at this institution serve on several regional and state committees committed to the expansion and growth of the system. We are called upon by the state of North Carolina, state and regional organizations, and national events planners to showcase the NCIH at our facilities and to lecture at various events and conferences in the United States. Course offerings mediated through Internet based instruction continue to expand each semester in various subject areas.

Courses: (12) Advanced Visual Basic (CSC239) Database Applications (CIC153) Desktop Publishing 1 (CIS165) Intro to Healthcare Management (HMT110) Introduction to Computers (CIS110) Introduction to Programming and Logic (CIS115) Introduction to the Internet (CIS172) Introduction to the Internet (CSC106) PC Operating Systems - DOS 6.22 (CSC147) Survey of Operating Systems (CIS130) Technical Support Functions I (CIS170) Visual Basic (CSC139)

Red Wing Technical College   (REWI)
308 Pioneer Rd. Red Wing MN 55066

Accred.: North Central Association of Colleges and Schools   (800)657-4849 (612) 385-6300 fax:(612) 385-6377
Email: saran@rdw.tec.mn.us   URL: http://www.rdw.tec.mn.us

Description: Red Wing/Winona Technical College is a public technical college dedicated to providing education for employment. Our Computer Careers Department specializes in providing training in the latest microcomputer programming and support technologies.

Courses: (7) C++ Windows Programming 1 (CC2521) Intro to C/C++ Programming (CC2511) Object Oriented Analysis & Design (CC2510) Object Oriented Analysis & Design (CC2510) Object Oriented C++ 1 (CC2512) Object Oriented C++ 2 (CC2512) Visual Basic (CC1812)

Rio Hondo College   (RIHO)

3600 Workman Mill Rd. Whittier CA 90601

Accred.: Western Association of Schools and Colleges

Email: howard@www.rh.cc.ca.us

(562) 692-0921   fax:--

URL: http://www.rh.cc.ca.us/html/virtural_college.htm

Description: Rio Hondo now offers the nation's most extensive online courses in Public Service. Rio Hondo College has developed an impressive educational complex which serves approximately 15,000 full and part time students in the regular credit program. We serve a constantly evolving community population which is economically and culturally diverse.

Courses: (39) Administration of Justice (AJ101) Administration of Justice (AJ102) Administration of Justice (AJ41) Advanced Investigative Techniques (PAC4328) Advanced Officer Development (PAC43001) Advanced Police Video/Photography (PAC4355) Advanced Security Investigation (PAC4354) Child Abuse (PAC4362) Community Oriented Policing (PAC43021) Community Relations (AJ105) Community Relations (PAC43003) Controlled Substances-Drugs (PAC43012) Crime Scene Investigation (PAC4317) Criminal Justice Policy (WWW3) Custodial Services in Corrections (PAC43031) Domestic Violence (PAC43025) EFF Guide to the Internet (WWW8) Emergency Operations Planning (PAC43055) Ethics in Law Enforcement (PAC43007) Gang Awareness (PAC43038) Health Issues for Peace Officers (PAC43032) Homicide Investigation (PAC4323) Information Sources on the Internet (PAC43036) InterNIC and 15 Minute Series (WWW5) Interview and Interrogation (PAC4320) Introduction to Corrections (CORR101) Investigative Report Writing (PAC43018) Justice Information & Statistics (WWW7) Justice Information Sources Online (WWW1) Juvenile Justice (PAC4336) Legal Aspects of Evidence (AJ104) Legal Update - Court Decisions (PAC43008) Office of Justice Programs (WWW2) Personal Emergency Planning (PAC43055) Stress and the Peace Officer (PAC4343) UN Crime and Justice Info. Network (WWW4) Understanding and Using the Internet (WWW6) Victimology (PAC43004) Workplace Violence (PAC43025)

Rio Salado College   (RISA)

2323 W. 14th Street Tempe AZ 85281

Accred.: North Central Association of Colleges and Schools

Email: mills@rio.maricopa.edu

(602) 517-8150 (602) 517-8540 fax:(602) 517-8129

URL: http://www.rio.maricopa.edu

Description: The prevailing philosophy at Rio Salado College is to "Let the college come to you." With 132 courses offered via distance (with 80+ on the Internet), and start dates of every two weeks, it is possible to start classes anytime during the year. Delivery modes include: print, mixed media (audio/video cassette, teleconference, computer) and Internet.

Courses: (106) Advanced Access Office '97 for Win95 (BPC217AM) Advanced DOS (CIS221) Advanced Word for Windows (BPC235DK) American Literature Before 1860 (ENH241) Arizona Constitution (POS221) Basic Medical Terminology (HCC100AD) Beginning WordPerfect Windows (BPC235DD) Business Communication (GBS233) Business Organization & Mgmt (MGT175) Business Statistics (GBS221) Business Systems Analysis and Design (CIS225) C Programming I (CIS162AB) Career Exploration (CPD102AB) College Mathematics (MAT142) Communication in Health Care Setting (HCC100AE) Computer Configuration and Enhancement (PC225) Computer Information Systems (CIS105) Computer Usage and Applications (BPC110) Computerized Accounting (ACC115) Contemporary Cinema (HUM210) CPR for Health Care Providers (HCC100AG) Critical and Evaluative Reading I (CRE101) Cultural and Social Anthropology (ASB102) Cultural Values in Education (EDU230) Current Topics in Computing (CIS280) Desktop Publishing (BPC128AC) Desktop Publishing - Word 7.0 (BPC128AE) Developmental Psychology (PSY240) Elementary Spanish I (SPA101) Elementary Spanish II (SPA102) Environmental Biology (IO105) Excel Spreadsheet (BPC114DE) First-Year Composition (ENG101) First-Year Composition (ENG102) Health Care Today (HCC100AA) Human Anatomy and Physiology I (BIO201) Human Anatomy and Physiology II (BIO202) Human Biology for Allied Health (BIO156) Human Relations in Business (MGT251) Integrated Studies (IGS290) Intermediate Algebra Accelerated (MAT122) Intermediate Spanish I (SPA201) Intermediate Spanish II (SPA202) Internet Web Publishing I (CIS233AA) Internet Web Publishing III (CIS233CA) Interpersonal Communication (COM110) Introduction to Art (ARH100) Introduction to Business (GBS151) Introduction to Cultural and Social Anthropology (ASB102) Introduction to Literature (ENH110) Introduction to Local Area Networks (CIS190) Introduction to Philosophy (PHI101) Introduction to Physical Geography (GPH111) Introduction to Psychology (PSY101) Introduction to Sociology (SOC101) Introduction to Statistics (PSY230) Introduction to the Supermarket Industry (SPM101) Introductory Accounting Lab (ACC250) Introductory Algebra (MAT092) Java Programming I (CIS163AA) LAN Operations and Concepts (CIS109) Law, Ethics, and Regulation in Issues (GBS205) Leadership for Front-Line Employees (TQM200) Legal, Ethical, and Regulatory Issues in Business (GBS205) Local Area Network Installation (CIS242) Local Area Network Planning and Design (CIS240) Magazine Article Writing (ENG235) Management and Leadership I (MGT229) Marine Biology (BIO183) Mathematical Concepts/Applications (MAT102) Medical Office - Vocabulary (OAS181) Medical Terminology (HIT170) Microcomputer Set Up & Maintenance (BPC125) Microcomputer Software Installation (BPC278) MS Access - Database Management (PC117DM) MS-DOS Advanced Desktop Publication (BPC238AA) MS-DOS Desktop Publication (BPC138AA) Office Automation Concepts (OAS250) Organizations, Paradigms, and Change (MGT172) Overview of the Community Colleges (EDU250) Personal & Workplace Safety (HCC100AC) Personal and Exploratory Writing (ENG217) Powerpoint (BPC120AE) Principles of Human Nutrition (FON241) Quality Customer Service (TQM101) Retirement Planning (CPD122) Small Business Operation (MGT253) Speed Reading (RDG105) Team Building Skills (HCC100AF) Teamwork Dynamics (TQM230) Technical Writing (ENG111) The Internet (BPC133DA) The Internet - Level I (BPC133AA) The Internet - Level II (BPC133BA) The Internet - Level III (BPC133CA) The Internet Web Publishing II (CIS233BA) UNIX Operating Systems (CIS122AC) Visual Basic Programming I (CIS159) Windows Operating System I (BPC121AE) Windows Operating System II (CIS122AE) Women and Men in a Changing Society (SOC212) Word for Windows (BPC135DK) WordPerfect for Windows (BPC135DD) Workplace Behavior in Health Care (HCC100AB) Workplace Resolution and Negotiation Strategies (CPD127) Writing For Quality Results (TQM105)

Roane State Community College   (ROAN)

Distance Learning 276 Patton Lane Harriman TN 37748

Accred.: Southern Association of Colleges and Schools

Email: online_dl@a1.rscc.cc.tn.us

(423) 882-4602 (423) 882-4611 fax:(423) 882-4683

URL: http://toccc.rscc.cc.tn.us/rscctocc.htm

Description: The Roane State Distance Learning program, through the CyberCollege, College at Home or College at Work video/audio/Internet program, Interactive Distance Education Access courses (IDEA), or through its affiliation with the Tennessee On-line Community College Consortium (TOCCC) allows students to learn at a set time and speed that fits their current life condition. As state in Roane State's Statement of Mission: "At seven staffed centers, numerous teaching sites and with a wide range of distance learning offerings, the college is a leader in responding to student needs.

Courses: (11) Composition I (ENG101) Deming Quality Management Philosophy (BUS210) Elementary Ethics (PHL121) General Psychology I (PSY101) Global Quality Imperative (BUS213) Improvement Using Gemba Kaizen (BUS214) Introduction to Technical Writing (ENG231) Music Appreciation (MUS130) Quality Systems Development (BUS217) Statistical Process Control (BUS290) Teaming and Group Dynamics (BUS230)

Rochester Institute of Technology   (ROCH)

Distance Learning Office 25 Lomb Memorial Drive Rochester NY 14623

Accred.: Middle States Association of Colleges and Schools   (800) 225-5748 (716) 475-6186 fax:(716) 475-5077
Email: disted@rit.edu   URL: http://www.rit.edu/

Description: Distance Learning at RIT offers students the opportunity to study at one of the nation's leading universities from anywhere in the world! Rochester Institute of Technology has distinguished itself as one of the premiere distance learning programs in the nation. Since 1979, when RIT offered its first distance learning course, the Institute has been a leader in the use of electronic forms of communication for course interaction. Distance Learning gives students the flexibility to earn a quality education where and when it suits their schedules. RIT's distance learning courses have the same objectives, rigorous work load, tuition and academic credit as its on-campus courses. Delivery methods are driven by the needs of the learner, the learning situation, and objectives of the course. Today, nearly 4000 students across the United States and overseas enroll each year in RIT's distance learning programs. Uses First Class.

Courses: (24) American Politics (051321190) Comp Concepts & Software Systems (060241090) Contemporary Science - Oceanus (069223490) Data Comm & Comp Networks (060241190) EHS Project Management (063075090) Emergency Planning & Methodology (069447190) Gov't & Politics of Russia & the CIS (051344290) Health Care Quality Assurance (063543190) Intro. to Computers & Programming (069225090) Introduction to Programming (060220890) Marketing on the Internet (010544090) Mass Communication (053548290) Medicare/Medicaid (063579891) Networking Technology (061447790) Organizational Communication (053541590) Programming Design & Validation (060221090) Project Management (063049090) Reengineering Health Care Systems (063579890) Remed Invest & Corrective Action (063044490) Reusable Software Design (060272590) Specifictn & Design of Info Systems (060282190) Sports Physiology & Life Fitness (069233190) Statistical Quality Control II (030773190) Survey of Health Care Systems (063531090)

Rogers State University   (ROGE)

c/o The Electronic University Network 1977 Colestin Road Hornbrook CA 96044

Accred.: North Central Association of Colleges and Schools   (800) 225-3276 (541) 482-5871 fax:(541) 482-7544
Email: euncouncil@aol.com   URL: http://www.wcc-eun.com/ru

Description: Rogers University - Claremore is part of the Oklahoma State System of Higher Education, located in Claremore, OK (birthplace of Will Rogers), about 15 miles northeast of Tulsa. Rogers U. offers courses for credit, taught by regular faculty, through the Electronic University Network. Courses include videotapes produced at KRSC-TV, the college's educational television station, as well as productions from other telecourse-producing colleges. Degrees offered include AA in Liberal Arts, AA in Business Management, and AS in Computer Science.

Courses: (37) Accounting II - Managerial (ACCT2203) American Federal Government (POLSC1113) American History I to 1865 (HIST2483) American History II from 1865 (HIST2493) Art History II - 1400-1850 (ART2723) Astronomy (PHYS2003) Basic Mathematics (MATH0013) C Programming (CS2223) C++ Computer Programming (CS2323) CAD Fundamentals (CAD2114) Chemistry (CHEM1115) College Algebra (MATH1513) Contemporary Marketing (BMA2143) Creative Writing (ENGL2023) Economics I - Macroeconomics (ECON2113) Economics II - Microeconomics (ECON2114) Elementary Algebra (MATH0113) English Composition I (ENGL1113) English Composition II (ENGL1213) Financial Accounting (ACCT2103) General Environmental Biology (BIOL1134) Human Geography (GEOG2243) Humanities I (HUM2113) Humanities II (HUM2223) Intermediate Algebra (MATH0213) Intro. to Computer Programming (CS2113) Introduction to Accounting (ACCT1113) Introduction to Business (BMA1203) Introduction to Psychology (PSY1113) Medical Terminology (NURS1103) Microcomputer Applications (CS2113) Operating Systems (CS2153) Principles of Management (BMA2013) Principles of Sociology (SOC1113) Social Ethics (PHILO2213) Systems Analysis and Design (CS2133) Visual Basic (CS1133)

Salve Regina University   (SALV)

c/o The Electronic University Network 1977 Colestin Road Hornbrook CA 96044

Accred.: New England Association of Schools and Colleges   (800) 225-3276 (541) 482-5871 fax:(541) 482-7544
Email: euncouncil@aol.com   URL: http://www.wcc-eun.com/salve/

Description: The Master of Arts in International Relations is designed for graduates seeking a broader and deeper understanding of the contemporary world, to help prepare them for their role in the increasingly interdependent world of the 21st century. The chief focus of the program is a search for new avenues to global harmony and justice. Courses in the program, however, are designed to meet the individual needs of students and help them prepare for or enhance their careers in government, international organizations, business, finance, teaching, research or further study. The Master of Arts in Human Development is intended to provided the student with an opportunity to integrate the growing body of theoretical formulations and research findings concerning human development. The Renaissance Person was scholar, artist, merchant, and what-have-you all rolled into one. She or he was a person who knew as much about mathematics and engineering as about poetry and music. She or he was sensitive yet pragmatic, a person who was eager to explore every facet of his or her human potential. This is the objective of the Master of Arts program in Human Development. It is an education in how people can fulfill themselves -- spiritually, emotionally, and intellectually. You will learn new ways of thinking and learning and how to help others think and learn for themselves. The program is very flexible. Working with your own program committee, you will help design the program that is best for you

Courses: (17) Africa and the Global Perspective (INR524) Central and South America (INR561) Central Asia and India (INR535) China, Japan, and the Pacific Rim (INR528) Contemporary International Issues (INR568) Development - Adulthood to Aging I (HDV539) Development - Adulthood to Aging II (HDV540) Ethical Perspectives on Global Issues (HUM501) Foundations of International Relations (INR502) Great Writers (HUM503) Infancy to Adolescence (HDV519) International Law (INR504) North America in the New World (INR550) Psychology of Personality (HDV541) Research Seminar (HUM500) Russia and Eastern European Politics (INR518) The Middle East (INR586)

Shawnee Community College   (SHAW)

8364 Shawnee College Road Ullin IL 62992

Accred.: North Central Association of Colleges and Schools   (800) 481-2242 (618) 634-2242 fax:(618) 634-9028
Email: mariab@shawnee.cc.il.us   URL: http://www.shawnee.cc.il.us
Description: Shawnee Community College is your community college! You can succeed in reaching your educational goals conveniently and at the lowest possible cost here. My challenge to you is to start reaching for your dreams now. We are ready to help you succeed. Call or come in to the main campus near Ullin or any of our extension centers located in Anna, Cairo or Metropolis, Illinois. Our students represent all ages and educational backgrounds. You may begin by taking one course or start a degree program. Our articulated courses are fully transferable when you are ready to move on to a four year college or university. Our occupational programs will qualify you for immediate employment. Shawnee Community College adult education classes provide courses to upgrade reading, writing and mathematical skills, achieve a GED certificate or pursue a personal interest, such as starting up a small business. In fact the Small Business and Workforce Development Center Staff are here to meet any business training need. Start fulfilling your dreams today with a quality education close to home!
Courses: (2) Data Communications (COM0230) English Composition (ENG0112)

Southwest Missouri State University   (SOMI)

College of Continuing Education 901 S. National St. Springfield MO 65804

Accred.: North Central Association of Colleges and Schools   (888) 767-8444 (417) 836-6015 fax:(417) 836-6016
Email: tmr832t@wpgate.smsu.edu   URL: http://www.smsu.edu/online
Description: SMSU Online is an Internet-based instruction program coordinated through the College of Continuing Education and the Extended University. We offer quality instruction and a low cost to students. Because we value our online students, we have placed an emphasis on student support services, many of which are available via the Internet.
Courses: (3) Management Information Systems (CIS661) Organizational Communication (COM638) Religion and Human Culture (REL580)

State University of New York   (SUNY)

The SUNY Learning Network SUNY Plaza S-510 Albany NY 12246

Accred.: Middle States Association of Colleges and Schools   (800) 875-6269 (518) 443-5331 fax:(518) 443-5167
Email: contacts@sln.suny.edu   URL: http://www.sln.suny.edu/sln
Description: The SUNY Learning Network is a growing consortium, currently with 20 campuses in the SUNY System, who have joined together to offer graduate and undergraduate online courses. The on-line courses are available to degree seeking students or to students who simply want to take courses for personal development (non-matriculated students). Credits earned in the program are fully transferable; degrees earned in the program are SUNY degrees. You can also earn credits by combining traditional on-campus courses and distance learning studies from the colleges participating in the SUNY Learning Network. The SUNY Learning Network uses a new type of software called groupware and the Internet. Groupware creates an electronic forum where students and professors working at a distance can work and learn collaboratively, sharing documents, graphics, and images. Being able to work collaboratively with others as part of a team is becoming a highly prized skill in the workplace today. Each year new on-line courses will be developed and offered.
Courses: (193) Abnormal Psychology (SS155) Academic Writing I (ENGL101) Accounting for Decision Making-Concepts and Theory (ACC19571) Accounting I (BUS1404S) Advanced Ceramic Processing (CES510001) Advanced Composition (ENG200) Advanced Financial Accounting Theory (ACC68535) Advanced Fire Administration (264014) Advanced Income Tax Accounting (ACC61135) America Since 1970, The Mirror of the Movies (AHI315585) American Government and Politics (7721607) Assessment of Sociotechnological Problems and Issues (CEN580) Astronomy (1230101) Barrier Precautions and Infection Control Measures (DEN113) Basic Graphic Design (GC111) Basic Nutrition (FSA102) Basic Photography (GC126) Behavior Modification (PSY227Y02) Bioceramic Materials (CES486001) Biology of Nature (BIO103) Broadcast Journalism (BRC225) Broadcast News Writing (BRC326) Building Materials and Construction (FPT103) Business and Society in the Information Age (213254) Business Communications (BAUD101) Business Policy (214814) Business Statistics (BSAD221) Calculus I w/ Analytic Geometry (MAT171Y03) Calculus with Business Applications (MAT125) Carbohydrate Chemistry I (FCH540) Career and Life Planning for Returning Adult Students (CDL101) Child Psychology and Development (3837107) Children Literature (3551202) Clinical Pharmocology in Nursing (NUR211) Coaching Theory and Techniques (PPE209) Coed Personal Fitness (PE101) College Algebra and Trigonometry (MAT1593408) College Composition (ENG1011) College Writing (221624) Color and Design (GC125) Complete Manager (FSD24571) Computer Applications in Telecommunications (01920588R) Computer Programming II (CISY2133) Computing Fundamentals I (CSC1591887) Computing in Education I (ETAP5265024) Consumer Nutrition (HRMG110) Corporate Finance (213514) Creative Typography (GC210) Data Base Systems (CS532) Data Communications Concepts, Security and Management (273304) Dental Materials (DEN211) Dental Radiology (DEN111) Deregulation - Do Market Solutions Really Work' (213224) Developmental Psychology (PSY210Y05) Digital Electronics For Telecommunications (01915588R) Digital Illustration (GC141) Digital Imaging (GC142) Digital Typography (GC121) Direct Marketing (DMR110Y01) Diversity in the Workplace (213164) Eastern Religious Traditions (HIS305) Economics, Micro (212224) Educational Uses of the Information Highway (EST572) Emerging Infectious Diseases (1134501) Engineering Mechanics (Statics) (EGR271Y01) English Composition II (ENG102) Ethics (HUM13042S) Exercise Physiology (ES380) Fashion Business Practices (FM116) Fashion Merchandising Principles and Techniques (FM122) Financial Management (BFIN5257172) Food Service Preparation I (HRMG101) Freshman Seminar (FS100) Fundamentals of Law (LAW101) Fundamentals of Library and Information Science (CEL59130) General Internship (CEL200) Global Workplace and Employers, Workers & Organizations (263724) Golf Course Management (GLF130) Golf Shop Operation (GLF118) Hazardous Materials and the EMT (EMS113) Health Care Delivery in the United States (HSM30135) Healthcare Financing Issues (HCM194Y01) Human Behavior and the Organization (HMS250Y02) Human Genetics and Values (BIO144) Human Resource Management (213504) Human Sexuality (SOCE201) Imaging Processing (MAT433085) Information Literacy (LIB111) Introduction to Biology I (SCI 1103S) Intelligence and Mental Retardation (PSY223Y04) International Business (213314) Interpreting Statistics (MAT150) Introductory Sociology (SS161) Intro to Mass Media (TELC101601) Introduction to Airline Reservations Systems-SABRE (TVL210) Introduction to Astronomy (SCI1030S) Introduction to Calculus (272754) Introduction to Computer Science (CSC1518223) Introduction to Criminal Justice Systems (PSCJ101) Introduction to Criminalistics (CHEM131) Introduction to Fashion Industry (FM114) Introduction to Hospitality Industry (HRMG100) Introduction to Language Study (ENG201) Introduction to Microprocessors with Digital Logic (EGR279Y01) Introduction to Operating Systems (2143101) Introduction to Paralegalism (PARA101) Introduction to Psychology (PSYC103) Introduction to Radio and Television (13116) Introduction to Sociology (SOC110Y01) Introduction to Sociology (SOCI101) Introduction to Sports Medicine (PPE170) Introduction to Sports Science (PPE100) Introduction to Stock Market Investing (BUS107) Introduction to the Travel and Tourism Industry (TT130) Introductory Accounting 1 (212054) Introductory Accounting 2 (212064) Italian Syntax and Composition (ITL412) Juvenile Justice and Delinquency (264604) Language and Composition (ENGL101) Latin America on the Brink of the 21st Century (HUM215) Legal Research (PAL11271) Litigation/Civil Procedure (PARA205) Living with the Internet (CIS115) Management (BADM249) Management and Supervision (PT404) Management Information Systems (273654) Management of Health Services (253734) Managerial Leadership (214624) Managing Security Systems (CRJ302002) Marketing Principles (212414) Marketing Research (214924) Math

Applications I (06332588R) Math Concepts (MAT13071) Mathematics for Decision Making (271754) Mechanical Properties of Ceramics and Glass (CES562001) Media Economics (BRC320) Media in Teaching and Learning (ETAP5236741) Medical Terminology and Pharmacology (OT317) Merchandise Planning and Control (FM121) Microcomputer Applications (271454) National Parks Biology (SC119) News in Historical Perspective (243504) Online Fiction Workshop (ENG329001) Operating Systems (CS552) Operations Management (214204) Oral Anatomy and Physiology I (DEN112) Paradigms of Programming Languages (2132101) Personnel Management (MBA538) Perspectives on Death and Dying (HMS240Y01) Philosophy & Principles of PE & Athletics (PPE175) Physics I for Engineers & Scientists (PHY17101) Physics II for Engineers & Scientists (PHY17201) Pluralism and Diversity In America (PDA101) Polymer Properties and Technology (FCH552I) Pratique de L'ecriture (FRE312001) Preclinical Dental Assisting (DAS110) Principles of Accounting I (ACCT101) Principles of Biology I (BIOL101) Principles of Retailing and Business (RET101) Professional Communication (ENG250) Programming Languages (CS571) Psychology of Addictions (PSY234Y02) Psychology of Advertising (PSY240Y01) Psychology Principles I (PSY111) Public Relations (BU221) Publication Design (GC215) Regional Geography (SS172) Rock Music Style and Development (MUS11571) Rooms Division Management (HRMG103) Sanitation Techniques (HOT13271) Science of Human Movement (ES200) Script Writing (ENGL200) Selected Topics in Physical Studies (PPE240) Semiconductor Device Packaging (EE577) Social Research for Professionals (283504) Solid State Physics I (CES541001) Sport Psychology (PPE208) Sports Management (PPE215) State & Local Government (POLSC107) Statistics - An Activity Based Approach (272384) Stress Management (PEC253) Studio Procedures (GC131) Teachers in Context (ETAP5125022) Telecommunications (BRC330) Theoretical Foundations of Reading/Literacy (3479301) Topics in Art History (GC244) Topics in Computers & Society Information Superhighway (272154) Typography (0930702) U. S. Destinations & Domestic Ticketing (TT131) Women's & Family History in America (243254) World History 1 (242104) World Literature - Ancient World Through The Renaissance (11203) X-Ray Powder Diffraction (CHEM581B)

Strayer University   (STRA)

Distance Learning Center 8382-F Terminal Road Lorton VA 22079

Accred.: Middle States Association of Colleges and Schools
Email: psb@ns1.strayer.edu

(800) 422-8055 (703) 339-1850 fax:(703) 339-1852
URL: http://www.strayerdl.edu

Description: Classes on the Internet to fit your busy schedule. Whether at home, at work, or on the road - now you can take classes wherever you are. Improve your career without taking time off from work. Save travel time by attending class on your computer. For the busy working adult we believe that time spent on the job can be put towards Life Learning credit. All our classes are conducted in a "real-time" chat environment with classes being offered in the evenings and weekends.

Courses: (153) Accounting I (ACC101) Accounting II (ACC105) Accounting Information Systems (ACC564) Accounting Policy (ACC566) Accounting Theory (ACC415) Advanced Access Applications (CIS113) Advanced Accounting I (ACC401) Advanced Accounting II (ACC402) Advanced Accounting Theory (ACC563) Advanced Administration, Installation & Configuration (CIS280) Advanced Auditing (ACC562) Advanced Federal Taxation (ACC220) Advanced Managerial Accounting (ACC561) Advanced Structured COBOL (CIS249) American Literature (ENG220) Auditing I (ACC403) Auditing II (ACC405) Business Communication (ENG105) Business Communications (BUS490) Business Ethics (BUS290) Business Policy (BUS490) Business Policy (BUS490) C Programming Language I (CIS240) C Programming Language II (CIS241) Communication I (ENG102) Communication II (ENG106) Communication Software Update (CIS304) Communications III (ENG310) Communications III (ENG320) Comparative Philosophical Concepts (HUM205) Computer Architectures I (CIS312) Computer Programming Design (CIS110) Computerized Accounting (ACC208) Contemporary American Economic History (ECO200) Contract Administration and Management (BUS330) Contract and Purchasing Negotiation Techniques (BUS340) Cooperative Education in Accounting (ACC399) Cooperative Education in Business Administration (BUS399) Cost Accounting I (ACC225) Cost Accounting II (ACC325) Cost and Price Analysis (FIN230) Current Topics in Accounting (ACC291299) Current Topics in Business Administration (BUS291299) Current Topics in Computer Information Systems (CIS291-299) Data Communication (CIS185) Design and Implementation and TCP/IP (CIS300) Directed Study Project (ACC590) Directed Study Project (BUS590) Drama (ENG305) Econometrics (ECO470) Economic Development (ECO415) Economic Problems and Issues (ECO405) Economics and Management (ECO550) Economics of Energy (ECO440) Economics of Labor (ECO310) Economics of Transportation (ECO455) Economics of Urban Development (ECO425) Electronic Commerce (BUS213) Federal Acquisition Systems and Process (BUS209) Federal Personnel (BUS225) Federal Taxation (ACC215) Film and Society (ENG310) Financial Management (BUS534) Financial Management (BUS534) Financial Management (FIN300) History of Economic Thought (ECO400) Human Resource Management (BUS310) Human Resource Management (BUS530) Intermediate Accounting I (ACC200) Intermediate Accounting II (ACC205) Intermediate Accounting III (ACC305) Intermediate Macroeconomics (ECO302) Intermediate Microeconomics (ECO301) International Business Environment (BUS250) International Economics (ECO305) International Environment of Financial Management (ECO410) Internet Program Development (CIS309) Internet Security (CIS311) Internet Topics (CIS307) Introduction to Art, Music and Literature (HUM100) Introduction to Business (BUS100) Introduction to Business (BUS532) Introduction to Computer Information Systems (CIS105) Introduction to Computer Networking (CIS175) Introduction to Database Management Systems (CIS275) Introduction to Financial Accounting (ACC104) Introduction to Psychology (PSY105) Introduction to Public Finance (FIN250) Introduction to Sociology (SOC100) Introductions to Oracle (CIS276) Labor Relations (BUS405) Logic (HUM200) Macroeconomics (ECO102) Management (Internal) Auditing (ACC420) Management Communication (BUS531) Management Theory (BUS541) Management Theory (BUS541) Managerial Accounting (ACC560) Managerial Accounting (Accounting III) (ACC110) Microcomputer Applications in Business I (CIS107) Microcomputer Applications in Business II (CIS108) Microeconomics (ECO101) Money and Banking (ECO320) Networking Administration (CIS180) Non-profit/Municipal Accounting (ACC410) Object-Oriented Programming I (CIS265) Object-Oriented Programming II (CIS266) Oracle and PL/SQL (CIS305) Oral Communications (ENG221) Organizational Behavior (BUS520) Organizational Behavior (BUS520) Personal Financial Planning (FIN215) Philosophy, Religion, and Ethics (HUM400) Political and Economic Geography of the World (ECO105) Position Management and Classification (BUS215) Principles of Economics (ECO100) Principles of Economics (ECO250) Principles of Finance (FIN100) Principles of Investment (ECO150) Principles of Management (BUS200) Principles of Organizational Behavior (BUS105) Production and Operations Management (BUS540) Public Contracting (BUS350) Public Finance (ECO450) Public Relations (BUS300) Purchasing and Materials Management (BUS230) Recruitment and Placement (BUS220) Risk and Insurance (BUS305) Science and Society (HUM300) Senior Seminar in Business Administration (BUS499) Service and Support (CIS285) Short Story (ENG300) Small Business Management (BUS205) Structured COBOL (CIS248) Study of Africa, Asia, and Latin America (SOC300) Supporting Systems Management Servers (CIS302) Supporting Windows '95 (CIS182) Supporting Windows NT (CIS187) Systems Administration for SQL Server (CIS289) Systems Analysis & Design (CIS510) Tax Research and Planning (ACC565) TCP/IP for Windows NT (CIS287) The Individual and Society (PSY100) The Marketing Process (BUS533) The Origins of Western Culture (HUM310) Training and Development (BUS222) UNIX Operating System (CIS155) Using and Programming Access (CIS111) Visual Programming (CIS267) Windows NT Server Enterprise (CIS283) World Art (HUM103) World Literature (ENG225) World Literature (HUM104)

The Internet University - Accredited Course Providers

Syracuse University   (SYRA)
700 University Ave. Syracuse NY

Accred.: Middle States Association of Colleges and Schools   (315) 443-1127 (315) 443-3273 fax:(315) 443-4410
Email: online@uc.syr.edu   URL: http://www.suce.syr.edu/online/

Description: Syracuse University, a pioneer in distance education, has offered limited residency degree programs since 1996. As a further innovation in providing quality educational experiences to distant students, or students who cannot attend class for a variety of reasons, Syracuse's Continuing Education Division has begun to offer a select number of purely online courses each term, in cutting edge subjects not readily available from other web sources, taught by the same faculty who teach the courses on campus.

Courses: (12) Geography of Latin America (GEO3211) Government and Politics of Canada (PSC3311) Investing and Trading on the Internet (HSC0011) JAVA Programming for the Internet (CIS300) Online Fiction Workshop (ETS200) Social Influences on Human Sexual Behavior (PSY5771) Sociology of Evil (SOC4004) Sociology of the Internet (SOC4005) Strategies for Effective Communication (ETS400) The Politics of the Information Revolution (PSC3001) Travel the Lewis and Clark Trail (HSC0021) UNIX Operating System and Internet (CIS333)

Texas Technical University   (TETE)
Division of Continuing Education P. O. Box 42191 Lubbock TX 79409

Accred.: Southern Association of Colleges and Schools   (800) 692-6877 (806) 742-2352 fax:(806) 742-2318
Email: distlearn@ttu.edu   URL: http://www.dce.ttu.edu/

Description: Distance Learning, a unit of Extended Learning at Texas Tech University, is accredited by the Southern Association of Colleges and Schools. College courses are accredited by the appropriate academic department. High school courses are approved by the Texas Education Agency. Texas Tech University High School was established by the State Board of Education in Fall 1993 as a Texas public high school able to offer high school diplomas through Distance Learning.

Courses: (18) Abnormal Psychology (PSY4305) American Public Policy (POLS2302) Baseball History (HIST3339) Chemical Engineering Thermodynamics I (CHE3321) Child Psychology (PSY2301) Drugs, Alcohol, and Behavior (PSY4325) History of Texas (HIST3310) History of the United States to 1877 (HIST2300) History of the US Since 1877 (HIST2301) Internet for Educators (EDIT4000) Life Span Human Development (HD2303) Nutrition and Food (FN1410) Principles of Economics I - Micro (ECO2301) Short Story (ENGL3331) Sports and Recreation in the U.S. (HIST3338) US Government Organization (POLS1301) Western Civilization I (HIST1300) Western Civilization II (HIST1301)

The Graduate School of America   (TGSA)
330 Second Avenue South, Suite 550 Minneapolis MN 55401

Accred.: North Central Association of Colleges and Schools   (800) 987-1133 (612) 339-8650 fax:(612) 339-8022
Email: tgsainfo@tgsa.edu   URL: http://www.tgsa.edu/

Description: The Graduate School of America offers graduate degrees designed for mid-career learners. TGSA meets the needs of working professionals by combining time-honored educational practices with modern technology. Our instructional approach builds on the individual faculty tutorial, a teaching method long used in the great European universities. Through faculty-guided, self-directed study and the interactive capabilities of telecommunications and computer technology, The Graduate School is able to deliver an educational experience that is personal, convenient and of the highest quality. TGSA's online courses are all web-based. Materials and assignments are all downloaded from the web site. Students and faculty hold asynchronous (non-real time) discussions online and communicate through email.

Courses: (93) Accounting and Financial Management (OM815W) Advanced Marketing Management (OM853W) Advanced Study in Research Methods (RM502W) Applied Business Economics (OM854W) Biological Bases of Behavior (HS811W) Changing Patterns of the Educational Process (ED813W) Clinical Supervision (HS862W) Cognitive-Affective Bases of Behavior (HS812W) Collaborative Nature of Adult Education (ED836W) Compulsive & Addictive Behavior (HS875W) Compulsive Behavior & the Disturbance of Self (HS866W) Consulting Practice (OM879W) Curriculum Development (ED825W) Data Analysis & Statistics (RM500W) Decision Making Under Risk & Uncertainty (OM836W) Education and the Law (ED823W) Elementary School Administration (ED853W) Entrepreneurship (OM876W) Environmental and Societal Issues in Telecommunications (OM892W) Ethics & Social Responsibility (OM821W) Ethics and Social Responsibility in Distance Education (ED852W) Ethnic & Cultural Awareness (HS834W) Evaluating the Effectiveness of the Educational Process (ED814W) Finance (OM720W) Forecasting (OM861W) Funding of Educational Institutions (ED822W) General Management Perspectives (OM871W) Global Financial Management (OM721W) Grief and Bereavement Counseling (HS845W) Group Counseling and Psychotherapy (HS841W) Higher Education Administration (ED855W) Human Development and Behavior (HD501W) Human Resources Management (OM845W) Industry Structure, Roles and Change (OM889W) Instructional Design for Distance Education (ED846W) Instructional Design for Multimedia (ED847W) Integrative Management Project (RM810W) Intellectual Development Across the Lifespan (ED828W) International Business (OM838W) International Marketing Management (OM867W) Intranets and Electronic Commerce (OM894W) Introduction to Digital Transmission (OM883W) Introduction to Multimedia and Web-Based Instruction (ED720W) Issues in International Advertising (OM872W) Leadership Tools for Successful Project Management (OM885W) Leading the High Performance Organization (OM844W) Learning from an Interdisciplinary Perspective (ED827W) Life Planning & Career Development (HS879W) Managerial Accounting (OM868W) Managerial Communication (OM827W) Managing and Motivating Generation 'X' (OM831W) Managing Creativity (OM829W) Managing Information and Communications Technology (OM843W) Marketing Strategy and Practice (OM814W) Marriage & Family Systems (HS871W) Mental Health Counseling (HS821W) Network Management (OM888W) Network Technology (OM884W) Operations Management (OM855W) Organizational and Group Dynamics (OD501W) Overview of Distance Education (ED845W) Performance Management (OM869W) Personnel Administration (ED857W) Power & Politics in Organizations (OM834W) Principles of Educational Administration (ED820W) Principles of Learning and Instructional Design (ED851W) Process Management for Improved Performance (OM842W) Professional & Scientific Ethics (HS815W) Psychopathology, Assessment and Treatment (HS831W) Redefining the Workplace (OM874W) Regulatory Issues (OM891W) Secondary School Administration (ED854W) Social Influences of Behavior (HS813W) Strategic Planning (OM816W) Supervisory Principles (ED856W) Survey of Research in Societal and Cultural Change (SC501W) Survey of Research Methodology (RM501W) System Planning and Design (OM886W) Teaching and Learning with Diverse Populations (ED838W) Telecommunications Applications (OM893W) Telephony I (OM882W) The Climate and Structure of the Learning Environment (ED824W) The Counselor as Scientist-Practitioner (HS838W) The Four Levels of Evaluation (ED850W) The Future of Educational Institutions (ED815W) The Leadership Challenge (OM896W) The Politics of Higher Education (ED840W) Theories of Personality (HS814W) Theories of Psychotherapy (HS839W) Theory and Methods of Educating Adults (ED829W) Theory, Structure and Design of Organizations (OM846W) Total Customer Management (OM851W) Written Communications for Business (OM895W)

The Heritage Institute

(HEON)

Heritage Online 2802 E. Madison Ave., Suite 187 Seattle WA 98112

Accred.: Northwest Association of Schools and Colleges
Email: mail@hol.edu

(800) 445-1305 -- fax:--
URL: http://www.hol.edu/

Description: Welcome to Heritage OnLine. We specialize in Internet-assisted distance education for teachers. Our Vision is to see teachers and students across America using the Internet for learning in all subjects. Our current program has twenty active courses in a variety of subjects such as art, assessment, classroom management, education, foreign language, literature, math, science, social studies, writing and technology. All courses are available for Antioch University credit. Teachers enjoy the opportunity in our courses to explore the Internet for learning and to benefit from listserv discussions with other educators from around the country. With the recent addition of eight new on-line courses, educators now have Internet access to a variety of non-technical courses that are also offered by The Heritage Institute as Guided Independent Study (correspondence) courses. Teachers also appreciate our practical academic approach that brings coursework into their actual classroom teaching. Courses may be started at any time, are self-paced and are taught by instructors who combine expertise in their subject area with a knowledge of technology and the Internet. Most course information is accessible via the World Wide Web, and many courses may be completed by those with only email capability.

Courses: (20) Astronomy and the WWW (SC404I) Computer Enhancement of Classroom (CM400) Connecting With At-Risk Students (ED411S) Current Children's Literature (HU402V) Email Learning Across Curriculum (CM400L) Emerging Models of Assessment (ED412L) Foreign Language Learning on Net (ED408O) Grant Writing for Technology (BU400F) Integrating Art in the Curriculum (HU403D) Multimedia Across the Curriculum (CM400K) Museums in the Classroom (ED406M) Online Projects for Schools (CM400I) Portfolio Assessment (ED407Y) Real World Math via the Internet (ED408P) Research in the Classroom (ED409V) Science Study on the WWW (SC404J) Teaching Writing Online (ED409Q) Using News Media Across Curriculum (ED410S) WWW Page Construction (CM400H) WWW-Enhanced Student Writing (ED408N)

The University of Alabama

(ALAB)

Distance Education Office Box 870388 Tuscaloosa AL 35406

Accred.: Southern Association of Colleges and Schools
Email: disted@ccs.ua.edu

(800) 452-5971 (205) 348-5991 fax:(205) 348-0249
URL: http://ua1ix.ua.edu/~disted

Description: The University of Alabama's GOALS (Global Online Academic Learning System) program is Internet-based online instruction featuring courses delivered over the World Wide Web directly to the student's home or corporate desktop. Students receive instruction through an established and secured Internet site and are able to interact with instructors and complete lessons via electronic mail. The mission of online courses is to accommodate the educational needs of individuals who have access to and experience with a computer and the Internet. Electronic communication reinvents and enhances the student's learning experience. The same high standard of education that is imparted on The University of Alabama campus is now available to students online around the world. The registration process is handled by the Division of Distance Education.

Courses: (1) English Bible as Literature (EH363)

Thomas Edison State College

(THED)

DIAL 101 W. State St. Trenton NJ 08608

Accred.: Middle States Association of Colleges and Schools
Email: bursar@call.tesc.edu

(609) 292-4000 (609) 984-1150 fax:
URL: http://www.tesc.edu/tesc/online.html

Description: The Center for Distance & Independent Adult Learning (DIAL) provides Thomas Edison State College course options and approaches to learning that take place outside the traditional college classroom. Offering a flexible and accessible way of earning credit towards a college degree, DIAL courses have proven most successful with well-motivated, self-disciplined individuals who enjoy learning independently. On-Line Computer Classroom courses utilize computer communications to link distance learners with each other and faculty. On-Line courses allow interactive distance learning in a structured, semester-based format, but without imposing barriers of time and place. Courses include required on-line course discussions in which students participate on their own schedule, and written assignments that are sent to faculty via private e-mail.

Courses: (19) American Cinema (OLFIL110) Behavioral Science & Management (OLMAN352) Computers and Society I (OLCOS161) Computers and Society II (OLSOC160) Contemporary Ethics (OLPHI286) Eastern Religions (OLREL406) Global Environment & Change I (OLENS311) Global Environment and Change II (OLENS312) International Economics (OLECO490) Introduction to Marketing (OLMAR301) Introduction World Religions (OLREL405) Major Philosophers - Socrates-Sartre (OLPHI376) Marriage and the Family (OLSOC210) Principles of Management (OLMAN301) Social Psychology I (OLPSY370) Social Psychology II (OLPSY371) Systems & Management (OLMAN351) Topics in Management (OLMAN353) Western Religions (OLREL407)

Trinidad State Junior College

(TRIN)

600 Prospect St. Trinidad CO 81082

Accred.: North Central Association of Colleges and Schools
800-621-8752
Email: ptate@aol.com

719-846-5625 fax:719-846-5667
URL: http://writing.tsjc.cccoes.edu/CrWrAd/InternetCourses.html

Description: Trinidad State Junior College is the oldest two-year college in Colorado. It is located in the city of Trinidad, which lies on the edge of the foothills of the Sangre de Cristo mountain range. The climate is semi-arid, with plenty of sunshine. Online classes begin in late August and mid-January.

Courses: (6) Fiction Writing (ENG255) Film Studies (LIT103) Freshman Composition I and II (ENG121) Introduction to Literature (LIT115) Masterpieces of World Literature I & II (LIT201) Survey of British Literature I and II (LIT221)

The Internet University - Accredited Course Providers

UCLA Extension   (UCLA)

924 Westwood Blvd, Suite 650 Los Angeles CA 90024

Accred.: Western Association of Schools and Colleges   (800) 784-8436   fax:(310) 794-8424
Email: URL: http://www.then.com

Description: The Home Education Network is the leading online supplier of continuing higher education and is dedicated to providing busy professionals with the tools needed to pursue their lifelong learning objectives. By combining technological innovation with extraordinary customer service, we are committed to helping adult learners around the world access the best in educational resources - anytime, anywhere, at any stage in life. Since 1996, THEN has distributed 150 online courses through UCLA Extension, the nation's largest single-campus continuing higher education program. New courses are continually updated to our already comprehensive list.

Courses: (93) Academic Content via English (X325E) Accounting for Non-Accountants (X429) Advanced Writing for Grad School (X340E) Advertising Copywriting (X401B) American Culture (X325F) Basics of Budgeting (X430) Business Computer Programming (X41420) Business Computer Programming (X414B) Business Plan for New Media Venture (X402) Cultural Diversity in the Classroom (X325H) Cutting-Edge Documentation (X860) Data Modeling and Analysis (X418H) Developing a Business Plan (X497B) Developing Career Options (X765C) Developing Online Curriculum (X396F) Distance Learning Assessment Theory (X396G) East Asia for Educators (X400B) English Grammar and Usage (X340G) Entertainment Industry Careers (X474) Entrepreneurial Businesses Marketing (X497) Extended Preparation for the GMAT (X740) Extended Preparation for the LSAT (X740B) Facilitative Tools for Online Teaching (X396H) Fiction Fundamentals (X450E) Financing for Entrepreneurs (X897) Food and Beverage Management (X407) Fundamentals of Public Relations (X422) Grant Proposals (X480) Human Resources Management (X450J) Information Systems and Analysis (X418) Instructional Technology (X332) Intensive Grammar Review (X401) Intensive Grammar Review (X801) International Human Resources (X450D) Internet for Educators (X333B) Internet Publishing for Educators (X333) Internet Research for Online Courses (X396B) Intro to Client-Server Computing (X418C) Intro to International Business (X460) Intro to MIS (X418D) Introduction to C Programming (X418B) Introduction to Computing for Business (X414) Introduction to Online Technologies (X396C) Introduction to Screenwriting I (X451D) Introduction to Screenwriting II (X451E) Investing in Securities (X433) Java Programming Fundamentals (X418F) Javascript for Educators (X396D) Language Development and Acquisition (X325C) Language Structure and Usage (X325D) Library and Information Access Tools (X340C) Marketing Hospitality Services (X491B) Mathematics for Management (X110) MIS for Planning and Control (X418G) Models for Online Courses (X396) Nature Writing (X445) Networking for Career Advancement (X765B) Novel Writing I (X450G) Object-Oriented Programming C++ (X418J) Online Global Business Presence (X898) Poetry Workshop (X450F) Practicum in Online Teaching (X396E) Preparatory Writing for Grad School (X340D) Preparing for the TOEFL (X931) Principles of Accounting (X1A) Principles of Accounting 1B (X1B) Problem Solving and Critical Thinking (X340) Professional Novel Writing (X450C) Quantitative Reasoning Skills (X340F) Reading Comprehension (X340B) Real Estate Principles (X475) Recruitment, Interviewing, Selection (X450) Rewriting the Screenplay (X451) Screenwriters, Playwrights & Fiction (X450H) Self Managed Career (X765) Strategic Business Writing (X409) Teaching English Abroad (X325) Teaching English Language Development (X325G) Teaching English Language Learners (X325B) Teaching Exceptional Learners (X328) Technical Editing (X439) Technical Writing (X439B) Technology in K-12 Curriculum (X333C) Travel Journalism (X447) Visual Basic for Windows (X418E) Working with Boards and Volunteers (X413) Workplace Leadership and Influence (X491) Writing Comedy for Film and TV (X451B) Writing Effective Proposals (X439C) Writing for Episodic Television (X451C) Writing for Public Relations (X439D) Writing Nonfiction for Publication (X450B) Writing Spanish for Professionals (X400)

University of Alaska - Fairbanks   (ALFA)

Center for Distance Education P.O. Box 756700 Fairbanks AK 99775

Accred.: Northwest Association of Schools and Colleges   (907) 474-5353 —   fax:(907) 474-5402
Email: racde@uaf.edu   URL: http://uafcde.lrb.uaf.edu

Description: We believe you'll enjoy the convenience and flexibility of our independent learning program. No more night school! We offer a viable alternative to the professional working student. Our courses carry university credit and are applicable toward UAF degree and certificate programs. (Please note that a UAF degree cannot be earned solely through correspondence.) Our credits also may be transferred to other universities.

Courses: (96) Abnormal Psychology (PSY345) Alaska Native Claims Settlement (AKNP151) Alaska, Land and Its People (HIST115) American Government & Politics (PS101) Applying Telecommunications (ED593C) Basics of Investing (ABUS120) Beginning Ancient Greek I (FL193A) Beginning Ancient Greek II (FL193AA) Beginning Latin I (FL193B) Beginning Latin II (FL193C) Biological Psychology (PSY393) Business, Grant and Report Writing (ENGLF212) Business, Grant, and Report Writing (ENGL212) Calculus I (MATH200) Calculus II (MATH201) Calculus III (MATH202) Child Development (EC245) Computer Sci for Software Engineer (CS670) Concepts & Applications of Math (MATH131) Concepts of Math (MATH132) Drugs and Drug Dependence (PSY370) Education and Cultural Processes (ED610) Education and Cultural Processes (EDF610) Electronic Mail & Online Services (ED293A) Electronic Mail & Online Services (ED593A) Elementary Algebra (DEVM060) Elementary Probability and Statistics (STAT200) Elementary School Teacher Math I (MATH205) Elementary School Teacher Math II (MATH206) Elements of Physical Geography (GEOG205) Enjoying Jazz (MUS125) Family - Cross-Cultural Perspective (SOC242) Federal Aviation Regulations (AFPMF152) Film and TV Criticism (JB308) Functions for Calculus (MATH107) Fundamentals of Petroleum (SCIA101) Geography of Alaska (GEOG302) History of Alaska (HIST461) History of the Cinema (JB105) History of the US I (HIST131) History of the US I (HIST132) Individual, Society, and Culture (ANTH100X) Individual, Society, and Culture (SOC100) Intermediate Algebra (DEVM070) Intermediate Ancient Greek I (FL293) Intermediate Ancient Greek II (FL293B) Intermediate Exposition (ENGL213) Intermediate Latin I (FL293C) Intermediate Latin II (FL293D) Interrelation of Art, Drama, and Music (ART200) Intro to Mass Communications (JB101) Introduction to Anthropology (ANTH101) Introduction to Broadcasting (JB102) Introduction to Business (BA151) Introduction to Marine Biology (BIOL150) Introduction to Psychology (PSY101) Introduction to Sociology (SOC101) Introduction to the Internet I (ED293B) Introduction to the Internet II (ED293C) Introductory Geography (GEOG101) Library and Information Strategies (LS100) Lifespan Development Psychology (PSY240) Lit. of Alaska & Yukon Territory (ENGL350) Magazine Article Writing (JB311) Mass Media Law & Regulation (JB413) Methods of Written Communication (ENGL111) Modes of Literature (ENGL211) Music Fundamentals (MUS103) Narrative Art of Alaska Native Peoples (ENGLF349) Native Cultures of Alaska (ANTH242) Natural History of Alaska (BIOL104) Nature of Language (LING101) Oral Tradition and Folklore (ANTH230) Personality (PSY304) Pre Algebra (DEVM050) Preparatory College English (DEVE070) Principles of Advertising (BA326) Principles of Advertising (JB326) Principles of Economics (ECON200) Principles of Marketing (BA343) Private Pilot Ground School (AVTY100) Publishing, Production, and Theory (JB685) Real Estate Law (ABUS223) Review of Basic Geometry (DEVM081) Review of Elementary Algebra (DEVM061) Review of Intermediate Algebra (DEVM071) Science of Nutrition (HLTH203) Small Schools Curriculum Design (ED631) Social Institutions (SOC102) Survey of Energy Industries (PETE103) The Alaska Native Land Settlement (ANS310) The Exceptional Learner (ED375) Tourism Principles and Practice (BA160) Trigonometry (MATH108) Using the Internet (ED593B) Western Civilization I (HIST101)

University of California-Irvine   (CAIR)
UCI Extension P. O. Box 6050 Irvine CA 92616

Accred.: Western Association of Schools and Colleges   (949) 824-5414 (949) 824-6116 fax:
Email: oac@uci.edu   URL: http://www.unex.uci.edu/

Description: We're the continuing education branch of the renowned University of California, Irvine. For over 30 years, thousands of professionals have passed through our doors seeking career and personal enrichment. We offer prestigious instructors, solid curricula that includes more than 1,800 courses each year, and the opportunity to meet fellow learners who are dynamic, stimulating, and interesting to know.

The doors to UCI Extension also open to our acclaimed certificate programs and new specialized studies. These concentrated formats allow you to develop a specialty within your current field or transition to a new career.

And we have much, much more to offer you -- from our new online courses to ACCESS UCI and WOC career development -- from Custom Education and Training to English as a second language communication and culture courses.

Courses: (4) Fundamentals of Visual Basic (COM1) Fundamentals of Visual C++ (COM2) Fundamentals of Visual J++ (COM3) The Power of Macroeconomics (ACC1)

University of Central Florida   (FLCE)
4000 Central Florida Blvd. P. O. Box 160000 Orlando FL 32816

Accred.: Southern Association of Colleges and Schools   (407) 207-4910 (407) 823-2000 fax:–
Email: distrib@pegasus.cc.ucf.edu   URL: http://pegasus.cc.ucf.edu/~distrib

Description: Distributed Learning at UCF delivers university-level education beyond the constraints of time and space. Based on interactive computer-based communications over the global Internet, Distributed Learning brings the University of Central Florida to those who otherwise would not be able to attend classes on one of our central Florida campuses. By state-wide agreement, our University distance learning courses are limited to upper division and Graduate studies. Consequently, students must have completed substantial prerequisites prior to entry into web-based degree programs. Anyone who has been admitted to the University and has met the individual prerequisites for a particular class may enroll in that class.

Courses: (18) Advances in Vocational Education (EVT4368) Exceptional Children in the Schools (EEX5051) Fundamentals of Graduate Research (EDF6481) General Methods in Vocational Ed. (EVT3365) Healthcare Automation (HSA4193) Information Systems and Computer Applications in Medicine (HSA5198) Introduction to Women's Studies (WST3010) Leadership and Management Principles (NUR4932OE91) Measurement & Evaluation in Education (EDF6432) Nursing Research (NUR3165) Organized Crime (CCJ4641) Physiological Psychology (PSB3002) Police & Society (CCJ4105) Post Modernism in Theory and Practice (LIT4932) Principles of Vocational Education (EVT4065) Social Problems (SYG2010) Special Needs of Vocational Students (EVT3502) The Community College in America (EDH6053)

University of Colorado   (CUON)
CUOnline P.O. Box 173364 (Campus Box 144) Denver CO 80217

Accred.: North Central Association of Colleges and Schools   (888) 535-4490 (303) 556-6505 fax:(303) 556-4861
Email: djwalker@ouray.cudenver.edu   URL: http://www.cuonline.edu/

Description: CU Online is a virtual campus of the University of Colorado offering courses and providing student services via the WWW. CU Online currently offers a wide range of liberal arts courses both in core curriculum and electives in such areas as English, Sociology, Biology, History, Anthropology, Psychology, Philosophy, Economics and Music. These are the same quality courses that are taught on the CU Denver campus. Assignments are completed on the student's individual schedule within the time frame requirements of each course schedule. Technologies used include email, virtual classroom, listservs and threaded discussions.

Courses: (74) Advanced Composition (ENGL3084) Advanced Disease State Management I (PRDO5310) Advanced Disease State Management V (PRDO5350) Advanced Screenwriting (ENGL3418) Agents, Managers, Producers and Others (MUS3760) Analytical Geometry & Calculus I (MATH1401) Analytical Mechanics I (CE2121) Basics of Cancer Biology (BIOL1352) Beginning Latin (LATN1010) Behavioral Genetics (BIOL4104) Behavioral Genetics (PSY4104) Business Writing (ENGL3170) Child Socialization (SOC3550) Clinical Skills Foundations (PRDO5700) College Physics I (PHYS2010) College Physics Lab I (PHYS2030) Contemporary Social Issues (SOC2010) Contemporary Social Theory (SOC3161) Contemporary Sociological Theory (SOC5160) Core Composition I (ENGL1020) Core Composition II (ENGL2030) Cultural Diversity in the Modern World (ANTH3142) Data Communications (ISMG6120) Design and Production of Multimedia (MUME2000) Drama of Diversity (THTR3611) Dynamics (ME2033) Ethics and Society - The Person and the Community (PHIL1020) Fantasy Literature (ENGL4770) Financial Management (BUSN6640) Fundamentals of Communication (CMMU1011) Grant Writing for Non-Profits (PSC5830) History of Film (ENGL3065) Ideology and Culture - Racism and Sexism (PHIL3500) Immunology (PRDO5010) Independent Record Production (MUS3740) Intellectual Property Law (ARTS3150) Intelligent Agents (CSC5805) Interactive Multimedia Systems (ISMG6240) Intermediate Latin I (LATN2010) Introduction to Art (FA1001) Introduction to Biological Anthropology (ANTH1303) Introduction to Creative Writing (ENGL2154) Introduction to Human Origins (ANTH103) Introduction to Psychology I (PSY1000) Introduction to Psychology II (PSY1005) Introduction to Social Psychology (SOC2462) Introduction to Sociology (SOC1001) Introduction to Statistics (PSY2090) Introduction to The Music Business (MUS2700) Java Programming (CSC2801) Literature and Society of the Middle East (ENGL3300) Logic and Language (PHIL2441) Magazine Writing (ENGL3416) Mathematics for the Liberal Arts (MATH2000) Music Appreciation (PMUS1001) Music Fundamentals (PMUS1010) Principles of Economics - Macroeconomics (ECON2012) Principles of Microeconomics (ECON2010) Race and Ethnicity in the U.S. (SOC3020) Relationship of the Individual to the World (PHIL1012) Remarriage and Stepfamilies (SOC4600) Senior Seminar (SOC4831) Software Project Management (ISMG6260) Statics (ME2023) Statistics (SOC3121) Technical Report Writing (TC4120) Technical Writing (CMMU3154) Technical Writing (ENGL3154) Technical Writing (TC3154) Techniques For Improving Imagining Ability (ARCH6290) Telling Tales - Narrative Art in Literature and Film (ENGL1601) U.S. History Since 1876 (HIST1362) World History since 1500 (HIST1026) Writing Workshop - Poetry (ENGL3020)

University of Colorado-Boulder   (COBO)
Division of Continuing Education Campus Box 178 Boulder CO 80309
Accred.: Western Association of Schools and Colleges   (800) 331-2801 (303) 492-8757 fax:(303) 492-3962
Email: dunnjr@spot.colorado.edu   URL: http://www.colorado.edu/cewww/
Description: Busy people use Independent Study to earn credit toward a degree, to meet job requirements, to prepare for career change, or to satisfy an interest in the subject. Not tied to the calendar or the classroom, the courses are available for registration any time of the year. Independent Study requires motivation and self-discipline, but many people find that independent study provides an opportunity to combine course work with family and career responsibilities. You set an individual pace, working with an instructor by mail or email, using a study guide or online syllabus, text books and other materials. Some courses have additional material or media fees.
Courses: (24) Analyzing Society (SOCY1001) Biological Psychology 1 (PSYC2012) Biological Psychology 2 (PSYC2022) Bones, Bodies and Disease (ANTH2070) Children's Literature (EDUC4161) Communication and Society (COMM2400) Conflict Mgmt in Social Systems (SOCY4025) Cost Management 2 (ACCT3320) Criminology (SOCY4014) Deviance in U.S. Society (SOCY1004) Family and Society (SOCY4086) Intro to International Relations (PSCI2223) Introduction to Human Geography (GEOG1992) Managing Process Technology (MBAT6450) Organizational Communication (COMM4600) Principles of Macroeconomics (ECON2020) Principles of Microeconomics (ECON2010) Society, Ethics and the Professions (CSCI2830) Statistics & Research in Psychology (PSYC2101) The American Political System (PSCI1101) Topics in Writing - Culture (UWRP3020) Travel Journal Writing (ENGL3081) Western Civ 1 - Antiquity to 1600 (HIST1010) Western Civ 2 - 1500s to Present (HIST1020)

University of Denver, University College   (DEUC)
2211 S. Josephine St. Denver CO 80208
Accred.: North Central Association of Colleges and Schools   (800) 347-2042 (303) 871-3155 fax:(303) 871-3303
Email: ucolinfo@du.edu   URL: http://www.du.edu/ucol
Description: Dept. of Environmental Policy and Management offers online instruction emphasizing scientific, policy, economic, human relations and communication aspects of field. Personalized learning uses outcome based model. Students provided opportunity for discovery, participation in learning and time for reflection and assimilation. Primarily text based with Web links for any time and any place learning.
Courses: (13) Client and Relationship Management (TELE4804) Computer Networks I (CIS4815) Digital Telecommunications Networks (TELE4846) Electronic Communications (TELE4801) Electronics for Telecommunications (TELE4800) Information Industry Finance (TELE4822) Introduction to Computer Networks (CIS3813) Math for Information Technology (TELE3800) Principles of Telecommunications (TELE4810) Strategies for Telecommunications I (TELE4835) Technical Writing (COMM4120) Telecommunications Policy (TELE4830) Telephony I (TELE4811)

University of Iowa   (IOWA)
Guided Correspondence Study 116 International Center Iowa City IA 52242
Accred.: Middle States Association of Colleges and Schools   (800) 272-6430 (319) 335-2575 fax:(319) 335-2740
Email: credit-programs@uiowa.edu   URL: http://www.uiowa.edu/~ccp/gcs-catalog/
Description: University of Iowa Guided Correspondence Study (GCS) courses allow for independent, self-paced learning and personalized instruction. They are a great way to begin or continue your college education. The flexibility of the GCS format makes it an excellent choice for people with work or family obligations that make it impossible to attend daytime classes on campus. More than 160 courses are available, covering a variety of interest areas, chiefly in the liberal arts. A study guide replaces typical classroom meetings. Within the guide, you'll find commentary by the instructor, reading and mail-in assignments, study suggestions, instructions for completing the course, and information on taking exams in your area.
Courses: (11) American Music - Rock and Roll (045075) Elementary French I (009001) Internetworks in International Development (047150) Introduction to Sociology (034001) Microcounseling (07C178) Neurological and Behavioral Pathology (096119) Parent-Child Relationships (07E114) Pathophysiology (096118) Science Fiction (From Frankenstein to the Future) (008182) Social Problems (034002) Women, Medicine, and Society (131135)

University of Massachusetts - Dartmouth   (MADA)
Admissions Center 285 Old Westport Road No. Dartmouth MA 02747
Accred.: New England Association of Schools and Colleges   (508) 999-8605 –   fax:–
Email: webteam@mail.umassd.edu   URL: http://www.umassd.edu/cybered/distlearninghome.html
Description: Welcome to CyberEd, where you can take courses online, earn college credits, enjoy a quality learning experience, enroll in certificate programs, and interact with students from around the world.
Courses: (17) Advanced WebCraft Workshop (CMP310) Beyond HTML (CMP308) Creating Your Own Web Pages (CMP300) Find a Creative Job in the Real World (CMP325) General Chemistry I (CHM101) Intercultural Communications Skills (PRD22481) Introduction to Astronomy (PHY151) Marketing on the Internet (CMP305) Online Interpersonal Communications (CMP302) Personal Finance (FIN320) Photoshop Fundamentals (001) Planet Earth (PHY171) Preparing Images for the Web (CMO303) Technical and Business Writing (ENL600) Technical Writing (ENL650) The Holocaust (HST356) Women's Health (PSY490)

University of Massachusetts - Lowell   (MALO)
One University Avenue Lowell MA 01854
Accred.: New England Association of Schools and Colleges   (508) 934-2261 (508) 934-3939 fax:(508) 934-3086
Email: cybered@cs.uml.edu   URL: http://cybered.uml.edu/
Description: CyberEd is a means of delivering quality education from our desktop to yours! CyberEd is a selection of standard, full-credit University courses being offered to the global audience of the Web through the UMass Dartmouth and UMass Lowell Divisions of Continuing Education. CyberEd courses are delivered over the Internet. Students and faculty use the World Wide Web, email, chat and other Internet resources, to review assignments, collaborate on projects, collect reference materials and to complete homework. CyberEd courses provide many opportunities for students and faculty to interact and collaborate in a global classroom. CyberEd classes are kept to a size where professors can provide the same level of personal interaction they do in the traditional classroom.
Courses: (9) Business Writing (42224) C Programming (92267) C++ Programming (92268) Computer Algebra with Mathematics (92419) Total Quality Management (69275) UNIX Operating System (92311) UNIX Operating System (92312) Visual Basic (92220) Writing for Interactive Media (42221)

University of Minnesota (MINN)

Independent and Distance Learning 77 Pleasant St. SE Minneapolis MN 55455

Accred.: North Central Association of Colleges and Schools
Email: indstudy@maroon.tc.umn.edu

(800) 234-6564 (612) 624-0000 fax:(612) 626-7900
URL: http://www.cee.umn.edu/dis/

Description: Distance Education (DE) gives you the opportunity to take University of Minnesota credit courses without entering a classroom. Choose from hundreds of college courses, with convenient schedules and creative learning resources, including email, videos, World Wide Web technologies, and computer courseware. Study wherever and whenever you want--we bring the U to you.

Courses: (257) Accounting and Finance for Managers (ABUS3101) Accounting Fundamentals I (GC1540) Accounting Fundamentals II (GC1542) Adolescent Psychology (CPSY5303) African-American Literature (GC1816) American Constitutional History I (HIST5331) American Constitutional History II (HIST5332) American Cultures II (AMST1002) American Cultures III (AMST1003) American Government and Politics (POL1001) American History I (HIST1301) American History II (HIST1302) American Immigration 1884-1984 (HIST3910) American Indian History 1850 to the Present (AMIN3112) American Indian History I (15th Century to 1850) (AMIN3111) American Political Parties (POL5737) American Short Story (ENGL3455) Andersen and the Scandinavian Fairy Tale (SCAN3602) Asian-American Literature (GC1836) Beginning Finnish I (FIN1101) Beginning Finnish II (FIN1102) Beginning Finnish III (FIN1103) Beginning French I (FREN1101) Beginning French II (FREN1102) Beginning French III (FREN1103) Beginning German I (GER1101) Beginning German II (GER1102) Beginning German III (GER1103) Beginning Italian I (ITAL1101) Beginning Italian II (ITAL1102) Beginning Latin I (LAT1101) Beginning Latin II (LAT1102) Beginning Norwegian I (NOR1101) Beginning Norwegian II (NOR1102) Beginning Norwegian III (NOR1103) Beginning Russian I (RUSS1101) Beginning Russian II (RUSS1102) Beginning Russian III (RUSS1103) Beginning Spanish I (SPAN1101) Beginning Spanish II (SPAN1102) Beginning Spanish III (SPAN1103) Beginning Swedish I (SWED1101) Beginning Swedish II (SWED1102) Beginning Swedish III (SWED1103) C++ in Embedded Systems (IDLS0001) Calculus I (MATH1211) Calculus III (MATH1261) Cell Biology (BIOL5004) Civil War and Reconstruction (HIST3812) Collective Bargaining and Labor Relations (IR3007) Columbus and the Age of Encounter (HIST3700) Communication and Public Opinion I (JOUR5501) Comprehensive Introductory Physics with Calculus I (PHYS1311) Comprehensive Introductory Physics with Calculus II (PHYS1321) Comprehensive Introductory Physics with Calculus III (PHYS1331) Comprehensive Introductory Physics with Calculus IV (PHYS1341) Computer Systems Performance Analysis (CSCI5863) Computer Systems Performance Analysis (EE5863) Conservation of Natural Resources (NRES1201) Contemporary Political Ideologies (POL1041) Counseling Psychology-Integrative Career Planning (EPSY5400) Creating Social Studies Curriculum Materials (EDUC5666) Critical Reading and Writing for Management (COMP3022) Cultural Pluralism in American History (HIST1305) D. H. Lawrence and Freud (ENGL3910B) Deformable Body Mechanics (ENGR3016) Directed Studies in Stress Management (PSY3970) Document Design (RHET5581) Dying and Death in Contemporary Society (PUBH5040) Entrepreneurship and the Smaller Enterprise (MGMT3008) Environmental Problems (GEOG3355) Environmental Studies (BIOL3051) Ethics and Stakeholder Management (BGS3002) European Folktales (CLIT5414) European Heritage - Greece (HUM1111) European Heritage - Rome (HUM1113) Everpresent Past in Spanish and Portuguese Culture (SPAN3970) Expressionist Film in Scandinavia - Ingmar Bergman (SCAN3606) Family Systems (FSOS5200) Finance Fundamentals (BFIN3000) Fundamentals of Management (MGMT3001) Fundamentals of Music (MUS1001) Fundamentals of Music II (MUS1002) Gender Communication (COMM3220) General Biology (BIOL1009) General Physics (PHYS1104) General Physics (PHYS1105) General Physics (PHYS1106) Genetics (BIOL5003) Genetics (GCB3022) Geography of Latin America (GEOG3121) Geography of the United States and Canada (GEOG3101) German Authors and/or Topics in Translation (GER3610) Greek and Latin Terminology in Medical Sciences (CLAS1048) Greek and Roman Mythology (CLAS1042) Hemingway (ENGL3940B) Heredity and Human Society (BIOL1101) Historical Geology (GEO1002) Historical Perspectives and Contemporary Business Challenges (ABUS3011) History of American Foreign Relations 1760-1865 (HIST3881) History of American Foreign Relations, 1945-95 (HIST3883) History of Journalism (JOUR5601) How to Write a Business Plan and Financial Proposal (ABUS3501) Human Origins (ANTH1111) Human Sexual Behavior (FSOS5001) Humanities in the Modern West II (HUM1002) Humanities in the Modern West III (HUM1003) Infancy (CPSY3302) Intermediate Algebra I (GC0625) Intermediate Algebra II (GC0631) Intermediate Norwegian I (NOR1104) Intermediate Norwegian II (6307) (NOR1105) Intermediate Norwegian III (NOR1106) Intermediate Poetry Writing (ENGW3103) Intermediate Spanish I (SPAN1104) Intermediate Spanish II (SPAN1105) Intermediate Spanish III (SPAN1106) Intermediate Swedish I (SWED1104) Intermediate Swedish III (SWED1106) International Business (BGS3004) Introduction to Abnormal Psychology (PSY3604) Introduction to African Literature (AFRO3601) Introduction to American Literature (ENGL1016) Introduction to Basic Mathematics (GC0611) Introduction to Biological Psychology (PSY3061) Introduction to Business and Society (GC1511) Introduction to Criminology (SOC1300) Introduction to Drafting (DHA0620) Introduction to Ecology (EEB3001) Introduction to Financial Reporting (ACCT1050) Introduction to Geology (GEO1001) Introduction to Ideas of Statistics (STAT1001) Introduction to Judaism (JWST3034) Introduction to Logic (PHIL1001) Introduction to Management Accounting (ACCT3001) Introduction to Marketing (GC1551) Introduction to Mass Communications (JOUR1001) Introduction to Microcomputer Applications (GC1571) Introduction to Modern Drama (ENGL1019) Introduction to Modern Poetry (ENGL1017) Introduction to Personality (PSY3101) Introduction to Philosophy (PHIL1002) Introduction to Professional Editing (ENGW5401) Introduction to Psychology (PSY1001) Introduction to Psychology (PSY1001) Introduction to Retail Merchandising (DHA1211) Introduction to Social Development (CPSY3331) Introduction to Social Psychology (SOC5201) Introduction to Social Welfare and Community Services (SW1001) Introduction to the Religions of South Asia (RELS1031) Introduction to the Theatre (TH1101) Introduction to the Visual Arts (ARTH1001) Introductory Child Psychology (CPSY1301) Introductory Physics I (PHYS1041) Introductory Physics II (PHYS1042) Issues in Sustainable Agriculture (AGRO5500) James Joyce (ENGL5363) Journal and Memoir Writing (ENGW5201) Journal and Memoir Writing II (ENGW5202) Journaling into Fiction (ENGW3110) Judicial Process (POL3309) Landscape Gardening and Design (HORT1010) Latin American History 1929 to Present (HIST3403) Latin American History Colonial Period to 1800 (HIST3401) Latin Poetry - Cicero (LAT3105) Latin Poetry - Vergil's Aeneid (LAT3106) Latin Prose and Poetry - Caesar and Others (LAT1104) Life Span Growth and Development II (NURS3691) Lifespan Growth and Development I (NURS3690) Literary Aspects of Journalism (JOUR5606) Literature of American Minorities (ENGL1591) Literatures of the United States (GC1365) Madness and Deviant Behavior in Ancient Greece and Rome (CLAS5005) Magazine Writing (JOUR3173) Magic, Witchcraft, and the Occult in Greece and Rome (CLAS1019) Major American Writers - Fitzgerald and Hemingway (ENGL3410) Managing Information on the Internet (RHET3400) Middle Ages-Dostoevsky in Translation (RUSS3421) Modern Drama since 1920 (ENGL5175) Modern Physics (PHYS3501) Modern Women Writers (ENGL3920) Money and Banking (ECON3701) Multivariable Differential Calculus (MATH3251) Multivariable Integral Calculus (MATH3252) Northern Minnesota Women Myths and Realities (WS1990) One-Variable Differential and Integral Calculus I (MATH1251) One-Variable Differential and Integral Calculus II (MATH1252) Parent-Child Relationships (GC1722) Plane Geometry (GC0623) Playwriting I (TH5115) Practical Law (GC1534) Precalculus (MATH1201) Preparation for Writing Practice (ENGC0011) Preprofessional Writing for Business (ENGC3032) Principles of Chemistry (GC1166) Principles of Economics Macro (ECON1005) Principles of Macroeconomics (ECON1102) Principles of Management of Marketing (GC1553) Principles of Marketing (MKTG3000) Principles of Microeconomics (ECON1101) Psychological Anthropology (ANTH5141) Psychology of Human Development (GC1283) Racial and Ethnic Diversity in Families (FSOS5500) Reading French (FREN0001) Reading Spanish (SPAN0221) Readings in Swedish Literary Texts (SWED3670) Religions of East Asia (EAS1032) Russia and Environs (GEOG3181) Science Fiction and Fantasy (ENGL1020) Second Languages and Young Children (CI5620) Selections from Latin Literature (LAT1103) Shakespeare I (ENGL3241) Shakespeare II (ENGL3242) Short Calculus (MATH1142) Small Business Fundamentals (GC1513) Social Work with Involuntary Clients (SW5424) Sociolinguistics (LING5831) Sociology and Social Problems (SOC1100) Solar System Astronomy (GC1161) Statistics (GC1454) Stellar Astronomy (GC1162) Survey of American Literature to 1850 (ENGL3411) Survey of American Literature, 1850-1900 (ENGL3412) Survey of American Literature, 1900-1945 (ENGL3413) Survey of Civilizations in Ancient Asia (HIST1451) Survey of English Literature I (ENGL3111) Survey of English Literature II (ENGL3112) Teaching Labor Relations in the Schools (IR3000) Technical Writing for Engineers (COMP3031) Techniques of Literary Study (ENGL3008) The Avant-Garde (MUS3045) The Celtic World

(ENGL3910) The Changing Physical World (PHYS1003) The English Language (ENGL3851) The Life and Times of Peter the Great (HIST3700B) The Media in American History and Law (JOUR3007) The Nature of Human Language (LING1001) The Origin of English Words (ENGL3860) The Physical World (PHYS1001) The Short Story (ENGW3102) The United States Congress (POL3308) The United States in the 20th Century 1932-60 (HIST3822) The Woman Writer in 19th-Century Fiction (ENGL3940) The World Around Us (GEOG1302) Theory and Research in Audience Analysis (RHET8110) Trigonometry (MATH1008) Twentieth-Century American Music (MUS5702) U. S. in the 20th Century, 1890-1917 (HIST3821) Understanding Cultures (ANTH1102) Understanding War Causes and Consequences (POL3810) Women in Muslim Society (SOC3340) Writing about Literature (ENGC3011) Writing about Science (COMP3015) Writing for the Arts (COMP3013) Writing in the Social Sciences (COMP3014) Writing in Your Profession (RHET3562) Writing Practice I (ENGC1011)

University of Missouri   (MOCE)
Center for Independent Study Columbia, MO 65211-420 136 Clark Hall
Columbia MO 65211

Accred.: North Central Association of Colleges and Schools   (800) 609-3727 (573) 882-2491 fax:(573) 882-6808
Email: independ@ext.missouri.edu   URL: http://indepstudy.ext.missouri.edu

Description: The University of Missouri Center for Independent Study was established in 1911 to extend learning opportunities to students who cannot or choose not to attend traditional classroom courses. Today we are a leader in distance education, with more than 15,000 enrollments annually. By incorporating the latest technology in our program, we are able to provide online courses to students around the world.

Courses: (160) Abnormal Psychology (PS245) Accounting I (AC130) Accounting I (AC36) Accounting II (AC37) Administration of Programs for Children and Families (SO358) Adolescent Development (A208) Adolescent Psychology (PS271) African-American Literature (LI104A) Aging in Contemporary Society (SO410R) America, 1945 to the Present (HI308B) American Civilization (HI3) American Civilization Since 1865 (HI4) American Foreign Relations (IN361) American Government (GO1) American Literary Masterpieces (LI17) American Literature (LI175) American Poetry - A Survey (LI101A) Analytic Geometry and Calculus I (MA80) Analytic Geometry and Calculus II (MA175) Analytic Geometry and Calculus III (MA180) Animal Behavior (HO330) Applied Nutrition (HE212) Art Activities in the Elementary School (T230) Basic Home Horticulture (HO25) Career Planning for Adults (A170) Child Development (A207) Child Psychology (PS170) College Algebra (MA30) Computer Survival - Applications (CO100) Congressional Politics (PO231) Corrections (LE260) Creative Writing - Fiction (WR50) Creative Writing - Poetry (EN70) Criminology (CR211) Earth Science (EA56) Economics for Health Care Executives (EC201) Educational Measurement (A280) Elementary French I (LA1F) Elementary French II (LA2F) Elementary German I (LA1G) Elementary German II (LA2G) Elementary German III (LA3G) Elementary Latin I (LA1) Elementary Russian I (LA1R) Elementary Spanish I (LA110S) Elementary Spanish I (LA1S) Elementary Spanish II (LA2S) Elementary Spanish III (LA3S) Elementary Statistics (MA31) Elements of Calculus (MA61) Elements of Health Education (T85) Engineering Mechanics-Dynamics (EN150) Engineering Mechanics-Statics (EN50) English Literature I (LI131) Environmental Psychology (PS315) Ethics and the Professions (HU135) European Civilization 1715-Present (HI32) Experiencing American Cultures in the Contemporary Novel (LI101B) Exposition and Argumentation (SO20) Finite Mathematics (MA60) Formal Logic (LO160) Fundamentals of Extension Teaching of Adults (ED406) Fundamentals of Management (MA202) General Anthropology (AN1) General Biology (BI1) General Psychology (PS3) Genetics (SC224) Geography of Missouri (GE225) Geometric Concepts for Teachers (MA68) Gothic Fiction (LI101C) High School Journalism (JO380) History of Missouri (HI107) History of Modern Europe (HI2) History of Science (SC275) History of the Old South (HI254) Horse Production (HO325) Human Learning (ED212) Human Resource Management (MG310) Industrial Psychology (PS212) Insects in the Environment (SC110) Intensive Beginning Latin I (LA207L) Intercultural Communication (CO332) Intermediate Algebra (MA5) International Relations (IN55) Introduction to BASIC (CO71) Introduction to Business Law (LE254) Introduction to Criminology and Criminal Justice (CR010) Introduction to Economics II (EC202) Introduction to Educating the Gifted (ED489V) Introduction to Educational Statistics (A354) Introduction to Folklore (FO184) Introduction to Folklore (FO185) Introduction to Leisure Studies (HE327A) Introduction to Mental Retardation (L385) Introduction to Political Science (PO11) Introduction to Sociology (SO1B) Introduction to Special Education for Regular Educators (L312) Introduction to the American Economy (EC40) Introductory Astronomy (AS999) Introductory Meteorology (ME50) Introductory Meteorology (ME50) Issues and Trends in Reading Instruction (T420) Learning and Instruction (A205) Library Materials for Children and Youth (ED321) Literary Types (LI12) Literature of the New Testament (LI124) Literature of the Old Testament (LI125) Logic and Language (LO60) Major Questions in Philosophy (PH50) Making of Modern Britain (HI220) Meeting Affective Needs of Gifted Individuals (ED589JM) Money, Banking, and Monetary Theory (FI220) Multicultural Study of Children and Families (SO241) Music Appreciation (MU120) Number Systems and Applications (MA130) Operation of Therapeutic Recreation (HE327B) Organizational Analysis in Adult Education (K420) Organizational Theory (OR330) Personal and Family Finance (FI183) Photography for Teachers (T373) Physical Geography (GE111) Physical Geology (GE51) Principles of Finance (FI123) Principles of Marketing (MA204) Psychology and Education of Exceptional Individuals (PS313) Psychology of Sensation and Perception (PS220) Public Administration (A140) Regions and Nations of the World I (GE1) Regions and Nations of the World II (GE2) Revolutionary America, 1754-1789 (HI342) Rights of the Offender (LE345) Rural Sociology (SO1) Seminar in Curriculum and Instruction (T410) Shakespeare (LI135) Social Justice and Social Policy (SO310) Social Policy and Service Delivery in Social Work (SO410) Social Psychology (PS190) Social Welfare and Social Work (SO25) Surface Water Management (WA201) Teaching of Reading (T315) Teaching Reading in the Content Areas (T316) Technical Writing (EN161) The American Constitution (LE320) The American Health Care System (HE210HM) The Mechanical Universe (SC275B) The Politics of the Third World (PO350) The Secondary School Curriculum (T445) The Twilight of the Sioux (LI101D) The War in Vietnam and the U.S. (HI101) The War in Vietnam and the U.S. (HI161) The War in Vietnam and the U.S. (HI380F) Themes and Forms in Literature - Shakespeare (LI225) Theory and Concepts of Plant Pathology (HO305) Thinking and Cognition (PS356) Trigonometry (MA9) Urban Sociology (SE202) Urban Sociology (SO216) Women in Popular Culture (SO201) Women's Experiences in Modern Fiction (LI101E) Women's Experiences in Modern Fiction (LI101F)

University of Nebraska   (NEBR)
College of Human Resources & Family Science Economics Building Lincoln NE 68588

Accred.: North Central Association of Colleges and Schools   (402) 472-2913   fax:(402) 472-9863
Email: fmcs080@unlvm.unl.edu   URL: http://ianrwww.unl.edu/ianr/chrfs/exteduc.htm

Description: The M.S. degree through distance learning includes 36 hours earned in this manner: 18 credit hours in family & consumer sciences, 6 credit hours in textiles, clothing and design, 6 credit hours in nutritional science and dietetics, 3 credit hours in research methods and 3 credit hours in statistics. There is flexibility within the categories. The student will complete an Option III paper. The final exam is a written comprehensive. There is no residency requirement for this program. Starting Fall 1998, all class will be taught by Internet. One class will be taught each fall and spring semester and one class will be taught during a 5 week summer session. It will take four years to complete the program. You may take individual classes without being part of the masters program.

Courses: (17) Adolescent in the Family (FACS872) Computers in Food Service (NSD272) Consumer and Family Economics (FACS906) Contemporary Nutrition (NUTR800) Family - Cross-Cultural Perspective (FACS980) Family and Consumer Sciences (FACS815) Family Financial Management (FACS907) Family Strengths (FACS987) Human Nutrition & Health (NSD151) Instructional Theory in Family Sciences (FACS815) International Perspectives of Human Resources (FCS865) Nutrition Throughout Life Cycle (NUTR855) Praxis and Policy (HRFS900) Recent Developments in Textiles (TXCD811) Research Methods (HRFS875) Statistical Decision Making (BIOM896) Textile Economics (TXCD870)

University of Nevada-Reno   (NERE)
Independent Study by Correspondence P. O. Box 14430 Reno NV 89507
Accred.: Northwest Association of Schools and Colleges   (800) 233-8928 (702) 784-4652 fax:(702) 784-1280
Email: istudy@scs.unr.edu   URL: http://www.dce.unr.edu/istudy/
Description: Independent Study by Correspondence is a department in the university's Division of Continuing Education which offers an individualized method of learning. We are the sole provider of university credit through independent study by correspondence in the state of Nevada. We offer courses from the University of Nevada, Reno and the University of Nevada, Las Vegas, as well as high school credit courses, continuing education units and non-credit courses. Instruction is given by means of a course syllabus, textbooks, video and audio cassettes (where appropriate), and additional reference and instructional material. Some courses accommodate e-mail submissions via the Internet and one course is administered on the World Wide Web. If you wish to submit lessons for your course via e-mail, please contact the independent study office. If the format of your assignments accommodates e-mail transmission, we will mail you an instruction packet with information on how to proceed. We offer almost 100 high school and college courses. Many are available online.
Courses: (3) British History II for the Internet (C394) Journalism (C490) Mathematics on the WWW (C120)

University of North Alabama   (NOAL)
UNA Box 5195 Florence AL 35632
Accred.: Southern Association of Colleges and Schools   (800) 825-5862 (205) 765-4316 fax:
Email: swilson@unanov.una.edu   URL: http://www2.una.edu/histpolsci/sreb.htm
Description: UNA is a comprehensive regional state university, offering undergraduate and graduate degrees, and serving both residential, commuting, and extended campus learners. The University of North Alabama is a comprehensive regional state university offering undergraduate and graduate degree programs, serving residential and commuting students. UNA shares the broad purpose of all institutions of higher learning for the discovery, preservation, and transmission of knowledge through teaching, research, and public service. More importantly, UNA is earnestly committed to ensuring that all students receive full value for their investment of personal and family resources in obtaining a top quality university education . This claim is supported by a tradition, dating back to 1830, of providing high quality that is generally associated with private colleges and universities at the lower cost of a state-assisted public institution of higher education.
Courses: (2) American History to 1877 (HIST201) United States in the Modern Age (HIST202)

University of North Dakota   (NODA)
The Department of Space Studies P. O. Box 9008 Grand Forks ND 58202
Accred.: North Central Association of Colleges and Schools   (800) 828-4274 (701) 777-2480 fax:(701) 777-3711
Email: info@space.edu   URL: http://www.space.edu/
Description: The UND Master of Science degree in Space Studies is a unique and valuable educational experience, both for those seeking to enter this exciting field, and aerospace professionals who wish to expand their breadth of knowledge. However, due to existing employment and/or family commitments, many who would benefit from the program are unable to attend on-campus classes. For this reason, starting January 1996, the M.S. in Space Studies has been offered as a Distance Education program. We hope to reach aerospace professionals and pre-professionals who cannot come to North Dakota for the two-year conventional program. The goal of the Space Studies program is to offer, via modern distance learning techniques, a fully-accredited education with the same courses and the same level of opportunities for discussion, advisement and research as our campus students enjoy.
Courses: (24) Advanced Topics in Space Studies (SPST570) Asteroids, Meteorites, & Comets (SPST520) Commercialization of Space (SPST440) Earth System Science (SPST430) Global Change (SPST435) Human Factors in Space (SPST515) Individual Research in Space Studies (SPST593) Introduction to Orbital Mechanics (SPST500) Life In The Universe (SPST570B) Life Support Systems (SPST410) Mars (SPST570A) Observational Astronomy (SPST425) Remote Sensing Policy & Law (SPST575) Satellite Information Processing (SPST535) Soviet/Russian Space Program (SPST450) Space Policy & Internat. Implications (SPST545) Space Science and Exploration (SPST420) Space Studies Seminar (SPST590) Space Treaties & Legislation (SPST565) Space Vehicle Design (SPST405) Strategic Implications of Space (SPST555) Survey of Space Studies (SPST501) Technical Issues in Space (SPST525) Vehicles & Facilities Operations (SPST550)

University of Northern Colorado   (CONO)
College of Continuing Education 501 20th St. Greeley CO 80639
Accred.: North Central Association of Colleges and Schools   (800) 232-1749 (970) 351-2944 fax:(970) 351-2519
Email: spelis@cce.univnorthco.edu   URL: http://www.colorado.edu/cewww/catalog/lists/unc_list.html
Description: Busy people use Independent Study to earn credit toward a degree, to meet job requirements, to prepare for career change, or to satisfy an interest in the subject. Not tied to the calendar or the classroom, the courses are available for registration any time of the year. Independent Study requires motivation and self-discipline, but many people find that independent study provides an opportunity to combine course work with family and career responsibilities. You set an individual pace, working with an instructor by mail or email, using a study guide or online syllabus, text books and other materials. Some courses have additional material or media fees.
Courses: (1) Art History Seminar - Women Artists (ART680)

University of Oregon   (OREG)
Distance Education Program 1277 University of Oregon Eugene OR 97403
Accred.: Northwest Association of Schools and Colleges   (800) 824-2714 (541) 346-0696 fax:(541) 346-3917
Email: sgladney@continue.uoregon.edu   URL: http://center.uoregon.edu/disted/disted.html
Description: We provide online programs in collaboration with non-U.S. institutions who want teacher and/or student training in subjects such as English, technology, U.S. culture, and academic content areas (e.g. Pre-MBA). Courses can be structured online only, or with a face-to-face component.
Courses: (16) Alternative Energy Sources (PHY162) Cosmology and the Origin of Life (AST123) Diagnostic Procedures for Communication Disorders (CDS658) Geology of Oregon and the Pacific Northwest (GEO308) Geology of the National Parks (GEO303) Introduction to Comparative Politics (POL204) Introduction to Macroeconomics (ECON202) Introduction to Microeconomics (ECON201) Oceanography (GEO307) Physics of Energy and Environment (PHY161) Solar Energy [Alternative Energy Sources] (PHY162) Solar System Geology (AST121) The Fossil Record (GEO304) The Structure of English Words (LING150) United States Politics (POL201) Volcanoes and Earthquakes (GEO306)

University of South Carolina-Aiken (SCAI)
171 University Parkway Aiken SC 29801
Accred.: Southern Association of Colleges and Schools
Email: viviang@aiken.sc.edu

(803) 648-6851 fax:(803) 641-3461
URL: http://www.usca.sc.edu/201/index.htm

Description: USC Aiken is a fully accredited public senior institution in the University of South Carolina system, with nearly 3,000 undergraduate students and over 200 faculty. SCAI Welcome to APLS 201 on the internet. This On-line Distance Education (ODE) course is for students whose schedule or location or some other obstacle does not fit the traditional classroom setting and those students who enjoy learning on the World Wide Web (Web). It allows you to have almost daily interaction with your professors and with other students doing interesting assignments that are tied to current events.

Courses: (1) American National Government (APLS201)

University of South Florida (FLSO)
Florida Center for Instructional Technology 4202 East Fowler Avenue, EDU208B Tampa FL 33620
Accred.: Southern Association of Colleges and Schools
Email: barrona@mail.firn.edu

(813) 974-6099 (813) 974-6953 fax:(813) 974-7187
URL: http://www.usf.edu/CyberEd/

Description: The University of South Florida, one of the new universities created in the 20th century, is driving higher education on a fast track into the next millennium. You won't find ivy walls or weighty tradition here - rather a boundless optimism, vitality and can-do attitude indicative of its youth. The 13th largest university in the United States and still growing, USF has built a solid reputation as a leader in learning, offering comprehensive state-of-the-art, student-centered programs. With growing prestige and a dedicated faculty, including 73 Fulbright Scholars and 42 endowed chairs, USF has become a research powerhouse.

Courses: (9) Air Photo Interpretation (GEO4124) Coastal Geography (GEO4201) Geographic Technical Methodology (GEO4114) Introduction to Physical Geography (GEO3013) Occupational Information (VED510) Political Economy (U102) Society, Culture and the Environment (U101) Theatre History (THE3100) World Geography (GY102)

University of Southern Colorado (COSO)
Division of Continuing Education 2200 Bonforte Boulevard Pueblo CO 81001
Accred.: North Central Association of Colleges and Schools
Email: coned@meteor.uscolo.edu

(800) 331-2801 (719) 549-2316 fax:(719) 549-2438
URL: http://www.colorado.edu/cewww/

Description: Busy people use Independent Study to earn credit toward a degree, to meet job requirements, to prepare for career change, or to satisfy an interest in the subject. Not tied to the calendar or the classroom, the courses are available for registration any time of the year. Independent Study requires motivation and self-discipline, but many people find that independent study provides an opportunity to combine course work with family and career responsibilities. You set an individual pace, working with an instructor by mail or e-mail, using a study guide or online syllabus, text books and other materials. Some courses have additional material or media fees.

Courses: (11) Death and Dying in American Society (SOC491C) Grantsmanship (SOC491B) Health, Culture, and Society (SOC401) Human Sexuality and Social Behavior (SOC403) Marriage and Family Relationships (SOC231) Political Sociology (SOC355) Popular Culture (SOC308) Sociology of Religion (SOC491A) Urban Sociology (SOC354) Women in Contemporary Society (SOC491D) Working in Modern America (SOC431)

University of Washington (WASH)
Distance Learning P. O. Box 354223 Seattle WA 98105
Accred.: Northwest Association of Schools and Colleges
Email: --

(800) 543-2320 (206) 543-2310 fax:--
URL: http://www.edoutreach.washington.edu/dl/dl-about.htm

Description: Most UW Distance Learning courses are designed by the faculty who teach the same courses on the University of Washington campus. The instructors are familiar with student questions and needs and, with the help of educational designers, have developed the appropriate materials and methods to help students achieve the course objectives in a distance learning format. Each registrant receives a course guide containing the course outline, a list of required texts and materials, study instructions, supplementary information and specific lesson assignments. Sometimes additional media such as video or audio tapes or laboratory kits are required to further expand the scope of study. These materials provide a basic focus and discipline for your study, as well as a means of establishing and maintaining communication with your instructor.

Courses: (7) Adaptive Computer Technology (REHABC496) Communication for NonSpeakers (REHABC458) Composition - Exposition (ENGLC131) Computers and Rehabilitation (REHABC496B) Developing a C Application (C900) Intermediate Expository Writing (ENGLC281) Internet Curriculum Development (LIBRC498)

University of Wisconsin Colleges (WISC)
780 Regent St. Madison WI 53708
Accred.: North Central Association of Colleges and Schools
Email: pmcgrego@uwc.edu

(608) 262-9652 (414) 335-5200 fax:(414) 335-5220
URL: http://washington.uwc.edu/online/uwconline.htm

Description: The University of Wisconsin Colleges is the Freshmen/Sophomore transfer institution of the University of Wisconsin System. The Pilot Asynchronous (Web-based)course offerings will explore web based instruction with a variety of science, humanities and social science courses.

Courses: (8) Calculus Offered On Line (MATH221) Global Communications (COMM302) Interpersonal Relations (EDUC388) King Lear Online (ENGL0290) Resampling Statistics (EDUC796) Small Group Communication Lab (COMM380) Technology and Leadership (COMM303) The Interpersonal Internet (COMM385)

Walden University   (WALD)
c/o The Electronic University Network 1977 Colestin Road Hornbrook CA 96044

Accred.: North Central Association of Colleges and Schools

Email: euncouncil@aol.com

(800) 225-3276 (541) 482-5871 fax:(541) 482-7544

URL: http://www.waldenu.edu

Description: Walden University has been a pioneer and leader in graduate level distance education for the past 28 years. Founded in 1970, Walden was conceived as and remains an institution dedicated to providing the established professional with the opportunity to complete a challenging, accredited graduate degree without sacrificing family and career commitments. Social change is important to Walden's philosophy, as is assisting the mature student in understanding change within his or her field.

Courses: (9) Alternative School Reform (ECTI5120) Change Theory & Human Behavior (ECTI5130) Computers in Education (ECTI5220) Educ. in Environment of Change (ECTI5125) Educational Decision Processes (ECTI5115) Educational Innovations & Tech (ECTI5200) Family and Societal Factors in Ed. (ECTI5110) Learning and Technology (ECT15100) Outcome-Based Assessment (ECTI5135)

Waukesha County Technical College   (WAUK)
800 Main Street Pewaukee WI 53072

Accred.: North Central Association of Colleges and Schools

Email: sgoran@waukesha.tec.wi.us

(888) 892-9282 (414) 691-5578 fax:(414) 691-5047

URL: http://www.waukesha.tec.wi.us/online.html

Description: Waukesha County Technical College is now offering associate degree level courses for full credit as part of the OnLine Program. There are a number of WCTC Associate Degrees that can be earned entirely by Internet Distance Learning. You do not need to be "on campus" when you attend the "online program" by means of the internet. Earn credit from online courses that may be transferable to other colleges and universities. WCTC OnLine Program is ideal for the independent learner. Online courses can offer the motivated learner flexibility.

Courses: (23) Business Law I (102160007) Contemporary Business (102100) Develop Your Own Business Plan (145465) Economics (809195016) Equine Genetic Principles (091112) Ethics (809158007) International Business (138150003) International Marketing (138155) Introduction to Financial Planning (114105004) Introduction to Sociology (809196016) Job Search (102113013) Learn About the Internet on the Internet (103413) Loan Servicing (115101001) Math Principles (804160008) Online Book Club (801645001).Psychology of Human Relations (809199016) Real Estate Finance (194184003) Real Estate Fundamentals (194180006) Real Estate Law (194182003) Retirement Planning/Employee Benefits (114120003) Workplace Violence (001) Writing in the Workplace (801463002) Written Communications (801195019)

Western Illinois University   (WEIL)
1 University Circle Macomb IL 61455

Accred.: Northwest Association of Schools and Colleges

Email: IS-Program@wiu.edu

(309) 298-2496 (309) 298-2133 fax:–

URL: http://www.wiu.edu/

Description: Western Illinois University's commitment is to provide the premier undergraduate education among all public universities in Illinois, and, in selected disciplines, far beyond Illinois' borders. Established in 1899, Western Illinois University's main campus is located in Macomb, a picture-perfect rural city 240 miles southwest of Chicago and 160 miles north of St. Louis. The WIU Regional Center is located 80 miles north of Macomb in Moline and serves the Quad Cities area.

Courses: (113) Abnormal Psychology (PSY424G) Advanced Fire Administration (IND481) Advanced Organizational Behavior (MAN350) Age of Enlightenment (HIS426G) American Government and Politics (POL122) American History Since 1877 (HIS106) American History to 1877 (HIS105) American Law (HIS303) American Nature Writing (ENG400G) Analytic Approaches to Public Fire Protection (IND482) Anthropology of Religion (ANT324) Anthropology of Women (ANT315) Applications of Fire Research (SOC487) Astronomy (GEO325) Biology of Aging (BIO420G) Broadcasting and Society (COM323) Bureaucracy and Formal Organization (SOC330) Child Nutrition and Health (HEA303) Civil War and Reconstruction (HIS415G) Climatology (GEO327) College Writing I (ENG180) Commodity Markets and Futures Trading (AGR447G) Community (SOC312) Conservation and Management of Natural Resources (GEO426G) Consumer Behavior (FIN333) Consumer Economics (FAM331) Crime and Police (HIS310) Development of Mutual Resources Parenting (FAM426G) Disaster and Fire Defense Planning (SAF477) Elementary French I (LANF121) Elementary French II (LANF122) Elementary Spanish I (LANS121) Elementary Spanish II (LANS121) Environmental Geology (GEO375) Ethics and Social Responsibility (MAN481) Fire Dynamics (IND444) Fire Prevention Organization and Management (IND484) Fire Protection Structures and Systems Design (IND443) Fire-Related Human Behavior (IND481) Gender Roles (SOC360) Human Biology (BIO304) Human Resource Management (MAN353) Immunology (BIO434) Incendiary Fire Analysis and Investigation (IND486) Intermediate French I (LANF223) Intermediate French II (LANF224) Intermediate Spanish I (LANS223) Intermediate Spanish II (LANS224) International Business (FIN317) International Marketing (FIN417) International Tourism (REC462) International Trade - Inside the Global Economy (ECO470) Introduction to Finance (FIN311) Introduction to Nutrition (HEA109) Introduction to Organic Evolution (BIO319) Labor Institutions and Public Policy (ECO340) Leisure Services for the Elderly (REC452G) Literature of the Americas (ENG400A) Magazine and Feature Writing (ENG330) Management and Organizational Behavior (MAN349) Managerial Economics (ECO332) Managerial Issues in Hazardous Materials (SAF478) Managing in Organizations (MAN420) Market Logic (AGR459G) Marketing Grain and Livestock Products (AGR442G) Marketing Principles (FIN327) Minority Peoples (SOC300) Modern Drama (ENG360) Modern English Grammar (ENG370) Modern Political Theory (POL382) Money, Banking, and Credit (ECO325) Moral Philosophy (PHI330) Operations Management (MAN352) Options on Futures (AGR456G) Outdoor Recreation Perspectives (REC376) Personal Financial Planning (FIN301) Personal Nonfiction (ENG400B) Personnel Management for the Fire Service (IND483) Philosophy of Law (PHI420) Planet Earth (GEO422) Political and Legal Foundations of Fire Protection (IND485) Political Geography (GEO444G) Preparation for Marriage and Family (FAM321) Principles of Real Estate (FIN321) Promotional Concepts (FIN331) Psychology of Adulthood and Aging (PSY423G) Race to Save the Planet (BIO422) Real Estate Finance and Investment (FIN421) Religion in America (PHI301) Retailing Management (FIN343) Reviewing and Criticism (ENG405) Risk Management and Insurance (FIN351) Scientific and Technical Writing (ENG381) Seasons of Life (PSY423) Shakespeare (ENG412) Short Story (ENG300) Social and Psychological Aspects of Apparel (HEA313) Sociology of Mental Health (SOC424) Statistical Methods for Experimental Sciences (FIN470) Studies in American Drama (ENG341) Studies in American Poetry - Voices and Visions (ENG335) Technology and Society (HIS312) The Adult Years (PSY423) The American Revolution and the New Nation (HIS413G) The American West (HIS308) The Community and Fire Threat (SOC488) Tourism (REC362) Twentieth Century Europe (HIS429G) U.S. Foreign Policy (POL331) U.S. Military History (HIS304) United States and Canada (GEO461G) Women in Religion (PHI303) Writing in the Humanities and Social Sciences (ENG380)

Wichita State University   (WIST)
Office of University Communications 1845 N. Fairmount Wichita KS 67260

Accred.: North Central Association of Colleges and Schools
Email: riordan@feist.com

(800) 516-0290 (316) 978-5735 fax:(316) 978-3776
URL: http://www.twsu.edu

Description: The University, situated in south central Kansas in the state's largest metropolitan area, boasts an unrivaled advantage. Nestled in Wichita's northeast neighborhood, WSU offers its students educational, economic, and entertainment opportunities common in larger cities while retaining the friendliness typical of smaller cities. Students can work while attending the University and gain that "cutting edge" over other university graduates seeking employment after graduation. The connections students make with possible employers and with the city gives our students an advantage.

Courses: (4) Breastfeeding and Human Lactation (NUR001) Information Systems and Health Care I (NUR775) Information Systems and Health Care II (NUR776) Psychology of Personality (PSY324)

Yavapai Community College   (YAVA)
1100 East Sheldon Street Prescott AZ 86301

Accred.: Western Association of Schools and Colleges
Email: registration@yavapai.cc.az.us

(520) 776-2150 (520) 634-7501 fax:–
URL: http://ycnotes.yavapai.cc.az.us/courses.nsf

Description: Yavapai College, a fully accredited college in the Arizona Community College System, provides educational opportunities to residents in an 8,100 square mile service area. Yavapai College students pursue academic or professional-technical studies leading to transfer to four-year colleges or universities, associate degrees, certificates or special interest courses.

Courses: (7) Art History I, Prehistoric-Middle Ages (ART200) Basic Police Armorer Certification (GST160) Collage with Digital Techniques (ART165) English Composition I (ENG101) Home Page Design and Presentation (ART108) HTML Tags for Page Design (ART109) Native American Literature (ENG239E)

College and University URL's

The Internet University - College URL's

Abilene Christian Univ. - TX
http://www.acu.edu/

Abraham Baldwin Coll. - Tifton GA
http://stallion.abac.peachnet.edu/

Academy of Art Col - SF CA
http://www.academyart.edu/

Adams State Coll. - Alamosa CO
http://www.adams.edu/

Adelphi Univ. - Garden City NY
http://www.adelphi.edu/

Agnes Scott Coll - Decatur GA
http://www.scottlan.edu/

Air Univ. - Montgomery AL
http://www.au.af.mil/

Alabama A+M U - Normal AL
http://www.aamu.edu/

Alabama State U. - Montgomery AL
http://www.alasu.edu/

Alaska Pacific U - Anchorage AK
http://www.alaska.net/~apu/

Albany Coll. Pharmacy - NY
http://panther.acp.edu/

Albany State Col - Albany GA
www.alsnet.peachnet.edu/

Albertson Col - Caldwell ID
http://www.acofi.edu/

Albertus Magnus C - New Haven CT
http://www.albertus.edu/

Albion Col - Albion MI
http://www.albion.edu/

Albright Col - Reading PA
http://www.alb.edu/

Alcorn State Univ. - Lorman MS
http://academic.alcorn.edu/

Alderson-Broaddus C - Philippi WV
http://www.mountain.net/ab/

Alfred Univ. - Alfred NY
http://www.alfred.edu/

Alice Lloyd Coll. - Pippa Passes KY
http://www.aikcu.org/Cols/AliceLloyd/alc.html

Allegheny Col - Meadville PA
http://www.alleg.edu/

Allegheny U. Health Sci. - Phila. PA
http://www.allegheny.edu/

Allentown Col - Center Valley PA
http://www.allencol.edu/

Alma Col - Alma MI
http://www.alma.edu/

Alvernia Col - Reading PA
http://www.alvernia.edu/

Alverno Col - Milwaukee WI
http://www.alverno.edu/

Ambassador Univ. - Big Sandy TX
http://www.ambassador.edu/

American Grad Sch. - Glendale AZ
http://www.t-bird.edu/

American Int'l Coll. - Springfld MA
http://www.aic.edu/

American Univ. - Wash. DC
http://www.american.edu/

Amherst Col - Amherst MA
http://www.amherst.edu/

Anderson Col - Anderson SC
http://www.icusc.org/anderson/achome.htm

Anderson Univ. - Anderson IN
http://www.anderson.edu/

Andrews Univ. - Berrien Springs MI
http://www.andrews.edu/

Angelo State Univ. - San Angelo TX
http://www.angelo.edu/

Anna Maria Col - Paxton MA
http://www.anna-maria.edu/

Antioch Col - Yellow Springs OH
http://Col.antioch.edu/

Antioch Univ. - Marina del Rey CA
http://www.antiochla.edu:7901/

Antioch Univ. - Keene NH
http://www.antiochne.edu/

Antioch Univ. - Seattle WA
http://www.seattleantioch.edu/

Appalachian State U - Boone NC
http://www.appstate.edu/

Aquinas Col - Grand Rapids MI
http://www.aquinas.edu/

Arizona State U East - Tempe AZ
http://www.asu.edu/east/

Arizona State U West - Tempe AZ
http://www.west.asu.edu/

Arizona State Univ. - Tempe AZ
http://www.asu.edu/

Arkansas State Univ. - State U AR
http://www.astate.edu/

Arkansas Tech U - Russellville AR
http://www.atu.edu/

Armstrong State U - Savannah GA
http://www.armstrong.edu/

Art Academy of Cincinnati - OH
http://www.tso.org/gcccu/artacademy.html

Art Center Col - Pasadena CA
http://www.artcenter.edu/

Art Institute of Seattle - Seattle WA
http://www.ais.edu/

Asbury Col - Wilmore KY
http://www.asbury.edu/

Asbury Theological - Wilmore KY
www.ats.wilmore.ky.us/

Ashland Univ. - Ashland OH
http://www.ashland.edu/

Assumption Col - Worcester MA
http://www.assumption.edu/

Athena Univ. - Columbia MO
http://www.athena.edu/

Atlantic Union Col.-S.Lancaster MA
http://www.atlanticuc.edu/

Auburn Univ. - Montgomery - AL
http://www.aum.edu/

Auburn Univ. - Auburn U AL
http://www.aubum.edu/

Audrey Cohen Col - NY NY
http://www.audrey-cohen.edu/

Augsburg Col - Minneapolis MN
http://www.augsburg.edu/

Augusta Col - Augusta GA
http://webserv.educom.edu/members/InterimPages/412Interim.html

Augusta State Univ. - Augusta GA
http://www.ac.edu/

Augustana Col - Sioux Falls SD
http://www.augie.edu/

Augustana Col - Rock Island IL
http://www.augustana.edu/

Aurora Univ. - Aurora IL
http://www.aurora.edu/

Austin Col - Sherman TX
http://www.austinc.edu/

Austin Peay State U - Clarksville TN
http://www.apsu.edu/

Averett Col - Danville VA
http://www.averett.edu/

Avila Col - Kansas City MO
http://www.avila.edu/

Azusa Pacific Univ. - Azusa CA
http://www.apu.edu/

Babson Col - Babson Park MA
http://www.babson.edu/

Baker Col - Flint MI
http://www.baker.edu/

Baker Univ. - Baldwin City KS
http://www.bakeru.edu/

Baldwin-Wallace Col - Berea OH
http://www.baldwinw.edu/

Ball State Univ. - Muncie IN
http://www.bsu.edu/

Baltimore Hebrew U - MD
http://www.bhu.edu/

Bank Street Col - New York NY
http://www.bnkst.edu/

Baptist Bible C. - Clarks Summit PA
http://www.bbc.edu/

Barat Col - Lake Forest IL
http://www.fihe.org/fihe/corporate/illinois/il-barat.htm

Barber-Scotia Col - Concord NC
http://www.theology.org/APCU/bsc.htm

Bard Coll -Annandale-on-Hudson NY
http://www.bard.edu/

Barnard Col - New York NY
http://www.barnard.columbia.edu/

Barry Univ. - Miami Shores FL
http://www.barry.edu/

Bassist Col - Portland OR
http://www.bassist.edu/

Bastyr Univ. - Bothell WA
http://www.bastyr.edu/

Bates Col - Lewiston ME
http://www.bates.edu/

Baylor Coll. of Dentistry - Waco TX
http://www.tambcd.edu/

Baylor Coll. of Medicine - Waco TX
http://www.bcm.tmc.edu/

Baylor Univ. - Waco TX
http://www.bcm.tmc.edu/

Beaver Col - Glenside PA
http://www.baylor.edu/

The Internet University - College URL's

Belhaven Col - Jackson MS
http://www.beaver.edu/

Bellarmine Col - Louisville KY
http://www.bellarmine.edu/

Bellevue Univ. - Bellevue NE
http://bruins.bellevue.edu/

Belmont Abbey Coll. - Belmont NC
http://www.bac.edu/

Belmont Univ. - Nashville TN
http://acklen.belmont.edu/

Beloit Col - Beloit WI
http://stu.beloit.edu/

Bemidji State Univ. - Bemidji MN
http://bsuweb.bemidji.msus.edu/

Benedict Col - Columbia SC
http://www.icusc.org/benedict/bchome.htm

Benedictine Col - Atchison KS
http://www.benedictine.edu/

Bennett Col - Greensboro NC
http://www.bennett.edu/

Bennington Col - Bennington VT
http://www.bennington.edu/

Bentley Col - Waltham MA
http://www.bentley.edu/

Berea Col - Berea KY
http://www.berea.edu/

Berklee Coll. of Music - Boston MA
http://www.berklee.edu/

Berry Col - Mount Berry GA
http://www.berry.edu/

Bethany Col - Bethany WV
http://info.bethany.wvnet.edu/

Bethany Col - Scotts Valley CA
http://www.bethany.edu/

Bethany Col - Lindsborg KS
http://www.bethanylb.edu/

Bethel Col - Mishawaka IN
http://www.bethel-in.edu/

Bethel Col - North Newton KS
http://www.bethelks.edu/

Bethel Col - St. Paul MN
http://www.bethel.edu/

Bethune-Cookman C - Dayt. Bch FL
http://www.bethune.cookman.edu/

Biola Univ. - La Mirada CA
http://www.biola.edu/

Birmingham-Southern C. - AL
http://www.bsc.edu/

Black Hills State U - Spearfish SD
http://www.bhsu.edu/

Blackburn Col - Carlinville IL
http://www.mcs.net/~kwplace/bc.htm

Bloomsburg Univ. - Bloomsburg PA
http://www.bloomu.edu/

Bluefield State Coll. - Bluefield WV
www.bluefield.wvnet.edu/

Bluffton Col - Bluffton OH
http://www.bluffton.edu/

Bob Jones Univ. - Greenville SC
http://www.bju.edu/

Boise State Univ. - Boise ID
http://www.idbsu.edu/

Boston Architect'l Ctr - Boston MA
http://www.the-bac.edu/

Boston Col - Chestnut Hill MA
http://infoeagle.bc.edu/

Boston Grad. School - Brookline
http://www.bgsp.edu/

Boston Univ. - Boston MA
http://web.bu.edu/

Bowdoin Col - Brunswick ME
http://www.bowdoin.edu/

Bowie State Univ. - Bowie MD
http://www.bsu.umd.edu/

Bowling Green State Univ. - OH
http://www.bgsu.edu/

Bradley Univ. - Peoria IL
http://www.bradley.edu/

Brandeis Univ. - Waltham MA
http://www.brandeis.edu/

Brenau Univ. - Gainesville GA
http://www.brenau.edu/

Brescia Col - Owensboro KY
http://brescia.edu/

Briar Cliff Col - Sioux City IA
http://www.briar-cliff.edu/

Bridgewater Coll. - Bridgewater VA
http://www.bridgewater.edu/

Bridgewater State C - B'water MA
http://www.bridgew.edu/

Brigham Young Univ. - Provo UT
http://www.byu.edu/

Brigham Young Univ. - Oahu HI
http://www.byuh.edu/

Brown Univ. - Providence RI
http://www.brown.edu/

Bryant Col - Smithfield RI
http://www.bryant.edu/

Bryn Mawr Col - Bryn Mawr PA
http://www.brynmawr.edu/

Bucknell Univ. - Lewisburg PA
http://www.bucknell.edu/

Buena Vista Univ. - Storm Lake IA
http://www.bvu.edu/

Butler Univ. - Indianapolis IN
http://www.butler.edu/

CA Baptist Coll. - Riverside CA
http://www.ci.riverside.ca.us/docs/baptist.html

CA Coast Univ. - Santa Ana, CA CA
http://www.calcoastuniv.edu/

CA Coll. of Arts Crafts - Oakland
http://art.aicad.org/aicad/brief/ccac.html

CA Col for Health Sciences -
http://www.cchs.edu/

CA Institute of Tech. - Pasadena CA
http://www.caltech.edu/

CA Institute of the Arts - Valencia
http://www.calarts.edu/

CA Lutheran U - Thousand Oaks CA
http://robles.callutheran.edu/

CA Maritime Academy - Vallejo CA
http://www.csum.edu/

CA Pacific Univ. - San Diego CA
http://www.groupweb.com/cpu/cpu.htm

CA Polytechnic - San Luis Obispo
http://www.calpoly.edu/

CA State Polytech - Pomona CA
http://www.csupomona.edu/

CA State U - San Marcos CA
http://coyote.csusm.edu/

CA State U - Turlock CA
http://lead.csustan.edu/

CA State U - Los Angeles CA
http://www.calstatela.edu/

CA State U - Bakersfield CA
http://www.csubak.edu/

CA State U - Chico CA
http://www.csuchico.edu/

CA State U - Carson CA
http://www.csudh.edu/

CA State U - Fresno CA
http://www.csufresno.edu/

CA State U - Long Beach CA
http://www.csulb.edu/

CA State U - Northridge CA
http://www.csun.edu/

CA State U - Sacramento CA
http://www.csus.edu/

CA State U - San Bernardino CA
http://www.csusb.edu/

CA State U - Fullerton CA
http://www.fullerton.edu/

CA State U - Hayward CA
http://www.mcs.csuhayward.edu/

CA State U - Seaside CA
http://www.monterey.edu/

Cabrini Col - Radnor PA
http://www.cabrini.edu/ •Caldwell Col - Caldwell NJ
http://www.caldwell.edu/

CA U of Pennsylvania - California
http://www.cup.edu/

Calumet Coll. - Whiting IN
http://birch.palni.edu/~jcampbell/ccsj/ccsj.htm

Calvin Col - Grand Rapids MI
http://www.calvin.edu/

Cameron Univ. - Lawton OK
http://www.cameron.edu/

Campbell Univ. - Buies Creek NC
http://www.campbell.edu/

Campbellsville Coll. - C'ville KY
http://www.campbellsvil.edu/

Canisius Col - Buffalo NY
http://www.canisius.edu/

Capital Univ. - Columbus OH
http://www.capital.edu/

Capitol Col - Laurel MD
http://www.fga.com/capcol/

Cardinal Stritch C. - Milwaukee WI
http://www.stritch.edu/

Carleton Col - Northfield MN
http://www.carleton.edu/

Carlow Coll. - Pittsburgh PA
http://www.carlow.edu/

Carnegie Mellon - Pittsburgh PA
http://www.cmu.edu/

Carroll Col - Waukesha WI
http://carroll1.cc.edu/

Carroll Col - Helena MT
http://www.carroll.edu/

Carson-Newman - Jefferson City TN
http://www.cn.edu/

Carthage Col - Kenosha WI
http://www.carthage.edu/

Case Western - Cleveland OH
http://www.cwru.edu/

Castleton State Coll. - Castleton VT
http://www.csc.vsc.edu/

Catawba Col - Salisbury NC
http://www.catawba.edu/

Catholic U of America - Washington
http://www.cua.edu/

Cazenovia Col - Cazenovia NY
http://www.cazCol.edu/

Cedar Crest Col - Allentown PA
http://www.cedarcrest.edu/

Cedarville Col - Cedarville OH
http://www.cedarville.edu/

Centenary Coll. - Shreveport LA
http://www.centenary.edu/

Central Baptist Col - Conway AR
http://www.centralonline.org/

Central Bible Coll. - Springfield MO
http://www.cbcag.edu/

Central Col - Pella IA
http://www.central.edu/

Central CT State U - New Britain CT
http://www.ccsu.ctstateu.edu/

Central Methodist C. - Fayette MO
http://www.cmc.edu/

Central Michigan U - Mt Pleasant
http://www.cmich.edu/

Central Missouri State Warrensburg
http://cmsuvmb.cmsu.edu/

Central Washington U - Ellensburg
http://www.cwu.edu/

Centre Col - Danville KY
http://www.centre.edu/

Chadron State Col - Chadron NE
http://www.csc.edu/

Chaminade Univ. - Honolulu HI
http://www.pixi.com/~chaminad/

Champlain Col - Burlington VT
http://www.champlain.edu/

Chapman Univ. - Orange CA
http://www.chapman.edu/

Charleston Southern Univ. - SC
http://www.icusc.org/chas_sou/cshome.htm

Charter Oak State C - Newington CT
http://www.ctstateu.edu/~chartoak/index.html

Chatham Col - Pittsburgh PA
http://www.chatham.edu/

Chesapeake Col - Wye Mills MD
http://www.chesapeake.edu/

Cheyney Univ. - Cheyney PA
http://www.cheyney.edu/

Chicago State Univ. - Chicago IL
http://www.ncsa.uiuc.edu/Edu/ILM/data/org/IBHE
/Chistate/Chistate.htm

Chicago-Kent C of Law - IL
http://www.kentlaw.edu/

Christendom Coll. - Front Royal VA
http://www.crnet.org/christdm/christdm.htm

Christian Brothers U - Memphis TN
http://www.cbu.edu/

Christian Theological - Indianapolis
http://www.cts.edu/

Christopher Newport - Newp. News
http://www.cnu.edu/

Cincinnati Bible Coll. - OH
http://www.tso.org/gcccu/cintibib.html

Citadel - Charleston SC
http://www.citadel.edu/

City Univ. - Renton WA
http://www.cityu.edu/inroads/welcome.htm

Claflin Col - Orangeburg SC
www.icusc.org/claflin/cchome.htm

Claremont Grad. Sch. - CA
http://www.cgs.edu/

Claremont McKenna - CA
http://www.mckenna.edu/

Clarion Univ. - Clarion PA
http://www.clarion.edu/

Clark Atlanta Univ. - Atlanta GA
http://www.cau.edu/

Clark Univ. - Worcester MA
http://www.clarku.edu/

Clarke Col - Dubuque IA
http://www.clarke.edu/

Clarkson Col - Omaha NE
http://www.clarksonCol.edu/

Clarkson Univ. - Potsdam NY
http://www.clarkson.edu/

Clayton State Col - Morrow GA
http://www.csc.peachnet.edu/

Clemson Univ. - Clemson SC
http://www.clemson.edu/

Cleveland Inst. of Music - OH
http://www.cwru.edu/CIM/

Cleveland State U - Cleveland OH
http://www.csuohio.edu/

Clinch Valley Col - Wise VA
http://www.clinch.edu/

Coastal Carolina U - Conway SC
http://www.coastal.edu/

Coe Col - Cedar Rapids IA
http://www.coe.edu/

Cogswell Polytech - Sunnyvale CA
http://www.cogswell.edu/

Coker Col - Hartsville SC
http://www.coker.edu/

Col. School of Mines - Golden CO
http://gn.mines.colorado.edu/

Colby Col - Waterville ME
http://www.colby.edu/

Colby-Sawyer Col.-New LondonNH
http://www.colby-sawyer.edu/

Colgate Univ. - Hamilton NY
http://www.colgate.edu/ •

Coll. of Art + Design - Detroit MI
http://www.ccscad.edu/

Coll. of Saint Catherine -St Paul MN
http://www.stkate.edu/

Col. of Saint Scholastica - Duluth
http://www.css.edu/

Coll. of St. Benedict - St. Joseph MN
http://www.csbsju.edu/

Coll. of the Atlantic - Bar Harbor
http://www.coa.edu/

Col. of William + Mary - W'msbrg
http://www.wm.edu/

Col Misericordia - Dallas PA
http://www.miseri.edu/

Col of Aeronautics - Flushing NY
http://www.mordor.com/coa/coa.html

Col of Charleston - Charleston SC
http://www.cofc.edu/

Col of Eastern Univ. - Price UT
http://www.ceu.edu/

Col of Marin - Kentfield CA
http://www.marin.cc.ca.us/

Col of New Rochelle - NY
http://www.cnr.edu/

Col of NJ - Trenton NJ
http://www.trenton.edu/

Col of Notre Dame - Belmont CA
http://www.cnd.edu/

Col of Notre Dame - Baltimore MD
http://www.ndm.edu/

Col of Ozarks - Point Lookout MO
http://www.cofo.edu/

Col of Saint Francis - Joliet IL
http://www.stfrancis.edu/

Col of Saint Rose - Albany NY
http://www.strose.edu/

Col of Santa Fe - Santa Fe NM
http://www.state.nm.us/csf/

Col of Wooster - Wooster OH
http://www.wooster.edu/

Colorado Christian U-Lakewood CO
http://www.ccu.edu/

Colorado Col - Col. Springs CO
http://www.cc.colorado.edu/

Colorado State U - Fort Collins CO
http://www.colostate.edu/

Columbia Col - Chicago IL
http://www.colum.edu/

Columbia Pacific U - San Rafael CA
http://www.itstime.com/cpu/

Columbia Southern U - Orn Bc AL
http://www.colsouth.edu/

Columbia U Col - Takoma Park MD
http://www.cuc.edu/

Columbia Univ. - New York NY
http://www.columbia.edu/

Columbus C of Art/Design - OH
http://www.ccad.edu/

Columbus State Univ. - GA
http://www.colstate.edu/

Conception Seminar - MO
http://www.msc-net.com/~/cabbey/seminary.html

Concord Col - Athens WV
http://www.concord.wvnet.edu/

Concordia Col - Austin TX
http://austin.concordia.edu/

Concordia Col -
http://cuis.edu/www/cus/cuny.html

Concordia Col - Ann Arbor MI
http://www.ccaa.edu/

Concordia Col - Seward NE
http://www.ccsn.edu/

Concordia Col - Moorhead MN
http://www.cord.edu/

Concordia Col - St. Paul MN
http://www.csp.edu/

Concordia Col - Portland OR
http://www.cu-portland.edu/

Concordia Col - Bronxville NY
http://www.cuis.edu/www/cus/cuny.html

Concordia Univ. - River Forest IL
http://www.curf.edu/

Concordia Univ. - Irvine CA
http://www.cui.edu/

Concordia Univ. - Mequon WI
http://www.cuw.edu/

Connecticut Coll. - New London CT
http://camel.conncoll.edu/

Converse Col - Spartanburg SC
http://www.icusc.org/converse/cchome.htm

Cooper Univ. - New York NY
http://www.cooper.edu/

Coppin State Col - Baltimore MD
http://coeacl.coppin.umd.edu/

Corcoran School of Art - Wash. DC
http://www.corcoran.org/

Cornell Col - Mount Vernon IA
http://www.cornell-iowa.edu/

Cornell Univ. - Ithaca NY
http://www.cornell.edu/

Cornerstone Coll. - Grand Rapids MI
http://www.grfn.org/~cstone/

Covenant Coll. - Lookout Mountain
http://www.covenant.edu/

Creighton Univ. - Omaha NE
http://www.creighton.edu/

Criswell Col - Dallas TX
http://www.criswell.edu/

Crown Col - Saint Bonifacius MN
http://www.crown.edu/

Culver-Stockton Coll. - Canton MO
http://www.culver.edu/

Cumberland Coll. - Williamsbg KY
http://www.cumber.edu/

Cumberland Univ. - Lebanon TN
http://members.aol.com/cumbrlndu/cumberland.edu/index.htm

CUNY - - Baruch Col New York
http://www.baruch.cuny.edu/

CUNY - Brooklyn NY
www.brooklyn.cuny.edu/

CUNY - City Col NY
http://www.ccny.cuny.edu/

CUNY - Staten Island NY
http://www.csi.cuny.edu/

CUNY - Hunter Col NY
http://www.hunter.cuny.edu/

CUNY - John Jay Coll. NY
http://www.jjay.cuny.edu/

CUNY - Lehman Coll. NY
http://www.lehman.cuny.edu/

CUNY - Medgar Evars C NY
http://www.cuny.edu/Cols/frames/eversf.html

CUNY-NYC - Brooklyn NY
http://www.cuny.edu/Cols/frames/nytechf.html

CUNY-Queens - Flushing NY
http://www.qc.edu/

CUNY-York - Jamaica NY
http://www.york.edu/

Curry Col - Milton MA
http://www.curry.edu:8080/

Daemen Col - Amherst NY
http://www.daemen.edu/

Dakota State Univ. - Madison SD
http://www.dsu.edu/

Dakota Wesleyan U - Mitchell SD
http://www.dwu.edu/

Dallas Baptist Univ. - Dallas TX
http://www.dbu.edu/

Dallas Theo. Seminary - Dallas TX
http://www.dts.edu/

Dana Col - Blair NE
http://www.dana.edu/

Daniel Webster Col - Nashua NH
http://www.dwc.edu/

Dartmouth Col - Hanover NH
http://www.dartmouth.edu/

Davenport Col - Grand Rapids MI
http://www.davenport.edu/

David H. Myers Coll - Clevelnd OH
http://ellen.dnmyers.edu/

David Lipscomb U - Nashville TN
http://www.dlu.edu/

Davidson Col - Davidson NC
http://www.davidson.edu/

Davis and Elkins Coll. - Elkins WV
http://www.dne.wvnet.edu/

Defiance Col - Defiance OH
http://www.defiance.edu/

DeKalb Col - Clarkston GA
http://www.dc.peachnet.edu/

Delaware State U - Dover DE
http://www.dsc.edu/

Delaware Valley C - Doylestown PA
http://silo.com/delval/

Delta Col - U Center MI
http://www.delta.edu/

Delta State Univ. - Cleveland MS
http://www.deltast.edu/

Denison Univ. - Granville OH
http://louie.cc.denison.edu/

Denver Seminary - Denver CO
http://www.gospelcom.net/densem/

DePaul Univ. - Chicago IL
http://www.depaul.edu/

DePauw Univ. - Greencastle IN
http://www.depauw.edu/

Detroit Col - Dearborn MI
http://www.dcb.edu/detroit.html

DeVry Institute - Atlanta - GA
http://www.atl.devry.edu/

DeVry Institute - Chicago - IL
http://www.chi.devry.edu/

DeVry Institute - Columbus - OH
http://www.devrycols.edu/

DeVry Institute - Dallas - Irving TX
http://www.dal.devry.edu/

DeVry Institute - DuPage - IL
http://www.dpg.devry.edu/

DeVry Institute - Kansas City - MO
http://www.devry.edu/kans.htm

DeVry Institute - Long Beach - CA
http://www.devry.edu/long.htm

DeVry Institute - Phoenix - AZ
http://www.devry-phx.edu/

DeVry Institute - Pomona - CA
http://www.pom.devry.edu/

Diablo Valley Coll. - Pleas. Hill CA
http://www.dvc.edu/

Dickinson Col - Carlisle PA
http://www.dickinson.edu/

Dickinson State U - Dickinson ND
http://www.dsu.nodak.edu/

Dillard Univ. - New Orleans LA
http://www.dillard.edu/

Dixie Col - St. George UT
http://sci.dixie.edu/

Doane Col - Crete NE
http://www.doane.edu/

Dominican Col - Orangeburg NY
http://www.dc.edu/

Dominican Col - San Rafael CA
http://www.dominican.edu/

Dordt Col - Sioux Center IA
http://www.dordt.edu/

Dowling Col - Oakdale NY
http://www.dowling.edu/

Drake Univ. - Des Moines IA
http://www.drake.edu/

Drew Univ. - Madison NJ
http://www.drew.edu/

Drexel Univ. - Philadelphia PA
http://www.drexel.edu/

Drury Col - Springfield MO
http://www.drury.edu/

Duke Univ. - Durham NC
http://www.duke.edu/

Duquesne Univ. - Pittsburgh PA
http://www.duq.edu/

Earlham Col - Richmond IN
http://www.earlham.edu/

East Carolina Univ. - Greenville NC
http://www.ecu.edu/

East Central Univ. - Ada OK
http://www.ecok.edu/

East Stroudsburg State Univ. - PA
http://www.esu.edu/

East Texas Baptist U - Marshall TX
http://www.etbu.edu/

East Texas State U - Commerce TX
http://www.etsu.edu/

East TN State U - Johnson City TN
http://www.etsu-tn.edu/

East-West Univ. - Chicago IL
http://www.eastwest.edu/

Eastern Col - St. Davids PA
http://www.eastern.edu/

Eastern CT State U - Willimantic CT
http://www.ecsu.ctstateu.edu/

Eastern Illinois U - Charleston IL
http://www.eiu.edu/

Eastern Kentucky U - Richmond KY
http://www.eku.edu/

East. Mennonite U - Harrisonbg VA
http://www.emu.edu/

Eastern Michigan U - Ypsilanti MI
http://www.emich.edu/

Eastern Nazarene C. - Quincy MA
http://www.enc.edu/

Eastern NM Univ. - Portales NM
http://www.enmu.edu/

Eastern OR State - La Grande OR
http://www.eosc.osshe.edu/

Eastern Washington U - Cheney WA
http://www.ewu.edu/

Eastman Sch Music - Rochester NY
http://esm.rochester.edu/

Eckerd Col - St. Petersburg FL
http://www.eckerd.edu/

Edgewood Col - Madison WI
http://www.edgewood.edu/

Edinboro Univ. of Pennsylvania
http://www.edinboro.edu/

Elizabeth City State Univ. - NC
http://www.ecsu.edu/

Elizabethtown Col - PA
http://www.etown.edu/

Elmhurst Col - Elmhurst IL
http://www.elmhurst.edu/

Elmira Col - Elmira NY
http://www.elmira.edu/

Elon Col - Elon Col NC
http://www.elon.edu/

Embry-Riddle Aero U - Dayton Bch
http://macwww.db.erau.edu/

Embry-Riddle Aero U - Prescott AZ
http://www.pr.erau.edu/

Emerson Col - Boston MA
http://www.emerson.edu/

Emmanuel Col - Boston MA
http://www.emmanuel.edu/

Emmaus Bible Col - Dubuque IA
http://www.xicom.com/edu/emmaus/

Emory + Henry Col - Emory VA
http://www.ehc.edu/

Emory Univ. - Atlanta GA
http://www.emory.edu/

Emporia State Univ. - Emporia KS
http://www.emporia.edu/

Endicott Col - Beverly MA
http://www.endicott.edu/

Erskine Col - Due West SC
http://www.erskine.edu/

Eugene Lang Col - New York NY
http://www.newschool.edu/

Evangel Col - Springfield MO
http://www.evangel.edu/

Evergreen State Col - Olympia WA
http://www.evergreen.edu/

Fairfield Univ. - Fairfield CT
http://www.fairfield.edu/

Fairleigh Dickinson U - Teaneck NJ
http://www.fdu.edu/

Fairmont State Col - Fairmont WV
http://www.fairmont.wvnet.edu/

Faulkner Univ. - Montgomery AL
http://www.faulkner.edu/

Fayetteville State Univ. - NC
http://www.fsufay.edu/

Felician Col - Lodi NJ
http://www.felician.edu/

Ferris State Univ. - Big Rapids MI
http://about.ferris.edu/

Ferrum Col - Ferrum VA
http://www.ferrum.edu/

Fielding Institute - Santa Barbara CA
http://www.fielding.edu/

Fisk Univ. - Nashville TN
http://www.fisk.edu/

Fitchburg State Col - Fitchburg MA
http://www.fsc.edu/

Flagler Col - St. Augustine FL
http://www.flagler.edu/

Florida A+M Univ. - Tallahassee FL
http://www.famu.edu/

Florida Atlantic Univ. - Boca Raton
http://www.fau.edu/

Florida Gulf Coast Univ. - Ft. Myers
http://www.fgcu.edu/

Florida Institute of Tech - Melbourn
http://www.fit.edu/

Florida International Univ. - Miami
http://www.fiu.edu/

Florida Memorial Col - Miami FL
http://www.fmc.edu/

Florida Southern Col - Lakeland FL
http://snoopy.tblc.lib.fl.us/fsc/fsc.html

Florida State Univ. - Tallahassee FL
http://www.fsu.edu/

Fontbonne Col - St. Louis MO
http://www.fontbonne.edu/

Fordham Univ. - Bronx NY
http://www.fordham.edu/

Fort Hays State Univ. - Hays KS
http://www.fhsu.edu/

Fort Lewis Col - Durango CO
http://www.fortlewis.edu/

Framingham State Col - MA
http://www.framingham.edu/

Francis Marion Univ. - Florence SC
http://swampfox.fmarion.edu/web/UnivRel/urmain.html

Franciscan U of Steubenville - OH
http://www.franuniv.edu/

Franklin + Marshall C - Lancast. PA
http://www.fandm.edu/

Franklin Col - Franklin IN
http://www.franklincoll.edu/

Franklin Pierce Col - Rindge NH
http://www.fpc.edu/

Franklin Pierce Law - Concord NH
http://www.fplc.edu/

Franklin Univ. - Columbus OH
http://www.franklin.edu/

Franklin U Comp Sci - Columb. OH
http://www.cs.franklin.edu/

Freed-Hardeman U - Henderson TN
http://www.fhu.edu/

Fresno Pacific Univ. - Fresno CA
http://www.fresno.edu/

Friends Univ. - Wichita KS
http://www.friends.edu/

Frostburg State Univ. - MD
http://www.fsu.umd.edu/

Fuller Theological - Pasadena CA
http://www.fuller.edu/

Fullerton Col - Fullerton CA
http://www.fullcoll.edu/

Furman Univ. - Greenville SC
http://www.furman.edu/

Gallaudet Univ. - Washington DC
http://www.gallaudet.edu/

Gannon Univ. - Erie PA
http://www.gannon.edu/

Gardner-Webb U - Boiling Spgs NC
http://www.gardner-webb.edu/

Geneva Col - Beaver Falls PA
http://www.geneva.edu/

George Fox Col - Newberg OR
http://www.gfc.edu/

George Mason Univ. - Fairfax VA
http://www.gmu.edu/

George Washington Univ. - DC
http://gwis.circ.gwu.edu/

Georgetown Col - Georgetown KY
http://www.gtc.georgetown.ky.us/

Georgetown Univ. - Washington DC
http://www.georgetown.edu/

GA Baptist Col of Nursing - Atlanta
http://www.gbcn.edu/

Georgia Col - Milledgeville GA
http://www.gac.peachnet.edu/

Georgia Southern Univ. - Statesboro
http://www.gasou.edu/

Georgia SW State Univ. - Americus
http://gswrs6k1.gsw.peachnet.edu/

Georgia State Univ. - Atlanta GA
http://www.gsu.edu/

Georgia Tech - Atlanta GA
http://www.gatech.edu/

Georgian Court Col - Lakewood NJ
http://www.georgian.edu/

Gettysburg Col - Gettysburg PA
http://www.gettysburg.edu/

Glendale Univ. of Law - CA
http://www.glendalelaw.edu/

Glenville State Col - Glenville WV
http://www.glenville.wvnet.edu/

GMI Engineering - Flint MI
http://www.gmi.edu/

Goddard Col - Plainfield VT
http://www.goddard.edu/

Golden Gate Univ. - San Francisco
http://www.ggu.edu/

Goldey-Beacom Col - Wilmington
http://goldey.gbc.edu/

Gonzaga Univ. - Spokane WA
http://www.gonzaga.edu/

Gordon Col - Wenham MA
http://www.gordonc.edu/

Goshen Col - Goshen IN
http://www.goshen.edu/

Goucher Col - Baltimore MD
http://www.goucher.edu/

Governors State Univ. - U Park IL
http://www.govst.edu/

Grace Col - Winona Lake IN
http://www.grace.edu/

Grace Univ. - Omaha NE
http://www.graceu.edu/

Graceland Col - Lamoni IA
http://www.graceland.edu/

Grand Canyon Univ. - Phoenix AZ
http://www.grand-canyon.edu/

Grand Valley State U - Allendale MI
http://www.gvsu.edu/

Green Mountain Col - Poultney VT
http://www.vermontel.com/~admiss/greenmtn/ind
ex.htm

Greensboro Col - Greensboro NC
http://www.gboroCol.edu/

Greenville Col - Greenville IL
http://www.greenville.edu/

Grinnell Col - Grinnell IA
http://www.grin.edu/

Grove City Col - Grove City PA
http://www.gcc.edu/

Guilford Col - Greensboro NC
http://www.guilford.edu/

Gustavus Adolphus Col - StPete MN
http://www.gac.edu/

Gutenberg Col - Eugene OR
http://www.efn.org/~mscenter/guten

Gwynedd-Mercy Col - PA
http://www.gmc.edu/

Hamilton Col - Clinton NY
http://www.hamilton.edu/

Hamline Univ. - St. Paul MN
http://www.hamline.edu/

Hampden-Sydney Col - VA
http://www.hsc.edu/

Hampshire Col - Amherst MA
http://www.hampshire.edu/

Hampton Univ. - Hampton VA
http://www.cs.hamptonu.edu/

Hannibal-LaGrange C - MO
http://www.hlg.edu/

Hanover Col - Hanover IN
http://www.hanover.edu/

Hardin-Simmons U. - Abilene TX
http://www.hsutx.edu/

Harding Univ. - Searcy AR
http://www.harding.edu/

Hartwick Col - Oneonta NY
http://www.hartwick.edu/

Harvard Univ. - Cambridge MA
http://www.harvard.edu/

Harvey Mudd Col - Claremont CA
http://www.hmc.edu/

Hastings Col - Hastings NE
http://www.hastings.edu/

Haverford Col - Haverford PA
http://www.haverford.edu/

Hawaii Pacific Univ. - Honolulu HI
http://www.hpu.edu/

Hebrew Col - Brookline MA
http://shamash.org/hc

Heidelberg Col - Tiffin OH
http://www.heidelberg.edu/

Hellenic Sch of Theo - Brkline MA
http://www.drscc.com/clients/bti/schools/holycros/l
ibs/holycros.htm

Henderson State U. - Arkadelph AR
http://www.hsu.edu/

Hendrix Col - Conway AR
http://www.hendrix.edu/

Heritage Col - Toppenish WA
http://www.heritage.edu/

Hesston Col - Hesston KS
http://www.hesston.edu/

High Point Univ. - High Point NC
http://acme.highpoint.edu/

Hillsdale Col - Hillsdale MI
http://www.hillsdale.edu/

Hiram Col - Hiram OH
http://admission.hiram.edu/

Hobart + Wm Smith C - Geneva NY
http://hws3.hws.edu:9000/

Hofstra Univ. - Hempstead NY
http://www.hofstra.edu/

Hollins Col - Roanoke VA
http://www.hollins.edu/

Holy Cross - Worcester MA
http://www.holycross.edu/

Holy Names Col - Oakland CA
http://www.hnc.edu/

Hood Col - Frederick MD
http://www.hood.edu/

Hope Col - Holland MI
http://www.hope.edu/

Houghton Col - Houghton NY
http://www.houghton.edu/

Houston Baptist Univ. - Houston TX
http://www.hbu.edu/

Howard Payne Univ. - Brownwd TX
http://www.hputx.edu/

Howard Univ. - Washington DC
http://www.howard.edu/

Humbolt State Univ. - Arcata CA
http://www.humboldt.edu/

Huntingdon Col - Montgomery AL
http://www.huntingdon.edu/

Huntington Col - Huntington IN
http://www.huntcol.edu/

Huron Univ. - Huron SD
http://www.huron.edu/

Husson Col - Bangor ME
http://www.husson.edu/

Huston-Tillotson Col - Austin TX
http://www.htc.edu/

ICI Univ. - Irving TX
http://www.ici.edu/

Idaho State Univ. - Pocatello ID
http://www.isu.edu/

Illinois Benedictine Univ. - Lisle IL
http://www.ibc.edu/

Illinois Col - Jacksonville IL
http://www.ic.edu/

Illinois Institute of Tech - Chicago
http://www.iit.edu/

Illinois State Univ. - Normal IL
http://www.ilstu.edu/

Illinois Wesleyan U. - Bloomington
http://www.iwu.edu/

Immaculata Col - Immaculata PA
http://www.immaculata.edu/

Incarnate Word Col - San Antonio
http://www.iwctx.edu/

Indiana IT - Fort Wayne IN
http://www.indtech.edu/

Indiana State Univ. - Terre Haute IN
http://www.indstate.edu/

Indiana Univ. - Bloomington IN
http://www.indiana.edu/

Purdue U - Columbus IN
http://www.columbus.iupui.edu/

Indiana Univ. at Kokomo - Kokomo
http://www.iuk.indiana.edu/

Indiana Univ. Bloomington
http://www.indiana.edu/iub/

Indiana Univ. East - Richmond IN
http://www.iue.indiana.edu/

Indiana Univ. Northwest - Gary IN
http://www.iun.indiana.edu/

Indiana Univ. of Pennsylvania
http://www.iup.edu/

Indiana U. Southeast - New Albany
http://www.ius.indiana.edu/

Purdue U - Fort Wayne IN
http://www.ipfw.indiana.edu/

Purdue U - Indianapolis IN
http://indyunix.iupui.edu/

Indiana Univ./South Bend - IN
http://smartnet.iusb.indiana.edu/

Indiana Wesleyan Univ. - Marion IN
http://www.indwes.edu/

Inst for Christian Studies - Austin
http://www.ics.edu/

Institute of Paper Science - Atlanta
http://www.ipst.edu/

Inst of Transpersonal Psy - Palo Alto
http://www.tmn.com/itp/

Iona Col - New Rochelle NY
http://www.iona.edu/

Iowa State Univ. - Ames IA
http://www.iastate.edu/

Ithaca Col - Ithaca NY
http://www.ithaca.edu/

Jackson State Univ. - Jackson MS
http://www.jsums.edu/

Jacksonville State Univ. - AL
http://www.jsu.edu/

Jacksonville Univ. - Jacksonville FL
http://junix.ju.edu/

James Madison U - Harrisonburg VA
http://www.jmu.edu/

Jamestown Col - Jamestown ND
http://acc.jc.edu/

Jersey City State Col - Jersey City
http://www.jcstate.edu/

Jewish Theological Seminary - NY
http://www.jtsa.edu/

John Brown U. - Siloam Springs AR
http://www.jbu.edu/

John Carroll Univ. - U Heights OH
http://www.jcu.edu/

John F. Kennedy Univ. - Orinda CA
http://www.jfku.edu/

Johns Hopkins U. - Baltimore MD
http://www.jhu.edu/

Johnson + Wales U. - Providence RI
http://www.jwu.edu/

Johnson and Wales U - Charleston
http://www.sims.net/organizations/jwu-sc/jwu.html

Johnson Bible Col - Knoxville TN
http://www.jbc.edu/

Johnson C. Smith Univ. - Charlotte
http://www.jcsu.edu/

Johnson State Col - Johnson VT
http://www.jsc.vsc.edu/

Jones Col - Jacksonville FL
http://www.jones.edu/

Judson Col - Marion AL
http://home.judson.edu/

Judson Col - Elgin IL
http://www.judson-il.edu/

Juilliard School - New York NY
http://www.juilliard.edu/

Juniata Col - Huntingdon PA
http://www.juniata.edu/

Kalamazoo Col - Kalamazoo MI
http://www.kzoo.edu/

Kansas Newman Col - Wichita KS
http://www.ksnewman.edu/

Kansas State Univ. - Manhattan KS
http://www.ksu.edu/

Kansas Wesleyan Univ. - Salina KS
http://www.kwu.edu/

Kean Col of New Jersey - Union NJ
http://www.kean.edu/

Keene State Col - Keene NH
http://www.keene.edu/

Kennedy-Western U - Cheyenne WY
http://kw.edu/

Kennesaw State Univ. - Kennesaw
http://wwwcoles.kennesaw.edu/

Kent State Univ. - Kent OH
http://www.kent.edu/

Kentucky Christian Univ. - Grayson
http://www.kcc.edu/

Kentucky State Univ. - Frankfort KY
http://www.kysu.edu/

Kentucky Wesleyan - Owensboro
http://www.kwc.edu/

Kenyon Col - Gambier OH
http://www.kenyon.edu/

Keuka Col - Keuka Park NY
http://www.keuka.edu/

King Col - Bristol TN
http://www.king.bristol.tn.us/

King's Col - Wilkes Barre PA
http://www.kings.edu/

Knox Col - Galesburg IL
http://www.knox.edu/

Knoxville Col - Knoxville TN
http://falcon.nest.kxcol.edu/

Kutztown Univ. of Pennsylvania
http://www.kutztown.edu/

La Salle Univ. - Philadelphia PA
http://www.lasalle.edu/

La Sierra Univ. - Riverside CA
http://www.lasierra.edu/

Lafayette Col - Easton PA
http://www.lafayette.edu/

LaGrange Col - LaGrange GA
http://www.lgc.peachnet.edu/

Lake Forest Col - Lake Forest IL
http://www.lfc.edu/

Lake Superior State - S. St. Marie MI
http://www.lssu.edu/

Lakeland Col - Sheboygan WI
http://www.lakeland.edu/

Lamar Univ. - Beaumont TX
http://kw.lamar.edu/

Lambuth Univ. - Jackson TN
http://www.lambuth.edu/

Langston Univ. - Langston OK
http://www.lunet.edu/

LaSalle Univ. - Philadelphia PA
http://www.lasalle.edu/

Lawrence Tech U. - Southfield MI
http://www.ltu.edu/

Lawrence Univ. - Appleton WI
http://www.lawrence.edu/

Le Moyne Col - Syracuse NY
http://www.lemoyne.edu/

Lebanon Valley Col - Annville PA
http://www.lvc.edu/

Lee Col - Cleveland TN
http://www.lee.edu/

Lehigh Univ. - Bethlehem PA
http://www.lehigh.edu/

LeMoyne-Owen Col - Memphis TN
http://www.mecca.org/LOC/page/LOC.html

Lenoir-Rhyne Col - Hickory NC
http://www.lrc.edu/

Lesley Col - Cambridge MA
http://www.lesley.edu/

LeTourneau Univ. - Longview TX
http://www.letu.edu/

Lewis + Clark Col - Portland OR
http://www.lclark.edu/

Lewis Univ. - Romeoville IL
http://www.lewisu.edu/

Lewis-Clark State Col - Lewiston ID
http://www.lcsc.edu/

Liberty Univ. - Lynchburg VA
http://www.liberty.edu/

Life Col - Marietta GA
http://lifenet.life.edu/

Limestone Col - Gaffney SC
http://web.icusc.org/limestne/lchome.htm

Lincoln Memorial U - Harrogate TN
http://www.lmunet.edu/

Lincoln Univ. - Lincoln U PA
http://www.lincoln.edu/

Lincoln Univ. - San Francisco CA
http://www.lincolnuca.edu/

Lindenwood Col - St. Charles MO
http://199.217.137.67/

Linfield Col - McMinnville OR
http://www.linfield.edu/

Lock Haven Univ. - Lock Haven PA
http://www.lhup.edu/ •

Loma Linda Univ. - Loma Linda CA
http://www.llu.edu/

Long Island Univ. - Brooklyn NY
http://www.brooklyn.liunet.edu/cwis/bklyn.html

Long Island Univ. - Brookville NY
http://www.cwpost.liunet.edu/cwis/cwp/post.html

Long Island Univ. - Southampton
http://www.southampton.liunet.edu/sc_frame.htm

Longwood Col - Farmville VA
http://www.lwc.edu/

Loras Col - Dubuque IA
http://www.loras.edu/

Louisiana Col - Pineville LA
http://www.laCol.edu/

Louisiana State Univ. - Eunice LA
http://www.lsue.edu/

Louisiana State U - Baton Rouge LA
http://www.lsu.edu/

Louisiana State U - Alexandria
http://www.lsua.edu/

Louisiana State U - Shreveport
http://www.lsus.com/

Louisiana Tech Univ. - Ruston LA
http://aurora.latech.edu/

Loyola Col - Baltimore MD
http://www.loyola.edu/

Loyola Marymount Univ. - LA CA
http://www.lmu.edu/

Loyola Univ. - New Orleans LA
http://www.loyno.edu/

Loyola Univ. - Chicago IL
http://www.luc.edu/

Lubbock Christian Univ. - TX
http://www.lcu.edu/

Luther Col - Decorah IA
http://www.luther.edu/

Luther Seminary - St. Paul MN
http://www.luthersem.edu/

Lutheran Bible Inst - Issaquah WA
http://www.lbi.edu/

Lycoming Col - Williamsport PA
http://www.lycoming.edu/

Lynchburg Col - Lynchburg VA
http://www.lynchburg.edu/

Lyndon State Col - Lyndonville VT
http://www.lsc.vsc.edu/

Lynn Univ. - Boca Raton FL
http://www.lynn.edu/

Lyon Col - Batesville AR
http://www.lyon.edu/

Macalester Col - St. Paul MN
http://www.macalstr.edu/

MacMurray Col - Jacksonville IL
http://www.mac.edu/

Madonna Univ. - Livonia MI
http://www.munet.edu/

Maharishi U of Mgt - Fairfield IA
http://www.mum.edu/

Maine Col of Art - Portland ME
http://www.ime.net/gdmeca/

Maine Maritime Academy - Castine
http://www.state.me.us/maritime/mma.htm

Malone Col - Canton OH
http://www.malone.edu/

Manchester Col - IN
http://eris.manchester.edu/

Manhattan Col - Riverdale NY
http://www.manhattan.edu/

Manhattanville - Col Purchase
http://www.mville.edu/

Mankato State Univ. - Mankato MN
http://www.mankato.msus.edu/

Mannes Col of Music - New York
http://www.newschool.edu/

Mansfield Univ. - Mansfield PA
http://www.mnsfld.edu/

Marietta Col - Marietta OH
http://www.marietta.edu/

Marist Col - Poughkeepsie NY
http://www.marist.edu/

Marlboro Col - Marlboro VT
http://www.marlboro.edu/

Marquette Univ. - Milwaukee WI
http://www.mu.edu/

Mars Hill Col - Mars Hill NC
http://www.mhc.edu/

Marshall Univ. - Huntington WV
http://www.marshall.edu/

Mary Baldwin Col - Staunton VA
http://www.mbc.edu/

Mary Washington - Fredericksburg
http://www.mwc.edu/

Marycrest Internat U - Davenport IA
http://www.mcrest.edu/

Maryland Institute of Art - B'more
http://www.mica.edu/

Marylhurst Col - Marylhurst OR
http://www.marylhurst.edu/

Marymount Col - Tarrytown NY
http://www.marymt.edu/

Marymount Manhattan Col - NY
http://marymount.mmm.edu/home.htm

Marymount Univ. - Arlington VA
http://www.marymount.edu/

Maryville Col - Maryville TN
http://www.maryvilleCol.edu/

Maryville Univ. - St. Louis MO
http://www.maryvillestl.edu/

Marywood Col - Scranton PA
http://www.marywood.edu/

Massachuetts Col of Art - Boston
http://www.massart.edu/

MA Col of Pharmacy - Boston MA
http://www.mcp.edu/

MIT - Cambridge MA
http://web.mit.edu/

Mass Maritime - Buzzards Bay MA
http://www.mma.mass.edu/mma.html

Master's Col, The - Santa Clarita CA
http://www.masters.edu/

Master's Seminary - Sun Valley CA
http://www.mastersem.edu/

Mayo Foundation - (unknown)
http://www.mayo.edu/education/education.html

Mayville State Univ. - Mayville ND
http://www.masu.nodak.edu/

McKendree Col - Lebanon IL
http://www.mckendree.edu/

McMurry Univ. - Abilene TX
http://www.mcm.acu.edu/

McNeese State U - Lake Charles LA
http://www.mcneese.edu/

McPherson Col - McPherson KS
http://www.mcpherson.edu/

Medical Col of Georgia
http://www.mcg.edu/

Medical Col of Ohio
http://www.mco.edu/

Hahnemann Univ. - PA
http://www.mcphu.edu/

Medical Col of Wisconsin -
http://www.mcw.edu/

Medical Univ. of South Carolina -
http://www.musc.edu/

Memphis Col of Art - Memphis TN
http://www.mca.edu/

Menlo Col - Atherton CA
http://www.menlo.edu/

Mercer Univ. - Macon GA
http://www.mercer.peachnet.edu/

Mercy Col - Dobbs Ferry NY
http://www.mercynet.edu/

Mercyhurst Col - Erie PA
http://utopia.mercy.edu/

Meredith Col - Raleigh NC
http://www.meredith.edu/meredith/

Mesa State Col - Grand Junction CO
http://www.mesastate.edu/

Messiah Col - Grantham PA
http://www.messiah.edu/

Methodist Col - Fayetteville NC
http://www.apcnet.com/Methodist/Methodist.html

Metropolitan State Col of Denver
http://www.mscd.edu/

Metropolitan State Univ.
http://www.metro.msus.edu/

Miami Univ. of Ohio - Oxford OH
http://www.muohio.edu/

Michigan Christian - Rochester Hills
http://www.michristian.edu/

Michigan State Univ. - East Lansing
http://www.msu.edu/

Michigan Tech Univ. - Houghton MI
http://www.mtu.edu/

Mid-America Nazarene - Olathe KS
http://www.manc.edu/

Middle Tenn. State - Murfreesbor
http://www.mtsu.edu/

Middlebury Col - Middlebury VT
http://www.middlebury.edu/

Midland Lutheran Col - Fremont NE
http://www.mlc.edu/

Midwestern State U - Wich Falls TX
http://www.mwsu.edu/

Millersville Univ. - Millersville PA
http://marauder.millersv.edu/

Milligan Col - Milligan Col TN
http://www.milligan.milligan-Col.tn.us/

Millikin Univ. - Decatur IL
http://www.millikin.edu/

Mills Col - Oakland CA
http://www.mills.edu/

Millsaps Col - Jackson MS
http://www.millsaps.edu/

Milwaukee School of Engineering
http://www.msoe.edu/

Minneapolis Col of Art Design
http://www.mcad.edu/

Minot State Univ. - Minot ND
http://warp6.cs.misu.nodak.edu/

Mississippi Col - Clinton MS
http://www.mc.edu/

Mississippi State U - Miss. State
http://www.msstate.edu/

Miss. U for Women - Columbus
http://www.muw.edu/

Miss. Valley State U - Itta Bena
http://www.mvsu.edu/

Missouri Baptist C - Creve Coeur
http://mobap.edu/

Missouri Southern State - Joplin
http://www.mssc.edu/

Missouri Western State - St. Joseph
http://www.mwsc.edu/

Molloy Col - Rockville Centre NY
http://www.molloy.edu/

Monmouth Col - Monmouth IL
http://pippin.monm.edu/

Monmouth U - West Long Branch NJ
http://www.monmouth.edu/

Montana State Univ. - Bozeman MT
http://www.montana.edu/

Montana State Univ. - Billings MT
http://www.msubillings.edu/

Montana State Univ. - Havre MT
http://www.nmclites.edu/

Montana Tech - Butte MT
http://www.mtech.edu/

Montclair State Univ. - NJ
http://www.montclair.edu/

Monterey Inst of Int'l Studies - CA
http://www.miis.edu/

Montreat Col - Montreat NC
http://www.montreat.edu/

Moody Bible Institute - Chicago IL
http://www.moody.edu/

Moorhead State Univ. - MN
http://www.moorhead.msus.edu/

Moravian Col - Bethlehem PA
http://www.moravian.edu/

Morehead State Univ. - KY
http://www.morehead-st.edu/

Morehouse Col - Atlanta GA
http://www.morehouse.auc.edu/

Morgan State Univ. - Baltimore MD
http://www.morgan.edu/

Morningside Col - Sioux City IA
http://www.morningside.edu/

Morris Col - Sumter SC
http://www.icusc.org/morris/mchome.htm

Mt Holyoke Col - South Hadley MA
http://www.mtholyoke.edu/

Mount Ida Col - Newton Center MA
http://www.mountida.edu/

Mount Marty Col - Yankton SD
http://www.mtmc.edu/

Mount Mercy Col - Cedar Rapids IA
http://www.mtmercy.edu/

Mount Olive Col - Mount Olive NC
http://horizon.moc.edu/

Mount Saint Clare Col - Clinton IA
http://www.clare.edu/

Mt Saint Mary Col - Newburgh NY
http://www.msmc.edu/

Mount Saint Mary's - Emitsbrg MD
http://www.msmary.edu/

Mount Senario Col - Ladysmith WI
http://www.mscfs.edu/

Mount Univ. Col - Alliance OH
http://www.muc.edu/

Mount Vernon Col - Washington DC
http://www.mvc.edu/

Mt Vernon Nazarene - OH
http://www.mvnc.edu/

Muhlenberg Col - Allentown PA
http://www.muhlberg.edu/

Murray State Univ. - Murray KY
http://www.mursuky.edu/

Muskingum Col - New Concord OH
http://www.muskingum.edu/

National Defense U. - Washington
http://www.ndu.edu/

National Hispanic Univ. - San Jose
http://www.nhu.edu/

National Tech Univ. - Ft Collins CO
http://www.ntu.edu/

National Univ. - San Diego CA
http://nunic.nu.edu/

National-Louis Univ. - Evanston IL
http://nlu.nl.edu/

Naval Postgrade School - Monterey
http://www.nps.navy.mil/

Nazareth Col - Rochester NY
http://www.naz.edu/

Nebraska Wesleyan Univ. - Lincoln
http://www.nebrwesleyan.edu/

Neumann Col - Aston PA
http://www.neumann.edu/

New Church Coll. - Bryn Athyn PA
http://www.newchurch.edu/

New Col of California - San Fran
http://www.newCol.edu/

New England Conserv - Boston
http://copernicus.bbn.com/nec/

New England Inst Tech - Warwick
http://media1.hypernet.com/neit.html

New Hampshire Col - Manchester
http://www.nhc.edu/

NJ Institute of Tech - Newark
http://www.njit.edu/

NM Highlands U - Las Vegas NM
http://www.nmhu.edu/

NM Institute of Mining - Socorro
http://www.nmt.edu/

New Mexico State U - Las Cruces
http://www.nmsu.edu/

NM Western Univ. - Silver City NM
http://www.wnmu.edu/

NY Col of Podiatric Medicine
http://www.nycpm.edu/

New York IT - Old Westbury NY
http://www.nyit.edu/

New York Univ. - New York NY
http://www.nyu.edu/

NYU Grad Sch Arts + Sci - NY
http://www.nyu.edu/gsas/

Newberry Col - Newberry SC
http://www.newberry.edu/

Niagara Univ. - Niagara U NY
http://www.niagara.edu/

Nicholls State Univ. - Thibodaux LA
http://server.nich.edu/

Nichols Col - Dudley MA
http://www.nichols.edu/

Norfolk State Univ. - Norfolk VA
http://cyclops.nsu.edu/

North Adams State Col - MA
http://www.nasc.mass.edu/

N Carolina A+T Univ. - Greensboro
http://www.ncat.edu/

N Carolina Central Univ. - Durham
http://www.nccu.edu/

North Carolina State U - Raleigh
http://www.ncsu.edu/

NCarolina Wesleyan C - Rocky Mt
http://www.ncwc.edu/

North Central Bible C - Minneapolis
http://www.ncbc.edu/

North Central Col - Naperville IL
http://www.noctrl.edu/

North Dakota State Univ. - Fargo
http://www.ndsu.nodak.edu/

North Georgia Col - Dahlonega GA
http://www.ngc.peachnet.edu/

North Greenville Col - Tigerville SC
http://www.icusc.org/n_greenv/nghome.htm

North Park Theo Sem. - Chicago
http://www.npcts.edu/

Northeast Louisiana Univ. - Monroe
http://www.nlu.edu/

Northeastern Illinois U - Chicago
http://www.neiu.edu/

Northeastern State U - Tahleq. OK
http://www.nsuok.edu/

Northeastern Univ. - Boston MA
http://www.northeastern.edu/

Northern Arizona Univ. - Flagstaff
http://www.nau.edu/

Northern Illinois Univ. - DeKalb IL
http://www.niu.edu/

No Kentucky Univ. - Highland Hts
http://www.nku.edu/

Northern Michigan U. - Marquette
http://www-ais.acs.nmu.edu/

Northern State Univ. - Aberdeen SD
http://www.northern.edu/

Northland Col - Ashland WI
http://bobb.northland.edu/

Northwest Col - Kirkland WA
http://www.say64k.com/nwCol/

NW Missouri State U - Maryville
http://www.nwmissouri.edu/

Northwest Nazarene C - Nampa ID
http://www.nnc.edu/Homepage.html

Northwestern Col - Orange City IA
http://solomon.nwciowa.edu/

Northwestern Col - St. Paul MN
http://www.nwc.edu/

NW Michigan Col - Traverse City
http://www.nmc.edu/

Northwestern State U - Natchitoches
http://www.nsula.edu/

Northwestern Univ. - Evanston IL
http://www.nwu.edu/

Northwood Univ. - Midland MI
http://www.northwood.edu/

Northwood Univ. - West Palm Beach
http://www.northwood.edu/nu-fl.html

Norwich Univ. - Northfield VT
http://www.norwich.edu/

Nova Southeastern U - Ft Laud
http://www.nova.edu/

Nyack Col - Nyack NY
http://www.nyackCol.edu/

Oak Hills Bible Col - Bemidji MN
http://www.digitmaster.com/homepages/ohf/ohbc.html

Oakland Univ. - Rochester MI
http://www.acs.oakland.edu/

Oakwood Col - Huntsville AL
http://www.oakwood.edu/

Oberlin Col - Oberlin OH
http://www.oberlin.edu/

Occidental Col - Los Angeles CA
http://www.oxy.edu/

Oglethorpe Univ. - Atlanta GA
http://www.oglethorpe.edu/

Ohio Dominican Col - Columbus
http://www.odc.edu/

Ohio Northern Univ. - Ada OH
http://www.onu.edu/

Ohio State Univ. - Marion OH
http://beetle.marion.ohio-state.edu/

Ohio State Univ. - Columbus OH
http://www.acs.ohio-state.edu/

Ohio State Univ. - Lima OH
http://www.lima.ohio-state.edu/

Ohio State Univ. - Mansfield OH
http://www.mansfield.ohio state.edu/

Ohio Univ. - Athens OH
http://www.ohiou.edu/

Ohio Valley Col - Parkersburg WV
http://wvweb.com/www/OVCol/

Ohio Wesleyan Univ. - Delaware OH
http://www.owu.edu/

Oklahoma Baptist Univ. - Shawnee
http://www.okbu.edu/

Oklahoma Christian Univ. - Ok City
http://www.oc.edu/

Oklahoma City Univ. - Ok City
http://frodo.okcu.edu/

Okla Panhandle State - Goodwell
http://www.opsu.edu/

Oklahoma State Univ. - Stillwater
http://www.okstate.edu/

Old Dominion Univ. - Norfolk VA
http://www.odu.edu/

Olivet Col - Olivet MI
http://www.olivetnet.edu/

Olivet Nazarene Univ. - Kankak IL
http://www.olivet.edu/

Oral Roberts Univ. - Tulsa OK
http://www.oru.edu/

Oregon Institute of Sci - Beaverton
http://www.ogi.edu/

Oregon Health Sciences U. - P'land
http://www.ohsu.edu/

Oregon Institute of Tech - Klamath
http://www.oit.osshe.edu/

Oregon State Univ. - Corvallis OR
http://www.orst.edu/

Ottawa Univ. - Ottawa KS
http://www.ott.edu/

Otterbein Col - Westerville OH
http://www.otterbein.edu/

Ouachita Baptist U. - Arkadel AR
http://www.obu.edu/

Our Lady of Lake U - San Antonio
http://www.ollusa.edu/

Pace Univ. - New York NY
http://www.pace.edu/

Pacific Christian Col - Fullerton CA
http://pacificcc.edu/

Pacific Lutheran Univ. - Tacoma WA
http://www.plu.edu/

Pacific NW C of Art - Portland
http://www.pnca.edu/

Pacific Univ. - Forest Grove OR
http://www.pacificu.edu/

Pacific Univ. Col - Angwin CA
http://www.puc.edu/

Pacific Western Univ.
http://www.pwu.com/

Palm Beach Atlantic C - West Palm
http://www.pbac.edu/

Park Col - Parkville MO
www.uol.com/park/index.html

Parsons School of Design - NY
http://www.parsons.edu/

Peace Col - Raleigh NC
http://www.peace.edu/

Pembroke State Univ. - NC
http://www.pembroke.edu/

PA Col of Technology - Williamspt
http://www.pct.edu/

Pennsylvania State Univ. - U Park
http://www.psu.edu/

Pensacola Christian C - Pensacola
http://www.pcci.edu/

Pepperdine Univ. - Malibu CA
http://www.pepperdine.edu/

Peru State Col - Peru NE
http://www.peru.edu/

Philadelphia Col of Pharmacy - PA
http://www.pcps.edu/

Philadelphia Col of Textiles - PA
http://www.philacol.edu/

Phillips Univ. - Enid OK
http://www.phillips.edu/

Piedmont Col - Demorest GA
http://www.piedmont.edu/

Pillsbury Baptist Bible C - Owatona
http://www.pillsbury.edu/

Pine Manor Col - Chestnut Hill MA
http://www.pmc.edu/

Pittsburg State Univ. - Pittsburg KS
http://www.pittstate.edu/

Pitzer Col - Claremont CA
http://www.pitzer.edu/

Plymouth State Col - Plymouth NH
http://www.plymouth.edu/

Point Loma Nazarene C - S Diego
http://www.ptloma.edu/

Point Park Col - Pittsburgh PA
http://www.ppc.edu/

Polytechnic U. of NY - Brooklyn
http://www.poly.edu/

Polytechnic Univ - Farmingdale NY
http://rama.poly.edu/

Pomona Col - Claremont CA
http://www.pomona.edu/

Portland State Univ. - Portland OR
http://www.pdx.edu/

Prairie View A+M U. - TX
http://www.pvamu.edu/

Pratt Institute - Brooklyn NY
http://www.pratt.edu/

Presbyterian Col - Clinton SC
http://www.presby.edu/

Prescott Col - Prescott AZ
http://aztec.asu.edu/prescott.col/

Princeton Univ. - Princeton NJ
http://www.princeton.edu/

Principia Col - Elsah IL
http://www.prin.edu/

Providence Col - Providence RI
http://www.providence.edu/

Purdue Univ. - West Lafayette IN
http://www.purdue.edu/

Purdue U Calumet - Hammond IN
http://www.calumet.purdue.edu/

Purdue Univ. - Westville IN
http://www.purduenc.edu/

Quincy Univ. - Quincy IL
http://www.quincy.edu/

Quinnipiac Col - Hamden CT
http://www.quinnipiac.edu/

Radford Univ. - Radford VA
http://www.runet.edu/

Ramapo Col - Mahwah NJ
http://www.ramapo.edu/

Randolph-Macon Col - Ashland VA
http://www.rmc.edu/

Randolph-Macon Col - Lynchburg
http://www.rmwc.edu/

Reed Col - Portland OR
http://www.reed.edu/

Regent Univ. - unknown
http://www.regent.edu/

Regis Col - Weston MA
http://www.regis.edu/

Regis Univ. - Denver CO
http://www.regis.edu/

Rensselaer Polytech - Troy NY
http://www.rpi.edu/

Rhode Island Col - Providence RI
http://www.ric.edu/

R Island Sch of Design - Providence
http://www.risd.edu/

Rhodes Col - Memphis TN
http://www.rhodes.edu/

Rice Univ. - Houston TX
http://www.rice.edu/

Richard Stockton U - Pomona NJ
http://odin.stockton.edu/

Rider Univ. - Lawrenceville NJ
http://www.rider.edu/

Ringling School - Sarasota FL
http://www.rsad.edu/

Ripon Col - Ripon WI
http://www.ripon.edu/

Rivier Col - Nashua NH
http://www.riv.edu/

Roanoke Col - Salem VA
http://www.roanoke.edu/

Robert Morris Col - Coraopolis PA
http://www.robert-morris.edu/

Rochester Inst of Tech - NY
http://www.rit.edu/

Rockefeller Univ. - New York NY
http://www.rockefeller.edu/

Rockford Col - Rockford IL
http://www.rockford.edu/

Rockhurst Col - Kansas City MO
http://www.rockhurst.edu/

Rocky Mountain Col - Billings MT
http://www.rocky.edu/

Roger Williams Univ. - Bristol RI
http://www.rwu.edu/

Rogers Univ. - Bartlesville OK
http://www.rogersu.edu/bville/

Rogers Univ. - Claremore OK
http://www.rogersu.edu/cmore/

Rogers Univ. - Pryor OK
http://www.rogersu.edu/pryor/

Rogers Univ. - Tulsa OK
http://www.rogersu.edu/tulsa/

Rollins Col - Winter Park FL
http://www.rollins.edu/

Roosevelt Univ. - Chicago IL
http://www.roosevelt.edu/

Rosary Col - River Forest IL
http://www.rosary.edu/

Rose-Hulman IT - Terre Haute IN
http://www.rose-hulman.edu/

Rosemont Col - Rosemont PA
http://www.rosemont.edu/

Rowan Col of NJ - Glassboro NJ
http://www.rowan.edu/

Russell Sage Col - Troy NY
http://www.sage.edu/

Rutgers - Camden NJ
http://camden-www.rutgers.edu/

Rutgers - New Brunswick NJ
http://www.rutgers.edu/aboutru/campuses/newbrun.html

Rutgers - Newark NJ
http://www.rutgers.edu/aboutru/campuses/newark.html

Sacred Heart Univ. - Fairfield CT
http://www.sacredheart.edu/

Saginaw Valley State U UCenter MI
http://www.svsu.edu/

Saint Ambrose Univ. - Davenport IA
http://www.sau.edu/sau.html

St Andrew Presb. C - Laurinburg NC
http://www.sapc.edu/

Saint Anselm Col - Manchester NH
http://www.anselm.edu/

Saint Bonaventure Univ. - NY
http://www.sbu.edu/

Saint Cloud State U. - St. Cloud MN
http://www.stcloud.msus.edu/

Saint Edward's Univ. - Austin TX
http://www.stedwards.edu/home.htm

Saint Francis Col - Fort Wayne IN
http://stfrancis.sfc.edu/

Saint Francis Col - Loretto PA
http://www.sfcpa.edu/

St John Vianney Col - Miami
http://www.stthomas.edu/www/sjv_http/index.htm

Saint John's Col - Annapolis MD
http://www.sjca.edu/

Saint John's Col - Santa Fe NM
http://www.sjcsf.edu/

Saint John's Univ. - Colville MN
http://www.csbsju.edu/

Saint John's Univ. - Jamaica NY
http://www.stjohns.edu/

Saint Joseph Col - West Hartford CT
http://www.sjc.edu/

Saint Joseph's Col - Rensselaer IN
http://www.saintjoe.edu/

Saint Joseph's Col - Standish ME
http://www.sjcme.edu/

Saint Joseph's U - Philadelphia PA
http://www.sju.edu/

Saint Lawrence Univ. - Canton NY
http://www.stlawu.edu/

Saint Leo Col - Saint Leo FL
http://www.saintleo.edu/

Saint Louis Col of Pharmacy - MO
http://www.stlcop.edu/

Saint Louis Univ. - St. Louis MO
http://www.slu.edu/

Saint Martin's Col - Lacey WA
http://www.stmartin.edu/

Saint Mary Col - Leavenworth KS
http://www.smcks.edu/

Saint Mary's Col - Notre Dame IN
http://www.saintmarys.edu/

Saint Mary's C of Cal - Moraga
http://www.stmarys-ca.edu/

Saint Mary's C - St. Mary's City MD
http://www.msmary.edu/

Saint Mary's Col - Winona MN
http://www.mnsmc.edu/

Saint Mary's Univ. - San Antonio TX
http://www.stmarytx.edu

Saint Mary-of-the-Woods Col - IN
http://woods.smwc.edu/

Saint Meinrad Col - St. Meinrad IN
http://www.stmeinradcol.edu/

Saint Michael's Col - Colchester VT
http://waldo.smcvt.edu/

Saint Norbert Col - De Pere WI
http://www.snc.edu/

Saint Olaf Col - Northfield MN
http://www.stolaf.edu/

Saint Paul's Col - Lawrenceville VA
http://www.st.pauls.edu/

Saint Peter's Col - Jersey City NJ
http://www.spc.edu/

Saint Thomas Univ. - Miami FL
http://www.stu.edu/

Saint Vincent Col - Latrobe PA
http://www.stvincent.edu/

Saint Xavier Univ. - Chicago IL
http://www.sxu.edu/

Salem Col - Winston-Salem NC
http://www.salem.edu/

Salem State Col - Salem MA
http://www.salem-ma.edu/

Salem-Teikyo Univ. - Salem WV
http://stulib.salem-teikyo.wvnet.edu/

Salisbury State Univ. - MD
http://www.ssu.umd.edu/

Salish Kootenai Col - Pablo MT
http://www.skc.edu/

Salve Regina Univ. - Newport RI
http://www.salve.edu/

Sam Houston State U. - Huntsville
http://www.shsu.edu/

Samford Univ. - Birmingham AL
http://www.samford.edu/

Samuel Merritt Col - Oakland CA
http://www.peralta.cc.ca.us/merritt/merritt.html

San Diego State Univ. - CA
http://www.sdsu.edu/

San Francisco Art Institute - CA
http://rrose.sfai.edu/

San Francisco Conservatory - CA
http://www.sfcm.edu/

San Francisco State Univ. - SF CA
http://www.sfsu.edu/

San Jose State Univ. - San Jose CA
http://www.sjsu.edu/

Santa Clara Univ. - Santa Clara CA
http://www.scu.edu/

Sarah Lawrence Col - Bronxvlle NY
http://www.slc.edu/

Savannah Col of Art and Design
http://www.scad.edu/

School of Psychology - Chicago IL
http://www.csopp.edu/

School of Art Institute of Chicago
http://www.artic.edu/saic/saichome.html

Museum of Fine Arts - Boston MA
http://www.smfa.edu/

School of Visual Arts - New York
http://www.sva.edu/

Schreiner Col - Kerrville TX
http://www.schreiner.edu/

Scripps Col - Claremont CA
http://www.scrippscol.edu/

The Internet University - College URL's

Seattle Pacific Univ. - Seattle WA
http://www.spu.edu/

Seattle Univ. - Seattle WA
http://www.seattleu.edu/

Seton Hall Univ. - South Orange NJ
http://www.shu.edu/

Seton Hill Col - Greensburg PA
http://www.setonhill.edu/

Shawnee State Univ. - Portsmth OH
http://www.shawnee.edu/

Sheldon Jackson Col - Sitka AK
http://www.sheldonjackson.edu/

Shenandoah Univ. - Winchester VA
http://www.su.edu/

Shepherd Col - Shepherdstown WV
www.shepherd.wvnet.edu/

Shippensburg Univ. of PA
http://www.ship.edu/

Shorter Col - Rome GA
http://www.shorter.edu/

Siena Col - Loudonville NY
http://www.siena.edu/

Silver Lake Col - Manitowoc WI
http://www.sl.edu/slc.html

Simmons Col - Boston MA
http://www.simmons.edu/

Simon's Rock C - G. Barrington MA
http://www.simons-rock.edu/

Simpson Col - Indianola IA
http://www.simpson.edu/

Simpson Col - Redding CA
http://www.simpsonca.edu/

Sinte Gleska Univ. - Rosebud SD
http://sinte.indian.com/

Skidmore Col - Saratoga Springs NY
http://www.skidmore.edu/

Slippery Rock U. - Slippery Rock PA
http://www.sru.edu/

Smith Chapel Bible C - Tallahassee
http://www.specdata.com/cgbbs/scbc.html

Smith Col - Northampton MA
http://www.smith.edu/

Sonoma State Univ. - Rohnert Park
http://www.sonoma.edu/

South Carolina State U - Orangebg
http://www.scsu.edu/

SD School Mines + Tech - Rapid C
http://www.sdsmt.edu/

SD State Univ. - Brookings
http://www.sdstate.edu/

Southampton Col - Southampton NY
www.southampton.liunet.edu/

SE Missouri State U - C. Girardeau
http://www.semo.edu/

SE Bible Col - East Birmingham AL
http://www.sebc.edu/

Southeastern College - Lakeland FL
http://www.seCol.edu/

SE Louisiana U - Hammond
http://www.selu.edu/

SE Oklahoma State U - Durant OK
http://www.sosu.edu/

So Adventist Univ. - Coldale TN
http://www.southern.edu/

Southern California C - Costa Mesa
http://www.sccu.edu/

So Christian U - Montgomery AL
http://www.southernchristian.edu/

Southern CT State Univ. - N Haven
http://scwww.ctstateu.edu/

Southern Illinois U - Carbondale IL
http://www.siu.edu/cwis/

Southern Illinois - Edwardsville IL
http://www.siue.edu/

Southern Methodist Univ. - Dallas
http://www.smu.edu/

Southern Nazarene - Bethany OK
http://www.snu.edu/

So Oregon State Col - Ashland OR
http://www.sosc.osshe.edu/

So Polytechnic State U - Marietta
http://www.sct.edu/

Southern Univ. - Baton Rouge LA
http://www.subr.edu/

Southern Univ. U - Cedar City UT
http://www.suu.edu/

Southern Vermont Col - Bennington
http://www.sover.net/~svc/index.html

Southern Wesleyan U - Central SC
http://www.swu.edu/

Southwest Baptist U - Bolivar MO
http://www.sbuniv.edu/

SW Missouri State Univ. - Spr'field
http://www.smsu.edu/

Southwest State U - Marshall MN
http://www.southwest.msus.edu/

SW Texas State Univ. - San Marcos
http://www.swt.edu/

SW Adventist Col - Keene TX
http://www.swac.edu/

SW Assemblies of God - Waxah TX
http://www.sagu.edu/

SW Christian Col - Terrell TX
http://pubweb.acns.nwu.edu/~lwd003/swcc.htm

Southwestern Col - Chula Vista CA
http://swc.cc.ca.us/

Southwestern Col - Phoenix AZ
http://www.netwrx.net/swc/

Southwestern Col - Winfield KS
http://www.sckans.edu/

Southwestern Medical Ctr - Dallas
http://www.swmed.edu/

SW Oklahoma State - Weatherford
http://www.swosu.edu/

Southwestern U - Georgetown TX
http://www.southwestern.edu/

Spalding Univ. - Louisville KY
http://www.spalding.edu/

Spartanburg Methodist Col - SC
http://www.icusc.org/spartanb/schome.htm

Spelman Col - Atlanta GA
http://www.auc.edu/

Spring Arbor Col - Spring Arbor MI
http://www.arbor.edu/

Spring Hill Col - Mobile AL
http://www.shc.edu/

Springfield Col - Springfield MA
http://www.spfldcol.edu/

Stanford Univ. - Stanford CA
http://www.stanford.edu/

State U of W Georgia - Carrollton
http://www.westga.edu/

S. F. Austin State U - Nacogdoches
http://www.sfasu.edu/

Stephens Col - Columbia MO
http://www.stephens.edu/

Sterling Col - Sterling KS
http://www.stercolks.edu/

Stetson Univ. - Deland FL
http://thoth.stetson.edu/

Stevens Inst. of Tech - Hoboken NJ
http://www.stevens-tech.edu/

Stillman Col - Tuscaloosa AL
http://www.stillman.edu/

Stonehill Col - North Easton MA
http://www.stonehill.edu/

Strayer Col - Washington DC
http://www.strayer.edu/

Suffolk Univ. - Boston MA
http://www.suffolk.edu/

Sul Ross State Univ. - Alpine TX
http://www.sulross.edu/

Summit U Louisiana -New Orleans
http://www.summitunivofla.edu/

SUNY - Col of Ag+Tech - Morrisvil
http://www.snymor.edu/

SUNY Col of Tech - Farmingdale
http://www.farmingdale.edu/

SUNY/Alfred State Col - Alfred NY
http://www.alfredtech.edu/

SUNY/Col at Albany - Albany NY
http://www.albany.edu/

SUNY/Col - Binghamton NY
http://www.binghamton.edu/

SUNY/Col - Brockport NY
http://www.brockport.edu/

SUNY/Col at Buffalo - Buffalo NY
http://wings.buffalo.edu/

SUNY/Col at Cortland - Cortland
http://www.cortland.edu/

SUNY/Col at Fredonia - Fredonia
http://www.cs.fredonia.edu/

SUNY/Col at Geneseo - Geneseo
http://mosaic.cc.geneseo.edu/

SUNY/Col - New Paltz NY
http://www.newpaltz.edu/

SUNY/Col - Westbury NY
http://www.oldwestbury.edu/

SUNY/Col at Oneonta - Oneonta
http://www.oneonta.edu/

SUNY/Col at Oswego - Oswego NY
http://www.oswego.edu/

SUNY/Col at Plattsburgh - Platsbgh
http://www.plattsburgh.edu/

SUNY/Col at Potsdam - Potsdam
http://www.potsdam.edu/

SUNY/Col at Purchase - Purchase
http://www.purchase.edu/

SUNY/Col - Stony Brook NY
http://www.sunysb.edu/

SUNY/Col of Ag +Tech - Cobleskill
http://www.cobleskill.edu/

SUNY/Col of Enviro Sci - Syracuse
http://www.esf.edu/

SUNY/Empire State C - Saratoga Sp
http://www.esc.edu/

SUNY/Fashion Institute - New York
http://www.anewnet.com/usCol/nyfit001.htm

SUNY/Maritime Col - Throgs Neck
http://www.sunymaritime.edu/

Susquehanna Univ. - Selinsgrove PA
http://www.susqu.edu/

Swarthmore Col - Swarthmore PA
http://www.swarthmore.edu/

Sweet Briar Col - Sweet Briar VA
http://www.sbc.edu/

Syracuse Univ. - Syracuse NY
http://www.syr.edu/

Tabor Col - Hillsboro KS
http://www.tabor.edu/

Tarleton State U - Stephenville TX
http://www.tarleton.edu/

Taylor Univ. - Upland IN
http://www.tayloru.edu/

Teachers Col - New York NY
http://www.tc.columbia.edu/

Teikyo Marycrest U. - Davenport IA
http://geraldine.mcrest.edu/

Teikyo Post Univ. - Waterbury CT
http://www.teikyopost.edu/

Temple Univ. - Philadelphia PA
http://www.temple.edu/

Tennessee State Univ. - Nashville
http://www.tnstate.edu/

Tennessee Tech Univ. - Cookeville
http://www.tntech.edu/

Texas A&M - Laredo TX
http://www.tamiu.edu/

Texas A&M Univ. - Col Station TX
http://www.tamu.edu/

Texas A&M Univ. - Commerce TX
http://www.etsu.edu/

Texas A&M Univ.i - Corpus Christi
http://www.tamucc.edu/

Texas A&M Univ. - Galveston TX
http://www.tamug.tamu.edu/

Texas A&M Univ. - Kingsville
http://www.tamuk.edu/

Texas Christian Univ - Fort Worth
http://www.tcu.edu/

Texas Lutheran Univ - Seguin TX
http://www.txlutheran.edu/

Texas Southern Univ - Houston TX
http://www.tsu.edu/

Texas Tech Univ - Lubbock TX
http://www.ttu.edu/

Texas Tech U- Health Sci - Lubbock
http://www.ttuhsc.edu/

Texas Wesleyan Univ - Fort Worth
http://www.txwesleyan.edu/

Texas Woman's Univ - Denton TX
http://www.twu.edu/

The Univ Institute - Cincinnati OH
http://www.tui.edu/

Thiel Col - Greenville PA
http://www.thiel.edu/

Thomas A. Edison State - Trenton
http://www.tesc.edu/

Thomas Aquinas C - Santa Paula CA
http://www.ewtn.com/tac/

Thomas Col - Waterville ME
http://www.thomas.edu/

Thomas Cooley Law - Lansing MI
http://www.cooley.edu/

Thomas Jefferson U - Philadelphia
http://www.tju.edu/

Thomas More C - Crestvw Hills KY
http://www.thomasmore.edu/

Toccoa Falls Col - Toccoa Falls GA
http://toccoafalls.edu/

Tougaloo Col - Tougaloo MS
http://www.tougaloo.edu/

Touro Col - New York NY
http://www.touro.edu/

Towson State Univ - Towson MD
http://www.towson.edu/

Transylvania Univ - Lexington KY
http://www.transy.edu/

Trevecca Nazarene U - Nashville TN
http://www.trevecca.edu/

Tri-State Univ. - Angola IN
http://www.tristate.edu/

Trinity Christian C - Palos Hghts IL
http://www.tmty.edu/

Trinity Col - Washington DC
http://www.consortium.org/~trinity/home.htm

Trinity Col - Hartford CT
http://www.trincoll.edu/homepage.html

Trinity Col of Vermont - Burlington
http://www.trinityvt.edu/

Trinity Internatl U. - Deerfield IL
http://www.trin.edu/

Trinity Univ. - San Antonio TX
http://www.trinity.edu/

Troy State Univ. - Troy AL
http://www.troyst.edu/

Troy State Univ. - Dothan AL
http://www.tsufl.edu/

Troy State Univ - Montgomery AL
http://www.tsum.edu/

Truman State Univ - Kirksville MO
http://www.truman.edu/

Tucson Univ. - Tucson AZ
http://www.tucsonu.edu/

Tufts Univ. - Medford MA
http://www.tufts.edu/

Tulane Univ. - New Orleans LA
http://www.tulane.edu/

Tusculum Col - Greeneville TN
http://www.tusculum.edu/

Tuskegee Univ. - Tuskegee AL
http://www.tusk.edu/

Univ Col - Lincoln NE
http://www.uCol.edu/

Univ Col - Colville PA
http://www.ursinus.edu/

Univ Col - Pepper Pike OH
http://home.earthlink.net/~ursuline/

Univ Iowa Univ. - Fayette IA
http://www.uiu.edu/

Univ U - Jackson TN
http://www.uu.edu/

Univ Valley State Col - Orem UT
http://www.uvsc.edu/

Union Col - Schenectady NY
http://www.union.edu/

Union Col - Barbourville KY
http://www.unionky.edu/

Unity Col - Unity ME
http://www.unity.edu/

Univ. of Akron - Akron OH
http://www.uakron.edu/

Univ. of Alabama - Tuscaloosa
http://www.ua.edu/

Univ. of Alabama - Birmingham
http://www.uab.edu/

Univ. of Alabama - Huntsville AL
http://www.uah.edu/

Univ. of Alaska - Anchorage AK
http://www.jun.alaska.edu/

Univ. of Alaska - Fairbanks AK
http://www.uaa.alaska.edu/

Univ. of Alaska - Juneau AK
http://www.uaf.alaska.edu/

Univ. of Arizona - Tucson AZ
http://www.arizona.edu/

Univ. of Arkansas - Little Rock
http://www.ualr.edu/

Univ of Arkansas - Monticello AR
http://www.uamont.edu/

Univ of Arkansas - Little Rock AR
http://www.uams.edu/

Univ. of Arkansas - Pine Bluff AR
http://www.uapb.edu/

Univy of Arkansas - Fayetteville AR
http://www.uark.edu/

Univ of Baltimore - Baltimore MD
http://www.ubalt.edu/

Univ of Bridgeport - Bridgeport CT
http://www.bridgeport.edu/

Univ. of California - Berkeley CA
http://www.berkeley.edu/

Univ. of California - Davis CA
http://www.ucdavis.edu/

Univ. of California - Irvine CA
http://www.uci.edu/

Univ of California - Los Angeles CA
http://www.ucla.edu/

Univ of California - Riverside CA
http://www.ucr.edu/

Univ. of California - Santa Barbara
http://www.ucsb.edu/

Univ of California - Santa Cruz CA
http://www.ucsc.edu/

Univ of California - La Jolla CA
http://www.ucsd.edu/

Univ of California - San Francisco
http://www.ucsf.edu/

Univ of Central Arkansas - Conway
http://www.uca.edu/

Univ of Central Florida - Orlando
http://www.ucf.edu/

U of Central Oklahoma - Edmond
http://www.ucok.edu/

Univ of Charleston - Charleston WV
http://www.uchaswv.edu/

Univ. of Chicago - Chicago IL
http://www.uchicago.edu/

Univ of Cincinnati - Cincinnati OH
http://www.uc.edu/

Univ. of Colorado - Boulder CO
http://www.colorado.edu/

Univ. of Colorado - Denver CO
http://www.cudenver.edu/

Univ of Colorado - Co. Springs CO
http://www.uccs.edu/

U of Colorado Health Sci - Denver
http://www.hsc.colorado.edu/

Univ. of Connecticut - Storrs CT
http://www.uconn.edu/

Univ. of Dallas - Irving TX
http://www.udallas.edu/

Univ. of Dayton - Dayton OH
http://www.udayton.edu/

Univ. of Delaware - Newark DE
http://www.udel.edu/

Univ. of Denver - Denver CO
http://www.du.edu/

Univ of Detroit Mercy - Detroit MI
http://www.udmercy.edu/

Univ. of Dubuque - Dubuque IA
http://www.udq.edu/

Univ of Evansville - Evansville IN
http://www.evansville.edu/

Univ of Findlay - Findlay OH
http://www.findlay.edu/

Univ. of Florida - Gainesville FL
http://www.ufl.edu/

Univ. of Georgia - Athens GA
http://www.uga.edu/

Univ. of Great Falls - Great Falls
http://www.ugf.edu/

Univ. of Hartford - West Hartford
http://www.hartford.edu/

U of Hawai'i - Pearl City
http://www.uhwo.hawaii.edu/

Univ. of Hawaii at Hilo - Hilo HI
http://www2.hawaii.edu/~uhhilo/

U of Hawaii at Manoa - Honolulu HI
http://www.hawaii.edu/

Univ. of Houston - Houston TX
http://uhdux2.dt.uh.edu/

Univ. of Houston - Houston TX
http://www.cl.uh.edu/

Univ. of Houston - Houston TX
http://www.uh.edu/

Univ. of Idaho - Moscow ID
http://www.uidaho.edu/

Univ. of Illinois - Chicago IL
http://www.uic.edu/

Univ. of Illinois - Urbana IL
http://www.uiuc.edu/

Univ of Illinois - Springfield IL
http://www.uis.edu/

Univ of Indianapolis - Indianapolis
http://www.uindy.edu/

Univ. of Iowa - Iowa City IA
http://www.uiowa.edu/

Univ. of Judaism - Bel Air CA
http://www.uj.edu/

Univ. of Kansas - Lawrence KS
http://www.ukans.edu/

Univ of Kentucky - Lexington KY
http://www.uky.edu/

Univ. of La Verne - La Verne CA
http://www.ulaverne.edu/

Univ of Louisville - Louisville KY
http://www.louisville.edu/

Univ. of Maine - Augusta ME
http://www.uma.maine.edu/

Univ. of Maine - Orono ME
http://www.ume.maine.edu/

Univ. of Maine - Farmington ME
http://www.umf.maine.edu/

Univ. of Maine - Fort Kent ME
http://www.umfk.maine.edu/

Univ. of Maine - Machias ME
http://www.umm.maine.edu/

Univ. of Maine - Presque Isle ME
http://www.umpi.maine.edu/

U of M. Hardin-Baylor - Belton TX
http://www.umhb.edu/

Univ of Maryland - Baltimore MD
http://www.ab.umd.edu/

Univ of Maryland - Baltimore MD
http://www.umbc.edu/

Univ of Maryland - Col Park MD
http://www.umcp.umd.edu/

Univ of Maryland - Princess Anne
http://www.umes.umd.edu/

Univ of Maryland - Col Park MD
http://www.umuc.edu/

Univ of Massachusetts - Amherst
http://www.umass.edu/

U of Massachusetts - No Dartmouth
http://www.umassd.edu/

Univ of Massachusetts - Boston MA
http://www.umb.edu/

Univ of Massachusetts - Lowell MA
http://www.uml.edu/

Univ. of Memphis - Memphis TN
http://www.memphis.edu/

Univ. of Miami - Coral Gables FL
http://www.miami.edu/

Univ. of Michigan - Flint MI
http://www.flint.umich.edu/

Univ. of Michigan - Dearborn MI
http://www.umd.umich.edu/

Univ of Michigan - Ann Arbor MI
http://www.umich.edu/

Univ of Minnesota - Crookston MN
http://www.crk.umn.edu/

Univ. of Minnesota - Duluth MN
http://www.d.umn.edu/

Univ. of Minnesota - Morris MN
http://www.mrs.umn.edu/

Univ of Minnesota - Minneapolis
http://www.umn.edu/tc/

Univ. of Mississippi - U MS
http://www.olemiss.edu/

Univ. of Missouri - Columbia MO
http://www.missouri.edu/

Univ of Missouri - Kansas City MO
http://www.umkc.edu/

Univ. of Missouri - Rolla MO
http://www.umr.edu/

Univ. of Missouri - St. Louis MO
http://www.umsl.edu/

Univ. of Mobile - Mobile AL
http://www.umobile.edu/

Univ. of Montana - Missoula MT
http://www.umt.edu/

Univ of Montevallo - Montevallo AL
http://www.montevallo.edu/

Univ. of Nebraska - Kearney NE
http://www.unk.edu/

Univ. of Nebraska - Lincoln NE
http://www.unl.edu/

Univ. of Nebraska - Omaha NE
http://www.unomaha.edu/

Univ. of Nevada - Las Vegas NE
http://www.nscee.edu/

Univ. of Nevada - Reno NE
http://www.scs.unr.edu/

Univ of New England - Biddefd ME
http://www.une.edu/

Univ of New Hampshire - Durham
http://www.unh.edu/

Univ of New Haven - West Haven
http://www.newhaven.edu/

Univ of New Mexico - Albuquerque
http://www.unm.edu/

Univ of New Orleans - New Orleans
http://www.uno.edu/

Univ of Newport - Newport Bch CA
http://www.newport.edu/

Univ of North Alabama - Florence
http://www.una.edu/

Univ of North Carolina - Asheville
http://www.cs.unca.edu/

Univ of North Carolina - Chapel Hill
http://www.unc.edu/

Univ of North Carolina - Charlotte
http://www.uncc.edu/

U of North Carolina - Greensboro
http://www.uncg.edu/

U of North Carolina - Wilmington
http://www.uncwil.edu/

Univ of North Dakota - Grand Forks
http://www.und.nodak.edu/

Univ of North Florida - Jacksonville
http://www.unf.edu/

Univ of North Texas - Denton TX
http://www.unt.edu/

U of N.TX Health Sci - Fort Worth
http://www.hsc.unt.edu/

Univ of Northern CA - Petaluma CA
http://www.uncm.edu/

U of North Colorado - Greeley CO
http://www.univnorthco.edu/

Univ of Northern Iowa - Cedar Falls
http://www.uni.edu/

Univ. of Notre Dame - ND IN
http://www.nd.edu/

Univ. of Oklahoma - Norman OK
http://www.uoknor.edu/

Univ. of Oregon - Eugene OR
http://www.uoregon.edu/

Univ. of Pennsylvania - Phila.
http://www.upenn.edu/

Univ of Phoenix - San Francisco CA
http://www.uophx.edu/

Univ. of Pittsburgh - Pittsburgh PA
http://www.pitt.edu/

Univ. of Pittsburgh - Bradford PA
http://www1.pitt.edu/~bradford/

Univ. of Pittsburgh - Greensburg PA
http://www.pitt.edu/~upg/

Univ. of Pittsburgh - Johnstown PA
http://www.pitt.edu/~upjweb

Univ. of Portland - Portland OR
http://www.uofport.edu/

Univ of Portland (Eng.) - Portland
http://www.up.edu/

Univ of Puget Sound - Tacoma WA
http://www.ups.edu/

Univ. of Redlands - Redlands CA
http://www.uor.edu/

Univ of Rhode Island - Kingston RI
http://www.uri.edu/

U of Richmond - U of Richmond VA
http://www.urich.edu/

Univ of Rio Grande - OH
http://www.urgrgcc.edu/

Univ of Rochester - Rochester NY
http://www.rochester.edu/

Univ of Saint Thomas - Houston TX
http://basil.stthom.edu/

Univ of Saint Thomas - St. Paul MN
http://www.stthomas.edu/

Univ of San Diego - San Diego CA
http://www.acusd.edu/

U of San Francisco - San Francisco
http://www.usfca.edu/

U of Science + Arts - Chickasha OK
http://mercur.usao.edu/

Univ. of Scranton - Scranton PA
http://www.uofs.edu/

Univ of Sioux Falls - Sioux Falls SD
http://www.thecoo.edu/

Univ of South Alabama - Mobile AL
http://www.usouthal.edu/

Univ of South Carolina - Columbia
http://www.csd.scarolina.edu/

Univ of South Carolina - Aiken SC
http://www.usca.sc.edu/

U of South Carolina - Spartanburg
http://www.uscs.edu/

Univ. of South Dakota - Vermillion
http://www.usd.edu/

Univ. of South Florida - Tampa FL
http://www.usf.edu/

Univ. of Southern CA - Los Angeles
http://cwis.usc.edu/

Univ. of So. Colorado - Pueblo CO
http://meteor.uscolo.edu/

Univ. of S. Indiana - Evansville
http://www.usi.edu/

Univ. of S. Maine - Gorham ME
http://www.usm.maine.edu/

Univ of S. Mississippi - Hattiesburg
http://www.usm.edu/

Univ of SW Louisiana - Lafayette
http://www.usl.edu/

Univ of Tampa - Tampa FL
http://www.utampa.edu/

Univ of Tennessee - Chattanooga TN
http://www.utc.edu/

Univ of Tennessee - Knoxville TN
http://www.utk.edu/

Univ. of Tennessee - Martin TN
http://www.utm.edu/

Univ of Tennessee - Memphis TN
http://www.utmem.edu/

Univ. of Texas - Edinburg TX
http://www.panam.edu/

Univ. of Texas - Arlington TX
http://www.uta.edu/

Univ. of Texas - Richardson TX
http://www.utdallas.edu/

Univ. of Texas - El Paso TX
http://www.utep.edu/

Univ. of Texas - Austin TX
http://www.uTexas.edu/

Univ. of Texas - San Antonio TX
http://www.utsa.edu/

U of Texas - Health Sci. - Houston
http://www.uthouston.edu/

U of TX - Health Sci. - San Antonio
http://www.uthscsa.edu/

Univ. of Texas at Brownsville
http://www.utb.edu/

U of Texas Health Ctr at Tyler
http://pegasus.uthct.edu/

Univ. of Texas Medical - Galveston
http://www.utmb.edu/

Univ. of Texas - Odessa TX
http://www.utpb.edu/

Univ. of the District of Columbia
http://www.udc.edu/

Univ. of the Ozarks - Clarksville AR
http://www.ozarks.edu/

Univ. of the Pacific - Stockton CA
http://www.uop.edu/

Univ. of the South - Sewanee TN
http://www.sewanee.edu/

Univ. of Toledo - Toledo OH
http://www.utoledo.edu/

Univ. of Tulsa - Tulsa OK
http://www.utulsa.edu/

Univ. of Utah - Salt Lake City UT
http://www.utah.edu/

Univ. of Vermont - Burlington VT
http://www.uvm.edu/

Univ. of Virginia - Charlottesville VA
http://www.virginia.edu/

Univ. of Washington - Seattle WA
http://www.washington.edu/

Univ. of W. Alabama - Livingston
http://www.westal.edu/

Univ. of West Florida - Pensacola FL
http://www.uwf.edu/

Univ. of Wisconsin - Madison WI
http://wiscinfo.wisc.edu/

Univ. of Wisconsin - Eau Claire WI
http://www.uwec.edu/

Univ. of Wisc - Green Bay WI
http://www.uwgb.edu/

Univ. of Wisconsin - La Crosse WI
http://www.uwlax.edu/

Univ. of Wisconsin - Milwaukee WI
http://www.uwm.edu/

Univ. of Wisconsin - Oshkosh WI
http://www.uwosh.edu/

Univ. of Wisconsin - Kenosha WI
http://www.uwp.edu/

Univ. of Wisconsin - Platteville WI
http://www.uwplatt.edu/

Univ. of Wisconsin - River Falls WI
http://www.uwrf.edu/

Univ. of Wisconsin - Stevens Point
http://www.uwsp.edu/

Univ. of Wisconsin - Menomonie WI
http://www.uwstout.edu/

Univ. of Wisconsin - Superior WI
http://www.uwsuper.edu/

Univ. of Wisc. - Whitewater WI
http://www.uww.edu/

Univ. of Wyoming - Laramie WY
http://www.uwyo.edu/

USAF Academy - Col. Springs
http://www.usafa.af.mil/

US Coast Guard Acad - N London
http://www.dot.gov/dotinfo/uscg/hq/uscga/uscga.html

US International U - San Diego CA
http://www.usiu.edu/

US Mer Marine Ac - Kings Point NY
http://www.usmma.edu/

US Military Academy - West Point
http://www.usma.edu/

US Naval Academy - Annapolis MD
http://www.nadn.navy.mil/

US Sports Academy - Daphne AL
http://www.sport.ussa.edu/

USAF Inst Tech - Wright-Pat AFB
http://www.afit.af.mil/

Utah State Univ. - Logan UT
http://www.usu.edu/

Valdosta State Univ - Valdosta GA
http://www.valdosta.peachnet.edu/

Valley City State U - Valley City ND
http://www.vcsu.nodak.edu/home.html

Valparaiso Univ - Valparaiso IN
http://www.valpo.edu/

Vanderbilt Univ. - Nashville TN
http://www.vanderbilt.edu/

Vassar Col - Poughkeepsie NY
http://www.vassar.edu/

Vermont Tech - Randolph Center VT
http://www.vtc.vsc.edu/

Villa Julie Col - Stevenson MD
http://www.vjc.edu/

Villanova Univ. - Villanova PA
http://www.ucis.vill.edu/

Virginia Commonwealth - Richmnd
http://www.vcu.edu/

Virginia Intermont Coll - Bristol VA
http://www.vic.edu/

Virginia Military Inst. - Lexington
http://www.vmi.edu/

Virginia State Univ. - Petersburg
http://www.vsu.edu/

Virginia Tech Univ. - Blacksburg
http://www.vt.edu/

Virginia Wesleyan Col - Norfolk
http://www.vwc.edu/

Viterbo Col - LaCrosse WI
http://www.viterbo.edu/

Voorhees Col - Denmark SC
http://www.icusc.org/voorhees/vchome.htm

Wabash Col - Crawfordsville IN
http://www.wabash.edu/

Wagner Col - Staten Island NY
http://www.wagner.edu/

Wake Forest U - Winston-Salem NC
http://www.wfu.edu/www-data/start.html

Walden Univ. - Minneapolis MN
http://www.waldenu.edu/

Walla Walla Coll. - Col Place WA
http://www.wwc.edu/

Walsh Univ. - North Canton OH
http://www.walsh.edu/

Warner Pacific Col - Portland OR
http://www.warnerpacific.edu/

Warner Southern C. - Lake Wales FL
http://www.warner.edu/

Warren Wilson Col - Asheville NC
http://www.warren-wilson.edu/

Wartburg Col - Waverly IA
http://www.wartburg.edu/

Washburn Univ. - Topeka KS
http://www.wuacc.edu/

Washington + Lee U - Lexington VA
http://www.wlu.edu/

Washington and Jefferson - PA
http://www.washjeff.edu/

Washington Bible Col - Lanham MD
http://www.bible.edu/

Washington Col - Chestertown MD
http://www.washcoll.edu/

Washington State Univ. - Pullman
http://www.wsu.edu/

Washington State Uni - Spokane
http://www.spokane.wsu.edu/

Wash State U - Tri-Cities - Richland
http://www.tricity.wsu.edu/

Wash State U - Vancouver
http://vancouver.wsu.edu/

Washington Univ. - St. Louis MO
http://www.wustl.edu/

Wayland Baptist U - Plainview TX
http://www.wbu.edu/

Wayne State Col - Wayne NE
http://www.wsc.edu/

Wayne State Univ. - Detroit MI
http://www.wayne.edu/

Waynesburg Col - Waynesburg PA
http://www.waynesburg.edu/

Webb Institute - Glen Cove NY
http://webb-institute.edu/

Webber Col - Babson Park FL
http://www.webber.edu/

Weber State Univ. - Ogden UT
http://www.weber.edu/

Webster Univ. - St. Louis MO
http://www.websteruniv.edu/

Wellesley Col - Wellesley MA
http://www.wellesley.edu/

Wells Col - Aurora NY
http://www.wells.edu/

Wentworth Institute - Boston MA
http://www.wit.edu/

Wesley Col - Dover DE
http://www.wesley.edu/

Wesleyan Col - Macon GA
http://www.wesleyan.peachnet.edu/

Wesleyan Univ. - Middletown CT
http://www.wesleyan.edu/

West Chester U of PA - West Chester
http://www.wcupa.edu/

West Coast Univ - Los Angeles CA
http://katz.wcula.edu/

West Liberty State C - West Liberty
http://www.wlsc.wvnet.edu/

West Texas A+M Univ - Canyon TX
http://www.wtamu.edu/

West Virginia State Col - Institute
http://www.wvsc.wvnet.edu/

West Virginia Univ - Morgantown
http://www.wvu.edu/

West Virginia Univ - Parkersburg
http://www.wvup.wvnet.edu/

WV Inst. of Tech - Montgomery WV
http://wvit.wvnet.edu/

WV Wesleyan Col - Buckhannon
http://www.wvwc.edu/

Westbrook Col - Portland ME
http://www.une.edu/wc/mewomwr.html

Western Baptist Col - Salem OR
http://www.wbc.edu/

West. Carolina U - Cullowhee NC
http://www.wcu.edu/

Western CT State Univ - Danbury
http://www.wcsu.ctstateu.edu/

Western Illinois Univ. - Macomb
http://www.wiu.edu/

Western International U - Phoenix
http://www.wintu.edu/

Western Kentucky U - Bowling Grn
http://www.wku.edu/

Western MD Col - Westminster
http://www.wmc.car.md.us/

Western Michigan U - Kalamazoo
http://www.wmich.edu/

Western Montana Col - Dillon MT
http://www.wmc.edu/

West. N. England C - SpringfieldMA
http://www.wnec.edu/

Western NM Univ. - Silver City
http://www.wnmu.edu/

Western Oregon State - Monmouth
http://www.wosc.osshe.edu/

Western State Col - Gunnison CO
http://www.western.edu/

Western Washington U - Bel'ham
http://www.wwu.edu/

Westfield State Col - Westfield MA
http://www.wsc.mass.edu/

Westminster Choir C - Princeton NJ
http://www.rider.edu/www/westminster/index.html

Westminster C - N. Wilmington PA
http://keystone.westminster.edu/

Westminster Coll. - Salt Lake City
http://www.wcslc.edu/

Westminster Col - Fulton MO
http://www.westminster-mo.edu/

Westminster Theo. Sem. - Ph. PA
http://www.wts.edu/

Westmont Col - Santa Barbara CA
http://www.westmont.edu/

Wheaton Col - Wheaton IL
http://www.wheaton.edu/

Wheaton Col - Norton MA
http://www.wheatonma.edu/

Wheeling Jesuit Univ. - WV
http://www.wjc.edu/

Wheelock Col - Boston MA
http://www.wheelock.edu/

Whitman Col - Walla Walla WA
http://www.whitman.edu/

Whittier Col - Whittier CA
http://www.whittier.edu/

Whitworth Col - Spokane WA
http://whitworth.edu/

Wichita State Univ. - Wichita KS
http://www.twsu.edu/

Widener Univ. - Chester PA
http://www.widener.edu/

Wilberforce Univ - Wilberforce OH
http://www.wilberforce.edu/

Wilkes Univ. - Wilkes Barre PA
http://www.wilkes.edu/

Willamette Univ. - Salem OR
http://www.willamette.edu/

Wm Howard Taft U - Santa Ana CA
http://www.taftu.edu/

William Jewell Col - Liberty MO
http://www.jewell.edu/

William Mitchell C - Saint Paul MN
http://www.wmitchell.edu/

William Paterson Col - Wayne NJ
http://pioneer.wilpaterson.edu/

William Penn Col - Oskaloosa IA
http://www.wmpenn.edu/

William Woods Univ. - Fulton MO
http://www.wmwoods.edu/

Wil'ms Baptist C - Walnut Ridge AR
http://wbc2.wbcoll.edu/

Williams Col - Williamstown MA
http://www.williams.edu/

Wilmington Col - New Castle DE
http://www.wilmington.edu/

Wilmington Col - Wilmington OH
http://www.wilmington.edu/

Wilson Col - Chambersburg PA
http://www.wilson.edu/

Wingate Univ. - Wingate NC
http://www.wingate.edu/

Winona State Univ. - Winona MN
http://www.winona.msus.edu/

Winston-Salem State U. - NC
http://voyager.cs.wssu.edu/

Winthrop Univ. - Rock Hill SC
http://www.winthrop.edu/

Wittenberg Univ. - Springfield OH
http://www.wittenberg.edu/

Wofford Col - Spartanburg SC
http://www.wofford.edu/

Woodbury Univ. - Burbank CA
http://www.woodburyu.edu/

Worcester Polytech - Worcester MA
http://www.wpi.edu/

Wright State Univ. - Dayton OH
http://www.wright.edu/

Xavier Univ. - Cincinnati OH
http://www.xu.edu/

Xavier U of LA - New Orleans
http://www.xula.edu/

Yale Univ. - New Haven CT
http://www.yale.edu/

Yeshiva Univ. - New York NY
http://www.yu.edu/

York Col of Pennsylvania - York PA
http://www.yorkcol.edu/

Youngstown State U - OH
http://gateway.cis.ysu.edu/ •

Your Guide To On-Line College Courses

The Internet University - INDEX

Your Guide To On-Line College Courses

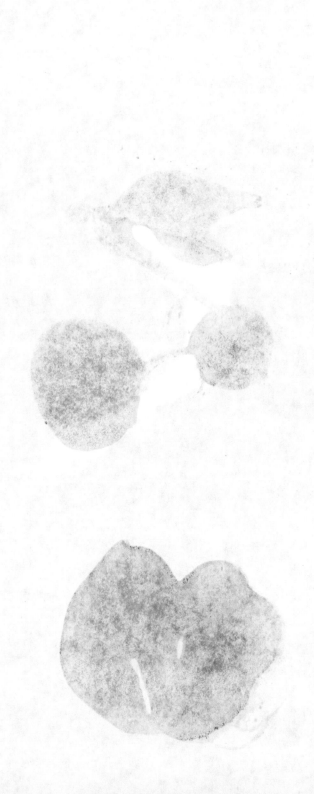

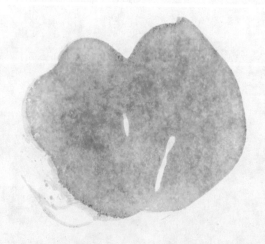